D0417016

Trumpets of Glory

Trumpets of Glory

Fourth of July Orations, 1786-1861

Henry A. Hawken, Ph.D

PUBLISHER

The Salmon Brook Historical Society
Granby, Connecticut
1976

Society publication assisted by
ARBA and ARBCC funds.

Library of Congress Catalog Card Number: 76-1784

Manufactured in the United States of America
First printing

Table of Contents

Preface

Since the United States observes the Bicentennial of the American Revolution in 1976, it is perhaps fitting that we take a fresh approach to the Fourth of July oration during the significant National Period. The romantic preoccupation of Centennial "bibliologists" like Frederick Dawson Stone of the Historical Society of Pennsylvania, or Frederick Saunders of the now dissolved Astor Library in New York City, certainly must be guarded against. And even the tentative checklist of oration pamphlets, compiled in the twentieth century by Walter Stanley Biscoe and Joseph Gavit of the New York State Library, has rather obvious shortcomings as a critical bibliographical tool.

Seven years of my research will furnish the reader with necessary background details on specific orations. He will be able to scan pamphlet texts, knowing that such versions are edited to read better in the absence of any manuscript draft. And where a draft, stenographic transcript, or other relevant document is extant, he can gain accurate insight into the orator's revision process, grasping why partisan contexts might indeed render commemorative ideals less than honorific to some mass audience. Regardless of how generalized the diction in the orator's final draft, the reader will be able to ascertain the precise manner in which revisions do (or do not) approximate linguistic spaciousness as defined by modern critics of nineteenth-century oral style (e.g., Richard M. Weaver, Barnet Baskerville, Howard H. Martin, et al.). In short, this edition should serve as an illustrative casebook of sorts.

Four chapters deal with the evolving antislavery movement, from Colonization and/or immediatism to transcendental protest and western support for civil war. Another chapter treats advocacy of Mr. Madison's unpopular war in 1812, another breaking ground on internal-improvements projects during the 1820's, and yet another "centennial" celebrations held prior to the national 1876 year. Two chapters, as one might expect in a democratic society with aspirations, delve into the effectiveness of fledgling orators Daniel Webster and George Bancroft, while the tenth chapter in this exposition focuses upon the media-selling of Davy Crockett by an obliging Whig ghostwriter. Five distinct manuscript texts comprise the Appendix, followed by a critical reading list and index for easy reference. Wherever pertinent, explanations of editorial method are designed to facilitate reading of speech texts, with some meaningful editorial synthesis being sought between nineteenth-century oral emphasis and modern usage.

The American Revolution Bicentennial Commission has generously provided a grant to assist in publication of this edition. Several persons have proffered encouragement to see me through the rigors of research and writing: Harry R. Lanser, president of the Salmon Brook Historical Society (1972-1976); Brewer G. Dean, of Combustion Engineering, Windsor, Connecticut (former president of the Salmon Brook Historical Society); Thomas Blanding of the Thoreau Lyceum; Robert P. Hay of Marquette University; R. David Henderson of Eastman Kodak, Farmington, Connecticut; and Rush Welter of Bennington College. And several libraries have opened stack areas for my research needs, namely, the American Antiquarian Society, Library of Congress, Pennsylvania State Library, Yale University, Dartmouth College, and Connecticut Historical Society. Any errors of fact or interpretation remaining in the edition are, of course, my sole responsibility.

Henry A. Hawken, Ph.D.

Granby Ct.
March 1976

Chapter 1

Daniel Webster's Fourth of July Oration, 1800

On the same day Henry Clay addressed the citizens of Lexington, Kentucky, junior Daniel Webster delivered his initial Fourth of July oration a thousand miles away in Hanover, New Hampshire. Indeed, young Webster, only eighteen at the time, may not have been the first choice of the Federal Club at Dartmouth College, sponsors of the Independence Day exercises. For according to a brief announcement in the *Dartmouth Gazette* of July 23, Webster's appointment as orator came only after considerable *bustle*, leaving open the possibility that some seniors in the Federal Club like Joseph Warren Brackett, Tristram Gilman, Cyrus Perkins, Benjamin Clark, or George Herbert,[1] perhaps better able to discourse on "principles of civil polity" than a junior classman, declined to accept and third-man-down Webster agreed to speak.

Quite obviously in his role as correspondent "Icarus" for the *Gazette*, Webster was ambitious enough to sort out his general reading and promote those patriotic themes which always seemed to satisfy Federal audiences on the Fourth. There was a rural hankering after refined expression and status, known about firsthand by orator Clay in frontier Kentucky, in his background. Webster taught school both before and after Dartmouth, reputedly standing on a big rock in the pasture and practicing sections of imaginary speeches upon farm animals when home from Dartmouth.[2] His reading might be termed atypical homespun Boscawen-Elms Farm, running the gamut from the family Bible to neoclassical worthies on the Continent—orators like Cicero and Burke and such writers as Virgil, Shakespeare, Bacon, Milton, Cervantes, Pope, Addison,

---

1 George Cheyne Shattuck, "To the Literary Executors of the late Mr. Webster" [1853], Shattuck Papers, Massachusetts Historical Society (Boston). Shattuck qualifies young Webster's status in the Club, noting that he was "a prominent member, although junior to the others."

2 Frances Ann Johnson, *Daniel Webster, Statesman* (Littleton, N.H.: Courier Printing, 1953), p. 7.

Watts, and Johnson.[3] By his own admission, the youth rather jauntily admired orators who "shook the fabric of imperial power" with their "lightning" periods.[4]

Yet, whether first or last choice, provincially homespun or not, Webster was intent upon tailoring inspirational phrases to suit a partisan occasion. In fact, one sophomore who sat through the oration identified such components in Webster's "vein of mother wit" as "quickness of apprehension," "retentive memory," "ready invention," and "habitual preparation," though minimizing the important elocutionary canon of delivery for the sake of a novice's diligent "habit."[5]

We can almost visualize young Webster late in June, sitting by candlelight in the small south chamber he rented upstairs from innkeeper George Foote,[6] and composing to please an avowedly Federal audience from college and town, not all of whom needed automatically imbibe a novice's partisan generalizations. For despite the partisan nature of an occasion which freely joined paeans praising Mother Columbia with trumpeted demands for a national purpose, demands addressed to Federal sons like departed Washington and then President John Adams,[7] the audience was sufficiently broad to include students, professors, and officials, all from Dartmouth, and Revolutionary veterans, adolescents, the aged, and toddlers, many of them townspeople.[8]

Webster's oration at the Hanover meetinghouse followed a prayer of invocation offered by Reverend John Smith of the Dartmouth faculty.[9] And apart

---

3 Rufus Choate, "On the Death of Daniel Webster," quoted in Hoyt Hopewell Hudson, "Daniel Webster," in *A History and Criticism of American Public Address*, ed. William Norwood Brigance (New York: Russell, 1960), II, 670, n. 4; Horatio King, "An Hour with Daniel Webster," *Magazine of American History*, 27 (June 1892), 460; Lorenzo Sears, *The History of Oratory from the Age of Pericles to the Present Time* (Chicago: S. C. Griggs, 1896), p. 339; Esther G. Stevens, *Daniel Webster's Heritage* (Franklin, N.H.: n.p., 1957), pp. 20-21.

4 Icarus, "Poem on Fear," *Dartmouth Gazette*, 28 Oct., 1799.

5 Shattuck Manuscript [1853]. Despite laudatory references to a "worthy subject" and an almost customary "pathway to the first place in his country;" Shattuck deletes a sentence indicating that a frolic or troublesome period awaited Webster. Editor Moses Davis specifically ruled out any "Bacchanalian revel," or even any "Epicurian repast," in the *Gazette* for July 7, so the frolic detracting from what Davis and other audience members expected to be a "rational" oration and ceremony might be Webster's fault alone. Assuming of course that an inexperienced youth, not accomplishing his purpose in speaking, would not "always" be prepared to meet with a frolic or adverse reaction. The relevant Shattuck passage reads: "Quickness of apprehension enabled Webster to acquire knowledge rapidly and with ease. His retentive memory held it for use. A ready invention fitted whatever was in his store house to the time and occasion. Habitual preparation secured success in whatever he undertook. His tasks accomplished, he was always ready for a frolick. His words flowed as from a vein of mother wit."

6 Francis Lane Childs, *The Webster Cottage and Those Who Lived There* (Hanover: Hanover Historical Society, 1969), pp. 6, 8, 27-28, incl. photograph of Webster room on fourth side of photo section.

7 "Two Odes Sung on the Fourth of July," *Dartmouth Gazette*, 7 July, 1800.

8 Reverend Joseph Banvard, *The American Statesman: or Illustrations of the Life and Character of Daniel Webster, Designed for American Youth* (Boston: Gould and Lincoln, 1859), p. 83.

from a rather heroic capsule history of the American Revolution, pretty much standard fare on the Fourth, it was correspondent Icarus who played to the audience assembled, certainly one much broader and perhaps less partisan than a novice might anticipate. For audience members of the Federal intelligentsia, who idled their leisure hours away on campus by scanning the *Gazette*, could apply a nonpartisan grain of salt over a sociable tavern mug or in heated debates of the United Fraternity and Federal Club.

Icarus grew accustomed to characterizing President Adams as an Atlas vindicating proud Columbia—constantly bearing up under both oppression and corruption, "Firm as 'the rock on which the storm shall beat.' "[10] Nor was Washington any less "lilylivered"[11] in his actions, braving "big thunders" and the "red wave" of an apocalyptic flood to "point each danger to our infant realm."[12] Washington urged Columbia to stand firm against factious Europe's "embattled millions" or "thronged cohorts," carrying "the sword of freedom in the day of battle" even from the grave.[13] Beneath this Columbia imagery, however, Icarus's concern lay with justifying possible American intervention to rebuff French tyranny,[14] thus eliminating exorbitant payments of half a billion dollars fictively necessary to establish paper constitutions on the Moon,[15] and preserving intact Federal control of a Senate over which opposition candidate Jefferson presided.[16]

If young Webster miscalculated in presuming his audience to be as partisan as the occasion allowed, the immediate comments of editor Moses Davis in the *Gazette* were extremely flattering. Davis admitted that the oration may only have "entertained" and not have persuaded, yet he felt the "spirited patriotic" effort quite pertinent to an occasion "unusual" in its "apparent" patriotism. Davis conceded the oration like most others was "composed on very short notice," yet the product of friend Webster was not that of an orator by default, doing "honor to grey headed patriotism" and crowning "with new laurels the most celebrated orator of our country."[17]

---

9 *Gazette*, 7 July, 1800.

10 Icarus, "Poetical Epistle dated 11 Feb.," *Dartmouth Gazette*, 21 Feb., 1801.

11 Icarus, "Question—by a Jacobin," *Dartmouth Gazette*, 13 Dec., 1800.

12 *Gazette*, 21 Feb., 1801.

13 *DW* to James Hervey Bingham, 5 Feb., 1800, in *The Private Correspondence of Daniel Webster*, ed. Fletcher Webster (Boston: Little Brown, 1857), I, 79, text revised slightly for "accurate observer" Icarus's piece, *Dartmouth Gazette*, 17 Feb., 1800.

14 Icarus, "War," *Dartmouth Gazette*, 25 Nov., 1799.

15 Satirical letter from Secretary Le Garde to Citizen Blanchard the Aeronaut, n.d., in Icarus, "Lunar Expedition," *Dartmouth Gazette*, 24 Feb., 1800.

16 Icarus, "Response to Moses Davis dated 27 Nov., 1799," *Dartmouth Gazette*, 6 Dec., 1800.

17 *Gazette*, 7 July, 1800.

And other Webster critics have been equally generous in their comments. Indeed, they tolerate as part of a statesman's accomplishments what Webster in 1829 regarded as stylistic defects detracting from the "true power" of ideas.[18] Style itself is not a fault in the Hanover oration, these critics say, because of young Webster's flowering simplicity of expression—a "weighty"[19] and "straightforward,"[20] "crisp"[21] and "axiomatic"[22] simplicity which enabled him to achieve "complete clarity of utterance, even in the discussion of abstruse topics."[23] Very much as with advocating some Teutonic germ theory of migration and settlement, they seek to cultivate young Webster's mind and make it all the more formidable. The vital "essential substance" of a towering Mont Blanc,[24] "rich veins" of New Hampshire marble able to be worked into some "smooth" and "beautiful" Apollo Belvidere, and a first "few grains" of the "abundance of pure gold" in the American Dream[25] all represent a kind of romantic germ device used by the critics.

But it is Reverend Benjamin Franklin Tefft who culls the most words in defending Webster's youthful mind against the premise that "mature productions have reflected an unreal splendor upon the promise of his youth." Tefft crystallizes such germ allusions as a fountainhead and the track of time into a generous statement about the mind which spoke to the Hanover audience. Young Webster is credited with a "vigorous" and "skillful" intellect *a priori*, a mind "not customarily occupied with the trivial concerns immediately about it, but going out, even then, to think upon, to study, to comprehend the world."[26] And Reverend Joseph Banvard generously manages to render Webster's elocutionary manner more palatable to his youthful readers, granting the "manly" gesture, "eloquent" eye, and "impassioned" tones required for a "full appreciation" of the oration.[27]

Yet Webster could find very little merit in his performance, and appeared

---

18 "Autobiography" in *Correspondence*, ed. Fletcher Webster, I, 11.

19 Horatio Alger, Jr., *From Farm Boy to Senator: Being the History of the Boyhood and Manhood of Daniel Webster* (New York: J. S. Ogilvie, 1882), p. 90.

20 Sears, *loc. cit.*; Charles Francis Richardson, "Address," in *The Proceedings of the Webster Centennial*, ed. Ernest Martin Hopkins (Hanover: Homer Eaton Keyes, 1902), p. 46.

21 John Bach McMaster, *Daniel Webster* (New York: Century, 1902), p. 56.

22 Richardson, *loc. cit.*

23 McMaster, *loc. cit.* An article in the *Western Monthly Magazine*, 2 (Aug. 1833), 338, expresses simplicity in terms of "strength, clearness, and common sense."

24 Henry Cabot Lodge, *Daniel Webster* (Boston: Houghton Mifflin, 1883), p. 23.

25 Banvard, *loc. cit.*

26 *Life of Daniel Webster* (Philadelphia: Porter and Coates, 1854), I, 64, 77-78.

27 Banvard, *loc. cit.*

more troubled by the Hanover oration than by his Fourth of July address at Salisbury five years later. His private secretary, Charles Lanman, in a book published the year Webster died, refused to impart any personal insight to his regret that the Hanover text never was included in a late edition of Webster's works.[28] And Webster himself on July 7, 1802, perhaps already composing his Fryeburg oration, also endeavored to keep his feelings under control when congratulating friend Thomas Merrill on the early first-choice selection of an Independence Day orator for Hanover, and wishing the 1802 Hanover speaker "better success" in the appearance.[29] Why any better success than the romanticized youth adored by the critics, however?

The crowning blow to young Webster really was the poor sales response to the pamphlet edition. Editor Davis never excerpted the pamphlet in the *Gazette* after printing it, and may even have put his best face on a rather glib satisfaction at agreeing to print the Hanover oration.[30] The series of advertisements run in the *Gazette* certainly are most revealing. Not only were several buyers tardy in returning their subscription lists to Davis,[31] but the Webster pamphlet sold very slowly. Even when subscribed for at a reasonable price of 12½ cents per copy, a good number undoubtedly gathered dust in the *Gazette* office. As late as November 1, editor Davis pleaded with *Gazette* readers in a fourth and final version of the pamphlet advertisement: "Give Ear! Those subscribers for Mr. *Webster*'s 4th of July Oration, who have not taken their books, are requested to call immediately and receive them."[32]

Disappointing sales might be traced in part to the excesses of Webster's youthful chauvinism, rendered more egregious by faulty diction in print, especially when the broad audience expected a mature essay on civil government. Webster's brother Ezekiel, speaking as a Dartmouth graduate at Salisbury on the Fourth two years after Daniel, touched upon the fallacy of such excesses: "But we mistake our interest, and we mistake our character, when we

---

28 *The Private Life of Daniel Webster* (New York: Harper Brothers, 1852), p. 30. Nor does David A. Harsha offer any commentary in *The Most Eminent Orators and Statesmen of Ancient and Modern Times* (New York: Scribner, 1855), pp. 435-36.

29 Letter from Fryeburg, Me., to Thomas A. Merrill, Hanover, in *Correspondence*, ed. Fletcher Webster, I, 117.

30 *Gazette*, 7 July, 1800.

31 Triangular-asterisked note directly below advertisement in *Gazette* for July 14. The note from Davis reads, "Those who hold subscription papers are desired to send them to the Printer; and subscribers are requested to call for their books."

32 The first and last versions of the advertisement were carried consecutively in four issues, while the second and third versions ran only once. The dates-of-issue for each version are: #1 July 14 thru Aug. 4, #2 Aug. 25, #3 Oct. 6, and #4 Oct. 13 thru Nov. 1. And the last two versions substantially repeated clause 2 of the note quoted above, the final version prefixing "Give Ear!" for added effect. Davis's Printing Office was not specified as the place to call for the pamphlets, however, in these last two abbreviated versions.

quit the sober, temperate deductions of reason, and yield to the tossings and vagaries of unlicensed fancy."[33] And Webster himself, only too well aware of his youthful error, could still bend the truth a bit in a three-hour session with Harvard's Cornelius Conway Felton, five weeks before death. For classicist Felton virtually worshipped the ailing Marshfield baron as a native specimen of Grecian excellence.[34]

To sustain his reputation in Felton's eyes, Webster conveniently recalled a review of the Hanover oration by "great" writer Joseph Dennie in a "literary paper" which Dennie presumably had to edit in 1800.[35] Webster's resort to Dennie's good name, and his classical, if not statesmanlike, resolve to be a good man and remedy the oration's stylistic defects, effectively concealed the complete scope of his error at Hanover. Webster went on to tell Felton the alleged substance of Dennie's critique: "He praised parts of the oration as vigorous and eloquent; but other parts he criticized severely, and said they were mere *emptinesses. I thought his criticism was just:* and I resolved that whatever else should be said of my style, from that time forth there should be no *emptiness* in it."[36]

But the facts suggest otherwise. Whatever Webster's intentions were of bettering himself by addressing "common men" in a more "intelligible" style,[37] he rather craftily transposes a review of his 1806 Federal Fourth of July oration at Concord,[38] perhaps attributable to Dennie that year, to Hanover and Dennie circa 1800. For Webster's Federal oration at Concord revolved around a similar partisan occasion and was excerpted in the *Dartmouth Gazette,* something

33 *An Oration, Delivered at Salisbury, New-Hampshire, July 4th, 1807* (Concord: George Hough, 1807), p. 4.

34 Summary of "Athens and the Great Spirits of Her Ripened Age," Address Delivered by Felton to the Phi Beta Kappa Society at Amherst College, 9 Aug., New York *Herald* (d), 13 Aug., 1854. Felton's remark likening Webster to orator-of-action Demosthenes, "extolled to the highest heavens of rhetorical eloquence" according to the *Herald* correspondent, seems to presage Richardson's observation that young Webster in the Hanover oration occasionally suggested "that power in which he surpasses Demosthenes, Cicero, and Burke," an allusion to simplicity incidentally not paraphrased by McMaster. Richardson, McMaster, *loc. cit.*

35 McMaster uses the qualifier "presumably," and Lathem "evidently," regarding Webster's reliance upon Dennie. A thorough perusal of the *Port-folio, Gazette of the United States,* for which no semiweekly edition was issued after Sept. 18, 1793, *Farmer's Museum,* and *Dartmouth Gazette,* not neglecting possibilities in any Dennie/Webster correspondence, fails to verify the complete accuracy of Webster's narrative as reported. McMaster, p. 58, n. 1; Edward Connery Lathem, "Daniel Webster's College Days," *Dartmouth Alumni Magazine,* 45, No. 1 (Oct. 1952), 22.

36 *American Whig Review,* 10 (Dec. 1852), 483. Felton skeptically writes that Webster was "mistaken" in asserting rather defensively about the Hanover oration, "It was printed, and I have a copy of it now—the only copy in existence."

37 *Ibid.*

38 "Review of Concord Oration," *Monthly Anthology and Boston Review,* 3 (Aug. 1806), 442. Obviously the content of this review does not precisely fit into the Dennie review criteria, since Webster had to make his "emptiness" rationale plausible to an Eliot Professor of Greek Literature at Har-

editor Davis did not do six years earlier. The Concord oration actually was the first Independence Day address Webster could reflect back on without any serious misgivings.

Why the transfer, however, in light of Webster's routine at Dartmouth? Although not published until 1803, the *Monthly Anthology and Boston Review* in which the Concord review appeared was the "literary paper" Dennie's *Gazette of the United States* was not. And the Federal Club at Dartmouth probably subscribed to the Philadelphia *Gazette* in 1800.[39] enabling member Webster to savor Dennie's accounts of the Andrews-Abercrombie Fourth of July controversy over Britain,[40] not to mention two satirical extracts from Dennie's former paper, the *Farmer's Museum or Literary Gazette* in Walpole, also relating to Britain.[41] Perhaps, almost unwittingly, this half-truth protected Webster's career from future inquiries about the original performance and text, encouraging romanticists to spawn more favorable interpretations of the Hanover oration and grant him the patriarch status his seventy odd years somehow denied.

The following text polishes Webster's diction,[42] and the elocutionary content of paragraphs 10 thru 13 will become slightly more evident when read along with the Mason oration in the Appendix.

---

vard, especially when Felton already sensed Webster's defensive error concerning the "only copy." Still, some parallels are discernible with reference to topics of praise and criticism, though not relating to "severe" comments from a knowledgeable critic which would create sympathy for youthful errors. In the Concord review, "emptiness" is a bit misleading, because simplicity (brevity, sententious) is unacceptable to the critic, while florid fancy used in moderation (purity), really not too far removed from several excesses at Hanover, merits the critic's approval. And the critic has vacillating praise for an absence of what went wrong at Hanover, not really being able to distinguish an acceptable "publick harangue" on the Fourth from unacceptable "rancorous colourings of party spirit, which are wholly inconsistent with true eloquence." Webster would have found these intellectual strains quite attractive after his Hanover experience. And assuming he made a conscious effort to acquire and master stylistic simplicity in his ceremonial oratory, such an influence may not have become apparent until after 1806, certainly not at Hanover in 1800 as critics tenaciously assert to bolster post-romantic points of view. In this regard, see Current's "good enough" statement of continuity and Nagel's emphasis upon the "lifetime philosophy" of a developing "high priest." Richard N. Current, *Daniel Webster and the Rise of National Conservatism* (Boston: Little Brown, 1955), p. 7; Paul C. Nagel, *This Sacred Trust: American Nationality, 1798-1898* (New York: Oxford University Press, 1971), p. 37.

39 Shattuck manuscript. Shattuck writes, "Among the aspiring spirits in the college a Federal Club had been formed to take newspapers and discuss politicks."

40 "More *Aurora* Falsehood," *Gazette of the United States and Daily Advertiser* (Philadelphia), 11 Oct., 1800; "Extract of a Letter from New-England," *Gazette of the U.S. and Dly Advertiser*, 9 Sept., 1800. Dennie writes regarding the Fourth and William J. Duane's *Aurora*, "It is natural, and it may be very proper, to view the fourth of July as a festal day, but it is unjust, illiberal, and impolitic, ostentatiously to indulge a sort of annual acrimony against England, with whom we are now connected by public ligaments, and by the more binding ties of national attachment, and mutual interest."

41 *Ibid.*, 30 Aug., 21 Oct., 1800.

42 Polishes, that is, compared with the standard Davis text rept. in facsim. form by *Bay State Monthly*, 1 (June 1884), iv ff., and *Granite Monthly*, 7 (July and Aug. 1884), 264 ff.

An oration delivered by Daniel Webster on the Fourth of July, 1800, at Dartmouth College (Hanover, N.H.), a pamphlet edition of the speech manuscript being published on the fourteenth by Moses Davis, editor of the local Dartmouth Gazette, *to which young Webster submitted articles under an "Icarus" pseudonym. Since Webster's speech manuscript is no longer extant, perhaps actually being "burned" by his own hand not long after publication of Davis's pamphlet, two sentences in the edited text below point up revision-process relationships with an "Icarus" essay in the* Gazette *for February 17, 1800. Other word relationships should likewise become evident to the reader. For example, an oralized "ball" in sentence 6 of paragraph 8 at first glance merely seems to connote an earthly globe, even if extending grandly "from pole to pole" when national commercial prosperity is considered. Yet when the national naval presence in* **"thunder** *around* **ball"** *is compared with* **"thunder** *of* **cannon"** *in the final sentence of paragraph 12, young Webster clearly has in mind a rhetorical cannon "ball" of sorts thunderously vindicating American honor, though the first definition (or generalized battle location) is by no means necessarily excluded from his diction. The true irony of such diction, oralized really beyond the brink of chauvinism, though not without some skill, is that correspondent Icarus's fledgling wings failed him in the heat of personal inadequacy when addressing the Hanover audience. Although Icarus's oration droned on, apparently without interruption, in the noon heat of a New-England meetinghouse on that summer day, young Webster suffered the unfortunate consequences of overdoing on a trial flight, perhaps even burning his manuscript when grasping mediocre implications in less than flattering appraisals from audience members. In reading through the text below, the reader will not exactly relish the task of testing this inner turmoil of aspirant Icarus against the romanticized story of early consistent success, parroted with a campaign type of adulation by many of Webster's contemporaries. For, whether prepared to strut his rhetoric on the local stage or not, the fact that young Webster came to understand his shortcomings at Hanover and Salisbury on the Fourth made him better aware of his capabilities as a speaker. Correspondent Icarus matured, phoenix-like, to use a worn metaphor from the Fourth, in the years after 1806. And not even tales of a Dartmouth diploma renounced at Commencement, inaccurate as they were, could eclipse the youthful lesson Webster learned at Hanover on the Fourth.*

1 Countrymen, brethren, and fathers, we are now assembled to celebrate an anniversary, ever to be held in dear remembrance by the sons of freedom. Nothing less than the birth of a nation—nothing less than the emancipation of three millions of people from the degrading chains of foreign dominion—is the event we commemorate! Twenty-four years have, this day, elapsed since united Columbia first raised the standard of Liberty and echoed the shouts of Independence. Those of you who were then reaping the iron harvest of the martial field—whose bosoms then palpitated for the honor of America—will (at this

time) experience a renewal of all that fervent patriotism—of all those indescribable emotions which then agitated your breast! As for [those of] us who were either then unborn, or not far enough advanced beyond the threshold of existence to engage in the grand conflict for Liberty, we now most cordially unite with you to greet the return of this joyous anniversary—to hail the day that gave us freedom- and hail the rising glories of our country! On occasions like this, you have heretofore been addressed from this stage on the nature, the origin, the expediency of civil government.—The field of political speculation has here been explored by persons, possessing talents to which the speaker of the day can have no pretensions. Declining, therefore, [to recite] a[nother] dissertation on the principles of civil polity, you will indulge me in [my task of] slightly sketching [up]on those events which have originated, nurtured, and raised to its present grandeur the empire of Columbia.

2 As no nation on the globe can rival us in the rapidity of our growth since the conclusion of the Revolutionary War—so none, perhaps, ever endured greater hardships and distresses than the people of this country previous to that period. We behold a feeble band of colonists, engaged in the arduous undertaking of a new settlement in the wilds of North America. Their civil liberty being mutilated, and the enjoyment of their religious sentiments denied them in the land that gave them birth, they fled their country—they braved the dangers of the then almost unnavigated ocean—and sought on the other side [of] the globe an asylum from the iron grasp of tyranny- and the more intolerable scourge of ecclesiastical persecution! But gloomy indeed was their prospect [of success] when [they] arrived on this side [of] the Atlantic. Scattered in detachments along a coast (immensely extensive) at a remove of more than three thousand miles from their friends on the Eastern continent, they were exposed to all those evils and endured all those difficulties to which human nature seems liable. Destitute of convenient habitations, the inclemencies of the seasons attacked them—the midnight beasts of prey prowled terribly around them—and the more portentous yell of savage fury incessantly assailed them! But the same undiminished confidence in Almighty God, which prompted the first settlers of this country to forsake the unfriendly climes of Europe, still supported them under all their calamities, and inspired them with [a] fortitude almost divine. Having a glorious issue to their labors now in prospect, they cheerfully endured the rigors of the climate—[they] pursued the savage beast to his remotest haunt —and stood undismayed in the dismal hour of Indian battle!

3 Scarcely were the infant settlements freed from those dangers which at first environed them, ere the clashing interests of France and Britain involved them anew in war. The colonists were now destined to combat with well-appointed, well-disciplined troops from Europe. And [all] the horrors of the tomahawk and the scalping knife were again renewed [for them]. But these frowns of fortune, distressing as they were, might have been met without a sigh and endured without a groan had not imperious Britain presumptuously arro-

gated to herself the glory of victories achieved by the bravery of American militia! "Louisburgh must be taken- Canada attacked- and a frontier of more than one thousand miles defended by untutored yeomanry—while *the honor of every conquest* must be ascribed to *an English army*!" But while Great Britain was thus ignominously stripping her colonies of their well-earned laurel, and triumphantly weaving it into the stupendous wreath of her own martial glories, she was unwittingly teaching them to value themselves and effectually to resist (in a future day) her unjust encroachments.

4 The pitiful tale of taxation now commences.—[And] The unhappy quarrel which issued in the dismemberment of the British empire has here its origin. [For] England, now triumphant over the united powers of France and Spain, is determined to reduce to the condition of slaves her American subjects. We might now display the legislatures of the several states (together with the general Congress) petitioning- praying- remonstrating—and like dutiful subjects humbly laying their grievances before the [British] throne. On the other hand, we could exhibit a British Parliament assiduously devising means to subjugate America—disdaining our petitions- trampling on our rights- and menacingly telling us, in language not to be misunderstood, "Ye *shall* be slaves!"—We could mention the haughty- tyrannical- perfidious Gage at the head of a standing army—we could show our brethren attacked and slaughtered at Lexington- our property plundered and destroyed at Concord!—Recollection can still pain us with the spiral flames of burning Charleston- the agonizing groans of aged parents- the shrieks of widows, orphans, and infants!—Indelibly impressed on our memories still live the dismal scenes of Bunker's awful mount[ain], the grand theater of New England bravery—where *slaughter* stalked- grimly triumphant—where relentless Britain saw her soldiers- the unhappy instruments of despotism- fallen in heaps beneath the nervous arm of injured freemen!—There the great Warren fought- and there alas he fell!—Valuing life only as it enabled him to serve his country, he freely resigned himself [to his fate]- a willing martyr in the cause of Liberty- and now lies encircled in the arms of glory!

Peace [be] to the patriot's shades—let no rude blast
Disturb the willow, that nods o'er his tomb,
Let orphan tears bedew his sacred urn,
And fame's loud trump proclaim the hero's name,
Far as the circuit of the spheres extends.

5 But, haughty Albion, thy reign shall soon be over;-thou shalt triumph no longer. Thine empire already reels and totters—thy laurels even now begin to wither- and thy fame decays! Thou hast at length roused the indignation of an insulted people—thine oppressions they deem no longer tolerable. [For] The 4th day of July, 1776, is now arrived. And America, manfully springing [up] from the torturing fangs of the British lion, now rises [equally] majestic in the pride of her [own] sovereignty—and bids her eagle elevate his wings!—The solemn

Declaration of Independence is now pronounced amidst crowds of admiring citizens by the supreme council of our nation, and received with the unbounded plaudits of a grateful people. [For] That was the hour when heroism was proved—when the souls of men were tried! It was then, ye venerable patriots—it was then you stretched [forth] the indignant arm and unitedly swore to be free! Despising such toys as subjugated empires, you then knew no middle fortune between Liberty and death. Firmly relying on the patronage of Heaven, unwarped in the resolution you had taken, you (then undaunted) met- engaged- defeated the gigantic power of Britain—and rose triumphant over the ruins of your enemies!—Trenton- Princeton- Bennington- and Saratoga were the successive theaters of your victories!—And the utmost bounds of Creation are [now] the limits to your fame.—The sacred fire of freedom, then enkindled in your breasts, shall be perpetuated through[out] the long descent of future ages—and burn with undiminished fervor in the bosoms of millions yet unborn!

6 Finally—to close the sanguinary conflict- to grant America the blessings of an honorable peace- and clothe her heroes with laurels—Cornwallis- at whose feet the kings and princes of Asia have since thrown their diadems- was compelled to submit to the sword of our father, Washington!—The great drama is now completed—our Independence is now acknowledged- and the hopes of our enemies are blasted forever!—Columbia is now seated in the forum of nations, and the empires of the world are lost in the bright effulgence of her glory. Thus, friends and citizens, did the kind hand of [an] overruling Providence conduct us- through toils, fatigues, and dangers- to Independence and peace. If piety be the rational exercise of the human soul- if religion be not a chimera- and if the vestiges of heavenly assistance are clearly traced in those events which mark the annals of our nation, it becomes us on this day- in consideration of the great things which the Lord has done for us- to render the tribute of unfeigned thanks to that God, who superintends the universe and holds aloft the scale that weighs the destinies of nations! The conclusion of the Revolutionary War did not conclude the great achievements of our countrymen. Their military character was then, indeed, sufficiently established. But the time was coming which should prove their political sagacity.

7 [For] No sooner was peace restored with England- the first grand article of which was the acknowledgement of our Independence- than the old system of confederation,-dictated at first by necessity, and [actually] adopted for the purposes of the moment,-was found inadequate to the government of an extensive empire. Under a full conviction of this [shortcoming], we then saw the people of these states engaged in a transaction which is undoubtedly the greatest approximation towards human perfection the political world [has] ever yet experienced. And which, perhaps, will forever stand on the history of mankind without a parallel! A great republic, composed of different states whose interest (in all respects) could not be perfectly compatible, then came deliberately forward—discarded one system of government- and adopted another without the

loss of one man's blood. There is not a single government now existing in Europe which is not based in usurpation, and established (if established at all) by the sacrifice of thousands. But, in the adoption of our present system of jurisprudence, we see the powers necessary for government voluntarily springing from the people—their *only proper* origin, and directed to the public good—their *only proper* object! With [a] peculiar [sense of] propriety, we may now felicitate ourselves on that happy form of mixed government under which we live. [For] The advantages resulting to the citizens of the Union from the operation of the federal Constitution are utterly incalculable. And the day when it was received by a majority of the states shall stand on the catalogue of American anniversaries—second to none but the birthday of [our] Independence!

8 In consequence of the adoption of our present system of government, and the virtuous manner in which it has been administered by a Washington and an Adams, we are (this day) in the enjoyment of peace while war devastates Europe. We can now sit down beneath the shadow of the olive—while her cities blaze- her streams run purple with blood- and her fields glitter [like] a forest of Bayonets![1] The citizens of America can (this day) throng [into] the temples of freedom, and renew their oaths of fealty to Independence—while Holland- our once sister republic- is erased from the catalogue of nations—while Venice is destroyed- Italy ravaged—and [while] Switzerland,-the once happy- the once united- the once flourishing Switzerland,-lies bleeding at every pore!—No ambitious foe dares now invade our country—no standing army now endangers our Liberty!—Our commerce, though subject in some degree to the depredations of the belligerent powers, is extended from pole to pole!—And our navy, though just [now] emerging from nonexistence, shall soon vouch for the safety of our merchantmen—and bear the thunder of freedom around the [cannon's] ball! Fair Science, too, holds [forth] her gentle empire amongst us. And almost innumerable altars are raised to her divinity from Brunswick to Florida. Yale, Providence, and Harvard now grace our land. And Dartmouth, towering majestic above the groves which encircle her, now inscribes her glory on the registers of fame!—Oxford and Cambridge, those oriental stars of literature, [surely] shall now be lost while the bright sun of American Science displays his broad circumference in uneclipsed radiance!

9 Pleasing, indeed, were it [for me] here to dilate on the future grandeur of America. But we forbear—and pause for a moment to drop the tear of affection over the graves of our departed warriors. Their names should be mentioned on every anniversary of Independence, [so] that the youth of each successive generation may learn not to value life [more] when held in competition with their country's safety. Wooster, Montgomery, and Mercer fell bravely in battle, and their ashes are now entombed on the fields that witnessed their

---

1 These three "her" references are to Europe.

valor. Let their exertions in our country's cause be remembered while Liberty [still] has an advocate- or gratitude a place in the human heart! Greene, the immortal hero of the Carolinas, has since gone down to the grave,-loaded with honors and high in the estimation of his countrymen. The courageous Putnam has long [since] slept with his fathers. And Sullivan and Cilley, New Hampshire's veteran sons, are *no more* numbered with the living. With hearts penetrated by unutterable grief, we are at length constrained to ask, "Where is our Washington!-where the hero who led us [on] to victory!-where the man who gave us freedom!—Where is he who headed our feeble army when destruction threatened us—who came upon our enemies like the storms of winter- and scattered them like leaves before the Borean blast!—Where, Oh my country, is thy political saviour!-where, Oh humanity, thy favorite son!"—[And] The solemnity of this assembly- the **lamenta**tions of the American people will answer, "**Alas**,- **he is** now **no more**;- the Mighty is fallen!"[2]

10 Yes, Americans, your Washington is gone; he is now consigned to dust and "sleeps in dull, cold marble." *The man*—who never felt a wound but when it pierced his country—who never groaned but when fair freedom bled—is now forever silent!—Wrapped in the shroud of death, the dark dominions of the grave long since [have] received him, and he rests in undisturbed repose. Vain were the attempt to express our loss—vain the attempt to describe the feelings of our souls!—Though months have rolled away since he left this terrestrial orb and sought the shining worlds on high, yet the sad event is *still remembered* with increased sorrow!—The hoary-headed patriot of '76 *still tells* the mournful story to the listening infant—'til the loss of his country touches his heart- and patriotism fires his breast!—The aged matron *still laments* the loss of *the man*—beneath whose banners her husband has fought- or her son has fallen!—[And] At [such mention of] the name of Washington, the sympathetic tear *still glistens* in the eye of every youthful hero! Nor does the tender sigh yet cease to heave in the fair bosom of [many of] Columbia's daughters.

Farewell, Oh Washington, a long farewell!
Thy country's tears embalm thy memory;
Thy virtues challenge immortality;
Impressed on grateful hearts, thy name shall live,
'Til dissolution's deluge drown the world!

11 Although we must feel the keenest sorrow at the demise of our Washington, yet we console ourselves with the reflection that his virtuous compatriot- his worthy successor,-the firm- the wise- the inflexible Adams,-*still survives*!—Elevated by the voice of his country to the supreme executive

---

2 The prior Icarus fragment reads "it is true, **alas**! most **lamenta**bly true, that **Washington,** the great political cement, **is no more**!"

magistracy, he constantly adheres to her essential interests—and with steady hand **a** CONFRONT[S] **b** draws the disguising veil from ☆ the intrigues of foreign **a** POLITICIANS **b** enemies- ☆ and the **a** DESIGNS **b** plots ☆ of domestic foes. Having the honor of America always in view, never fearing (when wisdom dictates) to stem the impetuous torrent of popular resentment, he stands [alone] amidst the fluctuations of party and the explosions of faction—unmoved as Atlas "While storms and tempests thunder on its brow,/ And oceans break their billows at its feet." Yet all the vigilance of our Executive, and all the wisdom of our Congress, have not been sufficient to prevent this country from being in some degree agitated by the convulsions of Europe. But why shall every quarrel on the other side [of] the Atlantic interest us in its issue!—Why shall the rise (or depression) of every party there produce *here* a corresponding vibration!—Was this continent designed as a mere satellite to the other! Has not Nature *here* wrought all her operations on her broadest scale? [And] Where are the Mississippis and the Amazons- the Alleghenies and the Andes of Europe, Asia, or Africa? The natural superiority of America clearly indicates that it was designed to be inhabited by a nobler race of men—possessing a superior form of government- *superior* patriotism- *superior* talents- and *superior* virtues!—Let then the nations of the East vainly waste their strength in destroying each other!—Let them aspire at conquest and contend for dominion 'til their continent is deluged in blood!—But let none,-however elated by victory, however proud of triumphs,- ever presume to intrude on the neutral station assumed by our country!

12 Britain, twice humbled for her aggressions, has at length been taught to respect us. But France, once our ally, has dared to insult us. She has violated her obligations—she has depredated our commerce—she has abused our government- and riveted the chains of bondage on our unhappy fellow citizens!—Not content with ravaging and depopulating the fairest countries of Europe—not yet satiated with [all] the contortions of expiring republics- [all] the convulsive agonies of subjugated nations- and [all] the groans of her own slaughtered citizens—she has spouted her fury across the Atlantic!—And the stars and stripes of Independence have almost been attacked in *our* harbors!—When we have demanded reparation [for wrongs done others], she has told us, "Give us *your money*- and we will give you *peace*!"—Mighty nation- magnanimous republic,-let her fill her coffers from those towns and cities which she has plundered—and grant *peace* (if she can) to the shades of those millions whose death she has caused! But Columbia stoops not to tyrants; her sons will never cringe to France. [For] neither a supercilious, five-headed Directory nor the gasconading pilgrim of Egypt will ever dictate terms [of surrender] to sovereign America!—The thunder of our cannon shall insure the [total] performance of our treaties- and fulminate destruction [up]on Frenchmen—'til [many an] old ocean is crimsoned with blood and gorged with [the bodies of French] pirates!

13 It becomes us, on whom the defense of our country will ere long devolve, this day most seriously to reflect on the duties incumbent upon us.

[For] Our ancestors bravely snatched expiring Liberty from the grasp of Britain—whose touch [still] is *poison.* Shall we now consign it to France—whose embrace is *death*! We have seen our fathers, in the days of Columbia's trouble, assume the rough habiliments of war- and seek [out] the hostile field. Too full of sorrow to speak, we have seen them wave a last [fond] farewell to a disconsolate- a woe-stung family—we have seen them return,-worn down with fatigue, and scarred with wounds,—or we have seen them perhaps *no more*!—For us they fought- for us they bled- for us they conquered!—Shall we (their descendants) now basely disgrace our lineage- and pusillanimously disclaim the legacy bequeathed us!—Shall we pronounce the sad valediction to freedom- and immolate Liberty on the altars our fathers have raised to her? "No!"—The response of a nation is "No!"—Let it be [so] *registered* in the archives of Heaven! —Ere the religion we profess and the privileges we enjoy are sacrificed at the shrines of despots and demagogues, let the pillars of Creation tremble—let world be wrecked on world- and systems rush to ruin—let the sons of Europe be vassals—let her hosts of nations be a vast congregation of slaves!—But let us who are this day *free,*- whose hearts are [as] yet unappalled, and whose right arms are [as] yet nerved for war,- assemble before the hallowed temple of Columbian freedom—and swear to the God of our fathers "*to preserve* it secure- or *die* at its portals!"

Chapter 2

Richard Rush's Fourth of July Oration, 1812

Two factors led chairman John P. Van Ness and the Committee of Arrangements,[1] meeting at Davis's Hotel on June 16 for the "usual and necessary" celebration program,[2] to settle on Richard Rush as the orator who might best "promote unanimity and harmony" on behalf of President James Madison and another war against Britain.[3] A war declared on Thursday, a scant two days after the Committee met, but perhaps even more significant, the very same Thursday Rush's acceptance of the Committee's assignment for the Fourth formally was announced.[4]

Factor one leading to Rush's selection by the Committee obviously centered on his ethos as a speaker. Head comptroller under Albert Gallatin in the Treasury, Rush had acquired a working knowledge of American grievances, countersigning departmental warrants and communicating policy to federal district attorneys and customs collectors so as to ensure uniform judicial and commercial compliance with various nonimportation laws passed by Congress.[5] A body which, incidentally, updated the 1809 and 1811 laws yet again on the

---

1 Nine men assisted chairman Van Ness on the Committee: Joseph Gales Jr., secretary, and vice-presidents John Davidson, James H. Blake, Robert Brent (replaced by John Graham, shortly after the meeting of Tuesday-16 June), Charles Carroll, Thomas Tingey, Walter Jones Jr., Elias B. Caldwell, and Edward Coles. *National Intelligencer* (tw, Washington D.C.), 20 June and 2 July, 1812.

2 *National Intelligencer* (tw, WDC), 16 June, 1812.

3 *National Intelligencer* (tw), 20 June, 1812. For a comparison of Rush's harmonious purpose with that of Timothy Dwight at New Haven, see Paul C. Nagel, *This Sacred Trust: American Nationality, 1798-1898* (New York: Oxford University Press, 1971), p. 27.

4 *National Intelligencer* (tw), 18 June, 1812.

5 WDC, 26 April, 1812, *RR* to Charles Jared Ingersoll, Philadelphia, Ingersoll Papers, Historical Society of Pennsylvania (Philadelphia); Rush, "Circulars to District Attornies of the United States,

sixth after Rush spoke. A bureaucratic official, able to back up idle rhetoric with a personal knowledge of conditions presumably justifying more than unorganized skirmishing against Britain, what Rush termed "a ground of dignified justification,"[6] really impressed the Committee as most apt to inspire and persuade Administration partisans, if not lukewarm Federalist congressmen. Although the hall of the House of Representatives could only be used from ten o'clock until noon, and subject to last-minute congressional change,[7] Rush, for Committee members, was one of a very few bureaucrats able to address the question of why the United States need have been so illy prepared to wage war against Europe's major maritime power. A realistic patriotic premise, which had made the vote in favor of declaring war rather close in both the House and Senate on June 18.[8]

A second factor inclining the Committee toward Rush, and quite decisive in their selection, involved a manuscript for an essay, tentatively titled "No Longer Colonies" and labeled as "anti-Brittania" in focus (by lessening war's horrors, Federalists who ran from the issue might reconsider their position), which the comptroller had been composing since mid-May in consultation with President Madison, Gallatin in Treasury, and Attorney-General William Pinkney.[9] Rush left little doubt that some propaganda tract was needed to consolidate support for a congressional declaration of hostilities, when sounding out friend Charles Jared Ingersoll on the pamphlet idea late in April. He defined the 32-expounder, reasoned rationale that, Administration supporters at least might hope, would rival propagandists Thomas Paine and William Cobbett: "Call the pamphlet 'No longer Colonies.' It will be a simple, appropriate, dignified name. Under it, you may bring [in] pride, sovereignty, nationality, republican-

---

dated 15 May, 5 Oct., and 16 Oct.," *National Intelligencer* (tw), 20 Oct. and 3 Dec., 1812; Rush, "Circular to Collectors, with general Oct. date," *Intelligencer* (tw), 15 Oct., 1812. Historical Society of Pennsylvania (Philadelphia) cited hereafter as PaHi.

6 WDC, 9 July, 1812, *RR* to John Binns, Philadelphia, Simon Gratz Collection-PaHi.

7 *National Intelligencer* (tw), 2 and 4 July, 1812.

8 Fon W. Boardman Jr., *America and the Virginia Dynasty, 1800-1825* (New York: Henry Z. Walck, 1974), pp. 36-38. Although a juvenile title neglecting to mention the Rush oration, Boardman ably relates inadequate preparation for war to the closeness of the congressional vote.

9 WDC, 29 April, 23 and 24 May, 2 and 17 July, 1812, *RR* to Charles Jared Ingersoll, Philadelphia, Ingersoll Papers-PaHi. Rush began composing "No Longer Colonies" in earnest no later than 21 May, when friend Ingersoll read a pro-Administration address to a First Congressional District rally in the yard of the Pennsylvania statehouse (text in *National Intelligencer* [tw], 26 May). And Rush's attitude toward the Ingersoll address reveals the rationale behind the genesis of his own "Colonies" manuscript: "It has given already a visible impulse to publick feeling here, and must, will, whip up the sluggish movements of the government itself .... It is a grand intellectual explosion, which, taking place in the centre [of the republican party], will reverberate to the extremities. Think what an example it will be to other meetings—which it will be sure to create, and to which it will impart the tone of fervid patriotism and a magnanimous boldness. The open language which it speaks is above all praise, and happily rebukes the mealy-mouthed restraint of Washington in times like these .... For it is things even more than words; it is logick, all over, as well as rhetorick; the scope of its argument takes in everything, yet happily, forcibly, luminously, condensed. It is fuel as well as blaze, consuming while it crackles."

ism; thoughts that breathe and words that burn. You may, and you can, thunder and lighten- be all fire and eloquence; and yet be chaste and classic, argumentative (that is, by single strokes), solid and convincing . . . A style like Cobbett's or Paine's would suit admirably, but that is not your's, and you must not attempt it. But be plain, avoid unusual words and *involution* of sentence [structure], as hundreds of plain people must read it, or have it read to them. 'Common Sense' was once read from the pulpit by a clergyman."[10]

But acceptance of the Committee's assignment meant that Rush had to trim the "Colonies" manuscript, then some 50 or 60 imaginary printed pages long and taking an "insufferable" two hours to recite, down to a more manageable hour's delivery time.[11] The revision process, of which unfortunately no evidence remains, surely must have been vexing and formidable. Primarily because the orator now was compelled to do the week's concentrated labor in cutting that he had resolved to avoid by gradually writing the master "Colonies" piece over a two-month period.[12] So extensive was the cutting procedure, in fact, that even after producing a "shockingly mangled" oration draft via "such erasing, transposing, altering, interlining, abbreviating, [and] blotting [as] you never saw," Rush's patience began to wear a bit thin when still having to recopy the speech

10 WDC, 26 April and 2 Aug. 1812, *RR* to Ingersoll, Philadelphia, Ingersoll Papers-PaHi. Orator Rush, though not completely successful, endeavored to motivate friend Ingersoll to write the tract he had in mind by summoning some "Lighten[ing]"-type argument: "If done better than I could do it, it would flash like light from above. It would hit between wind and water; never did a stronger opportunity invite, call, implore. It might be made a second 'Common Sense' . . . . Trust to me for [publicizing] its success, and I too shall have half the merit, as my father before me had in bringing out [Paine's] 'Common Sense'." Ingersoll may well have repeated the allusion to Paine taking up father Benjamin's idea for a tract, when urging total victory in short order over Britain at Philadelphia on the Fourth: "The war of the American Revolution was said by one of its principal supporters to be a *bold* speculation. And perhaps the present conflict is not less so. But, [when] in danger and in doubt, to be *bold* is always the best policy." And he discerned the same propagandistic boldness, when excerpting the "elaborate and excellent" Rush oration for John Binns's *Democratic Press:* "Mr. Rush takes a *bold,* nervous, and striking view . . . , exposes in strong but dignified language . . . . Mr. Rush speaks out in a language which, we trust, will become more familiar, 'til at last, if we may be indulged in the figure, it shall be the political vernacular of North America . . . . The whole speech is remarkable for plain vigorous diction, apposite and pungent illustrations, decided but decorous denunciation of American provocations to war, and just and sound political sentiments." Indeed, orator Rush could be nothing but pleased that friend Ingersoll looked so favorably upon the bold rhetorical strategy, writing on 2 Aug. in this vein: "Nothing could have been better than what you said of it in the *Press.*" Ingersoll, *An Oration, Delivered at Mr. Harvey's Spring Garden, before A Very Numerous Meeting of Democratic Citizens, July 4, 1812* (Philadelphia: John Binns, 1812), p. 8. text first printed in Binns's *Democratic Press for the Country* (d), 7 July; "Ingersoll critique," *Democratic Press* (d) and *Press for the Country* (d), 24 July, 1812.

11 WDC, 2 July, 1812, *RR* to Ingersoll, Philadelphia, Ingersoll Papers-PaHi. Two hours, of course, was the total elapsed time specified by the Committee when requesting use of Representatives' Hall for the morning of the Fourth.

12 WDC, 26 and 29 April, 1812, *RR* to Ingersoll, Philadelphia, Ingersoll Papers-PaHi. Perhaps none too eager to abandon "indispensable business and studies" in the comptroller's office, much less peremptorily for a week of intensive composition ("rasp, measure, and polish"), Rush dealt quite guardedly with the "No Longer Colonies" proposal when writing friend Ingersoll. In fact, late in April, his hypothetical acceptance of composing the tract himself was enough mocking and irresponsible to amount to a rejection: "I declare that, could I but escape to Bladensburgh [Md.] for a week, I would strain my little utmost, day and night, to fire it off."

draft into readable form only two days prior to the Fourth.[13] He doubtless was spurred on in recopying the draft, by the realization that President Madison himself had suggested the proportional advantages inherent in making a call to glorious deeds animatedly confirm the concept of a "genuine, popular, democratical government." And with Madison present in the audience, bureaucrat Rush could anticipate being complimented at the White House evening reception, held after a Committee banquet in Tench Ringgold's Ropewalk, for inspiring to "great deeds" and "prospects of glory" on the national anniversary.[14]

As if the orator did not have difficulty enough in reading through the recopied oration draft, after Justice Gabriel Duvall recited the Declaration of Independence,[15] chairman Van Ness and his "zealous" Committee never really did accomplish getting the oration printed before Congress adjourned. Indeed, the printer, not necessarily affiliated with secretary Gales of the Committee, did not start work on it until the ninth. But even then, smarting under procedures usually discriminating against sloppy novice orations ever being printed, Rush remained trapped in the cutting process—"living by the press" and interpreting still more revisions for the hapless compositor. All the while, reflecting upon how vastly improved the procedure might be if John Binns in Philadelphia had brought out an uncut "No Longer Colonies" text, leaving the orator free to speak without worrying about the "Colonies" tract being rendered any less oral or animated than Madison partisans desired.[16] By the seventeenth, one day before Roger C. Weightman in Washington City and Joseph Milligan in Georgetown began retailing the oration pamphlet for 25 cents per single copy,[17] the printer's work was completed, allowing orator Rush to mail out complimentary copies.[18]

13 WDC, 2 July, 1812, *RR* to Ingersoll, Philadelphia, Ingersoll Papers-PaHi; WDC, 9 July, 1812, *RR* to John Binns, Philadelphia, Simon Gratz Collection-PaHi.

14 WDC, 29 April 1812, *RR* to Ingersoll, Philadelphia, Ingersoll Papers-PaHi; "Letter to editor John Binns, datelined WDC-5 July," *Democratic Press* (d, Philadelphia), 8 July, 1812; WDC, 17 July, 1812, *RR* to Madison, White House, Gratz Collection-PaHi. The theme, in which the President saw such advantages, really pervades much of the oration, and is rather succinctly stated in paragraphs 32 and 33.

15 *National Intelligencer* (tw), 2 and 8 July, 1812.

16 WDC, 9 July, 1812, *RR* to Binns, Philadelphia, Gratz Collection-PaHi; WDC, 2 Aug., 1812, *RR* to Ingersoll, Philadelphia, Ingersoll Papers-PaHi. The orator's attitude, regarding style, impact, and Binns printing the uncut tract, can be glimpsed in his letter to the editor of the *Democratic Press* on the ninth: "I, too, made a speech: 'a long talk'- dry enough, I fear. My aim was to give it the texture of a special plea, without it[s] coldness . . . . I should have wished you to publish it; but I am in the hands of the Committee, of course . . . . They still urge me [on], and you know enough of authors to infer that this will not offend."

17 *National Intelligencer* (tw), 18 July, 1812.

18 WDC, 17 July, 1812, *RR to Ingersoll, Philadelphia, Ingersoll Papers-PaHi; WDC, 17 July, 1812, RR* to James Madison, White House, Gratz Collection-PaHi.

Three Federalists are known to have received copies, autographed with customary honored "respects" from the orator. Rush's own father, Benjamin, treasurer of the United States Mint and not out-of-touch with policy in the comptroller's office, was irritated that his son chose to include the Gadsden and Hancock anecdotes from personal family letters in paragraphs 35 and 36 of the oration. Friend Ingersoll associating the quoted martial ardor of merchants Christopher Gadsden and John Hancock with Benjamin's "surviving-patriot" name could hardly be prevented. But permitting the reading public at large to speculate about and possibly undermine Benjamin's noncommittal stance on the war, what the orator's bias rather neatly described as his father's determination "to *draw in* [away] *from* all [persons] that may *draw down upon* him any [partisan] strife," was an eventuality son Richard probably failed to reckon with, when cutting "No Longer Colonies" for the Committee.[19]

John Adams was kind enough to applaud the Hancock anecdote for decorum's sake, orator Rush readily conceding that the oration expressed a rationale at odds with the elder Adams's liberal Federalist views.[20] Yet Adams's Brahmin leanings, tears and tenderness being part of a cultivated gentleman's excited "sensibility" on the Fourth, never truly could accept merchant Hancock for the benevolently generous republican both Rushes, father and son, seemingly characterized the ostentatious millionaire as being. Indeed, the elder Adams's subdued response became rather obvious, when bringing up a Revolutionary veteran's "odd" appraisal of the orator, which, Brahmin that he was, Adams could not take too seriously. Was the former President, firmly ensconced in a gentry class he respected, supposed to rush into accepting the logical consequences of Rush's "Colonies" argument, exclaiming with the deluded nostalgia of some aged officer, "This young gentleman makes my old blood fly through my veins, as it did when I was young?"[21]

Rush had to admit that such compliments were "merely constrained" at

---

19 WDC, 2 Aug., 1812, *RR* to Ingersoll, Philadelphia, Ingersoll Papers-PaHi. For example, editor Isaac W. Hill of the *New Hampshire Patriot*, though not bothering to identify the source of the anecdotes, did utilize them to inveigh: "Let the sordid souls who advocate peace on the most degrading terms of servility—let those who terrify our women and men/children with the story of our towns being burnt [down] about our ears, and who tell us we ought to submit to the most ignominious, slavish bondage [in order] to preserve them,—reflect on *the magnanimous declaration of Gadsden, the disinterested patriotism of Hancock*, and blush for their coward, corrupted hearts." *N-H Patriot* (Concord), 4 Aug., 1812.

20 *Ibid.:* WDC, 18 July, 1812, *RR* to Adams, Quincy Mass., in *Pennsylvania Magazine of History and Biography*, 60 (Oct. 1936), 434. Rush confided his recognition of the elder Adams's true beliefs to friend Ingersoll: "If *I* drove J[ohn]. A[dams]. from the Capitol, I fain would hope it was by *point-blank shot*. But to show you that I bear him no personal gall (more especially, as he visits us when here), while I have so plainly fired away at all his sentiments, I have sent him a copy of my logical bombardment, with a polite note saying that I know with *what candor liberal minds receive all sentiments, though opposite from their own*! Now this he *must* take politely, however he may *feel*."

21 Quincy, 31 July, 1812, Adams to RR, WDC, in *Pennsylvania Magazine of History and Biography*, 60 (Oct. 1936), 435. The elder Adams concluded his response to Rush's oration on a somewhat equivocal note, "I dare not say, even to you at this time, what I think and what I know."

best.[22] And the third Federalist to be sent a copy, Virginia congressman James Breckenridge, a man of "mongrel uncertain mind"[23] whom Rush thought incompetent to write the "No Longer Colonies" tract, likewise forwarded apparently flattering comments, which friend Ingersoll subsequently may have misplaced.[24]

Seven Administration supporters are known to have received pamphlets. Among them, Madison, Gallatin, and Pinkney. Pinkney even turning down an appointment as Baltimore-celebration orator to be present in the hall of the House, with other Cabinet members, when Rush spoke.[25] Friend Ingersoll received a hefty parcel of copies to distribute in Philadelphia (Rush had "some qualms" about "too many separate packages" disrupting the mails),[26] though *Democratic-Press* editor John Binns did receive the single copy via the mail which the orator had promised.[27] A number of copies from the Ingersoll parcel were quite possibly consigned to area bookstores, at the same two-bits price prevailing in Washington. Three Philadelphia shops did in fact retail the oration. Bradford and Inskeep, 4 Third Street,[28] and Moses Thomas, 52 Chestnut Street,[29] both starting sales on the twenty-first. With Birch and Small, 37 Second Street, carrying it nine days later.[30]

As former President supporting Madison on the war issue. Thomas Jefferson received his copy of the oration in the mail on the twenty-third.[31] But the titular Democratic Republican realistically might at least hope that a Satanically weakened mother country was at the heart of Rush's "Colonies" reasoning: "Every day's history proves, more and more, the wisdom and salutary result of

22 WDC, 19 Aug., 1812, *RR* to Ingersoll, Philadelphia, Ingersoll Papers-PaHi.

23 WDC, 29 April, 1812, *RR* to Ingersoll, Philadelphia, Ingersoll Papers-PaHi.

24 WDC, 19 Aug., 1812, *RR* to Ingersoll, Philadelphia, Ingersoll Papers-PaHi. Rush did not value Breckenridge's penmanship very highly, either: "Breckenridge might as well have paid [me] compliments in Slavonic or Erse [Irish], as [in] his own handwriting, and therefore . . . most judiciously employed an amanuensis . . . . He knows he can't write a line that anybody can read."

25 *Federal Gazette and Baltimore Daily Advertiser*, 27 June and 1 July, 1812; WDC, 17 July, 1812, *RR* to Madison, White House, Gratz Collection-PaHi; Ernest L. Hettich, comp., "Exhibition Commemorating the 150th Anniversary of the Adoption of the Declaration of Independence, 1776-1926," *Bulletin of the New York Public Library*, 31 (Nov. 1927), 935.

26 WDC, 17 July, 1812, *RR* to Ingersoll, Philadelphia, Ingersoll Papers-PaHi.

27 WDC, 9 July, 1812, *RR* to Binns, Philadelphia, Gratz Collection-PaHi.

28 *Freeman's Journal and Philadelphia Mercantile Advertiser* (d), 21 July, 1812.

29 *Aurora, General Advertiser* (Philadelphia) and *Democratic Press* (d), 21 July, 1812.

30 *Poulson's American Daily Advertiser* (Philadelphia), 30 July, 1812.

31 WDC, 18 July, 1812, *RR* to Jefferson, Monticello Va., Thomas Jefferson Coolidge Collection, Massachusetts Historical Society (Boston).

that measure [Declaration of Independence written by himself]—by developements [daily occurring] of the degeneracy of the British nation, and of its rapid decline towards some awful catastrophe, from which [fate] their injustice and the favor of Heaven have separated us."[32] And after forwarding a specimen pamphlet to editor Isaac W. Hill in Concord, New Hampshire,[33] Rush could not object to the oration pamphlet being reissued at half-price by Hill's *Patriot* on the first of September, with even greater savings given to Administration partisans buying in quantity (12½ cents when buying one copy only, 8⅓ cents per dozen copies purchased, and 6 cents per hundred).[34]

The Democratic-Republican press publicized the orator's role, equating the summary effectiveness of a "master stroke" with a partisan brand of patriotic zeal, never nearly as "uniform" or "disinterested" as artistic objectivity properly demanded.[35] Pro-Administration Washington papers had to make the oration "elegant" and "animated" enough to fit into "a sublime spectacle." Son Richard necessarily was cast as following in father Benjamin's greater reputation, and addressing a grass-roots yeomanry which, assuming ceremony to be an extension of partisanly intense feeling, might not tolerate Federalist congressional opposition to Madison's war. The "son of *another patriot* of the Revolution" was, in effect, speaking out to "our constitutional rulers, the sons and disciples of Washington, Franklin, Adams, Hancock, Mercer, and the other *fathers* of the nation, to an audience . . . composed, as it were, of *the United States.*"[36]

An anonymous correspondent wrote a graphic promotional critique for John Binns's Philadelphia *Democratic Press*, pitting the orator's pathos, made more partisanly righteous by a marked response from the ladies, against detestable opposition to the war, as epitomized by Federalist congressman John Randolph from Virginia. After characterizing Rush's immediate audience as a "mass of intellect" worthy to honor "Athens or Rome in their proudest days," the correspondent partisanly proceeded to heighten the response of "brilliant" ladies and military escorts: "There was great expectation from Mr. Rush, but in sober truth he distanced all expectation. Every bosom swelled with indignation, expanded with patriotism, or glowed with emulation at the will of the orator. Aye, and many a beauteous eye was wet [with tears] at the pathetic

32 Monticello, 2 Aug., 1812, Jefferson to RR, WDC, Coolidge Collection, Massachusetts Historical Society.

33 *New-Hampshire Patriot* (Concord), 4 Aug., 1812.

34 *New-Hampshire Patriot*, 1 Sept., 1812. The reissue advertisement applied a promotional label of "excellent" to Rush's oration.

35 WDC, 6 June, 1812, *RR* to Albert Gallatin, WDC, Gallatin Papers, New-York Historical Society (NY City); *New-Hampshire Patriot*, 4 Aug., 1812.

36 *National Intelligencer* (tw), 8 July, pooled account also in *Universal Gazette*, 10 July, 1812.

recital of our country's wrongs. Federalism, and even John Randolph of Roanoke, were riveted with attention, if not transfixed by some 'compunctious visitings of conscience.' Our female friends were so fascinated by the manner and the matter, that they regretted when the oration was concluded, and declared as a common sentiment that they could have listened for another hour with delight."[37]

The correspondent's "fervent" partisan line was rather obvious to Henry K. Helmbold of the satirical Philadelphia *Tickler*, who joined the Washington press in being concerned about some impact beyond the immediate audience. An oration on the Fourth during wartime, for gallant satirist Helmbold, supposedly stirred men to take up arms against the enemy, and unredressed American grievances were not to be groaned about by the weaker sex "from one extremity of the Tiber to the other."[38] And in an attempt to increase the orator's secondary audience, later in July, Administration editors like William J. Duane of the Philadelphia *Aurora* took pains to emphasize that suspension of the British Orders in Council on June 16 was a gesture as much "cunning perfidy" as Napoleon's Cadore letter, purporting to repeal the Berlin and Milan decrees.[39] Indeed, listing twenty grievances in support of Rush and war, editor Duane hawkishly took up friend Ingersoll's vision of total victory over Britain: "Montreal occupied, by the American flag before the 20th [of] September—the measure is practicable, and wants nothing but the will to accomplish it."[40]

Rush was quite contented with the publicity as he sorted through comments in some twenty-three letters and clippings on the nineteenth of August.[41] Yet he valued a partisan martial consensus more highly than any commemorative means, however "good" for a divided republic-at-war the "Colonies" comparison actually might prove. Madison and the Democratic Republicans as a political party were beneficiaries on a national occasion, in Rush's eyes at least, of what seemed more a political tract partisanly masquerading as oral panegyric: "The republican part of the nation just wanted such a little thing at the moment I threw it out, which has occasioned it to be received with more than due éclat . . . . It is a fact to mark the rising spirit of the times. At any 'common' season, a pamphlet of ten times its merit would not excite half its interest."[42]

37 "Letter of 5 July," *Press* (d), 8 July, 1812.

38 *The Tickler*, 20 July, 1812.

39 *Aurora, General Advertiser* and *United States Gazette for the Country* (Philadelphia), 30 July, 1812; *New-Hampshire Patriot*, 4 Aug., 1812.

40 *Aurora, General Advertiser*, 30 July, 1812; Ingersoll, *Oration Delivered at Mr. Harvey's*, pp. 5-6.

41 WDC, 19 Aug., 1812, *RR* to Ingersoll, Philadelphia, Ingersoll Papers-PaHi.

42 WDC, 2 Aug., 1812, *RR* to Ingersoll, Philadelphia, Ingersoll Papers-PaHi.

Still, with the flowering of the orator's governmental service, father Benjamin's coattails gave way to critics mentioning son Richard's own innate patriotism and ability, the oration as a "*large* addition" to a "*rising* reputation" rather remarkably demonstrating an unsurpassed "*perfect* knowledge" of the "*whole* subject" of impressment.[43] And, moreover, critics in retrospect identified orator Rush more with a nonpartisanly nationalistic occasion, the oration being the "masterly production" or "patriotic model" able to bring across anti-British "national classicality" for less factious schoolchildren.[44] The reader may care to compare Rush's stance with Cadwell's advocacy of the divisive Mexican War in the Appendix.

---

43 "Biographical sketch of Rush," *United States Magazine and Democratic Review*, 7 (April 1840), 305.

44 *Ibid.*; John J. Harrod, *The Academical Reader* (Baltimore, 1831), cited in Ruth Miller Elson, *Guardians of Tradition: American Schoolbooks of the Nineteenth Century* (Lincoln: University of Nebraska Press, 1964), p. 109; Passage cited in n. 43 paraphrased into "Rush obituary," New York *Herald* in *Butte Democrat* (Oroville, Cal.), 3 Sept., 1859.

An oration delivered by Richard Rush on the Fourth of July, 1812, in the Hall of the House of Representatives (D.C.), two pamphlet editions subsequently being issued—the first on the eighteenth by the Committee of Arrangements through an unidentified Washington printer, and the second on September 1 at Concord (N.H.) by Isaac W. and Walter R. Hill, an edition placing partial segments of the text in proper order after their insertion in Isaac's New-Hampshire Patriot *on August 4, 11, and 18. The complete text of the first edition was reprinted in the* Aurora, General Advertiser *(d. Philadelphia) on the twenty-fourth and twenty-fifth, the triweekly* National Intelligencer *(D.C.) on the twenty-eighth, and the* Universal Gazette *(also D.C.) on the thirty-first. The* Democratic Republican *(Walpole, N.H.) of August 10 and the* North Star *(Danville, Vt.) of August 15 reprinted extracts from the* Patriot *issue of August 4, prior to their organization into the second edition, the* Star *reprinting Isaac Hill's introductory commentary and the full excerpt.*

1 Sensibly as I feel, fellow citizens, the honor of having been selected to address you, on such an occasion as this, I am no less sensible of the difficulties of the task [facing me]. Not that there is anything intrinsically arduous in a celebration, in this form, of the most brilliant political anniversary of the world. But, as the [festive] subject has been repeatedly exhibited under so many points of view, I am apprehensive of tiring, without being able to requite the attention with which you may be good enough to honor my endeavors. The fruitful subject must still sustain me. And I proceed with unfeigned diffidence, and the most profound respect for this distinguished and enlightened assembly, to perform the office assigned me. During each return of this day, for nearly thirty successive years, our country [has] rested in all the security and all the blessings of peace. But the scene and the aspect are [now] changed. The menacing front of war is before us—to awaken our solicitudes- to demand, at the hands of each citizen of the republic, the most active energies of duty- to ask, if need be, the largest sacrifices of advantage and of ease! The tranquility- the repose- the enjoyments- the schemes- the hopes of peace are, for a while, no more! [and] These, [along] with their endearing concomitants, are to give place to the stronger and more agitating passions—to the busy engagements- to the solemn and anxious thoughts- to the trials- to the sufferings that follow in the train of war!

2 Man in his individual nature becomes virtuous by [waging] constant struggles against his own imperfections. His intellectual eminence, which puts him at the head of [all] created beings, is attained, also, by long toil and painful self-denials—bringing with them, but too often, despondence to his mind- and hazards to his [physical] frame. It would seem to be a law of his existence that *great* enjoyment is only to be obtained as the reward of *great* exertion! She shall go "to a wealthy place," but her way shall be [only] "through fire and through water." It seems the irreversible lot of nations that their permanent well-being is to be achieved, also, [only] through severe probations. [For] Their origin is often

[found] in agony and blood—and their safety [again is] to be maintained only by constant vigilance- by arduous efforts- by a willingness to encounter danger- and by actually and frequently braving it! Their prosperity- their rights- their liberties are, alas, scarcely otherwise to be placed upon a secure and durable basis. [And] It is in vain that the precepts of the moralist (or the maxims of a sublimated Reason) are leveled at the inutility, if not the [very] criminality, of wars—in vain that eloquence portrays- that humanity [obligingly] deplores- the misery they inflict! If the wishes of the philanthropist could [but] be realized—then, indeed, happily for us- happily for the whole human race—they would be banished forever from the world! But while selfishness, ambition, and the lust of plunder continue to infest the bosoms of the rulers of nations, wars *will* take place! They always *have* taken place. And the nation that shall at this day hope to shelter itself, by standing in practice on their abstract impropriety, must expect to see its very foundations assailed—assailed by cunning and artifice- or by the burst and fury of those fierce, ungoverned passions which [even] its utmost forbearance would not be able to deprecate or appease! It would [most] assuredly fall (and with fatal speed), the victim of its own impracticable virtue.

3 Thirty years, fellow citizens, is a long time to have been exempt from the calamities of war. Few nations of the world, in any age, have enjoyed so long an exemption. It is a fact that affords, in itself, the most honorable and incontestible proof that those who have guided the destinies of this [republic] have ardently cherished peace. For it is impossible but that, during the lapse of such a period, abundant provocation must have [been] presented, had not our government and people been slow to [incite] wrath- and almost predetermined against [ensuing] wars. It is a lamentable truth that, during the whole of this period, we have been the subjects of unjust treatment at the hands of other nations- and that the constancy of our own forbearance has been followed up by the constant infliction of wrongs upon ourselves. When,-let us ask with exultation,—when have ambassadors from other countries been sent to our shores [in order] to complain of injuries done by the American states!-what [one] nation have the American states plundered!-what [one] nation have the American states outraged!-upon what rights have the American states trampled! In the pride of justice and of true honor, we answer—"None!" But we have sent forth, from ourselves, the messengers of peace and conciliation, again and again, across seas and to distant countries—to ask- earnestly to sue- for a cessation of the injuries done to us! They have gone charged with our well-founded complaints—to deprecate the longer practice of unfriendly treatment- to protest, under the sensibility of real suffering, against that course which made the persons and the property of our countrymen the subjects of rude seizure and rapacious spoliation! These have been the ends they were sent to obtain—ends too fair for protracted refusals- too intelligible to have been entangled in evasive subtleties- too legitimate to have been neglected in hostile silence! When their ministers have been sent to us, what [in fact] has been the

aim of their missions? To urge redress for wrongs done to them, shall we again ask? No, the melancholy reverse. For, in too many instances, they have come to excuse- to palliate- or even to endeavor in some shape to rivet those [wrongs] inflicted by their own sovereigns—*upon us*!

4 Perhaps the annals of no [other] nation, of the undoubted resources of this, afford a similar instance of encroachments upon its essential rights—for so long a time- [and] without some exertion of the public force [being made] to check or to prevent them. The entire amount of property of which, during a space of about twenty years, our citizens have been plundered,-alternately by one- or the other (or by both) of the two great belligerent powers of Europe,- would form, could it [but] be ascertained, a curious and perhaps novel record of persevering injustice on the part of nations professing to be at peace. Unless recollection be awakened into effort, we are not ourselves sensible (and it requires, at this day, some effort to make us so) of the number and magnitude of the injuries that have been heaped *upon us*! They teach in pathology that the most violent impressions lose the power of exciting sensation, when applied gradually and continued for a long time. This [precept] has been strikingly true in its application to ourselves as a nation. [For] The aggressions we have received have made a regular and the most copious part of our national occurrences- and stand incorporated, under an aspect more prominent than any other, with our annual history. Our state-papers have scarcely, since the present government began, touched any other subject. And our statute book will be found to record, as well, the aggressions themselves,-as [much as any] peaceful attempts at their removal in various fruitless acts of legislative interposition. It may strike even the best informed with a momentary surprise,-when it is mentioned that for eighteen successive years the official communication from the head of the Executive Government to both Houses of Congress, at the opening of the annual Sessions, has embraced a reference to some well-ascertained infringement of our rights as an independent state. Where is the parallel of this in the history of any nation- holding any other than a rank of permanent weakness or inferiority! As subsequent and superior misfortunes expel the remembrance of those [nations] which have gone before, so distinct injuries,-as we have progressively received them-have continued to engross, for their day, our never-tiring remonstrances.

5 Still, it may be said, we *have* been prosperous and happy. So we have, relatively [speaking]. But we have [most] assuredly been abridged of our full and rightful measure of prosperity! Of a nation composed of millions, calamitous indeed beyond example would be its lot if, in its early stages, the domestic condition of all (or the chief part) of its inhabitants was in any sensible degree touched with misery- or overwhelmed with ruin. This [premise] marks the fall of nations—it is not the way in which national misfortunes and an untoward national fate begin to operate. We protest against the principle which inculcates constant submission to wrongs! To ourselves- to our posterity—this

[advice] is alike due. With what palliation would it be replied, to the plunder of a rich man, that enough [treasure] was left for his comfortable (or even easy) subsistence! If our ships are taken, is it sufficient that our houses are left! If our mariners are seized, is it a boon that our farmers- our mechanics- our laborers are spared—that those [barons] who sit behind the barriers of affluence are safe! To what ultimate dangers would not so partial an estimate of the protecting duty open the way? Happily, we trust, the nation,-on a scale of more enlarged equity and wiser forecast,-has judged (and has willed) differently. [For] Having essayed its utmost [effort] to avert its wrongs by peaceful means, it has determined on appealing to the sword. Not on the still higher one[scale].-that longer submission to them[wrongs] holds out a prospect of permanent evil- a prospect rendered certain by the experience we have ourselves acquired,—that forbearance for more than twenty years has not only invited a repetition, but an augmentation of trespasses increasing in bitterness as well as [in] number- increasing in the most flagrant prostrations of justice,-presumptuously avowed, at length, to be devoid of all pretext of moral right,-and promulgated as the foundation of a system- intended to be as permanent as its elements are depraved!

6 It is cause for the deepest regret, fellow citizens, that while we are about to enter upon a conflict with one nation, our multiplied and heavy causes of complaint against another should remain unredressed. It adds to this regret that, although a last attempt is still pending, the past injustice of the latter nation, wantoning also in rapacity, leaves but the feeblest hope of their satisfactory and peaceful adjustment. Some [citizens] there are,-who shrink back at the [very] idea of war with Britain,—war with the nation from which *we* sprung- and where still sleep the ashes of *our* ancestors—whose history is *our* history- whose firesides are *our* firesides—whose illustrious names are *our* boast- whose glory *should be* our glory! Yes, we feel these truths. We reject the poor definition of "country," which would limit it to an occupancy of the same little piece of earth. A common stock of ancestry- a kindred face and blood- the links that grow upon a thousand moral and domestic sympathies *should* indeed reach farther,- and might once have been made to defy [even] the intermediate roll of an ocean to sunder them apart. But who was it that first broke these ties—who was it that first forgot- that put to scorn such generous ties?

7 Let their own historians- their own orators answer! Hear the language of a member of the British House of Commons, in the year 1765: "They—children planted by *your care*? No, *your oppression* planted them in America! They fled from *your tyranny* into an uncultivated land,-where they were exposed to all the hardships to which human nature is liable,—to the savage cruelty of the enemy of the wilderness- a people the most subtle and the most formidable upon the face of the earth!—And yet they met all these hardships with pleasure, -compared with those they suffered [under] in their own country- where they *should* have been treated as friends. They—nourished by *your indulgence*? No, they grew by *your neglect*! When you began to care about

them, that *care* was exercised in sending persons to rule over them,-who were the deputies of some deputy- sent to spy out their liberty- to misrepresent their actions- to prey upon their substance,—men whose behavior has caused the blood of those sons of liberty to recoil within them! They—protected by *your arms*? They have nobly taken up arms in *your defense-* have exerted their valor amidst their constant and laborious industry for the defense of a country,-the interior of which has yielded [up] all its little savings to *your* enlargement- while its frontier was drenched in blood!" Yes, who was it, we ask, [that] first tore [apart] such generous sympathies? Let the blood of Concord and of Lexington again answer! Our whole country converted into a field of battle—the bayonet thrust at *our* bosoms! And for what [reason]? For asking only the privileges of Britons- while they claimed "to bind us *in all cases whatsoever*!" Against all that history teaches, will they raise *upon us* the crime of rending these ties? They compelled us into a rejection of them all,-a rejection to which we were long loath,—by their constant exercise of unjust power- by laying *upon us* the hand of sharp, systematic oppression- by attacking us with fierce vengeance! With [all] the respect due from faithful subjects (but with the dignity of freemen), did we, with long patience, petition- supplicate- for a removal of our wrongs—while new oppressions, insults, and hostile troops were *our answers* [from them]!

8 When Britain shall pass from the stage of nations, it will be indeed with her glory- but it will also be with her shame. And with *shame* will her annals in nothing more be loaded than in this [respect]. That,-while in the actual possession of much relative freedom at home,-it has been her uniform characteristic to let fall, upon the remote subjects of her own empire, an iron hand of harsh and vindictive power. If, as is alleged in her [evolving] eulogy, to touch her soil proclaims emancipation to the slave, it is more true that,-when her sceptre reaches [out] over that confined limit,-it thenceforth (and as it menacingly waves throughout the globe) inverts the rule that would give to her soil this purifying virtue. Witness Scotland—towards whom her treatment, [up] until the union in the last century, was marked (during the longest periods) by perfidious injustice or by rude force,-circumventing her liberties- or striving to cut them down with the sword! Witness Ireland,-who for five centuries has bled—who, to the present hour, continues to bleed under the yoke of her galling supremacy,—whose miserable victims seem, at length, to have lain down- subdued and despairing- under the multiplied inflictions of her cruelty and rigor! In vain do her own best statesmen and patriots remonstrate against this unjust career,-in vain put forth the annual efforts of their benevolence- their zeal- their eloquence,—in vain touch every spring that interest- that humanity- that the maxims of everlasting justice can move,-[all in an attempt] to stay its force and mitigate the fate of Irishmen! Alas, for the persecuted adherents of the Cross she leaves no hope. Witness her subject millions in the East—where, in the descriptive language of the greatest of her surviving orators, "sacrilege, massacre, and perfidy pile up the somber pyramids of her renown!"

9 But all these instances are of her fellowmen—of merely coequal (perhaps unknown) descent and blood,-coexisting from [the beginning of] all time with herself- and making up, only accidentally, a part of her dominion. We ought to have been *spared*—the otherwise undistinguishing rigor of this outstretched sceptre [of hers] might have still have *spared us*! [For] We were descended from *her own* loins, -bone of *her* bone- and flesh of *her* flesh,—not so much a part of her empire, as a part of *herself*- her *very self*! [And] Towards *her own* [offspring], it might [perhaps] have been expected she would relent. [Since] When she invaded *our* homes, she [presumably] saw *her own* countenance-heard *her own* voice- beheld *her own* altars [to worship]! Where was then that pure spirit,-which she *now* would tell us sustains her, amidst self-sacrifices, in her *generous* contest for the liberties of *other* nations? If it [at least] flowed in her nature, here [in America] it might have delighted to beam out—here was [some] space for its saving love!—The true mother chastens, not destroys, the child. But Britain, when she struck [out] at us, struck at *her own* image—struck, too, at the immortal principles which her Locke's- her Milton's-and her Sydney's taught! And the fell blow severed us forever [from her] as a kindred nation! The crime is purely *her own*—and *upon her*, not us, be its consequences and its stain [cast].

10 In looking at Britain,-with eyes less prepossessed than we are apt to have from the circumstance of our ancient connection with her,-we should see indeed her common lot of excellence, [up]on which to found [our] esteem. But it would lift the covering from deformities which may well startle and repel [us]. A harshness of individual character, in the general view of it, which is perceived and acknowledged by all Europe—a spirit of unbecoming censure,-as regards all customs and institutions not their own-a ferocity in some of their characteristics of national manners,-pervading their very pastimes,—which no other modern people are endowed with the blunted sensibility to bear [up under]—an universally self-assumed superiority- not innocently manifesting itself in speculative sentiments among themselves,-but unamiably indulged [in] when [chatting] with foreigners (of whatever description) in their own country,—or when they themselves are the temporary sojourners in a foreign country—a code of criminal law that forgets to feel [sympathy] for human frailty,-that sports with human misfortune,—that has shed more blood in deliberate judicial severity, for two centuries past (constantly increasing, too, in its sanguinary hue), than has ever been sanctioned by the jurisprudence of any ancient or modern nation civilized and refined like herself—the merciless whippings in her army,-peculiar to herself alone—the conspicuous commission and freest acknowledgement of vice in her upper classes—the overweening distinctions shown to opulence and birth,-so destructive of a sound moral sentiment in the nation,—so baffling to virtue:—these are some of the [character] traits that rise up to a contemplation of the inhabitants of this isle- and are adverted to,-with an admission of qualities that may spring up as the correlatives of some of

them,-under the [critical] remark of our being prone to overlook the vicious ingredients, while we so readily praise *the good* that belongs to her.

11 How should it fall out that this nation,-more than any other that is ambitious and warlike,-should be [totally] free from the dispositions that lead to injustice- violence- and plunder,—and [from] what[ever] rules of prudence should [allow us to] check our watchfulness (or allay our fears) in regard to the plans [which] her conduct is the best illustration of her having so steadily meditated towards us? Why not be girded as regards her attacks [upon us]- wary as regards her intrigues- alarmed as regards her habit of devastation and long-indulged appetite of blood! Look at the Marine of Britain—its vast- its tremendous extent! What potentate upon the [face of the] earth wields a [naval] power that is to be compared with it! What potentate upon the earth can move an apparatus of destruction,-so [utterly] without rival,—so little liable to any counteraction! The world, in no age, has seen its equal. [For] It marks [the inauguration of] a new era in the history of human force—an instrument of power and of ambition- with no [ultimate] limits to its rapid and hideous workings but the waters and the winds. Why should she impiously suppose the ocean to be *her own* element! Why should she claim the right to give law to it- anymore than the eagle [pretends to claim] the exclusive right to fly in the air! If ever there was a power formidable to the liberties of other states- particularly those afar off [geographically from her]- is it not *this*! If ever there was a power which other states should feel [fore]warned [enough] to behold with fearful jealousy,-and anxious to see broken up,-is it not *this*! The opinion,-inculcated by her own [self-]interested politicians and journalists,—that such a force is designed to be employed only to mediate for the rights of *other* nations,—can hold no sway before the unshackled reflections of a dispassionate mind. All experience- all knowledge of man [simply] explode the supposition.

12 So, more particularly, does the very growth and history of this extraordinary power itself. [For] It has swelled to its gigantic size- not through any concurrence of fortuitous or temporary causes,-but through long-continued (and the most systematic) national views. It was in the time of her early Edward's that she first began, arrogantly, to exact a ceremonious obeisance from the flags of *other* nations. Since which [time], the entire spirit of her navigation laws- her commercial usages- her treaties- have steadily looked to the establishment of an overruling Marine. *This* is the theme from which her poets insult the world,-by singing "Britannia's *is* the sea- and not a flag but by [her] permission waves!" It is the *great* instrument of annoyance [held aloft] in the hands of her ministers—with which they threaten,-or which they wield to confirm [the allegiance of] allies,—to alarm foes,—to make *other* states tributary to their manufacturing- their commercial- or their warlike schemes!—Even the multitude in their streets,-[especially] their boys- [both] the halt and the blind,-learn [to sing] it in the ballads and at every carousal! "*Rule* Britannia" is the loud acclamation- the inspiring sentiment- the triumphant echo of the scene!

The end,-so long pursued, with a constant view to unlimited empire, throughout that element which covers two-thirds of the globe,-has [at last] been obtained. And Britain finds herself, at this era, the dreaded mistress of the seas. With what rapacious sway she has begun to put forth this arm of her supremacy, we, fellow citizens, have [now] experienced—while the flames of Copenhagen have lighted it up to Europe in characters of a [still] more awful glare.

13 When the late Colonel Henry Laurens left England in the year 1774, he had previously waited [up]on the Earl of Hillsborough in order to converse with him on American affairs. In the course of [their] conversation, Colonel Laurens said [that] the duty of three-pence-a-pound on tea (and all the other taxes) were not worth the expense of a war. "You mistake the cause of our controversy with your country," said his Lordship. "You spread *too much canvas* upon the ocean. Do you [really] think we will *let* you go on with *your navigation*- and *your forty thousand seamen*!" The same hostile spirit to[wards] our growing commerce has actuated every minister (and every Privy Council and every Parliament) of Great Britain since that time. And it is the [very same] spirit she [today] manifests towards *other* nations! The recent declarations,- made upon the floor of the House of Commons- in debate upon the Orders in Council,-add a new corroboration to the proofs that this monopolizing spirit has been one of the steady maxims- *designed* to secure and uphold *her absolute* dominion upon the waves. But to that [Supreme] Being,-who made the waters and the winds for the common use of [all] His creatures,-do we owe it *never* to forego *our equal* claim to their immunities!

14 In entering upon a war, it is our chief consolation,-that will give dignity to the contest- and confidence to our hearts,-to know that, before God and before the world, our cause *is just.* [Yet] To dilate [up]on this head[ing], altho[ugh ever] so fruitful, would swell to undue limits this address- and betray a forgetfulness of the informed (and anticipating) understandings of this assembly. [Suffice it to say,] Our provocation consists of multiplied wrongs—of the most numerous injuries- of the most aggravated insults! [And] They have been fully placed before the world in the recent, authentic declarations of our government. In these declarations will be read the solemn justification of what we have done. And our posterity will cling to them as a manly, yet pure and unblemished, portion of their inheritance. In the language of one of them,-flowing from the highest and the purest source- founded on authentic history- which exhibits a state-paper alike distinguished by its profound reasoning, its elevated justice, and its impressive dignity,-we have "beheld, in fine, on the side of Great Britain, a state of *war against the United States*; and, on the side of the United States, a state of *peace towards Great Britain*!"—It is the same pen, too,—which has been officially employed for so many years in combating our wrongs,- and [in] striving for their pacific redress- with a constant and sublime adherence to the maxims of universal equity, as well as of public law,—which now solemnly declares our actual situation!

15 Can Americans, then, hesitate [about] what part [they are] to act [out]? Whither would have fled the remembrance of their character and deeds,- whither soon would flee their rights- their liberties,—where would be the spirits- where the courage of their slain fathers! Snatched and gone from *ignoble* sons? What should we *answer* to the children we leave behind,-who will take their praise or their reproach from the conduct of their sires (and those sires *republicans*),—who- rejecting from the train of their succession the perishing honors of a ribbon or a badge- are more nobly inspired to transmit the unfading distinctions that spring from the *resolute* discharge of all the patriot's high duties! Why should we *stay* our arm *against* Britain- while she wars *upon us*! Are we *appalled* at her legions—do we *shrink back* at her vengeance? No, fellow citizens—*no*! We have faced [up to] those legions- braved and triumphed over that vengeance! Powerful as she is old,-[both] in arms and in discipline,-upon the plains of America has she [already] once learned that her ranks can be subdued- and her high ensign fall! Not in a boastful [vein], but in a temper to encourage [ourselves], would we speak it. British valor has *yielded* to the equal, spontaneous valor,-[a valor nothing] but the more indignant [kind of] fire,—which [only] freedom and a just cause could impart when opposed to the hired forces of an unjust king! And is there [anything] less to inspire [us] now?- let a few short reflections determine. While I abstain from any enumeration of the [various] other encroachments of Great Britain *upon us* as an independent nation,-through their successive accumulations—until they have ended [up] in *making the whole trade* of our country, in substance- and in terms [deplorably] *colonial* suffering it to exist (and to exist *only*) where it subserves *her own* absorbing avarice (or what she calls her "retaliating vengeance"),-I must nevertheless solicit your indulgence to pause with me, for a little while, [and reflect] upon a single wrong.

16 The seizure of the *persons* of American citizens,-under the name and the pretexts of impressment- by the naval officers of Great Britain,-is an outrage of that kind which makes it difficult to speak of it in terms of appropriate description. For *this*,-among other reasons,—that the *offense itself* is new! It is probable that the most careful researches into history,-where, indeed- of almost every form of rapine [practiced] between men and between nations- is to be found the melancholy record,- will yet afford no example of the systematic perpetration of an offense of a similar nature (perpetrated, too, under a *claim* of right). To take a just (and no other than a serious) illustration, the only parallel to it is to be found in the African slave trade. And if an eminent statesman of England once spoke of the latter as the *greatest practical* evil that had ever afflicted mankind, we may be allowed to denominate the former [*as*] the *greatest practical* offense that has ever been offered to a civilized and independent state [like ourselves]! [For] With the American government, it has been a question of no party [at fault being recognized]- or of [there being] no day [for arbitration and reconciliation]. At every period of its administration, the odious practice has been constantly protested against- and its discontinuance been demanded

under every form of pacific remonstrance [available to us]. [And] With all our statesmen,-while [thus busily] engaged in exercising the public authorities of the nation,-it has been deemed (if not otherwise to have been abrogated) *Legitimate* cause for war!

17 The only imaginable difference, among any of them, [really] has been as to the *time* when it would be proper [for us] to use this imperious resort [to arms].—As if the *time* was not *always* at hand for a nation to redeem such a stain upon *its vitals,*—and as if an encroachment of *this* nature does not become [all] the more difficult to beat back with *each* [passing] year- and with *each* [and every] instance in which it is permitted! But it best accorded with the genius of our [form of] government,-with its love of peace (and perhaps with what was *due* to peace),-to attempt, at first, its *pacific* removal. General Washington, when [still] at the head of the government, is known to have viewed it with [all] the sensibility that such an indignity could not [but] fail to arouse in his bosom. And had he lived until this day,-to see it [go] not only unredressed and unmitigated- but [cunningly be] increased amidst all the amicable efforts, on our part, for its cessation,—there is the strongest reason for supposing that his just estimate of the nation's welfare- that his lofty and gallant spirit- would have stood forth ([even] had it been but the single grievance [mentioned]) [as] the *manly* advocate of its extirpation *by the sword*! But if our submission to it, [for] so long, has incurred a just reproach, happily it is in some measure assuaged in the reflection,-that our forbearance will serve to put us more completely *in the right* at this eventful period.

18 That our enemy has invariably *refused* to accede to such terms as were [directly] answerable to the indispensable expectations of our own government (as the organ of a *sovereign* people)—upon this head[ing] is a point susceptible of entire proof. Avoiding [all] other particulars, it will be sufficient to introduce [but] a single one. It is a fact- which the archives of our public departments will [amply] show- that,-in order to take *from* Great Britain the *remnant* of *her own* excuses for seizing our ships in search of *her own* [men],-it was proposed to her that the United States would forbear to receive her seamen on board of their vessels,—provided she, in her turn, would *abstain* from receiving our men on board of hers. This [arrangement] would wholly have destroyed the insulting claim set up by her [in order] to break in with armed men *upon our vessels,* -[an act committed] while "peaceably" sailing on the ocean- under color of "forcibly" taking *her own* mariners! For the regulation, if adopted, would have given the previous assurance that *her own* [men] were *not* there to be found! But this proposal (it is also a fact) she *declined.* As rapacious of [our] men [as she is]- as greedy of riches and grasping at [absolute] dominion,-she *neglected* to avail herself of a regulation that would curtail *her* in this new species of plunder,—this plunder in the flesh and blood of *freemen*- of which *she* has afforded the first example (in all time) to the eyes of an insulted world! But it forcibly marks the devouring ambition of her naval spirit—and that

[spirit in effect being],-if public law is [to be] ridiculed- justice scoffed at- sovereignty prostrated- and humanity [otherwise] made to shudder and to groan,—still, *her ships must have men*!

19 Under a mere[ly] personal view of this outrage (and considering it [up]on the footing of a moral sin), it *is* strictly like the African slave trade. [For] Like that, it breaks up [entire] families- and causes [their] hearts to bleed! Like that, it tears the son [away] from the father,-the father from the son! [And] Like that, it makes orphans and widows,-takes the brother [away] from the sister,—seizes up the young man [of the family] in the health of his days- and blasts his hopes *forever*! It is worse than the slavery of the African, for the African is *only* made to work under the lash of a taskmaster. Whereas the citizen of the United States, thus enslaved [at the hands of Britain], receives also the lash on [exhibiting] the slightest lapses from a rigorous discipline—and is moreover exposed to the bitter fate of fighting against those,-towards whom he has no [real] hostility,—perhaps his own countrymen it may be- [even] his own immediate kindred. This is *not* exaggeration, fellow citizens,—it *is* reality and fact!

20 "But," say the British, "we want *not your* men,—we want *only our own*! *Prove* that they are *your's*- and we *will* surrender them up [to you]!" Baser outrage, [what an] insolent indignity,-that a freeborn American [citizen] must be made to *prove* his nativity to those who have previously *violated his liberty*! Else he is to be held *forever* as a slave. That before a British "tribunal" (a [single] British boarding officer), a freeborn American must be made to seal up the vouchers of *his* lineage—to exhibit the records of *his* baptism (and *his* birth)— to establish the [racial] identity that binds *him* to *his* parents- to *his* blood- to *his* native land,—by setting forth, in odious detail, *his* size- *his* age- the shape of *his* frame,-whether *his* hair is long or cropped,-*his* marks (like [brands upon] an ox- or a horse of the manger)!—[And] that *all this* must be done as the *condition* of his escape from the galling thralldom of a British ship! Can we hear it, can we *think* of it- with any other than indignant feelings at *our* tarnished name and nation! And suppose, through this degrading process, *his* deliverance [is] to be effected. Where [then] is *he* to seek *redress* for the [more] intermediate [sort of] wrong! The unauthorized seizure and detention of any piece of property, [even though] a mere trespass upon goods, will always lay the foundation for some (often the heaviest) retribution- in *every* well-regulated society. But to whom- or where- shall our imprisoned citizen,-when the privilege of shaking off *his* fetters has at last been accorded to *him*,-turn for *his redress*—where look to reimburse the stripes (perhaps the wounds) *he* has received, [particularly] *his* worn spirit- *his* long, inward agonies? No, the public code of nations recognizes *not* the penalty! For to the modern rapaciousness of Britain [alone] it was reserved to add, to the dark catalogue of human sufferings, this flagitious crime.

21 But why be told that, even on [the basis of] such proofs, our citizens will be released from their captivity? We have long and sorely experienced the

impracticable nature of this boon- which, in the imagined relaxation of her deep injustice, she would affect to hold out [to us]. Go to the office of the Department of State,-within sight of where we are [now] assembled,-and there see the piles—of certificates and documents—of affidavits- records- and seals—[every last one] anxiously drawn out and folded up to show *why* Americans should *not* be held as slaves,—and see how they rest (and will forever rest)- in *hopeless neglect* upon the shelves! Some defect in form [perhaps]- some impossibility of filling up all the crevices which British exaction insists upon being closed,—the uncertainty if (after all [is said and done]) they will ever reach their point of destination,—the climate (or the sea) where the hopes of gain or the lust of conquest are impelling, through constant changes, their ships,—the probability that the miserable individual to whom they are intended- as the harbinger of liberation from his shackles- may [already] have been translated from the first scene of his incarceration to [yet] another (from a 74[-gun] to a 64- from a 64 to a frigate),-and thus [on] through rapid, if not *designed*, mutations- a practice which *is known* to exist:—these are [, every one,] obvious causes of [our] discouragement,- by making the issue at all times doubtful- [even] most frequently *hopeless*! And this [impact] Great Britain cannot but know! She *does know* it! And with *deliberate* mockery,-in the composure with which bloated power [alone] can scoff at submissive and humble suffering,-has she continued to increase and protract our humiliation (as well as our suffering)- by [making constant] renewals of the visionary offer!

22 Again, it is said that our citizens resemble *their* men,-look like *them* in their persons- speak [much] the *same* language,—that [any close] discriminations are difficult or impracticable [to make- far away from port upon the high seas],—and therefore, it is [asserted], they are "unavoidably" seized. Most *insulting* excuse! And will they [dare to] impeach that God who *equally* made us both—who forms our features- molds our statures- and stamps us with a countenance that turns up[wards] to [worship] His goodness,-in adoration and love! [What an] *Impious*- as well as insulting [excuse]! The leopard [surely] cannot change his [black] spots- or the Ethiopian his [black] skin,-but we- *we* are [told] to put off *our* bodies (and become [racially] unlike *ourselves*) as the price of [obtaining] *our* safety! Why should [some perceived] similarity of face yoke *us exclusively* with [such an] ignominious burden—why because *we* were once descended from them should *we* be made (at this day- and *forever*) to clank [their] chains! Suppose [that] one of their subjects landed upon *our* shores.—[And) let us suppose him [to be] a prince of *their* blood.—Shall we [proceed to] seize upon him to mend *our* highways—shall we draft him for *our* ranks! Shall *we* subject him, in an instant, to all the civil burdens of duty- of taxation- of every species of aid and service (that grow out of the *allegiance* of the citizen),-until he can send across the ocean for the registers of *his* family and birth! What has her foul spirit of impressment to answer to this [parallel]? Why not *equally* demand, on our part, that *every* one of her [merchant] factors- who lands upon *our* soil- should bring a [sum of] protection in his pocket (or hang

one [moneybag] round his neck) as the price of *his* safety! [And] If this plea of monstrous outrage be only for one instant admitted, remember, fellow citizens, that it becomes as lasting- as monstrous. If our children (and our children's children and their children) continue to speak the same tongue- to hold the same [home] port with their fathers, *they also* will be liable to this [type of] enslavement—and the groaning evil [will] be coexistent with *British* power- *British* rapacity- and the maxim that the *British Navy must have men*! [For] If our men are [at all] like their's, it should form,-to any other than a nation *callous* to [principles of] justice- *dead* to [making any application of] the moral sense- and [,as a consequence,] *deliberately* bent upon plunder,-the very reason *why they should give up* the practice! Seeing that it is [so] intrinsically liable to [be distorted into a rationalization of] these mistakes—and that the exercise of what they call a "right," on their part, necessarily brings with it certain- eternal- and the most high-handed wrongs to us.

23 "*I am* a *Roman* citizen!—*I am a Roman citizen!*"-was an exclamation that insured [one's] safety- commanded respect- or inspired terror,-in *all* parts of the [ancient] world. And although the mild temper[ament] of our government exacts not all [of] these attributes, we may at least be suffered to deplore, with hearts of agony and shame, that while the inhabitants of *every other* part of the globe enjoy an immunity from the seizure of their *persons*,-except under the [obvious] fate of war- or by acknowledged pirates,-[an immuunity] even [extending to some of] the wretched Africans of late,—*to be an American citizen* has, for [the past] five-and-twenty years, been [little else but] the signal for insult- and the passport to [our] captivity! [Yet] Let it not be replied—that the men they take from us are "sometimes" *not* of a character (or description) [compelling enough] to attract the concern(or interposition) of the [American] government. [Even] If they were *all* so [regarded], it lessens in nowise the enormity of the outrage! It adds, indeed, a fresh indignity [but] to mention it! The sublime *equality* of justice [certainly] recognizes no such distinctions. And a government, founded upon the *great* basis of *equal* right, would [really] forget one of its fundamental duties if, in the exercise of its protecting power, it admits to a foreign nation the least distinction—between what [rights] it owes to the lowest and meanest- and the highest and most exalted of its citizens! Sometimes it is said—that but "few" of our seamen are in reality seized. [What a] Progressive and foul aggravation—to *admit* the crime- to *our* faces,—and [then] seek to screen its atrocity under [the guise of] its "limited" extent! Whence but from a source hardened with long rapine could such a palliation flow! It is false. [For] The files of that same department (its melancholy memorials) attest that there are thousands of our countrymen, at this [very] moment, [confined] in slavery in their ships! And if there were but one hundred- if there were but fifty- if there were but ten- if there were but *one* [of our men confined]—how dare they insult a *sovereign* nation with such an answer!

24 Shall I state to you a fact, fellow citizens, that will be sufficient to rouse not simply your indignation- but your *horror*? (And would that I could

[but] speak it, at this moment, to the whole nation, [so] that every American who has a heart to be inflamed with honest resentment might hear [me].) A *fact* that shows all the *excess* of shame,- that should flush *our* faces- at submission to an outrage so *foul!* I state to you- upon the highest and most unquestionable authority—that two of the nephews of *your* immortal Washington have been seized- dragged- made slaves of,-on board of a *British* ship! Will it be credited [with honor by any of us]? It is, nevertheless, true. [For] They were kept in slavery more than a year- and,-as the transactions of your government will show,-were restored to their liberty only a few months since! How, Americans, can you sit down [complacently any longer] under such indignities! [In obedience] To which of their princes- which of their nobles—to which of their ministers- or which of their regents—will you allow, in the just pride of men (and of *freemen*), that those [citizens] who stand in consanguinity to the illustrious founder of *your* liberties are *second* [best],-in all *their claims* to safety and protection! But we must leave the odious subject. It swells indeed, with ever "fruitful" expansion, to the indignant view. But while it animates- it *is* loathsome! [And] If the English say [that] it is *merely* an abuse,- incident[al] to a "right" on their part (besides denying forever the [legal] foundation of [any] such "right," [especially] where it goes to the [question of] presumptuous entry of *our own* vessels with *their* armed men),—shall we tolerate its exercise, for an instant, when manifestly attended with such a practical- unceasing- and enormous oppression *upon ourselves*!

25 This crime of impressment may justly be considered ([and] posterity will so consider it) as transcending the [total] amount of all the *other* wrongs we have received. Notwithstanding the millions [of dollars] which the cupidity of Britain has wrested [away] from us- the millions which the cupidity of France has wrested from us,-including her wicked burnings of our ships- adding [in], also, the wrongs from Spain and Denmark,—the sum of all should be estimated *below* this enormity [of impressment]. Ships and merchandise belong to individuals—and may be valued- may be endured as [proper] subjects for negotiation. But *men* are the [vital] *property* of *the nation* [and cannot be bargained in]! In *every* American face- a [vital] part of our country's sovereignty is written! It is the living *emblem* (a thousand times more sacred than the nation's flag itself) of its character- its independence- and its rights,-its quick and most dearly cherished *insignium*- towards which *the nation* should ever demand the most scrupulous and inviolable *immunity*.—being [wary and] instantly sensitive- under the "flagrant" indignity of [even] the slightest infringement of its beaming, vivid attributes of *sovereignty*! [For] Man was created in his Maker's own image,—"in the image of God created He him." [And] When He is made a slave, where shall there be [any relevant] reimbursement [for the crime]? No, fellow citizens, [it is only] under the assistance and protection of the Most High [that] the evil *must* be stopped! His Own image *must not* be enslaved! [For] It was, deservedly, the first-enumerated of our grievances- in the late solemn message from the first magistrate of our land! On

the eighteenth of June of this memorable year- we appealed *to the sword and to Heaven* against it! And we shall be [found] wanting to ourselves- to our posterity,-we shall never stand erect in our *sovereignty* as a *nation,*—if we return it to the scabbard- until such an infamy and a curse are finally (and effectually) removed!

26 The blessings of peace itself become a curse- a *foul* curse—while such a stain is permitted to rest upon *our* annals. *Never,* henceforth, must American ships [be allowed to] be converted into [a scene of confrontation] worse than butchers' shambles- for [purposes of] the inspection and seizure of [our] human flesh! We would appeal to the justice and humanity of their own statesmen—claim the [active] interference of their [abolitionist] Wilberforce's—invoke the [righteous] spirit of their departed Fox—call upon all, among them, who nobly succeeded in their long struggles against the African slave trade,—to stand up and retrieve the British name from the "equal" odium of this offense! [And] If it be true that injuries long acquiesced in lose the power of exciting [our] sensibility, it may [well] be remarked- in [an appropriate] conclusion of this hateful subject- how forcibly verified [as a truism] it [really] is,-in the [single] instance of robbing *us* of *our* [own] citizens. [For] When it happens that some of them are surrendered up on examination and allowance of "the proofs," it is not [at all] unusual to advert to it as an indication of the "justice and generosity" of the *British*! The very act which, to an abstract judgment, should be taken as stamping a seal [of ignominy] upon the outrage,-by the acknowledgment it implies, from *themselves,* of the [very existence of the] atrocity- [primarily] because [of] the [gross] unlawfulness of the seizure,-is thus converted into a medium of "homage" and of "praise!" [What] Inverted patriotism—[what] drooping- downcast honor,—to derive a "pleasurable" sensation from the insulting confession of [such] a crime!

27 Next to a just war, fellow citizens, we [prefer to] wage a defensive one. This [really] is its true and only character[istic]. *Our* fields were not indeed invaded—or *our* towns entered- and sacked. But still- it is purely a war of defense [we wage]. [For] It was to stop reiterated encroachment [upon our nationality that] we took up arms. Persons- property- rights- character- sovereignty- justice——all these [vital national qualities] were contumaciously invaded at *our* hands! Let impartial truth *say if it were* for [purposes of] ambition- or conquest- or plunder,-or through any false estimate of [national] character or pride,-[that] we appealed to the sword! No, Americans, [thrice] no! [Fellow] Republicans, there will rest *no* such blot upon *your* moderate- *your* pacific councils! [For] It is [but] an imperfect view of this question,-which takes as a "defensive" war only that which is entered upon when the assailant [already] is bursting through *your* doors- and leveling the musket at the bosoms of *your* women and children! Think *how* a nation may be abridged- may be [totally] dismantled- of its rights—may be cut down in [the exercise of] its [very] liberties,-this side of an open attack! The Athenian law punished seduction of female

honor more severely than it did [the open act of physical] force. And the nation that would adopt it as a maxim,-to lie [idly] by under whatever curtailments of its sovereignty [accumulate]- resolving upon no resistance until the actual "investment" of its soil [takes place],-might [well] find itself too fatally trenched [in] upon- too exhausted in resources- or too enfeebled in spirit,—[finally] to rouse itself when the foe was [discovered] rushing through the gates!

28 The war whoop of the Indian had indeed been heard in the habitations of our frontier. And it is impossible to abstain from imputing to the agency of our enemy this horrid species of invasion. Their hand *must be* in it! For although it may not be directly instigated by their government (on the "other" side of the water[,as the Indian might say]), yet past proofs make it- to the last degree- [quite] probable that the intrigues of *their* subagents in the Canada's *are* instrumental to the [acts of] wickedness. Nor will a rational mind hesitate [but] to infer,- that the same spirit which, from that quarter at least, could send- for the most nefarious purposes- a polished spy through[out] our [major] cities,—would also (varying the *form* of its inequity [on our frontier]) let loose *upon us* the hatchet- and the scalping knife! Great Britain, indeed, had *not* declared war *against us in form*- but she had made it *upon us in fact*! She had plundered us of *our* property—she had imprisoned *our* citizens! Nor can any accommodation now erase from our memories,-although it may from our public discussions,-the bloody memorials of her attack upon the [ship] Chesapeake.

29 Since, fellow citizens, [we recognize] that- through [the interaction of] these motives- a war with Britain has been *cast upon us,*- while bearing up against whatever pressures it may bring- with [all] the energy (and the hope) of our fathers,—let us deduce, also, this [measure] of consolation: that it will- more than anything else- have a tendency to break the sway which that nation is enabled to *hold over us*. I would address myself, on this point, to the candid minds of our countrymen—and [especially] to all such, among them, as have bosoms penetrated with a *genuine* love for our republican systems. We form- probably for the first time in all history- the [single] instance of a nation [being] descended (and politically detached) from another- but still keeping up the most intimate connections with the original (and once [inviolate]) parent [racial] stock. The similarity of our manners and customs- [stemming from] our language being *one* [in origin] (and our religion nearly *one*)—the *entire* [racial] identity- in individual appearance (and [really] in all things else)- which is spread before the American (and the English) eye—our boundless social intercommunication-[including] the very personal respectability, in so many instances, of those [residents] of that nation- who in such numbers[decide to] come to this [republic and settle down]—pecuniary connections so universal and unlimited- [making us as] dependent [as America now is] upon her [textile] loom- dependent upon her fashions [of dress]-dependent upon her judicature- dependent upon her [taste in] drama,-reading none but her books (or scarcely any others)- [and] taking up her character and actions chiefly at the hands of

her own annalists or panegyrists,—nothing, in fine, that comes from that quarter being regarded as "foreign,"-but ([we might] as well [include in this rule] her inhabitants- as her modes of life and all her usages([instead] being taken to be as of *our own*:—these complicated similitudes operate like cramps and holdings,-to bind us insensibly to her sides,—yielding to her an easy- an increasing- and an unsuspected ascendancy [over us]!

30 It may [perhaps] be said,-this is an advantageous ascendancy [to have],—that- as a "young" people- we may [better] profit from the intimacy—have *her* arts and *her* manners- copy *her* "many" meliorations of [national] existence- eat of *her* intellectual food- and get stamina [all] the more "quickly" upon [reaping] its nourishment! But stop, Americans. Do you not know that *this same people* are the subjects of an old and luxurious monarchy- [together] with all the corrupt attachments to which it leads! That- if not their duty- it *is* naturally *their practice*—to breathe [forth] the praise (and inculcate the love) of *their own* forms of polity! Do you not know that- if *not* the correlative duty- it *is* [just] as certainly their correlative *practice*—to deal out disapprobation (even contempt) for *our own* [civil polity]- and the habits which, [permitted to stand] alone, [forms such as] they *should* superinduce [in us]! And is there not [some] cause for [added] apprehension,-that the [very] superiority which we so easily (often so "slavishly") choose to *yield* her on all other points—that the moral prostration- in which we "consent" to fall [down] before her [royal] footstool—*may also* trench [in steadily] upon the reverence due *our own* public institutions,—producing results at which all our fears should startle [suddenly in recognition]! If, fellow citizens, our freedom- our republican freedom,-which to make lasting we should cherish with uninterrupted constancy and the purest love,-has a foe more deadly than any other,—it is probably this! *This* is the destroying spirit which can make its way,- slowly and unperceived- but surely and fatally! If we stood farther off (*much* farther off) from Britain, we should still be "near" enough to derive all that she has [that is] valuable—while we should be [rendered] more safe, [,thus removed at a distance,] from the poison of her political touch. Just as, at this day, we can draw upon the repositories of genius and literature among the ancients—while we escape the vices of paganism (and the errors of their misleading philosophy). But if Athenian citizens [now] filled our towns,-if we spoke their language- wore their [garment of] dress- took them [in]to our homes,-if we kept looking up to them with *general* imitation and subserviency,—[even] the [central] truths of Christianity themselves would be in danger of *yielding* to the adoration of the false [pagan] gods!

31 This war may produce- auspiciously and forever- the effect of throwing us [off] at a safer distance from so contaminating an intimacy— [of] making our liberty thrive more securely- and [making] ourselves more independent,- [both] privately and politically. From *no other* nation are we [now] in danger- in the same way. For, with *no other nation* have we the same affinities—but, on the

contrary, numerous points of [mutual] repulsion- that interpose as *our* [protective] guard. Let us have [but] a shy connection with *them all*! For history gives the admonition that, for the last twenty years, *every nation* of the world,-that has come too close in friendship with either our present enemy- or her neighbor [France] (the "ferocious giant" of the land[,quite hopefully]),-has lost its [fundamental] liberties- been prostrated [in national disgrace]- or been ravaged [without mercy]! After the war of our Revolution, we were still *so much* in the feebleness of youth as to take [back] the outstretched hand of Britain,-who could [in that way continue to] establish our [manufacturing] industry- shape our [personal] occupations- and give them (involuntarily to *ourselves*) the [colonial] *direction* advantageous to *her* views! But henceforth *we shall stand* upon a pedestal,-whose base is fixed *among ourselves,*—whence *we* may proudly look around and afar- from the ocean to the mountains- from the mountains to the farthest west— beholding *our* fruitful [agricultural] fields—listening to the hammer [and anvil] of *our* [home] workshops- the cheerful noise of [women operating] *our* looms [at home] ,—where the view, on all sides, of *native* numbers- opulence- and skill will enable *us* to stamp (more "at pleasure") [our very own imprint upon] the future destinies of *our happy land*! Possibly, also, the "sameness" of our pursuits in so many things with Britain,-instead of pointing to[wards] close connections with her (as *her* politicians so steadily hold up [for our example]),-will at length indicate- to the foresight of *our own* statesmen- unalterable reasons [tending] to[wards] an intercourse more restrained,—[even,] it may be, the [initial] elements of a lasting rivalship!

32 Animated by all the motives- which demand and justify this contest—let us advance to it with resolute (and high-beating) hearts- supported [only] by the *devotion to our beloved* country,-which [devout] wishes for her triumphs cannot [but] fail to kindle [in us]! Dear to *us* is *this beloved country-far* dearer than *we* can [begin to] express—[yet we can convey that she is dear to us] for [reason of] *all the true* blessings that flourish within her bosom,-[being, as she is,] the country of *our fathers-* the country of *our children-* the scene of *our dearest* affections,—[a sovereign republic] whose rights and liberties have been consecrated by the blood whose [swift] current [still] runs so fresh in *our own veins*! Who shall touch [the fabric of] such a country—and *not* fire the patriotism (and unsheath the swords) of *us all*! No, Americans. While you reserve *your* independent privilege,-of rendering at all times *your* suffrages as *you* please,-let our proud foe [on this point] be undeceived! Let her- let the world learn (now and *forever*),-that the voice of *our nation-* when once "legitimately" expressed- *is holy,—is imperious*! That it is a summons,-of *duty* to *every* citizen! That when *we* strike [out] at a foreign foe,-the *sacred* bond of "country" becomes the *pledge of a concentrated effort!* That in such a cause (and at such a crisis),-*we* feel with but *one heart-* and strike [out] with *our whole* [*united*] *strength! We* are the *only nation* in the world, fellow citizens,-where the people and the government stand in *all* things identified [as *one*],—where *all* the acts of the latter are immediately submitted to the *superior* revision of the for-

mer,—where *every* blow at the general safety becomes the *personal* concern of *each individual*! Happy people- happy government,—will you give up [lightly]- will you *not* defend *such* blessings!

33 We are, also, perhaps the *only genuine* republic which- since the days of the ancients- has taken up arms against a foreign foe,-in defense of its rights- and its liberties. [What an] Animating thought! Warmed with the [inspiring] fire of "ancient" freedom—may *we not* expect to see the valor of [the Greek forces at] Thermopylae and Marathon *again* displayed [in America]! The Congress of 1812,-[sitting] *here*- within these august walls [of the Capitol],-have proclaimed to the world,—that *other* feelings than those of servility- avarice- or fear pervade the *American* bosom! That in the hope and purity of youth,-*we are not debased* by the [doting] passions of a corrupt old age! That *our* sensibilities are,-*other than* sordid! That *we* are,-ambitious of [acquiring] the dignified port [and bearing] of *freemen*! That, while pacific [in outlook], we *know* the value of *national* rights and *national* justice—and,-with [all] the spirit due our lasting prosperity as a [sovereign] republic,—*design* to repel "authenticated" outrages [perpetrated] *upon either*! That we will (and *dare*) act,-as becomes a *free*- an *enlightened*- and a *brave* people! *Illustrious* Congress—[how] worthy [*we* truly are] to have *your* names recounted [in the same breath] with the illustrious fathers of *our* Revolution! For, [after all,] what grievances [really] *were* those,- that led [our fathers] to [advocate and commit] the *great* act which made us [into] a nation,—that have *not* been equaled [ever since] (shall I say "have not been *surpassed* [since]," [rather than using "equaled" in this instance]?)- [even] by those [very grievances] which moved [you as a Congress] to [enact] *your deed* [of declaring war against Britain]! And what noble hazards did *they* encounter—which *you ought not* [now] to brave!

34 If *we are not fully* prepared for war [at present], let the sublime spectacle be *soon* exhibited [-for all to see],-that a *free* (and a valiant) nation,-[so fortunate as to be blessed] with *our* [superior] numbers- and a *just* cause [like our own],—is *always a powerful* nation,—*is always ready to defend* its *essential* rights! [For] The Congress of Seventy-six declared [our] Independence- and hurled [its] defiance at *this same* insatiate foe (six-and-thirty years ago),-[when confronted] with an army of [some] seventeen thousand hostile troops- just landed *upon our shores*! And *shall we now* "hesitate,"-*shall we bow our* necks [down meekly] in "submission,"—*shall we* [*condescend to*] *make* an ignominious "surrender" of *our* birthright [as American citizens] (under the "plea" that *we are not* "prepared" to defend it)! No, Americans. Your's *has* been a pacific republic—and, therefore, has *not* [thus far] exhibited [any active design of] military preparation. But it *is a free republic*—and, therefore, will it now (as *before* [in Seventy-six]) *soon* [have at its] command battalions [of militia]- [the] discipline [of a maturing nation]- [individual acts of] courage! Could a [vain and haughty] General- of old[en days in Europe- perhaps not expect that],-by only stamping [his boot in displeasure up]on the earth,-[he

might] raise up [vast] armies [of peasants,—to protect the interests of the ruling nobility]! And shall a whole [united] nation of *freemen* [like ourselves]- at such a time [and crisis]-know *not where* to look for [its militia and recruits,-who, in turn, will learn to keep a sharp lookout for hired conscripts like] them! The *soldiers* of Bunker Hill- the *soldiers* of Bennington- the *soldiers* of [Tippecanoe and] the Wabash- the [gallant] *seamen* of Tripoli [and the Barbary Coast simply] contradict [the mercenary service] it [,as a proposition, demands of *freemen* like ourselves]!

35 By one of the surviving patriots of our Revolution, I have been told that- in the Congress of 1774,-among other arguments used- to prevent a war (and separation from Great Britain),—the danger of having *our towns* battered down (and burnt) was zealously urged [before the delegates]. The venerable Christopher Gadsden of South Carolina rose [from out of his seat]—and replied to it- in *these* memorable words: "Our seaport towns, Mr. President, *are* composed of brick and wood. If they *are destroyed,*-we have clay and timber *enough* in our country,—to rebuild them. But,-if the [very] *liberties* of our country *are destroyed,*—where [then] shall we find the materials *to replace them*!" Behold, in this [quotation],-an example of virtuous sentiment- *fit* to be imitated! Indulge me with [yet] another illustration of American patriotism,-derived from the same source. During the seige of Boston, General Washington consulted Congress- upon the propriety of bombarding the town. Mr. Hancock was then president of [the] Congress. [And] After General Washington's letter was read,-a solemn silence ensued [among the delegates]. This [lull] was broken [only] by a member making a motion,-that the house *should* resolve itself into a Committee of the Whole,—in order that Mr. Hancock might give *his* opinion upon the important subject- as *he* was so "deeply" interested from having all [of] *his* estate [and holdings] *in Boston.* After he left[his post on] the Chair, he [acceded to the member's request—and] addressed the chairman of the Committee of the Whole- in the following words: "It *is true,* sir,—*nearly all* the property I have in the world is in houses and other real estate- [all lying *with*]*in the town of Boston.* But,-if the expulsion of the British army from it (and the [very] *liberties* of our country) *require* their being burnt to *ashes,*—issue the order for that purpose *immediately*!"

36 What has ancient or modern story to boast [of],-beyond [offering, for our view,] *such* elevated specimens of public virtue? And *what inspiring lessons* of [national] duty *do they teach us*! War, fellow citizens, [really] is *not* the *greatest* of evils [facing us at the present time]. Long submission to [cumulative acts of] injustice is *worse*! Peace- a long peace,-a peace purchased by [paying the lesser price of] mean and inglorious sacrifices,—is *worse,*—*is far worse*! War takes away a [human] life- *destined* by Nature to [extend unto a person's] death—it produces- chiefly *bodily* evils [in everyone among us]. But when ignoble peace *robs us* of virtue- *debases* the [national] mind (and [in effect] chills its *best* feelings),-it renders life [but] a *living death* [for all among us],—and makes *us* [every bit as] offensive [as in death- only adding to the bur-

den by placing our "existence"] above [the plane of a burial] ground! The evils of ignoble peace are,-an *inordinate love* of money [and titled wealth]—[the divisive] rage of *party spirit,*—and a willingness to endure even [the onus] of *slavery* itself,-rather than [responsibly] bear [the distinct reality of pending] pecuniary deprivations (or brave [assorted] "manly" hazards)! The states of Holland and of Italy will be found- at several stages of their history- strikingly to exemplify this remark. [For] War in a *just* cause produces [a national sense of] *patriotism*! Witness the speech of Gadsden[,as excerpted above]. It produces [only] the most *noble* disinterestedness [and resourcefulness],-where [the issue of the vital fiber and destiny of *our* country is concerned! Witness the speech of Hancock [,likewise above]. It serves to destroy *party spirit,*-which *may* become *worse than war* [in its national impact]! [For] In war, death *is* produced [through an allegiance to national patriotism-] without personal hatred [entering in as a direct cause of the final act, regardless of however violent or self-confronting it might be]. But,-under the influence of [a] *party spirit* inflamed by [all] the *sordid* desires of an *inglorious peace,*—[only] the most *malignant* passions *are generated*—and *we hate* [one another, not in a general national way, but in a way far more intensely personal-really] with [passions akin to] the [intensely vindictive] spirit of [spiteful] *murderers*!

37 Could the departed heroes of the Revolution [but] rise [up] from their sleep,-and behold *their* descendants,—[alternately] hanging ("contentedly" [in the manner of some miser or actual owner]) over hoards of [British] money—or casting up British invoices [-as regularly received with British goods,-to be paid for, in full, out of their British hoards],—while *so long* a list of [vital national] wrongs *still* looked them in the face—calling [crying out] for *retribution,—what would they say*! Would they *not* hasten back to [the relative solitude of] *their* tombs,-now *more* welcome than ever,-since they [and the grave] would conceal-from *their* view- the *base conduct* of those sons,—for whom *they so gallantly fought,*—and *so gallantly fell!* But stop [and reflect for a moment]. Return-*return,-illustrious band,*—stay *and behold,—stay—and applaud* what *we too* are [now] doing! [For] *we* will *not dishonor your noble* achievements! *We* will *defend* the inheritance *you bequeathed us,-we* will wipe away *all past* stains [upon our national honor],—*we* will maintain *our* rights at [the cold steel of] *the sword,*—or- like you- *we will die* [in the cause and effort]! [And only] *Then* shall *we* render *our ashes worthy* to mingle with *your's* [in the grave]! *Sacred* in *our* [national] celebrations [ever] be *this day,*-[un]to the *end of time*! *Revered* [ever] be the *memories* of the statesmen and orators (whose *wisdom led* to the act of Independence),-and of the gallant soldiers (who [successfully] *sealed* it with *their blood*)!

38 May the fires of *their* genius and courage [ever] animate (and sustain) us- in *our* contest—and bring it to a *like glorious* result! May it [ever] be carried on,-with *singleness* [of national purpose shown] to[wards] the objects- that *alone summoned us* to [engage in] it,—as a *great and imperious duty* (irksome-

yet *necessary*)! May there [ever] be a willing (a *joyful*) immolation of *all selfish passions*,-[up]on the [sacred] altar of a *common* country [and national mission like our own]! May the *hearts* of *our* combatants [ever] be [made] *bold*—and-under [the blessing of] a propitious Heaven- *their swords* [be made to] *flash* "Victory!" May a speedy peace *bless us*,-and the passions of war [ever] *go off* [from the scene- once *our* victory is achieved],—leaving- in their place- a [yet] *stronger love* of country (and of *each other*)! *Then* may pacific glories,-accumulating (and *beaming*) from the *excitement* of the *national mind*,—*long be our's*!—A *roused intellect*- a *spirit* of *patriotic improvement*,-in whatever *can gild the American* name,—in *arts*- in *literature*- in *science*- in *manufactures*- in *agriculture*- in *legislation*- in *morals*—in imbuing *our admirable forms* of [civil] polity (with *still more and more* perfection),—may these *then* (and *long*) *be our's*! May *common* perils and *common* triumphs [ever] *bind us*- [the] *more closely* together! May the [resulting] era furnish [illustrious] names to [illuminate] *our* annals,-up[on] whom- "late time" a "kindling eye" shall [in-deed] "turn!" *Revered* [ever] be the *dust* of those who *fall* [in battle],—[ever] *sweet* [be] their *memories* [for us]!—Their *country vindicated*- their *duty done*,—an *honorable* renown- the *regrets* of a nation [united in peace]—[regrets including] the *eulogies* of friendship- the slow (and *moving*) *dirges* of [seasoned military veterans, in] the camp- the *tears* of [womanly] beauty,—all—*all will* [serve to] *sanctify their* [individual sacrifice and] *doom*!*Honored* [ever] be those [soldiers],-who *outlive the strife* of arms—*our rights* [having been] established-*justice* secured [for the nation]- a haughty foe taught to respect *the freemen* she had abused (and plundered)!—To [be able to] *survive* [and] to [enjoy] *such* recollections (and *such* a consciousness),—*is* there ([really] *can there be*) a *nobler reward*!

Chapter 3

Leonard Bacon's Fourth of July Oration, 1824 and 1825

The classification of sermons and orations, known contemporaneously as humanitarian "pleas for Africa," required that certain fundamental questions of moral responsibility be addressed by the speaker.[1] Particularly when a "plea" was delivered on the national anniversary of Independence, the orator had to measure inconsistent Christian conduct against a welfare-state patriotic guideline. The benevolent standard for white citizens' patriotic morality presumably being emphasized in terms of community services (an "*every*day duty for *every* man").[2] Such a determination indeed became quite essential in the light of generalized perversions of the oration medium as the 1820's unfolded, perversions rather deplored by one religious correspondent in 1824 as amoral weakness in "gasconading eulogiums, improbably anticipations, and universal denunciations of all sorts of government except our own."[3] And

1 Boston, 30 May, 1825, John Todd to LB, New Haven, Bacon Family Papers, Yale University Library (New Haven, Ct.); *Recorder and Telegraph* (Boston), 8 July, 1825. The majority of published sermons and orations benefiting the American Colonization Society did not, of course, have a formal "plea" designation in their titles. In addition to the pamphlet edition of Bacon's oration, printed by Thomas G. Woodward after the second delivery in 1825, two explicit exceptions to this implied "plea" rule are Edward D[orr]. Griffin, *A Plea for Africa: A Sermon Preached October 26, 1817, in the First Presbyterian Church in the City of New-York, before the Synod of New-York and New-Jersey, at the Request of the Board of Directors of the African School Established by the Synod* (New York: Gould, 1817); John Newland Maffit, *A Plea for Africa: A Sermon Delivered at Bennet Street Church, in Behalf of the American Colonization Society, July 4, 1830* (Boston: E. W. Crittenden, 1830). Bacon Family Papers (Yale Univ. Library) hereafter cited as Bacon Family Papers-Yale.

2 Bacon, "The Proper Character and Functions of American Literature," *American Biblical Repository and Classical Review*, 2nd Ser., 3 (Jan. 1840), 16.

3 D.R., "Remarks on the manner of celebrating our National Independence," *Christian Spectator*, 6 (1 June, 1824), 307.

any northern orator, speaking on behalf of the American Colonization Society, had to weigh moral repercussions when preparing his "plea." For if southern slaves, when emigrating north to obtain some "emancipated" status as freemen/laborers, were immorally discriminated against as fatalistic nuisances draining a thrifty Yankee community's social assets, what moral obligation had southern planters to accede to the Colonization Society's demand for even a token release of surplus slave labor?[4]

If state statutes in the South, immorally legislating "perfect ignorance" for blacks, were being impinged upon in this gratuitous process, really before the heyday of a pro-southern fugitive slave law and pacifist underground-railroad solution, what responsible role were auxiliary chapters of the parent Colonization Society in fact to play?[5] Slavery certainly had become a more integral part of an expanding southern economic apparatus by 1824, and many planters fronted self-righteous paternalism to rationalize stopping short of supplying the Colonization Society with slaves for Liberia. All dazzling biblical imagery alluding to horrors of the African slave trade aside, however, the effective province of the northern orator's "plea" turned more domestic than foreign in the 1820's, the orator arguing a good-works case to recognize civil rights of freed blacks in church parishes and more politicized sectors of northern communities. Indeed, the chain of events flowing from such pleas (and non-recognition of civil rights) often was so ironically defeatist, that its gradualist tone more than matched the parent Society's ineffectiveness in never really being able to requisition an adequate number of southern slaves for amicable resettlement in Liberia.

Leonard Bacon's "plea for Africa," delivered at Boston's Park Street Church on the non-Sabbath fifth in 1824, and repeated the next year on the Fourth at New Haven's Centre Church, offers a case in point of the moral limitations placed upon advocates for the American Colonization Society. When first drafting the oration in mid-June, 1824, Bacon, a novice licentiate from Andover Seminary,[6] seemingly sought to suppress his own "dark forebodings of failure" in "very elaborate" Alexandrian views, an attitude perhaps more morally propagandistic than cynically a statement from fact.[7] But he never confided such details to his mother, when writing about the responsible attitude with which he approached addressing the joint Congregational and Baptist observance at Sereno Edwards Dwight's church: "I felt myself obligated to devote

---

4 B.L., "Fourth of July,—African Colonization," *Recorder and Telegraph* (Boston), 17 June, 1825.

5 Bacon, "Report of a Committee appointed February 18, 1823, to inquire respecting the black population of the U.S.," Manuscript in Andover Newton Theological School (Newton Centre, Mass.), sentence printed in *Christian Spectator*, 5 (1 Oct., 1823), 541; A Fredonian, "Undated letter to editor," *The Intelligencer* (Lexington, Va.), 24 June, 1825. This Bacon reference cited hereafter as "Black Inquiry Committee Report," Andover Newton MS.

6 Boston *Recorder*, 5 June and 3 July, 1824.

7 Andover, Mass., 18 June, 1824, *LB* to Alexander C. Twining, New Haven, Bacon Family Papers-Yale.

considerable time to the composition of this address, both for the sake of the Colonization Society- whose cause I was to plead, and for the sake of my own reputation- which was very much at stake, and that of the Seminary- which was somewhat involved in my success. I succeeded, I believe, quite well as I had any reason to expect. The contribution [to the Colonization Society] amounted to 140 [or 142] dollars; and my performance has been spoken of by good judges in terms of approbation."[8]

Although Bacon may have been offered an agent's position in the Colonization Society as a result of the appearance, the Andover novice knew well enough to turn it down. Instead, heeding the advice of Andover mentors Ebenezer Porter and Edward Dorr Griffin, each a Professor of Sacred Rhetoric, that grudging approval of the oration necessarily committed him all the more to dedicated practice on the itinerant circuit ("preaching, preaching, preaching is the business for me"). Especially when, unordained licentiate that he was, Bacon obviously never dared confess every last scintilla of self-doubt, even to "very great friend" Porter: "They do not know, to be sure, all that I might tell them . . . ,-but still they can judge of my abilities better, in some respects at least, than I can; and, therefore, I cannot disregard their opinions in forming my determinations."[9]

If Bacon understandably found himself trying to cope with some lack of experience at Boston in 1824, circumstances surrounding his repetition of the "plea" in 1825 at New Haven were slightly more auspicious. But why the repetition? Bacon's inaugural sermon in Centre Church on the afternoon of March 13, 1825, provides a partial answer. For despite equating moral intensity ("fervor" and "boldness") with effective rhetorical purpose, there is an apparent assumption that beginning clergymen like himself are more prone to dabble in "hasty and careless composition." A corollary really of this inventive statement cautioning parishioners against taking exhibitionist sermonizing too seriously: "I say that if his sermons are such as an enlightened congregation ought to hear, the simple process of composition, especially in the earlier years of his ministry, must be no slight or momentary labor. But the process of composition is only a small part of what a minister must go thro[ugh]' in his study. So long as he continues to preach, he must be able to bring forth out of his treasure things new and old."[10] And when, on June 22, pressed by agent Ralph

8 Andover, 8 July, 1824, *LB* to Mrs. Alice Bacon, West Bloomfield, N.Y., Bacon Family Papers-Yale; Boston *Recorder*, 10 and 17 July, 1824.

9 Andover, 20 July, 1824, *LB* to Theodore D[wight]. Woolsey, New Haven, Bacon Family Papers-Yale. Most of Bacon's itinerant substitutions were in Massachusetts, towns like Medford, Quincy, and Salem, all within convenient traveling distance of Andover and metropolitan Boston. And on 28 Sept., he was ordained as an evangelist at Windsor, Connecticut, *Christian Spectator*, 6 (1 Nov., 1824), 607.

10 "Manuscript of part 2 of inaugural sermon," Bacon Family Papers-Yale. Bacon formally was installed as pastor by Rev. Joel Hawes of Hartford's First Church on 9 March, with this particular sermon being given morning (part 1) and afternoon on the following Thursday. *Christian Spectator*, 8 (1 April, 1825), 224.

Randolph Gurley of the Colonization Society for some song or ode, with which to memorialize "injured and benighted Africa" to a comfortably "enlightened, benevolent, and liberal public," Bacon decided to revive his old "plea" text, resolving to send a specimen copy from a forthcoming pamphlet edition of the oration along to Gurley toward the end of July.[11]

The morning of the Fourth found pastor Bacon offering up a benedictory prayer in the Methodist Church, after William Croswell recited a "poetic oration."[12] More a poem than an oration, incidentally, and lauded as "excellent" and "suited to the occasion" by a reporter for the *Columbia Register.*[13] Then, late in the afternoon, Bacon repeated his "plea" in Centre Church, not to any heterogeneous religious audience but one comprised mostly of his own parishioners. Of the three major New Haven papers, only the *Connecticut Journal* included some mention of the "plea" in covering local events-of-the-day. And since Bacon's oration came last in the *Journal* account, the reporter may have cited it more to emphasize the almost programmed tranquility of New Haven's celebration: "He was listened to, with great interest, by a large and respectable audience, who retired from the church highly gratified with the opportunity of commemorating the occasion in a manner so appropriate and so consonant to their feelings."[14]

When the pamphlet edition, sponsored locally by A. H. Maltby and Company, and printed by Thomas G. Woodward, came out on the twenty-sixth,[15] reviewers quickly took up the question of what means realistically were available

11 Washington, D.C., 21 April and 22 June, 1825, Gurley to LB, New Haven, Bacon Family Papers-Yale; Gurley, "Appeal to Christians in the United States, datelined Society office-27 June," *Daily National Intelligencer* (Washington, D.C.), 30 June, 1825. Bacon also was influenced in his decision by the fact that he never furnished Gurley with any sort of lengthy article, requested for the first issue of the Society's *African Repository and Colonial Journal.* Preferring, instead, to forward the text of his sermon eulogizing Rev. Samuel J. Mills, which Gurley devoted only a single page (63) to excerpting in the second *Journal* issue. And if forwarded by Bacon, as was not to be the case, any brief song or ode quite obviously would be printed in the *Intelligencer* or the Society's *Journal.* Georgetown, D.C., 11 Jan., 1825, Gurley to LB, Taunton, Mass./WDC, 8 March, 1825, Gurley to LB, New Haven, Bacon Family Papers-Yale.

12 *Connecticut Journal* (New Haven), 5 July, 1825.

13 *Register* (New Haven), 9 July, 1825.

14 "Independence," *Journal* (New Haven), 5 July, 1825. Even the final artillery salute strangely featured gratitude and quiescence. Immediately after the sentence quoted, the reporter concluded his account in this manner: "The day was closed with the evening salute. And we are gratified to say that the exercises of every description were terminated without accident, or any occurrence to mar the festivities of the occasion."

15 *Connecticut Herald* (New Haven), 2 Aug., 1825. Maltby and Company was a local book-stationery store, and its advertisement of the pamphlet in the *Herald* contained a humanitarian "plea" allusion from Proverbs (chapter 31, verse 9): "Open thy mouth, judge righteously, and *plead* the cause of the poor and needy."

16 Two identifications of these initials might conceivably be valid. Benjamin D. Hubbard permanently resided in New Haven when, as a senior, choosing not to graduate from Yale in the class of

to achieve the civilized ends postulated by orator Bacon. Correspondent B.D.H.[16] wrote local *Journal* editor Sherman Converse, a Bacon parishioner who may have heard the oration firsthand, about the pastor's "loud tone" which white public opinion in New Haven ought not disregard. Yet a strong hint of hypocrisy and racial discrimination could not be erased by the correspondent's setting out to rid the local community of a black social stain, which even then might be resistant to respectable "good wishes and good exertions" proffered by philanthropic whites: "Must they frequent, in numbers, the vile dramshops [barrooms] in some parts of the city, without [such] a louder warning voice [being heard]? Can no spirited or noble attempt be made to elevate their condition—either by teaching them lessons of morality and religion here, or by inducing them to go where they can be more respectable (to Haiti, or to Africa)? And is it wise or benevolent to say that nothing can be done, without further attempts? And if any are to be made, will the spirit of New Haven permit them to languish?[17]

Dr. Eli Ayres, veteran Liberian agent who had visited New Haven during August of 1824, inducing an inactive local auxiliary to remain active enough so as to have a committee of correspondence with the Colonization Society,[18] thought "young clergyman" Bacon and the oration able to stimulate a more active interest in community racial relations among whites. Far better able to deal with racial apathy locally, that is, than with what Ayres regarded as "an intolerable jealousy against elevating the character of the blacks" in the South.[19] Still, Ralph Randolph Gurley could not as easily eliminate southern auxiliaries from the purview of the oration, not only confirming that Bacon forwarded pamphlets to sympathetic Andover friends, but requesting a packet of pamphlets for his personal distribution to secretaries of southern chapters, including of course southern legislators in southern-oriented Washington. Gurley credited the "plea" with possessing enough rational argument, divine charity mitigating

---

1810. By 1825, assuming that he continued to reside locally or returned within the ten-year census period, Hubbard may have become a staffer on editor Converse's *Journal.* Or a second possibility suggests itself. The *Journal* compositor could have been guilty of a slight typo when initialing Benjamin L. Hamlen's name from the article submitted. Hamlen was a Centre parishioner at the time, and may have listened to Bacon's "plea" in the company of editor Converse. He had joined Centre during Nathaniel W. Taylor's ministry, becoming printer to Yale several years after Bacon's repetition of the oration. *Catalogue of the Officers and Students of Yale-College, November 1810* (poster/sheet); *Catalogue of the Members of the First Church in New Haven, from March 1, 1758, to May 1, 1847* (New Haven: B. L. Hamlin, 1847), p. 51.

17 *Journal* (New Haven), 26 July, 1825.

18 *Dly National Intelligencer* (WDC), 9 Sept., 1824; *Appendix to the Eighth Annual Report of the American Society for Colonizing the Free People of Color of the United States* (Washington City: James C. Dunn, 1825), pp. 47-48. Five local men served on the correspondence committee: Simeon Baldwin (chairman), Ralph I. Ingersoll (secretary), Rev. Harry Croswell, Rev. Claudius Herrick, and Timothy Dwight.

19 Baltimore, 4 Aug., 1825, Ayres to LB, New Haven, Bacon Family Papers-Yale.

"mere pathetic appeals," to placate a much lesser "degree of irritation and unkindness" in the South than Ayres discerned.[20]

Indeed, agent Gurley had absolutely no reason to find fault with any exhibitionist demonstration on Bacon's part, and viewed the oration as a tangible expression of national support, bringing sorely needed means, necessary for advancing what he persistently proclaimed to be the Society's "great and good cause," within reach of the organization's limited funds: "God forbid, that anything should disturb the harmony which is apparent, or prevent the citizens of these states from exhibiting themselves, as [if] in one mass of wisdom and strength, to effect a purpose most strictly national—which demands national means, and which must bring the richest contribution to our national honor." Concluded Gurley in a slightly condescending manner, "Africa, My Dear Sir, owes you much."[21]

If resident agent Gurley was preoccupied with fitting out a vessel scheduled to carry a minimal number of slaves to Liberia early in September,[22] agent Ayres in Baltimore tried out two communal possibilities for manumitted southern slaves on Bacon. One, a trading company in Liberia, which would have to fund transporting many more blacks to the Society's colony there.[23] Another, a domestic school and laboring community in Montgomery County, Maryland,[24] geared to generate similar funding, though sufficiently "respectable" and "public" not to antagonize northern philanthropists, and certainly never to be classed with Frances Wright's utopian schemes in Louisiana and Nashoba, Tennessee. But

---

20 There is a distinct possibility that Gurley acted out of some familiarity with a parallel southern distribution of a pamphlet edition of Bacon's 1823 Andover report. For one of the many reprints of an article describing Bacon's "interesting statement," read by him to the Colonization Society's Board of Managers meeting at the Washington City Hall on 2 June, see *National Intelligencer* (WDC) in Hillsborough [N.C.], *Recorder*, 2 July, 1823. Nor could the fact that New Haven carriage entrepreneurs James Brewster and John Cook did considerable business with the South have made Bacon any less desirable as a sectional conciliator in Gurley's eyes. Alice Dana Adams, *The Neglected Period of Anti-Slavery in America, 1808-1831* (Boston: Ginn, 1908), p. 66; Ellsworth Strong Grant, *Yankee Dreamers and Doers* (Chester, Ct.; Pequot Press, 1974), pp. 169-70.

21 Gurley, *A Discourse, Delivered on the Fourth of July, 1825, in the City of Washington* (Washington, D.C.: Gales and Seaton, 1825), pp. 9, 13, and 21; WDC, 30 July, 1825, Gurley to LB, New Haven, Bacon Family Papers-Yale; *African Repository and Colonial Journal*, 1 (Aug. 1825), 169. No record is extant of the precise amount of money contributed to the Colonization Society by the Centre congregation after Bacon's second delivery. But agent Gurley might conceivably have passed along some personal displeasure at the Centre total, when he wrote Bacon: "We have indulged the hope that the collections on the Fourth of July would amount to a large sum, but little has yet come into our treasury. What may we expect from New England? Did the churches and congregations in Connecticut generally comply with the recommendation of the [Presbyterian] Gen[eral] Association?

22 Gurley, "Notice appealing for donations, datelined Society office-28 July," *Dly National Intelligencer* (WDC), 29 July, 1825.

23 Bacon, "The Reports of the American Society for colonizing the free people of color in the United States (1818 through 1823)," *Christian Spectator*, 5 (1 Sept., 1823), 492.

24 Boston *Recorder*, 12 June, 1824.

transparent sectional problems in funding even rival fanatical projects like Wright's came to the fore, when Ayres found himself speculating over her success: "She has the promise from New York, that, if she gets the countenance of the South, she shall not want [for] funds."[25]

And agent Ayres rather narrowly regarded Bacon as one among several regional publicists, eligible to promote the advantages of Ayres's own vested interest in superintending the Society's Kosciusko communal project in Maryland.[26] He tentatively put his inquiry to Bacon in this light: "Will you please to inform me which three [news]papers would be best to advertise the property in;-to give it the greatest circulation through[out] the New England states.—I will advertise the property, and if I see any probability of succe[e]ding, I will then come on [up] to the North.—If some young clergyman from Andover [such as yourself] would take it up, and form his congregation [into one opinion on the matter], would it not be a great way to begin?—Please to give me your opinion on it."[27]

Jared Sparks in the *North American Review* likewise skirted realistic implications of existing means, when examining "glowing colors" in Bacon's "eloquent and animated" oration. The precise number of blacks actually resettled in Liberia could not be at issue. Rather, for Sparks, "good results" from the Colonization Society's civilized philanthropy were more than assured by a paramount theoretical purpose, benevolence inherent in "noble and generous objects." Bacon's oration, when read beyond the confines of New Haven, surely would gain new adherents, who in turn would contribute more funds, resettle more slaves, and justify philanthropists' faith in implementing any such attractive philosophical premise. Bacon's rhetorical message quite zealously flushed any satisfaction Sparks found in the establishment of a skeleton Liberian colony by the Society: "If one person only is sent away and prosperously settled in Africa, it is a benefit to this country, and a benefit to that [Africa], without doing any harm to either. If ten are sent, so much greater is the benefit. And if a colony is established, affording a home to hundreds and thousands, the gain is still increased in the same proportion. In short, much good is *certainly* done, and no harm can *possibly* follow. Such in reality are the facts of the case . . . ."[28]

But a reviewer for the *United States Literary Gazette*, another Boston periodical, conceivably mentors Griffin or Porter unable to forget some of

---

25 Baltimore, 4 Aug., 1825, Ayres to LB, New Haven, Bacon Family Papers-Yale.

26 Baltimore, ca. June, 1824, Robert G. Harper to Leonard Woods, Andover, Mass., in *North American Review*, 20 (Jan. 1825), 197-98.

27 Baltimore, 4 Aug., 1825, Ayres to LB, New Haven, Bacon Family Papers-Yale. The reader may care to consult Amicus, "Kosciusko School," *Freedom's Journal* (New York City), 8 and 15 June, 1827.

28 *Review*, 21 (Oct. 1825), 462-63.

Bacon's inexperience the previous year, refused to be inspired so readily. Even if the very same "glowing colors" labeled by Sparks were not symptomatic of "enormous deductions" novices took such delight in on the Fourth, Bacon's rational specificity was not all that persuasive, seeming "more philanthropic than practical." Bacon's shortcomings, for the reviewer, were virtually synonymous with the plight of the Society whose cause the orator flattered himself he was espousing. As the *Gazette* reviewer curtly surmised, when taking pastor Bacon to task in a note far less generalized than Sparks's benevolent logical progression: "Allowing that these means would effect the attainment of the ultimate object, we still want to know how we are to attain the *means*."[29]

To be persuasively effective, Bacon in his "plea" did not of course, strictly speaking, really have to mobilize some nonexistent consensus behind whatever modest regional means were being advocated by managers of the parent Society. The *Gazette* reviewer failed to perceive that Bacon, in spite of friend Gurley's southern aspirations for the oration, utilized the parent Society's name on the Fourth at New Haven to enhance unprejudiced verbal appeals in support of a purely local means.[30] Namely, the means of activating the local auxiliary of the parent Society into a "Connecticut Colonization Society," a step beyond the existing pro-forma correspondence committee.[31] And in the process of en-

29 *Gazette*, 3 (1 Oct., 1825), 30-31. Mentor Griffin, for example, may have previously communicated similar comments to Bacon. Edward Beecher, in the minutes of a New Haven "antislavery association" meeting attended by Bacon on 10 Aug., includes this sentence: "Letters from Messrs. Ayres, Griffin, and Gurley were read." Assuming that "Ayres" (nn. 19, 25, and 27) and "Gurley" (n.21) designate letters responding to the text of a "plea" pamphlet, forwarded to each by Bacon, any such letter from Griffin cannot be located, as likely as he was to be another recipient of a "plea" copy. The likelihood is that chairman Bacon wanted association members kept informed of liaison activity developing with the parent Society. And even a critical reaction from mentor Griffin would be one means to furthering that end. Bacon Family Papers-Yale.

30 Bacon, "Black Inquiry Committee Report," Andover Newton MS. For other literature treating Bacon's oration, see Leonard Woolsey Bacon, "The Services of Leonard Bacon to African Colonization," *Liberia Bulletin*, 1 (Nov. 1899), 6-7, and *Anti-Slavery before Garrison* (New Haven: Tuttle, Morehouse, and Taylor, 1903), pp. 26-27; Alice Dana Adams, *The Neglected Period of Anti-Slavery in America, 1808-1831* (Boston: Ginn, 1908), p. 66; Theodore Davenport Bacon, *Leonard Bacon: A Statesman in the Church* (New Haven: Yale University Press, 1931), pp. 191-92; and Robert Austin Warner, *New Haven Negroes: A Social History* (New Haven: Yale University Press, 1940), pp. 46-47.

31 Alexander C. Twining, "Minutes of antislavery-association meeting held 17 Aug.," Edward Beecher, "Minutes of meetings dated 24 Aug. and 13 Sept., 1825," Bacon Family Papers-Yale; Twining, "Draft of White Committee Report, ca. early Sept., 1825," Bacon Family Papers-Yale. At the association meeting on 24 Aug., Bacon successfully moved "that the White Committee be requested to report on the expediency of forming a young men's auxiliary Colonization Society- and to devise measures for organizing such [an auxiliary] society, if deemed expedient." The previous week, on the seventeenth, with Bacon tardy in attending, Theodore Dwight Woolsey's motion that "the members of the auxiliary soc[iety]. already existing in N[ew]. Haven be sounded [out] as to their feelings on the objects of the Col[onization]. Soc[iety]. was referred to the White Committee. Twining chaired the White Committee, assisted by Beecher and Henry White. And as read to the 13 Sept. meeting of the association by Twining, the Committee report concluded: "The attention of the committee was naturally directed towards a state-society. But, upon closely exam[in]ing this idea, we think that such a society would end in a name [only], and were of opinion that the formation of a [local] society in N[ew]. H[aven]. is at present discussion preferable; and that the formation of one efficient society in N[ew]. Haven would at present be preferable. A state association, if at any time expedient, would best be formed when a number of [local] subordinate ones existed in full vigor; and [if] an attempt at forming that[state] should fail, would tend to discourage all more private

couraging the formation of other local chapters throughout the state, not only using the Woodward pamphlet edition as the first in a series of promotional essays,[32] but actively soliciting an African school for Connecticut which would equal or surpass the model then in vogue at Parsippany, New Jersey.[33]

A movement to create a young men's "antislavery association" was indeed afoot in New haven shortly before Bacon repeated his oration.[34] And when voted chairman of the reactivated chapter formed on July 6, 1825,[35] qualified as he was to accept donations statewide for a Lancastrian school contemplated in Liberia,[36] the Centre pastor acquired another practical basis for continuing his keen personal interest in the welfare of the quarter of a million freed slaves resident at the North.[37] The central issue, for Bacon, was not how to head off an insurrectionary bloodbath by twelve million southern slaves more than two or

---

auxiliaries. The committee, therefore, as the result of their deliberations recommend—That the antislavery association direct their efforts to the simple point of establishing an auxiliary to the Colonization Soc[iety]., in the city of New Haven." The selection of "Connecticut Colonization Society" as an official title by the 13 Sept. meeting, i.e., over "Young Men's Auxiliary CS," kept the focus local and open to absorbing prejudiced "older men" into the chapter. That is, contrary to what, at first glance, seem "state" implications in members voting to select "Connecticut" over an explicit local "Auxiliary." And just prior to Bacon's motion at the 24 Aug. meeting, of course, the White Committee confirmed the local racial apathy to be remedied ("the colonization [correspondence committee], at present existing [locally], has done nothing, and is likely to do nothing").

32 Beecher, "Minutes of 13 Sept. meeting," Bacon Family Papers-Yale.

33 Bacon, "Black Inquiry Committee Report," Andover Newton MS.; Solomon Peck, "Report of Delegates appointed to consult with the Managers of the American Colonization Society, submitted June 23, 1823," Manuscript in Andover Newton Theological School; Georgetown, D.C., 11 Jan., 1825, Gurley to LB, Taunton, Mass./WDC, 8 March, 1825, Gurley to LB, New Haven; Boston, 30 May, 1825, John Todd to LB, New Haven; Beecher, "Minutes of 3 Aug. meeting"; New York City,5 Sept., 1825, E[lihu]. W. Baldwin to LB, New Haven, Bacon Family Papers-Yale. Locales, under consideration for an African school by the association, included New Haven itself (near Yale, which was part of Centre parish), Cornwall (near the Foreign Mission School, though a similar site in Britain might have accounted for the mention), and Farmington.

34 Entry dated 23 June, 1825, diary of Theodore Dwight Woolsey, Yale University Library. Although apparently not attending an informal discussion in Woolsey's room on 22 June, Bacon may have participated in another discussion held the folowing Wednesday (the twenty-ninth).

35 Beecher, "Minutes of 6 July meeting," Bacon Family Papers-Yale. Bacon, Beecher and Twining (both alternating as secretaries, with Twining permanent treasurer), Woolsey, and Luther Wright, joined after this first meeting by Henry White and Josiah Brewer, comprised the membership of the "antislavery association." And when the association approved the White Committee's report at the 13 Sept. meeting, what once had been a rather secretive club acquired some official recognition as the reactivated chapter Bacon preferred to head. The Centre pastor, for example, willingly took on the role of corresponding secretary at the 10 Aug. meeting, when asked "to obtain the English[British] publications on the subject of Slavery, embracing views of both sides of the subject."

36 C. Wright, "Appeal to the Benevolent People of New England, datelined Montpelier Vt.-22 Sept." *Christian Secretary* (Hartford), 17 Oct., 1825.

37 Bacon, "Black Inquiry Committee Report," Andover Newton MS., passage printed in *Christian Spectator*, 5 (1 Oct., 1823), 548. Bacon's estimate for freed slaves in the North as of 1823 was 238,000, a number based upon 1820 census figures according to his own admission. With an annual rate of increase for the southern slave population in the vicinity of 35,000, again according to Bacon, two years later (or five statistically) freed blacks in the North quite conceivably numbered closer to the quarter-million mark, an estimate approximately 15 percent of some 1,675,000 slaves then laboring at the South.

three generations hence, but how best to educate these northern freedmen who, at the risk of rendering learned theologians and prejudiced Yankee yeomen alike somewhat hypocritical, appeared undeservedly "ignorant and vicious, adding more to the poor rates of the parishes in which they reside than . . . to the income of the Government."[38]

But local racial apathy, if dented only temporarily by Bacon, ambitious Yale tutors, and an oration with a second year's exposure, persisted well into the 1830's in spite of the Centre pastor's efforts. Less than a year after repeating the oration, for example, Bacon lamented the New Haven auxiliary's reversion to "no very great progress," when opening a school locally for a disappointing handful of black adults.[39] And when, in 1831, Simeon S. Jocelyn broached the possibility in earnest of starting up an adequate "Negro College" in New Haven, a proposal originating at Philadelphia and perhaps more in keeping with Bacon's concept of an African school, Mayor Dennis Kimberly and seven hundred voters, including among them Ralph I. Ingersoll, whose "republican" prejudice had taken a different tack since his term on the old correspondence committee,[40] flatly rejected Jocelyn's argument and plan at a town meeting on September 10.[41] Indeed, the reader may want to compare Bacon's gradualist benevolence with Enoch Mack's immediate abolitionist stance in chapter 7.

38 Bacon, "Black Inquiry Committee Report," Andover Newton MS., passages printed in *Christian Spectator*, 5(1 Sept., 1823), 493; (1 Oct., 1823), 542 and 547.

39 New Haven, 23 Jan., 1826, *LB* to Theodore D[wight]. Woolsey, New York City, Bacon Family Papers-Yale.

40 *Connecticut Journal* (New Haven), 5 July, 1825. Ingersoll, present with James Brewster at the Mechanics' Society dinner in the Connecticut Hotel, gave as his toast: "Benjamin Franklin—distinguished alike for his mechanic powers and his *republican* integrity."

41 New Haven *Palladium* in *Dly National Intelligencer* (WDC), 20 Sept., 1831.

Sermon from Mark XII, 34 ("Thou art not far from the Kingdom of God") delivered twice in Boston by Leonard Bacon, Sunday-July 4, 1824, once in the afternoon at the Union Church on Essex Street, and again that evening at the First Baptist Church on Back Street, Incomplete Manuscript in Bacon Family Papers, Yale University Library (New Haven). Since the Fourth and the Sabbath fell on the same day in 1824, Bacon delivered his "plea" address on Monday-July 5, the official Independence Day in Boston, while giving this somewhat "elect" sermon twice on Sunday.

1 The Hebrew prophets very frequently speak of the new and perfect dispensation which was to be established by the promised Messiah, under the image of a Kingdom. Thus in the second Psalm, which even independently of the authority of Peter most evidently refers to Christ, God is introduced as saying, "I have set my King upon my holy hill of Zion," and as having promised to give to this King "the heathen" for his *inheritance*, and "the uttermost parts of the earth" for his *possession*. The celebrated and unquestionable prediction contained in the 9th chapter of Isaiah, declares that "unto us a son is given: and the government shall be upon his shoulder,"-and "Of the increase of *his* government and peace *there shall be* no end, upon the throne of David and upon his Kingdom, to order it, and to establish it with judgment and with justice, from henceforth even forever." The same prophet often kindles to rapture in anticipation of the day when "the Lord of hosts *should* reign in Mount Zion, and in Jerusalem, and before his ancients gloriously." David, too, in Babylon, foretold that the God of heaven was to set up a Kingdom which should *never* be destroyed. And on another occasion he beheld, in no dim or distant perspective, the coming of the Son of Man, to whom was given dominion, and glory, and a Kingdom, that all people, nations, and languages *should* serve him: "His dominion," says the prophet, "is an everlasting dominion which shall *not* pass away, and his Kingdom that which shall *not* be destroyed." And Micah describes the same period as a time when the Lord, having removed all the afflictions of his people, *should* reign over them in Mount Zion forever.

2 To these and similar predictions of the ancient prophets, the expression "Kingdom of God", and the synonymous phrases "Kingdom of heaven", "Kingdom of Christ", and- as it sometimes stands- simply "Kingdom", which are all so often repeated in the *New Testament*, most indubitably refer. Consequently we may say that the *primary* meaning of these expressions is the *reign* of God on earth, the *government* of heaven over the hearts of men, the dominion of the Messiah,-that is to say, the Christian dispensation. So, no doubt, the Jews understood them [to be] when John came, preaching in the wilderness of Judea, and saying, "Repent for the Kingdom of heaven is at hand— repent for the Messiah is coming to establish a new and glorious dispensation." So they understood them [to be] when Jesus himself passed through "every city and village, preaching and showing the glad tidings of the Kingdom of God,"-and when he sent forth at one time his twelve, and at another his seventy disciples, clothed

with miraculous power, to preach the Kingdom of God- that is, to proclaim the approaching dispensation of the Messiah. So ought *we* to understand it, when, in the words which our Redeemer taught us, we pray— "thy Kingdom come",- that is, let Christianity be triumphant—let the empire of Jesus be coextensive with the world.

3 From the primary import of these phrases, the transition is easy to another shade of meaning in which they are frequently employed. It is very natural that the expression, which in one place denotes the spiritual *reign* of God on earth, should elsewhere be made to signify the spiritual *Kingdom* over which he reigns;-that the dominion of Jesus over the hearts of men should sometimes be regarded as the same thing with the men in whose hearts that dominion is established;-or, in other words, that the same language should be **a** EMPLOYED **b** used☆to designate the Christian dispensation and the Christian Church. Thus, when Christ says- "No man having put his hand to the plough, and looking back, is fit for the Kingdom of God," by this phrase he denotes the true spiritual Church;-he means to teach us that no man who wavers and hesitates in his obedience to the gospel, is fit to be a Christian,-or, as he expressed the same principle on a different occasion- no man who hesitates to renounce the world, and all its bliss for him, is worthy to be his disciple. In the same way, when he tells Nicodemus- "Except a man be born of water and *of* the Spirit, he cannot **a** BE MY DISCIPLE **b** enter into the Kingdom of God," ☆-he means to impress upon him the conviction that he who would enter the church of the redeemed, *must not only be* baptized but regenerated- *must not only* make a profession of Christianity, but must also be renewed in the temper of his mind.

4 Very frequently the same forms of speech are used to denote the multiplied blessings that belong to all the true disciples of Christ;- with a more special, and sometimes with an exclusive, reference to the everlasting happiness beyond the grave. This is what the Savior has in view, when he says- "Blessed are the poor in spirit, for their's is the Kingdom of heaven." The poor in spirit are rich in all the blessings of the gospel. In the same sense are we to understand him when he tells his disciples- "Take no thought, saying, *What shall we eat?* or, *What shall we drink?*—but seek first the Kingdom of God, and his righteousness." Let your highest solicitude be to obtain that blessedness which God has promised to all the members of his spiritual Kingdom. And so [God promises] in such passages as the following:—"Fear not, little flock, it is your father's good pleasure to give you the Kingdom." "Many shall come from the east and west, and shall sit down with Abraham and Isaac and Jacob in the Kingdom of heaven." "Know ye not that the unrighteous shall not inherit the Kingdom of God?" In the two last instances- and indeed in other texts too many to be enumerated, these expressions manifestly designate simply the everlasting blessedness of the saints in Heaven.

5 The phrases which I have been attempting to explain, are no doubt occasionally used in a still greater diversity of significations. But, in most in-

stances, one of the three general meanings which I have enumerated, will be found to be the key to any passage in which either of these expressions may occur. I have been, thus, particular in the explanation of these forms of speech—more particular perhaps than was necessary to the perfect understanding of the text[Mark XII, 34]—under the conviction that many Christians, in reading their bibles, are wont to gather from these ever returning expressions only some general and indefinite **a** EXPRESSIONS **b** conceptions, ☆ -and in the hope that, though to some, all that I have said may be perfectly familiar, they will remember how many there are, to whom an explicit and intelligible statement of the various *meanings belonging* to any scriptural expression of frequent occurrence, may be an important and permanent advantage. Permit me, then, to recapitulate what I have said. With a very few exceptions, the words "Kingdom of God", or the words "Kingdom of heaven", wherever they are used in the Bible, mean either— (1) the Christian dispensation- the spiritual reign of God on earth, or— (2) the Christian Church- the community of true believers in Christ, or— (3) the blessings which God has promised in the gospel- particularly the everlasting blessedness of heaven.

6 Now in which of these three significations are we to understand the expression in our text? Undoubtedly in the second, for here, as in almost every other instance, the answer is perfectly **a** EASY **b** evident from the context. ☆ You can all easily recall the circumstances in which the words before us were spoken. The evangelist tells us that a certain scribe— who had stood by while the Saviour had confounded the malignity of the Pharisees, and exposed the artifices of the Herodians, and silenced the cavils of the Sadducees— was prompted by his admiration of the wisdom with which Jesus spake to ask him- "Which is the first commandment of all?" And when Christ had answered him by repeating the words in which Moses sums up the requisites of the moral law,-his reply indicated at once the ingenuousness of his temper and the soundness of his principles.[1] "Well, Master, thou hast said the truth: for there is one God; and there is none other but he: And to love him with all the heart, and with all the understanding, and with all the soul,-and with all the strength, and to love *his* neighbour as himself, is more than all whole burnt offerings and sacrifices." And when Jesus saw that he had answered discreetly, he said unto him- *"Thou art not far from the Kingdom of God*— you are almost my disciple- you are not far from becoming a subject of my spiritual dominion." Wearied as he was, with the malevolence of one party of his adversaries, and the base duplicity of another, and the infidel

1 These three "his" references are to the scribe, and the scribe's reply is quoted next by Bacon.

Leonard Bacon's "Plea for Africa," an address twice delivered on behalf of the American Colonization Society—first at the Park Street Church in Boston at 9:00a.m. on July 5, 1824, and repeated the next Fourth at 5:00p.m. in the Centre Church of New Haven, a pamphlet edition of the speech text being issued on July 26, 1825, in New Haven by Thomas G. Woodward. That very day, the twenty-sixth, promotion excerpts were included in the local Connecticut Journal, *followed shortly thereafter by reprints of excerpts in three religious titles outside the New Haven area—the* Connecticut Observer *(Hartford) on August 2,* Zion's Herald *in Boston on August 17, and the* Recorder and Telegraph *(also Boston) two days later. Incidentally, the previous year any such reprint schedule was sorely lacking. For example, the very same Boston* Recorder *on July 10, 1824, abstracted Bacon's "plea" remarks, but no reprints at all were carried by other papers of its reporter's summary. In fact, only a bare capsule notice of the Park Street meeting, likewise from the* Recorder *of the tenth, was reprinted by various religious papers, the* Christian Secretary *(Hartford) of the twenty-seventh being among them. Yet the following year, despite reprinting pages 19 thru 22 of T. R. Marvin's pamphlet edition of "The Social and Civil Influence of the Christian Ministry" in the May 9 issue (a sermon Bacon preached on February 6, 1825, in commemoration of the sixth anniversary of the Boston Young Men's Auxiliary Education Society), the* Christian Secretary *editor failed to follow up this and previous capsule coverage by excerpting Bacon's "plea" when the Woodward pamphlet actually became available in August. The most extensive excerpts during August, 1825, as might perhaps be anticipated, were reprinted by friend Gurley in the Colonization Society's monthly, the* African Repository and Colonial Journal *(D.C.). Although the monthly's circulation really did not exceed that of a quarterly like the* Christian Spectator *(New Haven), or of a standard weekly like the Boston* Recorder and Telegraph, *Gurley augmented the* Journal *reprints by forwarding a good number of "plea" pamphlets "with advantage" to "Secretaries of Aux*[*iliary*]. *Societies, especially in the South," while urging friend Bacon to maintain faith in the benevolent philanthropy of "reflecting and distinguished men throughout the country." Finally in the spring of 1826, after looking into sales in New York City and Princeton, New Jersey, Bacon apparently decided to make a "gratuitous distribution" of whatever "plea" pamphlets remained unsold. So much for identifying the delivery and distribution specifics of the address. Two passages in the following text indirectly link Bacon's inventive process with a missionary-committee report, prepared by him between February 18 and April 22, 1823, while still studying at what was then Andover Theological Seminary. The missionary committee, with Bacon, Solomon Peck, S. A. Cowles, and R. Washburn listed as members, had the Society for Inquiry concerning Missions as its parent group at Andover, and spokesman Bacon, in drafting the subcommittee's final report, responded to a resolution from the parent group calling for "immediate objects" and "most eligible means" to be searched out and implemented "in favor of the black population of our country." Several* *comparative symbols are used in editing both inventive-process passages:* **s** *represents the Woodward pamphlet text, in the absence of any speech manuscript in the Bacon Family Papers;* **m** *part 2 of Bacon's Andover report, as published in the* Christian Spectator *for October 1, 1823; and* m *the original manuscript of Bacon's report presently on file at Andover Newton Theological School in Newton Centre, Massachusetts. The reader should pay particular attention to larger segments, structured with* CAPITAL LETTERS *in sequence, and to smaller phrases in* Univers *type designated by bold arabic numerals common to these larger structured segments. That is to say, each similar phrase will be preceded by the identical arabic numeral (***1 2 3***, etc.), and each of the three key textual symbols (***s m*** m*) will break down into the usual* **a b c** *revisions. Segments set off and preceded by* **s** *enable the reader to continue on with the "plea" text.*

1 I come before you today, my friends and fellow citizens, [so] that I may plead for Africa. And as I could not ask for an audience more favorable than an assembly of American Christians, so I could not seek an occasion more auspicious than that which this anniversary has offered. Today we remember that we are Americans; the voice of jubilee is heard in our land from the ocean to the mountains. Eight millions of freemen are rejoicing in their liberty, and calling to mind those high recollections of the past that glorify our national history, and those loftier anticipations that light up before us the obscurity of the future. Sharing in the enthusiasm which the occasion inspires, we seem almost to forget our individual existence in the consciousness that we are members of a great and happy community. The man who rejoices today rejoices not in the enjoyments by which he is distinguished from his fellows around him, but in those common blessings which he shares with the meanest and the proudest of his countrymen! His personal joys and selfish purposes are forgotten for the moment, while his spirit rises to a wider range of thought and to the exercise of nobler affections. A nation utters her voice of gladness today, and he who rejoices with her rejoices in the happiness of thousands whom he has never seen, and with whom he has no fellowship but the fellowship of a common nature and the fellowship of a common country! I may hail the occasion, then, as auspicious to my cause, inasmuch as the feelings of patriotism, which it inspires in every bosom, are akin to those still nobler feelings which my argument must presuppose within you, and to which it must be mainly addressed. But still more may I congratulate myself that I am permitted to plead before those in whose hearts the enthusiasm of the patriot is blending today with the devotion of the Christian, and who have come up to the temple of God [so] that they may learn to sanctify the fervency of the one with the purity of the other.

2 We might dwell in our thoughts on those topics of exultation which the occasion affords—on the unrivaled prosperity of our country- and the perfect beauty of our political institutions—on the bright memory of the past- and the still brighter prospect of the future;-and from all these contemplations learn no

holier lesson than to indulge the unhallowed exultation of national pride, or to cherish the bloody fanaticism of national ambition! But there are other feelings, more dignified in their aspect and more ennobling in their influence, which the solemnities that now engage us are designed to awaken. We look back on the ages that are past. Two centuries ago this wide continent was a wilderness, unvisited and unexplored. Then came our Pilgrim fathers, and erected here the ensigns of their freedom and the altars of their religion. They contended with difficulties to which even fable can hardly yield a parallel. But their faith and courage and devotion were mightier than their trials. And in the midst of peril they became the founders of an empire. We look around on the present condition of our country. Our coast is adorned with an hundred cities all humming with the noise of trade, and our bays and rivers are sprinkled with the sails of commerce. Where the wilderness lay, in its dark and untrodden luxuriance, a thousand villages are smiling in the face of Heaven, and the fields are whitening for the harvest. The land where the Puritans found a refuge has become the home of freedom;-and, under the republican institutions which they established, eight millions of citizens are enjoying a political happiness such as the historian has never recorded, and (I may say) such as the philosopher has never imagined. The halls of science and the schools of elementary instruction, which the Puritans erected, are still the memorials of their wisdom. And the new efforts that are made, from year to year, for the advancement and for the general diffusion of knowledge testify that the men of this age have not entirely degenerated from the spirit of their fathers. And, above all, the religion of the Puritans, which kindled in them their stern spirit of independence and their ardent love of knowledge—the religion which led them over the wide (and then hardly navigated) waters of the Atlantic— the religion which made them heroes in enterprise and martyrs in endurance—that [same] religion is exerting over our national character, today, an influence more sacred and a dominion more powerful than it has [ever] possessed before since the time when our fathers lifted up their voices in the wilderness! And,-with no walls around them but the everlasting hills, and with no roof above them but the arch of Heaven,-[they] offered their simple and solemn worship to Him who dwelleth not in temples made with hands!

3 We look forward;-and it seems as if all that is inspiring in our history and all that is happy in our present condition were but the dawning of our day. We are in the very infancy of our being—and as no nation could ever boast of a history more abundant in high and holy remembrances than our's,-as no political institutions were ever so perfect, and no political happiness was ever so unmingled as our's,-so, to no people under Heaven, was it ever permitted to contemplate a prospect of future prosperity more magnificent than that which is opening before us! These lofty recollections, this thrilling consciousness, these inspiring hopes we need not check. For who hath forbidden us to indulge them? But in this consecrated place, as our national happiness rises before us in all its aspects of past and present and to come, we cannot fail to reflect [that] it is the

doing of Jehovah and it is marvelous in our eyes. The doing of Jehovah! Where now is the pride that was stirring within us? The doing of Jehovah! The thought raises us to a higher sphere of contemplation; it gives us a dignity of national existence which the unbeliever has never dreamed of. It connects us with the vast designs of that Eternal Providence which will rescue humanity from darkness and misery and death, and renovate our world in the image of Heaven. [For] It was God who "sifted a kingdom," the freest and noblest on the globe, and gathered out our fathers like the wheat from the chaff! It was God who defended them from the perils of the deep and the perils of the wilderness! It was God who made them to flourish, and broke the weapons that were formed against them! It is God who hath spread out our land like the garden of Eden, who hath made it [as] free as its winds and its waters, and filled it with the light of science and the glories of his own eternal truth! It is God who hath opened before us that high career upon which we are entering, and who hath given us renown among the nations! With these reflections teaching us to check the workings of our pride, extinguishing the fires of a lawless ambition, and elevating our contemplations to the grand purposes of God's benevolence, we feel that it is neither arrogance nor enthusiasm to say that He, whom the Puritans worshipped, brought them forth from their house of bondage and planted them here on the shores of New England, [so] that the nation which should spring from them might lead in the march of human improvement, and that the country, blessed in their prayers and hallowed by their graves, might send forth from its borders the institutions of freedom and the light of salvation to the ends of the world!

4 I say, then, my fellow Christians, it is right that you should seek to shed over your gladness the sanctifying influence of devotion, and to connect the associations of this day with those principles and efforts of benevolence that raise us to a fellowship with God. And, standing here to speak for Africa today, I will not affect a diffidence which I do not feel. For I know that with such a cause and on such an occasion I cannot plead before you in vain. I might indeed be diffident if it were my task to excite within you, by the powers of language and fancy, the feelings of a transient benevolence. Nay, I should despair of success if I imagined I had anything to do but simply to lay before you the degradation, for which I would engage your sympathies, and the plans of doing good, for which I would secure your efforts. In describing the misery of that devoted race whose cause it is my lot to advocate, I can only tell you a story of simple, unalleviated, unromantic wretchedness. [For] There [really] are no spirit-stirring associations to break the monotony of the description. I can tell of no distant and shadowy antiquity—[an era presumably] when Africa was the cradle of the human race- and the seat of science and arts and empire. I cannot compare the darkness, that is now resting on those tribes, with some [such] period of ancient glory. Nor can I enlighten the picture of their present degradation by alluding to some former age of Arcadian felicity. There [simply] are no lighter shades to variegate the gloom. [For] The wretchedness is so great

and so unmingled that the mind shrinks from the conception, and seems almost ready to take refuge in a vague and quiet incredulity. And when I have told you what this wretchedness is, my plea is ended for the present;-I shall urge no other argument.

5 The country for which I am pleading extends from the Desert of Sahara to the Cape of Good Hope, and from the Atlantic to the Indian Ocean. With the exception of (here and there) a tract of complete and desolate barrenness, this wide region is fertile almost without a parallel, and the exuberance of its productions is such as we can only with difficulty imagine. It is a country varied like our own fair land—with mountains- and forests- and watered by "Streams that to the sea roll ocean-like." Abounding in all the resources that might minister employment or sustenance to a civilized and happy population, it is occupied by fifty millions of men as wild as the forests which they inhabit, and almost as far removed, from the high character and high destiny of our nature, as the lion and the tiger with whom they contend for the mastery of the soil. They are men indeed with all the instincts of humanity, and they walk beneath their burning sky with the port and bearing of manhood. Their's are the affections of kindred—the love of country and of home- and the kindness of savage hospitality. But they *are* barbarians. And with the nobler instincts of our nature and the rude virtues of their condition, they combine all that is degrading in human imbecility and all that is horrible in human depravity—unrefined by civilization and unrestrained by the influence of Christian truth. They are men, indeed. And when individuals from among them have been placed in circumstances favorable to the development of their powers, they have fully vindicated their title to all the honors of our nature. But, in Africa, the basest superstition has conspired with the darkest ignorance to stupify the intellect, as well as to brutalize the affections. And, in both cases, their influence has been as deadly in its operation as it is unlimited in its extent. Now what one is there among you, my hearers, who needs to be informed that these fifty millions of immortal beings, thus brought down to the very level of the brutes that perish, have a claim upon the sympathies of Christians? Do you find it difficult to conceive of their condition? It is just what your's would be if all the arts and knowledge and refinement of our land were to vanish, and the darkness of paganism were to settle on all the shrines of our devotion! It is just what it must be where treachery and lust are unforbidden, where rapine and murder are unrestrained, and where all the horrors of a savage warfare are perpetual!

6 Yes, in Africa the horrors of savage warfare are perpetual. Not that these tribes are created with a peculiar ferocity of disposition. So far from it [being the case], their nature seems to possess an uncommon share of what is mild and amiable. And yet you might traverse the whole region of which I speak, and you would find it (in all its districts) a theater of terror, flight, conflagration, murder, and whatever is still more dreadful in earthly suffering. You

might come to one place where there was a village yesterday, and find only its smoking ruins and the calcined bones of its murdered population! You might pass on to another and think that here there must be peace! But while the inhabitants are beginning to gather around you with a timid curiosity, there is an outcry of alarm—the foe is upon them- their houses are in flames- their old men are smitten with the sword- their infants are thrown to the tigers- and their young men are swept into captivity! You might follow the captives- weeping-bleeding- to the seashore. And *there* is the slave ship. We have heard of the slave trade and of its abolition, and we have been accustomed to regard it as a thing of other years! We have heard that thirty years ago the slave trade did exist, and [that] its existence was the foulest blot upon the picture of our world! We have heard that those, who have been laboring for the abolition of this traffic, have gained many a signal triumph over the obstinacy of the interested and the prejudices of the ignorant! So that now the two most enlightened and commercial nations of the world—who have *one* origin- *one* language- *one* religion-and (we might almost say) *one* freedom—are also united in declaring the slave trade [to be] piracy, and have thus denounced it before the world as an outrage against the Law of Nations and of Nature! All this is true. And, at the same time, it *is* equally true that the slave trade is carried on at this hour with a cruelty (if possible) more intense and aggravated. [For] Every year no less than sixty thousand of its victims are carried in chains across the ocean! Now, while I am speaking to this happy assembly, there is weeping and lamentation under the palm trees of Africa. For mothers have been plundered of their children and will not be comforted! Today the slave ships are hovering over that devoted coast, from the Senegal to the Zaire. Tonight, as the African lies down in his cabin, he will feel no security. And, as he sleeps, he will dream of conflagration and blood till suddenly he awakes—and his roof is blazing above him- his wife is bleeding at his feet- his children lie fettered and helpless before him- and, ere he can grasp the weapons of despair, the cold steel of the murderer is in his vitals!

7 It would be utterly impossible for me, or indeed for any man, to transcend in description the actual horrors of this trade as they have been exhibited again and again in the testimony of sworn witnesses, and as many of you have seen them exhibited from the record of judicial tribunals. You cannot, therefore, suspect me of attempting to impose on your feelings. I wish only to impress it on your minds that the slave trade, though abolished by law, has never been suppressed in fact;-and then to leave it for you to judge whether the cruelty, of which you have so often heard, and which was so great when the traffic was acknowledged by law and defended by argument, is likely to be less [dire] now that the traffic has become contraband and the subject of universal execration. So that [perhaps now] the slavetrader is governed not only by the natural baseness of his cupidity, but by the terror of detection and the greater risk of loss, and by the consciousness of being outlawed from the sympathies of human society. This horrible commerce in the blood of men has existed for ages, and the consequence is that there are now descendants of Africa in every quar-

ter of the globe. For them I plead today, as well as for their brethren on their native continent. Because wherever the children of Africa are found, they are *one* nation—a separate- distinct- peculiar people.

8 I plead for the whole race. And my argument with you, in their behalf, is that wherever they are found they are partakers in the misery of one common degradation. To establish this I need not carry you [far away] out of the streets and lanes of our own city. You would scorn the imputation (and justly), if I should suggest that there is anything *here* which subjects the African to peculiar disadvantages. On the contrary, it would seem far otherwise inasmuch as slavery never existed here to any considerable extent, and for years it has been a thing unknown. Yet when you look over this city, what do you find to be the actual state and character of its colored population? How many of the privileges which belong to other classes of society do they enjoy! How much of the happiness in which you are now rejoicing is their's! How many of the motives which are urging you to honest industry or to honorable enterprise are operating upon them! Who among them ever aspires to wealth or office, or ever dreams of intellectual pursuits or intellectual enjoyment! In short, are they not in the estimation of the community (and in their own consciousness) aliens and outcasts in the midst of the people! Now I am willing that you should take the condition of the children of Africa *here* as a fair specimen of their condition, wherever they are scattered. I am willing you should believe for the moment that the negro is nowhere more ignorant, nowhere more despised or oppressed than here. But, at the same time, I ask you to remember that within our own borders there are nearly two millions of these beings—and in the archipelago of the West Indies not less than two millions more. And, then, when you have computed the amount of wretchedness which belongs to these four millions of degraded men, [I ask you] to judge for yourselves whether the subjects of this degradation have no claim [at all] on the sympathies and efforts of those, who have been taught to love their neighbor as themselves!

9 And yet such a computation would fall far short of the actual amount of that wretchedness which, if I could, I would set before you. Of these four millions, the vast majority are slaves. And what is it [like] to be a slave? We know what it is [like] to be free! We know what it is to walk forth in the consciousness of independence, and to act with the feeling that we are responsible only to our God and to the community of which we are equal members! We know the inspiration that attends the efforts of him who can act for himself—who labors for his family- who identifies his interests with the welfare of a nation- who spreads out his affections [all] over the wide world of being! But we know not what it is [like] to be a slave. We can conceive indeed of stripes, and corporeal endurance, and long days of burning toil. But how can we conceive of that bondage of the heart, that captivity of the soul, which make the slave a wretch indeed? His intellect is a blank, and we may perhaps form some conception of his ignorance! The capacities of his moral nature are a blank, and we

may perhaps imagine that blindness! But even when we have conceived of this intellectual ignorance and this moral blindness, we know not all the degradation of the slave. We sometimes find an individual whose spirit [totally] has been broken and blasted. Some affection which engrossed his soul, and with which all his other affections were entwined, has been withered—and his heart is desolate! The hope, on which all his other hopes were centered, has been destroyed—and his being is a wreck! If you have ever seen such a man—and noticed how he seemed to lose the high attributes of manhood- how his soul died within him- and he sunk down (as it were) from the elevation of his former existence—you may conjecture perhaps how much of the dignity and happiness of our nature, even in minds purified by moral cultivation and enlarged by intellectual improvement, depends on the love of social enjoyment and the softening influence of affection. And you may thus be able faintly to imagine the degradation of the slave whose mind has scarcely been enlightened by one ray of knowledge, whose soul has never been expanded by one adequate conception of his moral dignity and moral relations, and in whose heart hardly one of those affections that soften our character, or of those hopes that animate and bless our being, has been allowed to germinate!

10 You have seen, my fellow Christians, something of the misery of that continent and the degradation of that race for which I plead before you today. You have not seen it all, for it passes [beyond] the powers of human fancy to conceive, and (still more) of human language to describe. But the few familiar facts, which I have attempted to bring to your remembrance, are enough to awaken all the sympathies of men and all the benevolence of Christians. We have seen a *continent* of misery—a *race*- degraded from the level of humanity! And it remains for me only to show how we can operate to alleviate this misery, and to remove this degradation. The problem is to give peace and happiness to the continent of Africa, and to elevate all her children to the rank which God has given them in the scale of existence. As one of these objects cannot be gained without affecting the other, so if we would be successful in the pursuit of either, we must aim at the attainment of both. Cover Africa with the institutions of civilized freedom and fill it with the light of knowledge and religion, and the whole negro race is raised in a moment from its hopeless depth of degradation. And, on the other hand, give freedom and intelligence and all the rights and honors of humanity to the exiled descendants of Africa, and you have completely provided for the salvation of the continent from which they sprung. After we have examined briefly these two propositions, we shall be able more distinctly to perceive the importance of comprehending both the objects of which I have spoken, [with]in one system of exertion.

11 First, by civilizing and christianizing the African continent the degradation of Africans in other countries may be removed. Such a civilization of that continent implies, at its outset, the final abolition of the slave trade—in its progress, the erection of free, independent, and intelligent nations—and, in

its completion, all the industry and enterprise of a thronging, active, enlightened population. What will be the influence of such changes on the condition of this degraded race in other lands? Let the slave trade be abolished, and that which has been at once the cause of their present wretchedness (and one grand obstacle in the way of their improvement) is done away [with]. While these men are sold like cattle in the shambles, what can you do for the general elevation of their character! While thousands of fresh victims are continually poured in to swell the tide of misery, what can you do for the alleviation of this woe! Let the fountain be dried up from which the misery has flowed, and you may [expect to] operate on the evil to be remedied with some prospect of success! Let there be erected one free and intelligent African empire, and the reproach of the negro will cease! There is a scorn which follows the very name of an African; he is hunted down by a contempt which he can never escape. He is treated—whatever may be your opinion about his native character—he is in fact treated as an inferior being! He is one of that people who have been meted out and trodden down, plundered and sold, persecuted and oppressed from the beginning of time. And the consciousness (which he cannot evade) that he is despised by others teaches him at length to despise himself, and robs him of the dignity of human character! Now let there be erected one Christian African republic—powerful- enlightened- and happy like our's—whose flag shall wave in the breezes of every ocean—whose commerce shall carry wealth to every port—whose ambassadors shall demand respect in every capital—whose patriots and sages- whose poets and artists shall share the admiration of every people—and this reproach, degrading as crime and cruel as the grave, will cease! The negro, exulting in the consciousness of manhood, will stretch out his hand unto Him, who hath made of one blood all nations to dwell on the face of the earth!

12 A/AE**s** Once more **3**) let Africa be filled with the industry of a free and enterprising population, and slavery can exist no longer! This **2**) slavery is the bitterest ingredient in that misery which we deplore. In all that we have contemplated, there is **2**) nothing more oppressive to our best feelings than the thought that **2**) so many millions of our fellow men are the subjects of a **2**thralldom, which **2**despoils them of the attributes of **2**intellectual and **2**moral (and even of **2**social) existence, and makes them the **2**) mere machines of avarice. *But let Africa be civilized, and slavery must be annihilated!* It is a **5**principle which the progress of political science has clearly and indisputably established—a **5**principle that illustrates at once the wisdom of the Creator and the blindness of human cupidity- that it is cheaper to hire **6**) the labor of freemen than it is to compel **7**) the labor of slaves.AB/AF

m We have **1**) no room to enlarge on the political aspect of this subject. A/AEm That **2**) slavery is a great political evil is one of those general **5**propositions, which receive the unreflecting assent of the understanding without exciting any **1**) vivid conception or any marked emotion. That slavery diminishes the wealth of the community is indeed a 5proposition more specific than the former, but even this may be assented to by a mind which does not reflect on the meaning of the assertion, and which therefore does not know or care for the 1) importance of the truth it announces. But when we reflect that, other things being 4equal, the 3) wealth of a community depends on the amount of enterprise in that community, and remember that the very conception of an 3) enterpriseing slave involves an absurdity,- AB/AF[1]

ma We will only ask— BCm**b** when we ask ourselves ☆ where would be the enterprise and the **ma** wealth and the strength **mb** political wealth ☆ of *New* England, if her green hills and pleasant valleys were cultivated no longer by her own independent and hardy yeomanry, but by the degraded serfs of a Polish aristocracy,-

CD**s** From this principle it results that (the productions of slave labor can never enter into competition, on 4equal/terms, with the productions of 6) free labor. An illustration of this is furnished by the fact that the sugar of the West Indies, which is produced by 7) the labor of slaves, demands the assistance of a high protecting duty before it can contend in the English market with the sugar of the East, which is raised by the hands of freemen.)

CD**m** And what would not Virginia become, if she could exchange her four hundred and twenty-five thousand 7slaves for as many 6freemen who, in blood and complexion as well as in immunities and enjoyments, should be *one* with the proudest of her children?

CDm when we call to mind that (the West India planters have complained that their own produce, which is raised by 7) the labor of slaves,/ cannot come into competition on 4equal/terms with the produce of the East, which is raised by 6) free labor, and that remonstrances and petitions to this effect have been presented by the planters and their friends to the British Parliament,-)[2]

AE**s** We see, then, that the system of slavery can be supported in a country, only so long as the slaveholders can retain either a complete or partial monopoly of such articles as they are able to raise by the labor of their drudges. And thus, whenever the civilized and enterprising population of Africa shall send forth their productions to compete in every market with the sugar and cotton and coffee of the West Indies and southern America, the planters will be compelled, by that spirit of improvement which always springs from com-

---

1 In this instance and in the last two sections, Bacon apparently inserts material deleted from his "report" manuscript as printed on page 540 of the *Christian Spectator*. Amplification of slavery as a "great" evil, and of "enterprise" versus a slavery less competitive for the public good, enables Bacon to emphasize slavery as a moral and economic fallacy in capitalistic systems. Indeed, such amplification might incorporate more direct appeals to the rather apathetic audience Bacon takes somewhat for granted in his "report" manuscript.

2 Again Bacon inserts material which he apparently revised out of his "report" manuscript as printed on page 541 of the *Christian Spectator*.

petition, to substitute the cheaper process for the more expensive, to adopt the labor of freemen instead of the labor of slaves—in a word, to convert their slaves into freemen!AF

[m We have 1) no room to enlarge on the political aspect of this subject.] AEm when we go into 1) details like these, we know what we mean by the assertion that slavery diminishes the wealth of the community;-we know that, though it may enrich now and then an individual, it makes the public poor indeed;-and if we have anything of the spirit of patriotism, we are ready to do everything that can be done to remove this obstacle to the prosperity of our country.AF

The conclusion from the principle, which I have attempted to illustrate and apply, is let Africa be civilized and every African throughout the world will be made a freeman, not by some sudden convulsion demolishing the fabric of society, but by the tendencies of Nature and the arrangements of Providence slowly (yet surely) accomplishing the happiness of man. The change will be [as] certain, indeed, as the revolution of the seasons, but [yet as] gradual as the growth of an empire.

13 It is equally true, in the second place, that by elevating the character of Africans in foreign countries the civilization of their native continent may be greatly and rapidly promoted. If ever Africa is civilized, as it unquestionably will be, the change must be brought about by the return of her exiled children. Political revolutions, the progress of the Christian religion, and the establishment of colonies are the only important means of civilization with which history makes us acquainted. That any political revolution such as the extensive conquests of some foreign empire (or of some native tribe) will ever accomplish the renovation of Africa appears beyond the compass of probability, whether we consider the country to be overrun or the barbarians to be subjugated. That white men alone can never extensively propagate Christianity on those shores, and that colonies of white men can never flourish there, seems rational in itself and has been confirmed by the experience of former efforts. If ever Africa is civilized it must be by the return of her exiled children; and those exiles are even now beginning to return. They have planted their feet on the soil of their fathers, and they have found that the influences so deadly to the white man are powerless upon them. In the land of the slave trade they have set up the banner of freedom, and where they are building their homes and cultivating their fields the wilderness echoes to their songs, and the Sabbath smiles on their devotions. Now in what way can you more powerfully (or more directly) promote the civilization of Africa than by enlarging the views and elevating the character of her children here, and thus making them at once more anxious to enjoy and more able to improve the advantages which their country is offering them! Or how can you imagine a more splended contribution to the cause of human happiness than you might make, if you would train up (and send to Africa) such men as were the Pilgrims of Plymouth or the Puritans of New Haven—men with all that wisdom and all that dauntless piety- which gave renown to the Win-

throps and the Winslows- the Davenports and Hookers of our early history!

14 We see, then, that by civilizing Africa the degradation of Africans in other countries may be forever and completely removed. And by elevating the character of these exiles the civilization of their native continent may be easily effected. And if these two objects are thus intimately blended,-so that the first can be perfectly gained only by means of the second, and the complete attainment of the second is equally dependent on the first,-it requires no great sagacity to reach the conclusion that any efforts, which may aim at either, must be imperfect in themselves and inadequate to their end, 'til they shall become the parts of such a system of exertions as shall comprehend in its design the accomplishment of both. And it is equally evident that, whenever such a system shall be organized, everything that may be done to give new impulse to any one department of its operation will accelerate the motion (and increase the momentum) of the whole. I now proceed to say that those projects of benevolence towards Africa, to which the attention of the American public has already been invited, do in fact constitute such a system. [For] The means of elementary instruction and the apparatus of moral and religious culture, which are employed on our colored population, lie at the foundation of all African improvement. The societies for the abolition of slavery are continually urging the claims of these unfortunates with a zeal which scorns to be weary, and which gathers impulse from discouragement. [And] The scheme of an African seminary for liberal education, which has been as yet only slightly discussed, will not be forgotten. For there are men engaged in its behalf who will never rest, while God spares them to the world, till the chasm which they now lament shall have been filled up, and the school which they have projected shall be sending forth its pupils to become (throughout the earth) the noblest and most efficient benefactors of Africa. The efforts proposed for the improvement of Hayti may be expected, by and by, when the fever of novelty and the reaction consequent on its subsiding shall have passed away, to kindle among our blacks a spirit of enterprise, and ultimately to bestow on the subjects of Boyer the happiness of a civilized and Christian people, as well as the honors of an independent republic. And to consummate the system the institution, for which I am particularly desirous to excite your immediate interest, is sending back the descendants of Africa to the land of their fathers [so] that they may extend over the continent, which God has given them for their inheritance, the light and blessedness of Christian civilization.

15 After having detained you so long, I will not exhaust your patience by detailing the plans, or the history, or the prospects of the American Colonization Society. You know that its design is to establish on the coast of Africa colonies of free people of color from America. And, after what I have already said, I need not trace out the influence which the successful prosecution of this design must have on the civilization of that continent, or on the character and happiness of our own colored population.

s You can imagine for yourselves how such a colony—founded in the principles of American freedom- and supported by American liberality and enterprise—would grow and flourish, giving a new employment and a new direction to commerce, adorning with villages and cultivated fields the land that is now half-desolate with the ravages of the slave trade, and overspread with the untamed luxuriancy of the wilderness! You can imagine how the rude tribes, gazing with astonishment on the arts of a civilized community, would soon become desirous of sharing in a power so wonderful;- and, being cut off from that traffic in each other's blood by which they live, would gradually engage in those pursuits and acquire that knowledge with which a people must commence the career of improvement!

m We do not fear to say that, to the friends of missions, the Colonization Society presents a loud and imperative claim. Am There is a star rising on the brightness of Africa. It shall herald the full brightness of the morning. **m** The advantage of the Moravian missions, and of the modern missionary establishments in savage countries, is that they are in substance little colonies. ABm The establishment in Liberia is what the establishment in the Sandwich Islands would be with a hundred missionaries. BCm If you could carry from this country to **ma** the Sandwich m**b** those☆Islands a thousand **ma** civilized and educated natives, m**b** Owhyheeans who had been educated in America,☆ would you not think you had done much for Owhyhee? This is what can be done- **ma** and must be m**b** must be done- will be☆done for Africa. And will there not be an interest in the progress of **ma** the m**b** this☆work?

CD**s** You can imagine how (**1**) the light of **4**) Christian truth might be made to **2**) beam forth on the **3**) benighted pagans!)

CDm Will it not be delightful to watch the advances of the morning; to see (**1**) the light **2**) breaking in on one dark habitation of cruelty, and another; to see the shadows of heathenism fleeing away, and the delusions which have so long terrified the **3**) ignorant pagans vanishing; to see one tribe after another coming to **1**) the light of Zion and to the brightness of her rising; to see Ethiopa waking, and rising from the dust and **2**) looking abroad on the day, and stretching out her hands to God; and **1**) the daylight still spreading and kindling and brightening, 'til all the fifty millions of Africa are brought into "**1**) the glorious light and liberty of the sons of God"? Is there not enough in this to arrest the attention of the **ma** public m**b4** Christian public☆and to keep it fixed on this object with an untiring interest, 'til **ma** all shall be accomplished m**b** it shall attain its **4**) perfect accomplishment?☆)[3]

s You can imagine how the negro, here despised and broken-spirited, would there stand up in the full majesty of

3 Bacon telescopes this "light" metaphor for his speech, and inserts it to highlight the "manhood" appeal which concludes next.

manhood, and with the inspiration of all the motives that are stimulating you to enterprise and effort! You can imagine, too, how all this might operate for the improvement and happiness of the African who should remain among us, exciting him to industry, and bestowing upon him the consciousness of wider and higher capacities!

16 Leaving all this to your reflections, I will only say that, though the Society has contended from the beginning (and is still struggling) with grievous embarrasments, its disappointments have been fewer, its calamities less terrible, and its success more rapid than ever attended the progress of any similar enterprise. [For] It has obtained a rich and beautiful territory adequate to all its present purposes. [And] It has succeeded in planting there a colony, now consisting of nearly four hundred individuals, who are rapidly preparing the means of sustenance not only for themselves, but also for the thousands who are anxious to join them. So far as the experiment has been conducted, it has been successful. And all that the Managers now need for the rapid prosecution of their designs is the voice of public opinion to cheer them on, and to direct for their assistance the energies of our national councils—the contributions of the benevolent to give them strength—and the prayers of the churches to call down upon them the blessing of Heaven. The voice of public opinion in favor of this enterprise is becoming louder and louder! In every section of our country the ministers of Jesus have been pleading for it today. From hundreds of churches the cry of supplication has gone up to Heaven in its behalf! And not a few are the freemen who, in the midst of their rejoicing today, have remembered the miseries of Africa and offered their contributions for her relief. Can you withhold from such an enterprise *your* voice of approbation! Can you, if you pray for anything—can you refuse to pray for this undertaking! Can you look round on the abundance wherewith God has blessed you, and refuse to bestow some little offering in behalf of such a cause! I have now completed my design. [Yet] I have not indeed spoken of the awful curse of Heaven on our own land, or of the measures which *must* speedily be adopted for its complete and eternal abolition. These things, if God shall give me strength and opportunity, I will bring more distinctly to your notice at some future period.

17 All that I designed for this occasion I have done. I have set before you the condition and character of those for whom I plead. And I have told you how we may operate for the alleviation of that misery (and the removal of that degradation) which I have led you to contemplate. And, surely,-if it is the noblest attribute of our nature which spreads out the circle of our sympathies to include the whole family of man, and sends forth our affections to embrace the ages of a distant futurity,-it must be regarded as a privilege (no less exalted) that our means of *doing* good are limited by no remoteness of country or distance of duration. But we may operate, if we will, to assuage the miseries of another hemisphere or to prevent the necessities of an unborn generation! The time has been when a man might weep over the wrongs of Africa, and he might look for-

ward to weep over the hopelessness of her degradation 'til his heart should bleed. And yet his tears would be all that he could give her. He might relieve the beggar at his door, but he could do nothing for a dying continent! He might provide for his children, but he could do nothing for the nations that were yet to be born to an inheritance of utter wretchedness! Then, the privilege of engaging in schemes of magnificent benevolence belonged only to princes, and to men of princely possessions. But now the progress of improvement has brought down this privilege to the reach of every individual. The institutions of our age are a republic of benevolence, and all may share in the unrestrained and equal democracy. This privilege is our's! We may stretch forth our hand, if we will, to enlighten the Hindoo or to tame the savage of the wilderness! It is our's, if we will, to put forth our contributions and thus to operate (not ineffectually) for the relief and renovation of a continent, over which one tide of misery has swept, without ebb and without restraint, for unremembered centuries! It is our's, if we will, to do something that shall tell (on all the coming ages) of a race which has been persecuted and enslaved, trodden down and despised for a thousand generations! Our Father has made us the almoners of His love. He has raised us to partake, as it were, in the ubiquity of his own beneficence. Shall we be unworthy of the trust?-*God forbid!*

Chapter 4

George Bancroft's Fourth of July Oration, 1826

The critical question must be understood in its precise context: why did George Bancroft, speaking at Northampton, Massachusetts, on the national jubilee of Independence, endeavor to take some ceremonial middle ground between egalitarian Jeffersonian ideals, more a rationale for partisan aspirations when fed to a Jacksonian "common" electorate in the next half-century, and an elitist commercial ethic cherished by Puritan theocrats, obviously interested in perpetuating the stratified stewardship not even a banished Jonathan Edwards could fault that much.

Ceremonial ground, really, because critics tend to skip rather lightly over details of the occasion, to which Bancroft necessarily had to adapt, being more intent upon unraveling the veritable dogmatic thread capable of setting the orator far enough apart from partisan Federalist surroundings, and casting him among the literati classification merited by his romantic history during the 1830's. In effect, the critics make orator Bancroft in 1826 a partisanly enlightened protagonist contravening, however unintentionally or in good faith, traditional Puritan values at the very fabric of the Northampton community.[1]

When, in fact, principal Bancroft of Round Hill School, for much the same reasoning advanced the previous year on the Fourth by orator Osmyn Baker of the local law school (then operated by chairman Elijah H. Mills of the 1826 Committee of Arrangements in partnership with Samuel Howe), represented the

1 For major critical treatment of the oration, consult M. A. DeWolfe Howe, *The Life and Letters of George Bancroft* (New York: Charles Scribner's Sons, 1908), I, 185-88, and Russel B. Nye, *George Bancroft, Brahmin Rebel* (New York: Alfred A. Knopf, 1944), pp. 87-88. Three critics give less extensive treatment: Michael Kraus in "Bancroft, 1834-1934," *New England Quarterly*, 7 (Dec. 1934), 669; Arthur M. Schlesinger Jr. in his *Age of Jackson* (Boston: Little Brown, 1945), 159-60; John W. Rathbun in "Bancroft on Man and History," *Transactions of the Wisconsin Academy of Sciences, Arts, and Letters*, 43 (15 Sept., 1954), 68 n. 96, 69 n. 106, and 70 n. 111.

institutional morality and incumbent wealth most of all sought after by local Puritan elders in selecting their jubilee speaker.[2] Indeed, the Jeffersonian republicanism so dogmatically manipulated by Bancroft critics probably was less of a partisan influence, prompted more out of the orator's respect for agrarian beliefs held by farmers and artisans in the local Mechanic Association. An organization which sponsored an oration by James Hillhouse commemorating the Hampshire and Hampden Canal at Oliver Warner's Inn, before many "mechanics" attended Bancroft's oration at the Northampton meetinghouse.[3]

The rather neat extremity assumed by the critics, even with a distorted "half-serious" label, in accepting Bancroft's description of the oration ("radical, democratic, levelling, unrighteous") ignores several adaptive factors within the rhetorical context.[4] For instead of being the experienced speaker who would not lightly consider the extreme possibility of inspiring an excessively "sober" and "unexcitable" audience to renounce "hereditary usage and hereditary faith," Bancroft was more the hesitant beginner, aware of partisan prejudice detracting from "sublime good" on a ceremonial occasion, and determined to demonstrate, using local patriots Seth Pomeroy and Joseph Hawley as examples,[5] that revolutionary liberty and Edwards's Christianity were appropriate topics ("a few words of truth and kindness") when addressed to a mixed ceremonial audience ("the general ear").

Any democratic liberals ("friends of Jefferson") were perhaps as much partisan liabilities to attaining commemorative good.[6] And the difficulty of such an

---

2 At the 1825 celebration of the Fourth in Northampton, Isaac C. Bates, a member of the 1826 Committee with Mills, had toasted orator Baker in this vein: "The orator of the day—whose *moral worth* entitles him to our respect and esteem, and whose intellectual [worth], as this day exhibited, to our admiration and gratitude." And in 1824, Jonathan H. Lyman, not available to serve on the 1826 Committee since he died in the closing months of 1825, similarly had toasted orator A. A. Locke: "The orator of the day—the patriotism of Sparta, the taste of Athens, the *morals* of New England." *Hampshire Gazette* (Northampton), 7 July 1824, 6 July 1825, and "Common-schools toast #11," 12 July 1826.

3 "Temple of Liberty toast and postmaster Ferdinand H. Wright's response," *Hampshire Gazette*, 12 July, 1826. Insurance entrepreneur William Bliss, jubilee orator at Springfield, relied on industrial ingenuity and even internal improvements to assure the traditional viability of the oration vehicle. He gave as his toast, "Fourth of July orations—steampower for their manufacture, and waterpower for their delivery." Springfield *Republican*, 12 July, 1826.

4 Howe, I 187, and Nye p. 88, quoting Northampton, 1 July, 1826, *GB* to Sarah H. Dwight, Springfield, Bancroft Papers, Cornell University Library (Ithaca, N.Y.). Bancroft Papers (Cornell Univ. Library) hereafter cited as Bancroft Papers-Cornell.

5 Consult paragraph 13 in the oration for evidence of Bancroft's citing Pomeroy and Hawley. And for some interesting but obscure data on Hawley biography, see William Tudor's *Life of James Otis* (published by Wells and Lilly in Boston, extracted from Boston *Dly Advertiser* into *Hampshire Gazette*, 5 March; "Undated letter to editor Sylvester Judd Jr., commenting on Tudor's treatment of Hawley," *Gazette*, 16 April 1823), and Marion L. Starkey's recent article ("Hawley, Forgotten Patriot," *New-England Galaxy*, 2 [Spring 1961], 11-12 especially).

6 Northampton, 27 July and 29 Aug., 1826, *GB* to Edward Everett, Charlestown, Bancroft Papers, Massachusetts Historical Society (Boston).

adaptive process for a beginner, not Jeffersonian tenets harshly thrust in front of a hostile audience, led Bancroft to fear that the rhetorical impact, as lacking in vain "pleasure" and "glory" as the composition task proved to be, might not be uniformly or "commonly favorable" enough to satisfy most groups in a mixed jubilee audience. Viewed in this light, the intense description seized upon by critics conceivably might indicate Bancroft's frustration at resolving traditional sinner-elect categories, that is, in the sincerely patriotic Christian stance demanded by ceremony. And combined with a slight beginner's overstatement, of course, so as not to have stodgy banker-congressman Henry W. Dwight add to any onerousness in the task by bringing himself and daughter Sarah, or a jubilee socialite party of fifty other Springfield touring enthusiasts, to sit through the performance in the Northampton meetinghouse.[7]

Levi Lyman and the Board of Selectmen,[8] in collaboration with chairman Mills and the Committee they appointed to supervise arrangements for the celebration on the Fourth,[9] asked Bancroft to be jubilee orator late in March.[10] Yet the schoolmaster's acceptance was not formally announced until mid-May,[11] perhaps indicating considerable reluctance to speak on the part of Bancroft. Mills as chairman indeed wanted to make the jubilee celebration a proper Puritan occasion, Revolutionary example presumably reinforcing grateful Christian duty.

The "high and solemn duty" to be undertaken by the jubilee orator, according to Mills, who read the Declaration of Independence himself before Bancroft spoke, involved more traditional Christian exposition—"recounting the achievements, the sacrifices and sufferings of those [patriots] who participated in the mighty conflicts of the Revolution, of contemplating the widespread and growing prosperity of our beloved country, and of [contemplating] aspirations of thankfulness to that Almighty Being who protected us through[out] the glorious struggle, and who has conducted us to a height of prosperity, freedom, and happiness unexampled in the annals of the world."[12] And although a cityite dancing teacher named Guigon, one of several frequenting Northampton during the 1820's, may not have been too well-received when

7 Springfield, 30 June, 1826, Sarah H. Dwight to GB, Northampton, Bancroft Papers-Cornell; *GB* to Dwight, 1 July, 1826, Bancroft Papers-Cornell.

8 Four other selectmen served on the Board with First Selectman Lyman: Joseph Burnell, Jonathan Strong, Samuel Parsons, and John Wright. *Hampshire Gazette*, 29 March, 1826.

9 Six local residents assisted chairman Mills on the Committee: Isaac C. Bates, James Shepherd, Ferdinand H. Wright, Nathaniel Fowle, Charles E. Forbes, and Samuel F. Lyman. "Committee notice dated 20 June," *Hampshire Gazette*, 21 June, 1826.

10 Northampton, 28 March, 1826, Lyman to GB, Northampton, Bancroft Papers, Massachusetts Historical Society.

11 *Hampshire Gazette*, 17 May, 1826.

12 Mills, "Undated Committee notice," *Hampshire Gazette*, 28 June, 1826.

expecting local citizens to become the fashionable equivalent of students in fourteen classes at Round Hill,[13] Bancroft simply had to weigh in his mind the divinely orthodox propriety demanded in the jubilee oration by president Heman Humphrey of nearby Amherst College, invited to attend with some members of the student body,[14] and by local Congregational ministers Solomon Williams and Edward B. Hall, each of whom offered up a prayer at the meetinghouse ceremony.[15]

Key elements in preparation of the oration indeed suggest a beginner's effort to honor the occasion by adapting. Especially Bancroft's taking great care to speak attired in a proper equivalent of the black robe worn by clerics Williams and Hall.[16] His putting questions rather belatedly to Senator Robert Y. Hayne, whose son (and Congressman James Hamilton's)[17] attended Round Hill, lines of inquiry the South Carolinian thought awkward enough to cleverly sidestep, claiming that the necessary documentation was not readily at hand in Albany, New York.[18] His pausing to reflect at Seth Pomeroy's grave, a few days prior to the Fourth, perhaps out of more than some sentimental historical afflatus for Marshal-of-the-jubilee Thomas Pomeroy.[19] Above all, his apparent attempt to adapt Milton's prose style (Bancroft conceded the poet sometimes was guilty of "unsatisfactory reasoning") into verbalizations proper enough to suit the occasion. The orator, in effect, hoped to be regarded as a tasteful man properly inspired, guarding against standard excesses on ceremonial occasions—too ardent zeal, too brilliant an imagination, too superb diction, too elevated feelings, or too fiercely nationalistic a pride.[20]

Even to the point of receiving counsel from friend John Davis, who regretted a commitment in Boston made attending the event impossible, about the proper

---

13 "Round Hill School," *Hampshire Gazette*, 31 May, 1826; "Monsieur P. Guigon's advertisements of 24 May and 8 Nov.," 1826 *Gazette* issues under same date. The first ad promoted Guigon as having taught in New York City, the second crediting him with Boston as well.

14 Northampton, 1 July, 1826, *GB* to Sarah H. Dwight, Springfield, Bancroft Papers-Cornell; Humphrey, *Parallel between Intemperance and the Slave Trade—An Address Delivered at Amherst College, July 4, 1828* (Amherst: J. S. and C. Adams, 1828), pp. 3-4.

15 *Ibid.* (letter); David S. Whitney, "Sabbath-school meeting notices, dated 15 March and 18 April," *Hampshire Gazette*, 15 March and 19 April, 1826; Lewis Strong, "Sabbath-school report, dated March," *Gazette*, 28 March, 1827; Wanderer, "Travel account datelined Amherst-8 Aug.," New York *Observer* in *Gazette*, 30 Aug., 1826; "Fourth of July," *American Advocate* (Williamstown) in Greenfield *Gazette and Franklin Herald*, 3 July, 1827; Rev. William B. Sprague [of West Springfield], *Religious Celebration of Independence—A Discourse Delivered at Northampton, on the Fourth of July, 1827* (Hartford, Ct.; Goodwin and Company, 1827), pp. 23-25.

16 Worcester, 30 June, 1826, John Davis to GB, Northampton, Bancroft Papers-Cornell.

17 *Hampshire Gazette*, 6 July, 1825; Northampton, 20 July, 1827, Hamilton to Jackson election committee, Philadelphia, in *Gazette*, 8 Aug., 1827.

18 Albany NY, 25 June, 1826, Hayne to GB, Northampton, Bancroft Papers, Massachusetts Historical Society.

19 Northampton, 1 July, 1826, *GB* to Sarah H. Dwight, Springfield, Bancroft Papers-Cornell.

20 Springfield, 1 May, 1826, Sarah H. Dwight, to GB, Northampton, Bancroft Papers-Cornell; *GB* to Dwight, 8 May, 1826, Bancroft Papers-Cornell.

mode of oral delivery necessary to perfect such a style: "Speak slow, but neither too loud nor too low,-keep, if possible, your natural tone of voice.—My experience has led me to begin [an address] in rather a low tone, and I find myself naturally rising [to a] sufficiently high [tone] if I feel the subject.—Much, very much, depends on [your] hitting right in this [inspired] particular.—All this you [probably] know, without [taking] any hint from me, but we cannot always do as we would [want to when speaking], without learning how [by experience]."[21] If Bancroft ever felt that his adaptation would improperly fall on hostile ears at the meetinghouse, numerous ladies, prior to taking their afternoon tea on the green,[22] and partner Joseph G. Cogswell with some seventy Round-Hill declamation students, prior to leading more than a hundred of the school's finest to Talcott Mountain in Connecticut on the sixth,[23] certainly formed a sympathetic core of support to assuage the orator's fretful anxiety.

Reaction to Bancroft's appearance was quite subdued, that is, compared to the nonadaptive lack of popularity which critics couple with almost visionary implications. Editor Sylvester Judd Jr., of the local *Gazette*, thought the oration a "learned and eloquent" specimen from the traditional institutional leader so attractive to First Selectman Lyman and the Committee: "Of this, it is not our intention to say [anything] more than that, however high public expectation might have been raised by the reputation of the writer for talent and literary attainments, it was amply gratified. The oration . . . , we do not hesitate to assert, will fully vindicate its claim to a rank in the first class of similar productions." A banquet held at Warner's Inn, after the meetinghouse ceremony, found chairman Mills paying tribute to ornamental "jewel" Bancroft, who so aptly appeased many a local matron's "conscious pride" in all things properly classical and patriotic. And another dinner guest anonymously noted the propriety of the oration, when toasting the future centennial orator of Independence: "May he be able to give as faithful, and as glorious, an account of our country's progress and prospects, as that to which we have this day listened."[24]

Despite a generalized pragmatic allusion suggesting that Bancroft ventured "more largely . . . into the present state and prospects of the world" than other jubilee orators, an unidentified reviewer for the *United States Literary Gazette* in Boston considered Bancroft's commemorative focus in paragraphs 18 and 19 properly responsible to the occasion.[25] Bumping into the orator while visiting

---

21 Washington D.C., 8 March, 1826, Davis to GB, Northampton, Bancroft Papers-Cornell; Worcester, 30 June, 1826, Davis to GB, Northampton, Bancroft Papers-Cornell.

22 *Hampshire Gazette*, 12 July, 1826.

23 *Hampden Register* (Westfield) in *Hampshire Gazette*, 19 July, 1826. The *Register* reporter robustly chose to define "finest," a term he did not actually employ, in this manner: "The healthy appearance, the cheerfulness, the activity, and, what is more, the general decorum of the pupils furnish the best comment on the success which has attended the efforts of the founders of this school."

24 *Hampshire Gazette*, 12 July, 1826.

25 *U.S. Literary Gazette*, 4 (Sept. 1826), 429-31.

Northampton on the seventeenth, Rev. Francis W. P. Greenwood, associate pastor of King's Chapel in Boston, shared George Ticknor's view that any "liberal democratic" preferences were not tantamount to partisan bias, but had to be regarded in the context of "men and principles" honored by the occasion.[26] Indeed, editor Jared Sparks of the *North American Review* in Boston unofficially criticized Bancroft for not amplifying upon libertarian Simon Bolivar and the South American experience in paragraphs 6 and 7.[27] Even a conservative newlywed fresh from three years of travel on the Continent, Samuel A. Eliot, thought the piece suited enough to the occasion that he might "expect a gilt-edged copy directly" late in August, that is, after finding he was unable to stay in town to hear the speech.[28]

When issued on the twenty-first, the oration pamphlet retailed at 17 cents per single copy in Northampton, carried primarily by the *Gazette* office, Jonathan Smith, and Simeon Butler.[29] The same Butler bookshop, 108 Main Street, which helped supply the Bancroft edition of Frederic Jacobs's *Latin Reader* to novice classes at Round Hill.[30] Since Elisha Turner's bookstore and the *Gazette* office occupied the same brick building north of the courthouse,[31] however, Turner's shop probably was not as vigorous a sales outlet for the oration, perhaps not bothering to carry the pamphlet at all.

The text of Bancroft's oration below should enable the reader to distinguish between commemorative adaptation and subsequent partisan taint. The reader hopefully will be able to avoid an overlapping contextual error critics seem to fall into for the sake of biography. And the word "our" in front of "free institutions" (sentence 1, paragraph 8) is deleted from the text, because most pamphlets mailed out by Bancroft have "our" inked through.[32]

---

26 Northampton, 19 July, 1826, *GB* to Sarah H. Dwight, Springfield, Bancroft Papers-Cornell; Newport RI, 8 Aug., 1826, Ticknor to GB, Northampton, Bancroft Papers, Massachusetts Historical Society.

27 Boston, 31 July, 1826, Sparks to GB, Northampton (MS, at Mass. Historical Society), and *GB* to Sparks, 2 Aug., 1826, in *Correspondence of George Bancroft and Jared Sparks, 1823-1832*, ed. John Spencer Bassett (Northampton: Smith College, 1917), pp. 110-11.

28 Waltham, 25 Aug., 1826, Eliot to GB, Northampton, Bancroft Papers, Massachusetts Historical Society.

29 *Hampshire Gazette*, 19 and 26 July, 1826; *Hampden Journal* (Springfield), 2 Aug., 1826.

30 *Hampshire Gazette*, 20 April 1825 and 31 May 1826. Butler also carried the jubilee orator's book of poems two years earlier, with Round Hill just under way. *Gazette*, 22 Oct., 1823.

31 *Hampshire Gazette*, 17 Nov. and 1 Dec., 1824. Turner's shop opened for business in a room beneath the *Gazette* office east of the courthouse, i.e., before the proprietor followed editor Judd in moving into the newly constructed brick building one year later, *Gazette*, 8 Oct., 1823.

32 Bancroft oration pamphlet, p. 11 l. 5, Edward Everett Collection of Fourth of July Orations, Hamilton College Library (Clinton, N.Y.).

An oration delivered by George Bancroft on the Fourth of July, 1826, at Northampton (Mass.), pamphlet text issued on the twenty-first by Thomas Watson Shepard of Northampton. Five days later, on the twenty-sixth, the local Hampshire Gazette *reprinted excerpts of the Shepard pamphlet, along with a customary follow-up publication notice. Yet here one dominant practice in the regional distribution setup emerges. For no other regional newspapers ran reprints of the oration, even when advertising the pamphlet for sale in Boston at Cummings, Hilliard, and Company, as three of that city's dailies (*Advertiser, American Statesman, Evening Gazette*) indeed did on the twenty-ninth. Or even when other regional papers took some precedent from the* Hampshire Gazette*—advertising the pamphlet for sale at their own office, though not mentioning bookstore outlets unlike the local* Gazette. *Both the Greenfield* Gazette *(Ag 1) and the* Hampden Journal *in Springfield (Ag 2) followed such a procedure, never in fact reprinting any extracts from the Shepard edition to promote "home" office sales. But a few words are perhaps in order concerning partisan excerpts reprinted in Northampton and Springfield ten years after the event. A few sentences, placed within bold parentheses in the text below, were excerpted during 1836 by the editor of the local* Hampshire Republican *to demonstrate whig Bancroft's philosophical identity with the "common man" of Jackson and Van Buren. As the* Republican *editor put the point, rather than playing the part of the opportunist contender and vacillating between party loyalties to garner more votes as the election neared, the 1826 oration extracts "show that Mr. Bancroft was the advocate of* uncompromising democracy *ten years ago." And the* Republican *piece was reprinted in the Springfield* Hampden Whig *of November 2, perhaps as much to counteract a charge of demagoguery by the editor of the Springfield* Gazette. *Bancroft of course had delivered a second Fourth of July oration in Springfield that year, and the* Gazette *on the sixth editorialized regarding a "base counterfeit" and "spurious" logic inherent in Bancroft's oration. The opposition* Gazette *editor completely disregarded Bancroft's studies on the Continent in favor of what he felt to be the province of the "common man." For even a schoolmaster and historian with credentials abroad might dabble in a tainted brand of democracy "which spends itself in noisy, ostentatious and hollow-hearted professions of love for the people, which, with hypocrisy on the lip, and deceit in the heart, goes about insidiously enticing men with flattering words, to minister to its own selfish purposes." So wrote the editor of the* Gazette, *and he obviously did not directly address himself to the 1826 text subsequently excerpted in a more favorable light.*

1 Our act of celebration begins with God. To the eternal Providence,-on which states depend, and by whose infinite mercy they are prospered,-the nation brings its homage and the tribute of its gratitude. [All things being created] From the omnipotent Power, who dwells in the unclouded serenity of Being without variableness- or shadow of change, we proceed as [if] from The Fountain of good- The Author of hope- and The Source of order and justice—now that we assemble to commemorate the revolution, the independence, and the

advancement of our country! No sentiments should be encouraged on this occasion but those of patriotism and philanthropy. [For] When the names of our venerated fathers were affixed to the instrument which declared our independence, an impulse and confidence were imparted to all efforts at improvement throughout the world. The festival which we keep is the festival of freedom itself; it belongs not to us only, but to man. All the nations of the earth have an interest in [preserving] it—and humanity proclaims it sacred! In the name of *liberty*, therefore, I bid you welcome to the celebration of its jubilee—in the name of *our country*, I bid you welcome to the recollection of its glories- and [bid you to] joy in its prosperity—in the name of *humanity*, I welcome you to a festival which commemorates an improvement in the social condition [of man]—in the name of *religion*, I welcome you to a profession of the principles of public justice which emanate directly from God!

2 These principles are eternal, not only in their truth but in their efficacy. The world has never been entirely without witnesses to them. [And] they have been safely transmitted through the succession of generations—they have survived the revolutions of individual states- and their final success has never been despaired of! Liberty has its foundation in human nature—and some portion of it exists wherever there is a sense of honor. Are proofs of its existence demanded? As the mixture of good and evil is the condition of our earthly being, [so] the efficient agency of good must be sought for- even in the midst of evil— [so] the impulse of free spirits is felt in every state of society- and in spite of all constraint! There may have been periods in which the human mind has sunk into slothful indifference—the arm of exertion been paralyzed—and every noble aspiration hushed in the tranquility of universal submission. But, even in such periods, the world has never been left utterly without hope. And when the breath of tyranny has most effectually concealed the sun of liberty, and shrouded in darkness the magnificence of his beams, it has been but for a season. "Tomorrow he repairs the golden flood,/ And gilds the nations with redoubled ray."

3 Nature concedes to every people the right of executing whatever plans they may devise for their improvement, and the right of maintaining their independence. Of the exercise of these rights, there have always been examples. The innate love of national liberty proceeds [as] from an impulse, and waits only for an opportunity to demonstrate its power. It has aroused the brave and generous from the first periods of history to the present moment, and has been a principle of action under every form of government. It was this [liberty] which made Marathon the watchword of those who fight for their country. This [liberty] pointed the arrows of the Parthian—*this* lent an air of romance to the early history of the Swiss- and gained the battles of Morgarten and Sempach—*this* inspired the Dutch,-when their freedom was endangered by the arms of Louis XIV, and could be secured by no smaller sacrifice,-to lay the soil of Holland beneath the ocean—*this* blessed the banners that waved on Bunker Hill- and canonized the memory of those who fell as the elect martyrs (and witnesses) to

their country's independence—*this* made the French republic invincible when it stood alone against the world—*this*, which formerly at Pultowa had taught the Russians to fight, sacrificed Moscow [as] a splendid victim on the altar of national existence—*this* united the mangled limbs of Germany- breathed a spirit once more into the long divided members- and led them against the French as if impelled by the throbbings of one mighty heart! What need [do I have] of many words? This [liberty] made New Orleans a place of proud recollections—and, still more recently, has raised its boldest standard under the southern sky- and finished a career of victory in the field of Ayacucho!

4 The exercise of free principles in the internal improvement of states is more difficult and more rare, for it requires the continued efforts of prudence- favored by the possession of power—a clear insight into the relations and wants of social life—an enlightened age and a persevering policy. Yet almost the first demand of civilized man has been a legislation founded on the principles of justice. And the Roman law is still in force as the guarantee of private possessions in many of the most despotic countries of Europe. Some fixed constitution, men have always claimed. And wherever codes have been established, their tendency has been favorable to individual rights, personal security, and intellectual liberty. The general sentiment of mankind is expressed by the master spirits—in the works which are as monuments of the knowledge and aspirations of departed ages. Here there exists no difference of feeling [at all]. Liberty may have been contemplated under different aspects, but honor has never been refused to the celestial visitant. Milton, [other] than whom no man ever enjoyed clearer revelations of the light of poetry, appeals to the greatest bards (from the first to his own time) as the lovers and eulogists of liberty. Do you ask after the reasonings of mankind? To the contemplative man, there is no equivalent for freedom of thought and expression—freedom to follow the guidance of Reason- wherever she may lead—freedom to make an open profession of all deliberate convictions! The historians, the orators, the philosophers are the natural advocates of civil liberty. From all countries and all ages we have the same testimony. It is the chorus of the whole family of nations.

5 The events of the last fifty years lead us to hope that liberty, so long militant, is at length triumphant. From our own Revolution, the period derives its character. As on the morning of the nativity the astonished wizards hastened with sweet odors on the Eastern road, our government had hardly come into being- and the star of liberty [hardly begun to] shed over us its benignant light, before the nations began to follow its guidance- and do homage to its beauty. The French Revolution followed our own, and new principles of action were introduced into the politics of Europe. The melancholy events which ensued must be carefully distinguished from the original resistance to unlimited monarchy. The evils which resulted from anarchy in the royal councils should not be referred [for blame] to the influence of national principles. [For] The popular effort—which abolished the system of absolute rule and feudal subjection- which maintained the equal rights of man- which reclaimed the sovereign power

for the people, and established the responsibility of all public officers—a revolution which at once annihilated the distinctions of birth and gave a free course to the principles of liberty- to industry- and to truth—was worthy of the enthusiasm which it excited in the lovers of freedom! The representatives of the people were true—while the Nobles were false- and the King prevaricated! And, but for the coalition of the foreign powers against France, there is reason to believe the French Revolution would have been consummated with so much order, and followed by so much prosperity and happiness, that the neighboring nations must have been incited to imitate the example and peacefully reform their institutions.

6 The wars which followed were not without their use, for though they were conducted by an exasperated nation whose generous passion for liberty had become a frenzy, the armies of the republic were still arrayed against tyranny. The torch of freedom [still] was in their hands- though it had been seized with profane recklessness—the light did indeed glare with [such] a wild and terrific splendor- yet as it waved round the continent of Europe its beams reached [into] the furthest kingdoms, and startled tyranny in its securest recesses! Germany awakened as if to a new consciousness of being—Poland caught a momentary hope of restoration—Bohemia, Hungary, and the furthest East lifted up their heads- and listened for a season to the strains that told of independence, before they relapsed again into their ancient lethargy. A permanent consequence of the French Revolution has been the establishment of representative governments in some of the states of Europe. France may modify her institutions, but never will resign them. The free states of Germany may be overawed by surrounding power, and so—fail of developing their public life by [means of] the strict rules of liberty. But they will never part with their political knowledge. You might as well endeavor to tear the plough [away] from their peasantry, as [endeavor to take] the principles of freedom from their intelligent men! But whatever may be the chances that popular sovereignty will finally prevail in Europe, that continent is no longer to the world what she once was. [For] She has fulfilled her high destiny. She has been for many centuries the sole depositary and guardian of all that is most valuable in government, letters, and invention- in present enjoyment and religious hope. But human culture has at length been transplanted to other climes- and already grown to a more beautiful maturity. Whatever destiny may hang over Europe, mankind is safe. Intelligence and religion have found another home. Not only in our own free states [but elsewhere in America], the Cross is planted on each side [of] the Andes—and the rivers which empty into either ocean fertilize the abodes of civilization.

7 A more admirable and cheering spectacle, therefore, than Europe can offer is exhibiting in our own hemisphere. A family of free states has at once come into being, and already flourishes on a soil which ('til now) had been drooping under colonial thralldom. Our happiness is increased by the wide diffusion of the blessings of [such] free institutions. And it is a pleasing con-

sciousness that the example of our fathers taught these new republics what were their rights- and how they might [best] assert them. Their final success we [now] regard as certain—believing that the freedom of inquiry and of action will ensure the triumph of Reason- and the establishment of wise constitutions. Be it [true] that the new aspirants after liberty are impeded by the relics of colonial bondage, the influence of pernicious forms [of government]- which rested for support on the dominion of the mother country- cannot long survive the end of that dominion! Be it [true] that the literature of Spain contains no eloquent exposition of the principles of liberty, they [as aspirants] will find a good interpreter of them in their own breasts! Be it [true] that clear views of public economy and [public] administration are not yet commonly diffused, the people soon learn to understand their interests- and to devise the best means of advancing them! Be it [true] that their religion partakes of bigotry and an exclusive spirit, bigotry will yield to light! And far be it from us to condemn wantonly a form of Christianity which is adopted by half the Christian world. Be it [true] that their social life has not yet assumed a form corresponding with their political condition, the natural operation of civil equality and the success of unrestricted enterprise will remove all injurious distinctions! (Be it [true] that they are taunted with extravagance- and denounced as drunk with liberty, it is a very safe intoxication- and would to God all the nations of the earth might drink deeply of that cup!)Be it [true] that they have consistently practiced in the faith of man's natural equality, there is no reason to apprehend a confusion of justice from those who guarantee the rights of all the members of their community! And, finally, be it [true] that they who are now beginning to enjoy free constitutions are partly of mixed descent, will you not all coincide with me when I say,("We feel for man- not for a single race of men- and wherever liberty finds followers—as wherever Christ has disciples,-be it [true] that English or Indian-Spanish or African blood pours in their veins,—we greet them as brethren!")

8 I have glanced at the leading events in the history of the last half-century- and their aspect on the progress of free institutions. Time will not permit—nor does our purpose lead us to enumerate all the states which were doomed to perish- or those which were to rise from their ruins. No so short [a] period of history ever presented so many (or so mighty) revolutions—such grand displays of national force—armies so numerous- and yet so well disciplined—battles so skillfully conducted- and decisive of such vast interests! The stream of time which flowed through so many of the past centuries with a lazy current has at last rushed onwards with overwhelming fury—leaping down one precipice after another- destroying all barriers in its ungovernable swiftness- hurrying states and empires and nations along [in] its current—while the master minds [of nation states] were driven (they knew not whither) on waters through which they vainly endeavored to direct their course!

9 The age has been fertile in strange contrasts [inherent] in unforeseen and unparalleled events. [For] Europe is filled with the shadows of departed states- and the graves of ruined republics. In the North an adventurer of fortune

has succeeded to the Swedish throne- and the legitimate King lives quietly in exile. While in the rest of Europe the doctrine of the divine right [of rule] has been revived. Rome was once more made the head of a republic. The secular power of the Pope, [though] annihilated for a season, was restored by the help of Turks- Russians- and English—infidels, schismatics, and heretics [alike]. An army of Europeans, having in its [caravan] train a band of scientific men, pitched its victorious camp at the foot of the Pyramids. The solitary banks of the Nile again became the temporary abode of glory and civilization—and again the bands of armed men poured through the hundred gates of the long deserted Thebes. An empire which sends its caravans into Tartary and China exerts its influence in Paris and Madrid- and has its envoy at Washington. The whole East has been a scene of continued turbulence—'til at last a corporation of merchants, residing in a distant island, has reduced seventy millions of people to subjection. And, finally, to notice a singular fact in our own history, (he whose eloquent pen gave freedom its charter in the declaration of our independence—he who was the third to receive the greatest honor ever awarded by public suffrage) —he who in the course of his administration doubled the extent of our territory by a peaceful treaty—he (whose principles are identified with the character of our government- and whose influence [is identified] with the progress of civil liberty throughout the world) —after declining to be a third time elected to the highest station in the service of his country, has *not* preserved [up]on his retirement,-I will not say "fortune enough to bury him with honor,"—has *not* saved the means of supporting the decline of life with decency![1]

10 The system of states now united by diplomatic relations or commerce embraces the world. The productions and the manufacturers of all climes- the advances of intelligence and all useful inventions- are made universal benefits—the thoughts of superior men find their way over every ocean and through every country. Civilization has its messengers in all parts of the world—and there is a community of feeling among the lovers of truth- however widely their abodes may be separated. And in this system of states, an experiment is simultaneously making of the most various forms of government—and all [forms are] within the reach of [our] mutual observation. While the United States show to what condition a nation is carried by establishing a government strictly national, we have in Russia and in Hayti examples of a military despotism—in England a preponderating aristocracy—in France a monarchy with partial limitations—in Prussia an absolute monarchy- yet [still] dependent for its strength on the spirit of the people—in Naples the old-fashioned system of absolute caprice. Let [other] men reason if they will on the

---

1 The *Republican* editor does not excerpt what Bancroft regarded as Jefferson's primary achievement in office. While studying abroad at Göttingen some sixteen years earlier, for example, Bancroft made it known in his initial Fourth of July oration that Jefferson "gained for us the vast territory of the West, and this deed alone entitles him to the gratitude of his country and to a glorious monument in the history of the world."

different systems of government. The history of the age is showing from actual experiment which of them best promotes the ends of the social compact.

11 Thought has been active in our times, not with speculative questions [only]—but in devising [appropriate] means for improving the social condition [of man]. Efforts have been made to diffuse Christianity throughout the world. The cannibal of the South Sea forgets his horrid purpose- and listens to the instructions of religion. [In this respect,] the light of the Sabbath morn is welcomed by the mild inhabitants of the Pacific islands- and Africa and Australia have not remained unvisited. Colonies, which were first established on the Guinea coast for [the purpose of supplying] the traffic in slaves, have [now] been renewed—[but] for the more effectual suppression of that accursed trade. A curiosity which will not rest unsatisfied perseveres in visiting the unknown parts of the earth. The oceans have been so carefully explored by skillful navigators that we are well-acquainted with all their currents and their paths. And the regions which lie furthest from the ancient abodes of civilization have at last received its colonies. Not only the advancement of knowledge characterizes the age [in which we live], but its wide diffusion throughout all classes of society [is another characteristic]. The art of printing,-which has been in use less than four hundred years, and which- vast as its influence has already been- is just beginning to show how powerfully it can operate on society,-offers such means of extending knowledge that national education becomes everywhere possible. And while before this invention it was impracticable to impart literary culture but to a few, the elements of science can now be made universally accessible. The facts to which I have rapidly alluded show a gradual amelioration of the human condition- and the more complete development of the social virtues. And where is it that the hopes of philanthropy are most nearly realized?

12 I turn from the consideration of foreign revolutions to our own condition—and meet with nothing but what may animate our joy- and increase our hopes. The visions of patriotism fall short of the reality. [For] He who observes the air of cheerful industry and successful enterprise—the sobriety of order- the increasing wealth of our cities- the increasing productiveness of our lands- our streams crowded with new establishments- and the appearance of entire success stamped on every part of our country—will yet be amazed at the official documents in which the elements of this success are analyzed, and its [actual] amount made the subject of cool calculation! In whatever direction we turn our eyes, we find one unclouded scene of prosperity—everywhere [the] marks of advancement and increasing opulence. While the population of the United States is doubled in less than twenty-four years, its [working] capital is doubled in less than eleven. At the beginning of the [Revolutionary] war, the manufactures of the country could hardly be said to have had any considerable value. [But] during the last twelvemonth the value of goods manufactured in the United States has probably exceeded three hundred millions of dollars! The commerce of the country, soon after the Revolution, extended it is true to every important mart, though it was but the first effort of a nation without capital. But now,

when a large part of the commerce of the world is done by American merchants, our internal commerce surpasses our foreign even in tonnage—and still more in its value to the nation! Our thriving agriculture gives an air of magnificence to our lands, and after supplying our domestic wants leaves a large surplus for exportation. All our rural towns have an aspect [about them] of ease and comfort and prosperity. On our seaboard, the wealth and population are advancing with a rapidity surpassing [even] the most sanguine expectations! And the prospect that lies before us seems too brilliant to be realized,-when we observe a city like New York, already one of the largest on earth (and yet so new), its crowded wharves- its splended walk by the oceanside- its gay and busy streets so remarkable for the beautiful neatness of the buildings—its industry- its moral order- and its rapid growth proceeding from causes that still operate with undiminished force! These grand results are visible in the oldest part of our country—where the trees are older than the settlements- and men are older than the bridges and the roads. The changes in the West[ern United States] are known to be still more amazing. The hunter finds his way through a fertile region, and hardly has his good report been heard before it is gemmed with villages—and all the intelligence and comforts of cultivated life are at once introduced into the new haunts of civilization! The voice of Christian worship is heard to rise from crowded assemblies- in regions which have been first visited within our memories. Domestic trade is extending itself in every direction. Steamboats ascend even the most rapid rivers, whose banks have been but recently explored. And,-as they pass through the lonely scenes, now first enlivened by the echoes of social cheerfulness,-the venerable antiquity of Nature bends [down] from her awful majesty- and welcomes the fearless emigrant to the solitudes where the earth has for centuries been hoarding fertility!

13 I have spoken to you of the condition of our country at large, [and] I have called on you to observe its general prosperity. I will now limit the sphere of our view, [and] I will ask you to look around at your own fields and firesides—your own business and prospects. There is not one desirable privilege which we do not enjoy—there is not one social advantage that Reason can covet-which is not our's. I speak not merely of our equal rights to engage in any pursuit that promises emolument or honor. I speak also of the advantages which we are always enjoying—security in our occupations- liberty of conscience- the certain rewards of labor. [For] While there is general ease, the distribution of wealth has led to no great inequalities [throughout our country]. *All* our interests are thriving—the mechanic arts are exercised with *successful* skill—*improved* means of communication with the seaboard are opening [up] to our trade—the waters of our abundant streams are continually applied to *new* branches of business—an *equal* interchange of kindness is the general custom—moral order pervades an *industrious* population—*intelligence* is diffused among our yeomanry—the plough is in the *hands* of its owner—and the neat aspect of our farmhouses proves them [to be] the abode of contentment and *successful* diligence! Nor are we without our recollections. I never can think

without reverence of the spirited veteran **who,-on** the morning of **the seventeenth of June,** in the seventieth year of **his** age,-was hastening **on horse**back as a volunteer **to Bunker Hill** but,-coming to **Charlestown Neck**, and finding **the fire** from **the British ships** so severe that [any attempt at] **cross**ing was extremely dangerous,-cooly sent back the animal **which he had borrowed** of a friend—and- shouldering his musket - *marched over* **on foot**![2] When the Americans saw him approach, they raised a shout- and the name of *Pomeroy* ran along the lines. [And] Since the ashes of the gallant soldier do not rest among us, let us [all] the more do honor to his memory! We have raised a simple monument to his name in our graveyard, but his body reposes where he breathed out life [intent up]on his country's service—in the maturity of [his] years- and yet a martyr! Even before that time,-and before the hour of immediate danger when the boldest spirits might have wavered in gloomy uncertainty, and precious moments were wasting in indecision,-one of our own citizens (my friends, his memory is still fresh among us) had been the first to cry [out], in a voice which was heard beyond the Potomac, "We must *fight*!"—And when some [other] alternative was desired, and [some] reconciliation hoped [for] from inactivity and delay, [that citizen] clearly saw the absolute necessity of the case—and did but repeat, "We *must* fight!" It was in front of the very place where we are now assembled that the hearts of our fathers were cheered (and their resolution confirmed) by the eloquence of *Hawley*.

14 And what is the cause and the guarantee of our happiness? What but the principles of our Constitution! [For] When our fathers assembled to prepare it, the genius of history admitted them to [learn] the secrets of [their] destiny- and taught them by the failures of the past to provide for the happiness of future generations. No model was offered them which it seemed safe to imitate. [And] the Constitution established a government on entirely liberal principles such as the world had never beheld in practice. The sovereignty of the people is the basis of the system. (With the people the power resides- both theoretically and practically. The government is a democracy—a determined, uncompromising democracy administered immediately by the people- or by the people's responsible agents.) In all the European treatises on political economy, and even in the state-papers of the Holy Alliance, the welfare of the people is acknowledged to be the object of [all] government. We believe [it is] so, too. But (as each man's interests are safest in his own keeping, so in [a] like manner the interests of the people can best be guarded by themselves.) If the institution of monarchy were

2 In a Fourth of July oration at Worcester seven years later, Edward Everett acknowledges his indebtedness to Bancroft for providing him with a copy of a Seth Pomeroy letter dated May 8, 1745. Apparently while in process of composing his Worcester oration, Everett took Bancroft's Northampton pamphlet edition (received shortly after being printed) from his library shelf, and revised Bancroft's description of Pomeroy's feat to the less oral "**who, on the 17th of June,** 1775 dismounted and passed **Charlestown Neck, on his** way **to Bunker-Hill, on foot,** in the midst of a shower of balls, because he did not think it conscionable to ride General Ward's **horse, which he had borrowed,** through **the cross fire** of **the British ships** of war and floating batteries."

neither tyrannical nor oppressive, it should at least be dispensed with as a costly superfluity. (We believe the sovereign power should reside equally among the people) —we acknowledge no hereditary distinctions- and we confer on *no man* prerogatives or peculiar privileges! Even the best services rendered the state cannot destroy this original and essential equality. [For] Legislation and justice are not hereditary offices—*no one* is born to power- *no one* dandled into political greatness! Our government, as it rests for support on Reason and our interests, needs no protection from a nobility. And the strength and ornament of the land consist in its industry and morality- its justice and intelligence.

15 The states of Europe are all intimately allied with the church- and fortified by religious sanctions. We approve of the influence of the religious principle on public, no less than on private life—but we hold religion to be an affair between each individual conscience and God- superior to all political institutions and independent of them. [For] Christianity was neither introduced nor reformed by the civil power. And with us the modes of worship are in no wise prescribed by the state. (Thus, then, the people governs (and solely)—it does not divide its power with a hierarchy, a nobility, or a king. The popular voice is all powerful with us. This is our oracle—this we acknowledge is the voice of God!) Invention is solitary- but who shall judge of its results—inquiry may pursue truth apart [from public scrutiny]- but who shall decide if truth if overtaken? There is [really] no safe criterion of opinion but the careful exercise of the public judgment. And in the science of government, as elsewhere, the deliberate convictions of mankind reasoning [up]on the cause of their own happiness- their own wants and interests- are the surest revelations of political truth. The interests of the people are the interests of the individuals who compose the people. [And] If we needed no general government for [securing and enhancing] our private success and happiness, we [certainly] should have adopted none. It is created to supply a want and a deficiency. It is simply a corporation invested with limited powers for accomplishing specific purposes.

16 (Government is based upon population- not upon property. If they who possess the wealth possessed the power also, they would legislate in such a way as to preserve that wealth and power. And this would tend to[ward] an aristocracy.) We hold it best that (the laws should favor the diffusion of property and its easy acquisition—not the concentration of it in the hands of *a few*- to the impoverishment of the *many*. We give the power to *the many* in the hope (and to the end) that they may use it for their own benefit) —that they may always so legislate as to open the fairest career to industry- and promote an equality founded on the safe and equitable influence of the laws. We do not fear—we rather invite the operation of the common motives which influence humanity. If the Emperor of Austria takes care to do nothing against his trade as a king- if the Pope administers his affairs with reference to his own advantage, and that of the Romish Church- if the English aristocracy provides for the secure succession of hereditary wealth and power,-so, too, we hope- where the power resides with *the many*- that *the many* will be sure to provide for themselves—magistrates be

taken from the bosom of the people- to which they [must] return [for responsibility]—the rights of those who have acquired property [be] sacredly regarded—the means of acquiring it [be] made common to all—industry receive its merited honors—morality be preserved—knowledge universally diffused—and the worth of naked humanity duly respected and encouraged!

17 The laws of the land are sacred, [for] they are established by the majority for the general good. Private rights are [also] sacred, [for] the protection of them is the end of [all] law and government. When the rules of justice are trampled on, or the power of maintaining it [is] wrested from the hands of its appointed guardians, there is tyranny—let it be done where and by whom it may- in the Old World or in the New- by a monarch or by a mob. Liberty frowns on such deeds as attacks [made up]on her safety. For liberty knows nothing of [this] passion. She is the daughter of God- and dwells in unchanging tranquility beside His throne—her serene countenance is never ruffled by excitement—Reason and justice are the pillars of her [divine] seat- and truth and virtue the angels that minister unto her. When you come with violence and angry fury, do you pretend to come in her name? In vain [you come], [for] she is not there! Even now she has escaped from among you! Thus, then, our government is strictly national—having its origin in the will of the people- its object[ive] in their happiness- its guarantee in their morality. A government essentially radical in so far as it aims to facilitate the prompt reform of abuses—and essentially leveling [insofar] as it prohibits hereditary distinctions- and tends to diminish artificial ones.

18 Our government is called weak and said to rest on an insecure foundation, while in truth it is established on the firmest. It is [a result of] the deliberate preference of all its citizens, and self-balanced rests securely on its own strength. Our confidence in its durability is equal to our confidence that the people will always find such a system for their interests—and that liberty and intelligence will always be respected by a majority of mankind. [For] The will of the people created our Constitution, and *not* prescriptive right—*not* the condescension of an individual—*not* the terrors of religion as interpreted by a priesthood—*not* the bayonets of a standing army—*not* the duplicity of diplomatic chicanery—*not* the lure of mitres, coronets, and artificial distinctions! The wisdom of the people is our only- our sufficient- constitutional- frank pledge! Our moral condition is, then, indeed superior to that of the Old World- in the present or in any former age. We have institutions *more* free- *more* just- and *more* beneficent than have ever before been established. And [so] that our glory as a nation might in nothing be wanting, the men to whom the people first confided their interests,-they whose names stand *highest* in the annals of our glory—the *statesmen* by whose voice the pure spirit of the country expressed its desires—the *leaders* by whose bravery and skill our citizens were conducted to [attain] success in the contest for their rights,-were of undoubted integrity and spotless patriotism—men in whom the elements of human *greatness* were so

happily mixed that, as their principles were generous and elevated, so their lives were distinguished by a course of *honorable* action- and the sacrifice of private advantage to the *public good*! They united the fervor of genius with the magnanimity of character! And the lustre of their brilliant career was tempered by the republican simplicity of their manners! The names of Washington and Franklin recur as often as examples are sought of enlightened philanthropy- and a virtue almost superhuman. The political privileges of the people correspond with the moral *greatness* of our illustrious men. [And] Greece and Rome can offer no parallel to the one or the other.

19 In possession of complete personal independence, our religious liberty is entire—our press without restrictions—the channels of wealth and honor alike open to all—the cause of intelligence asserted and advanced by the people! In our houses- our churches- our halls of justice- our legislatures—everywhere there is liberty! The sublimest views of superior minds are here but homely truths—reduced to practice- and shedding a beneficent influence over all the daily operations of [our] life. Soul is breathed into the public administration by the suffrages of the people- and the aspect of our policy on the world is favorable to universal improvement. [For] The dearest interests of mankind were entrusted to our country. It was for her to show that the aspirations of former ages were *not* visionary—that freedom is something *more* than [just] a name—that the patriots and the states (that have been martyrs in its defense) were struggling in a sacred cause- and fell in the pursuit of a *real* good! The great spirits of former times looked down from their celestial abodes to cheer and encourage her in the hour of danger. The nations of the earth turned towards her as to their last hope. And the country has not deceived them. With unwavering consistency she has pursued the general good- and confirmed the national sovereignty—she has joined a decided will to a clear perception of her rights and duties—she has had courage [enough] to regulate her course by [relying upon] free principles (wherever they might guide)- and has proclaimed them to the world, as with the voice of an inspired man! Resolutely developing her resources and perfecting her establishments by the light of her own experience, she stands [forth] (in the eye of Heaven and the world) in all the comeliness and strength of youth,-yet swayed by a spirit of mature wisdom- exemplifying in her public capacity the virtues and generous affections of human nature—a light to the world- an example to those who *would* be free—*already* the benefactress of humanity- the tutelary angel of liberty! She advances in her course with the energy of rectitude and the calmness of justice. Liberty is her device- liberty is her *glory*- liberty is *the American policy*! This [liberty] diffuses its blessings throughout all our land—this [liberty] is cherished in our hearts- dearer than life, and dear as honor—this [liberty] is embedded in our soil more firmly than the ancient granite in our mountains! *This* has been bequeathed to us by our fathers—and, whatever may befall us, we will transmit the heritage unimpaired to the coming generation!

20 Our Service began with [some mention made of] God. May we not believe that He, who promises assistance to the humblest of us in our efforts to do His will, regards with complacency the advancement of the nation—and now from His high abode smiles [up]on us with favoring benignity. Trusting in the Providence of Him the Universal Father, let the country advance [onward] to the glory and prosperity to which, [ever] mindful of its exalted privileges, it aspires! Wherever its voice is heard, let it proclaim the message of *liberty*- and speak [out] with the divine energy of truth (be the principles of moral goodness consistently followed in its actions)! And while the centuries as they pass multiply its population and its resources, let it manifest in its whole history a devoted attachment to public virtue- a dear affection for mankind- and the consciousness of [fulfilling] its responsibility to the God of nations!

Chapter 5

John Quincy Adams's Fourth of July Oration, 1828

Two years after the nation's jubilee of Independence, John Quincy Adams, resolutely confirmed to be an establishment Yankee "none the worse for Uncle Sam" by a patriotic ditty at Boston,[1] together with 91-year-old Charles Carroll, an establishment figurehead one correspondent labeled the "ultimus Romanorum,"[2] so taboo for patriotic Whigs was any mention of not-so-strictly-accountable public goals serving private commercial interests, helped commence work on twin internal-improvements projects—the Chesapeake and Ohio Canal, and the Baltimore and Ohio Railroad.

But a democratic counter-revolution rapidly was setting in against whatever stationary concepts the establishment and its leaders could invoke on the Fourth. The chief persona of this disestablishment movement, spurred on really

---

1 "T'other Yankee Doodle—sung at celebration of Fourth in Boston," *The Marylander* (sw, Baltimore), 19 July, 1828.

2 C. of A., "Undated letter on Grand National Canal celebration," *Daily National Intelligencer* (WDC), 31 May, 1828. Carroll made a prior appearance in Baltimore, laying the foundation stone for the Phoenix Shot Tower on the morning of 2 June. And editor William Fry of the Philadelphia *National Gazette* heightened Carroll's stature on the Fourth, by contrasting it with inferior visions in the British motherland: "Gentlemen who were present . . . say that the thrice venerable man . . . executed the part which was assigned to him with a firm hand, an agile step, and a countenance of the brightest vivacity and pleasure. He stated, to the bystanders, his recollection of their now populous and beautiful city when it was scarcely farther advanced than the work of which he was laying the first stone (and when an anticipation of its extent and character, at this period, would have been deemed not less romantic than many persons supposed their hopes of the Railroad to be). His memory touched nearly the two extremities of its condition. How much more magnificent, if not more dear, his retrospect of the progress of the country, through all the stages, from his fortunate dawn of reason and public sentiment to his present maturity of years, reverence, and wisdom. How inferior to this, the vision which Burke imagined for the aged Bathurst, when he pictured the angel of his auspicious youth drawing up, 'amidst bright and happy scenes of domestic prosperity,' the curtain of futurity, and unfolding the rising glories of Great Britain. 'Fortunate man,' exclaimed the transcendant orator, 'he has lived to see them—fortunate, indeed, if he lives to see nothing that shall vary the prospect and cloud the setting of the day.' " *American and Commercial Daily Advertiser* (Baltimore), 31 May and 3 June, 1828; *Gazette and Literary Register* (d), 8 July, 1828.

by a reactionary press cleverly pitting a tough "hickory" Tennessee farmer against vulnerable and status-conscious "oak" Adams,[3] was none other than Andrew Jackson, heir-apparent to a grass-roots "beauty and booty" dating back to his anti-royal triumph at New Orleans. Indeed, candidate Jackson may well have been advised to strike a very low profile on the Fourth, forsaking ghostwriters Harry Lee and Edward Livingston, old reliables occasionally in residence at the Hermitage, for a "neighbor-and-friend" dinner nearby in Carthage, Tennessee.[4] Neither at Carthage, nor Lebanon on the second, nor Hartsville on the fifth did Jackson, in his cryptic remarks, even broach potentially troublesome topics like the recent tariff law or additional protective facets of Henry Clay's American System.[5]

President Adams, on the other hand, as chief executive officer of a federal establishment committed to subscribing $1,000,000 for some ten thousand shares of Canal stock, almost of necessity had to broach internal improvements at the Chesapeake and Ohio ceremonies. Yet the topic need not have been that vexing for Adams. The Canal ceremonies actually grew out of general illuminations marking passage of the Canal Bill on May 22, illuminations pooh-poohed as mere "outward manifestations" by Mayor Joseph Gales, Jr. of Washington City,[6] and a series of dinners at Cumberland, Maryland, on June 3, Leesburg, Virginia, a week later, and Georgetown, D.C., only two days before Adams formally was invited to speak on the Fourth.

The thematic structure of after-dinner speeches by legislative managers Andrew Stewart of Pennsylvania and Charles Fenton Mercer of Virginia, spanning

---

3 Songs containing such imagery literally abounded in the 1828 Presidential campaign. For verses sung to "Hurrah for the bonnets of blue," contrast a pro-Jackson "Huzza for the Hickory Tree" (A.N.P., New York *Enquirer* in *United States' Telegraph* [d, WDC], 24 Nov., 1827; *National Palladium and Freeman's Journal* [Philadelphia] in *Telegraph*, 6 May, 1828) with a "Song" by T.H. (*Democratic Press* [d, Philadelphia], 29 July, 1828). For pro-Adams "Live Oak Tree" variants sung to "Scots wa ha wi' Wallace bled," see *The Virginian* (sw, Lynchburg), 23 June; *Waldo Democrat* (Belfast, Me.), 23 July; *Kennebec Journal* (Augusta, Me.), 19 Dec., 1828. Compare a pro-Adams "Song" by J.H.S., sung to "William Reily" (*Virginia Herald* [sw, Fredericksburg], 26 July) with a Jackson "Song" tuned to "I've kiss'd and I've prattled with fifty fair maids" (Dover [N.H.] *Gazette* in Lancaster [Pa.] *Journal*, 7 Nov., 1828). For another Adams song, and an "Oak Tree" poem by Thadore datelined Waynesburg, Pennsylvania, 27 July, see *Torch Light and Public Advertiser* (Hagers-Town, Md.), 14 Aug., 1828. Contrast the Jackson "hickory" rationale ("An Allegory," *Western Argus* [Beaver, Pa.] in Pittsburgh *Mercury*, 8 Jan.) with anti-image Adams commentary (*American Sentinel* [Georgetown, Ky.], 28 June; Live Oak, "Poem dated 4 July." *Somerset Iris and Messenger of Truth* [Princess-Anne, Md.], 22 July; *We the People* [WDC], 11 Oct.; Olive, *The Marylander* [d, Baltimore], 15 Oct., 1828). For a "Kentucky hunter" image extremely congruous with an industrious farmer, see S. Woodsworth's song, "New Orleans; Or, Hunters of Kentucky," *Republican Compiler* (Gettysburg, Pa.), 10 Sept., 1828. And for four pro-Adams rebuttals against the "Tennessee farmer" image, consult New-York *American* (d), 14 July; *Miners' Journal and Schuylkill Coal and Navigation Register* (Pottsville, Pa.), 19 July; *American Mercury* (Hartford, Ct.), 19 Aug. replied to in Richmond [Va.] *Enquirer* (sw), 26 Aug.; *Daily Cincinnati Gazette*, 3 Sept., 1828.

4 *National Banner and Nashville Whig* (sw), 18 July, 1828; Nashville *Republican* in *United States' Telegraph* (d, WDC), 28 July, 1828.

5 *National Banner*, 11 and 15 July, 1828.

6 "Announcement from Mayor dated 23 May," *Dly National Intelligencer*, 24 May, 1828.

these three occasions, clearly reveals the commercial rationale Adams might perhaps have been expected to manifest in his remarks at the Canal ceremonies. Speaking at Cumberland, for example, Stewart, a Board member of the Canal Company, cited a mutuality of speculative interests between private and federal operatives: "I regard the great work . . . as no local concern. It is national, emphatically *national* in all its aspects. It presents not the ordinary case of the National Government aiding a private company to execute a local work, but it is the case of a private company aiding the National Government to execute a *national* work—a work calculated, above all others, to promote the national defense in war and the national prosperity in peace—a work which will remain a proud and permanent monument, to future generations, of the wisdom and munificence of the present—[and] which will remain a strong and enduring bond of national union when every other tie, which [presently] unites us, may be sundered [apart] and destroyed."[7]

And Mercer, president of the Canal Company, emphasized the idyllic glory and prosperity of the enterprise in terms of primitive "Cohongoronta" lore and a "practical standard of public and private morality"[8] handed down from George Washington's Potomac Company. Speaking at Leesburg, Mercer ebulliently claimed that a progressive stage of civilization was about to be encouraged, in the spirit of internal improvements, along the Chesapeake and Ohio Canal: "It smoothes the rough current of our majestic river, and promises to unlock, for our enjoyment, both the treasures of Nature and the inventions of art—to augment not only our wealth and comfort by opening [up] new avenues of commerce, but [also to augment] the security of our freedom by perpetuating our happy and glorious Union. Is this language extravagant? . . . Such was the opinion of Washington when the Indian canoe had but just disappeared from the bosom of the 'river of Swans'[Cohongoronta]. He but glanced with a patriot's eye, [down] through dim futurity, to that Fourth of July which has been appointed by the public anticipation for commencing the greatest enterprise that ever ennobled the labor of man."[9]

On June 28, Mayor Gales of Washington City and Major John Cox of Georgetown, acting in accordance with resolutions from their aldermen and common-council members,[10] visited Adams at the White House, and gained his formal acceptance of their invitation to speak and "give the first stroke of the

---

7 *Dly National Intelligencer*, 10 June, 1828.

8 *Dly National Intelligencer*, 1 July, 1828.

9 *Dly National Intelligencer*, 16 June, 1828; *Genius of Liberty* (Leesburg, Va.) in *Intelligencer*, 18 June, 1828. Readers interested in a current oralized history of the Canal should consult George W. "Hooper" Wolfe's *I Drove Mules on the C. and O. Canal* (Williamsport Md., 1969), along with various Supplements to the first printing.

10 "Washington-City ordinance dated 26 June" and "Georgetown ordinance dated 28 June," Georgetown *Columbian, District Advertiser, and Commercial Gazette* (sw), 1 July, 1828.

spade." Adams accepted "with great pleasure,"[11] perhaps partly motivated by the bitter electioneering already making its presence felt, a campaign in which learned Brahmins like himself never could hope to swing very many undecided votes while shunning such favorable public exposure. Nor was he any too eager to allow a single yeoman from candidate Jackson's rabble into the White-House reception on the Fourth, pricing billiard tables or some other ostentatious trapping which, whether real or imagined, would permit the Jackson press to polarize undecideds by casting him as a noncredible Brahmin flunkey-recluse. There indeed were definite advantages for Adams in the arrangements—addressing a carefully controlled crowd, at a site more than slightly removed from the White House, as a venerable spokesman for internal improvements, and canceling the usual reception in favor of a close-knit, informal party with key Marshals-of-the-day and Canal Company officers after returning from the ceremonies. The evening prior to the Fourth, friend Charles Fenton Mercer listened to Adams read through his final draft of the speech at the White House, and agreed to insert an appropriate preface in his own remarks introducing the President at the ceremonies. But Mercer quite understandably cautioned Adams against concluding the oration on a note of "good wishes for the success" of the Baltimore and Ohio Railroad,[12] especially since injunctions had been obtained in Maryland by both the Canal Company and Railroad over conflicting rights-of-way.[13]

Little Falls above Georgetown, the location for the ceremonies, was itself more than slightly ironic as a selection, because vehement partisan John Randolph and the American-System's Henry Clay had gone through the motions of a duel near there on April 8, 1826. Indeed, it perhaps was only fitting that pro-Adams editor Jonathan Elliot reported a Randolph-like figure, "endeavoring to kick up a *huzza for Jackson*," fleeing mutely for "the skirts of Georgetown,"

11 Charles Francis Adams, ed., *Memoirs of John Quincy Adams, Comprising Portions of His Diary from 1795 to 1848*, VIII (Philadelphia: J. B. Lippincott, 1876), 45. At a meeting of the Committee of Arrangements in the City Hall, held later the same day, where the Canal Company also had its office, Mayor Gales, editor of the *National Intelligencer* with William W. Seaton, announced Adams's acceptance in his role as Committee chairman, and placed this notice in the *Intelligencer* for 30 June: "The Citizens of the District . . . are invited generally to be present . . . . As many as can conveniently procure boats are invited to attend the procession by water . . . . The President of the United States . . . has accepted the invitation to attend on the occasion, and put the first shovel in the ground for this great work." Simultaneously, private invitations were sent out by Gales to members of the establishment like Peter Force, editor of the *National Journal*, whose presence at the ceremonies warranted more than a come-if-you-can-make-it notice in the press. Force Papers, Manuscript Division, Library of Congress.

12 *Ibid.*, 48-49.

13 "Injunction from Judge John Buchanan against Railroad, dated 10 June-Washington County," *American and Commercial Dly Advertiser* (Baltimore), 13 June, in *National Journal* (tw, WDC), 17 June, 1828; "Injunction from Chancellor Theodoric Bland against Canal Company, dated 23 June-Annapolis," *American and Commercial Dly Advertiser*, 25 June, 1828. Prior to the Fourth, two other injunctions were obtained by the Railroad against the Canal Company. And the legal issues were not resolved satisfactorily until late in 1831. See random coverage of this settlement in *Dly National Intelligencer*, 19 Sept., 10 Oct., 9 Nov., 1831 and 9 Jan., 1832.

when confronted with Adams and other members of the procession leaving the canalboats and joining forces on the field where the ceremonies were to take place.[14] District governmental officials, Canal Company officers and stockholders, and the Diplomatic Corps comprised Adams's establishment-oriented audience on the field, with several thousand spectators taking up positions on crests of nearby hills, some even accompanying Marines into trees for a better view though out of earshot.

As agreed the night before at the White House, Mercer prefaced his remarks when handing over a silver spade, what he rather wordily labeled as a "humble instrument of rural labor" symbolizing a "favorite occupation,"[15] to Adams. Seizing the propitious moment for posterity to remember, Mercer declared: "There are moments in the progress of Time which are the counters of whole Ages. There are events, the monuments of which, surviving every other memorial of human existence, eternize the nation (to whose history they belong) after all other vestiges of its glory have disappeared from the globe. At such a moment have we *now* arrived; such a monument we are *now* to found."[16]

Temporarily setting aside the spade handed him by Mercer, Adams began his fifteen-minute oration. He attempted to consolidate respect for a commercial ethic by combining biblical imagery[17] with George Berkeley's rationale for New-World entrepreneurs,[18] an establishment outlook long shared with father John[19] and in 1840 developed into a parallel "Society and Civilization" lecture.[20] Attempted is probably too objective a frame word, for Adams afterward wrote with

14 *We the People* (WDC), 12 July, 1828.

15 WDC, 1 July, 1828, Mrs. Louisa C. Adams to George Washington Adams, Boston, Adams Family Papers, Massachusetts Historical Society (Boston); *Dly National Intelligencer* and *Dly National Journal*, 7 July, 1828.

16 *Dly National Intelligencer* and *Dly National Journal*, 7 July, 1828.

17 "Paraphrase of first four and last eight verses of 104th Psalm," Martinsburg [Va.] *Gazette and Public Advertiser*, 24 July, 1828; "Paraphrase of 42nd Psalm," *Gazette and Public Advertiser*, 14 Aug., 1828. Adams refers in the *Memoirs* (8:48-49) to a "religious character" and "religious cast" being part of the substance of his oration.

18 Anonymous correspondent, "Background commentary on Berkeley's Verses on the Prospect of Planting Arts and Learning in America," *Political Arena and Literary Museum* (sw, Fredericksburg Va.), 1 Aug., subsequently reprinted by *Aurora and Pennsylvania Gazette* (d, Philadelphia), 9 Aug. and Charleston [S.C.] *Courier* (d), 27 Aug., 1828. Bishop Berkeley remained a patriotic source well into the nineteenth century. See, for example, his "Maxims Concerning Patriotism" in *American Whig Review*, 7 (Feb. 1851), 126-27, and in *United States Review*, 5 (Aug. 1855), 103-04. But the correspondent's commentary never really compares with such current evaluations as Rexmond C. Cochrane's brilliant analysis of the Berkeley poem, in *Huntington Library Quarterly*, 17 (May 1954), 229-49.

19 Charles Sumner, "Prophetic Voices about America: A Monograph," *Atlantic Monthly*, 20 (Sept. 1867), 279.

20 *American Review*, 2 (July 1845), 80-89. Although Condorcet, and not Berkeley, furnished the main source for this lecture, Wendell Glick's analysis is quite useful in exploring any secondary Berkeley parallel (*New England Quarterly*, 37 [March 1964], 3-17). Compare, especially, the urban-progressive implications of stage 4 (lecture) and step 3 (oration), determining how both might relate to Berkeley's observation of cyclical industrial depression and geopolitical finality.

considerable displeasure about "flowers of rhetoric" in the speech being dulled by "stammering and hesitation of a deficient memory."[21] Indeed, friend William Armstrong, Jr., a Virginia congressman witnessing the ceremonies, apparently lost some appreciation of the purposeful "exuberance"[22] of Adams's oration in the space of a single day. On the day of delivery, for example, Armstrong's "animated and *exceedingly* appropriate" description[23] very much paralleled the "animation" and "whole heart" terms employed in the official account.[24] By the fifth, however, Armstrong's "animated" gave way to "few pertinent remarks," and "exceedingly" no longer was underscored for emphasis.[25]

An incident involving an unforeseen tree root occurred in the course of Adams's oration, which certainly did not make his presentation any easier.[26] The orator's father, John, first President in the proud family line, occasionally had found his good sense of humor tested when narrating how, as a lad in the late 1740's, only two days of hard labor at ditching were sufficient to make him resume studying the establishment Latin grammar he felt too confining.[27] But now a bit more than boyhood pride was at stake in an election year. John's son, John Quincy, was the mature establishment figure addressing a restricted

---

21 *Adams Memoirs*, 8: 50.

22 James W[alter]. Thomas and T[homas]. J. C. Williams, *History of Allegany County, Maryland* (Cumberland: L. R. Titsworth, 1923), p. 224.

23 Armstrong, "Publicity letter for release, dated 4 July," *Scioto Gazette* (Chillicothe, Ohio), 17 July and *Illinois Intelligencer* (Vandalia), 2 Aug., 1828. The relevant sentence reads: "Mr. Adams . . . pronounced an animated and *exceedingly* appropriate address to the assembled multitude . . . ."

24 *Dly National Intelligencer* and *Dly National Journal*, 7 July, 1828.

25 WDC, 5 July, Armstrong to Charles Miner, WDC, in *Village Record or Chester and Delaware Federalist* (West-Chester, Pa.), 23 July, 1828. Miner, likewise a congressman, served as junior editor of the *Record* when Congress was not in session. Again, the relevant sentence: "Mr. A[dams]. made a few pertinent and exceedingly appropriate remarks to the assembled multitude . . . ."

26 Despite a fresh breeze and the temperature being near 60 degrees at the ceremonies, wife Louisa feared that heat and humidity would exact their "very pernicious effect . . . during the digging sce[ne]." WDC, 29 June, 1828, Mrs. Louisa C. Adams to Charles Francis Adams, Boston, Adams Family Papers, Massachusetts Historical Society.

27 George Whitney, *Some Account of the Early History and Present State of the Town of Quincy, in the Commonwealth of Massachusetts* (Boston: S. B. Manning, 1827), p. 52. A dialect song by B. in the Georgetown *Columbian* had both the President and Mercer busily ditching the route of the Canal. To assist the reader, several of the more troublesome dialect words are—*do/th*ough, *da/th*e, hee-han/heeing, kenne/kenning, 'speck/expect, stan/stand, ater/after, wuss/worse, grate/great, tak/take, and berry/very. The complete song follows: "Backside Georgetown da berry fine land, We want to get t'him by water; Berry small trade done dere just now, I 'speck he be grater. do, hereater. Eberybody want to get at de stuff, All make berry grate fuss, Sir; Who you tink shew 'em de way, Why Massa Charles Fenton Mercer. Massa Charles tell 'em dig grate long ditch, All same creek, full o'water, Flote down kenne, make plente rich, Dat de way dey gone to, do, hereater. Fourth day [o'] July berry grate day, Old Massa go—dat plese me, He tak shubbel and shew 'em de way, No stop him berry esy. Massa Phil want to tak away de ground—Dat make me laff, wuss and wusser, Cant stan hee-han with Old Massa John, And Massa Charles Fenton Mercer. Gess when Old Massa tak shubbel himself, Massa Phil berry glad to quit *railin*; Time come berry soon, we see de fine boats, Down Chespek Canal all sailin." *Columbian, District Advertiser, and Commercial Gazette* (sw), 4 July, 1828.

establishment audience on the Little-Falls field. And detestable Latin exercises were not necessarily sought after, even by the most ardent member of Johnny Q. Public, in a Presidential campaign.

At the midpoint of the President's oration, with cannon booming out salvoes down the Potomac to the Navy Yard, Greenleaf's Point, and Fort Washington,[28] much in the grand manner of dedicating the Erie Canal, Adams discovered that he could not dig into the earth with the spade because of the "large stump of a tree"[29] (not a more manageable root). After three or four futile tries, again in the language of the official account, Adams "threw down the spade, hastily stripped off and laid aside his coat, and went seriously *to work*."[30] Probably stimulated by the repetitive cannonading, and the fact they now were able to see what previously had been out of earshot, the multitude on the hilltops cheered his shovelful of ceremonial earth and perseverance.

Still, Adams was reluctant to concede that the "awkward" moment even approximated being a clumsy disaster ("gross and palpable failure"), strangely preferring to relish his instant popularity in the crowd's "eye and fancy."[31] Nor did his remarks answer a question perplexing the establishment itself. In the event that the Canal route never extended beyond Rock Creek at Georgetown to Tiber Creek (Tiber formerly named a sedgy, non-Roman "Goose"), how real in fact were the commercial benefits to be gained from District participation in Adams's commercial ethic? That is, if the glowing style could not even refurbish the old City Canal.[32] And especially with litigation over injunctions actively un-

---

28 *Dly National Intelligencer* and *Dly National Journal*, 3 and 7 July, 1828; Washington [City] *Chronicle*, 5 July, 1828.

29 *Adams Memoirs*, 8: 49.

30 *Dly National Intelligencer* and *Dly National Journal*, 7 July, 1828.

31 *Adams Memoirs*, 8: 50. Perhaps somewhat partial to the memory of candidate Jackson, Walt Whitman wrote an obituary evaluation of Adams for the New Orleans *Daily Crescent*, tracing Adams's lack of popularity to the non-innovative establishment the President represented: "John Quincy Adams was a virtuous man—a learned man . . . ; but he was not a man of the People. Never, at any time, did he heartily espouse the side of any of those hot struggles for the rights of men, as opposed to wealth and conservatism . . . . Is it wonderful, then, that he never was a popular man? Oh, the people know well enough who stand by them. Even if temporary circumstances . . . lead the masses for a moment to frown on those who really befriend them, there is always a chosen circle . . . who faithfully make headway for the truth and its dauntless leaders. Can anyone say that Mr. Adams . . . ever generated this sort of enthusiasm? No: it was not of him." Whitman, *The People and John Quincy Adams*, ed. William White (Berkeley Heights, N.J.: Oriole Press, 1961), consecutive pp. 17 and 19.

32 Two District residents addressed just such a question at the City Hall, shortly after Adams's appearance at the ceremonies. Namely, J. L. Skinner on 20 Aug., principal of an academy for young ladies, and Joseph H. Bradley on 1 Sept., secretary of the Franklin Insurance Company and treasurer of the Rockville and Washington Turnpike Road Company. And although a resolution purporting to implement an extension to the Tiber-Creek basin was passed, 4051 to 528, by a meeting of stockholders in the Canal Company at the City Hall on 17 Sept., work did not actually begin on deepening the Tiber basin until the fall of 1831. Deepening the basin, of course, was a prime condition for passing the resolution in the first place. *National Journal* (tw), 28 June, 1828; *Dly National Intelligencer*, 18 and 25 Aug., 11 and 19 Sept., 1828, 27 July and 7 Oct., 1831; Washington [City] *Chronic'e*, 30 Aug., 1828.

derway in Maryland, contrary to the goodwill claimed for the Baltimore and Ohio Railroad in his closing paragraph.[33]

The pro-Adams response to the oration certainly left much to be desired, doubtless because many Adams editors assumed that the official account, when reprinted, would pretty much speak for itself. By the ninth, for example, both the *Commercial Advertiser* in New York City and the *Aurora and Pennsylvania Gazette*, nearby in Philadelphia, drew upon the official account of the ceremonies. The *Advertiser* cited Adams's "energetic and dignified language" which seemingly defied misrepresentation by Thomas Ritchie's Richmond *Enquirer*, while William J. Duane in the *Aurora* took a liking to such "exhilarating and appropriate" language.[34]

Yet more Whig editors relied on Peter Force's separate commentary in the *National Journal*, a kind of editorial on the seventh accompanying the official account. Almost ironically, Force wrote of the ceremonies being inherently immortal due to "moral and physical opulence" and "lessons of wisdom and enterprise," benefits alleged to be more speculatively moral than any "ruins or solitary grandeur" glimpsed on a European tour. Indeed, so virtually assured was the establishment message that Force thought "not even the aid of the press" required to herald the effect intended of super-reverence for the orator, independent munificence for the entrepreneurs, and historical permanence for the event.[35]

Hezekiah Niles in his *Weekly Register* at Baltimore, eager to transform Adams from a grandiloquent establishment politician into an active spokesman, who kept "moving and working" to advance *productive industry*, downplayed Force's "happy" reference to the Baltimore and Ohio Railroad, and applied the term more generally to internal improvements benefiting "teeming millions."[36] The *American Traveller* in Boston borrowed Force's use of "liberal," but again a superlative "happiest" designated internal improvements generally.[37] The *Ohio State Journal* in Columbus appeared to second Force's qualifying a superlative "most chaste and felicitous," but when "eloquent and felicitous" was formulated, no really ardent Adams supporter

33 See n. 13 in this regard.

34 *Advertiser* (d); *Aurora* (d).

35 "Fourth of July, and Breaking Ground for the Canal," *Dly Journal*. The relevant Force commentary reads: "We will not say that it was the most chaste and felicitous address he ever delivered; but we will boldly say, that it will not suffer in comparison with any one he has previously given, or any other effort, be the source what it may. It was simple, pious, and liberal. Its allusions were apt, accurate, and beautiful. There was a sincerity in his manner, which made every sentence eloquent. The ornaments he used were judicious; and his liberal reference to the ceremony of laying the first stone of the railroad in Baltimore, invoking equal success on the two great works, was happy and acceptable."

36 *Register*, 12 July, 1828.

37 *Traveller* (sw), 15 July, 1828.

would dare question whether every last sentence and allusion in the oration was "apt" or sincerely "eloquent."[38] Or were Adams's supporters that devoid of reason?

And a correspondent of the Burlington *Free Press* in Vermont put Force's "pious and liberal" description of the oration to a partisan test: "What has Gen[eral]. Jackson done, I ask, to show the *Chief Magistrate of a great and growing Republick in the man himself, as was there shown?* Where has he shown the talent, the extension of views, the reading, the knowledge of history and governments, and, what is more, the real Americanism of soul (as here exhibited)? It will not be attempted; it would be 'Hyperion to a Satyr' to pretend any such comparison. I prophesy that the warmest admirers of Jackson will not undertake to bring him to this test. Nor, if they have remaining any respect for their own reputation, will they venture to ridicule the great historical transaction which has given occasion to these remarks."[39]

As reprints of the official account began to wane, however, late in July, Adams editors became less grandly able to compliment the oration.[40] No longer were internal improvements in general the issue, but Force's "felicitous" had to be partisan enough to defend Adams against charges of being an irreverential Unitarian who traveled on the Sabbath.[41] Even in the Southwest, where few newspapers carried the official account during August, Adams's "masterpiece" had to be defined from the perspective of "reverence" and "hoary age" somehow diminishing implications of a "vague and unmeaning display."[42] Still, perhaps the best evidence of the ineffectiveness of this Adams commentary is the fact that several editors, as the official account went out-of-print and election day neared, found it necessary to reprint criticism of a spurious schoolboy declamation by candidate Jackson,[43] even though the declamation appeared in print prior to the Fourth.[44]

The anti-Adams response to the oration indeed demonstrated the extent to which internal improvements could not be regarded as a nonpartisan issue.

---

38 "Internal Improvements," *Journal and Columbus Gazette*, 17 July, 1828.

39 One, "Prophecy—Mr. Adams will be the next President of the United States," *Press*, 25 July, 1828.

40 Consult notes 17, 18, and 23 for specific textual inserts during this period.

41 *Rhode Island American and Providence Gazette* in *Dly National Intelligencer*, 31 July, 1828.

42 Port-Gibson *Correspondent and Mississippi General Advertiser*, 9 Aug., 1828.

43 *Western Star and Lebanon* [*Ohio*] *Gazette* in: *The Marylander* (sw, Baltimore), 6 Aug.; *Our Country* (Hagers-Town, Md.), 16 Aug.; *National Journal* (tw, WDC), 28 Aug.; *Anti-Jacksonian* (Frederick-Town, Md.), 9 Sept.; *We the People* (WDC), 13 Sept.; Pittsburgh *Gazette*, 19 Sept.; *Bucks County Intelligencer and General Advertiser* (Doylestown, Pa.), 22 Sept.; Greensburgh [Pa.] *Gazette in Adams Sentinel* (Gettysburg), 15 Oct.; *The Virginian* (sw, Lynchburg), 16 Oct., 1828.

44 "Substance of General Jackson's Address to his Troops, before New Orleans (Designed as an exercise for youth)," Baltimore *Republican* in: *United States' Telegraph* (d, WDC), 23-24 June, not in two parts but repeated in each of these two issues; *Village Herald* (Princess-Anne, Md.), 1 July, 1828.

Duff Green in his *United States' Telegraph* derided Adams's remarks as those of a "political aspirant" justifying an "uneconomical application" of public funds to private interests, with elaborate "contingencies" in lucrative contracts making the rich even richer at the people's expense.[45] And a correspondent of Green's *Tell-lie-graph* (a Whig device), Dick Quiz,[46] likewise railed against a bloody partisan allusion to Jackson's coffin-handbill victims, an allusion read into Adams's first paragraph so as to transform the pompous theatricality of the official account into a liability. The cause célèbre to be exploited, for correspondent Quiz, was that of alien mercenaries being successfully rebuffed by yeoman Jackson at New Orleans. Not bereaved relatives of a few militiamen being trotted forth to point up faulty decisions at odds with the aristocracy's faith in national genius and industry. Quoting hardy Jackson supporters present at the ceremonies, Quiz endeavored to convey that Tennessee-farmer Jackson was no cruel slave-master to such hill spectators: "Of what consequence is it to us, said they, to subdue and improve the land, if an enemy is to come and make slaves of us to till it."[47]

To which the pro-Adams editor of the Georgetown *Columbian* replied by fashioning a witty verse out of Green's own mock Adams serial[48] and a doggerel chorus of the British nursery lullaby, "A frog he would a-wooing go."[49] The

---

45 *Telegraph* (d), 5 July, 1828.

46 For information concerning a parallel pseudonym, see Don Quizzicus, "Undated reply to Bombastes Furioso," *The Microscope* (Louisville, Ky.), 1 May, 1824. And for a definition of the nonsensical lampooning in "quiz" itself, consult the Cincinnati *Mirror and Western Gazette of Literature and Science*, 11 April, and the New York *Transcript* (d), 21 May, 1835.

47 *Telegraph* (d), 10 July, 1828.

48 Beaumont and Fletcher, "King John The Second, a Serio-Comico Tragedy," *Telegraph* (d), 20 May, 1828. The relevant affected disquisition by Professor Edward Everett goes: "Amo, Amas! Before a glass, To practice all my speeches; When sense absit, In place of Wit, Grace auditor reaches; Yankee quidem, Semper idem, Harum Scarum drive oh! Brag rag, very merry, handkerchief and white hand, Hic hoc horum genitivo. Can I decline A Priest divine, My vox is soft and tender, My sermo's grace, Is the nominative case, My text of the epicene gender; Snore 'em, bore 'em, Preach before 'em, Harum Scarum strive oh! Brag rag, very merry, handkerchief and white hand, Hic hoc horum genitivo. Greek and Latin I'm quite pat in, Potens in the forum, Auctors jubeo, Procul dubio Chief sum asinorum; Oh the natio! Quahs dash oh! I to cut contrive oh. Brag rag, very merry, handkerchief and white hand, Hic hoc horum genitivo. Pulpit fine oh! How I shine oh! Handkerchief quite handy, Ruffles white, My waistcoat tight, Dei gratia dandy; Deist quidem, Semper idem, Harum Scarum strive oh! Brag rag, very merry, lavender and kerchief, Hic hoc horum genitivo."

49 Two versions of this doggerel stanza/chorus come much later than 1828. And neither one is contained in a ca. 1800 sheet-music text of the song, printed at Boston by J. Hewitt (sheet text in Music Division, Library of Congress). In 1850, to cite the first version, the Boston *Museum* reprinted some lines added by a correspondent of *Notes and Queries* in London: "A frog he would a-wooing ride, With a rigdum bullydimy kymy; With sword and buckler by his side, With a rigdum bullydimy kymy. Kymyary kelta cary kymyary kymy, Strimstram paradiddle, larrabona ringting, Rigdum dullydimy kymy." And early in 1861, a correspondent for the Sacramento *Daily Bee* recalled a second version heard in town at Sam Wells's Melodeon: "There was a frog lived in the river, Kimo Kairo, Kimo Kairo, When it was cold he used to shiver, Kimo Kairo, Kimo Kairo, Slimslam funnediddle, radabone rigdum, Rigdum bullymiti kimo." *Museum*, 7 Sept.; Sycamore, "Sycamore looks 'round and makes a note on't—letter dated 12 Jan.," *Dly Bee*, 14 Jan.

satirical verse prefaced an anti-*Telegraph* commentary from the *Greene County Republican* in Catskill, New York,[50] "a decided Jackson paper" according to the *Columbian*. The verse went, "Brag rag very merry men and girls, Hic hoc horum Genetivo. Gen'ral Duff, Has got his puff, Rig tail bolimity kimo."[51] Clearly, in the partisan parlance of the campaign, mighty sorcerer Green was rigging his puffery and bully propaganda to the impressionable masses, who found it difficult to make merry when prodded by dull Latin derivatives in Adams's oration.[52] And even if a wagon driver's phonetic "wo hoy"[53] or a railroad engineer's phonetic "gee ho"[54] could be interpreted into the devilish "kimo," resorting to such nonsense words was more weakness than strength on the part of Adams editors.

Elsewhere, an equally "bully" Mordecai Manassa Noah took a dim view of the oration in his New York *Enquirer*. Instead of being delivered at a "grand" event truly worthy of the people, Adams's oration, prompted as it regrettably was for Noah by Mayor Gales's aristocratic "bull of etiquette,"[55] omitted key names like DeWitt Clinton and George Washington from step 3, an omission really castigated by Noah as the worst brand of *non-mi-ricordism*[56] for elec-

---

50 For the continuous context of this reprint, contrast pro-Jackson commentary from the Troy [N.Y.] *Sentinel* (in Greenfield [Mass.] *Gazette and Franklin Herald*, 17 June; *Somerset Iris and Messenger of Truth* [Princess-Anne, Md.], 15 July) with pro-Adams commentary in: Utica [N.Y.] *Sentinel and Gazette* (sw), 1 July; *Washington Whig* (Bridgeton, N.J.), 19 July; *L'Abeille* (d, New Orleans), 8 Aug., commenting on the *Republican* extract in the issue for the seventh; *The Virginian* (sw, Lynchburg), 18 Aug., 1828.

51 *Columbian, District Advertiser, and Commercial Gazette* (sw), 11 July, 1828. Immediately after formulating this verse, the editor commented: "General Duff Green, in his usual strain of discontented feeling, has attacked, and makes a pitiful fist in ridiculing, the late address of President Adams .... Will the General have the goodness to take some of the wholesome stomachic bitters of the following recipe (from the *Greene County Republican*, a decided Jackson paper). Probably it will serve to mitigate the sufferings of the mental dyspepsia, under which he evidently labors, and may have the tendency to enable him to disgorge the nausea produced by the honor conferred on Mr. Adams .... *Tase and try*, Before *you* buy."

52 Interpret the final two words of the verse as three, that is, bully, mighty (not the German mit-y); and kimo. For parallel usages of these words, consult "bully crew" (Boatman's Dance, *Susannah* p. 89), "bully boats" (Arkansas Trabeller, *Sable* p. 48), "mitty fine" (Good Bye John; Or, Them New-York Gals, *Susannah* p. 39), and a witch's chant of "Kemo; Kimo! Rumps-a-diddle soot bag; Kemo! Kimo! Wake snakes and June bugs!" (*Xlanties* p. 28) Thomas H. Elliott, *The Xlanties; Or Forty Thieves, A Musical, Satirical, and Quizzical Burlesque, In Two Acts* (Philadelphia: McLaughlin Brothers, 1857); Urastix Bust, *Charley Fox's Sable Songster, Containing Many of the Best Banjo Songs, Jokes, and Gems of Wit* (New York: Frederic A. Brady, 1859); *De Susannah, and Thick Lip, Melodist* (New York: T. W. Strong, ca. 1860).

53 St. Leger L. Carter, "The Wagoner," Easton [Pa.] *Centinel*, 14 Oct., 1831 and 25 Jan., 1833.

54 George Washington Parke Custis, "The Steam Coach," *Free Press* (Tarborough, N.C.), 1 May, 1829. Joseph Jefferson sang this song while performing in Custis's commemorative musical, "The Railroad," at the Baltimore Theater on 27 and 28 Oct., 1828. The reader also might want to consult "The Waterman," *Dutchess Observer* (Poughkeepsie, N.Y.) in Edenton *Gazette and North-Carolina General Advertiser*, 7 May, 1821.

55 N-Y *Enquirer* (d), 9 July, 1828.

56 This term is latinate slang for, "I value *my own* reputation enough to suppress memories or circumstances, not of my own doing, which threaten to minimize its stature." Consult the proper

tioneering purposes.[57] Even the normally pro-Adams New York *Statesman*, just two days after reprinting the oration, criticized the President's "inadvertent omission" of Clinton's name.[58] The Rochester *Daily Advertiser*, upstate in western New York, the day after the local *Telegraph* carried the oration, claimed that "general disgust" was excited by leaving out Clinton's name.[59] And the *Ulster Plebian* in Kingston, New York, the same day it ran the oration, likewise called attention to Adams's appearing to put Clinton "altogether in the shade."[60]

Indeed, a correspondent of the *Connecticut Herald* in New Haven extensively assailed the omission of Clinton. Observed correspondent Brutus, Adams never could hope to flatter himself by striking the pose of such a "father and founder" of internal improvements, as late as 1828: "It was DeWitt Clinton who gave this new era to his country—the *very man* whom the present Administration undertook to hunt down on the field of his fame. The present is truly the Age of Improvement, and might with great propriety be called the Clintonian Age; and probably, at some future day, will receive that designation. It is now the spirit of the Age to foster every undertaking which promises benefit to any portion of the community, by opening roads and canals. Not so when Mr. Clinton commenced his great work; then, every obstacle, which ignorance, prejudice, or malice could invent, was thrown in the way. He surmounted the whole, and carried his great system into operation in the face of an astonished world."[61]

Besides cutting into Clintonian Federalists' support for the President, Jackson editors set up convenient men of straw to ridicule, those few Adams supporters ardent enough to make "extravagant boasts" on behalf of the oration. The *Delaware Gazette* in Wilmington, for example, spun out Adams's language into a vaguely absurd style: "He roved through Egypt and Italy and Greece, talked of towers and temples and mausoleums and the [Great] Wall of China, and displayed his learning as much as possible; but, in some instances, expressed himself in a style so awkward that it is almost impossible to understand his meaning."[62]

Other Jackson editors contrasted paragraph 2 with aspirations of the "tag-rag-bobtail" yeomanry they desired to emphasize as backing their candidate.

definition of the term in: Plattsburgh [N.Y.] *Republican*, 18 June and 30 July, 1825; Reporter, "Court of Conscience—Trial of G. W. Turncoat, for violating an order of this Court," *Anti-Jacksonian* (Frederick-Town, Md.), 5 Aug., 1828.

57 N-Y *Enquirer* (d), 10 July, 1828.

58 N-Y *Statesman* (d), 11 July, 1828.

59 "Introduction to reprint of *Statesman* commentary," *Advertiser*, 17 July, 1828.

60 *Plebian*, 16 July, 1828.

61 "The New Adams Era," *Herald*, 22 July, 1828.

62 "Style," *Gazette* (sw), 15 July, 1828.

Commented the *Vermont Patriot and State Gazette* in Montpelier, the ego-satisfying "ink" of the oration in the official account seemed at cross-purposes, on the Fourth in an election year, with the Revolutionary "blood" which should have been unselfishly memorialized: "We had supposed that 'the right of self-government' was an inalienable right, possessed by every people, and founded on the broad principles of equity and justice. Nor did we suppose that this right could in any case, with propriety, be supposed to depend upon either the will or power of the people themselves, or upon the determination of any other nation. Will anyone doubt that the Irish people possess 'the right of self-government?' And yet everyone knows they have not the *power* to exercise that right. The idea that 'the right of self-government' is to be acquired by superior strength fully recognizes the principle of the *Divine Right of Kings,*—a principle which Mr. Adams will find is not very well approved of by the *republicans* of America."[63]

And a correspondent of the Troy *Budget* in New York reemphasized Adams's lack of sympathy for "simple republican government" in the northeastern states. Turning around the "greater" District residence phraseology in paragraph 6, correspondent Tompkins suggested that yeomen in New York and New England vote to remedy their being excluded from the seat of national power: "If we believe his own words, his fondness for that ten-mile square surpasses his attachment for any other place. Then, how are we to believe that, *even if he had* feelings in common with Americans, he has feelings in common with the people of the north and east? These local attachments are mentioned to show the absurdity of northern and eastern men supporting him from local views, or from local policy."[64]

Reaction to the oration spilled over into commentary on the spade root incident. Those Adams editors following up the official account's version of the incident emphasized Adams's republican demeanor and the philosophical continuity behind his act. Indeed, their incumbent was gifted with the "happy change" or "happy omen"[65] of a "great mind"[66] which never faltered when introducing the first internal-improvements resolution, twenty years previously in the United States Senate. For the perseverance in his act, whether described as "zealous devotion,"[67] "serious determination,"[68] "good earnestness,"[69] or

63 *Patriot*, 21 July, 1828.

64 *Budget* in *United States' Telegraph* (d), 2 Sept., 1828.

65 *We the People* (WDC) and *The Marylander* (sw, Baltimore), 5 July, 1828. On the eve of the Presidential election, editor Joseph Gales likewise traced Adams's role in supporting the Canal Company, destined to brighten "like unto gold seven times refined," back to "the first movement . . . as long ago as 1807." *Dly National Intelligencer*, 23 Oct., 1828.

66 Butler [Pa.] *Sentinel*, 26 July, 1828.

67 "Internal Improvements," Hingham [Mass.] *Gazette*, 25 July, 1828.

68 "Internal Improvements," *Saturday Evening Chronicle* (Cincinnati), 19 July, 1828.

69 *Pennsylvania Intelligencer* (Harrisburg), 15 July, 1828.

"still greater earnestness,"[70] spelled none other than success for the Canal project in Whig editors' minds. As the New York *National Advocate* almost nonchalantly put the point, Adams was a shrewd Yankee methodically conquering a root not readily to be denied: "It was covered with *Clay*, but with true Yankee spirit and perseverance he drove through it. He might just as well have turned a little to the right-hand or the left. But no, he had put his spade down, and *there* it must go in."[71]

Some Adams editors became quite ingenious in their efforts to cast the President as a plain everyday citizen at the ceremonies. The editor of the *Virginia Free Press* in Charlestown, for example, who resolutely turned two shovels of earth after Adams's oration, described the plain republican attire of "a drab coat, light-colored pantaloons, and white hat," and how the President's spadework was unquestionably "as familiar to him as that of the pen."[72] No gilded silver pen or spade to cheer Jackson supporters intended, of course. But Adams editors could simply never allow the President to play the titled monarch in the public eye. Adams had no need for a fill-in deputy when asked to do manual labor, as a monarch presumably would react if asked.[73] And he handled the spade enough like some Cincinnatus to merit further publicity as an "admirable subject for a painter."[74] Publicity more flattering and exclusive than intended for active distribution in the press, of course.

Although at long last giving credit to the DeWitt Clinton thought deliberately excluded from Adams's remarks by several Jackson editors, the Boston *Evening Bulletin* argued the quintessence of "practical republican" Adams to receptive Back-Bay readers: "What crowned monarch would have placed himself upon a level with the ordinary individuals of our species, and suffered his royal fingers to come in contact with that vulgar instrument (the spade)? And what imperial retinue ever attended a ceremony of this nature, involving the dignity of government in the fate of an undertaking which was to be executed by laboring yeomen and dirty handicraftsmen (and finally devoted to the dull and despicable concerns of trade)? Such occurrences, it is gratifying to observe, find no opponents, no revilers in any part of our land. For this circumstance we cannot be too thankful. It affords an unanswerable argument in behalf of the perpetuity of our Union. It shows, most conclusively, that there exists a *bond* that will endure for ages, in spite of our casual bickerings on questions of minor import (and in defiance of the clamorous contests of those who seek place, power, or emolument), through seas of popular turbulence and confusion—a bond that is

---

70 *Northampton Whig and Farmers' and Mechanics' Journal* (Easton, Pa.), 18 July, 1828.

71 *Advocate* (d), 11 July, 1828.

72 *Press and Farmers' Repository* in *Dly National Intelligencer*, 19 July, 1828.

73 *Manufacturers and Farmers Journal and Providence* [R.I.] *and Pawtucket Advertiser*, 14 July, 1828.

74 Lowell [Mass.] *Journal*, 18 July, 1828.

growing more strong and durable with every new ramification in the shape of a railroad or canal, from what quarter soever it may emanate."[75]

Jackson editors rather bitterly opposed their candidate's "republican" attributes being twisted by the Adams press. They proclaimed the President to be a doting old monarch, fated eventually to fall flat on his face despite managing just enough subnormal-reflex perseverance to stave off only a temporary failure at the ceremonies. Warned the editor of the *New Hampshire Spectator* in Newport about publicizing a "royal brother" to the detriment of diligent "farmer" Jackson: "Gen[eral]. Jackson is engaged on his farm constantly, turning up the turf and encountering roots, and makes no more fuss about it than our farmers do in Sullivan [County]."[76] Indeed, any painting done of Adams's "herculean but polite and gentlemanly slashes" would require an appropriation of no less than two thousand dollars from the very contingent funds considered suspect by Jacksonites.[77]

A conniving form letter was publicized by Jackson supporters in central and southeastern Pennsylvania, to make the President's attire at the ceremonies seem less appealing for "stupid" German voters. Allegedly, in the course of the "confidential" Adams memorandum from Philadelphia, sent as a cover letter to accompany "extra" newspaper issues containing the President's oration, a witness to the ceremonies approached the Whig-partisan narrator in a condescending sort of manner: "The gentleman said . . . he observed that his [Adams's] pantaloons were made in the old German style, and that he[Adams] wore them without suspenders, drew[drawn] tight 'round his hips and fastened with a leather string. He[gentleman] said he never saw a man look more like a German farmer in his life. There were several Germans present, and the President was talking Dutch in great style."[78]

Even Adams's organization of the oration, however rambling to opponents, related ultimately to Jacksonian ridicule of the incident. The Philadelphia *Gazette* made the transition and wry charge against the President: "Just figure to yourself, the President of the United States, in the midst of one of his highest flights of poetry, philosophy, and politics (forgetting, for a moment, the Pyramids of Egypt, the Great Wall of China, the Colossus of Rhodes, the march of mind, the perfectibility of our species, the lighthouses of the skies, and all other things terrestrial and celestial), throwing down his spade, laying aside his

75 "Internal Improvements," *Bulletin* (d), 18 July, subsequently excerpted in New-York *Gazette and General Advertiser* (d), 22 July; Albany [N.Y.] *Daily Advertiser*, 25 July, 1828.

76 "Royalty—His Majesty King John II," *Spectator* in Troy [N.Y.] *Budget* (sw), 5 Aug., 1828.

77 *Chautauque Republican* (Jamestown, N.Y.), 23 July, 1828.

78 Philadelphia, 11 July, Adams campaign worker to German farmer, Penn's Valley (northwest of Philadelphia), *Centre Democrat* (Bellefonte) in Harrisburg *Chronicle*, 4 Aug., 1828.

79 *Gazette and Daily Advertiser*, 10 July, 1828.

coat, and going *seriously* to work . . . . If there was the smallest spice of waggery in our composition, we should not be able to refrain from laughter at the sight of the picture . . . . But being as grave and considerate as any of the town-meeting orators, we only smile."[79]

Another Philadelphia editor, Stephen Simpson of the *Mercury*, apparently still smarting from charges that his oration, supposed to be delivered at the Lebanon-Garden celebration, had been censored by the Committee of Arrangements, presumably because of diatribes against Old-Federalist-Democrat Governor John Andrew Shulze,[80] bitterly lashed out at Adams as being "overworked" enough on the Canal to be stricken with a "Jackson horrors" malady.[81] The Columbia *Telescope* in South Carolina thought the incident symbolic of exactly how persistently dogmatic or "unconstitutional" the Administration could be, when using internal improvements as a national policy to beat down states' rights in the South.[82] And both the Hagerstown *Mail* in Maryland and Rochester *Advertiser* in New York charged Adams, through the incident, with being every bit the "turncoat" candidate Jackson was not, vigorously denying that their candidate had ever plotted treason with Aaron Burr on the Mississippi.[83]

---

80 Policy, "To the real Friends of Gen[eral]. Jackson," *Democratic Press* (d, Philadelphia), 30 June, 1828; Southwark, "Undated communication," *Press* (d), 3 July, 1828; "Simpson toast," *American Sentinel and Mercantile Advertiser* (d, Philadelphia), 9 July, 1828; "Item 8 commenting on Simpson toast—Jackson Lebanon Dinner," *Press* (d), 10 July, 1828; *Maryland Republican* (sw, Annapolis), 19 July, 1828. Simpson's effort to make the Fourth a partisan extension of candidate Jackson probably paralleled the bitter feeling claimed for the oration never delivered at Lebanon Garden. Prior to the Fourth, for example, Simpson editorialized in this vein: "Heretofore, we have kept this sacred day in [all its] festivity of heart, amidst the secure enjoyment of our rights, and the calm, the undisturbed possession of that liberty which confers on the people the sovereignty of dominion. Now the scene is reversed. We live in an era of usurpation. And we are called on to celebrate National Independence—with our hands manacled, our hearts crushed, and our rights betrayed, our sovereignty trampled in the dust and the voice of the majority stifled by corruption! Let us burst asunder these fetters of aristocracy. Let us rally [together] under the Declaration of our Rights, as did our noble and heroic forefathers in the glorious struggle of '76. Let the voice of an injured and insulted people pierce the Presidential Palace, and ring in the ears of guilty usurpation the knell of its approaching fate! Let us cry [out] to the people, from one end of the Republic to the other, 'Awake, awake-*now* is the appointed time!' Buckle on the armor of patriotism; grasp firmly the sword of freedom. Deliverance is at hand! Corruption trembles on her guilty throne! One blow, and the people stand redeemed in their native liberty, rights, and independence. It is a glorious sight—to behold a free and mighty people hail with loud hosannas of praise the day of their emancipation from thralldom! It is still more glorious to see an honest yeomanry strike the blow of retribution at usurping despotism, and vindicate the purity of elections by the ejection [from office] of their corruptors. Let us all unite, then, in doing honor to a day that comes like the harbinger of triumph to a people battling for their violated sovereignty. *Independence*—oh, how dear to the heart of man! *Liberty*—what a charm in the word, what a felicity in its enjoyment, what a fascination in its beams! To thee, *Jackson*, how much we owe [most] of all—thou who shone so bravely in the struggle that followed Independence, thou who gave us a *second era* of light and liberty! Be thy name the *watchword* on that day, be thy name the *precious jewel* in our cups. *Jackson and Liberty! Independence and Jackson!*" *Mercury* in Lancaster [Pa.] *Intelligencer*, 17 June, 1828.

81 *Mercury* in *Kentucky Gazette* (Lexington), 22 Aug., 1828.

82 *Telescope and South Carolina State Journal* in *Dly National Journal*, 28 July, 1828.

83 *Mail*, 19 July, 1828; *Daily Advertiser*, 21 July, 1828.

As treated by the Adams and Jackson presses, the spade root incident ensured that reprints of the oration would be caught up in petty bickering. To illustrate this point, the chronology of Baltimore *Patriot* and Dick-Quiz/*Telegraph* coverage of the incident is important. On the ninth, the regular evening and country editions of the Baltimore *Patriot*[84] ran a piece replying to some Jackson wag's alleged comment about a "hickory" root: "It may be so. But it must be observed *that stripping to it and a little manly exertion* very soon conquered even this 'Hickory' obstacle . . . . Let the friends of good order and civil rule (and of the prosperity of this nation) *strip to it,* and go to work manfully . . . , and they will certainly be successful. Let them not lay down the *spade* when they chance to meet with a *tough hickory root,* but lay down their *coats* and 'Go [to] it, Ned!' (as was said to Admiral Codrington, previous to the Battle of Navarin). And the 'Hickory' roots *that threaten to obstruct the internal improvement of the country* will easily and certainly be overcome." Quite obviously the *Patriot* scribe was straining a bit too much to compare Adams's predicament favorably with all the hoopla and fireworks in a Castle-Garden production of Edward Codrington at the "Battle of Navarino."

Three days later, Peter Force reprinted the *Patriot* piece in his *National Journal*[85] as confirming the "more than usual earnestness" of the President in the incident. Mass appeal faithfully qualified as "not so bad for all tow," when the New Brunswick *Fredonian*[86] in New Jersey reprinted the piece on the twenty-third. The very day that Force began the reprints, however, Jonathan Elliot paraphrased the same piece into an "Ominous!" commentary for *We the People:* "A Jackson wag, standing by, suggested that the obstacle was a 'Hickory' root. We have no objection to the idea. We *know* that 'Hickory' roots *are* in the way of the Canal, and that, for the prosperity of the great work of internal improvement, it only requires Mr. Adams' perseverance to dig them up, *root and branch*!"[87] By the fifteenth, another Adams campaign newspaper, the *Anti-Jacksonian* in Frederick, Maryland,[88] reprinted Elliot's paraphrase.

The following day, two Philadelphia editors, Jacob Frick of the *American*

---

84 *Patriot and Mercantile Advertiser.*

85 *Patriot* in *Dly National Journal.*

86 *The Fredonian* (New-Brunswick).

87 *We the People* (WDC), 12 July, 1828. In a passage immediately preceding these three sentences, Elliot notes: "A circumstance occurred, on the above occasion, too good to be lost. When Mr. Adams thrust the first spade into the earth, to break ground on this grand undertaking, it struck against a root that resisted two or three well-directed blows. With an animated face and his characteristic perseverance, as if determined not to be foiled, he unceremoniously threw off his coat and, applying the spade with redoubled vigor, he soon made 'the root' fly that baffled his first attempt to break ground. Sensible of the President's success (and viewing it as a *happy omen* for the progress of this truly national work), whilst he continued *to dig*, shouts and acclamations rent the air from ten thousand joyful spectators."

88 *Anti-Jacksonian* (Frederick-Town).

Sentinel and John Binns of the *Democratic Press*, locked horns[89] over the "royal" corollary that Adams of Braintree-Quincy once was promised in marriage, by father John, to a daughter of the King of England.[90] First the *Sentinel* commentary by Frick, then the Adams rejoinder by Binns in parentheses: "We are bound, out of sheer politeness, to return Alderman Binns our thanks for writing to the President—to ascertain whether it was a 'Hickory' root he encountered on the Fourth of July or not. Binns *says*, it was 'Hickory.' (He[Binns replying] never said anything about it. He left it, as a bone, for the Jackson men to gnaw and snarl and growl over.) If so, it only proves that, *go where Mr. Adams will*, he is *met* by 'Hickory.' (And if it [*Sentinel*] proves that [assertion], it further proves that, wherever Mr. Adams is met by 'Hickory,' he uproots and casts it out.) It is said that, just after the President entered the palace with the root in his hand, his son John [Quincy] met him and, eyeing the root, exclaimed, "Father, the house of Braintree is *done* [for]! You have let 'Hickory' into the palace already!' "[91] Of course, Jacksonites would never have contended that a "royal" daughter in the family diluted the haughty Braintree bloodroot.

Other newspapers like the Charleston *City Gazette* in South Carolina and the *Vermont Patriot and State Gazette* in Montpelier continued the response to "Ominous" and the Baltimore *Patriot*. The *Gazette* did little more than pass along a Jackson supporter's complaints about pro-Adams coverage of the incident.[92] But the *Vermont Patriot* directly sought to counter "Ominous." Concluded editor G. Washington Hill in a caustic vein, "The [publicity] tools of Mr. Adams declare that the obstruction was a 'hickory root,'—and that he actually dug through it, which they consider *ominous* of his future success in his exertions to gain a re-election. But whether he concluded to try another spot, or whether it in fact was a 'hickory root' (or some other root or no root at all), does not appear. It is quite possible, and not altogether improbable, that the failure was occasioned solely on account of Mr. Adams' being unused to the spade. For, it is to be presumed, he knew very little [about] what strength it required to make a proper use of the implements of husbandry. Viewing the obstruction to the progress of the spade to have been a 'hickory root,' which Mr. Adams subdued after pulling off his coat, his friends . . . set it down as one of the *signs* of the future triumph of the Coalition, provided Mr. Adams and his [Cabinet] Secretaries persevere in their desperate course, scour the country [over], make

---

89 *Sentinel and Mercantile Advertiser* (d), 11 and 17 July, 1828; *Press* (d), 15 and 18 July, 1828.

90 Philadelphia *Mercury* cited by *Illinois Intelligencer* (Vandalia) in *The Enquirer* (Knoxville, Tenn.), 23 April, 1828.

91 *Sentinel* (d) and *Press* (d), 16 July, 1828. For establishment implications present during the campaign in such "royal" Braintree symbolism, consult D. Henshaw (A Republican of the Jefferson School), *A Voice from the Interior: Who Shall Be President?—The Hero of New-Orleans, or John The Second, of the House of Braintree* (Boston: True and Greene, 1828), pp. 10-13. Also see notes 79 thru 81.

92 *Gazette and Commercial Daily Advertiser*, 15 July, 1828.

stump speeches, and bring the executive patronage to operate on the state elections. Query—if Mr. Adams is compelled to take off his *coat* of hypocrisy, before he can expect even to overcome the 'hickory roots,' how can he expect to resist that gigantic force, the voice of the people, which is collecting [together] to crush him at a [single] blow?"[93]

Jackson reaction to the incident began no later than the tenth, with Dick Quiz in Duff Green's *Telegraph*. For, the day after the Baltimore *Patriot* piece appeared in print, correspondent Quiz made known his desire to add some partisan "particulars" to the official account's version: "At the moment when Mr. Adams had taken the spade in hand, to give it one mortal plunge into the earth, it was suddenly arrested by a root which, on being inspected, a *bye*-stander cried out [to be] 'an *Old Hickory* root, by jingo!' This exclamation absolutely cowed his[Adams's] better part of man. The spade fell from his astonished hand to the earth. He looked with tears in his eyes at Mercer, who gave him a shrug of the shoulder in return, as much as [if] to say—'All *won't* do!' Gales sighed audibly, '*Grammercy*!'—and Southard fell back in a swoon. As soon as he [Southard] came to [be] himself, he cried out—'Confound this *Hickory!* Is it to foil us everywhere? It liked to have ruined me at Fredericksburg. It has stopped the President here and, I fear, will defeat poor Hal [Clay] in Kentucky.' 'Pull off your coat,' said Mr. Rush to the President. 'Cover the root with *Clay*, and twist the spade in diplomatic style around it!" Old Johnny Q. then took off his coat, and went to work *man*fully. 'How admirably he *cuts dirt*!'—said one of the [intellectual] parasites of the palace. 'By my faith and troth,' said an honest son of Erin, 'he *cuts dirt* very well here, to be sure. But, [I swear] by my soul, it's nothing [compared] to what he will do on the 4th of March next [,when retired from office by stout Irish ditchers]!' "[94]

On the eighteenth, the Albany *Argus* in New York carried a piece by an anonymous correspondent in Bridgewater,[95] Oneida County, lending greater satirical impact to Quiz's dialogue format. Unstable aristocrat Adams is speaking: "And now my spade has struck a hickory root. Oh, how I wish it was all *Clay* here. *Rush*, bring me a bottle of *Porter*! Oh, *Daniel, Web-stir* yourself! Oh, *Ever-yet* stand by me! How *Pleasant* it is for *Brothers* to dwell in unity. Ring the *Bell*, bring me more *Stores*! Tell the *Taylor* to take care of my coat! Hook my *Tracys*! *Tristram; Right* me up, for they have written me down! *Sargeant*, bring me a *Barber*, for my beard will be [too] long before I can get through this root! I

93 "The Hickory Root—*Ominous*," *Vermont Patriot*, 4 Aug., 1828.

94 *United States' Telegraph* (d).

95 Francis Egerton, the Duke of Bridgewater, was instrumental in getting the British Parliament to authorize a canal between Manchester and Worsley, in effect facilitating commercial traffic between Manchester and Liverpool. For further details on "Bridgewater" as a pseudonym, see Sandusky [Ohio] *Clarion* cited in Cleaveland *Herald*, 8 July, 1825. Also, see "Cross-Cuts and Rail-Roads Reconciled," *National Gazette and Literary Register* (Philadelphia) in Lancaster [Pa.] *Journal*, 17 June, 1825.

shall also want a *Cook*. Bring me *dusky Sally!* Call upon all the *Kings* of the Earth! Call *Col[onel]*. *Marble*, also, to write my epitaph! *Sic transit gloria mundi!*"[96]

By the fifth of August, editor Green of the *Telegraph* capitalized on a printing error in the Baltimore *Marylander*,[97] inquiring whether the Canal was a "patriotic" means or end for the President: "Mr. Adams' faith as to Internal Improvement was doubtful, and—he dug the dirt off of a hickory root."[98] To which Isaac Munroe dutifully replied in his Baltimore *Patriot*: "Not so, Duff. The hickory root lay across the path, and obstructed the course of Internal Improvement. And Mr. Adams removed it with the implements of Domestic Industry, plied by the sinews of American energy. But he did not attempt to dig the dirt off, Duff. That *were* a hopeless task." A reply carried throughout Maryland by such Adams titles as *Our Country*, the *Anti-Jacksonian*, and the Cumberland *Civilian*.[99] Indeed, Jackson reaction to the incident ended no earlier than August 11, when correspondent F. in the Albany *Argus*[100] resurrected spurious asides about Adams being "lugged" into and out of the Baltimore celebration,[101] and Clay being a better speaker than digger Adams for the Canal ceremonies.[102]

The leveling effect of the oration and spade root incident, dictated really by the dominant Jackson campaign-press, certainly was not the republican establishment image curried by Adams when consenting to appear at the ceremonies. Instead, the supposedly "conspicuous" role, replete as it was with his own verbalization of an establishment commercial ethic, turned out not to be so "nobly propitious" or rewarding for the President.[103] Even if Adams's oration at the ceremonies can be singled out as his only legitimate public ap-

---

96 *Daily Albany Argus*.

97 WDC, 12 July, *JQA* to Jonathan Nesbit, Sr., and William Knox, Baltimore, in *The Marylander* (sw), 16 and 19 July, 1828. The erroneous and first version reads: "Independence and union are the ends of internal improvement, and domestic industry, the means of the American Patriot . . . ." And the corrected version: "Independence and union are the ends, internal improvement and domestic industry, the means, of the American Patriot . . . ."

98 "Off Again!"

99 "A Mistake," *Patriot and Mercantile Advertiser* in *Anti-Jacksonian* (Frederick-Town), 12 Aug.; *The Civilian*, 14 Aug.; *Our Country* (Hagers-Town), 16 Aug., 1828.

100 "Digging." The single verse goes—"It is said when a certain great Railway began, Johnny Q. the first shoveling made,—He was wrong to attempt it, for Clay was the man: He knows how to *deal with the spade*!"

101 A Citizen of the Twelfth Ward, "Undated letter to Dabney S. Carr," Baltimore *Republican for the Country*, 18 July, 1828.

102 "A Difficult Case," *United States' Telegraph* (d), 29 May, 1828.

103 WDC, 14 July, 1828, *JQA* to Charles Francis Adams, Boston, Adams Family Papers, Massachusetts Historical Society.

pearance during the entire campaign,[104] the spade root incident, as interpreted and fanned among undecideds in the Jackson press, satirized the incumbent as too contented with the establishment dollar in such events, and consequently unable to continue in office without a popular mandate. For Jackson supporters, the President might as well have been some happy-go-lucky event-manipulator like Sam Patch—leaping on the Fourth at Passaic Falls, New Jersey (or a year later at "Little Falls" in Essex County), for a stipend of thirteen dollars. Money presumably handed over by proprietor T. B. Crane of Forrest Garden to give the Paterson factory mechanic a rewarding nip of local firewater.[105] Nor did the utter absence of any "rapid march" of internal improvements along the Canal route during the campaign enhance Adams's desirability for the mass electorate in the end.[106]

The three canal orations below all start work on projects part of a national era of internal improvements. DeWitt Clinton, Governor of New York, receives a standing tribute at Licking Summit. Oliver Wolcott, Governor of Connecticut, remains astride his horse while speaking at Southwick ponds. And Adams's situation with the spade at Little Falls is already known. An extensive table detailing the newspaper distribution for reprints of the Adams oration, July 7 thru August 13, 1828, may be found after the texts of the three orations.

---

104 Samuel Flagg Bemis, *John Quincy Adams and the Union* (New York: Alfred A. Knopf, 1956), p. 140. And despite no significant mention of the oration being made, the reader may also want to consult Florence Weston, *The Presidential Election of 1828* (Washington, D.C.: Ruddick Press, 1938).

105 "Patch cards, dated 2 and 15 July," Paterson [N.J.] *Intelligencer*, 2 and 16 July, 1828; *New Jersey Journal and Elizabethtown Gazette* in *Daily Chronicle* (Philadelphia), 25 July, 1828; "Patch card, dated 3 July," New York *Enquirer* in Newburyport [Mass.] *Herald* (sw), 10 July, 1829; "Andrew Kilpatrick cards, n.d.," *Democratic Press* (d, Philadelphia), 30 June and 9 July, 1829.

106 A Traveller, "The Spirit of Improvement is abroad upon the earth," *Dly National Intelligencer*, 2 May, 1831.

*Address delivered by John Quincy Adams at ceremonies commencing work on the Chesapeake and Ohio Canal, ceremonies held at the Little Falls near Georgetown, District of Columbia, July 4, 1828. Draft 1 from the Adams Family Papers, Massachusetts Historical Society (Boston); draft 2 from the Adams Papers in the Manuscript Division, Library of Congress. Most of the following text is draft 1 written in Adams's own script, with non-***ab** *revisions between drafts 1 and 2 designated by* Univers *type. A few interlinear revisions within draft 2 are identified by bold asterisks. But a word of explanation regarding Adams's second draft is perhaps in order. Draft 2 was transcribed from a previous version, probably draft 1 as extant in manuscript form, apparently not by Adams's son, who served as a private secretary at the time, but by some other person on the White House staff who would answer to the initials "L.P.", attached to the upper right-hand corner of the title sheet of the second draft. And at the risk of prolonging obvious details, once draft 2 was transcribed in someone else's script, Adams inserted the three revisions (noted by bold asterisks) in his own script.*

1 *****Friends and fellow Citizens.***** It is **a** NOW **b** nearly ☆ a full century, since Berkeley, Bishop of Cloyne, **a** CASTING **b** turning ☆ towards this fair land which we now inhabit the eyes of a prophet, closed a few Lines of **a** POETRY **b** poetical inspiration ☆ with this memorable prediction, "Time's noblest Empire is the last." A prediction which to those of us whose lot has been cast by Divine Providence in these regions, contains not only a precious promise, but a solemn injunction of duty *****since upon our energies and upon those of our posterity, its fulfil[l]ment will depend*****-For with reference to what principle could it be, that Berkeley proclaimed this, the last to be the noblest Empire of Time? It was as he himself declares [in his essay] on the transplantation of *Learning and the Arts* to America— Of Learning and the Arts of Peace- The four first Acts— the Empires of the old world and **a** THE OLDEN TIMES **b** of former ages, ☆ the Assyrian, the Persian, the Grecian, the Roman Empires, were Empires of conquest- **a** EMPIRES **b** Dominions ☆ of Man over Man— The Empire which his great mind, piercing into the darkness of futurity foretold in America, was the Empire of Learning and the Arts- The **a** EMPIRE **b** Dominion ☆ of man over himself and over physical Nature- It was the Empire acquired by the Inspirations of Genius and the toils of Industry— an Empire not watered with the Tears of the Widow and Orphan— not cemented in the blood of human victims— an Empire founded *but in harmony, not in discord*- of which the only spoils are the imperfections of Nature; and the victory achieved is the improvement of the condition of all— Well may this be termed nobler than the Empire of conquest, in which man subdues only his fellow man.

2 To the accomplishment of this great prophecy, the first necessary step was the acquisition of the right of self government by the People of the British

North American, Colonies,

draft a AND THIS UNION

draft b atchieved by the Declaration of Independence, and its acknowledgment by the British **a** GOVERNMENT **b** Nation. ☆ The second was the Union

of all those Colonies, under one general Confederated Government; a task more arduous, than that of the preceding separation, but which was at last effected by the present Constitution of the United States.

3 The third step, more arduous still than either or both the others, was that of which we, fellow Citizens, may now congratulate ourselves, our Country and the world of man, that it is taken- It is the **a** CONCENTRATION **b** adaptation ☆ of the powers physical, moral and intellectual of this whole Union, to the improvement of its own condition- to the improvement of its moral and political condition, by wise and liberal Institutions- by the cultivation of the Understanding and the Heart- by Academies, Schools and Learned Institutes. By the pursuit and patronage of Learning and the Arts— to the improvement of its physical condition, by associated labour to improve the bounties **a** OF NATURE **b** and to supply the deficienc[i]es of Nature- ☆ to stem the torrent in its course; to level the mountain with the plain; to disarm and fetter the raging surge of the Ocean—Undertakings, of which the language I now hold is no exaggerated description, have become happily familiar not only to the conceptions but [also] to the [practical] enterprize of our Countrymen— That, for the commencement of which we are here assembled, is eminent among the number- The project contemplates a conquest over physical Nature such as has never yet been achieved by man— The wonders of the antient world, the Pyramids of Egypt, the Colossus of Rhodes, the Temple of Ephesus, the Mausoleum of Artemisia, the Wall of China, sink into insignificance before it—Insignificance in the mass and momentum of human labour required for the execution- insignificance in the comparison of the purposes to be accomplished by the work when executed-

4 It is therefore a pleasing contemplation to those sanguine and patriotic spirits who have so long looked with hope to the completion of this great undertaking, that it unites the moral power and resources- first of numerous individuals, secondly of the Corporate Cities of Washington, Georgetown and Alexandria- thirdly of the great and powerful States of Pennsylvania, Virginia and Maryland- and lastly **a** OF THE WHOLE UNION. **b** by the subscription authorized at the recent Session of Congress, of the whole Union. ☆

5 Friends and fellow labourers, we are informed by the Holy **a** SCRIPTURES **b** Oracles of Truth, ☆ that at the Creation of man (male and female), the Lord of **a** CREATION **b** the Universe their Maker, ☆ blessed them, and said, unto them, "Be fruitful, and multiply, and replenish the earth— *and subdue it*"—To subdue the Earth was therefore one of the **a** PRIMITIVE **b** first ☆ duties assigned to man at his Creation **a** .BEFORE THE FALL **b** ;and now in his fallen condition ☆ it remains among the most excellent and virtuous of his occupations. To subdue the Earth

is preeminently the purpose of the undertaking, to the accomplishment of which the first stroke of the spade is now to be **a** GIVEN **b** struck— ☆ That it is to be **a** GIVEN **b** struck ☆ by this hand I **a** NOW CALL **b** invite ☆ you to witness— *(Here the stroke of the spade [will be made by me.])* And in **a** GIVING **b** performing ☆ this act I call upon you all to join me in fervent supplication to him from whom that primitive injunction came, that he would follow with his blessing this joint effort of our great community, to perform his will in the subjugation of the Earth for the improvement of the condition of Man— that he would make it one of his chosen instruments for the preservation, prosperity and perpetuity of our Union— that he would have in his holy keeping all the workmen, by whose labours it is to be completed— that their lives and their health may be precious, in **a** THEIR **b** his ☆ sight— and that they may live to see the work of their [own] hands contribute to the comforts, and enjoyments of millions of their Countrymen

INSERT DELETED: —and that at the last hour of their lives, followed **a** EVER **b** as the gospel promises ☆ by their works, they may be entitled to the blessing of the dead who die in the Lord.

6 Friends and brethren, permit me **a** IN CONCLUSION **b** further ☆ to say, that I deem the duty now performed at the request of the President and Directors of the Chesapeake and Ohio Canal and of the Corporations of the District of Columbia, one of the most fortunate incidents of my Life- Though not among the **a** DUTIES **b** functions ☆ of my Official Station, I esteem it as a privilege conferred upon me, by my fellow Citizens of the District- Called **a** BY THE DISCHARGE **b** in the performance ☆ of my **a** DUTIES **b** service ☆ heretofore as one of the Representatives of my native Commonwealth in the Senate, and now as a member of the Executive Department of the **a** UNION **b** Government, ☆ my abode has been among the inhabitants of the District longer than at any other spot upon Earth- In availing myself of this occasion to return to them my thanks for the numberless acts of kindness that I have experienced at their hands, **a** I MAY BE PERMITTED **b** may I be allowed ☆ to assign it as a motive operating upon the heart, and superadded to my official obligations for taking a deep interest in their welfare and prosperity. Among the prospects of futurity which we may indulge the rational hope of seeing realized by this junction of distant waters; that of the auspicious influence which it will exercise over the fortunes of every portion of the District, is **a** OF THE MOST CHEERING CHARACTER **b** one upon which my mind dwells with unqualified delight/pleasure— ☆ It is my earnest prayer that they may not be disappointed.

7 It was observed that the first step towards the

draft a ESTABLISHMENT OF A SYSTEM OF INTERNAL IMPROVEMENT, COEXTENSIVE WITH THIS UNION AND COUNTRY.

draft b

accomplishment of the glorious destinies of our Country;

was the Declaration of

Independence. That the second was the Union of **a** ALL THOSE COLONIES **b** these States ☆ under one federative Government. The third is **a** THE ACT IRREVOCABLY FIXED BY **b** irrevocably fixed, by the Act ☆ upon the commencement of which we **a** HAVE **b** NOW ARE **c** are now ☆ engaged—What time more suitable for this operation could have been selected than the anniversary of our great National festival- what place more appropriate from whence to proceed than that which bears the name of the great Citizen Warrior who led our armies in that eventful contest to the field, and who first presided as the Chief Magistrate of our Union- You know that of this very undertaking he was also one of the first projectors, and if in the world of Spirits, the affections of our mortal existence still retain their sway, may we not without presumption imagine that he looks down with complacency and delight upon the scene before and around us?

8 But while indulging a sentiment of joyous exultation, at the benefits to be derived from this herculean labour, of our friends and neighbours, **a** WE SHALL **b** let us ☆ not forget that the spirit of internal improvement is catholic and liberal- We hope and believe that its practical **a** PLEASURES **b** advantages ☆ will be extended to every indiv[id]ual in our Union- **a** WHILE **b** In ☆ praying for the blessing of Heaven upon our **a** LABOURS **b** task, ☆ we ask it with equal zeal and sincerity upon those of every other similar work in this **a** UNITED STATES; **b** confederation; ☆ and particularly **a** FOR **b** upon ☆ that which on this same day (and perhaps at this very hour) is commencing from a neighbouring City- It is one of the happiest characteristics in the principle of internal improvement, that the success of one great enterprize, instead of counteracting, gives instant assistance to the Execution of another- May they increase and multiply 'til, in the sublime language of Inspiration, "every valley shall be exalted, and every mountain and hill shall be made low- the crooked straight- the rough places plain"- **a** 'TIL **b** thus shall ☆ the prediction of the Bishop of Cloyne **a** SHALL BE **b** be ☆ converted from prophecy into History, and that in the Virtues and Fortunes of our posterity the last shall prove the noblest Empire of Time.

Address delivered by Governor DeWitt Clinton of New York at ceremonies breaking ground on the Ohio Canal, ceremonies performed at the Licking Summit near Newark, Ohio, July 4, 1825. An account of the ceremonies, first printed in the Ohio Eagle *(Lancaster) of the seventh, and reprinted by the Newark* Advocate *on the fourteenth and the Cleaveland* Herald *eight days later, not mentioning papers outside Ohio like* Niles' Register *in Baltimore, contains the only definitive version of this address. In fact, Clinton turned down an invitation from the Directors of the Farmington Canal in order to tour Ohio, Kentucky, and Pennsylvania on behalf of internal improvements. And before the Governor began speaking at the Summit site, several hundred members of the audience rose in tribute from sturdy wooden benches in front of the platform. Alfred Conkling, a witness of their gesture, simply had to describe the omen in terms worthy of his friend and the "grand" canal. For Conkling, only a "bright but transient vision, at once beautiful and sublime, of all that is most pure and exalted in man;—the silent, unpremeditated, spontaneous homage of the heart to virtue" placed the ceremonies in a "grand" enough perspective. Eulogy aside, however, Clinton directed the opening sentences of his address to those persons standing in tribute in front of the rostrum, faltering with some emotion as he spoke softly and almost indistinctly. Yet when the audience members sat down after Clinton's first few sentences, a reporter for the* Eagle *echoed the salient optimism which seemed to persist in the Governor's manner, observing that "his voice became loud and distinct, and his manner in the highest degree impressive." And two years later, on the morning of May 23, Clinton made good on his original invitation by pausing at the Southwick boundary while touring the Farmington Canal from New Haven to Barnet, Vermont.*

1 Fellow citizens, no language can describe the sublimity of this scene or the auspicious consequences of the proceedings of this day. I cannot restrain the expression of the feelings which animate my bosom on this occasion. The day which I have long looked for with extreme solicitude has at length arrived—a day of joy and congratulation to all the friends of freedom and union, and which will lay the foundations of both on an imperishable basis.

2 There is a peculiar fitness in the selection of this natal day of the American nation for the commencement of one of the greatest works of the age. If this day has established our freedom and given us a national being, it will also consummate the prosperity of the American people, and still further exalt our national character in the estimation of the civilized world.

3 The completion of this work will form a navigable communication between our Great lakes or Mediterranean Seas and the Gulf of Mexico, the Bay of New York, and the Gulf of St. Lawrence. It will open three avenues from our vast interior to the Atlantic Ocean. It will form a cordon of navigable circumvallation round the most fertile and extensive portion of the United States. Its blessings every man can foresee, but no human being can predict all the auspicious influences which will spring from this state of things.

4 It will unite the East and the West, the North and the South, by identity of interest, by frequency of communication, and by all the ties which can connect human beings in the bonds of friendship and social intercourse. The Union of the states will be as firm as the everlasting hills; and from this great epoch in our history, we may dismiss all fears of a dismemberment of the American republic!

5 As a channel of commerce, as a stimulus to manufactures, as a source of revenue, as an encouragement to agriculture it will excite into activity all kinds of productive and laudable industry, and diffuse a spirit of emulation and a power of exertion, of which nothing but actual experience can furnish an adequate idea! It will be a great school of ingenuity that will produce eminent engineers and mechanicians. It will be a guardian of morality by rousing the human mind from a state of torpidity and inactivity. But there are other considerations which press with irresistible force in estimating the merits of this great undertaking.

6 The history of Ohio from its forest state to the present period is without a parallel in the history of mankind. Her existence as a confederate state does not extend beyond twenty-three years, when her population did not exceed fifty thousand souls. And her first effective settlement reaches back little more than thirty years. She now has a population—moral, patriotic, and intelligent—of near eight hundred thousand human beings. And of the twenty-five millions of acres contained in her territory, perhaps not one-seventh part has been brought to a state of cultivation.

7 To what has this great increase of population been owing? To the unsurpassed fertility of your soil, to the undoubted salubrity of your climate. But above all to the moral power of freedom which animates all the energies of man, and furnishes inducements to activity that no other state of things can exhibit! With all these advantages, you have felt the paralytic effects of the want of markets for your surplus productions. Cut out from almost all profitable communications with the great market-towns of the Atlantic, your principal reliance has been on the consumption produced by emigration, and on the small profits elicited by distant, expensive, and difficult transportations. You will now have not only the markets of New Orleans and New York, but of Philadelphia, Baltimore, and Montreal! The canals of New York in their connection with the Susquehannah and Lake Ontario, which must speedily be formed, will furnish almost all these vast accommodations.

8 This great work will also confirm your patriotism and make you proud of your country. Every man of Ohio will say, not in a tone of rhodomontade, but in a spirit of temperate encomium: "See what my country has done in her juvenile state. And if she has achieved this gigantic enterprise in infancy, what will she not effect in the maturity of her strength, when her population becomes exuberant and her whole territory in full cultivation?" And your sister states

and the civilized world will be astonished. It will exhibit a spectacle unprecedented and amazing—an infant wielding the club of Hercules, and managing the lever of Archimedes with irresistible power! When the eagle in its first flight from the aerie soars to the heavens, looks at the sun with an unfailing eye, and bears in its talons the thunderbolts of Jove, who will not admire this sublime flight!

9 But I shall no longer engross your time, which has been more profitably directed to the very able and eloquent discourse just now pronounced.[1] Suffice it to say that all your energies will be awakened. That at the expiration of ten years from the completion of this work, a clear annual revenue of a million of dollars will be at your disposal, which will of course be applied to all beneficial purposes. That every citizen of Ohio will feel the exaltation of his country in the conduct of his own life, that your fame will be coextensive with civilized man, that the benedictions of the most remote posterity will follow you! That the wise and the good of all countries, and of all times, will look back to you with respect and will be ready to exclaim with the great Legislator of the Jews: "Blessed of the Lord be this land, for the precious things of Heaven, for the dew and *for the deep that coucheth beneath*, for the precious things of the earth and fullness thereof!"

1 Clinton does not refer to his own remarks here, but to the tribute paid by Thomas Ewing prior to this address. Indeed, many members of the audience may have been prompted to stand in honor of Clinton as a response to Ewing's tribute.

"Memorandum of an Address [,delivered by Governor Oliver Wolcott of Connecticut,] at the [state] line between Southewick [Mass.] and Granby [Conn.,] on the commencement of [*work on*] *the* Farmington Canal, *July 4th: 1825." Manuscript in the Wolcott Jr. Papers, Connecticut Historical Society (Hartford). Wolcott prepared two drafts of his address, and a final printed version was issued as part of an account of the canal ceremonies. A reporter, perhaps even the editor, for the* Columbian Register *(New Haven) apparently made an on-the-spot sketch of the ceremonies at Granby and Southwick ponds prior to inserting a copy submitted of the final version of Wolcott's address. Quite obviously the* Register *printed what seemed to be its very own reporter's account on the ninth. Yet when the* Connecticut Courant, *upstate in Hartford and much closer to the event itself, printed precisely the same account three days later, a formal dateline ("New Haven-July 12") rather strongly suggested that some pooled account may have been released to the press through superintendent James Hillhouse's office in New Haven. To a considerable extent, the* Register *account represented more of a consensus release, and certainly was not an unscrutinized sketch compiled by a "solo" reporter who gallantly received Wolcott's manuscript immediately after delivery of the address. Indeed, a possible parallel can be discerned between this "solo"-process pooled arrangement and the slightly varied pooled account of* National Intelligencer-National Journal *reporters covering the Chesapeake and Ohio Canal ceremonies. In days subsequent to the twelfth, of course, reprints of the pooled account ran in various towns along the projected route of the Farmington Canal. Canal meetings had in fact been held in New Haven, and in Northampton and Westfield, Mass., before the ceremonies even began. To offer but two examples of the reprint setup, the* Hampshire Gazette, *serving the canal terminus at Northampton, Mass., the day after the* Courant *printing (the thirteenth) cited the* Register *as its source. While the* Times and Advertiser, *back in Hartford once again, did not cite the* Register *as its source on the nineteenth, leading to the conclusion that the local* Courant *of the twelfth was its implied source. Still further evidence, perhaps, that both the* Register *and* Courant *printed a pooled account in the first place, despite a three-day disparity in the precise printing dates. In the following text, bold type designates words retained by Wolcott in drafts 1 and 2, hopefully better enabling the reader to focus on significant variations in Wolcott's revision process.*

1 Friends and Fellow Citizens. We are assembled on this Anniversary of our National Independence to perform an interesting ceremony:—The time, the circumstances and the object of our meeting are calculated to awaken recollections and to suggest thoughts, peculiarly impressive:—

draft a This day is to witness the **commence**ment of **a work, which** has for **its** object, a **practical** developement of **the resources of an extensive and flourishing**

portion of our common **Country**—

draft b

The **noble enterprize** of uniting the Valley of [the] Connecticut [River], with the City of New Haven, by a navigable Canal, **is this day** to be **commenced**;-

draft a **To me has been assigned the high honor, of first** putting **the hand of labor to** this **work;-**

draft b

To me has been assigned the high Honor of first applying **the hand of labor to a work, which** is **its**elf magnificent, though, as I believe, but the first of a series of like operations, which are to combine **the resources of an extensive and flourishing Country**.

draft a And while, as the Representative of **a** the Association, formed [to] **b** the Association, united to **c** the Association, constituted to **d an Association, which has united** its individual **talents, wealth** and exertions, to☆prosecute this **noble enterprize** "to *perfection*", I apply the implements of **labor** **a** in **b** to☆its first formation; I solicit, in **a** their **b** its☆behalf, the aid, the patronage, the support, the good wishes of every friend **a** of improvement, of his Country, **b** to public improvements, every man who loves his Country,☆every individual who has a mind to perceive and a heart to rejoice in the consequences **a** all resulting **b** which will result☆from its completion—

draft b

Under the auspices of **an** honourable **Association, which has united talents, wealth** and perseverance, and confiding in the skill and intelligence which I see assembled around me, I have repaired to this Station, here to manifest my conviction, that scientific investigations have already demonstrated that the enterprize is **practicab**le and my belief, that the requisite **labour**s will be continued with the characteristic energy of New England men, until the design shall be successfully consummated.

2 It is impossible to entertain doubts on either of these points:—

draft a Indeed, much *depends* on their efficient cooperation—

draft b

for permit me to enquire when, on any former occasion, have the enlightened Freemen of this region failed to accomplish their deliberate resolutions? or, when has their ardour been subdued by obstacles which it was possible to surmount?[1]

---

1 "Possible" reads "impossible" in the pooled text, corresponding with "impossible" in the first sentence of this second paragraph.

draft a

They **can retard,** if not prevent, its **a** final **b** entire ☆ execution—

draft b

Nothing **can** even **retard** the progress of our public improvements, but foreign War, or domestic dissentions. The first is improbable; the last may possibly create some temporary **embarrass**ments.[2]

draft a They can **embarrass** the operations of the Company, by **excit**ing **prejudices, imput**ing **mercenary motives, creat**ing local **jealousies, array**ing **a** formal **b** supposed **c imaginary** ☆ **counter-interests,** persuading **individual**s **to withhold necessary facilities,** or to demand **exorbitant remuneration for** the **surrender** of **them—**

draft b

Ignorance may **excit**e **prejudices,-** envy may **imput**e **mercenary motives;** may **creat**e sectional **jealousies;-array** the opposition of **im[a]ginary counter-interests;** or stimulete[stimulate] **individual** selfishness, **to withhold necessary facilities,** unless accompanied with **exorbitant remuneration**s for **surrender**ing **them.**

draft a None of these **events are however expected**- and they are only mentioned, **as** a **contrast to** what **will** follow from the adoption of **the** opposite **course of conduct—**

draft b

No sinistrous **events are however expected** in this quarter, and such have been recited, merely **as contrast**s **to** the **course of conduct**, which **will** be here exhibited.

draft a Relying up**on the sound sense and patriot**ism **of** those **among whom** they **are to** commence and continue **their operations**, which **a** thus **b** ,it is believed, ☆ will be evinced by a zealous cooperation, **this Association will proceed** to the contemplated work **with ardent hopes a ,and b** ;prosecute it ☆ with **an untiring Spirit—**and, with the blessing of a superintending Providence, will complete its **a** instruction **b** construction— ☆

draft b

Relying on the efficient aid, **the sound sense and** the **patriot**ic views **of** the people **among whom their operations are to** be conducted, **this Association will proceed with ardent hopes and an untiring spirit.**

3 Philosophy has proved, that animal vigor and health depend on the constantly reciprocating action of muscles, nerves, veins and arteries:- intellectual excitement is promoted by the activity of social intercourse, this intercourse is elevated and refined as it progresses through populous Cities,

2 "Even" reads "ever" in the pooled text.

flourishing Towns and prosperous Villages, until it vivifies the minutest ramifications of civilized life. Our experience has proved, that the interests of Science, agriculture, arts, commerce and manufactures are correlative, and that they are mutual aids to public industry and the common prosperity.[3] The present period appears to be the fulfilment of a divine Prediction, that "*many shall run to and fro and Knowledge shall be increased.*"

4 **draft a And while, in** common **with** this **great Nation, we a** commerate **b** commemorate ☆ **the** day, **which** gave to **us** that distinction,

draft b

And while in unison **with** our Countrymen from Maine to Missouri, **we** peal anthems of [con]gratulation in honour of **the** festival **which** constituted **us** a **great Nation,**

draft a may we not indulge the **hope, that this day** may **a** be the witness [to] **b also witness** ☆ **the** beginning **of an** enterprize, **which** is to **add to** its **strength and security—**

draft b

may we not indulge in a **hope, that this day** will **also witness the** commenc[e]ment **of an** equally durable work, **which** will **add to** the **strength and security** of this community;

that another link is to be attached to that Chain which surrounds and binds together the resources and interests of our beloved Country?[4]

draft b With such hopes and feelings, I now proceed to perform the duty assigned to me, leaving the many interesting reflections connected with this occasion, to the Gentleman who has been designated to address you.[5]

pooled draft b

With such hopes and feelings, I now proceed to perform the duty which has been **assigned to me**.

---

3 "The common prosperity" reads "the prosperity and power of states and nations" in the pooled text.

4 "That another link is to be attached" reads "and attach another link" in the pooled text.

5 Wolcott refers here to Jonathan H. Lyman, primary orator of the day.

Distribution list of newspapers reprinting Adams oration text, July 7 thru August 13, 1828

Newspaper title abbreviations

Amn American
Cent/Sent Centinel/Sentinel
Chron Chronicle
Co County
Comm Commercial
Comp Compiler
Dem Democratic
Gaz Gazette
Gen General
J Journal
Lit Literary
Merc Mercantile
Nat National
Pol Political
Reg Register
Rep Repository
St/U Sts State/United States

Random place abbreviations

Miss Mississippi, not Mo

O Ohio, not to be confused with a 0 quantity

WDC District of Columbia or Washington City, not to be confused with possible initials for a pseudonym or personal name

Editorial abbreviations

incl/excl included or including/excluded or excluding
Neutral/pro-Jackson titles not partisanly inclined to be **pro-Adams**
ed/eds edition(s)
evn evening edition
morn morning edition
fCtry/ctry paper for the Country or country edition
dly daily series
tw triweekly series
sw semiweekly series
w/wkly weekly series

Sequential tally symbols and framework

* next to a title or day indicates a significant variation in **D**istribution: **early***, **delay***, **neg**ative*, and **affil**iation*.
Also, **D*** accompanies a day heading in several instances.

f frequency or number of times (by title) with which Adams oration text is reprinted within a specified area on a given day

pr probable inclusion of Adams oration text in title and issue cited, since no bound file containing this issue is known to exist

pt only partial text of Adams oration reprinted in title and issue cited, this symbol and such a development being taken to indicate **peak** distribution

C/C Daily framework for sequential distribution tally, divided into **C**-anal areas/and areas other than C-anal not directly advocating internal improvements. The ten **C** locations in sequence are:

a. WDC-Md-Va (and W Va), Chesapeake and Ohio Canal 000
b. Pa-Del-NJ, related Chesapeake and Ohio Canal 000
c. Mass-Ct, New England and Adams's home state 00
d. NY-O, Erie Canal and Ohio Canal 00/

And the thirteen C locations in sequence would be:

a. NC-SC-Ga, Seaboard South 000
b. RI-NH-Vt-Me, New England 0000
c. Ind-Ky-Tenn, Border South 000
d. Miss-Ala-Fla, Gulf Coast South 000 =

0/29 possible locations, i.e., 10**C** + 13C + 6 locations not reprinting the Adams oration text at all.

To offer a simple example, 010 020 **3**0 0**4** (**4**)/001 0020 003 400 (4) indicates that, on a given day, the oration text was reprinted in one Md newspaper, two Del papers, three Mass papers, and four Ohio papers (4**C** locations), versus one Ga newspaper, two Vt papers, three Tenn papers, and four Miss papers (4C locations) = 8/29, 8 being standard type since **C** locations not greater than C locations. The bold type designates a **C** location with a **f**requency of 3 or higher, as well as a C location possessing a **f**requency of 2 or higher.

Distribution tally totals 195 titles (15**pr**/6**pt**)

C149, calculating number of days **C** locations have **f** of 3 or more (titles/days)

Mass	30f5	Ohio	16f2
Pa	27f4	WDC	7f1
NY	23f4	Ct	6f1
Md	18f3	NJ	5f0
Va	16f3	Del	1f0

C46, calculating days C locations have **f** of 2 or more (titles/days)

RI	6f2	Tenn	3f1
Me	6f1	Fla	2f1
Ky	6f1	NC	2f0
Vt	5f1	Miss	2f0
NH	5f1	Ind	1f0
SC	4f1	Ala	1f0
Ga	3f1		

Six locations having 0 titles and 0**f**
Ark, Ill, La, Mich, Mo, and Tex

C location aggregates in 149:
a. 41 b. 33 c. 36 d. 39
C location aggregates in 46:
a. 9 b. 22 c. 10 d. 5

Breakdown by region
New England area (categories c**C**, bC) = 58/195
Southern area (categories a**C**, acdC, and Del) = 66/195
Chesapeake and Ohio area (categories ab**C** and Ohio) = 90/195
Northern area (categories cd**C**, bC, Pa and NJ) = 128/195

Resolution of five stages into three cycles for analysis

Cycle 1 (stage 1 and 2, seven days) 69 titles, *area* measurement of .143 contrasted with .310, 4.16 daily mean or .143 of 29 locations, versus 8**C**/1C actual locations incl or .310 of 29. This predominately **C** cycle excl only Ct and Ohio in **C**, incl only RI in C.

Cycle 2 (stages 3 and 4, fourteen days) 115 titles, *area* measurement of .204 contrasted with .586, 5.92 daily mean or .204 of 29 locations, versus 8**C**/9C actual locations incl or .586 of 29. This cycle has a reasonably well balanced distribution, and is more extensive than either cycle 1 or cycle 3. WDC and Del excl in **C**, Ind-Miss-Ala-Fla excl in C.

Cycle 3 (stage 5, twelve days) 11 titles, *area* measurement of .039 contrasted with .241, 1.13 daily mean or .039 of 29 locations, versus 2**C**/5C actual locations incl or .241 of 29. C becomes dominant in this cycle; Pa and Ohio incl in **C**, Ky plus four locations excl from cycle 2 are incl in C here.

Distribution list proper for sequence in reprinting of Adams oration text, Jl 7 thru Ag 13, 1828, arranged by day and newspaper title

Stage 1, four days Jl 7 thru 10; 27 titles distributed over a 4.00 area incl 6**C** locations

D* JULY 7 M **4**/29 Both titles reprint text sources, with a weight factor of 3 allowing for a nationwide circulation in this and lesser series. 2 WDC/ Dly Nat Intelligencer, Dly Nat J; **4**/29 calculation based on **C**2 or one location being added to the weight factor of 3.

JULY 8 TU **C11 C351** 200 00 00 = **4**/29
3 WDC/ Nat Intelligencer tw, Nat J tw; Georgetown Columbian, DC Advertiser, and Comm Gaz
5 Baltimore/ Amn and Comn Dly Advertiser; Comm Chron and Balt Advertiser d **pr**; Gaz and Dly Advertiser; Patriot and Merc Advertiser (dly ctry and dly evn eds)
Alexandria, Va/ Phoenix-Gaz d
2 Philadelphia/ Nat Gaz and Lit Reg (d and tw)

JULY 9 W **C9 C04**1 100 00 **3**0 = **4**/29
3 Baltimore/ Comm Chron and Balt Advertiser fCtry **pr**; Gaz fCtry; Marylander sw
Rockville/ Md J and True Amn
Fredericksburg/ Va Herald sw
Philadelphia/ Poulson's Amn Dly Advertiser
3 NY City/ Comm Advertiser d; Evn Post; Statesman d

JULY 10 TH **C5 C**010 110 00 20 = **4**/29
Cumberland, Md/Civilian
Philadelphia/Gaz and Dly Advertiser
Wilmington/Del Wkly Advertiser and Farmer's J
2 NY City/Amn d; Gaz and Gen Advertiser d

Stage 2, three days Jl 11 thru 14; 42 titles distributed over a 4.33 area, incl 6**C** and 1C locations (3 **affil**, 2 **early**)

D* JULY 11 F **C**11/C2 00**4** 000 00 **7**0 (**2**)/000 **2**000 000 000 (1) = **3**/29 Next greatest distribution of 7 within a single location.
Fredericksburg, Va/ Pol Arena and Lit Museum sw
3 Richmond, Va/ **affil*** Enquirer sw **pro-Jackson;** Comm Comp (d and ctry eds) **pr**
2 Albany, NY/ **early*** Dly Advertiser; **early*** Morn Chron **pr** (See Rochester dly title under Jl 16.)
5 NY City/ Amn fCtry; Nat Advocate (d and ctry eds); Evn Post fCtry; Spectator (sw Comm Advertiser)
2 Providence/ R-I Amn and Providence Gaz sw, and Microcosm w under same title

D* JULY 12 SAT **C**20/C2 2**4**1 001 **10**, 0 20 (**6**)/000 **2**000 000 000 (1) = **7**/29
Greatest distribution of 10 within a single location.
2 WDC/ Chron; We the People
Annapolis/ Md Republican sw
Baltimore/ Niles' Wkly Reg
Cumberland/ **affil*** Md Advocate and Farmers' and Mechanics' Reg **pro-Jackson**

Easton, Md/ Gaz
Richmond, Va/ Constitutional Whig sw
9 Boston/ Advertiser (d and sw); Columbian Cent sw; Dly Comm Gaz; Courier (d and ctry eds); Mass J tw; Patriot and Merc Advertiser d, and Independent Chron and Boston Patriot sw under same title
Salem, Mass/ Observer
Trenton, NJ/ True Amn sw
Bridgeton, NJ/ **affil*** *Not* reprinted or summarized in Washington Whig
pro-Adams
Albany, NY/ Chron sw **pr**
NY City/ Statesman sw
2 Providence/ Lit Cadet and RI Statesman sw; Patriot and Columbian Phenix sw

JULY 14 M **C**6/C1 00**3** 000 **3**0 00 (**2**)/000 1000 000 000 (1) = **3**/29
Lynchburg/ Virginian sw
2 Norfolk, Va/ Amn Beacon and Nfolk and Portsmouth Dly Advertiser; Nfolk and Portsmouth Herald tw
2 Boston/ Comm Gaz sw; Courier sw
Salem, Mass/ Essex Reg sw
Providence, RI/ Manufacturers and Farmers J and Providence and Pawtucket Advertiser sw

Stage 3, three days Jl 15 thru 17; 56 titles distributed over a 10.33 area incl 8**C** and 6C locations (4 **peak**, 1 **delay**)

D* JULY 15 TU **C**13/C5 011 201 **4**1 **3**0 (**7**)/1**2**0 000**2** 000 000 (3) = **10**/29
Second greatest total distribution by number of locations.
Easton, Md/ Republican Star and Gen Advertiser
Norfolk, Va/ Amn Beacon and Va and N-C Gaz (ctry ed)
2 Boston/ **peak*** Amn Traveller sw **pt**; New-England Palladium and Comm Advertiser sw
Newburyport, Mass/ Herald sw **pr**
Salem, Mass/ Gaz sw
Hartford/ Ct Courant
Harrisburg/ Pa Intelligencer, and Farmers' and Mechanics' J
York, Pa/ Recorder
Newark/ Sent of Freedom and NJ Advertiser
Albany, NY/ Gaz (sw Advertiser)
2 Utica, NY/ Sent and Gaz (sw and w)
2 Portland/ Advertiser sw and Gaz of Me w under same title
Raleigh/ Reg and N-C Gaz sw
2 Charleston, SC/ Courier (d and tw)

D* JULY 16 W **C20**/C2 01**3 3**02 **43 4**0 (**7**)/011 0000 000 000 (2) = **9**/29 Third greatest total distribution by number of locations.
Frederick, Md/ Pol Examiner and Public Advertiser
Charlestown/ Va Free Press and Farmers' Rep
Wheeling/ Va Statesman
Williamsburg, Va/ Phoenix Plough-Boy **pr**
Northampton, Mass/ **peak*** Hampshire Gaz **pt**
2 Springfield, Mass/ Hampden J; **peak*** Republican **pt**
Worcester, Mass/ Nat Aegis
Bridgeport, Ct/ Republican Farmer
2 Norwich, Ct/ Canal of Intelligence; Courier
Gettysburg, Pa/ Adams Sent
Pittsburgh/ Statesman
Somerset, Pa/ Whig
New Brunswick, NJ/ Fredonian
Paterson, NJ/ Intelligencer
Ithaca, NY/ Republican Chron **pr**
Kingston, NY/ Ulster Plebian
Monticello, NY/ Sullivan Whig
Rochester, NY/ **delay*** Dly Telegraph
Charleston, SC/ Mercury d
Savannah, Ga/ Mercury tw **pr**

D* JULY 17 TH **C9**/C7 011 101 20 0**3** (**6**)/11**2** 1101 000 000 (6) = **12**/29 Greatest total distribution by number of locations.
Hagerstown, Md/ Torch Light and Public Advertiser
Martinsburg, Va/ Gaz and Public Advertiser
Amherst, Mass/ **peak*** New-England Inquirer **pt**
Boston/ Messenger fCtry (w Advertiser)
Indiana, Pa/ Ind and Jefferson Whig
Mount Holly/ NJ Chron
2 Cincinnati/ Dly Gaz, and Liberty Hall and Cinc Gaz w under same title
Columbus/ O St J and Columbus Gaz
Providence, RI/ Investigator and Gen Intelligencer
Portsmouth, NH/ Comm Advertiser
Waterville, Me/ Intelligencer
Fayetteville, NC/ Carolina Observer
Charleston, SC/ Mercury (ctry ed)
2 Savannah/ Georgian d; Republican tw **pr**

Stage 4, eleven days Jl 18 thru 30; 59 titles distributed over a 3.46 area incl 7**C** and 5C locations (7 **delay**, 2 **affil**, 1 **peak**)

JULY 18 F **C5**/C1 010 100 20 01 (**4**)/000 0010 000 000 (1) = **5**/29
Baltimore/ **delay*** Amn Farmer (See Baltimore titles for Jl 8, 9, and 12.)

Hingham, Mass/ Gaz
Taunton, Mass/ Commonwealth's Advocate
Pittsburgh/ Gaz
Cincinnati/ Gaz fCtry
Brattleboro, Vt/ Messenger

JULY 19 SAT **C**6/C4 000 100 **4**0 01 (**3**)/000 0111 010 000 (4) = **7**/29
Charlestown, Mass/ **peak*** Bunker-Hill Aurora and Farmers' and Mechanics' **J pt**
Haverhill, Mass/ Essex Gaz
Plymouth, Mass/ Old Colony Memorial
Worcester/ Mass Yeoman and Worcester Sat J and Advertiser
Harrisburg, Pa/ Argus
Lebanon, O/ Western Star and Leb Gaz
Amherst, NH/ Farmers' Cabinet
Windsor/ Vt Republican and Amn Yeoman, Windham, Windsor and Orange Co Advertiser
Eastport, Me/ Sent
Frankfort, Ky/ Commentator

D* JULY 21 M C1 1/29 Successive Mondays where number of titles limited to one or none; see two WDC reprint sources under Jl 7 M in this regard.
Concord/ NH J

D* JULY 22 TU **C**2/C5 000 000 01 01 (**2**)/000 0**23**0 000 000 (2) = **4**/29 **Only** instance of a C location having an **f** as high as 3.
Hartford, Ct/ Amn Mercury
Georgetown, O/ Castigator
Dover/ N-H Republican and Co Advertiser
Portsmouth, NH/ Times
Bennington/ Vt Gaz
Montpelier/ Vt Watchman and St Gaz
Rutland, Vt/ Herald

JULY 23 W **C**6/C1 000 **3**00 01 20 (**3**)/000 0000 010 000 (1) = **4**/29
New London, Ct/ Gaz and Gen Advertiser
3 Philadelphia/ **delay*** Dem Press (d and ctry eds); **delay*** U Sts Gaz d (See Philadelphia titles for Jl 8 thru 10.)
Albion, NY/ Orleans Advocate and Anti-Masonic Telegraph
Canandaigua, NY/ Ontario Rep
Maysville, Ky/ Eagle

JULY 24 TH **C**5 **C**000 **3**00 00 02 = **2**/29
Carlisle, Pa/ Herald
Lancaster, Pa/ Reporter

Milton, Pa/ St's Advocate
Chillicothe, O/ Scioto Gaz
Delaware, O/ Patron

JULY 25 F **C8**/C3 000 **3**00 10 0**4** (**3**)/000 0001 00**2** 000 (2) = **5**/29
Lowell, Mass/ J
Bedford, Pa/ Gaz
Greensburgh, Pa/ Gaz
Philadelphia/ **delay*** U Sts Gaz fCtry (See variant series of same title under Jl 23 above.)
Canton/ O Rep and Stark Co Gaz
Painesville, O/ Telegraph
Somerset/ Perry Record and O Whig
Xenia, O/ Western Cornet and Xenia Gaz
Augusta, Me/ Kennebec J
2 Nashville, Tenn/ **affil*** Nat Banner and Nville Whig (sw and w) **Neutral**

JULY 26 SAT **C3**/C2 000 200 00 01 (**2**)/000 0000 0**2**0 000 (1) = **3**/29
Butler, Pa/ Sent
Philadelphia/ **delay*** Dem Press w (See variant series of same title under Jl 23 and 25.)
Athens, O/ Mirror and Lit Reg
Georgetown, Ky/ Amn Sent **pr**
Mount Sterling, Ky/ Whig **pr**

D* JULY 28 M **C1** **1**/29 Successive Mondays where number of titles limited to one or none.
Doylestown, Pa/ Bucks Co Intelligencer and Gen Advertiser

JULY 29 TU **C2** C000 100 00 01 = **2**/29
Chambersburg, Pa/ Franklin Rep
Georgetown, O/ Western Aegis and Public Advertiser

JULY 30 W **C1**/C3 001 000 00 00 (**1**)/000 0001 011 000 (3) = **4**/29
Charleston/ **delay*** Western Virginian
Augusta/ Me Patriot and St Gaz
Lexington, Ky/ Reporter **pr**
Knoxville, Tenn/ Enquirer

Stage 5, twelve days Jl 31 thru Ag 13; 11 titles distributed over a .75 area incl 2**C** and 5C locations (1 **neg**, 1 **peak**)

JULY 31 TH **C1** **1**/29
Meadville, Pa/ Crawford Messenger

AUGUST 1 F **C**1/C1 2/29
Easton, Pa/ Northampton Whig and Farmers' and Mechanics' J
Huntsville, Ala/ **peak*** Southern Advocate **pt**

AUGUST 2 SAT **C2 1**/29
Piqua, O/ Gaz
St. Clairsville, O/ Nat Historian and St. Clsville Advertiser

D* AUGUST 4 M 0/29 Successive Mondays where number of titles limited to one or none.

AUGUST 5 TU C2 C000 0000 000 002 = 1/29
2 Pensacola/ Fla Argus and Pensacola Lit, Agricultural and Comm Reg; Gaz and Fla Advertiser

AUGUST 7 TH C1 1/29
Natchez, Miss/ Southern Galaxy

AUGUST 9 SAT C3 C000 0000 110 100 = 3/29
Lawrenceburg/ Ind Palladium
Paris, Ky/ Western Citizen **pr**
Port Gibson/ Correspondent and Miss Gen Advertiser

D* AUGUST 11 M 0/29 Successive Mondays where number of titles limited to one or none.

AUGUST 13 W 0/29
Little Rock/ **neg*** Ark Gaz does *not* include oration text as part of account of ceremonies reprinted from WDC Nat J.

Conclusions regarding characteristics of five stages, based in part on non-area variance in distribution:

Stage 1 Reprint process begins with publication of the Adams oration text on July 7 in two master WDC titles, but reprinting is confined to **C** locations as cyclical distribution table demonstrates. At no time is the Adams oration reprinted in a campaign pamphlet edition, quite possibly in light of the number of newspapers with an ample circulation carrying the text. Any editor along the reprinting route might have brought out a pamphlet edition from his own press to double or draw out the circulation of the text.

Stage 2 Reprinting spreads into upstate NY slightly ahead of schedule (2 **early**), with at least three papers temporarily suppressing party allegiances. Two pro-Jackson titles reprint the Adams oration text because of editorial stands in favor of internal improvements, a cause which candidate Jackson was not necessarily against. And one pro-Adams title does not reprint the oration because of space commitments to local Whig correspondents, none of whom even remotely allude to the Chesapeake and Ohio Canal ceremonies (3 **affil**).

Stage 3 Period of peak distribution (4 **peak**) covered in cyclical table, with some delay in reprinting evident in upstate NY (1 **delay**).

Stage 4 Some evidence of peak (1) and subdued partisanship (2 **Neutral**) continues from stages 2 and 3. But several pro-Adams titles in ab**C** distribution sectors (Baltimore, Charleston W*Va*, and Philadelphia) delay reprinting the Adams oration text to achieve a greater partisan impact—a development carrying over from stage 3, and yet very much at odds with touches of nonpartisanship here and in stage 2 (7 **delay**). By July 25, a pamphlet reprint of the Baltimore and Ohio Railroad ceremonies, taken mainly from the account printed in the *American and Commercial Daily Advertiser* of the seventh, appears in Baltimore at the bookstore of H. W. Bool, Jr., 60 Baltimore Street. Not only is the source date, July 7, identical with that for the Chesapeake and Ohio ceremonies, but the date of Bool's third and last advertisement in the *American* for the pamphlet, Aug. 15, approximates the end date of stage 5 or Aug. 13.

Stage 5 Some evidence of peak (1) lingers on. But the delay maneuver by pro-Adams editors like John Binns (Philadelphia *Democratic Press*) in stage 4 does not gain wide acceptance in western and southern locations. In fact, many editors apparently grasp the partisan implications of such delay tactics, and abstain altogether from reprinting any account of the Canal ceremonies, even in pamphlet form, at this late date. Indeed one editor in Little Rock, William E. Woodruff of the *Arkansas Gazette*, reprints the account of the ceremonies minus the "neat and appropriate speech, which is too long for insertion in our paper" (1 **neg**), perhaps one last hurrah for nonpartisanship in the 1828 campaign.

Chapter 6

David Crockett's Fourth of July Oration, 1834

Before reading through a purported text of David Crockett's after-dinner speech, allegedly delivered on the Fourth in 1834 at James Gregory's Hermitage Inn, Passyunk Road below Christian Street in Philadelphia, certain partisan-media attributes in Crockett's ethos as an orator must be understood. Attributes that threatened to transcend any traditional ceremonial nonpartisanship, for which the event itself never really was staged,[1] when publicized beyond the four[2] or five[3] hundred Whig faithful feasting at long tables and benches on the lawn outside the Inn.

Regardless of the precise extent of the orator's indebtedness to ghostwriters

---

1 The Hermitage-celebration Committee of Arrangements, for example, made no pretense about putting the event on a partisan key, especially when they had no reason to react to William L. Schaffer's short-lived "Philadelphia Association for celebrating the Fourth of July, without distinction of party." The Committee invited Crockett on 19 June to attend and partisanly "oppose Executive usurpation." Yet six days later, well within the time required for a letter from Philadelphia to reach Washington, Crockett apparently had not accepted the Committee's invitation, since he wrote James M. Sanderson, active in local Whig projects and superintendent of a reading room on the second floor of the Mercantile Exchange at the corner of Third, Walnut, and Dock Streets, regarding his determination to "perhaps spend" the Fourth in the city. *American Sentinel* (d, Philadelphia), 15 May, 1834; Philadelphia, 19 June, 1834, Sam[ue]l. Black, chairman, et. al. (incl., among nine other Committee members, George G. West, reader of John Adams's speech urging adoption of the Declaration of Independence, Committee-secretary George Norton, and vice-presidents James Maxwell, T[ruman]. M. Hubbell, and N. C. Foster, who introduced congressman Harmer Denny) to Daniel Webster, WDC, Webster Papers, Manuscript Division, Library of Congress; WDC, 25 June, 1834, *DCr* to Sanderson, Philadelphia, Ferdinand J. Dreer Collection, Historical Society of Pennsylvania (Philadelphia).

2 Philadelphia *Commercial Herald* in *United States' Telegraph* (d, WDC), 10 July, 1834.

3 Philadelphia *Inquirer and Daily Courier*, 7 July, pooled account also in *National Gazette and Literary Register* (Philadelphia), 8 July, 1834.

Mathew St. Clair Clarke[4] and Augustin S. Clayton.[5] Crockett's media-imprint clearly was stamped into the Hermitage speech message as reconstructed for the 1835 *Tour*.[6] A ghost process obviously more calculated and partisan, for example, than the rather haphazard satirical attempt, two years before the *Tour* came out, to incorporate some primitively convenient allusion about "Tennessee-Long-Face" Andrew Jackson into Black Hawk's lionized remarks on the Fourth at Allegheny College.[7] For the congressman, speaking on the national anniversary at the Hermitage Inn, found it necessary to pervert the occasion to serve his own partisan demagogic ends. In effect, following in the footsteps of Whig bankers, who quite properly feared austere consequences resulting from any diminution in congressional support for their Second United States Bank.[8] Unless presumably the "glorified popularity" of President Jackson and lackey "imps of famine" among the common man were not somehow actively countered.[9]

Indeed, the ghosted *Tour* version of Crockett's speech might well be a case in point of superimposed media-license. Although the ghosted version contains a superficially autobiographical hunting anecdote, much as the Baltimore *Saturday Visitor* had to include a wagoner anecdote in its questionable version (the reporter conceded it might be "more minute" and "more faithful") of the orator's "interesting digression" during an after-dinner speech to the Baltimore

4 WDC, 12 Jan., 1835, *DCr* to Edward L. Carey and Abraham Hart, Philadelphia, New-York Historical Society (NY City); Constance Rourke, "Davy Crockett: Forgotten Facts and Legends," *Southwest Review*, 19 (Winter 1934), 157-58, and *Davy Crockett* (New York: Harcourt Brace, 1934), pp. 265-66; Walter Blair, "Six Davy Crocketts," *Southwest Review*, 25 (July 1940), 459, and *Horse Sense in American Humor, from Benjamin Franklin to Ogden Nash* (Chicago: University of Chicago Press, 1942), p. 46; James Atkins Shackford, *David Crockett: The Man and the Legend* (Chapel Hill: University of North Carolina Press, 1956), pp. 258-63.

5 John D. Wade, "The Authorship of David Crockett's 'Autobiography,' " *Georgia Historical Quarterly*, 6 (Sept. 1922), 267-68.

6 This *Tour* abbreviated reference of course designates the 1835 ghosted narrative, published at Philadelphia and Baltimore by Carey and Hart. The complete *Tour* title is: *An Account of Col[onel]. Crockett's Tour to the North and Down East, in the Year of our Lord One Thousand Eight Hundred and Thirty-Four, His Object Being To Examine the Grand Manufacturing Establishments of the Country; and Also To Find Out the Condition of Its Literature and Morals, the Extent of Its Commerce, and the Practical Operation of "The Experiment," Written by Himself.* And the reader may care to consult a contemporary reference to Crockett's dashing off "a few hasty memoranda" for, of all things, a temperance speech (Crockett pseud., "Letter to editor Josiah P. Hetrich, datelined Easton-the seventeenth," *Northampton Whig* [Easton, Pa.], 17 Dec., 1833).

7 "Black Hawk-ism," *New-York and Richmond County Free Press* (Staten Island), 22 June, 1833; Presque Isle [Pa.] *Democratic Tornado* (satirical title) quoted by New York *Commercial Advertiser* in *Northampton Whig* (Easton, Pa.), 23 July, 1833.

8 Jean Alexander Wilburn, *Biddle's Bank: The Crucial Years* (New York: Columbia University Press, 1967), pp. 17-19.

9 WDC, 26 May, 1834, *DCr* to Joseph Wallis, Somerville Ala., TS copy, University of Texas Library (Austin); WDC, 27 May, 1834, *DCr* to T. J. Dobings, Brownsville Tenn., Indiana University Lilly Library (Bloomington); Crockett, "Remarks in House on Bill making appropriations for fortifications, dated 26 June," *Daily National Intelligencer* (WDC), 1 July, 1834.

Typographical Society,[10] the authentic speech-of-record by Crockett at the Hermitage probably was little better than an extemporaneous[11] partisan attack by a semiliterate against Jacksonite congressman Joel B. Sutherland.[12]

Crockett's toast and a local newspaper's commentary support this conclusion. Of the hierarchy of eighteen vice-presidents assisting celebration-president

---

10 "Crockett appearance of 30 Nov.," *Commercial Chronicle and Marylander* (Baltimore) in *Dly National Intelligencer*, 4 Dec., 1833; *Visitor* in *Evening Star* (New York City), 16 Dec., 1833. The wagoner anecdote featured persona Crockett didactically spinning out a mock-almanac, dialect yarn. "You see me here,—I'm but a plain-main man, and have got no education to boast of. Thirty-four years ago, gentlemen (now mind me, you what set up the types and publish papers, what I'm going to say is as true as the gospel),—thirty-four years ago, I visited this [h]ere same city.—I was then only thirteen years of age, and had just got education enough to spell 'baker.'—That was the biggist word I ever spell'd in them times.—I run away from my father, who used to keep a sort o[f] tavern by the roadside, for this reason. A pretty considerable-sized boy, somewhat *longer* than me, didn't like me nohow, and frequently rin[run] me [up] ag[a]in[st] the fence. So, I said, I'd *walk into him*.—And, I tell you, I did so,—for when I met him betwixt school hours, I *scratch'd him down* not [too] slow. After I'd *come over* the feller[fellow], I had to cut stick, but didn't make tracks for home. But [,instead,] went to a relation's [house], and staid[stayed] there 'til I thought the schoolmaster had cool'd down a leetle[little]. After awhile, he sent me word [that], if I'd come back to school, he'd gin me clear on a flogging[A] But I wasn't to be had.—So, my father bound me out [in service] to a cattle-dealer—and I *knocked about* for awhile with him. And then I run away ag[a]in, [be]cause I couldn't git[get] nothing to eat. After awhile, my father, who was a mighty poor man, binds me out [in service], ag[a]in, to a wagoner.—And this was the time I visited this very same city, and *knocked about* in some of these [same] streets. Gentlemen, what I tell you is as true as gospel (and you set up the types, you know, and let the people know all about these things). I wanted to go to sea when I arriv[*e*][B] at Baltimore, but the wagoner to whom I was apprenticed wouldn't gin me[C] my money. And so, though it went again[st] the grit, I had to make tracks towards home ag[a]in. But I'd no notion of going back. So, I cut stick, left the wagoner, and bound myself to [serve] the hatters' business in Virginny. The man failed, after I'd got [along] pretty well in business. And so, I had to *knock about* ag[a]in. I thought I'd go home. And so, I *scratch'd gravel* for Tennessee. When I *arriv*[*e*] home, nobody knowed me at first. But after awhile, sister recognized me. And so, I remained, as snug as a [rac]coon, at home for some time—tending horses and doing stable work. Gentlemen, I am speaking as true as gospel. I never had no education of any account. The biggist word I spelt [spell'd], when I was thirteen-years-old old, was *b-a*(bah)—*k-e-r*, 'baker.' " For a non-dialect recollection of wagoner Crockett, see Winchester [Va.] *Republican* in *Bucks County Intelligencer and General Advertiser* (Doylestown, Pa.), 16 May, 1831.

A "Gin me clear" is ghost vernacular for separate from peer objections to the schoolyard brawl, trusting in one thorough flogging with the schoolmaster's rod to reform the adolescent of aggressive traits, much as a cottin gin would separate fibers from undesirable seed and waste.

B There may be some latinate humor in having "arrived," literally coming ashore before venturing out to sea for the first time, particularly when the narrator already is so unsuccessfully jumping from one odd job to another.

C "Gin me" is ghost vernacular for cull me out, repeating the cotton-gin allusion.

11 Perhaps not wishing to suggest Crockett's authentic text, ghostwriter Clarke/Clayton labels the Hermitage oration as delivered "offhand" and by inference better able to be rewritten than a speech from manuscript. A term applied equally by the ghost to Crockett's two other speeches on the Fourth at Music Fund Hall and the Walnut Street Theater. Except that, at the Hermitage, "a great many ladies surrounding the stand" ("so many ladies" at Music Fund Hall) conceivably might be invented by the ghost to lionize Crockett in a manner dictating against readers expecting any excessively partisan speech. *Tour*, pp. 126, 130, and 139.

12 Both Bissell Brooke and James Atkins Shackford substantially accept the *Tour* ghost's version of the speech, Shackford even applying the same pseudo-press label ("tyranny, sword and purse, despotism, and independence") to all three Crockett appearances on the Fourth. Shackford, pp. 168-69; Brooke, "Philadelphia's Fourth of July, 1834, Described By A Famous American," *Hobbies*, 63 (Aug. 1958), 110-11.

Robert M. Carr,[13] who himself introduced Senator Asher Robbins of Rhode Island,[14] one, George Miller, introduced Crockett as a staunch Jeffersonian whose partisan views were "inflexible" enough to show up the paper tiger in Jackson's gold humbug.[15] Crockett's mere presence at the Inn suggested that he could not seriously be taken as "too independent to be led," or as "too sagacious to be cajoled," attributes supposedly assigned by Miller to a partisan whose vanity he sought to transform into another Jeffersonian thorn in Jackson's not so limitless crown of thorns.[16]

But the toast with which Crockett concluded his Hermitage remarks confirmed the partisan Sutherland message, only given fleeting mention in paragraph 5 of the stylized ghost version of the oration: "The Whigs of the First District—may they increase in numbers, and grow in strength, and teach their representative (Dr. J. B. Sutherland) to respect Whigism in preference to Jacksonism; and the next time he sells himself to the Kitchen Cabinet, it is to be hoped they may prove true to him."[17] And, though perhaps slanted a bit toward Jackson, the very first Philadelphia paper to report the celebration likewise confirmed that Crockett's toast mirrored some thematic structure in the authentic speech. Orator Crockett, according to the *Gazette and Universal Daily Advertiser* for the fifth, "gave the citizens of the First District such a picture of the conduct and treatment abroad of their representative (Joel B. Sutherland) as showed the latter in no very enviable light, and one too that will be remembered by them in Oct[ober]. next." A toast alone could not have begun to appeal to such personalized attitudes and voting behavior, even taking into consideration the Whig orientation of the immediate Hermitage audience.

Otherwise, the pre-*Tour* response to Crockett's Hermitage appearance was as disappointingly partisan as the probable speech-of-record. Local Whig editors

---

13 Besides the three vice-presidents cited in n. 1 and Miller, fourteen others served under president-of-the-day Carr: J. N. Scott, William F. Hughes, John L. Ferguson, David C. Landreth, William McAfee, Francis McBride, John Lentz, John Dillon, Thomas Patterson, George Richards, Robert Solts, John B. Smith, Thomas H. Femmington, and Martin Kochesperger. Philadelphia *Inquirer and Dly Courier*, 12 July, part 1 of pooled proceedings also in *United States Gazette* (d, Philadelphia), 14 July, 1834.

14 *Ibid.*

15 "The Progress of Humbug—humbug 10," *Delaware State Journal* (Wilmington) in *Dly National Intelligencer*, 29 July, 1834.

16 "Miller introductory toast," Philadelphia *Inquirer and Dly Courier*, 12 July, also in *U.S. Gazette* (d), 14 July, 1834. Miller's complete toast was: "The Honorable David Crockett, an inflexible democrat of the Jefferson school. Too independent to be led, too sagacious to be cajoled, he will always *go ahead* in the best service of his country."

17 *Ibid.*; *Tour*, pp. 134 and 138. The *Tour* ghost did not accurately transcribe the standard *Inquirer* version of Crockett's concluding toast. Above all, the ghost chose to omit two rather explicit references to Sutherland: "*May* the Whigs in the First District_____[*they*] **b** *grow in strength*, and **a** *increase in numbers*, and teach their representative [J.B.S.] to *know the difference between* Whigism *and* Jacksonism ((22 words omitted here))."

seemed unable to write off the notion that more than a few audience members conceivably might not have been sober enough to give the orator their undivided attention. Since the partisan personalities in the speech loomed large enough not to be paraphrased by sympathetic editors in the know, Crockett, complete with "unaffected and good-humored manner,"[18] was cast as a speaker sufficiently devout in his patriotism to gratify an audience, who also had to be cast as listening only with the "most profound"[19] and "close"[20] attention. The editor of the Nashville *National Banner* complained, with good reason, that Zachariah Poulson's local Whig account left him "totally in the dark as to what our patriotic member from the Shelby District *said* . . . on the occasion."[21] Nor did Crockett's remark on the sixth at Lancaster about speaking "himself hoarse in Philadelphia" help the *Banner* editor out of the predicament.[22]

If the Whig press carefully kept the wraps on Crockett's "double-nerved" sincerity,[23] Jackson editors were not at all reluctant to focus on the orator's opportunism, which they sensed to be so intensely partisan as not to qualify as a sincere motive for any ceremonial speech. Crockett admittedly might not even have passed for a mumbling sententious idol, to the avidly rancorous Jackson supporter.[24] Still, several opposition journalists were not entirely unaware of personalized partisan topics dragging Sutherland into the authentic speech. The Philadelphia *Star-Spangled Banner* may have thought Crockett and Thomas Chilton of Kentucky honest congressmen forsaking despot Jackson.[25] But the Jackson Administration's organ in Washington, the *Globe*, saw fit to include orator Crockett, as a recent recruit, among a coterie of miserable politicians "haranguing the Federalists of Philadelphia in partnership."[26]

The New York *Times*, successor to the Democratic *Standard*, also questioned Crockett's true motive, when perpetrating what the editor labeled as an intensely partisan farce at the Hermitage: "Crockett, let them say what[ever] they

---

18 *Poulson's American Daily Advertiser* (Philadelphia), 7 July, 1834.

19 Philadelphia *Commercial Herald* in *United States' Telegraph* (d, WDC), 10 July, 1834.

20 Philadelphia *Inquirer and Dly Courier*, 7 July, pooled account also in *National Gazette and Literary Register* (Philadelphia), 8 July, 1834.

21 *Banner and Daily Advertiser* (Nashville, Tenn.), 18 July, 1834.

22 *Columbia Spy* (Lancaster) in *Daily Evening Transcript* (Boston), 18 July, 1834.

23 "Joseph Martin toast at Hermitage," Philadelphia *Inquirer and Dly Courier*, 14 July, 1834, part 2 of proceedings not carried in *U.S. Gazette* (d).

24 "William McDonald toast at Democratic celebration, 2nd Congressional District," *The Pennsylvanian* (d, Philadelphia), 9 July, 1834; "Toasts by Thomas Hawkins and Joseph S. Dougherty at Democratic celebration, 1st Congressional District," *Pennsylvanian* (d), 16 and 19 July, 1834.

25 *Banner* in *Hampden Journal and Advertiser* (Springfield, Mass.), 3 Sept., 1834.

26 *Globe* (d), 10 July, 1834. Each "strange bedfellow" in the partisan group, namely, Crockett, Daniel Webster, and Duff Green, spoke at the Hermitage on the Fourth.

will, is the Magnus Apollo of the Bank party. He is the only man, of them all, who can keep his audience awake. When he is in want of a sentiment [to orate upon], he cuts a [farcical] caper; when he has nothing to say, he can at least grin. And he has an unblushing impudence which absolutely looks down all opposition."[27]

And the pro-Jackson Philadelphia *Aurora* more than hinted at contemptible acrimony, present in the orator lambasting Sutherland for official misconduct: "In what light is the *distinction* bestowed upon this gentleman[Crockett] to be viewed? Is it to do honor to great talents or great virtues? Has he contributed anything to [advance] science or general knowledge? What exploit has he performed? . . . What good has he done? . . . He can talk, in a vulgar [sort of] way, some blunt unmeaning things, . . . and rushes into the farther folly of talking upon topics of which he is wholly innocent of understanding . . . . If such a man could [but] feel the ignominy of such distinctions as he has received, he would blush at his own degradation, and that of Congress in one of its members."[28]

Yet what media-image of Crockett, if any, did the ghost then reconstruct the Hermitage oration to fit? Indeed, why would the ghost have to polish the nasty partisanship in the speech-of-record at all, when a complete rewrite might perhaps better bolster a media-imprint so firmly rooted in the popular mind as almost to spoof partisan vendetta? A media-imprint which clearly did not have to be overstated and pounded into the partisan psyche a la anti-Sutherland to win optimum public consumption.

For the very evening that Crockett attended the Walnut Street Theater, boisterously cheering on the acting company's repetition of "God Bless America," a "grand national anthem" included in the program to capture some small measure of patriotism displayed by personae Joseph Warren and Orloff Gabinski,[29] John C. Mossie was improvising orator Crockett's speaking manner in Bangor, Maine. Prior, that is, to spending late July and most of August entertaining the more affluent Whig gentry at their favorite Congress-Hall spa in Saratoga Springs, New York. A spa, incidentally, where numerous Mossie spectators arrived in the best fashion, riding the very first cars hauled "ahead" by the Saratoga and Schenectady Railroad's spanking new locomotive, christened "Davy Crockett" late in June.

Improvisator Mossie had in fact performed his Crockett sketch at Boston's Boylston Hall on May 6, with the congressman an honored guest in the audi-

---

27 *Times* in Boston *Morning Post*, 11 July, 1834.

28 *Aurora*, 19 July, 1834. For Walter Blair's somewhat oversimplified analysis of how Crockett-image 5, as publicized by the Whig press, never really could manage to absorb enough nonpartisan veracity from Crockett-image 1 in the popular mind, the reader may care to consult *Southwest Review*, 25 (July 1940), 457-59, and *Horse Sense in American Humor* (Univ. of Chicago Press, 1942), pp. 44-46.

29 *Pennsylvanian* (d), 4 July, 1834; Philadelphia *Gazette and Universal Dly Advertiser*, 5 July, 1834.

ence,[30] no doubt flattered by what the Whig press, writing up Mossie with a flair for Crockett's name, puffed as a puzzling but lifelike imitation of "an honest and fearless speaker."[31] Perhaps Mossie's act was so similarly ethos-enhancing as not to be mentioned at all in the *Tour*, a second narrative medium even if composed by the unidentified ghost. But one, quite obviously, in which stylistic technique could never be permitted to entertain readers at the expense of credible Whig-party doctrine.

Mossie's career spanned many facets that brought him into close contact with the media. He was a cub congressional reporter, eagerly caught up in seeking donations to aid victims of Poland's current spate of revolution.[32] Enterprising editor of a literary sheet written for a family readership and eschewing politics, titled the Louisville *Examiner* despite having no apparent connection with mercantile affairs.[33] And the rare playwright who found it necessary to promote his own work by appearing as a member of the cast (he wrote two melodramas, "Marco Savona" and "Francisco Roldan, or the Pirate King").[34] Publication of the *Tour* by Carey and Hart in 1835 may have adversely affected public interest in Mossie's Crockett sketch. At least by the advent of the 1837 New Year, drink

30 "Advertisement for 15th-night act, with separate Crockett notice," *Dly Evening Transcript* and Boston *Dly Advocate*, 6 May, 1834.

31 *Dly Evening Transcript*, 5 May, in *Dly News* (Albany, N.Y.), 13 May, 1834; New York *Transcript* (d), 8 May, 1834; New-York *Spectator* (sw), 15 May, 1834. The complete Crockett-Mossie dialogue, featuring a loose dialect antithesis in eh/ay, supposedly a faithful reproduction of their conversation on Sunday-4 May, went: Mossie—"Colonel, you have been the *greatest benefactor* I ever had. I have made hundreds [of dollars] by introducing you among my illustrations of orators." Crockett—"Among orators, eh? I was out of place, then. I have no *pretensions* to be an orator." Mossie—"You are something *better*, an honest and fearless speaker of your mind." Crockett—"Why, ay! I never was *scared* out of saying what I did think, nor ever will be."

32 "Report of 26 Oct. Polish rally," *Dly National Intelligencer*, 29 Oct., 1831; "Undated Mossie card," *Intelligencer* (d), 31 Oct., 1831; M[ossie], "Poland poem," *Intelligencer* (d), 4 Nov., 1831.

33 "Mossie *Examiner* promotional card, dated the thirteenth," *Dly Louisville* [*Ky.*] *Public Advertiser*, 13 Nov., 1832; *Public Advertiser* (d) and *Dly Louisville Herald and Commercial Gazette*, 3 Dec., 1832. The weekly *Examiner*, for which no single issue is known to be extant, commenced publication with the issue dated Saturday-1 Dec., running approximately seven months before editor Mossie departed for Virginia and the East. For three Mossie *Examiner* pieces, see "Disciple of Confucius," Cincinnati *Mirror and Ladies' Parterre*, 5 Jan., 1833; "Way of the World" (dialect poem), Greensborough [N.C.] *Patriot*, 12 June, 1833; "Roman Princes," Boston *Morning Post*, 29 May, 1834. And the reader may find it interesting to compare the "benefactor" frame of the passage in n. 31 with these six lines from Mossie's "Way of the World" poem: "When Tom was poor, I was his *benefactor*,—Tom drew the thirty thousand dollar prize, And, then became so *excellent* an actor, That, when I bowed, he gazed with *feigned* surprise, And lisped out drawlingly—to my amaze,—'I never *th*aw you, *th*ir, in all my day*ths*.' " Note possible structural parallels in the word "benefactor" itself, monetary benefit (thirty thousand/hundreds), the transition word "then," manner of expressing expertise achieved (excellent-feigned surprise/*superlative* great-*comparative* good-pretensions-scared), and timeless denial in the final period (never-all/ay, yes or always?-never-ever).

34 "Savona performances at Jefferson-Street City Theater on 27 April and 1 May," *Dly Louisville Herald and Commercial Gazette*, 25 and 30 April, and Louisville *Journal* cited in *Herald-Gazette* (d), 1 May, 1833; "Roldan performance at Cincinnati Citizens' Theater on 27 May," *The Republican* (d, Cincinnati), 25 and 27 May, and Cincinnati *Herald* cited in *National Banner and Nashville* [*Tenn.*] *Dly Advertiser*, 3 June, 1833.

and unpaid debts were to land him in New York City's Bridewell prison.[35]

Yet, in 1833 and 1834, Mossie's act helped create the favorable media-climate on which *Tour*-persona Crockett thrived. The thematic evolution of his treatment of orator Crockett was indeed rather simple: familiarity with almanac traits (half-horse, half-alligator, and whole-hog),[36] to the provincial "backwoodsman in Baltimore"[37] which he was not alone in performing, into dialect variations on orator Crockett's manner.[38] The effectiveness of Mossie's Crockett sketch clearly depended on the orator's "remarkable" or "renowned" cumulative reputation in the media.[39] So when not contrasting Crockett's oral congressional style with shrill-voiced "bully" and fellow Tennessean, Thomas D. Arnold,[40] or with ale-whetted, "treble-octave" sarcasms of Virginia's John Randolph,[41] the improvisator recited two affected-dialect Crockettiana pieces. Either an amusing "Defense of the Squatters," featuring eccentric dialect substitutions like *specific/Pa*cific, m*ou*ght/m*i*ght, s*a*ft/s*o*ft, and *ef*-fect/*af*fect,[42] or one of several Dutch stories told in Crockett's "queer quaint manner."[43]

---

35 Boston *Dly Advocate*, 11 Aug., 1835; New York *Transcript* in Pittsburgh [Pa.] *Mercury*, 25 Jan., 1837.

36 MOS[sie], "[Bedeviled] Editors—parts 1 and 2" (improvisation), *Dly National Intelligencer*, 16 and 18 Aug., 1831.

37 "Advertisement for act performed at Washington National Museum on the twenty-seventh," *Dly National Intelligencer*, 27 June, 1831.

38 In the act as performed in Nashville and Louisville, for example, Mossie first included the Crockett sketch when appearing before the Tennessee state legislature on 21 Sept., 1832. Indeed, the Crockett sketch may have been improvised in Washington or Baltimore at an earlier date, but no evidence supports such an assumption. And by 1 March, 1834, the sketch was enough a regular part of the act for Mossie to do a featured criticism on the orator's style, by "request" in advance from an audience member. "Ads for acts at Nashville Representatives' Hall on the twenty-first, and at Nashville Masonic Hall on 27 Sept." *National Banner and Nashville Dly Advertiser*, 21 and 26 Sept., 1832; "Preliminary notice of act at Louisville, ca. 1 Nov.," *Dly Louisville Public Advertiser*, 23 and 30-Oct. correction, 1832; "Ad for 9th-night act on the twenty-first at Clinton Hall in New York City," *Morning Courier and New-York Enquirer*, 21 Dec., 1833; "Ad for act at Troy Mayor's Courtroom," *Dly Troy [N.Y.] Press*, 28 Feb., 1834.

39 "4th-night ad for act on 3 Dec. at Clinton Hall," *Morning Courier and New-York Enquirer*, 2 Dec., 1833; "10th-night ad for Clinton-Hall act of the twenty-eighth," *Courier-Enquirer* (d), 28 Dec., 1833; "11th-night ad for act on the thirtieth at Masonic Hall in NY City," *Courier-Enquirer* (d), 30 Dec., 1833.

40 "Act Performed on 7 Dec.," *Morning Courier and New-York Enquirer*, 12 Dec., 1833; "Act of 22 April," *New England Galaxy* (Boston), 26 April, 1834.

41 "Ad for act at Boston Masonic Temple on 26 March," *Dly Evening Transcript*, 25 March, 1834; "Act of 2 May," *Evening Gazette* (Boston), 3 May, 1834.

42 "12th-night ad for Boston Masonic-Temple act of 29 April," *Dly Evening Transcript*, 26 April, 1834; "Act of 22 April in Boston," *New England Galaxy*, 26 April, 1834.

43 "11th-night ad for Masonic-Hall act of the thirtieth," New York *Standard* (d), 30 Dec., 1833. For sources on the impact of various Mossie performances, other than the usual list of improvisational topics submitted by the audience (the performer only selecting one at the close of the act), consult Admirer of Eloquence, "Undated letter," *Evening Star for the Country* (New York City), 13 Dec., 1833; Jurisconsultus, "Undated letter," *Dly Evening Transcript* (Boston), 27 March, 1834; and a third undated critique from a correspondent lacking any pen name or real identity, Newburyport [Mass.] *Herald* (d), 17 May, 1834.

But always, even at the risk of inviting charges of caricature,[44] or having partisan content supplant dialect manner,[45] Mossie both exploited and publicized Crockett for a "peculiar" brand of oratory,[46] a label occasionally applied by reporters to the improvisator's treatment of vehement Randolph as well.[47] In Crockett's case, however, a cunning vehemence, in the sense of being faddishly bold-and-blunt "ahead" or roughly effective in knock-me-down unsophistication, and never, with any demagogic crunch about to expose the speaker's true motive, failing to be shrewd enough to pass for commonsensically dry.[48] Despite the obvious elocutionary dialect and manner, Mossie's act certainly possessed a more substantial media-impact than this promotional "fluency" quotation from Crockett's persona might indicate, "A man may give you plenty of words and but few thoughts among the whole lot."[49]

Nor was Crockett the social realist to discourage other entertainers from capitalizing on his speaking manner in 1833 and 1834. No less than three times during 1834,[50] for example, he attended Thomas Danforth Rice's dialect ren-

---

44 "Act of 7 Dec.," *Morning Courier and New-York Enquirer for the Country*, 20 Dec., 1833; "9th-night ad for Clinton-Hall act of the twenty-first," *Courier-Enquirer* (d), 21 Dec., 1833; "Ads for Boston Masonic-Temple acts of 26 March and 11 April," *Dly Evening Transcript*, 25 March and 10 April, 1834.

45 *Evening Star* (NY City), 13 Dec., 1833; "Mossie Card dated 20 Dec.," *Morning Courier and New-York Enquirer*, 21 Dec., 1833.

46 "Crockett notice-invitation to Boylston-Hall act of the sixth," *Dly Evening Transcript* and Boston *Dly Advocate*, 6 May, 1834.

47 "Act of 7 Dec.," *Morning Courier and New-York Enquirer*, 12 Dec., 1833.

48 Mossie ads, nn. 30 thru 47 and 49. Readers interested in assessing whether Mossie perhaps directly influenced some perception of Crockett's oratory in the press, prior to publication of the *Tour* and apart from the usual "inimitable" comment from reporters about the Crockett sketch, may care to learn of these parallel Crockett evaluations by the media. *Dly National Intelligencer* (WDC), 22 June, 1831, "his discourses . . . not altogether *Ciceronian*, but to the point, short, *shrewd*, and few"// *Green River Gazette* (Bowling-Green, Ky.), 1 Nov., 1833, "no orator as [Felix] Grundy is, but a *right onward*, plain, *blunt* man"// *Evening Star* (NY City), 2 May, 1834, "delivered a few short and pithy sentences in his *quaint and original* style" (not "queer quaint" as in sentence cited by n. 43)// *Evening Gazette* (Boston), 10 May, 1834, "a plain, *sincere, peculiar* way . . . that, if not eloquence, is *very impressive*"//John Gadsby Chapman (WDC portraitist), June 1834, "told his stories with unhesitating *clearness of diction*, often embellished with *graphic touches* of original wit and humor, sparkling and even startling, yet never *out of place* or obtrusively ostentatious" (compare with media-implications of Crockett's "out-of-place" line in n. 31; Chapman quote in Curtis Carroll Davis, "A Legend at Full-Length," *Proceedings of the American Antiquarian Society*, 69 [21 Oct., 1959], 170).

49 "16th-night ad for Boston Boylston-Hall act of 12 May," *Dly Evening Transcript*, 9 May, 1834. For six Mossie improvisations not specifically relevant to any study of Crockett's oral style as interpreted by the media, consult "The Dream—parts 1 and 2," *Dly National Intelligencer* (WDC), 4 and 7 Oct., 1831; "Statesman or Politician," *Evening Star for the Country* (NY City), 31 Dec., 1833; "Jefferson toast at Washington's Birthday dinner in Troy House," *Dly Troy [N.Y.] Press*, 26 Feb., 1834; "Napoleon the Exile" (poem), *Dly Evening Transcript*, 28 April, 1834; "Junius" (poem), *Dly Evening Advertiser* (Portland, Me.), 19 June, 1834; "Dream of Malthus" (poem), *Evening Star* (NY City) in *National Banner and Dly Advertiser* (Nashville), 19 Dec., 1834, compared with "Malthusian Controversy" in the *Dly National Intelligencer* for 9 Sept., 1831.

50 "Ad for Rice act at Walnut Street Theater on the twenty-sixth," Philadelphia *Gazette and Universal Dly Advertiser*, 26 April, 1834; "Ad for Rice act at Tremont Theater on the eighth,"

dition of "Jump Jim Crow."[51] Indeed, so catching[52] was media-lion Crockett that, no later than July, Rice was including "Massah Davy and de koon" in his "Crow" performance, even when the congressman did not happen to attend.[53] In fact, the day after the Hermitage oration, Rice performed his "Massah Davy" routine at the Cincinnati Theater, along with a timely dialect tribute to the Fourth, and "Crow" vocalizations of lions "*Black Hawk* and him sweetheart" and "De dandy nigger *Cincernati*."

Twice during 1833 at the Nashville Theater, once on a Thursday, and again two days later on a Saturday,[54] Crockett had looked in on J. P. Brown's circus company (Thursday) and Bob Farrell's dialect vocalizing (both days) of his persona's lionhearted prowess in "Zip Coon."[55] A media-meeting of minds perhaps more fully realized when puffed in *Tour* environs by the *Constellation* and *Courier and Enquirer* in New York City,[56] and by the *American Saturday Courier* in Philadelphia.[57] Even "screamer" Nimrod Wildfire, a persona adapted for the stage as the "Kentuckian in New York" from James Kirk Paulding's "Lion of the West," evoked some comment from Whigs about Crockett's "honest heart, frank disposition, contempt of danger, and fondness for fun and frolic,"[58] when the congressman presumably agreed to "request" James H.

Boston *Dly Atlas*, 8 May, 1834; "Ad for Rice act at Cincinnati Theater on the twelfth," Cincinnati *Advertiser and Ohio Phoenix* (sw), 12 July, 1834.

51 For specimen dialect verses from the "Jim Crow" extravaganza, see "Crow's Visit [A]way Down East" (Baltimore *Genius of Comedy* in *Paul Pry* [WDC], 9 March, 1833).

52 For media-coverage of Crockett appreciating Rice's performance at the Walnut Street Theater, first of three attended by the congressman during 1834, consult Philadelphia *Inquirer* (d), 28 April, 1834; *Pennsylvanian* (Philadelphia) in New York *Standard* (d), 29 April, and *United States' Telegraph* (d, WDC), 3 May, 1834; Boston *Morning Post*, 1 May, 1834; Baltimore *Gazette and Advertiser* in Cincinnati *Mirror and Western Gazette of Literature and Science*, 10 May, 1834; Newburyport [Mass.] *Herald* (d), 14 May, 1834; *Paul Pry* (WDC), 17 May, 1834; *Tour*, pp. 32-34.

53 "Ad for Rice Act at Cincinnati Theater on the fifth," Cincinnati *Advertiser and Ohio Phoenix* (sw), 5 July, 1834; "Ad for Rice act at Jefferson-Street City Theater on the twenty-second," *Dly Louisville Public Advertiser*, 22 July, 1834.

54 "Rice act performed on 31 Oct.," *National Banner and Nashville Dly Advertiser*, 1 Nov., 1833; "Ad for Rice act of the second," *Banner-Advertiser* (d), 2 Nov., 1833.

55 For two specimen dialect verses, presumably from "Zip Coon" and not Rice's "Jim Crow," see Alexandria [Va.]*Phoenix-Gazette* in Cincinnati *Dly Whig and Commercial Intelligencer*, 19 July, 1837.

56 "Zip Coon v[ersu]s. Jim Crow," New York *Constellation* in Cincinnati *Advertiser and Ohio Phoenix* (sw), 13 Nov., 1833; *Morning Courier and New-York Enquirer for the Country*, 15 Nov., 1833; Nashville Theater, 22 Nov., Farrell to editor of *Atlas and Constellation*, NY City, in *National Banner and Dly Advertiser* (Nashville), 22 Nov., 1833; New York *Atlas and Constellation* in Plattsburgh [N.Y.] *Republican*, 14 Dec., 1833; Mobile Ala., April, Farrell to DCr, WDC, in *Banner-Advertiser* (d), 1 May, 1834.

57 *Courier*, quoting Nashville letter dated 20 Dec., 1833, in Mobile [Ala.] *Commercial Register and Patriot* (d), 6 Feb., 1834.

58 "Ad for Hackett performance on the twelfth," *Dly National Intelligencer*, 12 Dec., 1833.

Hackett's performance in the role at the Washington Theater later the same year.[59]

If entertainment-lion Crockett had any prayer of staying effectively credible, most of all in a campaign print struck after his defeat by Adam Huntsman, the *Tour* ghost's central task would entail making generalizations depersonalized enough to minimize Crockett's vindictiveness in the authentic speech at the Hermitage. The ghost ironically had to be a kind of party spokesman for the muted artificiality denounced, late in April, as inappropriate to the congressman's speaking by the local Whig press.[60] And the potential demagogic problem to be remedied, posed really by anyone ever being able to pin down the authentic Hermitage text, resulted from a "great and honest" personified curiosity[61] articulating, in an excessively personalized vein to an immediate partisan audience, remarks not necessarily "sensible and plain" enough to win respect for Whig dogma in any secondary *Tour* audience.[62]

Crockett's semiliterate irascibility as a speaker may have been implied by a critical undertone of severity, forcibleness, scorn, and even cursing, qualities which several Whig reporters conceded they observed.[63] But Democrats compared Crockett's vigorous, high-pressure partisanship[64] on the platform to George McDuffie, a fellow peripatetic[65] orator who favored a hotly vehement style, ranting anti-Jackson "evanescent bile" to Irish laborers on the Baltimore wharves.[66] Or the opposition compared Crockett's speaking to persona Punch, self-centeredly poking fun at society's ills and Judy, while insignificantly exercising mere caprice in a "glee" between acts at some theater.[67]

---

59 Cumberland, "Hackett-role commentary, dated 13 Dec.," *Dly National Intelligencer*, 16 Dec., 1833. Correspondent Gulliver made a comparable allusion to persona Wildfire and Crockett's ethos in the Boston *Dly Advocate* for 10 May, 1834: "I never saw our *Nimrod* of the West, but I conceive him to be a plain, honest man—a sort of rough diamond, or, to speak plainly, *common sense* personified in the plain garb and language of a Quaker . . . . The breed of these honest men has, I fear, run out [of existence] in Holland and Switzerland. And [they] are not quite so plenty in the Federal City [WDC], as in the days of our first President. But this is conjecture, mere guesswork."

60 *Commercial Intelligencer* (d, Philadelphia), 28 April, 1834; *United States Gazette* (sw, Philadelphia), 29 April, 1834; *Evening Star* (NY City), 30 April, 1834.

61 "Toast by anonymous guest at Whig celebration," *Hampden Whig* (Springfield, Mass.), 9 July, 1834; "Ghosted version of Crockett address at Music Fund Hall, 4 July," *Tour*, p. 126.

62 Philadelphia *Commercial Herald* in Dover [N.H.] *Enquirer*, 6 May, 1834.

63 *Commercial Intelligencer* (d), 28 and 29 April, 1834; Philadelphia *Inquirer* (d), 29 April, 1834.

64 *Dly Pennsylvanian* (Philadelphia), 29 April, 1834.

65 New York *Standard* (d), 3 May, 1834; *Dly Pennsylvanian*, 14 May, 1834; New York *Times* in Boston *Morning Post*, 11 July, 1834.

66 *Our Chronicle of '26. A Satirical Poem* (Boston: Wells and Lilly, 1827), pp. 13-14; *Commercial Chronicle and Marylander* (Baltimore) in Philadelphia *Gazette and Universal Dly Advertiser*, 29 April, 1834; *Dly Pennsylvanian*, 1 and 2 May, 1834; "Correspondent's letter datelined Baltimore-26 April," Newburyport [Mass.] *Herald* (d), 2 May, 1834.

67 *Dly Pennsylvanian*, 2 May, 1834; "Advertisement for 'Punchinello' performance at Mobile Theater on 26 May," Mobile [Ala.] *Commercial Register and Patriot* (d), 24 May, 1834; George L.

The ghost, in effect, fictively had to recreate Crockett's Hermitage text to fit a media-occasion, much as he obviously had to rectify the erroneous attribution of a Crockett speech to an out-and-out thief by the pro-Whig New York *Journal of Commerce*.[68] And even in such a confidence-man[69] type of partisan context, demagogic rumblings never ceased to be heard. Was orator Crockett tantamount to a personified Merry-Andrew ploy, "as contagious as the clatter of a barnyard fowl?"[70] Did his speaking excite frivolous laughter more by "peculiarly droll manner" than by argumentative substance?[71] And, in the end, was he so "brimful of honesty" that he could afford to denigrate opponents "without the least concealment?"[72]

In recreating the Hermitage oration, the ghost cleverly endeavored to make an increasing tolerance for partisanship on the Fourth an acceptable means for concealing Crockett's personalized attack against Sutherland. Successful or not when judged in modern-day terms, the Philadelphia *Tour* audience had to grasp that Crockett and the Whigs deserved a better media-fate than being linked[73] with John Pluck, a local hostler at Snare's Tavern, corner of Third and Callowhill Streets. With the ghost to defend his media-image, Crockett at least would not periodically be confined to the Blockley almshouse.[74] Even though a lame duck in Congress after Huntsman's victory, Whig bankers realized the importance to the party in not allowing Crockett to suffer any similar defeat. The

---

Barnett, "A Disquisition on Punch and Judy [1837] Attributed to Charles Lamb," *Huntington Library Quarterly*, 25 (May 1962), 231 and 233.

68 *Journal of Commerce* (d), 2 May, 1834, speech text reprinted locally the next day in NY *Standard* (d), NY *Spectator—Extra* (tw), *Man* (d), *Sun* (d), and excerpted the next day in NY *Transcript* (d).

69 *Ibid.* The thief almost ironically overplays his role, by concluding his speech before the police magistrate on this generalized and demagogic note: "I don't believe that the currency can be ever restored to the [prosperous] state it was [in], for we have lost *confidence* in each other, and everything like *confidence* is at an end."

70 New York *Standard* (d), 2 May, 1834.

71 New York *Journal of Commerce* (d), 2 May, 1834.

72 Brooklyn [N.Y.] *Evening Star* in Providence [R.I.] *Dly Journal*, 5 May, 1834.

73 *Pennsylvanian* (Philadelphia) in *United States' Telegraph* (d, WDC), 3 May, 1834; Boston *Dly Advocate*, 5 May, 1834; Salem [Mass.] *Gazette*, 6 May, 1834; New York *Times* in *Dly Louisville Public Advertiser*, 23 May, 1834; "Letter datelined Louisville-16 July," *Kentucky Gazette* (Lexington), 19 July, 1834. About the time the *Tour* was in process of being composed, for example, the Boston *Whig* ran this counter-Pluck dialogue, spoken allegedly between Crockett and a northern damsel at a soiree hosted by ghostwriter-candidate Clarke. Lady—"And where is it you board, sir?" Crockett—"I do not board in the [same] place my predecessor did, for I never could endure the farce to which he submitted." Lady—"And where did he board?" Crockett—"Oh, he boarded with a blacksmith, and slept in the coal-yard, and paid [for] his board by blowing and striking and shoeing horses, after the House [of Representatives] had concluded each day's business." *Whig* in *Dly Herald* (Newburyport), 30 Jan., 1835.

74 *Genius of Liberty* (Leesburg, Va.) in *We the People* (WDC), 20 Sept., 1828; *Saturday Chronicle* (Philadelphia) in Pittsburgh *Mercury*, 31 Aug., 1836.

media-persona in the *Tour* would not give way to an anti-militia fantastical. He would not be a hapless victim of alcoholism, a not so very "great" vocabulary unable to deny charges of corruption by plain people,[75] or gross accoutrements that only accented inadept rotundity.[76] He would not be satirically lionized on tour at 12½ cents a head, oblivious even to steamboat passengers nominating him for Vice-President only because the boat happened to be named "Washington."[77] His media-image was too valuable to be buried in a mediocre ghosted autobiography of Pluck's whole sordid campaign episode.[78]

Nor, in the interest of preserving his media-image intact, would Crockett have to play some front-porch monkey regarding impressions of his Hermitage appearance. There was little need for him to remain silent, on exhibit inside the front doorway to the Philadelphia Museum like an orangoutan,[79] when the ghost easily might alter subjective impressions of the authentic speech. For much as the Democratic press likened Crockett to the most objectionably im-

---

75 *Saturday Evening Post* (Philadelphia), 21 May, 1825; A Calm Observer, "Colloquy Extra—Dialogue between Major General J[ohn]. F[ox]. Pluck and Brigadier General A[lbert]. S[mith]. No-Pluck," *Bucks County Intelligencer and General Advertiser* (Doylestown, Pa.), 22 June, 1829.

76 Pluck's accoutrements were, in effect, those of a satirical demagogue. A white charger not so gallant when assigned to support his stoutly inactive physique (drink in 1825 and 1826 had yet to ravage Pluck). A blue trooper's uniform so small as to be confining and uncomfortable, certainly not up to making any real battle charge (the socially gallant charge suggested the satire). A chapeau quite reminiscent of pandering pimps, resplendent with game feathers, horse trappings from the stable where he worked, and curtain tassels from bars in the vicinity of Snare's Tavern. A discarded shoe, borne aloft on a stick, for his troop's ensign, but a playbill in place of the American flag perhaps better suggested satire in the public mind. And, as if rotundity were not enough of a problem already, two-pound iron spurs replete with tinkling bells sounded his every move on the parade-ground. For his own personal weapons, mostly for promotional display and of little real use, Pluck retained a gun nearly eight feet long and a sword upwards of one yard in length. While the ragamuffins, supposedly to benefit from his elect tutelage under the current state law, were forced to fend for themselves at Bush Hill with tree branches, cornstalks, and even surplus laths doubling as walking sticks. The satire decimating Pluck's character indeed had a maze of detail to work from, much as the British ridiculed victorious Americans after the Revolution on the stage. Except that, with Pluck, he was more the pawn manipulated by anti-militia forces who twice secured his election as Colonel. In that sense, he was satirized even more for an extremely hollow triumph. *Democratic Press* (Philadelphia) in Cleaveland [Ohio] *Herald*, 10 June, 1825; *Freeman's Journal* (New York City) in New-York *Mirror and Ladies' Literary Gazette*, 20 May, 1826; Philadelphia *Gazette and Advertiser* in *Adams Sentinel* (Gettysburg, Pa.), 24 May, 1826; New-York *National Advocate*, 24 May, 1826; *Massachusetts Spy* (Worcester), 16 Aug., 1826; New York *Courier* in *Evening Gazette* (Boston), 19 Aug., 1826.

77 New York *Statesman* in Utica *Sentinel and Gazette* (sw), 15 Aug., 1826; *Massachusetts Spy* (Worcester), 16 Aug., 1826; *Manufacturers and Farmers Journal and Providence* [*R.I.*] *and Pawtucket Advertiser*, 28 Aug., 1826; *Columbian Centinel* (Boston), 30 Aug., 1826; *Star and North-Carolina State Gazette* (Raleigh), 3 Nov., 1826.

78 *Narrative of the Life of the Celebrated John Pluck, Colonel of the Eighty-Fourth Regiment, Penn[sylvani]a. Militia, Accompanied by a Full-Length Portrait; (in his military costume) Interspersed with Anecdotes, illustrative of his Great Military Talent; and Treating Of his career in Çivil Life, previous to his elevation to the dignified station, which he now fills with such universal éclat and self-satisfaction, As Dictated by Himself* (Philadelphia, 1826), pp. 5-16. Although the demagoguery of Pluck was never actively polished by this pamphlet, which obviously could not approach circulation figures for the *Tour*, note the similar "himself" ghost here and in n. 6.

79 "Jonathan's visit to the Philadelphia Museum" (poem), *Wilmingtonian* (Del.) in Lancaster [Pa.] *Journal*, 2 April, 1824.

pulsive baboon or kangaroo,[80] Americans on the national anniversary in 1834 were prone to equate their own partisan aspirations with a primitive, media-howling "rocket" from the Tennessee canebrake.[81] But only if excessively personalized speech content were given substance by a Whig ghostwriter would demagogue Crockett enable the party to achieve the full media-exposure desired with the *Tour.*

When studying the personified partisan clash below, the reader must evaluate Crockett's ghosted Hermitage text as the personified media-position it indeed is. Contrary to first impressions, both the Cincinnati and Louisville inserts may be as much calculated media-positions as imperfect oral transcripts of what orator Crockett actually said.

80 *Dly Pennsylvanian*, 3 May, 1834; Nashua *Gazette and Hillsborough County Advertiser* cited in *New-Hampshire Statesman* (Concord), 17 May, 1834; Baltimore *Republican* in *New-Hampshire Gazette* (Portsmouth), 20 May, 1834.

81 "Davy Crockett" (poem), *West Tennessean* (Paris) in *Free Press* (Tarborough, N.C.), 18 Jan., 1828, the rocket verse, which concludes the poem, reading—"And when he gets to Congress hall, He'll burst out like a *rocket*; He'll make you stare and know he's there, Huzza, my immortal Crockett!"; "Anecdote of a Monkey," *Northampton Whig and Farmers' and Mechanics' Journal* (Easton, Pa.), 12 May, 1829; Western District, "Undated advertisement extraordinary, alluding to Crockett partisanly labeling congressman John C. Wright of Ohio as 'a monkey with spectacles on,' " Jackson [Tenn.] *Statesman* in *Morning Courier and New-York Enquirer for the Country*, 17 June, 1831; *Crockett Life* (Cincinnati—containing the W.D. monkey allusion just cited, except that Wright's name not specified, a duel rather than defeat or fleeing the probable action, and no mention of spectacles made) excerpted in *Traveller, Family Journal, Spirit of the Times, and Life in New-York* (NY City), 29 June, 1833; Mary Howitt, "The Monkey" (poem), Cincinnati *Mirror and Western Gazette of Literature and Science*, 6 June, 1835; "Monkey Orators," *Merry's Museum*, 6 (Sept. 1843), 24; "The Preaching Monkey," *Home Gazette* (NY City or San Francisco?) in *Flag of our Union* (Boston), 26 Aug., 1854.

Address delivered by David Crockett at the Hermitage Inn on Passyunk Road in Philadelphia, July 4, 1834, touched up by Crockett in collaboration with a ghostwriter, and included in An Account of Col[onel]. Crockett's Tour to the North and Down East *issued by Carey and Hart during 1835. In the following framework, the Hermitage text is compared with contemporaneous passages from two other Crockett speeches, one delivered at Cincinnati (***C***) on July 12 and another in Louisville (***L***) five days later. And, providing suitable contrast to such a Whig line, a speech attributed to Crockett by the Washington correspondent of the New York* Standard, *and "reported in anticipation" on January 11 so as to cast Crockett as a backwoods demagogue, a buffoon who "has the same right to play his antics as the congressional tragedy hero has to mount his high horse, and talk grandiloquently and pathetically about the ruin of the country." Editor Henry Hone of the* Standard *made this observation in the issue dated January 15, the day after publication of his correspondent's fictive piece on the "Deposite Question." The* Standard *text divides into three segments, labeled* SA, B, and C. *And reporter E. P. Cranch transcribed Crockett's Cincinnati remarks for the July 15 issue of the* Democratic Intelligencer and Commercial Advertiser, *while the Louisville "verbatim" paragraph appeared in the July 19* Journal *as part of a reporter's synopsis.*

1 Fellow citizens of Philadelphia, I am at a loss for language, suitably to express my thanks for the sentiments contained in the Toast which you just drunk. They demand a reply from me, and I sincerely regret my inability, adequately to discharge my duty.

The times, however, call for everyone to speak out and give his opinions of the true state of the country. "Circumstances alters cases!" I would have once thought it degrading to a gentleman to go into another's District, and make a political speech. But on the celebration of this day, in such times as these, it becomes every public man to let his sentiments be known—to speak *to* the people, *at* the people, and *for* the people, and *not for* ourselves!

C But, gentlemen, time and circumstances bring things to pass, and make it necessary for me to do things which would be degrading to them [another's constituents] at other times and under other circumstances. Time has been when I would have considered it degrading to go into another man's District, and address his constituents upon politics. But I consider the time has come when every public servant is indebted to his country—to speak out and sound the alarm and let the country know the situation it is in!

And therefore I'll "go ahead." You gentlemen have just heard read that glorious article, the Declaration of Independence. What caused that Declaration to be made? It was from such times and circumstances as the present.

2 In 1776, King George brought oppression upon the American Colonies, to such an extent that they could no longer bear it. The citizens of this country

laid their petitions at the foot of His Majesty's throne, and they were treated with silent contempt. He went on with his oppressions until loyalty was exhausted, and the best patriots that ever lived assembled in yonder Statehouse where they pledged, to one another and to the world, *their* lives, *their* fortunes, and *their* sacred honor that we should be free. Free from what? Why, free from despotism, and from British tyranny, and free from the Government of One Man!

C We had our George [the] Third. He had his reign, and what was it? He brought distress on this country and this colony. They had laid their petitions before him, they had humbled themselves at the foot of the throne. And what respect did they get? None! They and their petitions were treated with contempt. He saw our fathers take up the sword and pledge *their* lives, *their* fortunes, and *their* sacred honor that they would be rid of the Government of One Man! They declared war, they swore they would be free, and they *were* free! They and their children for fifty-eight years have been free.

3 Well, sirs, what was the consequence? War ensued, and thousands of our noble ancestors fell before the British arms, fighting [to] their death to obtain a government of Constitution and laws. The horrors of war did not make them stop 'til they obtained their object. We gained it and have lived more than fifty years, the happiest people under the sun. Look back only a few months since, and you saw this country blessed with the best circulating medium in the world. You saw our commercial men busily engaged in carrying our produce to the ends of the Earth. The seas were spotted with our ships all making a reasonable profit. Your manufactories were engaged busily employing everyone that wanted to work. And they also were once more about to flourish and extend their benefits to the whole country. Where now is your circulating medium? It is stamped with the curse of Executive folly! Your ships are calling home to be chained and rot at your wharves! And your manufactories are paralyzed and many of them breaking up! And what is all this for? Just to gratify the ambition of One Man, that he may wreak his vengeance upon the United States Bank because it refused to lend its aid in upholding his corrupt party! I consider, gentlemen, that in 1834 the same page has opened in our political history that did in 1776.

SB I argee in this way.—The Bank of the United States is the Treasury, and the constertution ses no money shall be drawn out of the Treasury but accordin to law; and it is as plain as a streak o' lightnin, as I said before, that the President, and the Secretary, and Mister **Kindle**,[1] and nobody else, can't draw a dollar out of the Bank if we don't make the law. They needn't tell me there wasn't any bank when the constertution was made; and that there wasn't any bank [as of] the last war; and that there wasn't any law tellin where the money should be kept afore 1816; and that there aint any law now telling what shall be the Treasury. They needn't tell me, that old Washington, and old Jefferson, and all them [who] are revolutioners, could take the money as old Jackson has did and put it jest where they pleased. It only shows they didn't understan the constertution, Mister Speaker. "Every gineration grows wiser and wiser," my grandmother use[d] to say, and I can tell, Mister Speaker, when this gineration got a leetle wiser than any one afore. You know, some old Congress about the year 1749 made a law to establish the Treasury Department, which telled about a Secretary, a Controller, a Register, a Treasurer, an **Odditor**,[1] and so forth. This was all nonsense, becorse, there wer[e]n't any Treasury then. The year arter the war, you know, the Treasury was created. But it's mighty queer that not one on' [th]em in that Congress, Mister Clay or Mister Calhoun, desperate l[e]arned and wise as they're got since, understood it [at] all. They thought and so did everybody that it was only a Bank they were creatin, when it was the Treasury. I'll tell you **to a primin'**[2] when the truth was first found out. The money was put in the Treasury (which everybody thought was a Bank), and the Treasurer, as they call him, drawed checks as if it had bin on a bank, and Mister Biddle paid 'em. But he or't not [to], becorse they didn't tell us as how the money was called for accordin to law. But when old Jackson comed in, he turned out the old Treasurer and put in a new one; and becorse he was afear[e]d his new Treasurer would take all the money out of the Bank with his checks, he made him send the warrants to the Bank and tell Mister Biddle not to pay any more of the Treasurer's checks. As soon as Mister Biddle see'd one of the warrants come to the Bank, says he, "*Oh ho,* I see how it is—*the Bank is the Treasury.*" So in anno dumino 1829, Mister Biddle got to be a *leetle* wiser than anybody ever was afore! The Senate, I reckon, has got to be about as wise as Mister Biddle, and we are gittin wise mighty fast in this [h]ere House. Mister Speaker, they say Mister Biddle lends the public money out of the Treasury to the Brokers, and Marchants, and Printers, and Members of Congress, and other big varmints, and that this aint accordin to the constertution. I say he has a right to lend every dollar of the money if he chuses. The constertution don't say no money shall be *lent* out of the Treasury but accordin to law, but that it shall not be *drawed out.* Mister Speaker—the pea vine is most trimendiously thick about these parts, and I don't think I'll foller that-are[there] trail any furder. My fren from Pheladelphy (Horace Binney) can tell how it is. Mister Speaker, I say old Jackson had no right to remove Mister Duane because he was *the Secretary of the Bank,* the Bank bein the Treasury; nor to appoint Mister Taney, because the Bank didn't want any such Secretary. But there's no use talkin about it. I motion, Mister Speaker, that all the laws about the Treasury but the law makin the Bank ar[e] unconstertutional, there bein no Treasury but the Bank, and or't to be repealed. Then there'll be no Secretary for old Jackson to turn out, and

1 Characterization of Fourth Auditor Amos Kendall as a distinctive bureaucrat with a disproportionate ("odd") influence ("kindle") over Jackson.

2 Vernacular meaning "for certain." Crockett's marksmanship and credibility both an issue.

Mister Biddle, I'll bet fifty **bearkins**,[3] will not draw the money out but accordin to law, only he will lend it to us and our frens when we want it. Mister Speaker, I have got a *leetle* wiser than Mister Biddle, and I'll tell ye how it is. I say the Treasury can't be put down, because the constertution ses no money shall be drawn from the Treasury and so forth. If the Treasury be put down there'll be no Treasury to draw money from, and [then] what is your constertution good for? It's all nonsense to talk about recharterin the Bank, because it is the Treasury and don't need recharterin any more than Congress needs recharterin. It will last as long as the constertution without any patchin of ours!

4 We have seen petitions signed by hundreds of thousands laid before your Congress, praying for relief and warning them of the danger. What has become of them? They were conveyed away to a committee selected by our hireling Speaker, with his written promise in his pocket to pay him for his servility. He came there for the purpose of raising committees, all in favor of the views of the "Greatest and Best," and he filled expectation. He has got his reward according to his works. He stuck by the pocket-flaps! You are never again to hear from your petitions. And still, this is what they call the days of Democracy. Good God, deliver me from such democracy!

C Gentlemen, this old, superannuated *government* (he calls himself The Government) sanctions the meanest action of his hirelings. There was his Speaker with his pay in his pocket, who packed his committees. Gentlemen, he was looking across the Atlantic. They wanted to pass a vote of thanks for his services, and your humble servant wanted to know what the country had to thank him for. They wanted me to glorify him, but they had too honest a cynic among them to take glory for granted! The Plenipotentiary-elect was looking across the Atlantic. He couldn't see his own country. He wanted to please the Kitchen Cabinet and the "Greatest and Best."

5 Sirs, I consider that Andrew Jackson has gone further than ever King George did. He has even closed the door of the Palace against the bearers of your petitions, and refused them entrance into His Majesty's presence.

C We see ourselves arrived at a crisis when One Man can hold the sword in this hand, and the power in that, and bid defiance to Congress and to the nation. That man is Andrew the First, King of this country. A King we couldn't think so hard of across the Atlantic. But to have a King in our own country putting up his will against the whole country, and declaring that unless two thirds of Congress will vote for a measure he will veto it, is worse than George [the] Third or any other King of England would dare to do. My friends, it would cost him not only his

---

3 "Bearskins" the word intended here. Would Crockett wager even family members, and to the point of "skinning" or ruin or death at that, in order to curry favor with Whig managers?

cap, but his *head* with it. But with Andrew the First it is *my* will, *my* Secretaries, *my* Congress, *my* Government, *My People*! This is the "Great Roman Patriot!" This is the "Hero of Two Wars," this is the "Greatest and Best" of mankind—the "*Great* Tennessee Farmer!"

And what is more degrading than all is to see a perfect hireling, a slave to party, supporting kingly principles in sight of the house where that glorious article was penned. This looks to me entirely out of the question. Have the citizens of this patriotic city, yea, the place where the first sentence of that paper was heard, have they forgotten the blood and treasure that our forefathers sacrificed to redeem them from the Government of One Man? I cannot and *will not* believe it possible that the people of the First District of the great state of Pennsylvania can be imposed on, any longer, by a slave to party upholding and supporting the most tyrannical measures! Yea, gentlemen, [I mean some]one who will sell himself and bow down to Andrew Jackson for the sake of an office, and of whom I heard it said in the House, when thirty votes were given him for a certain office, "That reminds me of the thirty pieces of silver." Will you permit yourselves [any] longer to be imposed upon? Gentlemen, you may think I am meddling with the election of your Representative, and this is true. And if you knew that, gentlemen, as well as I do, you would never blame me. However, as to that I take the responsibility. For I am determined to do my duty to my country, let the consequences be as they may.

6 I do believe the country is ignorant of its true situation. Andrew Jackson has, this day, every dollar of the Treasury under his control. And with a set of minions or slaves around him to sustain him in an open violation of the laws and Constitution of the country, what is to enlighten the people? Hireling presses all over the country, bought up by post offices and post-office contracts and extras and other fat offices, are ready to hand out to the people such stuff as is favorable to their party only, and reject the truth.

C But the people are ignorant; they will still "Huzza for Jackson." They have been used to it so long. If you go into the country and tell the people of these things—abuses, extravagances, usurpations and all—and prove every word you say, "Oh," say they, "Jackson has been in office a long time, he must be doing what's right." But I will put the documents into every hole and corner of the country! I will show the people how Andrew Jackson is surrounded by a set of the most cursed scoundrels that ever moved. And the old man suffers himself to be a perfect tool in their hands to deceive and ruin the country, and to destroy its peace and harmony! But I for one love my country. I'll speak my mind. I'll proclaim the truth, and the people shall know what I've seen and heard!

L Gentlemen, I am a plain blunt man, and I see everything with my own eyes. I do not look through any man's spectacles. But General Jackson does, and that political Judas, Martin Van Buren, has had the glasses so exquisitely engraved that the "Greatest and Best" sees nothing but *glory*, when the old dotard thinks he is looking through the *clear* glass! Gentlemen, I have discovered this since my residence in Washington, that Andrew Jackson, or his wire-workers (it is all one), care nothing for law nor the Constitution. [Just] so their ends are attained, it may go to the devil for them! The feeling became so strong, during the last session of Congress, that I could not help uttering that it was useless to sit there for the purpose of making laws for Jackson to trample on. He had, contrary to law, taken the money from the strongbox and placed it where the light-fingered gentry, who hang upon his skirts like the flies on the fox in the fable, goading the old fellow to death, may handle the cash! What was the use to make laws for appropriations? They had the cash and could appropriate it. And they would take very good care to appropriate a goodly part to their own purposes.

C Why, in my District we never used to ask for more than a little horse Mail. A pocket handkerchief would have carried all we wanted. But when Davy Crockett was beat and a Jackson man came in, we had a four-horse Stage stretching all over the country. "Oh, what a fine President is Jackson,"said they. "Oh," says I, "you poor devils, you will have to pay for it!" Well, so after a while they have a Coach from Reynoldsburgh to Paris, from Paris to Dresden, and thence straight to Mills Point. But they left out Troy, and the people of Obion County began to talk about leaving out [Jackson candidate] Fitz[gerald]. Mr. Barry immediately ordered his contractors to run anywhere to git Fitz[gerald] in. So he run the Coach fifteen miles out of the way to Troy 'til the election was over, and then withdrew every Stage from the District, except one running straight thro[ugh]. Troy had not even a horse Mail, tho[ugh] a county town, and they had to write to me at Washington. And I had to gog the Postmaster General's elbow and make him give them a Mail!

SC My fren from Pheladelphy (Horace Binney) needn't lead us [on] a long hunt around the heads of the Missouri, and Yaller Stone, and Arkansaw; for I see that's the campin ground we'll all cum to at last—that is, us frens. Old Jackson needn't think he can do everything. I telled my constituents I was for him; but I was only throwin a club to t[he] 'other side of the tree to make the squirrel hop round so I could get a good **crack**[4] at him. I'm a match for old Jackson and them too, if they don't mind. Mister Speaker, you've heard of the **Big Mammoth** who knocked off the **thunder** with his head when all the rest were shot by **Old Manito** at the **Big Bone Lick**.[5] He, ye know, got hurt at last, jumpt

4 "Crack" a shot dependent on a combustible mixture or "smart chance" of black powder.

5 Big Mammoth here not a mastodon elephant, but a mammoth boar which subsists on wood and travels only by day, lounging upright against rocks or tree trunks at night. The Sioux regarded Big Mammoth as an evil spirit or "Match Matchi Manitou," and Old Manito presumably is a type of father figure or Great Spirit. Big Bone Lick was an actual site in Kentucky where fossilized mastodon bones were unearthed during the 1820's and 1830's. And "thunder" probably refers to earthquakes, which the Sioux believed periodically killed and/or displaced whatever mammoth boars still survived extinction.

over the Ohio and streaked it beyond the big Lakes at sich a rate that lightnin couldn't catch him.—*He's dead, I killed him.*—When my constituents turned me out of Congress beca[u]se I woul[d]n't vote to dower the widder Old Jackson **wanted to marry**,[6] I thought I'd go and see if I cou[ld]n't find this big varmint. So I took my rifle and tomahawk and knife, with a **smart chance**[4] of powder and lead, and off I starts. About a million of miles beyond Lake Superior as well as I can judge (my Pheladelphy fren knows **Jografy**[7] and can tell whereabouts), I see'd one evenin a hill ahead without any brush on'[i]t, and pretty soon I see'd the settin sun shine under it like, and then I see'd it move. "Ar[e] ye there, my Old Feller?" ses I. His teeth was bad and he was pullin up the Oak Trees and swollerin them, roots and all, for his supper. I *Know*[e]d it was no use to shoot at him. So I cut a pole fifty yards long and tied my Knife to the end on[i]t. While he was asleep that night, I got right afore him and staid there 'til it was sunrise when he got up. I then stept up and as soon as he see'd me he shut his eyes, and ses I with a voice that made his ears flop, "You ugly old varmint, if you don't stand still I'll swaller ye in a minute."—So he stood as still as a rock 'til I jest walked up and cut his **jigular**[7] with my Knife. **When**[8] I slung him acrosst my shoulder and flung him into Lake Superior, where you may see his bones now if you'll only look 'til you find 'em. Mister Speaker, the chaps here looks as if they didn't believe me! It's amazin strange; for they believe much bigger stories when the Lawyers tell 'em. Aint it so Mister Binney? But if they won't believe this, I shan't make 'em believe the Bank's the Treasury, and so my hunt's out.

7 Look back to the days when Andrew Jackson was aspiring to the place which he now fills, and you saw the whole continent convulsed with the hue and cry that Adams (and Clay) was indulging in a system of extravagance that would speedily bankrupt the nation.

C Gentlemen, you have heard a great hue and cry [raised] against Clay and Adams for extravagance. They were wasting the public treasure, they were squandering the people's money.

They were hurled from office without ceremony, and the reformers and retrenchment-gentry rode into their seats. And the dust they had kicked up was so great the people's eyes were blinded! But, gentlemen, that dust has blown off.

And what is our situation [now] compared with the Administration of Adams and Clay? During that time, the expenditures ranged from ten to thir-

---

6 Wanted to marry off to Secretary of War John Henry Eaton, referring to Peg O'Neale whose first husband, purser John Timberlake, widowed her by committing suicide aboard ship. Also part of the context here is the Whig claim that Jackson was on intimate terms with Rachel Donelson, the President's only wife, before she separated from Lewis Roberts/Robards in Mercer County, Kentucky.

7 "Jografy" and "jigular" connote two related meanings. Not only do earthquakes jiggle and unsettle the mammoth boar, but narrator Crockett's perspective may be more than slightly jogged in favor of friend Binney. And "jigular" of course is synonymous with the bloody plight of any barnyard chanticleer after decapitation. "Geography" and "jugular" the words intended.

8 Is "when" any less credible and decisive than "then?"

teen millions of dollars. And what is it now under these reforming and retrenchment gentlemen? It is from eighteen to twenty millions! Will you take this for retrenchment? You may, I *will not*! Nor can I be made to believe that the people will think so when they come to understand it.

C What has he[Jackson] done? Adams spent from ten to thirteen millions. But Captain Jackson spent from eighteen to twenty-two millions per annum! What think you of old Roman retrenchment? It is as true as the Lord's Gospel. He has actually increased your expenses for you to *eighteen or twenty-two* millions!

No, gentlemen, it is like what the devil said when he was shearing the hog, "Great cry and little wool."

8 I was one that was deceived, among many others, and was made to believe that Adams (and Clay) was two of the greatest scoundrels on the face of the Earth. I joined the band and raised the war whoop against them. And finally we succeeded in putting them down, thus supposing we were serving the Lord (and General Jackson). But I found by personal acquaintance of those gentlemen that they had been grossly misrepresented, and [I] saw it was a political speculation—a fuss kicked up just to promote a certain set of men's own interests. I came into Congress in 1827 as honestly the friend of Andrew Jackson as any man in the world. But when I found that his whole object was to serve party and wreak his vengeance upon those who had voted against him, my bristles begun to get up. I inquired of myself if this was the *true* republican principle. When I saw honorable members creeping round the House with papers to recommend some man to office, and that his qualifications were overlooked and his Jacksonism wrote in capitals, when I saw them, also, like jackals in the night, prowling after those poor fellows in office who dared to think that we were *wrong* (and they were right), and who done their duty to their country faithfully, I said to myself: "God never made man upright to act so. I can't go it, there's no principle in this thing!" I stopped and looked and inquired the straight road. I found I was off the path, turned round, went home, and took a fresh trace. I had to pay for all this dearly. Every press denounced me as bought over [to the Whig side]. No matter! My bear-hunting knees were too stiff to bend to power. They hit me uncommon hard at home, but I bore it and fought shy 'til I got them out of wind, and then brought them to a parley.

9 You all know they turned me out of Congress, and often when in the woods with two companions that will never give a fellow up in the tryingest times, a *just* God and a *clear* conscience, I laid down my gun, called in the pups, and thought over everything. One evening, late, while I was sitting so, my oldest of the pack put his paw on my knee and seemed whining for me to go. "Well," said I to him, "honest old Tiger, you never cried on a false trail. Neither will your master. You always hold like death; when you take, you grip. So will I. You never forsook your master, though I have used you hard sometimes. So, by the help of God, I will not forsake my old constituents. And if I can only succeed in making them know one half of what I have seen of men and things at

Washington, they'll go right!" I sprung to my feet, begun a new campaign, and here I am again representing the same honest boys who go *for keep* when the country's stakes are up! I had hard work. But I stood up to the rack, fodder or *no fodder*. I told them I was fighting for my own liberty to vote as I pleased, and fighting for them also to do as they pleased. I only asked them to support principles, *not* men. And so they did and *will do* it again.

SA Mister Speaker, "I go the whole hog." I say the Bank is the [T]reasury, and I'll make it as plain as a streak of lightnin on a black cloud. Mister Speaker—I'll tell you a story. My dogs and I went out huntin bears one mornin. We thundered along through the woods as if all Niagara was comin, 'til all at once my dogs stopped under a smashing big sugar tree most as big as the Rotundo, only a mile higher. Four of my nabors comed up with their rifles jest as I did, and we peered away up into the clouds among the limbs and leaves to see what's there. At last I spied the feller through the leaves a mile and a half high, a little black speck, sorter like a grain o' powder in my *white* dog's hair. Ses I, "My sweety, see how I'll fetch you down in less **than**[9] no time." So I drawed up and cracked away. What du [you] think, Mister Speaker? I'll be shot if there didn't come tumbling down a damned **insingnifisant.**[10] black, leetle damned *hedgehog*! I felt mighty sheepish like, and I see'd my dogs' ears and tails drop down like frozed corn leaves in a sunshiny mornin. But my nabors beginned to laff, and that made me mad. "Ye damned rascals," ses I, "d[u]'ye say that aint *a bear*?" "I'll be infernally damned," ses I, "if it isn't a bear; and if anybody ses it aint, I'll knock him into a greese spot in a minit less **then**[9] no time!" For, ye see, I was as mad as a **painter**[11] with his leg broke. So they sorter stuck their grins in the fur eends of their mouths and sneaked away like; but nobody ever said it wasn't a bear arter that. Mister Speaker, there's nothin like *rammin down* argument with *force*; and I tel[le]d Mister Biddle so when I see'd him in Pheladelphy. I begin to like the big lawyers amazin [well]. They're jest like us backwoodsmen. They mind the law jest as long as they please an[d] no longer. Only we cus[s] the law, out and out, when we don't mean to mind it and there's an end on'[i]t; but they *talk it away* in speeches as long as the Missouri. I don't like that—it is too **teagious.**[12] They go away up and around the head of every branch, and creek, and river they come to that seems to be in a bit of [a] flurry; but we jump right in and ar[e] over in no time. But we all come to the same camp at last. My Philadelphy fren (Horace Binney) went up one side of the Creek and come down t[he] 'other, arter bein gone two or three days, and jumpt

9 Does inserting "then" instead of "than" here detract from Crockett's credibility as narrator?

10 "Insingnifisant" a portmanteau amalgam of non-singing and non-significant.

11 Vernacular for panther, but does Crockett's temper interfere even with his stance as "painter" or narrator?

12 Can narrator Crockett sincerely play the eccentric who exclaims "tea" and "Gee!" to demagoguery? "Tedious" the word intended here.

acrosst every branch that comed in his way, without **wettin**[13] his feet; but I was tired **watin**[13] for him!

10 I have the consolation to believe I did my duty before God and my country, which I consider a rich reward, better than gold or silver can procure. I am now about to close. And from the manner in which I have said all, you will be satisfied that an apology was due from me. Nothing could have prompted me to speak as I have done but a pure sense of public duty. Every man ought to sound the alarm and wake up the people to see their danger. This day is a day on which every patriot ought to rejoice, and [it] ought never to be forgotten! Yet I fear that the spirit of patriotism, which on this day first kindled in the bosoms of our illustrious fathers, is fast extinguishing by the party that rules the destinies of this nation. God grant it may revive.

13 "Waiting" obviously intended here, but how might "wading" coupled with "waitin" lessen Crockett's credibility?

Address delivered by Asher Robbins at the Hermitage Inn, July 4, 1834, text printed in the Philadelphia Inquirer and Daily Courier *of the eighteenth, and the first four paragraphs reprinted in the Boston* Daily Atlas *for the twenty-second. Robbins' treatment of the topic of national glory in this Hermitage text is but a precursor to a much fuller analysis of the "glory of a national literature," made by him before the Phi Beta Kappa Society at Brown University on September 3, approximately two months after his Philadelphia appearance. Indeed, there is very little doubt that Robbins consistently values the Athenian oratory of Isocrates and Demosthenes, placing their culture on a pedestal literally as high as his "towering and heaven-kissing" simile. Yet, apart from the partisanship which enters into the Hermitage address, Robbins felt American oratory dim and puerile in comparison with that of Athens. And he told his Brown listeners that individual students had to rely upon their own "natural genius" while educational institutions brought their oratory courses closer to the Athenian model.*

1 Fellow citizens, we still hold our national independence, so gloriously acquired and so gloriously maintained. Our national banner, wherever it floats in the breeze—in whatever sea, on whatever coast, in the sight of whatever foreign nation, whether civilized or barbarian—it receives the homage of their distinguished respect! Nor does the ocean bear on her bosom nor fan with her breezes a prouder ornament, nor wear one with more pride than the star-spangled banner of the United States! Though our nation as a nation has achieved for herself this pride of place on the list, and in the eyes of independent nations, yet when we look at home and within our own borders and ask where are those liberties whose spirit won that independence, and that glorious rank among nations, we are compelled to say that they are in the grasp of the iron hand of despotism. Yes, the man we have made our President has made himself our despot, and the Constitution now lies a heap of ruins at his feet.

2 If those liberties are not wrested from his grasp (nor to be wrested), let us never celebrate another anniversary of our Declaration of Independence. For what signifies our independence as a nation if as a people we are not free? If we are to live in servitude, what matters it whether that servitude be national or colonial? If we are to bear the burthen of tyranny, what matters it where the seat of that tyranny is—whether here at home or abroad in Great Britain? If we are to have a tyrant, what matters it whether that tyrant be a George the Third or Andrew the First? Bondage is bondage wherever the locality of the despot is; indeed, the more remote, the better for one I should like it, or rather the less I should dislike it.

3 From the beginning of his dynasty, our despot has gone on from one act of usurpation to another and another, 'til by his seizure of the control of the public treasure he has consummated his despotism over the liberties of this country. By that one and the same act, he gave the finishing stroke to those liberties and destroyed the prosperity of the country in all its branches. Some

have said, by way of some excuse for him, that he did not intend this consequence to that prosperity—that this consequence was unforeseen and unexpected by him. For one, I am not slow to give him credit for ignorance in this case, nor in any case! I well know how large a credit for that article is due to him in all cases; for I have had frequent occasion to observe how extremely limited his intelligence is, and that his comprehension is on a still smaller scale. Yet if his ignorance did not foresee the consequences to arise from his lawless and reckless act of seizing upon the control of the public treasure—yet when they had arisen and were before his eyes in the distress of his country, he could not be so blind as not to see them! Yet how has he regarded them? Why, he has regarded them with a cool contempt covered by an affected incredulity as to their existence; manifesting that if he was ignorant of, he was also perfectly reckless of those consequences.

4 It is strange that this man is not better understood than he seems to be. He is a tyrant in grain if ever Nature made a tyrant. He is carried to his arbitrary acts by the natural temper of his mind, which is to the last degree arbitrary; and it is as inflexible as it is arbitrary. As to those relentings of Nature at the unexpected and unintended evils resulting from a proposed course of action, they are feelings wholly unknown to his nature, and they interpose no impediment whatever to his course. None! When the way to his object lies through the Constitution, the Constitution has not the strength of a cobweb to restrain him from breaking through it. Nay, if the way to his object lay through the vitals of his country, and that country was on her knees to him, in tears, imploring for life itself—spurning her prayer he would march direct to his object over the bleeding and mangled corpse of his country! Persuade the ravenous tiger to give over the pursuit of his prey, persuade the ferocious tornado to stay his course and spare his desolation, but never think of moving Andrew Jackson from his purpose—however atrocious that may be, or however wide-wasting and desolating in its consequences! For "The Furies that relentless breast have steeled,/ Cursed with a heart, unknowing how to yield." Such is the man from whose grasp the people have to wrest their liberties. Yes, they have their liberties again to conquer, not on the field of battle as heretofore (as I would hope, though it may come to that extremity), but on the election field.

5 It seems incongruous with the nature of this festive occasion to dwell upon our painful situation as a nation, and upon the feelings which that situation invokes. And I would fain flatter myself that it is unnecessary at least, unnecessary to confine ourselves to those topics. For the people everywhere seem to be awake to that situation, and alive to the call it makes upon their patriotism to rally to the rescue of their liberties. I have no doubt they stand ready, and are waiting only for the time and the signal of battle to win the battle—to hurl from power the usurpers of power, to replace in competent and faithful hands the affairs of the nation, and to recommit our country to that stream of prosperity which was rapidly bearing her onward to her high and glorious destinies! It would seem then not uncongenial with this festive occasion, even at this time,

forgetting for a moment the present if we can, to indulge a little in anticipations of the future.

6 Let us then suppose the dark clouds which now obscure our sun to be dispersed. That the vessel of state is again under prosperous way before wind and tide, under the direction of a skillful and trustworthy commander. What then would be our appropriate theme on this occasion? Especially here in the city of Philadelphia founded by her own immortal Penn, that great apostle of peace whose simple ethics were so admirable for their effect on the economy of human life, and the health and happiness of his infant colony. The city too of the immortal Franklin, the votary equally of science and freedom, of whom it was said he wrested from the lightning its bolt, and from the tyrant his sceptre. Of whom it may be said that whenever and wherever science shall boast of her children, she will never fail to point to her Franklin with an "Ecce meum filium." And that at the same time freedom will say with the same designation, "Et meum." A city too whose foundations for science, for literature and the arts, are so ample and their endowments so munificent and magnificent, and whose citizens have made and are making such advances therein, that that theme should be the means of embellishing the fame of our country! For we are compelled to confess that the great desideratum of our country is the glory of literature and the fine arts. The glory of arms we have, the glory of civil institutions we have, the glory of science and the useful arts we have, but the glory of literature and the fine arts we have not! That glory not only immortal in itself, but by which and by which alone every other species is rendered immortal. For suppose the literature of Greece and of Rome had never been, what should we know of the ancient world? It would have been to us a blank; time like the universal deluge would have obliterated to us every trace of that world, as that deluge has done of the antediluvian. Then "Hoe tibi erunt artes, Romane."

7 The glory of arms is not to be coveted. But if it were, its pursuit at some hereafter is to be interdicted to our country by her position and her growing grandeur. Our nation was born with the parts and the proportions of a giant; and when these parts and proportions shall be fully developed she will be the most gigantic of nations! We can have no occasion for foreign conquest, and our gigantic power will overawe the world and guard our peace against all possible fears of invasion! Then our future ultimate condition is to be a state of peace, and our pursuits the arts of peace. We will look to Philadelphia for our lead in that pursuit, and particularly in the pursuit of the glory attendant on literature and the fine arts. For she has the means, if she have the will (and I have no doubt she has the will), to become another Athens: the Athens of the modern and the Western world. Of Athens, that wonderful city!

She appears to me like a towering monument, standing on the waste of time to mark the astonishing heights to which the human faculties may be carried.

Brown University version of same sentence:

See, too, in the midst of that constellation of glories, the city of Athens! standing, as it were, on the waste of time, like a towering and heaven-kissing monument, to mark the sublime heights to which the human faculties may be carried;—those peerless heights to which none before, none since, have ascended.

Let your city then, Oh ye Philadelphians, take the glory of Athens as the gage and measure of your emulous and aspiring ambition.

Chapter 7

Enoch Mack's Fourth of July Oration, 1838

Who were the more fanatical abolitionist railers expounding "immediate" emancipation for blacks during the late 1830's? And what antislavery tenets, if any sound strategy in fact prompted such emotive tirades at all, were their discourses on a typical national anniversary designed to communicate?

Consider Enoch Mack, unknown for the most part as a Freewill-Baptist minister in Dover, New Hampshire—a fanatical case in point. Mack, for all of his neglect at the hands of rationally-biased historians, had attained some small prominence when attending the 1833 Philadelphia antislavery convention as a county-level manager from Wilkes-Barre, Pennsylvania.[1] And, once moved to Dover in 1835,[2] he actively had participated in supervising the rather modest scope of Freewill-Baptist foreign missionary work. Serving his denomination both as corresponding secretary and Board agent for its Foreign Missionary Society, administrative posts which, if he had not already done so, literally obligated him to ascertain the viability of abolitionist thinking in Britain, especially policy toward the British West Indies, compared with operations domestically in America.[3]

---

1 *Proceedings of the Anti-Slavery Convention, Assembled at Philadelphia, December 4, 5, and 6, 1833* (New York: Dorr and Butterfield, 1833), pp. 4 and 10.

2 Rev. G. A. Burgess and Rev. J. T. Ward, *Free Baptist Cyclopaedia* (Chicago, Ill.: Free Baptist Cyclopaedia Company, 1889), p. 352.

3 "Minutes of Ninth General Conference, Greenville, Rhode Island, Oct. 4-10, 1837," in *Minutes of the General Conference of the Freewill Baptist Connection* (Dover: Freewill Baptist Printing Establishment, 1859), p. 145; "Report of Foreign Mission Society meeting at Lewiston, Maine, on 31 Aug.," *Morning Star* (Dover), 3 Oct., 1838. Somewhat contrary to the statement by Burgess and Ward that Mack resigned as pastor to devote full time to these posts, the available evidence does not support any implied total disassociation from local parish business. At least not thru the Fourth in 1838. And Burgess and Ward only specify a resignation "subsequent" to Mack's 1835 ordination, not any precise year. The lack of a precise year, of course, contributing to the apparently erroneous implication in their biographical sketch on Mack. Burgess-Ward source in n. 2 above.

Mack was prone to equate the ongoing British emancipation experience with evangelical Christianity,[4] a salvation process he preferred to America's non-militant and unrealistic apathy, thinking nationalistically in terms of a predatory flag whose repressive symbolism divinely had to be avenged. And his intense language should not mask the harsh antislavery premise: "Oh, our country, shame to thy false boast of liberty. [What] Deepest effrontery to earth and Heaven. Rather, strike the eagle off from thine [own] escutcheon, and paint the vulture—tearing [out] the vitals [and] drinking up the heart's blood of thy enslaved millions. Strike out the sky-blue lines, and draw [in] shades of deepest darkness in their place. Such as that [dark flag], in which [folds] the souls of thine [own] enslaved are wrapped with watchful vigilance. Let thy stripes of red remain, or paint them of a deeper gore. More faithfully to represent that bloody scourge, bathed in helpless man's and in resistless woman's gore. Thus change thy standard. Hold it up before the nations, professing it [as] thine own. And no more shall nations hiss thee, nor Heaven's wrath enkindle against thee, for *hypocrisy* persisted in. For *then* will nations see, and the King of kings will see, in thee, *profession true to character*."[5]

Indeed, the Freewill-Baptist doctrine of egalitarian salvation by "immediate" repentance and conversion,[6] a "harmonious" chain linking God's will with humanity and seldom, if ever, failing to be benevolently "golden" or direct enough,[7] tended to make true believers like Mack prone to anticipate "immediate" agitation in violent events, whether the burning of Pennsylvania Hall in Philadelphia[8] or the print-shop slaying of martyr Elijah P. Lovejoy in Alton, Illinois.[9] Pro-slavery mobocrats, presumably to blame for the spate of violence Mack had weathered when Rev. George Storrs, agent for the state antislavery

---

4 Newbury Vt., 24 May, 1838, *EM* to William Burr, Dover, in *Morning Star* (Dover), 20 June, 1838.

5 Mack, "Corresponding Secretary's report" in *Sixth Annual Report of the Freewill Baptist Foreign Mission Society* (Dover: *Morning Star* Office, 1839), p. 8.

6 Mack, "Agent's account of visit to Berwick/North Berwick, Maine, dated 23 thru 26 March," *Morning Star*, 11 April, 1838. As he preached the evangelical gospel, black Freewill-Baptist pastor Robert Tash, in Mack's eyes, furnished a veritable model for such a salvation process: "The preacher of color sounded . . . the trumpet of *free salvation*, the duty of immediate repentance and faith, the will of God that all sinners should repent *now*,—that the 'Lord's time,' in regard to the sinner's repentance and conversion, is always *now*—and that the sinner is guilty (and more guilty) by every moment's delay in coming to Christ."

7 Mack, "The Golden Chain," *Freewill Baptist Quarterly Magazine*, 2 (June 1840), 134.

8 For a juvenile propaganda version of the "last great mob" terminating antislavery meetings at Pennsylvania Hall, consult *Slave's Friend*, 4 (no. 2/1839), 4-11.

9 Mack, "Hymn eulogizing Lovejoy," *Morning Star*, 6 Dec., 1837. The militant tenor of the final two verses is quite revealing: "Avenging God, though justly o'er Our guilty land thy judgments lower, Thou will not on the guiltless pour That storm in retribution's hour. Repentance grant, and—when the stain Of martyr's blood is washed away, And [has] rent [apart], forever, slav[e]ry's chain,—Bring [forth] freedom's full and golden day."

society, spoke at Dover early in 1836,[10] performed their acts little caring that Mack viewed such malevolent irresponsibility as a portent of God's "immediate" intervention and vengeance. And all the more reason, not so incidentally, for Mack's believing that only an intense brand of advocacy would reflect God's "free" will in the Dover community. Especially when intense advocacy gave an evangelical believer like Mack the opportunity of sensationally equating God's omnipotence with the "immediate" evil to be remedied. Namely, sweeping deliverance of *all* slaves in the South from oppression by hellishly self-righteous masters.

While traveling through eastern Vermont late in June, 1838, for example, Mack obviously relished the task of rationalizing mob violence at Pennsylvania Hall into an intensely realistic oratory asking God's deliverance: "My soul chilled with horror in contemplation of this outrage. My hopes that repentance and favor would soon be found by our guilty nation (hopes which I had so fondly cherished, of late) were blasted. The spirit of slavery seemed more rampant and determined than ever, and scenes of wide desolation and of blood seemed to be approaching. The unrestricted reign of anarchy seemed [to have] begun . . . . But, in the midst of this horrid scene, and these dark bodings, a gleam of hope sprung up—a gleam of hope, even in flames of the fair temple kindled by the dark fiend of slavery himself. Prove a blazing torch which, unto all the world, reveals the hideousness of that monster which has lighted it . . . . That temple, if it had been spared, might have proved a source from whence streams of moral light might have flowed for years to come. But, methinks, that literal flame will prove more effectual. It shines the world around,—and here, in the full illumination, appears revealed the odious monster—revealed so fully, as that light doth make him manifest. A general detestation must rise [up] against him—in every heart not lost to virtue, not dead to patriotism, and true to humanity . . . . God will bring deliverance. And if we have become . . . a nation speaking such great swelling words of vanity, as makes it necessary that we should be humbled in our own sight, and in the eyes of the world, perhaps these works of deep shame and degradation are permitted [to occur] by Him, who holds the destiny of all in his own hands, for [the purpose of] producing that humiliation. Oh, may we soon humble ourselves, [so] that in due time we may be exalted."[11]

Language so declamatorily intense as to be overdone? And never truly "realistic" to a modern reader, not privileged to be steeped in the sentimentally obscure perspective of some bygone era? Unromantic escapism, perhaps, but

10 n.p., 18 Jan., 1836, Storrs to James Horace Kimball, Concord, in *Herald of Freedom* (Concord), 23 Jan., 1836. On the evening of 19 Aug., 1835, mobocrats already had been charged with preventing a speech by Storrs at the Congregational meetinghouse in neighboring Great Falls. Storrs managed to give his speech in Dover, however, the jostling and threat of violence coming only as the meeting dispersed. Great Falls *Journal*, 22 Aug., 1835.

11 Newbury Vt., 24 May, 1838, *EM* to William Burr, Dover, in *Morning Star*, 20 June, 1838.

queries not necessarily true to the mark. The executive committees of local antislavery societies in Dover and Great Falls selected Mack to make separate orations on the Fourth during 1838, because his exuberant rhetoric fit into an expansionist scenario they momentarily found rather worthwhile. As the 1838 national anniversary drew near, abolitionists indeed became quite intent upon cultivating non-timid ministers on a local level who might evoke some semblance of revolutionary fervor from the working masses.[12]

George Thompson might have been the inspirational British-antislavery-agent personified, lecturing six times in Dover and once in Great Falls early in February, 1835, even before pastor Mack arrived from Wilkes-Barre.[13] Yet Mack's participation in county-level antislavery committees (protesting against the Arkansas constitution, or favoring a propaganda depository for Dover),[14] coupled with his perennially optimistic appraisal of British emancipation, ideally suited him for the role of a spontaneous local orator whose fervor, recapturing Thompson's appearances at Dover and Great Falls, would not depend upon some formal agency assignment from Concord, Boston, Philadelphia, or New York City. Spontaneity was a particularly significant factor, since its presence, to any appreciable extent, could enable abolition strategists to develop a republican-oriented hinterland constituency.[15]

Yeoman hill-farmers uncorruptedly close to the soil,[16] or white-slave textile workers, many of them young girls lured off the farm, in milltowns like Dover

---

12 Plymouth N.H., 26 April, 1838, Nathaniel P. Rogers to Rev. Henry B. Stanton, NY City, in *The Emancipator* (Boston), 7 June, 1838; Rogers, "The Cause Dying Away, datelined Hebron-9 July," *Herald of Freedom* (Concord), 14 July, 1838.

13 Dover *Enquirer*, 3 Feb., 1835; Great Falls *Journal*, 7 and 14 Feb., 1835; Dover, 10 Feb., 1835, unidentified person to editor of *New Hampshire Observer*, Concord (letter not printed by *Observer*), printed in *Herald of Freedom* (Concord), 7 March, 1835. Thompson's precise speaking schedule in each town was: Great Falls, 7 Feb. evning; Dover, 5 evn, 6 evn, 8 morn-afternoon-evn, and 9 evn. Three periodical articles analyzing broader aspects of the Thompson tour are: Janet Wilson, "The Early Anti-Slavery Propaganda," *More Books*, 19 (Dec. 1944), 395; John L. Myers, "The Beginning of Anti-Slavery Agencies in New York State, 1833-1836," *New York History*, 43 (April 1962), 163; C. Duncan Rice, "The Anti-Slavery Mission of George Thompson to the United States, 1834-1835," *Journal of American Studies*, 2 (April 1968), 22.

14 Asa Freeman, Albert G. Fenner, and Mack, "Resolutions of Arkansas committee, appointed by Dover citizens meeting on 25 April," *Herald of Freedom* (Concord), 14 May, 1836; John M. McCrillis, Nathan W. Scott, and Mack, "Report of depository committee, appointed by Strafford County antislavery convention at Gilmanton Centre on 27 April," *Herald of Freedom*, 7 May, 1836.

15 Chelsea Vt., 21 May, 1838, *EM* to William Burr, Dover, in *Morning Star*, 13 June, 1838. Compare the tenor of this Mack description with his hinterland allusion in paragraphs 9 and 10 of the oration text: "No state, in general, seems to exemplify these principles so fully as Vermont. Here she dwells, upon her fertile hills and amidst her valleys, remote from the noise and strife of commerce, drawing her subsistence and her needful comforts from exhaustless resources . . . . Her religion, her humanity, and her patriotism unbribed—her mental vision clear as the light of liberty, in which she has ever dwelt,—from her calm and retired position, she contemplates the condition of her country. Looking forth from her hills and her mountains, free as the winds that breathe around them . . . , she considers the practices of her southern sisters. And she knows those practices to be as opposite to republican freedom and Christian liberty, as darkness [is] to light, as hell to Heaven."

16 Plymouth N.H., 26 April, 1838, Nathaniel P. Rogers to Rev. Henry B. Stanton, NY City, in *The Emancipator* (Boston), 7 June, 1838.

and Great Falls,[17] offered an "immediate" northern example of labor adversely impacted by textile magnates processing heinous southern raw materials.[18] And of the two towns where Mack spoke on the Fourth, Great Falls was the most agreeably inclined to a militant antislavery attitude. Dover, more a town where even the wife of Congregational minister David Root, president of the local ladies antislavery society, was a willing absentee, along with both vice-presidents under her, when many rank-and-file members attended Mack's oration in town.[19]

Still, pastor Root was a more significant factor in the rhetorical context than his wife. For his prominence, in effect, helped determine how Mack might prove desirable as an anniversary orator, concern for a grass-roots evangelical humanity making lesser local men like Mack appear spontaneous. It was Root, not Mack, who had brought Thompson and Rev. Amos A. Phelps to Dover-Great Falls,[20] despite being unsuccessful in getting either man to speak again at Dover on the Fourth, the same year, as part of a joint antislavery celebration by societies from Dover-Great Falls and South Berwick, Maine.[21] Root, not Mack, had attended the regional antislavery convention at Boston on May 25, 1836, proclaiming his faith in a reformative language of vindication for abolitionists,[22] a "plain" style of speaking well enough tempered with "cogent reasoning" to have him address Dartmouth students three years later.[23]

And Root, not Mack, most impressed Rev. Henry B. Stanton, during Stanton's lecture visit to Dover, August 26 thru 28, some two months after Mack gave his oration. Having addressed delegates to a western New York antislavery convention at Lockport on the Fourth, utilizing a five-link inferential chain from the Declaration of Independence (without Freewill-Baptist salvation) to illustrate the economic subservience of Yankee peddlers hawking wares like basswood pumpkin seeds, wooden nutmegs, and tin horns on southern tours[24]

---

17 R., "Undated communication," *The Ultimatum* [New London, Ct.], 1 (July 1838), 2; William Goodell, "To the Laboring People of the Free States," *The American Anti-Slavery Almanac, for 1838* (Boston: D. K. Hitchcock, 1838), p. 41.

18 Chelsea Vt., 21 May, 1838, *EM* to William Burr, Dover, in *Morning Star*, 13 June, 1838.

19 Dover *Gazette*, 3 July, 1838; Nathaniel P. Rogers, "Fourth of July," *Herald of Freedom* (Concord), 13 July, 1839; Manuscript, vol. 1 of "Records of the Ladies Anti-Slavery Society of Dover, 1835-1846," New Hampshire Historical Society (Concord).

20 Dover, 22 and 25 Jan., 1835, Root to Phelps, Boston, Phelps Papers, Boston Public Library.

21 Dover, 24 May, 1835, Root to Phelps, Boston, Phelps Papers, Boston Public Library.

22 *Proceedings of the New England Anti-Slavery Convention: Held in Boston, May 24, 25, and 26, 1836* (Boston: Isaac Knapp, 1836), pp. 38-40.

23 Hanover, 7 July, 1839, Francis Atkinson Freeman (son) to Asa Freeman (father), Dover, Jonathan Freeman Family Papers, New Hampshire Historical Society (Concord). Root delivered two discourses in Hanover on the seventh, perhaps a traditional sermon in the morning, and the lecture requested by the local antislavery society in the afternoon. See n. 14 for evidence of the father sharing a committee assignment with Mack.

24 *Friend of Man* (Utica, NY), 1 Aug., 1838.

(predating, of course, the legitimate plight of northern textile millhands, many none-too-taciturn feminists),[25] Stanton did recognize that both men kept the antislavery cause in "vigorous health" at Dover. Yet "indefatigable friend" Root, for Stanton, seemed the prominent organization man which propagandist Mack was not: "He[Root] is just what I think an antislavery clergyman should be. He is an abolitionist in the pulpit as well as the convention, on the Sabbath as well as other days . . . . He treats this society[American Antislavery] just as he does the Bible, Missionary, Tract, and Education Societies. He marshals them all under the same banner. No dodging, no flinching, no apologies. He is a noble man."[26]

Late in August, on the twenty-first, Mack continued to be cast in the lesser role of a spontaneous orator. As one among many vice-presidents attending the state antislavery convention in Concord, he proposed a resolution which partly suggested his role on the Fourth. Even if the resolution never quite measured up to a similar one passed by Root at the 1836 Boston regional convention.[27] Mack's resolution, unanimously adopted by county-level delegates, observed that "the nature and interest of the cause of emancipation require that its advocates should carry forward the enterprise in the spirit of *humble solemnity*."[28] The greater the enormity of slavery's "blight and curse" upon northern textileworkers, the greater presumably the need for intense advocacy by spontaneous local orators, their mission to shock reticent communities into dealing with the moral issue. Or so abolition strategists might at least fondly hope, assigning all of militancy's progressively "immediate" advantages unto themselves.

But the Fourth celebrations at Dover and Great Falls, much less minor evangelical orator Mack, were hardly the watershed type of loci necessary to test out such a holy generalization. Inasmuch as Freewill-Baptist pastor Joshua Quimby, speaking on the Fourth to his monthly parish meeting, in a presumably hinterland community like Lisbon, New Hampshire, utterly avoided mentioning slavery's moral havoc at all,[29] even within Mack's own denomination, perhaps, the oration at Dover and Great Falls was more a fanatical exception than any strategic norm for abolitionists. Indeed, the only

---

25 Consult, for example, the publicized feminist protest against layoffs and wage reductions by the management of the Cocheco Manufacturing Company in Dover. Dover *Gazette* in Boston *Commercial Gazette* (sw), 6 March, 1834.

26 NY City, 1 Sept., 1838, Stanton to Joshua Leavitt, Boston, in *The Emancipator* (Boston), 6 Sept., 1838. On the afternoon of 26 Aug., Stanton listened to Root delivering an antislavery discourse.

27 Root had proposed this resolution at the morning session of 25 May: "Resolved, that inasmuch as the principles and measures of abolitionists are based upon the word of God, it is the duty of the ministers of the gospel, and Christians generally, to come to the aid of this great enterprise of delivering [up] the captives of this land." See n. 22-p. 38 reference above.

28 *Herald of Freedom* (Concord), 25 Aug., 1838.

29 Lisbon, 13 Aug., 1838, James Parker to EM, Dover, in *Morning Star*, 29 Aug., 1838.

review of Mack's oration, penned by Oliver Johnson in the *Liberator*,[30] appeared to assume that the piece, however much a "faithful" or "interesting" treatment of pro-slavery "hypocrisy," never would topple partisans from power, when those politicians believed themselves every bit as remote as any handful of militant converts to radical abolitionism. A follow-up appeal for popular support, presumably the raison d'être behind Mack's oration in the first place, which incidentally was not excerpted in the *Liberator*, had to be included by Johnson as one of two sentences comprising his brief notice: "Our friends in the granite state ought to send copies . . . to those fierce Whigs and Democrats, who believe that buying and selling human flesh, and compelling laborers to work without pay, are practices consistent with the professions of this *republican* nation."[31] Johnson, however, may have mentioned the oration only to reinforce editor William Lloyd Garrison's dislike for Rev. Hubbard Winslow, Boston municipal orator on the Fourth and "self-styled evangelical" pastor of Bowdoin Street Church,[32] who permitted slaveholders like Elipha White, Presbyterian minister serving John's Island near Charleston, South Carolina, to preach from his not-so-free pulpit while summering in New England.[33]

The oration pamphlet was distributed by the Freewill-Baptist organ in Dover, the *Morning Star*, aided by the usual Dover bookstores, and by F. B. Moses in Great Falls. Also, by D. D. Holmes and Company in Lowell, Massachusetts,[34] another milltown with a Freewill-Baptist parish.[35] Indeed, the reader may want to compare Mack's ineffective spontaneity with the historical generalization that anti-fusion "fanatic" Thomas Starr King, by means of his Sacramento oration twenty-three years later, kept California loyal to the Unionist war-machine during a Civil War whose consequences were more dreaded than "immediate" in 1838.

---

30 [William H.] B[urleigh]., "Announcement of William Lloyd Garrison's temporary retirement," *Pennsylvania Freeman* (Philadelphia), 21 June, 1838.

31 *The Liberator* (Boston), 31 Aug., 1838.

32 Garrison, "Fourth of July oration at Marlboro' Chapel," *The Liberator*, 13 July, 1838; Johnson, "Boston Municipal Celebration, and the Rev. Orator Hubbard Winslow [at Old South Church]," *Liberator*, 20 July, 1838. For one antislavery correspondent's counter-militant letter citing the Garrison oration, consult commentary by "J.H." in *Vermont Telegraph* (Brandon), 8 Aug., 1838.

33 "Another Such Preacher," *The Liberator* in *Human Rights*, 4 (Aug. 1838), 4.

34 *Morning Star*, 29 Aug., 1838.

35 Lowell *Mercury* in *Yeoman's Gazette, Mechanic's Journal, and Middlesex Advertiser* (Concord, Mass.), 5 May, 1832.

"The Revolution Unfinished, or American Independence Begun," an address delivered twice by Rev. Enoch Mack on the Fourth of July, 1838—once in the morning at Dover, New Hampshire, before a joint meeting of the adult male, ladies', and juvenile antislavery societies, and again that afternoon before the sole adult male antislavery organization in neighboring Great Falls (or Somersworth). Late in August, a pamphlet edition of the address was printed by the Dover Morning Star, *a local religious paper on which Mack served as a special correspondent. Yet the* Star *never ran any column text initially, or even follow-up excerpts once the pamphlet was printed. Nor did any publication notice or excerpts appear in friend Nathaniel P. Rogers'* Herald of Freedom *in Concord, the state* Baptist Register, *or the* Baptist Missionary Magazine *in Boston. And the* Freewill Baptist Quarterly Magazine *in Dover, to which Mack contributed articles as well, did not commence publication of its first issue until June of the following year. Perhaps it is noteworthy, however, that, in addition to brief notices published by the* Star *and Garrison's* Liberator *in Boston, two twentieth-century works cite Mack's address, namely, David M. Ludlum's* Social Ferment in Vermont, *page 199, note 1, and Dwight L. Dumond's comprehensive* Bibliography, *page 77. The reader may care to ponder how "revolution unfinished" in Mack's speech title might suggest some participation in the temperance movement, despite Mack's entire address containing only the faintest glimmer of King Alcohol in one almost melodramatic reference to "revelry" wasted on "drunken Bacchus" in "temples towering to the clouds" (paragraph 8), and in another rather standard transition (paragraph 19) browbeating any recalcitrant listeners "drinking thus of slavery's cup." For Mack's clerical duties in Dover and training as a physician led him to edit a "rumseller's" pro-temperance paper there, while Rev. Samuel Joseph May, an antislavery agent who probably came to know Mack when preaching immediate emancipation in New Hampshire during the 1830's, gave a strikingly similar "second revolution" as the title, in 1855, of an exclusively Maine-Law Fourth of July oration delivered at Dryden, New York. An oration, incidentally, making no allusion at all to the peculiar institution of slavery, printed in a pamphlet edition by the Syracuse* Evening Chronicle, *much as the* Star *had done for Mack, and conjuring up visions of Mack's antichrist counterpart in "physicians of the Soul" who invoke wine "to fortify themselves for the labors of the pulpit" (page 6). Mack's title apparently demonstrates that "revolution" as a term applied equally to antislavery and temperance on the Fourth of July. One further editorial note before closing this introduction. No revision-process comparisons are made in the text below, because two Mack letters to* Star *editor William Burr, datelined Chelsea, Vt.-May 21 and Newbury, Vt.-May 24, reveal no significant revisions in this address, even when Mack describes the import of significant events like Lovejoy's murder and the conflagration at Pennsylvania Hall.*

1 Fellow citizens, the loud pealings of artillery with which the morning's dawn has been saluted—the voice of [con]gratulation heard throughout our

land—and the general demonstration of cheerfulness and joy, beaming on millions of countenances and bursting [forth] from millions of hearts—tell [us of] the recurrence of that day hailed as the birth of our nation's freedom. On this day, the people of our land in ten thousand convocations commemorate an era deemed the most important that has occurred in the history of this nation. *We* too have thought [it] proper to assemble on this day, and in the name of liberty. But it is not to pervert liberty to excess and riot, to senseless mirth and maniac revelry [,that we assemble]. Nor have *we* met to worship at the shrine of an ideal goddess, the personification of liberty. For, fair and beautiful as may appear the ideally embodied spirit of abstract freedom, *we* cannot make to her our devotional offerings—*we* cannot worship the creature—*we* are not idolaters—and *we* will contemplate liberty, beautiful and glorious as she may by herself appear, only in connection with her *Author.* In the name of true freedom's Author *we* assemble—before His throne *we* bow—to Him *we* render our praise and address our prayer. [All] In the name of Him who, from the throne of the universe, appeared upon earth to proclaim liberty to the captives, and the opening of the prison to them that are bound; who in the sublimity of moral conquest overcame an opposing world, and triumphed over death and hell personally (and as the Omnipotent helper and deliverer of His followers). And who has ascended to the throne of His glory, whereon He sits today, carrying forward by the dispensations of His providence the might of His spirit, the power of His truth, the institutions of His Church, and the agency of His intelligent creatures, that redemption for effecting which He came to earth—the redemption of man from the power of Satan (the dominion of sin and death), and from the oppression of his fellow man. In His name and in His presence are *we* met; and for the interests of such liberty as He dispenses will *we* deliberate.

2 That liberty was of Him which spake through our fathers, in Congress assembled at Philadelphia 1776, on the Fourth of July—the day our nation celebrates- the day *we* celebrate. Then, speaking through our fathers there, the spirit of true liberty declared all men created free and equal—endowed with the inalienable rights of life, liberty, and the pursuit of happiness. And, speaking still further through them, the spirit of freedom declared that these states virtually were and ought to be free. Three-score years have rolled away since the genius of true liberty uttered this declaration of the freedom of the people of these United States through their representative body. And has the event proved this nation to be really free? Is this now indeed a free nation?

3 The loud and joyous acclaim with which this day through following years has been hailed—the proud boast of independence which has been heard throughout our land, and which our nation has trumpeted to the ends of the earth—the roar of cannon- the demonstrations of joy- the convivial celebrations- the swellings of oratory- the songs of jubilee- and the bursts of sentiment which echo over our land and are rife throughout our nation, even as it is *this day*—all seem to testify that the declaration of our fathers,-that this nation

was of right free and independent,-has been maintained, and successfully and practically substantiated—and that the sentiments, which on that day gave birth to a new and free nation, are perpetuated and venerated and cherished and gloried in. And we might well suppose that those sentiments, uttered by our nation on the Fourth of July '76, uttered so firmly on the day of her birth, and for which *this day* has ever since been hailed and celebrated as a national jubilee by the whole nation—we might well suppose that, favored by providence as she has been- triumphant in war and prosperous in the arts of peace—we might well suppose that those sentiments, then bursting forth to life and ever since cherished and fostered, would ere now have been matured to the most complete, full, and practical freedom. So that every individual of this wide republic, by this day, would breathe an atmosphere of pure, uncontaminated freedom—and would be, *this day*, sitting under the spreading branches, sharing the protecting shelter and cheering shade, and feasting upon the blissful fruits of liberty's tree, planted so long ago, and apparently maturing so fast and flourishing so thriftily. But it is not indeed so! So far from this, that instead of meeting on this day in celebration of a general, equal jubilee such as impartial humanity might hail with joy, unmingled with a sigh or tear—we are compelled, while listening to the plainest dictates of patriotism, humanity, and religion (influences from which we wish not independence), to meet as an antislavery association- an anti-*American* slavery association- an anti-*United States* slavery association!

4 The clank of chains on inoffensive human limbs we hear. Responsive to the cannon's roar and loud huzza for liberty, *this day* there rises to our ears the horrid clangor of rattling chains upon the limbs of thousands, hundreds of thousands, ten hundred thousands,-twice, yea thrice, ten hundred thousands of our own countrymen! Our countrymen in chains! Yes, and heavier chains than these never galled the limbs, and bound and lacerated the hearts of bondmen. Behold how bitter is the toil (and all unpaid) to which these millions are bowed down. The scourge is lifted over them—and the wild shriek of agony arises, responsive to the whip's shrill crack! And blood is flowing from the gashed back of the helpless victim, and curdling with horror in the veins of humanity witnessing such fiendish cruelty! And lo, all deeds of cruelty, of torture and of blood and death,-that tyranny and wanton cruelty and lust unbridled, and malice and revenge, unchecked and unrestrained, can prompt those to commit who have the power,-are practiced here—an ample field, where every evil passion of the heart most deeply depraved may riot to satiety, and glut itself to surfeiting!

5 What have these millions done, [so] that they have forfeited the birthright which our national Declaration asserts to be the heritage of all [citizens]? They [certainly] have forfeited it by no misdemeanor. [For] The [very] chains were put upon their limbs while yet they hung upon their mothers' breasts, or slept in harmless infancy within the cradle.—Nay, they were claimed [by others] and doomed to slavery while yet unborn! Where then [lies] our nation's

Declaration, on which she sprang into being? [Especially] The principle from which she broke allegiance with her fatherland: "All are born *free and equal*; endowed by their Creator with *life and liberty, inalienable rights.*" What has become of that principle? What [exactly] has their Declaration effected? Dismemberment from the mother country and exemption from British taxation! And is this all? Exemption from taxation—is this all that our fathers meant by freedom? What [say you], was it bondage with them to pay a tax to Britain? And is this freedom—the subjection of one-sixth part of the nation to [the] most abject slavery, in which not a trifling tax is claimed, but both body and soul are seized and consigned from birth to unremitting, ceaseless toil, and to debasing darkness!

6 But is it said, that notwithstanding [the fact that] some millions groan in slavery in this nation, yet many millions more enjoy that freedom in its fullness declared by our fathers to be the gift of God, the inalienable birthright of every human being? [Presumably] a sentiment in defense of which they pledged their lives, their fortunes, and their sacred honor, and in vindication of which they fought and bled and died.—Is it said, that although our nation enslaves some millions of the descendants of Africa (those of dusky hue), she yet affords true freedom to the descendants of Europe (those of a white countenance), and [might it not be said] that especially the northern states are truly free?—Let us see. Look halfway back through the year of our national existence just closed—halfway back to our last national anniversary of boasted independence. Here lies the amiable, the good, the noble *Lovejoy*, bleeding-slain—his body deeply gored with mortal wounds—his fond and faithful wife a widow—his child an orphan—and his country deprived of one of her truest sons—the Christian Church bereft of one of its best members! And wherefore have they slain him? Say what has been his crime! No crime hath he committed? Then wherefore did they slay him! Was not his right to life inalienable? Our fathers said, "All men possess that right, *inalienable*." Then wherefore did they take his life away by violence? Was his complexion black, or was he in that portion of our country deemed less the abode of freedom than some other states? His countenance was white—pure European in descent- American by birth—born, educated, and murdered within states deemed preeminently free! Who slew him, then? The rampant spirit of dark and bloody slavery! Why did slavery slay him? Because he pled the cause of righteous freedom. And slavery murdered him to still his voice, [so] that it no more might speak the truth! But wherefore was he not protected from the bloody grasp of the monster by our country's laws? Slavery controlled the laws! But wherefore did the executioners of law yield up the laws to slavery? Why wielded they not the law's strong arm, in sure protection of a citizen so outraged and so guiltless? Because he spoke for freedom and advocated the cause of righteous liberty! Where then is the freedom of the white man, and [particularly] of the white man in states deemed freest? What freedom have we if we may not *speak*? Freedom to speak have we—to speak for anything- for everything *but* freedom! Freedom to speak for

slavery- for infidelity- for every vice- for anything *but* freedom's cause! And freedom have we to speak against anything *but* cruel, bloody slavery! Lovejoy spake against it.—Lovejoy pled for the groaning slave's emancipation—he pled for the suffering dumb who could not plead for themselves.—And for this he bleeds! Last anniversary he was nobly acting a righteous part for his God and country. Today his body lies entombed. And his murderers go at large unpunished,-because they slew him in support of slavery,-because they did it against an advocate for freedom!

7 But is not this occurrence—far towards the [western] extremity of our nation—removed far from that *heart* where we may suppose liberty to dwell in [all] her strength, while the spirit of slavery might only encroach upon our nation's borders where the pulsations of freedom might be expected to be more feeble, and where slavery might more readily fasten its influences? May we not hope that the heart is yet sound! Would it be possible that in the Atlantic cities where our freedom was cradled, that slavery, especially in the free states, can exist or be in any wise predominant? And now, as the fiendish yell of Lovejoy's murderers dies away in silence—as he sinks to his gory grave—and as the widow's wail of anguish and the orphan's cries of grief are hushed to the deep still sigh of more lenient sorrow—may we not hope that from this *heart* of our nation will be rallied and thrown forth to its farthest extremities the vital influences of freedom, such as will restore (and more than restore) the utmost border from the deadly influences of slavery so horribly predominant there!—Lo, what light is that which spreads its lurid brightness along the evening sky and o'er the Atlantic region and the free states! What bursting flames are those arising from that famed and beauteous city, the place of Penn, of Franklin—yea, the seat of [the] Congress of '76 and July 4th- where liberty was born- our nation's freedom by our fathers was declared! Is it a flame by patriots enkindled, a mighty, Heaven-piercing and earth-illuminating bonfire on freedom's altar?—As if by such a flame the nation might be warned to patriotism still more ardent, the chill of slavery be driven from its encroachment upon her distant borders,-and Columbia's zeal for liberty be proclaimed to all the nations! Not such that light—not such that flame. 'Tis freedom's fairest, most peculiar temple upon *slavery's altar* burning! That demon dark—that genius diabolical, of fetters- chains- scourges- lust- and every wrong and bloody outrage—he it is applies the torch, and that with open front and with a hand deliberate and unconcealed!

8 But where is freedom's law, enacted for her own protection? Where is the power to whom its execution is entrusted [so] that the incendiary demon, slavery, is permitted to consume without a covert freedom's temple? That power has sold itself to slavery, to permit that raging spirit to do as it doth list, unchecked and unobstructed! But was not that temple built and owned by men whose skin is white—and was it not within a state called free- the city where our nation's liberty was born? 'Tis even so! Where then is freedom *for* the white

man—and in freest states and cities- erst deemed sacred to her memory and reign? Are they not free to build, in [a] lawful way and peaceably to occupy, a temple for their peaceful convocations? They are free to build a temple—if it be *not* built and consecrated unto freedom! They are free to meet in any convocation—if they meet *not* in the name of liberty! They may erect and consecrate as many temples as they list—to anything *but* freedom! They may build up temples towering to the clouds—to drunken Bacchus- to licentiousness- to infidelity- to slavery- to anything *but* liberty! They may meet for revelry and foul debauch by day and night!—They may assemble for [the] hearing and utterance of blasphemies against God and His record and His son in the halls of infidelity!—They may meet for [the] furtherance of slavery's cause—in any place- at any time!—They may meet for any purpose and in any cause *but* for the purpose of speaking and hearing of liberty, and *but* for the furtherance of freedom's cause! To do this they are *not free*—but free to everything and every cause besides.

9 But, still, may we not hope to find at least some blest, secure retreats, where freedom holds her peerless umpire and reigns in all her blessedness? Is it not so among New England's hills and dales and in her uncontaminated villages? Surely, we might hope that here freedom yet may breathe! Are *we* [as] citizens of New England not free? Are not our laws made by ourselves—by our own servants well paid for all their work indeed- but delegated to serve us as our representatives and lawmakers? Our representatives, New Hampshire's representatives in Congress—our paid (and well-paid) servants to make our laws- servants just such as *we ourselves* have chosen! Do you hear what these well-paid servants of your election say? Be astounded, ye crowned despots of the Old World! Our servants speak to us as *ye* have not spoken to your subjects, [declaring] "You shan't petition!" Humbly, indeed—as if *we* were rather *their* servants- as if they were our absolute lords.—And as on bended knee we approach and offer our petition—our petition that our own territory- our own capital- the capital of our nation- may be made free, that it may be rescued from the odium- the guilt- the cruelty of hellish slavery— "*Avaunt*," they say, "we will not hear! Be gone with such a theme! Petition, pray to us for whatever else you will, and we will hear you. But ask no boon for freedom! We will not hear. Pray for anything besides—petition against what[ever] else you will—and we will hear,-we will receive your prayer for our consideration. But ask us nothing for freedom's cause—pray not one word against slavery! We will not *consider* it, we will not *receive* it; we will *hear* no word of it—*Avaunt*! We have naught to do with liberty, justice, truth, and mercy for those guilty of a skin not colored like our own—nor [for] those who plead their cause—further than to receive their votes and money, [entrusted] to seat and to support us here where we may serve the noble southron. We've sold ourselves to serve—to crouch unto the noble South- to lick the very dust at the feet of the noble southron! And in the great political market we have sold our constituents with ourselves unto the lordly

South. We've made the bargain! They with all their chivalry are to support our party, and we receive the stamp of slavery upon our doughy faces, and sell our state to go for slavery and to put down those fanatics who are still so disloyal to the noble South as to utter sentiments in *earnest* which our fathers, July 4th '76, spoke only as a mere *rhetorical* flourish. Be silent, then, constituents—white slaves with us—and let the black slave wear his chain, at least 'til your's is broken!"

10 Is this our case today? Is this the degraded condition of the inhabitants of New Hampshire's hills and dales and villages? 'Tis even so! Then wherefore speaks that cannon's roar in bellowing vauntings of our liberty—and wherefore that acclaim of freedom around festive boards? And wherefore waves a banner on which *liberty* is written? Because we are free from British rule—of Britain we are independent- we pay to her no taxes- no, nor do we share her liberty! Do I speak, against my country, treason? I say we share not Britain's *liberty*! Who will arise and call this [a] treason or libel on republican America? Then, in defense I point you to the martyred Lovejoy's grave! I point you to the ashes and the blackened ruins of Pennsylvania Hall! I point you to your own petitions trampled, unread, beneath the feet of Congress, and yourself spurned from your suppliant posture at its feet—[both resulting] if you but lisp the name of freedom or utter one complaint against earth's worst oppression! I point you to the standing pledge of our nation's Chief Magistrate: to crush at once by mighty veto any act of yours that, otherwise, might loose the chain from limbs in *your own* District; to knock on [its] head by veto the child of equal, righteous liberty—if in our nation's capital it should [happen to] be born!

11 I point you now to England. Through all her realm, you hear the voice of freedom in general acclamation urging the immediate emancipation of all the bondmen of that realm, and of all the world! And there in England and her colonies, freedom's advocates are free to plead her cause. No deadly weapon, there, is aimed at him who speaks for freedom. Even he, pursued and hunted from our shores, by citizens of republican America who sought his life because he spoke for liberty—he, the stranger-advocate of freedom, who to save his life fled from republican America's hospitality (by which he was assailed) back to the asylum of the monarch-land where,-now as he before was always free to do,- *Thompson* traverses the kingdom in its length and breadth, sounding a trumpet whose thundertones are heard to Britain's farthest isle and in the farthest state in Christendom! And *there* no violence awaits him—*there* he can speak for liberty—*there* he can plead the cause of the crushed and bleeding slave, and find protection—*there* he is hailed and honored by all, from the humble peasant to the noblest peer in all the realm! And *Lovejoy*- our own Lovejoy—laid low in his yet fresh grave (his martyr-grave)- gored with wounds by reigning slavery inflicted, from whose bloodthirsty rage *this* land afforded no protection—Lovejoy might have spoken *there* in England- might have spoken freely- and would have spoken safely.

12 Look to England yet again. Hear, from the ample, splendid halls of her famed London down to the chapel and the lecture-room of her obscurest hamlet, ringing forth the world around, the eloquence of freedom's advocates. And they are free to occupy those halls in freedom's cause. No brand is *there* applied—no conflagration tells to earth and Heaven that slavery's bloody and incendiary genius triumphs *there*! Look once again to Britain,-and behold the nation asking of their Queen and Parliament a boon—a mighty boon for *freedom*. And lo, their Sovereign, peers, and representatives respectfully receive- respectfully consider their petition! And yet once more look you to Britain—her islands and her provinces- close by and joining our own borders. See you that vessel freighted at our capital, at Washington, with groaning slaves for some of our more southern cities. If but the favoring wind of Heaven arise and force that vessel on a British isle—that moment the slave cargo is all changed to freemen. If, guided by the polar star, a slave of ours elude the chase of bloodhounds and the grasp of citizens more cruel still than hounds, and place his foot one inch beyond the limits of our own republic (and on British ground)—that moment he emerges from the slave up to the freeman!

13 This is some part of British freedom. This much we wish our nation had—with *all that is republican*, which we possess besides—while all that accords not with *true* republicanism would we discard. We want her *freedom* only- *not* her chains. And we *are* free from Britain's chains! In this, well may our land rejoice—but soberly- rationally- consistently- righteously- and religiously. Well may we celebrate *this Fourth*! The principles asserted by our fathers on this day (in Congress '76) have freed us from the British yoke. In this do we rejoice! These principles well carried out will *free us from ourselves*. In this still more do we rejoice! These principles, [as] far as our patriot fathers carried them, broke loose, forever from our shores, the grasp of Albion's tax-gripping hand. These principles, pushed completely through our land by us, their children (favored of Heaven as our fathers were), will unlock all fetters and sunder every chain from limb and lip and press—[and] would change at once three million slaves to freemen- and save our twenty million freemen from being [any] longer slaves!

14 Come we up, then, to resume the work our fathers well began- but dying left unfinished. [For] while altho[ugh] they left us free, they left a portion of the occupants and native-born of our own soil in chains. And while we, their descendants, have not pushed forward the car of liberty to consummation through[out] our whole land—while we have been rejoicing over the achievements of our fathers for us, and minding or caring only for our own freedom neglectful of the groaning slave— [all] at once we find the car of freedom has rolled back, and we arouse and see that *we ourselves* are well nigh slaves! The chain is on our tongues, the shackle on our press, the weapon of death aimed at our hearts, the torch applied to our temples, the ear of our Congress shut up against our prayers, and the veto of our Chief Magistrate ready-lifted to demolish at a blow any act that we might gain, to rescue our own

capital from being made the abode and national marketplace of slavery! Arise we then, both to retrieve our own lost or much endangered liberty, and to break the more cruel and deadly bonds of the American slave. We stand beside the slave—our fate, if not our choice, doth place us there. He must be freed, or we must become (more than we already are) slaves! There's [simply] no [other] alternative. 'Tis fixed in the Law of Nature—and it is *just* in the dispensations of Divine Providence. They that show not mercy shall *not* have mercy! [And] If we refuse to give liberty to the slave when we may [do so], it is *just* that *we ourselves* be [relegated to] bondmen.

15 Here then is cause for us to rise—the groaning, perishing slave's emancipation, and our own (and our children's) rescue from threatened bondage- and deliverance from oppression already felt. But where shall we strike first—directly for ourselves, or at once and mainly for the slave? We strike for the slave—his case is more urgent than our's! Our's is bearable for a little while—his is intolerable for one single moment! Besides, were we to pursue the other course we should fail altogether. Caring [only] for ourselves, the slave has remained in his chains, and fetters have become forged for us and almost fixed upon our limbs. But now, [presumably] caring for the slave, his chains shall be broken, and the power that breaks his chains will assuredly make us free indeed. Come we up, then, to the rescue—strike we *for* the slave! We make his cause our cause—we remember him in bonds as bound with him—we know not a backward course [to take] in [all] this work—we enlist 'til victory is complete- or 'til death release us from the service! Nor find we cause to relax our efforts—nor can we allow ourselves to become weary in the work! Our hearts are set upon it- our hands are put to it- our pledge is given—or, if not, we will here today (as our fathers of '76) make our appeal to Heaven for the rectitude of our cause- and pledge to it "our lives, our fortunes, and our sacred honor!" Nay, more than this we pledge that bond which in creation and redemption makes every man our brother, and demands of us that we love him as ourselves and do to him as we would have him do to us! Hear it, then, ye of our fellow citizens who excuse yourselves from this cause—consenting to be sold by your party leaders who barter both themselves and us as they would merchandise- and trifle with our dearest rights as toys! Hear it, ye who bargain us away to lordly southrons—hear it, southron!—We declare we will never rest until the slave leaps forth from all his chains—*a man*- a freeman! For Zion's sake and for the sake of humanity, we will not hold our peace until the bondman's soul shall find release from that fell grasp that binds it to the dust, and rises in its dignity to act as an intellectual and moral agent—to drink in the light of gospel truth,-to hear unfettered (and unfettered to obey) the mandates of his God—to toss abroad his freed arms,-and lift up his rejoicing head in praise to Him by whom he is delivered!

16 The cause in which our fathers [en]listed—our freedom from the unjust claims of Britain—was a noble cause. Our cause is greater- nobler still!

What was that oppression against which they declared, compared with that which we encounter? The "little finger" of American oppression is "heavier than Great Britain's loins." If Britain "scourged [us] with whips," slavery's scourge is [that of] *scorpions*! Did Britain make of our fathers merchandise, and count them with their wives and children nothing more than goods and chattels—parted- bought- and sold at [a stranger's] pleasure! Did Britain shut [out] the light of science and the Gospel from their sight- and wrench from them the Bible! Ah, did she deny to them the right to make petition to the throne or Parliament—a right denied in this our government- not only to the slave but unto us called freemen! And could our fathers appeal in confidence to Heaven, in attestation of the justice of their cause, and trust in God to aid them in their conflict? Much more may we! And arising in the ardor of their hearts and braving every hardship, were they blest of Heaven with victory? Much more may we hope to be! Far more abundantly is this His cause than that in which they strove. More mighty are the weapons of our warfare than those which they employed. *Their's* were carnal weapons— *our's* spiritual and mighty through our God- [even] to [the] pulling down of strongest holds! *Prayer* and *truth*—prayer which moves the *Arm* Almighty- truth set home upon the heart by Him whose *Spirit* is Omnipotent—these are the mighty levers- these the mighty engines which in confidence we ply!

17 But are there some—freedom's friends professed [and] sons and daughters of New England—[who are] not enlisted- and who applaud our fathers too? Where [then] is consistency! What [is it they do]! Approve—applaud with roar of cannon and the general huzza year after year—the lesser and more distant good- and yet oppose the present greater [good]? 'Tis as the building of the ancient prophets' monuments- while yet they kill the living ones! Perchance they have [some] objections to this cause. Then come and bring them forward, [my] friends. Bring forth your reasons- your strongest reasons bring—and set them in array with all your weaker ones. Summon them all up, and let us see if we can look a host so formidable in the face. And here they come—amalgamation- division of the Union- can't take care of themselves- they'll come among us- a[re]n't prepared for freedom- they'll cut their masters' throats- we've nothing to do with the South- it's [really] a political question- it makes [for] division in the churches! Are these all? Why, these are not *realities*—in these there is no substance!—These are naught but airy phantoms- conjured up (we can hardly tell how) before your illusory imagination! Sure[ly] your mental vision is disordered. Just take advice—apply to your mind's eye a little ointment- just one grain's weight of *common sense*—and this fantastic host will vanish like a troop of goblins (as our legends tell) at break of morning. Or if you do not fancy a remedy so simple, then we entreat you to take one spark of true humanity along with you- and follow us. And while we try to lift the curtain and reveal to you the foul- the cruel- and the bloody abominations of that system involving millions in deepest woe—Oh, let that spark of fellow-feeling kindle up even to the glow of natural affection (not to speak of Christian love),

and your objections shall be as so many flaxen fibers before the glowing furnace's flame! But if these remove not your objections- we have one thing more. [And] that is the Law of Heaven—the plain- the Golden Rule,-"What things soever you would have men do to you- do thou the same to them." Then, we must put you who object against immediate emancipation—abolition *now*- this moment- and *forever*—we must put you in the poor slave's place!

18 Ah, the enslaver has seized you—secured you as his property- soul and body—to sell you- work you- whip you- torture you just as he lists, be he humane- cruel- infidel or villain! So, also, of your wife- your children—your parents- brothers- sisters. He sets you up at auction. You stand upon the platform in the marketplace—the bidders come around and feel your joints- examine well your limbs- and shake your frame to see if you are put together well and likely to be a bargain at three, five, eight, ten, or fifteen hundred dollars. And now you are knocked off to go with your new master to Virginia. The beloved wife of your bosom is put up next.—She undergoes the same rude scrutiny with aggravated indignities—and is struck off to a purchaser from the sugar plantations of Louisiana. Next come your children. Some may be bidden off by a Missouri planter—perchance your own master may buy one—and you may be a witness to its sufferings beneath the heavy task and bloody scourge.—But the sale completed,-your chains and handcuffs put securely on,-you are ready for the start with your respective masters for your different and widely distant fields of toil and suffering and torture—*for life*. Now you must take the final farewell of wife and children. But how shall I describe (or how can you conceive) the depth of such distress! Heartstrings now are breaking! But the last embrace of lacerated, despairing affection must be short—your drivers will not wait for long adieus. [For] They [already] have mounted their steeds.—The loud signal crack of the brandished whip tells you that the last moment is come- and you must part! You have broken [away] from the arms of wife and children, frantic with grief, and started on your march. Should you stop to cast one lingering look [back], the lacerating lash will remind you that you are the property of another man! And, by and by, the last receding wailings and screeches of agony and despair from your wife and children are lost- *forever* lost in [the] distance! Perhaps your aged mother is in the same gang- chained in the same coffle with you. Infirm- faint- weary- and sick—she sinks in the toilsome way. Still she must go [on]! And while you see the aged form of her who bore, sustained, and loved you lacerated by the lash, you may not remonstrate on penalty of bitterest punishment! And while your thoughts turn to follow your beloved wife- severed [from you] *forever*- you know she is to be the prey- the resistless prey- to owner's and driver's lusts- the subject of toil and cruelty! And your children, too, are doomed *for life* to bondage—debarred from science- forbidden to read the Bible- exiled *forever* from a father's heart and mother's care!

19 This is slavery as slavery abounds in these United States. And now, objecting friend, as you are drinking thus of slavery's cup, what wouldst thou have

thy neighbors do for thee- thy wife- thy children- thy parent? Would you have them make objections against the immediate abolition of slavery? Would you have them turn away on the other side, excusing themselves by such objections as these of yours? Oh, your soul would be shocked and sickened by such mockery of common sense- and such outrage against common humanity- and such utter disregard and violation of the Law of Christ! Cast from thee, then, objections so unworthy—be at least *a man*- if *not* a Christian! Repent all past participation in the system—all excuses- all apologies! Come up and stand forth boldly, valiantly among those who have already enlisted and who are pressing forward to certain victory and glorious triumph! Come, timely join this righteous cause—conscience shall approve- honorable success shall attend [your effort]!—And when before the Judgment Seat you stand beside the spirit of the slave, he shall witness there that thou on earth didst mercy show!—And He *The Judge*—who to the merciful shows himself merciful—will there (before all worlds) thy labor of humanity and Christian love *approve*!

Chapter 8

William Henry Seward's Fourth of July Oration, 1840

Although not a formal historical discourse, but somewhat less conspicuous as an after-dinner speech, William Henry Seward's centennial tribute at Cherry Valley, New York, was integrally related to various bicentennial/centennial town orations preceding much more widespread reliance upon such a medium by town boroughs in America's heartland, on the Fourth during the 1876 centennial year. Seward's oration really was rather typical in its attempt to find some ancestral common ground in principles of the Enlightenment. Principles that hopefully might enable the orator to minimize national animosity, a phenomenon so very prevalent on the Fourth when political rewards were at stake in a campaign year.

Yet all town "centennials" especially those bi-"centennial" celebrations in New England prior to 1835, were not necessarily observed on the Fourth. On May 21, 1823, for example, Nathaniel Appleton Haven Jr., orator at Portsmouth, New Hampshire, uncovered nationalistic "prejudice and obloquy"[1] surrounding merchant-adventurer John Mason, original proprietor of Pascataquack. The Portsmouth bicentennial audience, for orator Haven, had to be more tolerant and weigh libertarian demands against the non-exploitative "daring spirit" and "keen sagacity" of proprietor Mason: "When, therefore, *rent* was demanded of them[Colonists] for lands which they had reclaimed from a state of nature, and measures were taken to eject them from their dwellings to enforce it's payment,-all their passions were awakened- they resisted, to a man-they combined together- and by continual struggles, at length succeeded in confirming their own title. No occurrence in the whole history of the Colony, from

1 *New Hampshire Republican* (Dover) in Portsmouth *Journal of Literature and Politics*, 31 May, 1823.

it's first establishment to the commencement of the Revolution, so deeply affected and agitated the minds of the people. It was, in their apprehension, a struggle not only for property, but for liberty. And whatever opinion may now be entertained of the means employed to ensure success, we cannot but rejoice that the Colonists gained the victory—that they made themselves and their posterity Lords of the Soil, instead of remaining the tenants of a distant Proprietor. Yet now, that the contest is over;-now that passion and feeling have subsided- if we examine the question impartially, we shall find that, like most other controversies, there is an appearance of equity on both sides. Mason was undoubtedly a benefactor to the Colony. It owes him it's first establishment; and it is indebted to him for the first materials of that commerce, which has ever since been among the principal causes of it's prosperity. In fine, in reviewing his whole conduct towards the Colony, and judging of his pretensions by the law of England as then established, he was a man 'more sinned against, than sinning.' "[2]

Josiah Quincy, bicentennial orator at Boston on September 17, 1830, the current-style calendar equivalent of the seventh in 1630, when Trimountain had been renamed Boston, amplified "glory" as defined in his 1826 Fourth of July oration[3] so as to preserve the conservative legacy of Governor John Winthrop.[4] Instead of visible monuments vulgarly alluded to by numerous other orators on the Fourth, however dross or even progressive the ideal lesson to be learned, the less visible truth in Winthrop's virtues as a leader meant considerably more to orator Quincy: "These virtues, indeed, are not seen charactered in breathing bronze, or in living marble. Our ancestors have left no Corinthian temples on our hills, no Gothic cathedrals on our plains, no proud pyramid, no storied obelisk, in our cities. But mind is there. Sagacious enterprise is there. An active, vigorous, intelligent, moral population throng our cities, and predominate in our fields—men, patient of labor, submissive to law, respectful to authority, regardful of right, faithful to liberty. These are the monuments of our ancestors. They stand, immutable and immortal—in the social, moral, and intellectual

---

2 "Oration, Delivered by Nathaniel Appleton Haven, Jr. at Portsmouth New Hampshire, May 21, 1823, Two hundred years from the landing of the first Settlers," Manuscript in New Hampshire Historical Society (Concord). For a standardized printing of this passage, see George Ticknor, *The Remains of Nathaniel Appleton Haven, with a Memoir of His Life* (Cambridge, Mass.: Hilliard, Metcalf, and Company, 1827), pp. 10-11, noting the typo (not "it" but "its") in line 11 of the latter page.

3 Quincy, Mayor of the City, *An Oration, Delivered on Tuesday, the Fourth of July, 1826. It Being the Fiftieth Anniversary of American Independence, before the Supreme Executive of the Commonwealth, and the City Council and Inhabitants of the City of Boston* (Boston: True and Greene, 1826), pp. 6-9.

4 Quincy, President of Harvard University, *An Address to the Citizens of Boston, on the XVIIth of September, M-DCCC-XXX, The Close of the Second Century from the First Settlement of the City* (Boston: J. H. Eastburn, 1830), pp. 18-19.

condition of their descendants. They exist in the spirit which their precepts instilled, and their example implanted."[5]

Edward Everett, bicentennial orator at neighboring Charlestown on June 28 (old-style, the seventeenth in 1630 when Winthrop landed on Ten Hills), and at Newburyport on May 26 five years later,[6] emphasized the bold traits of "commercial adventure" and "self-denying enthusiasm" which orators on the Fourth sometimes overlionized.[7] Charlestown never indeed did celebrate its bicentennial on the Fourth in 1829, the previous year.[8] And orator Everett took great pains in his introduction there, while amplifying a brief historical sketch from his 1828 Fourth of July oration,[9] to distinguish between a tastefully binding heritage and chauvinism noncredibly overdone: "Were these celebrations a matter of mere ceremony, or of official observance, their multiplication would be idle and oppressive. But they are all consecrated to events of real interest . . . . They are just tributes to the memory of worthy men, to whom we are under everlasting obligations. They furnish fit occasions for inculcating the great principles, which led to the settlement of our happy country. And by connecting some interesting associations with the spots [made already] familiar to us by daily visitation, they remind us that there is something worthy to be commemorated in the soil which we inhabit, and thus furnish food for an enlightened patriotism. The genius of our institutions has made this the chief means of perpetuating, by sensible memorials, the fame of excellent men and great achievements."[10]

Even Rufus Choate's "lofty and luxuriant"[11] figure on the Garden of Eden at the Ipswich bicentennial, celebrated on August 16, 1834, did not subordinate intellectual monuments to less enduring "grand festivals of the goddess of reason" or some "impious dream of human perfectibility."[12] Pride in liberty

---

5 Quincy, *Bicentennial Address*, pp. 9-10.

6 *Daily Herald* (Newburyport, Mass.), 29 May, 1835.

7 Everett, *An Address Delivered on the 28th of June, 1830, the Anniversary of the Arrival of Governor Winthrop at Charlestown, Delivered and Published at the Request of the Charlestown Lyceum* (Charlestown, Mass.: William W. Wheildon, 1830), pp. 25-33. Although not a centennial oration, another historical discourse sponsored by a lyceum is Redmond Conyngham, *An Address on the Early Settlement of the Valley of Pequea, Delivered . . . at the Lyceum Celebration, Fourth of July, 1842, at Paradise, Pennsylvania* (Published for Paradise Lyceum, 1842), pp. 3-5.

8 *Bunker-Hill Aurora* (Charlestown), 6 thru 27 June, 1829.

9 Everett, *An Oration Delivered before the Citizens of Charlestown on the Fifty-Second Anniversary of the Declaration of the Independence of the United States of America* (Charlestown: Wheildon and Raymond, 1828), pp. 40-41.

10 Everett, *Bicentennial Address*, p. 4.

11 Salem [Mass.] *Register* in *Dly Herald* (Newburyport), 19 Aug., 1834.

12 Choate, *The Colonial Age of New England: Address Delivered . . . upon the Centennial Celebration of the Settlement of Ipswich, Massachusetts, 16 August 1834* (Boston, 1928), p. 20.

during the Colonial Age, for orator Choate, certainly was not so glorious or grandiose as to be provincially contradictory of Enlightenment teachings. An excess of pride, perhaps, but pride of intellect and faith in Reason, not pride in unrestrained nationalistic passion: "The wilderness and the solitary place were glad for them, and the desert rejoiced and blossomed as the rose. The land was a desolate wilderness before them—behind them, [the land was] as the Garden of Eden. How glorious a triumph of patience, energy, perseverance, intelligence, and faith! And then how powerfully, and in how many ways, must the fatigues, privations, interruptions, and steady advance (and ultimate completion) of that long day's work have reacted on the character and the mind of those who performed it. How could such a people ever again (if ever they had been) be idle, or frivolous, or giddy, or luxurious! With what a resistless accession of momentum must they turn to every new, manly, honest, and worthy labor! How truly must they love the land for which they had done so much! How ardently must they desire to see it—covered over with the beauty of holiness and the glory of freedom, as with a garment! With what a just and manly self-approbation must they look back on such labors and such success! And how great will [the consciousness of] such pride make any people!"[13]

And no later than 1839, towns in the Northeast began to merge exercises on the Fourth with an observance of the centennial marking their settlement or incorporation. Considerably removed from the specter of illegal aliens and anarchist deportations in the twentieth century, town centennial orators were relatively content to place immigration patterns in a native ambience not always inimical to Old-World origins. Both Hampstead, New Hampshire, and Petersham, Massachusetts, were in fact tied very closely to British origins.[14] "Kingstown" or Palmer, Massachusetts, on the other hand, was first named for settler John King, and not out of gratitude to any proprietary British monarch.[15] "Cushnoc" or Fort Western in Augusta, Maine, demonstrated America's evolving independence during the French and Indian Wars,[16] as did the settling of Lebanon, New Hampshire, by residents of a similarly named town in Connecticut (the precise date, coincidentally, of Governor Benning Wentworth's

---

13 *Ibid.*, p. 19.

14 Isaac W. Smith, *Address Delivered July 4th, 1849, at the Centennial Celebration of the Incorporation of the Town of Hampstead, N.H.* (Manchester: James O. Adams, 1849), p. 13; Edmund B[urke]. Willson, *An Address Delivered in Petersham, Massachusetts, July 4, 1854, In Commemoration of the One Hundredth Anniversary of the Incorporation of That Town* (Boston: Crosby, Nichols, and Company, 1855), p. 31 and Appendix E.

15 Thomas Wilson, *An Historical Address Delivered at Palmer, Mass., July 5, 1852, In Commemoration of the Centennial Anniversary of the Incorporation of the Town* (Lowell: S. J. Varney, 1855), pp. 12-15.

16 Nathan Weston, *Oration at the Centennial Celebration of the Erection of Fort Western, on the Anniversary of American Independence, July 4, 1854* (Augusta, Me.: William H. Simpson, 1854), pp. 5-6.

charter was July 4, 1761).[17] Windham, Maine, initially named New Marblehead, derived its name from Thomas Chute and other "old" Marblehead grantees in Massachusetts.[18]

Moreover, Cherry Valley, New York, where Seward addressed a centennial banquet after the formal ceremony, traced its origins back to Scotsman John Lindesay, and Londonderry immigrants settling a colony in southern New Hampshire from Ireland.[19] William W. Campbell, centennial orator at the morning ceremony on the green in front of the local Academy, captured the legacy carved out by such humble immigrants in what once had been an "unbroken wilderness," fraught with romantic primeval pitfalls periling the weak-of-heart.[20] Indeed, the necessary lesson to be imparted by formal centennial discourses, for orator Campbell, was one of immigrants in America achieving the very "enlightened" traits and opportunities too often denied them by an overeducated proprietary class in the Old World: "It has become my duty, as it is my pleasure, to make up that record which may aid in fixing this day as a landmark for the guidance and direction of those who may come after us. If, in the brief review of the century which is just passing away, I shall present no gorgeous spectacle—no long train of titled lords and warrior knights,—I may be able to sketch characters which shall commend themselves [to us] by their intelligence, their morals, their courage, and their undying patriotism. Plain and humble though they may have been, and confined within a narrow sphere of action, they [all] were eminent in their respective stations. They discharged, with ability, the duties which devolved upon them,—and have passed away and left their impress upon this, the place of their and your habitation."[21]

In effect, Seward's commemorative task at the centennial dinner, much as with Daniel Webster at the Portsmouth bicentennial dinner and Samuel Swett

17 Rev. D. H[owe]. Allen, *July Fourth, 1761: An Historical Discourse in Commemoration of the One Hundredth Anniversary of the Charter of Lebanon, N.H., Delivered July 4th, 1861* (Boston: J. E. Farwell, 1862), pp. 6-9. Although not a historical discourse, another oration at the same celebration is J[ames]. W[illis]. Patterson, *An Oration in Commemoration of the One Hundredth Anniversary of the Charter of Lebanon, N.H., Delivered July 4th, 1861* (Boston: J. E. Farwell, 1862), pp. 5-10, citing Enlightenment principles.

18 Thomas Laurens Smith, *A Historical Address, Delivered on the Fourth of July, 1839, at the Centennial Anniversary, of the Settlement of Windham* (Portland, Me.: Arthur Shirley, 1840), pp. 4-8. As early as 8 Aug., 1829, obviously not on the Fourth, Ebenezer L. Finley celebrated Baltimore's centennial by delivering an oration at cornerstone-laying ceremonies for the Baltimore and Susquehanna Railroad. See the text of his remarks in *Commercial Chronicle and Daily Marylander* (Baltimore), 11 Aug., 1829.

19 "Centennial Address by William W. Campbell," *The Centennial Celebration at Cherry Valley, Otsego Co[unty]. N.Y., July 4th, 1840* (New York: Taylor and Clement, 1840), pp. 7-11. Pamphlet hereafter cited as *Centennial Celebration*.

20 *Ibid.*, pp. 9-10.

21 *Ibid.*, p. 7.

at two[22] Newburyport dinners, was to honor the "dearest associations"[23] or "high and holy character"[24] attaching to a fledgling Anglo-Saxon settlement. What the Committee of Arrangements termed "the sufferings, perils, and fortitude of the Pioneers of this then extreme western frontier," when inviting the Governor to attend the centennial ceremonies at Cherry Valley.[25]

Judge Jabez Delano Hammond, a member of the Committee, introduced Seward and related this commemorative purpose to the bitter partisan attitude spawned in New York by the log-cabin Presidential campaign. The audience at the banquet, catered by local innkeeper J. R. Wilkins, and attracting native sons from Albany, New York City, Troy, Schenectady, and Schoharie,[26] were asked by the Judge to regard Seward as a nonpartisan orator tastefully celebrating the centennial event: "Party jealousies and political differences, those smaller evils which always accompany that best gift of Heaven (liberty), can have no place here. All of us admire the fortitude, and lament the sufferings, and venerate the virtues, and exult in the success of the patriotic Pioneers. All rejoice in the Independence of this country, and all cordially approve of the principles which excited our fathers to declare that Independence. To add still higher to the enjoyment of the festivities of the day, we have been honored with the presence of . . . His Excellency, the Governor of the state. He, too, who is emphatically the representative of the whole people of New York, on this—our national jubilee,—has chosen to repose himself upon this quiet spot in the troubled ocean of political life. Although at other times the spirit of party may howl around, *here*—on this hallowed day, without one discordant note,—all hearts unite in the shout for Independence, Liberty, Union, and the Constitution . . . . I propose to you the health of our fellow citizen, William H. Seward—Governor of this state, of the empire state . . . . No higher evidence can be furnished of exalted talents and distinguished personal merit than an election, to the first office in the state, by the voluntary suffrages of a great, free, intelligent, and virtuous people."[27] And Seward concluded his oration by

22 Joseph H. Bragdon, comp., *A Report of the Proceedings on the Occasion of the Reception of the Sons of Newburyport Resident Abroad, July 4th, 1854, by the City Authorities and the Citizens of Newburyport* (Newburyport, Mass.: Moses H. Sargent, 1854), pp. 59-61.

23 *New Hampshire Republican* (Dover) in *New-Hampshire Gazette* (Portsmouth), 3 June, 1823. Also, since the piece comments on Old-World implications present in Webster's concluding quotation from Oliver Goldsmith, consult "New-England" by correspondent D., Portsmouth *Journal of Literature and Politics*, 5 July, 1823.

24 *Dly Herald* (Newburyport), 4 June, 1835.

25 Cherry Valley, 10 June, 1840, [Dr.] William Campbell, Jabez D. Hammond, James Brackett, Joseph Phelon, J. E. Cary, David H. Little, Mason Fitch, James Hetherington, Benjamin Davis, A. Belknap, O. A. Morse, and Ezra Trull to WHS, Albany, Seward Papers, University of Rochester Library. Seward Papers (Univ. of Rochester Library) cited hereafter as Seward Papers-Rochester.

26 Cherry Valley *Gazette*, 8 July, 1840, in *Centennial Celebration*, p. 4.

27 *Centennial Celebration*, pp. 32-33.

proposing a toast, in a similar nonpartisan vein, buoyantly declaring that Cherry Valley's settlers exhibited "intelligence and virtues . . . of most thrilling interest in the history of the state."[28]

Yet such sentiments really belied partisan circumstances which almost, at the last possible moment, made the Governor decide not to attend the ceremonies. For despite a gala log-cabin raising celebration in town on June 19,[29] the Whigs and Seward were distinctly in the minority as a political party in Otsego County.[30] Not only did Democrat James Hetherington, chosen town supervisor during the spring election, serve on the Committee of Arrangements. But the Committee had taken it upon itself to invite Seward's Democratic opponent in the upcoming state election, William C. Bouck.[31] Even wise, old Democrat, Levi Beardsley, who much to his chagrin found his chance remarks on July 24 at a Tippecanoe log cabin in New York City distorted out of all proportion by a partisan Whig press,[32] was issued an invitation by the Committee.[33] And in spite of the fact that neither Bouck nor Beardsley ever attended the event, two local Whigs, Committee member James Brackett and Willard Trull, advised friend Thurlow Weed to convince Seward not to come. This really as the Committee surely was in process of receiving the Governor's own letter of acceptance.[34]

Both local men, Trull in particular, discerned "bad motives,"[35] and presumably other negative-image hazards of a Democratic snare, should the Governor appear at the dinner and be introduced by Jabez Hammond. Of course, the Judge probably would not even mention the snare in his introduction. Trull wrote friend Weed: "The idea of inviting the Governor . . . was first started by Judge Hammond and some of his Loco Foco com-

---

28 *Ibid.*, p. 40.

29 Albany *Evening Journal*, 30 May and 24 June, 1840.

30 *Freeman's Journal* (Cooperstown), 9 March, 1840; Albany *Evening Journal*, 28 March, 1840. Although winning re-election based on returns elsewhere in New York, Seward's November vote tally for Otsego County (4762) did not exceed other Whig candidates: Senate (4785), minus 23; House of Representatives (4831), minus 69; and President (4856), minus 94. And Seward's margin of loss was the greatest for any major race in Otsego County: Seward-Governor (928) versus Senate (891), plus 37; House (781), plus 147; and President (724), plus 204. The presumption is that any nonpartisanship in the Governor's appearance at the centennial did not carry over to the November election. *Evening Journal*, 20 Nov., 1840.

31 Fulton, 26 June, 1840, Bouck to Committee, Cherry Valley, in *Centennial Celebration*, p. 43.

32 Cherry Valley, 29 July, Beardsley to Richard B. Connolly, New York City, New York *Evening Post* in Buffalo *Weekly Republican*, 6 Aug., 1840.

33 Oswego, 29 June, 1840, Beardsley to Committee, Cherry Valley, in *Centennial Celebration*, pp. 44-45.

34 Albany, 22 June, 1840, *WHS* to [Dr.] William Campbell et al. (Committee), Cherry Valley, Seward Papers-Rochester.

35 Cherry Valley, 27 June, 1840, Brackett to Weed, Albany, Weed Papers, University of Rochester Library. Weed Papers (Univ. of Rochester Library) cited hereafter as Weed Papers-Rochester.

panions who [like] Judas Ik[s]c[ariot], would betray the best man in the country if they thought any political capital could be made thereby . . . . Should the Governor attend, Hammond, Dr. Little, and others of the Van Buren school would be the first to cry mad dog, and it will be paraded in the columns of ev[e]ry Loco Foco [news]paper in the state, charging him with political designs."[36]

Late in June, meanwhile, Seward was penning letters of regret to a dozen committees throughout New York, declining each invitation to speak by citing his apparent commitment to attend the centennial at Cherry Valley.[37] With the oration drafted by June 29, leaving only some minor polishing on the manuscript to be done with private secretary Samuel Blatchford at Auburn on the second, Seward was understandably reluctant to give much substance to the "undefinable apprehension" relayed by friend Weed.[38] Even though Weed rather dutifully wrote Mark H. Sibley, scheduled to speak on the Fourth at the Tabernacle in New York City,[39] that the Governor might better campaign partisanly on Sibley's behalf than feign any nonpartisan stance at the centennial dinner.[40] As Seward viewed the matter, the day prior to departing Auburn by rail, any "close quarters," to be resolved in his own mind, stemmed from possible Whig non-attendance at the ceremonies being blindly encouraged by Whig partisan fears. And if not present at the dinner, he, as the most titular Whig of everyone invited by the Committee, being relegated to an uncomfortable position of undependability and national disrespect in the partisan Democratic press.

Seward made his feelings known to friend Weed, concerning the partisan implications of his not attending the centennial ceremonies: "I [will] come to be hung up in Loco Foco [news]papers as having been deterred by friends or opponents from keeping such an engagement. I do not believe a word in the fears

---

36 Cherry Valley, 27 June, 1840, Trull to Weed, Albany, Weed Papers-Rochester. David H. Little, "Dr. Little" to Trull, served on the Committee of Arrangements with Hammond, and read the Declaration of Independence before William W. Campbell spoke at the morning ceremony.

37 Auburn, 25 June, 1840, *WHS* to O. A. Bowe, Little Falls, and Auburn, 27 June, 1840, *WHS* to Chenango County Committee, n.p., Seward Papers-Rochester; Auburn, 2 July, 1840, *WHS* to Weed, Albany, Weed Papers-Rochester.

38 Auburn, 8 July, 1840, *WHS* to Weed, Albany (en route to Auburn), Weed Papers-Rochester.

39 *Evening Signal* (New York City) in Troy *Daily Whig*, 8 July, 1840. Sibley subsequently canceled out of his appearance because of illness, and John O. Sargent took his place, delivering some remarks at the Tabernacle with a meager six hours to prepare. Such a feat becomes even more noteworthy when it is considered that, on 27 June, Richard M. Blatchford had informed Seward about how "Sibley groans dreadfully at the labor attending his preparation of his speech." New York City, Blatchford to WHS, Auburn, Seward Papers-Rochester.

40 Albany, 1 July, 1840, Weed to WHS, Auburn, Seward Papers-Rochester. Weed turned around a bit on this point, having previously become quite reconciled to Seward's refusing to campaign for Sibley early in July: "Sibley will be sadly disappointed, but there is no help for it. I know you would help if it were possible. I sincerely hope you will obtain such relaxation [at Auburn] as is necessary to restore your health." Auburn, 25 and 26 June, 1840, *WHS* to Weed, Albany, Weed Papers-Rochester; Albany, 28 June, 1840, Weed to WHS, Auburn, Seward Papers-Rochester.

of Trull and Brackett, and I think they expose themselves to share any mortification in which I have no disposition to share.—There is nothing embarrassing about it, except that, after [their] having written such letters, they and the Whigs may not expect me [to appear at all]."[41]

And if the Governor still had any serious reservations to weigh in the balance on the morning of the third, the fact that he never was able to discuss them with Lewis Averill at St. Johnsville probably hardened his determination to continue on to Cherry Valley.[42] Lewis, as the brother of William Holt Averill of Cooperstown, was of course quite familiar with potential political consequences flowing from any centennial appearance. But, correct as Seward was in his resolve to attend the centennial, he missed seeing Lewis when the Averill brother spent the third proudly conveying a homemade log cabin via wagon train to the Whig celebration in Little Falls.[43]

Indeed, the effective nonpartisan tenor of Seward's oration may be realized by carefully examining a probable sore point, the anecdote in paragraph 4 pertaining to an unlikely "Muscat of Siam." There are two quite different meanings here: one so jocose as to be ineffective, the other not sufficiently partisan to interfere with the orator's commemorative purpose.

On June 24, within a day or two of when Seward actually began drafting the oration, friend Weed's Albany *Evening Journal* reprinted a description of a Siamese prince (Chaw Fah) from the Boston *Missionary Herald*. As missionary Robinson quickly perceived, Prince Chaw Fah was "very enthusiastic in imitating everything foreign, especially American." An American eagle, American stable, American trees and vines. The backward, even slavish, parallel to American nationality and the Fourth was extremely obvious. But if Muscat were combined with Siam, Seward perhaps hoped when first groping around for some suitable word association, might not such a ridiculous title (Muscat of Siam) suggest the travels of Joel Benedict Nott throughout Asia and Egypt?[44] For Joel, eldest son of Union College president Eliphalet Nott, had been born at Cherry Valley and named for his mother's Connecticut-schoolmaster father (Joel Benedict).[45] He was a Chemistry professor turned well-

---

41 Auburn, 2 July, 1840, *WHS* to Weed, Albany, Weed Papers-Rochester. Seward's precise phraseology after "expect me" was: "I have determined to go at 8 to-morrow morning, stop at Averills and advise with him—[and] probably go on to Cherry Valley, but if not I shall go to Albany. I cannot, as things stand, remain here- nor go elsewhere than to Cherry Valley or Albany.—It is close quarters- but I do not fear to show myself in any place.—All goes well here- courage will be right."

42 St. Johnsville, 11 July, 1840, Averill to WHS, Auburn, Seward Papers-Rochester.

43 *Herkimer County Journal* (Little Falls) in Albany *Evening Journal*, 22 July, 1840.

44 Boston *Commercial Gazette* (sw), 3 Sept., 1835.

45 "Rev. Doctor Nott," *Parthenon* (Union College) in *Daily National Intelligencer* (Washington, D.C.), 29 July, 1833.

to-do Guilderland Whig.[46] But, even more important, Joel often was mistaken for his stay-in-America father (Eliphalet) while abroad.[47] Would not Eliphalet, former principal of the Cherry Valley Academy, and speaker with William W. Campbell at the morning ceremony in front of that same building, fairly chortle with delight when exposed to such ponderous ambiguity in Seward's remarks at the centennial dinner?

Quite possibly not. Instead of suggesting the magical generalized meaning which residents of the South preferred to associate with Arabian topics,[48] the mere mention of Muscat in New York conjured up notions of a fresh controversy, with some partisan clash over a few rather ugly social issues.[49] Any controversy over reciprocating the Imaum of Muscat's gifts might be minimized, orator Seward perhaps reasoned, if "Sultan" (from Sultan*ee*, the name of the ship transporting gifts back and forth) were linked with Muscat. Opulence and despotism would then more properly be aligned with Arabian ignorance, and American nationalism more credibly be made an extension of the European Enlightenment. At least in the hope of maintaining unprejudiced harmony at the centennial dinner. And Seward, in his final version of the Eastern-Prince anecdote, accordingly revised the hazardous "Muscat of Siam" to a less general "Sultan of Muscat."[50] It was indeed much too hazardous, for Seward, to risk losing the goodwill gained from boatman Eliphalet[51] when narrating the Fulton anecdote in paragraph 3.

Despite friend Weed's concern, no partisan vitriol in fact greeted the Seward oration. No "Promethean fire" sarcastically intensifying patriotic wit, like that employed to puff the oratory of Patrick Henry's Whig descendant after the Poughkeepsie celebration,[52] where editor Weed spent the Fourth, marred the nonpartisan impact Seward endeavored to achieve at the Cherry Valley centennial dinner. Orator Seward was quite pleased that his "brief" remarks met

---

46 Utica *Sentinel and Gazette*, 21 Feb., 1826; Albany *Evening Journal*, 14 July, 1840; *Centennial Catalog, 1795-1895, of the Officers and Alumni of Union College in the City of Schenectady, N.Y.* (Troy: Times Printing House, 1895), p. xii; Codman Hislop, *Eliphalet Nott* (Middletown, Ct.: Wesleyan University Press, 1972), p. 599, n. 8.

47 "Correspondent's communication datelined Malta, 26 Nov., 1834," Boston *Commercial Gazette* cited in *Paul Pry.* (Washington, D.C.), 28 March, 1835; Boston *Commercial Gazette* (sw), 3 Sept., 1835.

48 Vincenzo Maurizi (pseud. Shaik Mansur, for initials "V.M."), *The History of Seyd Said, Sultan of Muscat* (London 1819, trans. from Italian manuscript), excerpted in *Southern Literary Register* (Columbia, S.C.), 29 Sept., 1820.

49 New-York *Mirror*, 27 June, 1840; New York *Sun* in *Daily Troy Budget*, 16 July, 1840; *Empire State* (New York City) and Boston *Notion* (large folio), 18 July, 1840.

50 Cherry Valley *Gazette*, 22 July, in Albany *Evening Journal*, 24 July, 1840; *Centennial Celebration* reprint, p. 38.

51 James Brewster, "Eliphalet Nott as a Steamboat Owner and Shipbuilder," *Union Alumni Monthly*, 24 (Dec. 1934), 50.

52 Troy *Dly Whig* and Albany *Evening Journal*, 6 July, 1840. William C. Preston, Senator from South Carolina, was the descendant of Patrick Henry and orator at the Poughkeepsie celebration.

with such a "hearty" and "very kind" response. Regardless of however "unstudied" the oration may have seemed to him, when compared to the Campbell and Nott discourses at the morning ceremony.[53]

Eliphalet Nott pronounced the oration as "very good," to friend Weed,[54] and the editor of the local *Gazette* similarly thought Seward's remarks "very eloquent."[55] Only James Brackett, whose partisan fears Seward largely discounted in attending the ceremonies, managed to buttonhole the single Cooperstown Whig who would rather basely, if not once again vaguely, grumble about the orator's "demagogic conduct."[56] And Seward's nephew, Frederick, an editorial staffer on friend Weed's *Journal* during the 1850's, favorably paraphrased two segments from the oration into his gay-nineties commemorative study of the Governor's career.[57]

---

53 Auburn, 8 July, 1840, *WHS* to Weed, Albany (en route to Auburn), Weed Papers-Rochester; Auburn, 7 June, 1844, *WHS* to James Brackett et al., Cherry Valley, in George E. Baker, ed., *The Works of William H. Seward* (New York: J. S. Redfield, 1853), III, 502.

54 Schenectady, 7 July, 1840, Nott to Weed, Albany, Weed Papers-Rochester.

55 Cherry Valley *Gazette*, 8 July, 1840, in *Centennial Celebration*, p. 5.

56 Cherry Valley, 17 July, 1840, Brackett to WHS, Auburn, Seward Papers-Rochester.

57 Frederick W. Seward, *William H. Seward: An Autobiography from 1801 to 1834, with a Memoir of His Life, and Selections from His Letters, 1831-1846* (New York: Derby and Miller, 1891), p. 489. One specimen, taken from each segment and compared with a corresponding passage in *Centennial Celebration*, serves to illustrate Frederick's juxtaposed paraphrase technique. Symbols **ABC** indicate sentence order, while double parentheses set off two sentences deleted by FWS. **Segment 1**—FWS version: "**A** Only a hundred times has the scythe passed over this valley since your ancestors pursued their weary way up the Mohawk, and over these hills, and planted here the first settlement of the Anglo-Saxon race west of the Hudson. **B** Yet, a hundred years is no unimportant portion of time. **C** In a single century four thousand millions of human beings appear on the earth, act their busy parts, and sink into its peaceful bosom." *Centennial* version: "**B** Yet a hundred years is no unimportant portion of time. ((It includes the periods of four generations.)) **C** In a single century four thousand millions of human beings appear on the earth, act their busy parts and sink into its peaceful bosom. ((A little more than half that period carries us back to the time when this great and free empire, now respected in every land, had no place among the nations of the earth.)) **A** Only a hundred times has the scythe passed over this valley since your ancestors pursued their weary way up the Mohawk and over these hills, and planted here the first settlement of the Anglo-Saxon race west of the Hudson." See sentences 2 thru 5 in paragraph 1, counting up from sentence 1 immediately after the second detailed passage in the oration text. Italics in segment 2 are used to designate specific word variants. And double parentheses again set off material deleted without ellipses by FWS. **Segment 2**—FWS version: "That century dawned upon one *broad* scene of war, extending throughout ^**A** Europe, ______ into Asia and Africa, and even this ______ remote continent. ^**B** No nation ______ escaped the *tread of hostile armies*, and few *were* exempt from revolution. ^**C** Some maintained their sovereignty, some *secured* their independence; but others *had* gone down forever." *Centennial* version: "It dawned upon one *blood*[*y*] scene of war, extending throughout **A** ((England, Russia, Prussia, Poland, Spain, Bavaria, Sardinia and France. Through a period of eighty years, with the occasional intervals of partial peace, the fires of war burned over the continent of)) Europe *after extending desolation* into Asia, Africa, and even this *new and* remote continent, **B** ((until within our own recollection the world's great disturber was confined on the rock of S[ain]t. Helena, and the exhausted nations found repose and peace.)) No nation *has* escaped the *evils of war*, and few *have been* exempt from revolution. **C** ((*Hostile armies have overrun* France, Holland, Saxony, Belgium, Bavaria, Sardinia, Spain, Portugal, Italy, Austria, Hungary, Prussia, and other German States, Poland, Russia and Switzerland, Egypt and Persia, and all the States of North and South America.)) Some maintained their sovereignty, some *received* their independence, but others *have* gone down forever." Consult sentences 4 thru 9 in paragraph 2 of the oration text. Very few, if indeed any, revisions in Seward's manuscript can justify the implementation of such favorable editorial license in the oration. *Centennial Celebration*, pp. 35-36.

Address delivered by William H. Seward at ceremonies commemorating the first centennial anniversary of the settlement of Cherry Valley, New York, ceremonies held July 4, 1840. After delivery at the centennial dinner, the Seward manuscript text initially was printed in the Cherry Valley Gazette *on the twenty-second, and then reprinted by friend Weed's evening and semiweekly Albany* Journal *on the twenty-fourth (also in the weekly* Journal *one day later), and by Greeley's* New-Yorker *downstate in New York City on August 1. Subsequently during 1840, the Seward text was incorporated in a formal pamphlet edition of the Cherry Valley proceedings, published at New York City by Taylor and Clement. But two omissions are perhaps as illuminating as this rather expected litany of reprints. First, the text never was reprinted in the* Otsego Republican *(Cooperstown) for the twentieth or twenty-seventh, as apparently promised in a summary account inserted from the Cherry Valley* Gazette *on July 13. Seward's manuscript galley did not arrive at the* Gazette *office in neighboring Cherry Valley until the fifteenth, necessitating the culprit delay since it was the* Gazette *editor himself who, on July 8, first promised to include Seward's address "in our next paper" (or, as events turned out, the very same day Seward's galley arrived). Given this time lag and space problems connected with coverage in a campaign, the three* Journal *reprints, combined with the* Gazette *printing and developing interest in some formal pamphlet, made sufficient inroads into the* Republican *editor's readership to make him heed opposition "Loco-Foco" leanings, and in effect waive any genuine inclination to reprint the Seward text by the twenty-seventh. Besides,* Republican *readers would have been just as interested in a party, given on the sixth in Seward's honor, at the Point on Lake Otsego near Cooperstown. Yet no extensive account, or even summary of possible remarks by the Governor, ever appeared in the* Republican. *And secondly, both the Fulton and Eastern-Prince anecdotes in paragraphs 3 and 4 were omitted by George E. Baker from page 227 in the third volume of his 1853 edition of Seward's* Works. *The following text is based upon a manuscript draft in the Seward Papers at the University of Rochester Library. Two passages treat Seward's composition process in some detail, words in* SIX POINT CAPITALS *designating what Seward regarded as "imperfect" base revisions preceding the final version in ten point type. And the final text, read by itself, should give a smooth and correct reading in each revision-process passage.*

1 Our's is a country in which all that is old is yet new/

We may deceive ourselves with the belief that we have antiquity, **a** AS WE CANNOT RECCOMEND OURSELVES WITH RUINS **b** BUT WE FIND NO WHERE THE RUINS OF ANTIQUITY **c** but we no where find its ruins. ☆ I have been impressed with this **a** WHEN I SEE THE PROSPEROUS CITIZENS OF THIS PROSPEROUS REGION ENGAGED [IN] **b** WHEN I HAVE WITNESSED **c** in looking on upon ☆ the celebration of the foundation of this **a** INTERESTING SETTLEMENT WHERE I SEE **b** beautiful town as an ancient event while all around me are ☆ the evidences of **a** INCREASE **b** youthfulness ☆ and prosperity.

INSERT DELETED: I return my great acknowledgements for **a** THE HONOR YOU HAVE SHOWN [ME] **b** your kind reception. ☆

I have always desired to see this place **a** WHICH WAS THE EARLIEST SETTLEMENT OF THE ANGLO-SAXON COLONISTS WEST OF THE HUDSON RIVER. A SPOT/SCENE/SIGHT [MADE MEMORABLE] **b** so long an outpost of civilization in the Western forests. ☆ **a** THE SCENES MADE MEMORABLE **b** ITS HISTORY HAS BEEN MADE MEMORABLE **c** Your annals have been made interesting ☆ by the fortitude, energy, and enterprise of **a** THE/ITS PIONEERS **b** your forefathers, ☆ and memorable by the perils, privation, and desolation of savage warfare-

I have desired to see for myself the valleys of Otsego through which the Susquehannah extends his arms and entwines his fingers with the tributaries of the Mohawk, as if to divert that gentle river from its allegiance to the Hudson- If I could have chosen the time for a visit here, it would have been on this occasion. When the political excitement, unavoidable in a country where the conduct of rulers is watched with the jealousy of freedom, is temporarily allayed and the discordant elements of party strife are hushed under the influence of recollections of a common ancestry, and common sufferings in the cause of liberty.

Our eloquent and gifted Orator has given us your **a** DOMESTIC NARRATIVE **b** entire local and domestic history. ☆ **a** SO FILLED THE EVENTS OF ITS [HISTORY WITH INCIDENTS WHICH?] **b** IS IT NOT STRANGE SO MANY THRILLING INCIDENTS **c** Does it not seem strange that so many extraordinary changes, so many important events, and so many thrilling incidents ☆ have occurred in the lapse of an hundred years! An hundred years, how short a period. That life is considered short which does not **a** EMBRACE HALF OF [THAT PERIOD?] **b** reach fifty years ☆ and that one is only very long which comprises an hundred. An hundred years! an hundred times this period of twelve months which the earth requires for the irrigation of its soil and the production of fruits, an hundred times this circle of three hundred and sixty five days, days that **a** PASS LIKE [BY?] SO UNNUMBERED AND LEAVE NO MEMORIAL/IMPRESSION BEFORE THE MEMORY **b** so often pass like a dream and are unnoted but by their loss. ☆ Who that places a tomb stone in the village church yard to the memory of a departed friend **a** DISCOVERS **b** would not sigh to think ☆ that that monument of his affection **a** HAS FALLEN AND THE GRAVE OF HIS FRIEND BE[COME UNDISTINGUISHED?[**b** will fall to the earth and his friend occupy an undistinguished grave ☆ within an hundred years?

Who that establishes a constitution or invents an engine or teaches a new science or founds a new sect would be content that his community, his invention, his science, or his creed should give place to new discoveries within an hundred years. Yet an hundred years is no unimportant portion of time. It includes the periods of four generations- In a single century Four thousand millions of human beings appear on the earth, act their busy parts, and sink into its peaceful bosom. A little more than half that period carries us back to the time when this great and free empire, now respected in every land, had no place among the nations of the

Earth. Only An hundred years ago your ancestors pursued their weary way up the Mohawk and over these hills, and planted here the first settlement of the Anglo Saxon race West of the Hudson.[1] They found the Six nations here as confident of perpetual enjoyment of this fair land as we now are- And yet so soon the tide of civilization has flowed over this valley, and filled the valleys of the Ohio and the Wabash and the Mississippi and the Missouri, and now scaracely [scarcely] the name of the Six nations remains- Only twice an hundred years have elapsed since the first navigator entered the Bay of New York, and not four centuries have passed since Columbus astonished the world with the discovery of this great continent. It is only ten centuries since all Europe, moved by wild fanaticism, poured her embattled hosts upon the fields of Palestine, and less than sixty times an hundred years, according to our accustomed chronology, carry us back to the epoch when there [was] no time nor light nor life nor earth nor Heavens, and God said let all these be, and they were-

2 We have reviewed the record of the past 100 years concerning the inhabitants of this beautiful valley. What is its more general history and what is its promise of the future- Alas! That it must be said although the spirit of Christianity has diffused a wider and warmer influence than ever before, yet the last century like the fifty seven that preceded it has been filled with the calamities of mankind. It dawned upon one broad scene of war extending throughout England, Russia, Prussia, Poland, Spain, Bavaria, Sardinia, and France. Through a period of Eighty years, with occasional intervals of partial peace, the fires of war burned over the Continent of Europe, often extending desolation into Asia, Africa, and even this new and remote continent, until within our own recollection the World's great Disturber was confined on the rock of St. Helena and the exhausted nations found repose and peace. No nation has escaped the evils of war, and few have been exempt from Revolution. Hostile armies have overrun France, Holland, Saxony, Belgium, Bavaria, Sardinia, Spain, Portugal, Italy, Austria, Hungary, Prussia and other German States, Poland, Russia and Switzerland, Egypt and Persia, and all the States of North and South America. Some maintained their sovereignty, some received their independence. Others regained their lost independence but others have gone down forever- No wonder that the pious and benevolent Poet exclaimed, "My ear is pained, my soul is sick/ With every day's report of outrage and oppression/ With which earth is filled." The occupation of man has been war, his ambition conquest, his enjoyment rapine and bloodshed.

3 Yet dark as the picture of the last century seems, it is relieved by lights more cheering than any that have shone upon our race in the previous course of

1 "The first settlement of the Anglo Saxon race West of the Hudson" may derive from "the earliest settlement of the Anglo Saxon colonists West of the Hudson river," a phrase not part of the final text in the first detailed passage above.

time- The human mind has advanced with unparallelled rapidity in discoveries in science and the arts. Civilization has been carried into new regions and has distributed, more equally than ever heretofore, the enjoyments and comforts of life. The education which an hundred years ago was a privilege of the few is now acknowledged to be the right of all. What were luxuries an hundred years ago are common enjoyments now. A renovating spirit is abroad in the world. The slave trade, an hundred years ago regarded as lawful Commerce by all Christian nations, is now denounced as Piracy by most civilized states, and the rights of man are secured by benign and wholesome laws. All expense and delay in passage and transportation from place to place are an incumbrance upon human labor. Yet it seems as if it were but yesterday since we learned that burthens may be more cheaply carried on parallel iron rails than on the rough and unequal surface of the ground, and now rail roads are common thoroughfares and animal force is too feeble an agent for locomotion. A Gentleman upon whom age seemed to have lightly laid his hand, a few days ago, told me that, less than forty years since, he dined with Chancellor Livingston at Paris. The party was composed of statesmen and men of science- The patience of the guests was exhausted by a visionary youth named Fulton, who engrossed the conversation by an argument to prove that, if he could obtain a small fund, he could construct a boat to be propelled by the power of steam, and navigate the Hudson River with the velocity of four miles an hour- Those who reflect upon the rapidity with which intelligence- social, commercial, and political- is diffused throughout our country and the civilized world can hardly believe that an hundred years ago scarcely a dozen vessels arrived in all our ports from Europe, and that seventy years ago mail coach[e]s were unknown. The object of all government is the welfare of the governed- yet it is only sixty five years since this model of practical, permanent, and free Republican Government was set up here for the maintenance of American liberty, and to animate the hopes and efforts of mankind. The religion of the cross is carried forth, and more effectively than under the banner of Constantine or even the preaching of the Apostles- The philosophy of Bacon and the Newtonian and Copernican systems were taught an hundred years ago, and Alchemy, after long abuses of the credulity of mankind, had introduced the elements of Chemistry, but the practical advantages resulting from all these sciences have been realized chiefly within an hundred years.

4 I lately met the Secretary of an Eastern Prince. He was a man of education and refinement, and had been selected by his Master to make a gorgeous present of Eastern luxuries acceptable to the President of the United States- We were standing near an almost speaking bust of Washington. I asked him if he knew the likeness. He answered in the negative- I told him that it was Washington, the deliverer- the Father of our Country, but he had never read- had never heard of Washington. I confess that I was astonished to find a man who had never read or heard of Washington, but I was no longer surprised that the Mus-

cat of Siam was a Despot and his subjects slaves.[2] If the principles of civil liberty are so imperfectly understood now, what could have been the condition of human rights before the days of Sicard. LaFayette, Wilberforce, Paine, Jefferson, Hamilton, and Washington. How obscure must have been the science of laws before Beccaria, Montesquieu, Puffendorf, Blackstone, Bentham, and Livingston reduced it to form and symmetry. How limited would be our knowledge of History if we were deprived of the writings of Rollin, Robertson, Leland, Hume, Gillies, Littleton, Priestley, Marshall, Russell, Roscoe, Gibbon, Henault, Halem, and Raynal. How has the human mind been enlightened, in that most mysterious of all mysteries itself, by the philosophy of Stewart, Reid, and Browne. How have theology and moral science been enriched by Edwards, Jenyns, Paley, Zimmerman, Johnson, and Ferguson- In Natural Philosophy what a blank would be produced by striking out the discoveries of Herschel, Halley, Franklin, Davy, Rumford, Galvani, and Delonti- How profitless would be our researches in Natural History without Linnaeus and Buffon for our guides— What would we have known of political economy but for the writings of Malthus, Smith, and Say- We can scarcely conceive of literature destitute of the works of Cowper, Pope, Thompson, Beattie, Gray, Gay, Goldsmith, Johnson, McPherson, Roscoe, Scott, Burns, Goethe, Byron, and Moore- In even such a superficial review as this of the contributions of the last century to the Knowledge, virtue, and happiness of our race, we forget that the human mind has been two thirds of the whole period stretched in extreme tension in the excitement of war, and that what it has accomplished in the way of science and art has been done in its occasional seasons of repose from the study and occupation of arms. That what has been expended in establishing schools, colleges, and seminaries, and in making roads and canals, has been only what has been saved from the prodigality of war- Happy, thrice happy will it be for us and for mankind if we extract from the history of the last century its true philosophy- Among its instructions are of a certainty these truths. That peace is indispensable to the improvement and happiness of man. That improvement is his highest duty, and arts not arms his right occupation. That Republican Governments, resting upon equal and universal suffrage, can alone secure an exemption from the ambition of conquest and the popular discontents which involve Nations in foreign wars and civil commotion. That a Republican Government, resting upon universal and equal suffrage, can only be maintained in a community where education is universally enjoyed, and where internal improvements bind together the various portions of the country in a community of interest and affection. Let us then extend our system of schools and our churches and take care that every child in

2 Quite obviously the Near-Eastern potentate of Muscat would be an "Imaum," and the Far-Eastern ruler of Siam or Thailand a "King." There logically is no such official as a country of a country, only a single titled person in charge of a territorial entity. But Seward conceivably may have intended a humorous figure here relating to the extensive travels of Joel Benedict Nott, travels upon occasion mistakenly attributed to Joel's father, Eliphalet, a featured centennial speaker present at the dinner.

the state, whatever be his faith, his language, his condition, or his circumstances or those of his parents, is brought to the instruction of those schools and churches- Let us do this and let us put on steam upon the land and steam upon the rivers and upon the sea, and the glorious career upon which our country has just entered will continue to be more successful and more glorious still. Those who shall celebrate the next centennial anniversary will bless our memories, and the great prediction of our religion will no longer seem apocryphal that a time is coming when the nations shall live in peace and the Knowledge of the Lord shall extend over the whole earth.

Chapter 9

Henry David Thoreau's Fourth of July Oration, 1854

Quite central to any understanding of the rhetorical context, to which Thoreau presumably had to adapt when delivering "Slavery in Massachusetts," is a possible confusion of the drafting chronology. Inasmuch as critics are a little too much devoted to events heightening *Journal* coherence, specifically, the hypothetical "Carrying off of Simms" lecture title.

For despite *Journal* references to a "feeling invitation," perhaps more soul-like gut reaction than a formal speaking appearance (in the sense of pgr 3), and three stalwart Concord family names Thoreau picked up (Buttrick, Davis, and Hosmer, though plural to allow for a course of action), references allegedly proving that some preliminary "Simms" manuscript was available for a Concord meeting of May 3, 1851, the "late" Concord meeting alluded to by Thoreau in paragraph 1 might be that held in March 6, 1854. To get an indication of the time frame involved, compare "late" (pgrs 1/33) and "last" (pgrs 6-7/46) with "three years" (pgrs 6/12).[1] Thoreau obviously had very little interest in attending the "adjourned" Concord coalition meetings of June 22 and 23, which friend Emerson attended and addressed (pgrs 2/26).[2]

---

1 Leo Stoller, *After Walden: Thoreau's Changing Views on Economic Man* (Stanford, Cal.: Stanford University Press, 1957), pp. 137-38; A Citizen of Concord, "A Voice from the Old North Bridge,—Old Concord Wide-Awake on the Nebraska Question," *Weekly Commonwealth* (Boston), 18 March, 1854. Thoreau alternates two verb tenses—past tense for both 1851 and recently, and present tense with minor conditional modifications for now-narrative. Hence, assuming the "Slavery" text to be integrated and polished subsequent to invention in the *Journal*, indicators other than verb tense can only distinguish between past (1851) and recent-past (March thru 23 June, 1854) time.

2 Northampton *Courier*, 27 June, 1854; *The Liberator* (Boston), 30 June, 1854; C.B., "The Adjourned Meeting at Concord, datelined Concord-23 June," *Weekly Commonwealth* (Boston), 1 July, 1854; *Daily National Era* (Washington, D.C.), 1 July, 1854.

Several non-tense elements in the text indeed suggest a preliminary "Slavery" manuscript being prepared for March 6, 1854. Mention of Nebraska (bill signed May 30) and exclusion of the fugitive slave law (pgrs 1-2). More "regret-refer" relevance to Anthony Burns's arrest and rendition (May 24 thru June 2) than to Thomas M. Simms in the waning days of April, 1851 (pgr 1). And the speaker's rather hesitant approval of "special town meetings," increasing in frequency as argument over Kansas-Nebraska became more intensely politicized, meetings which he hoped might pass resolutions denying the issue on the basis of non-politicized moral values (pgr 24).

Yet the tedious chore of getting *Walden* to the printers cannot obscure two *Journal* entries apparently supporting such an altered time frame. Take February 18, 1854, as an example. Thoreau conceivably was prodded into composition by perusing a few printed speeches on the Kansas-Nebraska Bill, those by Salmon P. Chase and Charles Sumner probably included. He thought mostly in terms of reacting against dishonest politicians crudely trifling with what he came to regard as a burgeoning slavery-evil. Burgeoning, that is, because he eventually was compelled to consider even "country" yeomen of Concord and Boxboro-Acton as prejudiced "apes and baboons," fodder-type prey to be victimized immorally by politicians and their "stale jokes and vulgar wit."[3] And his *Journal* entry for March 1, unlike the April 8 "contents" index better suited to revising *Walden*,[4] conceivably might include a single "Slavery" draft. That is, a draft produced by adapting acceptable *Journal* sentences into some preliminary manuscript, subsequently discarded much as *Journal* sentences hacked out with scissors were tossed into the wastebasket during the 1840's.[5] Indeed, this time frame would perhaps better explain contemporaneous availability of a "Slavery" draft. And critics might not have to wrestle with why or if Bronson Alcott, who never went to Framingham on the Fourth but pasted the *Liberator* text into his diary, extended an unlikely speaking invitation to Thoreau at Walden pond on the evening of July 2.[6]

Nor should the fact that orator Thoreau borrowed so extensively from his *Journal* necessarily eliminate any interpretation of narrative orality from the *Liberator* text, or, for that matter, minimize counter-Walden relevance to an Independence-Day context. A context equivalent, namely, to the perceived attitudes of five or six hundred abolitionists attending the Massachusetts Antislavery Society's rally at the Harmony-grove dell, their numbers swelled by

---

3 *Journal*, ed. Bradford Torrey and Francis Allen (1906; rpt. Dover Publications, 1962), VI, 129.

4 *Ibid.*, 190.

5 *Ibid.*, 146; Walter Harding, "A Check List of Thoreau's Lectures," *Bulletin of the New York Public Library*, 52 (Feb. 1948), 83, and "The Influence of Thoreau's Lecturing upon his Writing," *N.Y.P.L. Bulletin*, 60 (Jan. 1956), 74.

6 Entries dated 2 and 4 July, 1854, Journal of Amos Bronson Alcott, Houghton Library-Harvard University (Cambridge).

spectators in search of holiday recreational distractions—heat-taming ploys like promenading through shaded walk with drink in hand, boating with the family on Framingham pond, or placing the children on swings.[7] Relevance to the occasion predominated, of course, with orality but a sophisticated cohesive factor in Thoreau's presentation.[8]

The orator, in effect, was endeavoring to protest Burns's rendition in vigorously introspective transcendental terms, a stance he hoped even a city audience would recognize as a constructive activist step beyond the "mourning" called for on the Fourth by an executive subcommittee of the Boston Vigilance Committee.[9] Weigh, for example, Thoreau's abject refusal to stoop to mourning by patriotically sectarian "Americans," while pleading for introspective mourning by Judgmentally humanistic individuals (pgrs 31-33).[10] Also, consider his reliance on Bunyan and Dante to envision an "onward and upward path" akin to the most sensitive patriotic mourning (pgrs 46-47),[11] as well as his "rising"-banner allusion to not treading upon reputable individual liberty (pgr 19).

Still, the subcommittee's circular must be placed in perspective. The Common Council in Providence, Rhode Island, had decided on June 12 to rescind its order against appropriating $2,000 for a civic celebration of the Fourth.[12] An about-face rendering the subcommittee's circular, totally premised on the obsolete order and mailed out concurrently with the new decision on the twelfth, rather without meaning in populous Massachusetts towns like Lynn and Marblehead.[13] Nevertheless, the subcommittee did gain a proper "mourning"

---

7 Leicester Mass., 28 July, 1852, Samuel May Jr. to William Lloyd Garrison, Boston, in *The Liberator*, 30 July, 1852; Lowell *Daily Journal and Courier* and New-York *Evening Times*, 5 July, 1854; "Telegraph dispatch, datelined Framingham-4 July," New York *Herald* (d), 6 July, 1854; *Weekly Commonwealth*, 8 July, 1854; *National Aegis* (Worcester), 12 July, 1854; *Liberator*, 21 July, 1854.

8 Readers unfamiliar with Thoreau's persistent contempt for overly-adapted oral discourse may care to consult his entry under 27 Feb., 1851, *Journal*, ed. Torrey and Allen (1906; rpt. Dover, 1962), II, 170; the "Reading" chapter in *Walden* (New York: Bramhall House, 1951), pp. 117-18; and "Life without Principle," delivered 26 Dec., 1854, at New Bedford, *Atlantic Monthly*, 12 (Oct. 1863), 484.

9 The commentary of four correspondents is helpful in linking this mourning context with the Fourth: One of the Three Thousand and Fifty, "A Day of Public Prayer," *The Independent* (New York City), 15 June, 1854; B.P.L., "Independence Day," Dedham *Gazette*, 1 July, 1854; [William James] W[atkins]., "The Celebration," *Frederick Douglass' Paper* (Rochester, NY), 6 July, 1854; E[dmund]. Q[uincy]., "The Fourth of July," *National Anti-Slavery Standard* (NY City), 15 July, 1854.

10 Truman Nelson, "Thoreau and John Brown," in *Thoreau in Our Season*, ed. John H. Hicks (Amherst: University of Massachusetts Press, 1966), pp. 143-44. Nelson's essay is not reprinted from the commemorative issue of the *Massachusetts Review* (Thoreau Society Booklet #17).

11 Egbert S. Oliver, "Thoreau and the Puritan Tradition," *Emerson Society Quarterly*, 44 (3rd Quarter 1966), 84.

12 Worcester *Daily Spy*, 7 June, 1854; *Rhode Island Freeman* (Providence), 16 June, 1854.

13 *The Liberator*, 16 June, 1854; New York *Herald* (d), 17 June, 1854; *Bay State* (Lynn), 29 June, 1854.

response of sorts when antislavery speakers complemented a few area civic celebrations on the Fourth. Among them, Ohio's Joshua R. Giddings at the Beneficent Congregational Church in Providence,[14] subcommittee-member Rev. Theodore Parker at the Purchase-Street Christian Church in New Bedford,[15] no civic orator officially having been designated for either city, and municipal-orator Rev. Andrew L. Stone from Park Street Church at the pavilion on the Boston Common.[16] Francis Jackson, another subcommittee member and president of the state antislavery society's Board of Managers, assisted by Board-secretary Robert F. Wallcut, organized the Framingham rally, with Wendell Phillips, a featured speaker at the rally, likewise on the subcommittee issuing the circular.

Advertisements for the rally indeed took up the rhetorical "disgrace and humiliation" theme contemplated in the circular.[17] Instead of some partisan Free-Soil or Independent-Democrat celebration of the Fourth, a mode of "Americanism" disliked for markedly different reasons by Thoreau and Stephen A. Douglas,[18] spectators on June 21 were advised to commute by train from Boston, Worcester, or Milford, purging themselves of "deceptive glorying" in perverse antislavery liberty and resolutely reflecting upon "deep humiliation" needed to remedy the "disgrace and shame" of governmental authority gone

14 "Phonographic transcript of Giddings oration by J. C. Thompson Jr.," Providence *Daily Tribune*, 11 July, 1854.

15 *Daily Evening Standard* (New Bedford), 21, 27, and 29 June, 3 and 5 July, 1854; Truman Nelson, *The Sin of the Prophet* (Boston: Little Brown, 1952), pp. 370-73. Contrary to Nelson's literary license, in having Parker conceptualize a "whale pod" whose entrails symbolically suggest Garrison's "sacrificial fire" of the U.S. Constitution, Parker spoke in New Bedford at four o'clock in the afternoon. And, consequently, though Parker formerly had been scheduled to speak at nine o'clock in the morning, could not be present at Framingham, as Nelson has him doing, when Thoreau delivered "Slavery in Massachusetts."

16 Stone, *An Oration Delivered before the Municipal Authorities of the City of Boston, at the Celebration of American Independence, July 4, 1854* (Boston: J. H. Eastburn, 1854), pp. 36-38. Compare Stone's concept of a mourning eloquence, credibly detached from partisanship, with Cassius M. Clay's insistence at Chicago that "rhetorical flourish" was not applicable to egalitarianism in the Declaration of Independence ("Sketch of Clay address on the Fourth before Young Men's Association," *Daily Democratic Press* [Chicago, Ill.], 6 July, 1854). For illustrative antislavery commentary by two correspondents on Stone's oration, see H[arriet]. B[eecher]. S[towe]., "Report datelined Andover-13 July," *Dly National Era* (WDC), 17 July, and D.Y., "Report datelined Boston-17 July," *National Anti-Slavery Standard* [NY City), 22 July, 1854. A slanted report in the Newburyport *Daily Herald* of the eighth depicted only a few scattered sentimental ladies as in fact mourning: "The silly suggestion of the ultra abolitionists, with respect to celebrating the Fourth as a day of mourning, was adopted by some weak sisters. At South Hadley, the village bell was tolled in the morning, the rooms of the Female Seminary were dressed in black, and the young ladies wore mourning badges. Similar pieces of folly were practiced at South Reading and Scituate." And a correspondent, in a report datelined Boston-6 July and printed by the New York *Journal of Commerce* (d) on the eighth, likewise postulated that "universal mourning" was not realistically implemented by the "most fanatical" Framingham rally.

17 *The Liberator*, 16 June, 1854.

18 Douglas, *Speech . . . at the Democratic Celebration of the Anniversary of American Freedom, in Independence Square, Philadelphia, July 4, 1854* (Philadelphia, 1854), p. 5.

wrong.[19] Another advertisement, dated June 30, conveyed much the same "full and earnest" antithetical appeal: "The times demand humiliation, not exultation,-heartfelt contrition, not 'the loud huzza',-the tolling of bells, not the ringing of merry peals,-the most direct and efficient action to cause 'liberty to be proclaimed, throughout all the land, to all the inhabitants thereof,' not vain boasting in regard to what our fathers achieved in the Revolutionary struggle."[20]

And a broadside, making fairly certain that ribald verses were suppressed during the rally, also emphasized that mourners soberly had to comprehend the divine scope of "moral power" and renounce patriotic exuberance, usually associated more with "brave and free" delusions on the Fourth. It was the mother country's turn to "jeer and hiss" repressive Colonial administrators, and *Liberator*-editor William Lloyd Garrison, to the tune of "Auld Lang Syne," demanded sincere mourning in Massachusetts and other New England states: "She [America] may not, must not thus rejoice, Nor of her triumphs tell:—Hushed be the cannon's thundering voice, And muffled every bell!"[21]

Thoreau expressly wanted to avoid condoning the patriotic glory claimed for nationalism, whether popular sovereignty or manifest destiny.[22] But, given this mourning context, Thoreau's "Slavery" remarks were germane enough to the rally to cast him as a sincerely conscientious reformer.[23] A reformer utilizing the positive introspection or virtuous "aboriginal civility" earlier described in neo-patriotic terms by Bronson Alcott, who lauded him as humanity's "independent of independents," a self-reliant "Revolution in himself . . . more than '76."[24]

The orator's transcendental outlook was by no means incompatible with an enlightened brand of individual patriotism. Not only is purposeful mourning explicitly countenanced in paragraphs 12 thru 15 relating to Simms's rendition.[25]

---

19 "Ad," Worcester *Dly Spy*, 21 June, 1854.

20 *The Liberator* and Boston *Evening Transcript*, 30 June, 1854.

21 Anonymous writer for Framingham celebration, "Fourth of July—1854: Tune, 'Lenox'," and Garrison, "Independence Day," *Hymns and Songs for the Anti-Slavery Celebration of the Declaration of Independence, at Framingham, July 4, 1854* (Boston: Prentiss and Sawyer, 1854). An extremely minute coincidence regarding the first tune cited might interest the reader here. Charles L. Remond, the president of the Essex County Antislavery Society who spoke after Garrison at the morning session, had "Lenox" for a middle name.

22 Concord, 7 Feb., 1855, *HDT* to Thomas Cholmondeley, Shropshire Eng., in F. B. Sanborn, "Thoreau and His English Friend Thomas Cholmondeley," *Atlantic Monthly*, 72 (Dec. 1893), 744.

23 Providence, 14 Oct., 1854, A. Fairbanks to HDT, Concord, in *The Correspondence of . . . Thoreau*, ed. Walter Harding and Carl Bode (Washington Square: New York University Press, 1958), pp. 345-46.

24 Odell Shepard, ed., *The Journals of Bronson Alcott* (Boston: Little Brown, 1938), pp. 238-39.

25 Michael Glenn Erlich, "Selected Anti-Slavery Speeches of Henry David Thoreau, 1848-1859: A Rhetorical Analysis," Diss. Ohio State 1970, pp. 210, 217, and 221; Alfred A. Funk, "Henry David Thoreau's 'Slavery in Massachusetts,' " *Western Speech*, 36 (Summer 1972), 165.

And, drawing the mourning allusion out into time-present, also in paragraph 41. But Thoreau in paragraph 6 completely disassociates himself from former Governor George S. Boutwell, who dodged implications of the Burns case by addressing the Worcester-North Agricultural Society at Fitchburg on the Fourth.[26] Even the water lily in paragraphs 50 and 51 reveals a narrative sincerity paralleling Rev. Henry Ward Beecher's "floral fanaticism" of June 28,[27] prior to addressing parishioner Charles A. Avery and other Painesville, Ohio, citizens opposed to making patriotic glory part of their observance on the Fourth.[28]

Thoreau doubtless traveled the roughly ten miles to the Framingham site via horse-drawn carriage, setting out from Concord at eight o'clock sharp rather than taking the 9:25 excursion train from Boston.[29] And he addressed the rally during the afternoon, after an hour's break for "refreshment and social recreation," the third person to speak following Wendell Phillips and Stephen S. Foster.[30]

The response to Thoreau's oration indeed revolved around the intensely controversial partisan milieu in which his activist mourning sought to operate, what Moncure D. Conway of Virginia regarded as the problem posed by the orator's "Disunionist sympathy" being important enough to undermine pacifist manner and intent ("serene unconsciousness of anything shocking").[31] Editor Garrison loyally felt the oration to be "racy and ably written,"[32] while Horace Greeley in the New York *Tribune* endeavored to place possible confusion with political advocacy ("*genuine* higher-law speech") within a less "unctious" mourning context. Thoreau's remarks, for editor Greeley, possessed "a rare piquancy and telling *point*, which none but a man thoroughly in earnest, and regardless of 'self' in his fidelity to a deep conviction, ever fully attains."[33]

Rev. Thomas W. Higginson, friend of the regional emigrant aid society's Eli

---

26 Worcester *Dly Spy*, 29 June, 1854.

27 Beecher, "Report datelined Painesville, Ohio-30 June," *The Independent* (NY City) in *Kennebec Journal* (Augusta, Me.), 21 July, 1854; Richard Tuerk, "Man and Nature in 'Slavery in Massachusetts,' " *Concord Saunterer*, 7 (March 1972), 9-10.

28 Painesville *Telegraph*, 7 June and 5 July, 1854.

29 Entry dated 4 July, 1854, *Journal*, ed. Torrey and Allen (1906; rpt. Dover, 1962), VI, 384; "Ad," *The Liberator*, 30 June, 1854.

30 *The Liberator*, 7 July, 1854. Two other references mentioning Thoreau's appearance at the rally are the *Liberator* summary in *National Anti-Slavery Standard* (NY City), 15 July, 1854, and a separate summary in the *Proceedings of the Massachusetts Anti-Slavery Society's Annual Meetings, 1854 thru 1856*, the latter reference reprinted in *Thoreau Society Bulletin*, NS 1 (Fall 1971), 7.

31 Moncure Daniel Conway, *Autobiography, Memories, and Experiences* (London: Cassell and Company, 1904), I, 162-63.

32 *The Liberator*, 7 July, 1854.

33 "A Higher-Law Speech," N-Y *Daily Tribune*, 2 Aug., 1854, reprinted in Walter Harding, "Thoreau and Horace Greeley," *Thoreau Society Bulletin*, 1 (April 1945), 3.

Thayer in Worcester,[34] and still under grand-jury suspicion as a conspirator in the amateurish non-rescue of Burns, likewise thought the oration pertinent enough to mourning, since it did typify a "surpassing literary statement" making truth "more manifest" on the national anniversary.[35] And the editor of the New Orleans *Picayune* saw obvious advantages in ignoring Thoreau's idealistic dissatisfaction with the Boston press. Instead, he excerpted paragraphs 16 and 19 from Greeley's *Tribune*, and labeled them "bricks from Babel" by an "elegant" orator presumptuously out-of-place as an effective mourner.[36] Only the editor of the *National Anti-Slavery Standard*, still laboring under the false impression that Thoreau was a "mere satellite and imitator" of Emerson, needed some reassurance, perhaps from correspondent Edmund Quincy, before partially reprinting the *Liberator* text.[37]

---

34 In this vein, one of many periodical articles quoting some segment of "Slavery in Massachusetts" is Cora Dolbee, "The Fourth of July in Early Kansas, 1854-57," *Kansas Historical Quarterly*, 10 (Feb. 1941), 36.

35 Newburyport, 13 Aug., 1854, Higginson to HDT, Concord, in *Thoreau Correspondence*, ed. Harding and Bode (Washington Square: New York University Press, 1958), p. 336. For Higginson's letter declining to attend the Framingham rally, see Rockport Mass., 28 June, H. to Garrison, Boston, in Margaret Munsterberg ed., "Letters by . . . Higginson," *More-Books*, 22 (Feb. 1947), 53.

36 "Refined Oratory," *Daily Picayune* (evening edition only, New Orleans La.), 9 Aug., 1854. On 13 July, both the morning and evening editions of the *Dly Picayune* carried the Framingham telegraphic report. But the *Picayune* staff grossly distorted the authentic version by having abolitionists "muster all colors" at the rally, tantamount of course to enlisting a measly six hundred not-so-fresh (or black) recruits for spectator service, and be addressed by "poor wretch" Garrison and "raver" Phillips of the same "kidney" (not "class"). Another southern paper, the Charleston *Mercury* (d) for the tenth, may deliberately have dated the telegraphic report 5 June-Boston, rather than 4 July-Framingham. Three random national versions, with noteworthy variations, are: *Daily Union* (WDC), 8 July, misspellings in Framing*ton* and Beman/Remond; Boston *Atlas* in *National Aegis* (Worcester), 12 July, the "usual" style of such a rally's speeches described as "ultra in the extreme," though Thoreau not mentioned; *Daily Morning Post* (Pittsburgh), 8 and 13 July, first version pretty much a standard reprint, but version two a Democratic partisan charge accusing Whigs of coalescing with Garrison, and his "outrageous desecration" of the Fourth in burning the U.S. Constitution. For the authentic version of the telegraphic report, see n. 7.

37 "Words That Burn," *Standard* (NY City), 12 Aug., 1854.

"Slavery in Massachusetts," an address delivered by Henry David Thoreau at Framingham Grove on the outskirts of Boston, July 4, 1854. The text of Thoreau's manuscript, as most readers are probably well aware, first was printed in Garrison's Liberator *(Boston) on the twenty-first, reprinted in full in Greeley's* Daily Tribune *(NY City) on August 2, and then partially reprinted by the* National Anti-Slavery Standard *(also NY City) ten days later. However, neither the* Semi-Weekly Tribune *(Ag 4) nor the* Weekly Tribune *(Ag 5) reprinted the speech text, perhaps because of contemporaneous excerpts already scheduled from "hermit" Thoreau's* Walden. *Although the revision-process text which follows incorporates Moncure Conway's oral sentence at the start of paragraph 1, the reader may prefer to go on to paragraph 4 after scanning the oral tenor of this Conway version, and briefly comparing it with sentence 2-paragraph 1 thru paragraph 3 (or Thoreau's written introduction). And the reader should ponder whether any additional gray-tinted segments were omitted by Thoreau in his oral presentation at Framingham. In the text below, Thoreau borrows certain* words *directly from his* Journal, *while other* words *bear no direct relationship to any 1851 or 1854* Journal *passages. Selected sentences, set off from the final draft as printed in* The Liberator, *point up process variations in pencil that Thoreau apparently jotted down in his* Journal, *somewhat haphazardly in the margins or between inked lines, prior to settling upon some final speech draft, no manuscript or galley proof for which is known to exist. The effect intended in making such textual comparisons is for the reader to grasp process implications inherent in Thoreau's alternate oral revisions. Hopefully the reader will glimpse a more sophisticated rhetorical dimension behind Wendell Glick's rather staid generalizations. Faced with a manuscript apparently discarded by editor Garrison shortly after the first printing, and with a probable galley text for the 1866* Yankee *reprint, reflect upon whether Glick falters a bit in his misleading use of "haste" in preparation and "many essentially unchanged"* Journal *entries, not to mention his machine collation of compositors' nuts-and-bolts errors as if they were relics of Thoreau's nonexistent speech manuscript or corrected galley proof. See pages 333-35 in Glick's* Reform Papers *in this regard.*

1 **Conway's version of oral introductory sentence:**

Fellow citizens, you have my sympathy; it is all I have to give you, but you may find it important to you.

I lately attended a meeting of the citizens of Concord, expecting, as one among many, to speak on the subject of slavery in Massachusetts; but I was surprised and disappointed to find that what had called my townsmen together was the destiny of Nebraska, and not of Massachusetts, and that what I had to say would be entirely out of order. I had thought that the house was on fire, and not the prairie; but though several of the citizens of Massachusetts are now in prison for attempting to rescue a slave from her own clutches, not one of the speakers at that meeting expressed regret for it, not one even referred to it. It was only the disposition of some wild lands a thousand miles off, which appeared to concern them. The inhabitants of Concord are not prepared to stand by one of their own bridges, but talk only of taking up a position on the highlands beyond the Yellowstone River. Our Buttricks, and Davises, and Hosmers are retreating thither, and I fear that they will have no Lexington Common between them and the enemy. There is not one slave in Nebraska; there are perhaps a million slaves in Massachusetts.

2 They who have been bred in the school of politics fail now and always to face the facts. Their measures are half-measures and make-shifts, merely. They put off the day of settlement indefinitely, and meanwhile, the debt accumulates. Though the Fugitive Slave Law had not been the subject of discussion on that occasion, it was at length faintly resolved by my townsmen, at an adjourned meeting, as I learn, that the compromise compact of 1820 having been repudiated by one of the parties, "Therefore, the Fugitive Slave Law must be repealed." But this is not the reason why an iniquitous law should be repealed. The fact which the politician faces is merely that there is less honor among thieves than was supposed, and not the fact that they are thieves.

3 A I had no opportunity to express my thoughts at that meeting, will you allow me to do so here?

4 Again it happens that the Boston Courthouse is full of armed men, holding prisoner and trying a MAN, to find out if he is not really a SLAVE. Does anyone think that Justice or God awaits Mr. Loring's decision? For him to sit there, deciding still when this question is already decided from eternity to eternity, and the unlettered slave himself, and the multitude around, have long since heard and assented to the decision is simply to make himself ridiculous. We may be tempted to ask from whom he received his commission, and who he is that received it; what novel statutes he obeys, and what precedents are to him of authority. Such an arbiter's very existence is an impertinence. We do not ask him to make up his mind, but to make up his pack.

5 I listen to hear the voice of a Governor, Commander-in-Chief of the forces of Massachusetts. I hear only the creaking of crickets and the hum of insects, which now fill the summer air. The Governor's exploit is to review the troops on muster days. I have seen him on horseback, with his hat off, listening to a chaplain's prayer. It chances that is all I have ever seen of a Governor. I think that I could manage to get along without one. If *he* is not of the least use to prevent my being kidnapped, pray of what important use is he likely to be to me? When freedom is most endangered, he dwells in the deepest obscurity. A distinguished clergyman told me that he chose the profession of a clergyman, because it afforded the most leisure for literary pursuits. I would recommend to him the profession of a Governor.

6 **Pierpont Morgan Journal:** ink ~~draft~~ **versus** pencil ~~draft~~

There is such an office if not such a man as the Governor of Massachusetts— What has he been about the last fortnight? He has probably had as much as he could do to keep on the fence during this moral earthquake. It seems to me that no ~~such~~ keener satire, no ~~such~~ more cutting insult could ~~be~~ have been offered to that man than just what happened— ~~this~~ the absence of all inquiry after him in this crisis. The most and the worst I know of this Governor is that he did not make himself known and attractive

improve that opportunity to make himself known and worthily known. It app[e]ars to have been forgotten that there was such a man or such an office. Yet no doubt he has been endeavoring to filling the Gubernatorial chair all the while— One Mr. Boutwell— so named ~~perchance~~ methinks because he goes about well to suit the prevailing winds. He is no Governor of mine[;] he does not govern me.

Speech text compared with manuscript passage above:

Three years ago, also, when the Simms' tragedy was acted, I said to myself, there is such an officer, if not such a man, as the Governor of Massachusetts,—what has he been about the last fortnight? Has he had as much as he could do to keep on the fence during this moral earthquake? It seemed to me that no keener satire could have been aimed at, no more cutting insult have been offered to that man, than just what happened—the absence of all inquiry after him in that crisis. The worst and the most I chance to know of him is that he did not improve that opportunity to make himself known, and worthily known. He could at least have *resigned* himself into fame. It appeared to be forgotten that there was such a man, or such an office. Yet no doubt he was endeavoring to fill the gubernatorial chair all the while. He was no Governor of mine. He did not govern me.

7 But at last, in the present case, the Governor was heard from. After he and the United States Government had perfectly succeeded in robbing a poor, innocent black man of his liberty for life and, as far as they could, of his Creator's likeness in his breast, he made a speech to his accomplices at a congratulatory supper!

8 I have read a recent law of this state, making it penal for "any officer of the Commonwealth" to "detain, or aid in the detention," anywhere within its limits, "of any person, for the reason that he is claimed as a fugitive slave." Also, it was a matter of notoriety that a writ of replevin to take the fugitive out of the custody of the United States Marshal could not be served, for want of sufficient force to aid the officer.

9 I had thought that the Governor was in some sense the executive officer of the state; that it was his business, as a Governor, to see that the laws of the state were executed; while, as a man, he took care that he did not, by so doing, break the laws of humanity; but when there is any special,

important use for him, he is useless, or worse than useless, and permits the laws of the state to go unexecuted. Perhaps I do not know what are the duties of a Governor; but if to be a Governor requires to subject one's self to so much ignominy without remedy, if it is to put a restraint upon my manhood, I shall take care never to be Governor of Massachusetts. I have not read far in the statutes of this Commonwealth. It is not profitable reading. They do not always say what is true, and they do not always mean what they say. What I am concerned to know is, that that man's influence and authority were on the side of the slaveholder, and not of the slave— of the guilty, and not of the innocent— of injustice, and not of justice. I never saw him of whom I speak; indeed, I did not know that he was Governor until this event occurred. I heard of him and Anthony Burns at the same time, and thus undoubtedly most will hear of him. So far am I from being governed by him. I do not mean that it was anything to his discredit that I had not heard of him, only that I heard what I did. The worst I shall say of him is, that he proved no better than the majority of his constituents would be likely to prove. In my opinion, he was not equal to the occasion.

10 The whole military force of the state is at the service of a Mr. Suttle, a slaveholder from Virginia, to enable him to catch a man whom he calls his property; but not a soldier is offered to save a citizen of Massachusetts from being kidnapped! Is this what all these soldiers, all this *training* has been for these 79 years past? Have they been trained merely to rob Mexico, and carry back fugitive slaves to their masters?

11 These very nights, I heard the sound of a drum in our streets. There were men *training* still; and for what? I could with an effort pardon the cockerels of Concord for crowing still, for they perchance had not been beaten that morning; but I could not excuse this rub-a-dub of the *trainers*. The slave was carried back by exactly such as these, i.e., by the soldier, of whom the best you can say in this connection is that he is a fool made conspicuous by a painted coat.

12 Three years ago, also, just a week after the authorities of Boston assembled to carry back a perfectly innocent man, and one whom they knew to be innocent, into slavery, the inhabitants of Concord caused the bells to be rung and the cannons to be fired, to celebrate their liberty— and the courage and love of liberty of their ancestors who fought at the bridge. As if *those* three millions had fought for the right to be free themselves, but to hold in slavery three millions others. Now-a-days, men wear a fool's cap, and call it a liberty cap. I do not know but there are some, who, if they were tied to a whipping-post and could get but one hand free, would use it to ring the bells and fire the cannons, to celebrate *their* liberty. So some of my townsmen took the liberty to ring and fire; that was the extent of their freedom; and when the sound of the bells died away also; when the powder was all expended, their liberty went off with the smoke.

13 The joke could be no broader, if the inmates of the prisons were to subscribe for all the powder to be used in such salutes, and hire the jailors to do the firing and ringing for them, while they enjoyed it through the grating.

14 This is what I thought about my neighbors.

15 Every humane and intelligent inhabitant of Concord, when he or she heard those bells and those cannons, thought not with pride of the events of the 19th of April, 1775, but with shame of the events of the 12th of April, 1851. But now we have half buried that old shame under a new one.

16 Massachusetts sat waiting Mr. Loring's decision, as if it could in any way affect her own criminality. Her crime, the most conspicuous and fatal crime of all, was permitting him to be the umpire in such a case. It was really the trial of Massachusetts. Every moment that she hesitated to set this man free— every moment that she now hesitates to atone for her crime, she is convicted. The Commissioner on her case is God; not Edward G. God, but simple God.

17 I wish my countrymen to consider, that whatever the human law may be, neither an individual nor a nation can ever commit the least act of injustice against the obscurest individual without having to pay the penalty for it. A government which deliberately enacts injustice, and persists in it, will at length ever become the laughing-stock of the world.

18 Much has been said about American slavery, but I think that we do not even yet realize what slavery is. If I were seriously to propose, to Congress, to make mankind into sausages, I have no doubt that most of the members would smile at my proposition, and if any believed me to be in earnest, they would think that I proposed something much worse than Congress had ever done. But if any of them will tell me that to make a man into a sausage would be much worse,—would be any worse than to make him into a slave,—than it was to enact the Fugitive Slave Law, I will accuse him of foolishness, of intellectual incapacity, of making a distinction without a difference. The one is just as reasonable a proposition as the other.

19 I hear a good deal said about trampling this law under foot. Why, one need not go out of his way to do that. This law rises not to the level of the head or the reason; its natural habitat is in the dirt. It was born and bred, and has its life only in the dust and mire, on a

level with the feet, and he who walks with freedom, and does not with Hindoo mercy avoid treading on every venomous reptile, will inevitably tread on it, and so trample it under foot,–and Webster, its maker, with it like the dirt-bug and its ball.

20 Recent events will be valuable as a criticism on the administration of justice in our midst, or rather as showing what are the true resources of justice in any community. It has come to this, that the friends of liberty, the friends of the slave, have shuddered when they have understood that his fate was left to the legal tribunals of the country to be decided. Free men have no faith that justice will be awarded in such a case; the judge may decide this way or that; it is a kind of accident, at best. It is evident that he is not a competent authority in so important a case. It is no time, then, to be judging according to his precedents, but to establish a precedent for the future. I would much rather trust to the sentiment of the people. In their vote, you would get something of some value, at least, however small; but, in the other case, only the trammeled judgment of an individual, of no significance, be it which way it might.

21 PROBABLE *since two pages of Journal missing*

It is to some extent fatal to the courts, when the people are compelled to go behind them. I do not wish to believe that the courts were made for fair weather, and for very civil cases merely,—but think of leaving it to any court in the land to decide whether more than three millions of people, in this case a sixth part of the nation, have a right to be freemen or not! But it has been left to the courts of *justice*, so-called— to the Supreme Court of the land— and as you all know, recognizing no authority but the Constitution, it has decided that the three millions are, and shall continue to be, slaves. Such judges as these are merely the inspectors of a pick-lock and murderer's tools to tell him whether they are in working order or not, and there they think that their responsibility ends. There was a prior case on the docket which they, as judges appointed by God, had no right to skip; which having been justly settled, they would have been saved from this humiliation. It was the case of the murderer himself.

22 PROBABLE *since two pages of Journal missing*

The law will never make men free; it is men who have got to make the law free. They are the lovers of law and order who observe the law when the government breaks it.

23 Among human beings, the judge whose words seal the fate of a man furthest into eternity is not he who merely pronounces the verdict of the law, but he, whoever he may be, who from a love of truth, and unprejudiced by any custom or enactment of men, utters a true opinion or *sentence* concerning him. He it is that *sentences him*. Whoever has discerned truth has received his commission from a higher source than the chiefest justice in the world, who can discern only law. He finds himself constituted judge of the judge.—Strange that it should be necessary to state such simple truths.

24 PROBABLE *since two pages of Journal missing*

I am more and more convinced that, with reference to any public question, it is more important to know what the country thinks of it, than what the city thinks. The city does not *think* much. On any moral question, I would rather have the opinion of Boxboro' than of Boston and New York put together. When the former speaks, I feel as if somebody *had* spoken, as if *humanity* was yet and a reasonable being had asserted its rights,—as if some unprejudiced men, among the country's hills, had at length turned their attention to the subject, and by a few sensible words redeemed the reputation of the race. When, in some obscure country town, the farmers come together to a special town meeting to express their opinion on some subject which is vexing the land, that, I think, is the true Congress and the most respectable one that is ever assembled in the United States.

25 PROBABLE *since two pages of Journal missing*

It is evident that there are, in this Commonwealth at least, two parties becoming more and more distinct— the party of the city, and the party of the country. I know that the country is mean enough, but I am glad to believe that there is a slight difference in her favor. But, as yet, she has few, if any, organs through which to express herself. The editorials which she reads, like the news, come from the seaboard. Let us, the inhabitants of the country, cultivate self-respect. Let us not send to the city for aught more essential than our broadcloths and groceries, or if we read the opinions of the city, let us entertain opinions of our own.

26 Among measures to be adopted, I would suggest to make as earnest and vigorous an assault on the Press as has already been made, and with effect, on the Church. The Church has much improved within a few years; but the Press is almost without exception corrupt. I believe that, in this country, the Press exerts a greater

and a more pernicious influence than the Church did in its worst period. We are not a religious people, but we are a nation of politicians.

Pierpont Morgan Journal: ink versus pencil draft

We do not much care for- we do not read the Bible— but we do care for and we do read the newspaper- We do not lose our vile deeds because they are put away in it/. It is a bible which we read every morning and every aftern[o]on standing and sitting—riding and walking- It is a bible which every man carries in his pocket and which lies on every table and counter which the mail and thousands of missionaries are continually dispensing— It is the only book which America has printed and is Capable of exerting an almost inconceivable influence for good or for bad. The ?) editor is preacher whom you voluntarily support. Your tax is commonly one cent daily— and it costs nothing for pew-hire.

Speech text compared with manuscript passage above:

We do not care for the Bible, but we do care for the newspaper. At any meeting of politicians,—like that at Concord the other evening, for instance,—how impertinent it would be to quote from the Bible! how pertinent to quote from a newspaper or from the Constitution! The newspaper is a Bible which we read every morning and every afternoon, standing and sitting, riding and walking. It is a Bible which every man carries in his pocket, which lies on every table and counter, and which the mail, and thousands of missionaries, are continually dispensing. It is, in short, the only book which America has printed, and which America reads. So wide is its influence. The editor is a preacher whom you voluntarily support. Your tax is commonly one cent daily, and it costs nothing for pew hire.

But how many of these preachers preach the truth? I repeat the testimony of many an intelligent foreigner, as well as my own convictions, when I say that probably no country was ever ruled by so mean a class of tyrants as, with a few noble exceptions, are the editors of the periodical press in *this* country. And as they live and rule only by their servility, and appealing to the worst and not the better nature of man, the people who read them are in the condition of the dog that returns to his vomit.

27 The *Liberator* and the *Commonwealth* were the only papers in Boston, as far as I know, which made themselves heard in condemnation of the cowardice and meanness of the authorities of that city, as exhibited in '51. The other journals almost without exception, by their manner of referring to and speaking of the Fugitive Slave Law, and the carrying back of the slave Simms, insulted the common sense of the country at least. And for the most part they did this, one would say, because they thought so to secure the approbation of their patrons, not being aware that a sounder sentiment prevailed to any ex-

tent in the heart of the Commonwealth. I am told that some of them have improved of late; but they are still eminently time-serving. Such is the character they have won.

28 But, thank fortune, this preacher can be even more easily reached by the weapons of the reformer than could the recreant priest. The free men of New England have only to refrain from purchasing and reading these sheets, have only to withhold their cents to kill a score of them at once. One whom I respect told me that he purchased Mitchel's *Citizen* in the cars, and then threw it out the window. But would not his contempt have been more fatally expressed if he had not bought it?

29 Are they Americans, are they New Englanders, are they inhabitants of Lexington and Concord and Framingham, who read and support the Boston *Post, Mail, Journal, Advertiser, Courier*, and *Times*? Are these the flags of our Union? I am not a newspaper reader and may omit to name the worst.

30 Could slavery suggest a more complete servility than some of these journals exhibit? Is there any dust which their conduct does not lick and make fouler still with its slime? I do not know whether the Boston *Herald* is still in existence, but I remember to have seen it about the streets when Simms was carried off. Did it not act its part well— serve its master faithfully? How could it have gone lower on its belly? How can a man stoop lower than he is low, do more than put his extremities in the place of the head he has, than make his head his lower extremity? When I have taken up this paper, with my cuffs turned up, I have heard the gurgling of the sewer through every column. I have felt that I was handling a paper picked out of the public gutters, a leaf from the gospel of the gambling-house, the groggery, and the brothel harmonizing with the gospel of the Merchants' Exchange.

31 The majority of the men of the North and of the South and East and West are not men of principle. If they vote, they do not send men to Congress on errands of humanity, but while their brothers and sisters are being scourged and hung for loving liberty—— I might here insert all that slavery implies and is,——it is the mismanagement of wood and iron and stone and gold which concerns them. Do what you will, Oh Government, with my wife and children, my mother and brother, my father and sister, I will obey your commands to the letter. It will indeed grieve me if you hurt them, if you deliver them to overseers to be hunted by hounds or to be whipped to death; but, nevertheless, I will peaceably pursue my chosen calling on this fair earth until perchance, one day, when I have put on mourning for them dead, I shall have persuaded you to relent. Such is the attitude, such are the words of Massachusetts.

32 Rather than do thus. I need not say what match I would touch, what system endeavor to blow up,—but as I love my life, I would side with the light and let the dark earth roll from under me, calling my mother and my brother to follow.

33 I would remind my countrymen that they are to be men first, and Americans only, at a late and convenient hour. No matter how valuable law may be to protect your property, even to keep soul and body together, if it do not keep you and humanity together.

34 **Houghton printed Journal text:**

I do not believe that there is a judge in this country prepared to decide by the principle that a law is immoral and therefore of no force.

Speech text compared with Houghton passage above:

I am sorry to say that I doubt if there is a judge in Massachusetts who is prepared to resign his office, and get his living innocently, whenever it is required of him to pass sentence under a law which is merely contrary to the law of God.

I am compelled to see that they put themselves, or rather are by character in this respect, exactly on a level with the marine who discharges his musket in any direction he is ordered to. They are just as much tools and as little men. Certainly they are not the more to be respected, because their master enslaves their understandings and consciences instead of their bodies.

35 The judges and lawyers,—simply as such, I mean,—and all men of expediency try this case by a very low and incompetent standard. They consider not whether the Fugitive Slave Law is right, but whether it is what they call *constitutional*. Is virtue constitutional, or vice? Is equity constitutional, or iniquity? In important moral and vital questions like this, it is just as impertinent to ask whether a law is constitutional or not, as to ask whether it is profitable or not. They persist in being the servants of the worst of men and not the servants of humanity. The question is not whether you or your grandfather, seventy years ago, did not enter into an agreement to serve the devil, and that service is not accordingly now due; but whether you will not now, for once and at last, serve God,—in spite of your own past recreancy, or that of your ancestor,—by obeying that eternal and only just CONSTITUTION which He, and not any Jefferson or Adams, has written in your being.

36 The amount of it is, if the majority vote the devil to be God, the minority will live and behave accordingly, trusting that some time or other, by some Speaker's casting vote perhaps, they may reinstate God. This is the highest principle I can get out of or invent for my neighbors. These men act as if they believed that they could safely slide downhill a little way— or a good way— and would surely come to a place, by and by, where they could begin to slide up again. This is expediency, or choosing that course which offers the slightest obstacles to the feet, that is, a downhill one. But there is no such thing as accomplishing a righteous reform by the use of *expediency*. There is no such thing as sliding uphill. In morals, the only sliders are backsliders.

37 Thus we steadily worship Mammon, both school and state and church, and the seventh day curse God with a tintamar from one end of the Union to the other.

38 Will mankind never learn that policy is not morality— that it never secures any moral right but considers merely what is expedient, chooses the available candidate who is invariably the devil.—And what right have his constituents to be surprised because the devil does not behave like an angel of light? What is wanted is men, not of policy, but of probity— who recognize a higher law than the Constitution or the decision of the majority. The fate of the country does not depend on how you vote at the polls

Pierpont Morgan Journal: pencil draft **continued, same sentence**

[—] but on how you vote every where [,] and though you should have removed to solitary confinement [up]on which [the] manner of men [depends?]

Speech text, markedly different version:

— the worst man is as strong as the best at that game; it does not depend on what kind of paper you drop into the ballot-box once a year, but on what kind of man you drop from your chamber into the street every morning.

39 What should concern Massachusetts is not the Nebraska Bill, nor the Fugitive Slave Bill, but her own slaveholding and servility. Let the state dissolve her union with the slaveholder.

Houghton printed Journal text:

She can find no respectable law or precedent which sanctions its continuance.

Speech text compared with Houghton passage above:

She may wriggle and hesitate, and ask leave to read the Constitution once more; but she can find no respectable law or precedent which sanctions the continuance of such a union for an instant.

40 Let each inhabitant of the state dissolve his union with her, as long as she delays to do her duty.

41 The events of the past month teach me to distrust fame. I see that she does not finely discriminate, but coarsely hurrahs. She considers not the simple heroism of an action, but only as it is connected with its apparent consequences. She praises, 'til she is hoarse, the easy exploit of the Boston Tea Party, but will be comparatively silent about the braver and more disinterestedly heroic attack on the Boston Courthouse, simply because it was unsuccessful!

42 Covered with disgrace, the state has sat down coolly to try for their lives and liberties the men who attempted to do its duty for it. And this is called *justice*! They who have shown that they can behave particularly well may perchance be under bonds for *their good behavior*.

Pierpont Morgan Journal: pencil draft **INSERT**

And the one whom truth requires at present to plead guilty is perchance the one who is preeminently innocent-

Comparison with speech text version:

They whom truth requires at present to plead guilty are of all the inhabitants of the state preeminently innocent.

While the Governor and the Mayor and countless officers of the Commonwealth are at large, the champions of liberty are imprisoned.

43 Only they are guiltless who commit the crime of contempt of such a Court. It behooves every man to see that his influence is on the side of justice, and let the courts make their own characters. My sympathies in this case are wholly with the accused, and wholly against the accusers and their judges. Justice is sweet and musical, but injustice is harsh and discordant. The judge still sits grinding at his organ, but it yields no music and we hear only the sound of the handle. He believes that all the music resides in the handle, and the crowd toss him their coppers the same as before.

44 Do you suppose, that that Massachusetts which is now doing these things,—which hesitates to crown these men, some of whose lawyers and even judges perchance may be driven to take refuge in some poor quibble, that they may not wholly outrage their instinctive sense of justice,—do you suppose that she is anything but base and servile, that she is the champion of liberty?

45 Show me a free state and a Court truly of justice, and I will fight for them if need be; but show me Massachusetts, and I refuse her my allegiance and express contempt for her courts!

46 The effect of a good government is to make life more valuable,—of a bad one, to make it less valuable. We can afford that that railroad and all other merely material stock should lose some of its value, for that only compels us to live more simply and economically; but suppose that the value of life itself should be diminished. How can we make a less demand on man and Nature, how live more economically in respect to virtue and all noble qualities than we do?

Houghton printed Journal text:

Every man in New England capable of the sentiment of patriotism must have lived the last three weeks with the sense of having suffered a vast, indefinite loss.

Speech text compared with Houghton passage above:

I have lived for the last month,—and I think that every man in Massachusetts capable of the sentiment of patriotism must have had a similar experience,—with the sense of having suffered a vast and indefinite loss.

Pierpont Morgan Journal: pencil draft **INSERT**

At last it occurs to him that what he has lost is a country. I did not know at first what ail[e]d me.

Comparison with speech text version:

I did not know at first what ailed me. At last it occurred to me that what I had lost was a country.

I had never respected the government near to which I had lived, but I had foolishly thought that I might manage to live here, minding my private affairs, and forget it.

Pierpont Morgan Journal: pencil draft **INSERT continued**

It is the discovery of what kind of men your countrymen are.

For my part, my old and worthiest pursuits have lost I cannot say how much of their attraction, and I feel that my investment in life here is worth many percent less since Massachusetts last deliberately sent back an innocent man, Anthony Burns, to slavery. I dwelt before, perhaps, in the illusion that my life passed somewhere only *between* heaven and hell, but now I cannot persuade myself that I do not dwell *wholly within* hell. The site of that political organization called Massachusetts is to me morally covered with volcanic scoriae and cinders, such as Milton describes in the infernal regions.

v **Pierpont Morgan Journal:** ink ~~draft~~ **versus** pencil draft

If ~~hell is~~ there is any hell more unprincipled than our rulers and ~~our~~ we the people- ~~I feel curious to visit it~~ it occurs to me to visit it out of mild curiosity.

Speech text compared with manuscript passage above:

If there is any hell more unprincipled than our rulers and we the ruled, I feel curious to see it.

Life itself being worth less, all things with it, which minister to it, are worth less. Suppose you have a small library, with pictures to adorn the walls— a garden laid out around, and contemplate scientific and literary pursuits, etc., and discover all at once that your villa with all its contents is located in hell, and that the justice of the peace has a cloven foot and a forked tail— do not these things suddenly lose their value in your eyes?

47 I feel that to some extent the state has fatally interfered in my lawful business. It has not only interrupted me in my passage through Court Street on errands of trade, but it has interrupted me and every man on his onward-and-upward path, on which he had trusted soon to leave Court Street far behind. What right had it to remind me of Court Street? I have found that hollow, which even I had relied on for solid.

48 I am surprised to see men going about their business as if nothing had happened. I say to myself— "Unfortunates, they have not heard the news!" I am surprised that the man whom I just met on horseback should be so earnest to overtake his newly-bought cows running away, since all property is insecure and if they do not run away again, they may be taken away from him when he gets them. Fool, does he not know that his seed corn is worth less this year— that all beneficent harvests fail as you approach the empire of hell? No

prudent man will build a store-house under these circumstances, or engage in any peaceful enterprise which requires a long time to accomplish. Art is as long as ever, but life is more interrupted and less available for a man's proper pursuits. It is not an era of repose. We have used up all our inherited freedom. If we would save our lives, we must fight for them.

49 I walk toward one of our ponds, but what signifies the beauty of Nature when men are base? We walk to lakes, to see our serenity reflected in them; when we are not serene, we go not to them. Who can be serene in a country where both the rulers and the ruled are without principle? The remembrance of my country spoils my walk. My thoughts are murder to the state and involuntarily go plotting against her.

50 But it chanced the other day that I secured a white water-lily, and a season I had waited for had arrived. It is the emblem of purity. It bursts up so pure and fair to the eye, and so sweet to the scent, as if to show us what purity and sweetness reside in, and can be extracted from, the slime and muck of earth. I think I have plucked the first one that has opened for a mile. What confirmation of our hopes is in the fragrance of this flower! I shall not so soon despair of the world for it, notwithstanding slavery and the cowardice and want of principle of Northern men. It suggests what kind of laws have prevailed longest and widest and still prevail, and that the time may come when man's deeds may smell as sweet. Such is the odor which the plant emits. If Nature can compound this fragrance still annually, I shall believe her still young and full of vigor, her integrity and genius unimpaired, and that there is virtue even in man too, who is fitted to perceive and love it. It reminds me that Nature has been partner to no Missouri Compromise. I scent no compromise in the fragrance of the water-lily. It is not a *Nymphoea Douglassii*. In it, the sweet and pure and innocent are wholly sundered from the obscene and baleful. I do not scent in this the time-serving irresolution of a Massachusetts Governor, nor of a Boston Mayor. So behave that the odor of your actions may enhance the general sweetness of the atmosphere, that when we behold or scent a flower, we may not be reminded how inconsistent your deeds are with it; for all odor is but one form of advertisement of a moral quality, and if fair actions had not been performed, the lily would not smell sweet. The foul slime stands for the sloth and vice of man, the decay of humanity; the fragrant flower that springs from it for the purity and courage which are immortal.

51 Slavery and servility have produced no sweet-scented flower annually to charm the senses of men, for they have no real life: they are merely a decaying and a death offensive to all healthy nostrils. We do not complain that they *live*, but that they do not *get buried*! Let the living bury them; even they are good for manure.

Oration delivered by Wendell Phillips at Framingham Grove, July 4, 1854, text printed in The Liberator *(Boston), July 14.*

1 I do not know, ladies and gentlemen, that you will like the *first* part, at any rate, of my speech, which is merely to deliver a message to you, from one who is going just now to invade your seats, in behalf of the antislavery cause. I come to tell you that Abby Kelley Foster is to be among you; and what she comes for, you know very well. It is for "the sinews of war"—for the means of carrying this enterprise throughout the state. God has given us a text in the late events in the city of Boston, and now our object is to take out the burthen of that rebuke and preach a sermon upon it in every great town in Massachusetts. Massachusetts is ready to hear. The public ear was never so thoroughly aroused and awake as it is at this moment; you all know it; and in one form or another, either by our organization or by some other means, if we love the antislavery agitation we are bound to make use of this summer when public attention is so much aroused, to press upon all those who are turning their eyes for the first time to the claims of the slavery question, the nature and importance of that question, and prepare them for their duties, civil and political as well as religious, on this question. We are importuned from every town in the Commonwealth to send them lecturers; and if you will give us the means, we will try to do it. We will try to make Massachusetts worthy of the name she has always taken to herself of an antislavery state. We will try to make her worthy to send back *Charles Sumner* to the Senate, if they shall think him worthy of expulsion. I wish they would expel him; it would teach Massachusetts where she stands before the National Government.

2 I should prefer, Mr. Chairman, to make a speech entirely on the subject of money. I really do not feel any great interest in any other part of the question at this moment. I do not believe in an antislavery which undertakes to listen or to make speeches, just now. I have had enough on that. What we want in reality is a spot, however small—whether it be the state of Massachusetts or half of it—which we can truly say is a free state; of which we can say that a fugitive slave is safe there; that, no matter how many laws are made to the contrary, Constitution or no Constitution, law or no law, the moment a slave sets his foot on that soil he never goes back. That is what we want to make Massachusetts. We never shall make her that by undertaking to think that she is so when she is not. My friend, Mr. Conway, who has just addressed you, described us rightly as just as much slaves as the parties in whose behalf we move. I am sorry to dissent in any degree from the remarks with which Mr. Garrison introduced this meeting. I do not agree with them. I do not fully believe with our eloquent Senator at Washington that Massachusetts ever was entirely an antislavery state, or indeed that there ever was such a state in this country. The truth is there is more real antislavery [sentiment] in this country now than there ever was before. We may thank God, everyone of us, that we have lived to see the day when there was so much antislavery [sentiment] in the city of Boston that it took

two thousand armed men to carry a slave out of its streets. The day was, when we were boys, that they took a fugitive slave into a back parlor and sent him home without its being considered as a piece of news, even in the newspapers. The day was when no man entered a courtroom where a fugitive was being tried, when no lawyer volunteered his services, no judge hesitated an hour. Old Judge Davis, (to whom the Sims Commissioner refers in one of his recent letters), sent back a fugitive and not ten men in Boston knew of it;—and that was not more than thirty years ago. Antislavery is now at a great deal higher growth than ever before.

3 I think that the Fourth of July never was a day of Liberty—never until the abolitionists used it. The Declaration of Independence is not a Declaration of Liberty; it is what it purports to be, a Declaration of *Independence* and nothing more. It undertook to separate the connection betwixt the colonies and Great Britain. It ends off by declaring that, therefore, "they are, and of right ought to be—states without slavery in them?" Not at all: states where every man is a freeman? Not a bit of it—these colonies "are, and of right ought to be, *free and independent States*." That is what they fought for; that they got. Seven years they fought for it, and they succeeded; and ever since these states have been "free and independent" of all foreign power. That is what our fathers went to war for, and that they got. But it is not true, it cannot be made out from history that our fathers had any hatred of African slavery in 1776. It is not in the record. The allusion to the slave trade in the Declaration of Independence, as one of the grievances forced upon the colonies by the King, was struck out of that instrument. Our fathers had just as much hatred of slavery as the Whigs of Boston have today;—that is, they hated slavery abstractly; they were willing that slavery should perish; but they were not willing to make a sacrifice for it. They would sacrifice neither the commerce nor the union of the country, neither the wealth nor the strength of the colonies for the sake of abolishing slavery. They had the same hatred of slavery that the *Daily Advertiser* has today;—that is, a hatred that will round beautiful periods against it; that will make good speeches against it; but not a feeling that will sacrifice anything for the antislavery cause; and there never was any such feeling in the country until the antislavery enterprise created it.

4 The fourth day of July has been exactly what our fathers made it—the jubilee of a nation for its independence. It becomes us, their children, to take one step further than they dared to take, and to add to Independence, *Liberty*—which they dared not add. They did not dare to risk the union of the country, they did not dare to risk their material prosperity for the slave question. There were a few leading men that did: Jefferson, Adams, Wythe, Jay, and some other distinguished men. So there are, now; in exactly the same circumstances. This is the use I wish to make of the lesson: Do not imagine, because there are a few leading men whose names are to go down to posterity, who are in favor of freedom—do not imagine, because *Chase* and *Hale* and *Sumner* and our friend here, *Garrison*, will leave their names for posterity, to love and reverence as

lovers of liberty—that it is any proof that Massachusetts, at the present moment, is an antislavery state; neither was it the case in '76 because John Hancock and Sam Adams and John Lowell and Josiah Quincy and a few other men hated slavery.

5 The reason Burns went back from Boston was because the men of Boston were willing he should go—there is no other reason; and we have nothing to do but to stand here, day and night, and preach that lesson without intermission. The reason the slave is sent back is because the men of Massachusetts will it—nothing else. If it had not been so, why didn't you give us a Governor and not a dish of skimmed milk in his place? Had we had a Massachusetts Governor that week, Burns need not have gone back! Had we had a Mayor of Boston instead of an uncooked hasty-pudding, Burns need not have gone back! If we had had a will throughout the Commonwealth that would have undertaken to say, "The law shall not be executed!" Burns would not have gone back! If there had been an arrest at Richmond, Virginia, or at Charleston, South Carolina, where do you suppose their Governors would have been?—in those cities, or somewhere else addressing a Sunday School? If you are really abolitionists, give us a Governor that has outgrown the Sunday School; give us somebody who can do something else than address a Bible Society when the laws of Massachusetts are trodden underfoot!

6 There is no reasonable hope of the success of the antislavery enterprise, until you make up your minds that it is not somebody else, but you, that return fugitive slaves. It is not Colonel Suttle of Virginia; it is not Franklin Pierce nor Caleb Cushing at Washington; it is *Massachusetts* that owns Massachusetts; and if you that vote every year in November for laws and lawmakers choose to make this an antislavery state, you can do it next November [in] spite of all the Caleb Cushings or Franklin Pierces that the Government can buy up!

7 I am not going to make a long speech; but I will tell you the work which I would point out for abolitionists to do this summer—the work which will make Massachusetts what she boasts herself to be, an antislavery state. When it is done, I will be proud of the old Bay State. I used to be proud of her. Time was when I took on my lips the name of the old Commonwealth, with a glow of conscious pride that gave depth to the tones of my voice and an added pulse to the heart. I was proud of her; but, my pride all vanished when I saw that old Indian on her banner go floating down State Street with the slave brigade, with Ben Hallett and the United States Marshal and a chained slave beneath him. I have lost all pride in Massachusetts 'til she redeems herself from that second day of June.

8 Now, my friends, I will tell you what is left for us to do. Let us take this summer to roll up a petition, that shall be a hundred thousand strong, to the Legislature that is to assemble in January, asking them to turn *Edward Greeley Loring* out of the office of Judge of Probate. If we do not do that, we shall not be

a *decent* state to begin with. The second thing is, let us ask them for a law by which any man who helps in any way the return of a fugitive slave shall be forever disqualified from leaving office in Massachusetts. Let us ask them for a law that shall direct the judges of the Commonwealth to issue a writ of *habeas corpus* just as often as the United States Marshal arrests a slave, no matter if they have to issue a hundred in a week, and take him out of his hands. Let us learn of South Carolina, and nullify the Fugitive Slave Bill on the soil of Massachusetts. If the present Supreme Court would not do it, amend the Constitution and *elect* another. When we are an antislavery state, that is what we are to do.

9 It is in vain to make national parties. It is in vain to get up Liberty Parties and Free Soil Parties, stretching from the old Bay State back to the Mississippi. National politics is not possible. The Government has got the better of us. Slavery has got fifty million dollars of revenue to spend every year: *fifty millions of dollars*! We live in a country where if you put a dollar on the other side of hell, the Yankees will spring for it at the risk of tumbling in. We live in a land of money—you know it; and do you suppose that a Government with fifty millions of dollars to spend every year cannot buy up enough men in a year to carry any vote they wish to? How many men does it take in the city of Washington to carry any vote? Not more than thirty. This very year on the Nebraska question the votes of white men, white *Democrats*, were bought cheaper in the city of Washington than you could buy black slaves. It is a literal fact that Democratic votes were bought cheaper in Washington for the Nebraska Bill than an able-bodied slave thirty years old! Now, do you believe that a Government with fifty millions of dollars to spend annually can be checkmated? Never! The only way to checkmate it is to checkmate it at home. Massachusetts is our's, if we choose to make it so. We can nullify this Fugitive Slave Bill. We can put on that Supreme bench judges who will laugh to defiance the Congress of the United States when they undertake to carry a fugitive slave out of Massachusetts!

10 Give me an antislavery state, and I will leave it to antislavery Yankees to find out a way. Do you suppose the men who make wooden nutmegs and cheat all the South are not sharp enough to outwit us because her people are shrewder than Yankees? No! It is because we love to be cheated on this question; it is because our politicians are willing to compromise, and have been ever since '76. I will set a Yankee to have his way, and [you] find the means to have it against the world. And yet you tell me to believe in an antislavery New England that has been outwitted for sixty years! I don't believe it. I believe that when New England wants a thing, and wants it *with a will*, she will have it! The only reason why she has not had antislavery legislation is because she has not wanted it. One man has been making brooms on the banks of the Connecticut, and another manufacturing cotton in Lowell, and another curing fish on the seaboard, and another making shoes up and down the county of Essex, and,

provided they made money enough, they let the Government have its way. And then we send Mr. Sumner to Washington, and we send gentlemen to deliver Fourth of July orations to make it out that Massachusetts is an antislavery state. She is not! But the time has gone by when you can smuggle a slave out of the state. Thank God, you have got to smother down the antislavery sentiment of '54 with two thousand armed men in State Street before you can carry a slave from Court Square to T-wharf. That is growth. There is another evidence of growth. The spear of antislavery rebuke has pierced through even the hide of *George T. Curtis*, and proved that there is a living spot of moral life even in his body. It has disproved the old doctrine of Total Depravity. The old physicians used to say, "Experimentum in corpore vili;"—you must try experiments on a worthless thing. We followed the counsel. We tried an experiment on the most worthless thing we could get, and the antislavery spear has pierced through the hide of *George T. Curtis* and proved, by these very letters he writes, that there is a moral live spot even in him; and, therefore, we may hope for all above him!

11 The great difficulty here in Massachusetts is we are so fond of praising ourselves; so fond of rejoicing at the indignation that we feel; so fond of the afterthought of next week; of telling how indignant the "rural" districts of the state are at the kidnapping of a slave in Boston. I met a man, a week after Burns was surrendered, and he asked me, "Mr. Phillips, was Burns really a Baptist minister?" Said I, "He was, sir, a Baptist exhorter regularly licensed." "Well," said he, "I didn't take much interest in the case; but when I heard that Major General Edmands had sent back a brother Baptist, I couldn't sleep." He took no interest in the man—it was in the *Baptist*! He heard the mere fact of a human being surrendered as a chattel—and he went about his business; but when he heard that one Baptist had surrendered another Baptist, *it disturbed his slumber!* That is, to some extent, a fair specimen of much of the antislavery excitement we hear of about us. A week after Burns was sent away, we went down into State Street with a petition asking for the removal of *Edward Greeley Loring* from office, and we asked the gentlemen of State Street to sign it;—(they were the very men who had volunteered, among themselves, to rescue Burns and to tar and feather Suttle),—but six days had rolled away, and they were not ready even to sign a petition to remove Loring from his office as Judge of Probate! So much had their zeal cooled down in a single week. This is the antislavery sentiment of Massachusetts.

12 We shall never get any better until we see ourselves in an honest glass; until we get out of this habit of praising ourselves. The people of Massachusetts are not abolitionists—but [only] a very small portion of them. The state is a proslavery state as a whole. The Fourth of July is a proslavery day—a day meant to commemorate the independence of thirteen states, in every one of which there were slaves when the Declaration was issued; and not one of which took the slightest measure, for four years afterwards, to free a slave.

13 Now, gentlemen, I know that I might make a much more acceptable speech to you today. I might make a speech that should raise your plaudits, perhaps, by praising some of our antislavery men and measures. I could praise, as he deserves, your favorite Massachusetts Senator, Mr. *Sumner*, who has made a noble speech, and has grown an inch at least in moral stature within the last fortnight; but that is not what we want. I have had enough of antislavery plaudits. I lost my relish for them when I saw a whole city lying prostrate at the feet of a Virginia slavehunter. We have got to begin over again, from the root. We do not want reformation; as Mr. Conway says, we want a *revolution*—just as real and far more radical than that which our fathers undertook to make.

14 Then there is another thing as your work for this summer. Turn out Loring as the first thing; get a statute that shall nullify the slave law as a second;—the third is this: appoint officers and elect a Governor and Legislature that shall be Massachusetts men. It would have been a refreshing sight if, any time during those seven days of anxiety and trial, we could have seen a *man* in Boston. You could not find one. You could not find a *man* who would take the slightest responsibility. The Mayor could not do anything unless Mr. Hillard told him;—and Mr. Hillard could not say anything unless the Mayor asked him;—the Sheriff could not do anything unless Attorney-General Clifford advised it;—and Attorney-General Clifford could not give any advice unless the Governor asked him;—and the Governor had gone up to Worcester and nobody could find him! During that whole week, a dozen *men* employed the greater part of their time in hunting up Massachusetts officers and beseeching them to do something. They all acknowledged that something ought to be done, but nobody could settle [on] who ought to do it! We want a *real* Governor and Mayor, and you can make them! We want a *real* antislavery Legislature, not one that *talks* antislavery! We want South Carolina [to come] over again on the side of liberty. I like her pluck. When she did not fancy Mr. Hoar, she turned him out of the state. I am for turning out the *men* we do not like, not talking about them. I am for having half a dozen *men* wait on the slavehunter, when he comes to Boston on his infamous errand, and escort him to the boundary line between this state and Rhode Island; and then bid him a polite farewell. Then we can afford to despise Caleb Cushing, and not 'til then.

15 When we get antislavery law officers, we will find antislavery law enough. Chief Justice Shaw can outwit Caleb Cushing any day, and not get up 'til twelve o'clock in the morning besides. We have got Massachusetts lawyers as sharp as Philadelphia ones, if you will only show them you want them to exert their shrewdness. Our judges have law enough; it is the people behind them that is wanted;—it is South Carolina on the side of liberty; it is Virginia in favor of the black man having his rights! In the meantime, Massachusetts is a peddling state—sells her wares in the best market and looks out she don't offend her customers; and then comes home and congratulates herself that she is so *very*

antislavery because *Charles Sumner* has made a good speech in Congress! Yes, we can make good speeches enough, good resolutions enough; what we want is a good executive here at home!

16 We have had a Free Soil Party in this state. They undertook to nominate Martin Van Buren for President; they did not elect him. Any party that undertakes to get up a national movement will be bought up, because slavery is inside the Government fortress and has fifty millions of dollars to spend annually; and you never yet saw the land where, if you wanted a mean thing done and had the money to pay for it, you could not find mean *men* to do it.

17 I know I am talking of very low motives; but I am talking to Yankees; I am talking to Americans in the nineteenth century; I am talking of the *men* who put Franklin Pierce into office; I am talking plain, matter-of-fact [events] that we meet every day. You will never have an antislavery Government while slavery has fifty millions of dollars to spend every year—she can buy us up. They say it cost "mighty dear" to get Burns back. *Fifty thousand dollars*!—horribly dear! I think it was very cheap. She bought all Boston for fifty thousand dollars and we threw the Governor in. She had our regiment, our Mayor, our Court-house, our judiciary, the whole Commonwealth—she only paid fifty thousand dollars for it! *Cheap as dirt!* Why, she can afford to buy states up at that rate for any length of time to come. If it costs only fifty thousand dollars to buy Boston, what hope have we? And yet it is literally true that for that [sum] the United States Government bought the city.

18 My friends, I am now going to give place to others; but let me urge every man who loves the antislavery cause to confine his attention to his own state. State politics are within our control. We can put a Legislature into that Statehouse that shall hermetically seal Massachusetts against the slavehunter; and the moment we set the example Ohio, Michigan, and young Iowa and Wisconsin will follow; and state by state we can defy the Fugitive Slave Bill. Try a little *nullification* on our side! Why, we are very slow scholars. The South has been teaching us for forty years and yet we won't learn! She says—"Gentlemen, imitate me! I never let United States law get executed when it don't please me—why do you?"

19 My Free-Soil friends who are listening to me are anxious to put another Senator into the United States Senate, and to put Representatives into the House. I entreat them to forget Congress for a little while. We can do nothing there; it is beyond our reach. The National Government has beaten us. It is a melancholy fact—but it *is* a fact. She has written *Nebraska* over the tomb of our hope; she will soon add *Cuba* to the legend; and then she will revive the slave trade;—very little doubt of it. But in the meantime, though you cannot affect Congress, you can do this: With proper effort this summer, we can put a Legislature into that Statehouse in Boston which shall give us a series of statutes

better than Connecticut, better than Rhode Island, which will make it utterly impossible to execute that law in the state of Massachusetts. When we have done that, we can defy Congress. When we have made her a free state, we can begin to think of [the] outside. "Charity begins at home!" You know, farmers say, the man who takes a large farm never cultivates it faithfully; and the antislavery idea, if it undertakes to cultivate a nation, fails. Confine your efforts, friends, to a small Commonwealth, and we can plough deep and have a rich harvest! I mean what I say. I believe that the politics of antislavery—if there be any politics with antislavery—is *nullification.* That is the only politics that is possible in the present aspect of affairs. I commend it to you for your serious *work*—not consideration; to the efforts, the continued labor of this summer, so that we may really be able to boast of an antislavery government here in the Commonwealth next fall.

Chapter 10

Thomas Starr King's Fourth of July Oration, 1861

In the spring of 1860, an enterprising minister, Thomas Starr King by name, took leave of Boston's Hollis-Street parish. After venting the customary complaints about accommodations on Cornelius Vanderbilt's steamers during the voyage from New York via Aspinwall, he stepped ashore on what surely seemed a stark San Francisco waterfront, accepting in person the pastorate of California's only Unitarian Church, an organization far more heavily in debt than perhaps he ever realized.

California itself by the Fourth holiday, one year later, in a sense had to journey back to the East, at least to sustain any sentiment for carrying on the war effort of Union forces against a Confederate secessionist clique. And what better selection for such an oratorical emigré could the executive committee of the Sacramento Union Club make than pastor King? For not only was King well-versed in adapting Revolutionary lore to popular audiences, who just might share substantial empathy with the Union war effort if the proper chord were struck in the state capital. King was renowned, as well, as the proponent of a "living" Christian ethic, a standard presumably at odds with the "debauching influence" on "sensitive minds" perpetrated by "grandiloquent and undiscriminating" anniversary orations, replete as he preferred to believe with "senseless sentimentalism."[1]

Throughout California in 1861, Union Clubs were inviting clergymen like King to venture beyond the traditional prayer on the Fourth, instead, reading through the Declaration of Independence with bravura or declaring for the

---

1 *Patriotism—A Discourse Delivered before the Ancient and Honorable Artillery Company, on Their CCXIII Anniversary* (Boston: A. Tompkins, 1851), p. 9; *An Oration Delivered . . . at Fulton, Oswego Co., July Fourth, 1855* (Fulton, N.Y.: T. S. Brigham, 1855), pp. 3 and 6.

Union in the featured oration. Hiram Cummings read the Declaration at Oroville, Osgood C. Wheeler with King at Sacramento.

But seven clergymen joined King as orators. John W. Ross, former Sacramento minister, addressed Yreka citizens in response to an invitation from William S. Moses, president of the Union Club there.[2] Abram H. Myers traveled from San Francisco to address the celebration at Volcano in Amador County,[3] while Benjamin Brierly spoke to a hometown celebration at Nevada City initiated by the local Union Club.[4] Edward S. Lacy, among the very first to flag his church in San Francisco, delivered both prayer and oration on the Fremont estate in Mariposa County, responding to an invitation from estate manager Trenor W. Park, president of the Bear Valley Union Club.[5] One correspondent described Lacy's oration as "a bold, defiant vindication of the present Administration in conducting the war to a successful termination."[6]

Samuel B. Bell, still acting the part of a steward despite his recent resignation from the Oakland Presbyterian Church to run for State Assembly as a Republican, spoke in Marysville before a celebration sponsored by the local Union Club. Bell's intense advocacy of the war effort apparently did not satisfy any abstract solidarity demands of the occasion. For Douglas Democrats regarded him as an orator who stirred up war with a fervency as intense as "white heat," striking down with basely metallic disdain "the infatuated participants in an insane rebellion."[7] Nor did fellow Republicans fail to find fault with Bell's exulting in war as "a lucky occasion for thrashing people who will be [the] better for it." Waxing "funny," relating "amusing" anecdotes, and exciting "much merriment" simply could never minimize the vindictiveness of such a holy implication, suggesting as it did a steward irrationally bent upon extending the war into California against Breckinridgers and Knights of the Golden Circle.[8]

David A. Dryden, in an oration at Stockton, also evoked some controversy when listeners understood him as asserting that "the signers of the Declaration *lied*" if all men, white or black, were not in fact political equals. And when con-

---

2 Sacramento *Daily Union*, 6 July, 1861. Cummings served the Brick Congregational Church in Oroville. Wheeler did not have an active parish, but was secretary to the State Agricultural Society in Sacramento, with an office in the Agricultural Hall building where King spoke. And Ross served the Methodist Episcopal Church in Yreka.

3 *Evening Bulletin* (San Francisco), 25 June, 1861. Myers served the English Evangelical Lutheran Church in San Francisco.

4 *Morning Transcript*, 6 July, 1861. Brierly served the Baptist Church in Nevada City.

5 *Evening Bulletin* (SFrc), 9 July, 1861. Lacy served the First Congregational Church in San Francisco.

6 Las Mariposas, "Letter dated 6 July," *Daily Alta California* (San Francisco), 9 July, 1861.

7 *Daily National Democrat*, 6 July, 1861.

8 *Daily Appeal*, 6 July, 1861.

fronted with warnings of a "second Mexico" resulting from "filthy Chinese heathen" being enfranchised with whites, Dryden issued a card upping the holy implication to "monstrous *lie*" if the Declaration did not justify the racial equality demanded in God's name.[9]

S. S. Wheeler, orator at Centreville in El Dorado County, likewise was compelled to issue a card when he found that his temperance address was not at all well-received by Union Club adherents. Wheeler made a rather sweeping allusion in his oration to demon rum "soaking" Daniel Webster and Stephen A. Douglas, but it was his reference to ministers exploiting "the sins of another [social] ball under the covert of a patriotic celebration" that roused the ire of Unionist parishioners at a local indignation meeting four days later.[10]

And William C. Bartlett, orator in Santa Cruz at a celebration initiated by the local Union Club, sought to justify holy retribution against the Confederacy: "Is any man, by the highest standard of Christian morality, bound to stand still in the streets and let an assassin hack and hew him to pieces, when his wife and children call on him to preserve the faculties and the life which God has given him for his sake and for their sakes? Shall the best Government under the heavens stand defenseless and be hacked and hewn to pieces when God and twenty-five millions, and the spirits of the great army of patriots in glory, call on that Government to strike for self-preservation—by all that is precious in the past and fearful in the present and grand in the future?"[11]

Although not always immediately apparent, King and his compatriots thought it prudent to revivify the lapsing ideality[12] of the Fourth of July oration, officiating as they preferred at the "altar of American Union" to achieve a "new and potent spirit" which would render obsolete "old thoughts in strange and fantastic garbs of magniloquence."[13] Indeed, one of King's parishioners, speaking at San Francisco on the Fourth, depicted this rhetorical strategy for a "new and loftier" patriotism in terms of his pastor's recent sermon, "Religious Lessons from Mount Shasta." Inveighed disciple Edward Tompkins regarding God's fearful link with patriot humanity, "Will the hearts that leaped at the magnificent picture fail to remember now, that if we are true to our whole duty,

---

9 Stockton *Daily Argus*, 17 and 24 Aug., 1861; *Daily San Joaquin Republican*, 21 and 25 Aug., 1861. Dryden served the Methodist Church in Stockton.

10 *Weekly Mountain Democrat* (Placerville), 20 July and 3 Aug., 1861.

11 *Pacific Sentinel* (Santa Cruz), 11 July, 1861. Bartlett served the First Congregational Church in Santa Cruz.

12 "A Vision of the Future," *Daily Appeal* (Marysville), 5 March, 1861; "The Micawber Policy," San Francisco *Daily Times*, 16 April, 1861; "The Outburst of Loyalty," *Daily Bee* (Sacramento), 28 May, 1861; "Oh, What A Glorious Day Is This!"—Sacramento *Daily Union*, 4 July, 1861; "The National Anniversary," *Dly Union*, 4 July, 1862.

13 *Morning Transcript* (Nevada City), 6 July, 1861.

that we can rear a moral Shasta of patriotism and devotion to country that will not only tower towards, but into Heaven?"[14]

Yet if King advocated such an ethic, his controversial preeminence on the Union lecture circuit sealed his selection as orator at Sacramento. For even prior to commencing his lecture tour of northern California, late in May, friend N. A. Haven Ball[15] and Francis Tukey,[16] Grand Marshal of the Sacramento celebration and a member of the Union Club's executive committee, seriously advanced King's name for orator. And King consented to speak when a literary subcommittee of the Union Club took the steamer downriver and formally put the request to him at his residence, 831 Bush Street in San Francisco.[17] In fact, King's selection as orator took on greater prominence as the Union Club's executive committee supplanted a rival citizen's group, and when Brigadier General E. V. Sumner declined a similar invitation because already committed to review the First Division of the California Guard at the San Francisco celebration.[18]

---

14 *Daily Alta California* (San Francisco), 6 July, 1861. Tompkins, King's parishioner and orator at the Metropolitan Theater, formerly was a law partner of Daniel S. Dickinson in Binghamton, New York. And a second "Shasta" reference from King may occur in James G. Howard's oration at Iowa Hill, Placer County. Howard recalls that during his boyhood years, on the Fourth, an aged chaplain, "with locks streaming over his shoulders as blanched as Mount Shasta," made the appointed temperance speaker "quail into abject apology." He describes how the chaplain "reared his frame . . . to the altitude of its prime," a transformed "Shasta" allusion perhaps. Howard's description of the chaplain's prime role in war virtually seems a capsule statement of the Christian ethic: "He had been the earnest associate of the wise and valiant ones, who had fought a good fight and had passed away to the god of battles. As their chaplain, he had pointed their drooping eyes to Heaven; and yet, upon emergency, had he mingled with a stout arm in the thickest of the bloody carnival. Somehow, he thought the men of the Revolution, in wreck of fortune and protraction of suffering and sacrifice of life, were not entirely selfish. Principle and posterity were involved in the struggle and the carnage." *Golden Era* (San Francisco), 14 July, 1861.

15 Although not on the Union Club executive committee, Ball helped arrange King's speaking appointments in Sacramento. For example, King wrote him on 15 Nov., 1860, finalizing arrangements for a 23 Jan. performance of "Individual Power and Its Voices" before the Sacramento Library Association: "I will go for you at any time you say, after the middle of January . . . . If you know anybody else that wants to give me $100 etc. [plus expenses] for a lecture, send them along, and you shall have the blessing . . . of Your young and *old* friend, T.S.K." Ball was active in numerous civic organizations—the Library Association, the State Agricultural Society, the Howard Benevolent Association, and the Pioneers. And as Musical Director of the Philharmonic Society, he participated in the ceremonies when King spoke on the Fourth. Letter in Ball Papers, California Historical Society (San Francisco).

16 Tukey probably made King's acquaintance while organizing patriotic celebrations in Boston during the late 1840's, prior to coming out West. And his statement on 4 June as temporary chairman of the Republican County Convention reveals some rapport with King's militant Unionist stance: "I recollect when a man, not a Republican, but a vile Abolitionist, talked about severing this Union, and I was in the mob that mobbed him for it. Think of it as you will, I gloried in it then, and I glory in it now. I care not what his creed or profession was; when he proposed to dissolve this glorious Union, we boys mobbed him. We put him under the pump and pumped on him. We did it at the head of old State Street, in Boston, where even before the Revolution the first blood was shed on the question of who should rule, King or Country. We pumped on him to wash out his very grievous sin. From that day to this, I have always opposed every man, in every place, at all times and on all occasions, who dared to utter a sentiment against this glorious Union." Sacramento *Daily Union*, 5 June, 1861.

17 Sacramento *Dly Union*, 23 May, 1861.

18 *Dly Union*, 16, 21, 27, and 29-30 May, 1861; *Daily Bee* (Sacramento), 24 June, 1861.

Even as King began to speak at Sacramento on the Fourth, however, the vigilant Zouave on the Union badge[19] he sported must have symbolized in the minds of many audience members, similarly attired, the militant direction implicit in his rhetorical exposure since arriving in California. The militancy of such a context at times certainly verged upon becoming a secular liability. When King accepted the Union Club's invitation, for example, rumors were rampant in San Francisco that he would, once again, address the Episcopal Mission Sunday School on the Fourth.[20] Indeed, behind the card King had issued in the *Alta*, the previous year, lay a heated doctrinal controversy with Rev. S. Chipman Thrall.[21] Thrall, president of a standing committee sanctioned by the Episcopal Bishop, William Ingraham Kip, had alleged that pastor King wanted to deliver a doctrinal "address" rather than any staple "oration."[22] The controversy continued well into 1861, King delivering several doctrinal sermons, January thru April. On April 29, he gave a benefit performance of his "Socrates" lecture for Rev. George B. Taylor, a casualty of the dispute because of subsequent prayers, Taylor never having offered up any introductory prayer nor even graced the Sunday School ceremonies with his presence. And when Rev. A. C. Edmunds enlarged the *Star of the Pacific* from eight to twenty-four pages quarto in March, King was not reluctant to send in a doctrinal article or two.[23]

---

19 *Daily Appeal* (Marysville), 23 June, 1861; *Dly Union* and *Dly Bee*, 25 June, 1861.

20 *Daily Alta California* (San Francisco), 27 May, 1861.

21 *Dly Alta California* (SFrc), 2 July, 1860; *Daily Morning Call* (San Francisco), 3 July, 1860; *The Pacific* (San Francisco), 5 July, 1860; San Francisco, 4 June and 2 July, 1860, *TSK* to Randolph Ryer, New York City, King Papers, Bancroft Library-University of California (Berkeley). Thrall served Trinity Church in San Francisco.

22 SFrc, 27 June, 1860, Thrall to Rev. George B. Taylor, Marysville, in *Report of the Ecclesiastical Trial of the Rev. Geo. B. Taylor, upon a Presentment from the Standing Committee of the Protestant Episcopal Church, of the Diocese of California, for an Alleged Violation of the Canons of the Church* (San Francisco: David M. Gazlay, 1861), p. 19. Rev. William H. Hill, who offered up a prayer at the flag-raising ceremonies prior to King's 1861 Fourth of July oration, was Taylor's counsel, even though his duties as counsel were somewhat circumscribed. Hill served the Grace Episcopal Church in Sacramento.

23 *Star of the Pacific and Herald of Reform* (Petaluma) cited in *Pacific Expositor*, 3 (July 1861), 37. One incident perhaps illustrates how doctrinal matters did not absent themselves from the lecture circuit. At San Jose in mid-May, posters advertising appointments by King and Alexander Montarg, the living skeleton and natural violinist performing with Bassett's circus troupe, were so intertwined, in at least a single instance, that King's intellectually "spooney" head merged with the gaudy presentation of Montarg's body. The going rate for both performers was a dollar a head, and yet a Catholic professor at Santa Clara College, a more orthodox violinist than Montarg, refused to part with his violin for money. Observed the San Francisco *Evening Journal*, "That cherished instrument is more than two hundred years old, and he has refused to sell it for three thousand dollars, which enormous sum was actually offered by another *virtuoso*." And King passed up the Universalist Convention at Sacramento to lecture in San Jose, perhaps prompting delegates to go on record as resolving he "deliver the occasional sermon at its next session, to be held at Auburn, on the third Tuesday in April next." Touchstone, "Letter dated 11 May," *Daily Alta California* (San Francisco), 12 May, 1861; Sacramento *Daily Union*, 15 May, 1861; SFrc *Journal* in *Sonoma County Journal* (Petaluma), 28 June, 1861.

But the persistent flaw in King's reputation as a lecturer centered around mundane matters of secessionist hisses and personal fees interfering with charitable goals. When King delivered "Books and Readings" and "Substance and Show" to San Francisco audiences, for example, *Le Mineur*, the *California Demokrat*, and the *Abend Post* seriously questioned his racial sincerity, and demands were made that he atone for the not-so-plain "bookworm" remark by means of a lecture engagement to benefit the German Relief Society's project of rescuing immigrant washerwomen from menial labor and destitute children.[24] King was equally "starr" or obstinate in not heeding the suggestion, preferring to donate what friends labeled as unspecified sums out of his own pocket, only after hearing out the merits of an individual request face-to-face in private.[25] The reception of King's "Webster" lecture, before the Mercantile Library Association in San Francisco, likewise was marred by an audience member subsequently protesting against any fee being paid out "for a lecture in respect to the duty of the Federal Government to coerce the Seceding States into submission."[26]

24 A reporter for the *Evening Bulletin* made a close synopsis of the damaging "bookworm" remark, when King delivered "Books and Reading" on 17 Jan. before the Mercantile Library Association: "In the Imperial Library at Paris, the largest in the world, there are 800,000 volumes and 100,000 manuscripts. 'Art is long, and time is fleeting.' The reader who had begun in the reign of King David to read them, if he stopped only on Sundays, to rest his eyes and go to church, would be tonight about checking the last volume. Set a single copy of all the books that have been printed, side by side, and they would reach from the vineyards of Los Angeles to the snowy beard of Mount Shasta. No man lives, no German professor (the juices of whose body are a decoction, in equal parts, of tobacco juice and beer) can in all his lifetime read through half the volumes of your Mercantile Library. A hundred volumes might be selected, which, if read with care during their leisure hours, would make men of average brains better informed than are any, except those who are supereminent, in knowledge. Not the sort of specific knowledge which the great German grammarian in Latin craved, who in his old age remarked that, if he were to live life over again, he would devote himself entirely to the dative case." "Oh, Mrs. Jellyby!"—Red Bluff *Beacon*, 9 Jan., 1861; "A Word for the Poor Washerwomen," *Daily Morning Call* (San Francisco), 20 Jan., 1861; "Booribooza Gha," San Francisco *Evening Journal* in *Daily National Democrat* (Marysville), 15 Sept., 1861; Choyno, "Letters datelined San Francisco, 21, 24, and 31 Jan.," *Daily Appeal* (Marysville), 23 and 26 Jan., 2 Feb., 1861; New Bonnet, "That Starr King again, Drat Him!"—*Bulletin* (SFrc), 4 Feb., 1861. The editorial fray between Dr. Loehr of the *California Demokrat* in San Francisco and John Ross Browne, European correspondent for the Sacramento *Union*, heightened the controversy over implications present in King's remark. Browne, "Letter on German customs dated Dec., 1860," *Dly Union*, 5 Feb., 1861; *Demokrat* in *Union*, 18 Feb., 1861.

25 When King gave "Substance and Show," at the Mission-Street Methodist Episcopal Church eleven days later (repeated from a performance the previous year in SFrc), the *Bulletin* reporter took down the new "starr" passage verbatim: "*I am a German myself!* My grandfather was an emigrant from Germany. He did not learn English until after he was twenty-one, and he kept the true patriotic devotion to good tobacco-smoke and beer. My whole baptismal name, Thomas Starr, the name of my grandfather, comes straight from Saxony, although I regret to say that the word 'starr' means, in my native tongue, *stiff*, *stubborn*, *obstinate*, and *wrong-headed*. Every German will bear witness that this is true. And I shall be true to the suggestions of the name, and remain stiff and obstinate in my reverence and gratitude for the genius, learning, and service of the Professors of my fatherland." San Francisco *Abend Post* (d), 5 and 13 March, 1861; John O. S-----, "How a Clergyman Spends his Money," *Bulletin*, 29 March, 1861.

26 A Member of the Mercantile Library Association, "Letter dated ca. 19 March," *Bulletin* (SFrc), 3 April, 1861.

The very day, in fact, that King found it advisable to disclose bits of data about his lecture fees, Frank M. Pixley, editor of the San Francisco *Times* and a Republican candidate for Attorney General accompanying Rev. Lacy to Bear Valley on the Fourth, enlisted King's name in an effort to revive the chances of Caleb T. Fay and the Union slate in a municipal election.[27] And the *Mountain Democrat* and *Republican* in Placerville perpetuated the fee controversy by wrangling over King's remark to a Republican Victory Celebration, held at Platt's Hall the evening of September 4 to applaud Leland Stanford's election as Governor. *Democrat* editor Dan Gelwicks and Thomas Fitch, editor of the *Republican* and orator before the Episcopal Mission Sunday School in San Francisco on the Fourth, never really could pin down the formidable humor of "Let the war go on, damn the *expense*!" or "Damn the *expense*, so long as the people foot the bill!" versus "Let the war go on, damn the *secessionists*!" King presumably intimated the more Union-serving "secessionist" slogan, according to the San Francisco *Daily Mirror*.[28]

The essential elements in this secular faux pas can better be understood by examining King's "Life and Character of Washington" as an interactive model. A Marysville press that earlier advertised his "White Hills" gift book as on sale for theatergoers at S. G. Williams bookstore,[29] conceivably to reduce the fee King asked for lecturing, became quite divided over an *Express* demand that King avoid "occasional slight slurs and insinuations."[30] The *Appeal* eagerly conceded the "Washington" lecture to be "one great *slur* all through,"[31] and the *Express* responded in kind: "Had he delivered his political harangue in the Theatre or on a street corner, where it would have been less inappropriate but none the less offensive, we venture to say the audience would have given vent to their feelings, and hissed him down."[32] The *National Democrat* noted that a scheduling change was agreed to by the sponsor of King's lecture: "If it was a lecture proper to be hissed, why did those for whose benefit (to-wit, the Odd Fellows' Association) it was delivered, consent to the substitution of it for the lecture on Books and Reading?"[33] But A. N. Francisco in the Sonora *Union*

---

27 *Dly Times*, 21 May, 1861; San Francisco *Evening Journal* in *Daily San Joaquin Republican* (Stockton), 23 May, 1861; Critic, "Letter datelined San Francisco, 22 May," San Jose *Tribune*, 24 May, 1861. Pixley's allegation concerning an evening sermon should not be confused with King's debt sermon, delivered the morning of the same day (Sunday-28 April). And despite Pixley's publicity, Fay lost out to People's Union candidate H. F. Teschemacher in the mayoral contest.

28 *Mirror* in *Daily Appeal* (Marysville), 7 Sept., 1861; *Weekly Mountain Democrat* (Placerville), 5 Oct., 1861; Placerville *Republican* in *Daily National Democrat* (Marysville), 19 Oct., 1861.

29 *Dly Appeal* and *Daily California Express*, 10 Jan., 1861; *Dly National Democrat*, 10 and 11 Jan., 1861.

30 *Dly California Express*, 28 Feb., 1861.

31 *Dly Appeal*, 1 March, 1861.

32 *Dly California Express*, 2 March, 1861.

33 *Dly National Democrat*, 3 March, 1861.

Democrat thought hanging a fanatical priest like King, "talking so glibly about butchering and strangling secessionists," preferable to hissing.[34] Commentators in Marysville attacked King's fee. Was $100 or $150 per lecture really that much different from a Yankee peddler's trick of passing off oats as shoe pegs?[35] The *Appeal*, unable to deny that King's lecture was the "all-absorbing topic of conversation on the street," endeavored to play down any secessionist whining "here and there" about the "sordid and narrow channel" of fees.[36]

At the very same time editor James L. Hart's proposal for a northern tour[37] provoked some controversy over the "Washington" lecture between the *Beacon* and *Independent* in Red Bluff,[38] the Stockton press brought hisses into focus as part of King's lecturing strategy. The *Republican* advised that such exciting political subjects be "kept out of the lecture room and the social circle."[39] To which the *Argus* deviously responded by bringing in free love as practiced among Oberlin College's abolitionist reformers: "As well might the Free Lovers of Oberlin, of Ohio, extend their licentious doctrines, and where a public lecturer should denounce their immorality, flare up and hiss and threaten him as one who attacks religious sects!"[40] And when Pennsylvania native W. B. Norman, along with four other Democratic hissers (strangely not five Douglasites but a "dozen Southerners or less," gauged by a crusader intent upon giving "cracks on the raw" and otherwise humiliating "Southerners . . . in the gutter"), received refunds at the door after walking out on King, the *Argus*, though grandiosely claiming "extraordinary efforts were made to purchase up hissers," loyally emphasized only one offer as being refused, certainly not the five refunds.[41]

The *Argus* fee rationale surprisingly voided the "White Hills" gift book discount, initially so promising in Marysville: "In these days of the hurry of business and of feverish unrest for the masses (even the intelligent and educated masses), first-class public lecturers are a great blessing to the community. The people can well afford to support them liberally, [so] that they may get the

---

34 *Union Democrat* in *Dly California Express*, 14 March, 1861; San Francisco *Daily Times*, 16 March, 1861.

35 *, "T. Starr King's Lecture" and Citizen, "Starr King's Lecture," *Dly California Express*, 2 March, 1861; Oberlin *vel* Canada South, "That Diabolical Parson," *Dly National Democrat*, 3 March, 1861.

36 *Dly Appeal*, 3 March, 1861.

37 *Northern Argus* (Horsetown), 2 March, in *Semi-Weekly Independent* (Red Bluff), 5 March, 1861.

38 *Beacon*, 6 March, 1861; *Independent*, 8 March, 1861.

39 *Daily San Joaquin Republican*, 7 March, 1861.

40 *Daily Argus*, 9 March, 1861.

41 *Dly Argus*, 8 and 9 March, 1861; San Francisco, 10 March, 1861, *TSK* to Randolph Ryer, New York City, King Papers, Bancroft Library- University of California (Berkeley).

results of their reading and reflection in [a] condensed and pleasing style, without the heavy cost of the books that have been boiled down, devoured, and digested, and [without] the outlay of valuable time consumed in the process. Cheap, dirt cheap at ten times the price, that is, if knowledge and pleasure are worth anything. They are ordinarily purchased, at firsthands, at high figures, but are distributed to the masses by gifted lecturers at what would be ruinously low rates, if there were not so many to pay for them. Under these circumstances, the question is not whether we can afford to attend lectures, but whether we can afford to stay away."[42] Oblivious to the possibility any lecturer's ego could be deflated, the *Argus* dared disunionists to hiss King when he delivered "Washington" in Sacramento.[43]

No "discordant hiss," to be sure, was heard by a loyal *Union* reporter in Sacramento,[44] but a correspondent of the San Francisco *Times* wrote about a boycott by state bureaucrats, natives of the South conceivably sensitive to the German question.[45] Approximately one month later, a Sacramento correspondent for the *Pacific Sentinel* observed that, for the first time apparently, several ladies walked out on King "in a perfect fury of rage and scorn,"[46] some indication perhaps of any boycott continuing in effect through King's oration on the Fourth. The Nevada City press made fun of the fact that a "faint hiss" from the audience never really compared with the croaking chorus greeting "boss frog" King from nearby ponds. Still, a German shopkeeper refused to purchase a lecture ticket for "Washington," his twenty-first since moving into town, from promoter Rev. William Grove Deal, presumably because no lottery-type benefit had been "drawed" when attending less controversial events with the previous twenty tickets.[47] The inference was unmistakable—a lottery-fee "draw" lining King's own pocket, with the German question sweetening the pot.

---

42 *Argus*, 8 March, 1861.

43 *Argus*, 22 March, 1861.

44 *Daily Union*, 23 March, 1861. The reporter's account was glowing and slightly drawn out: "The lecturer was greeted at times with the heartiest and, it might be said, almost irrepressible applause. The feeling was general that the lecture ought to be delivered in every county of this state, and indeed of the Union."

45 Pequod, "Letter dated 23 March" *Daily Times*, 25 March, 1861.

46 Gus Gaston, "Letter dated 4 May," *Sentinel* (Santa Cruz), 9 May, 1861. King delivered his "Battle of Lexington" lecture before the Sacramento Library Association on the third. And, though the two events are not related, he rather cockily wrote Rev. William Rounseville Alger about "hair-trigger Southernism," the very day Gaston appeared in print: "We have saved California. From the white Sierra to the white-edged Sea the villains are prostrate. We dance on their heads. Their fangs are smashed. They are an awful race, shallow, hard-hearted, and vile. We must flog them for their [own] good, and then throw them off. I dread yet some compromise, that will enable them to come back with lordly step into Congress and a civilization to wh[ich]. they do not belong." San Francisco, 9 May, 1861, *TSK* to Alger, Boston, Western Americana Collection, Beinecke Library-Yale University (New Haven, Ct).

47 *Democrat* (tw), 11 April, 1861; *Journal* in *Daily National Democrat* (Marysville), 13 April, 1861,

And at Yreka on his northern tour, late in May, King discovered that secessionist banker George Greathouse created a "rich muss" by supressing advertisements of the "Washington" lecture. So meticulous was King that Greathouse misled him by sending routine replies not only to his letter of acceptance, but to a follow-up message by telegraph giving the precise hour of arrival in Yreka. King's scheduling talents triumphed in the end, of course. Gamblers with hawk's eyes and bankrupt planters, slightly more repentant after working one last slave, presumably were prodded by King to recollect Unionist "mines of knowledge" forsaken for gold. Yet the harsh reality of banker Greathouse could not be ignored when King wrote parishioner Robert B. Swain, defeated earlier as candidate for president of the San Francisco Mercantile Library Association: "The secessionists circulated stories that I was a peddler of abolition, a political preacher, a black-hearted scamp, and other pleasant phrases. They even tried to corrupt the Dutchmen of the Brass Band and prevent them from playing, but their success was not great."[48]

This was the insidious partisan milieu which ensnared orator King, a few minutes before noon on the Fourth, as he mounted the rostrum in the pavilion on the first floor of Agricultural Hall. Sacramento was fairly ablaze with partisan Unionist activity. Loyal members from Union Clubs throughout Sacramento County were in King's audience, men from places with stout names like Sutterville, Franklin, American, Richland, Alder Creek, and Prairie City.[49] Yet of the fifteen hundred spectators King addressed, one thousand were ladies seated before males sought out a vacant chair "decently and in order."[50] Indeed, the sister of Rev. J. M. Windsor, fellow Unitarian minister expelled from a parish in Charleston, South Carolina, because of antislavery opinions entertained while in the North, might well have been numbered among the ladies.[51]

A plethora of heroic adjectives sallied forth in response to King's oration, every last one femininely in line with the majority of his audience. The speech "abounded in true and genuine, loyal and patriotic sentiment,"[52] and was the "thrilling, soul-stirring, patriotic, and eloquent effusion" expected,[53] ap-

---

48 Dutch Flat *Enquirer* in Shasta *Courier*, 4 May, 1861; *L'Echo du Pacifique* (San Francisco) in *Dly National Democrat* (Marysville), 6 Sept., 1861; Yreka, 29 May, 1861, *TSK* to Swain, SFrc, in Swain, *Address before First Unitarian Society of San Francisco, in Memory of Their Late Pastor, Rev. Thomas Starr King, March 15, 1864* (San Francisco: Frank Eastman, 1864), p. 20.

49 *Daily Bee* (Sacramento), 29 June, 1861.

50 *Dly Bee*, 3 and 5 July, 1861; Sacramento *Daily Union*, 4 July, 1861.

51 Sacramento *Dly Union*, 26 Jan. and 22 June, 1861.

52 *Dly Bee*, 5 July, 1861.

53 Observer, "Letter dated 5 July," *Daily Morning Call* (San Francisco), 6 July, 1861.

propriately "splendid"[54] and "superb."[55] Rev. John Augustine Benton, whose prayer for a "broader zeal and livelier interest"[56] preceded King's remarks, followed up by delivering a parallel sermon entitled "The Present Condition of the Country," though Benton's purpose in Sacramento Sunday evening was not to protest the lack of any donations for California Volunteers at the pavilion ceremonies.[57] Even James Anthony of the Sacramento *Union* could find common ground with Leander Quint, temporary chairman of the Union Democratic State Convention in session at Agricultural Hall some two hours after King spoke, premised on a somewhat vague "deep meaning" of whatever Anthony considered King's demand for Union-consensus Congressmen to involve.[58]

Benjamin P. Avery, editor of the Marysville *Appeal* and Republican candidate for State Printer, honored King's tardy copyright "notice," taken out on the fifth in Judge Ogden Hoffman's Court at San Francisco, printing only a bon-mot excerpt from the stenographic transcript of the oration, originally published as two bulky paragraphs in editor Anthony's *Union Supplement* of the sixth.[59] And when announcing the lecture which King adapted from his Sacramento oration for delivery before the San Francisco Mercantile Library Association on the ninth, almost as an afterthought the *Alta* sought to minimize the copyright issue by transforming friend Jessie Benton Fremont's "forty nights in succession" into "a hundred times with pleasure and gratification."[60]

A controversy with the Sacramento *Union* definitely burgeoned when King stated his case, on the ninth, in a preface to his lecture at the Academy of Music. Had editor Anthony any right to print a stenographic transcript, not mutually agreed upon, of the entire oration? King preferred that only a superficial synopsis be printed, much as with "Washington," "Battle of Lexington," and "Union and War," implying that certain textual variants in a transcript not reviewed by the orator might jeopardize delivery to subsequent audiences. A mere handful of secessionists walking out on any recitation at variance with such a published

---

54 *Daily National Democrat* (Marysville), 7 July, 1861.

55 L., "Letter dated 4 July," *Daily Alta California* (San Francisco), 6 July, 1861.

56 Sacramento *Dly Union*, 6 July, 1861.

57 Rebecca, "Letter datelined San Francisco, 24 June," *Evening Bulletin* (SFrc), 24 June, 1861; Sacramento *Dly Union*, 8 July, 1861; *Dly San Joaquin Republican* (Stockton), 12 July, 1861.

58 "The Convention editorial" and "First Day Proceedings" *Dly Union*, 6 July, 1861; *Union*, 15 and 29-31 May, 11 July, 1861.

59 "Telegraph dispatch to editor datelined Sacramento, 5 July-2:00p.m.," *Evening Bulletin* (SFrc), 5 July, 1861; *Daily Appeal* (Marysville), 9 July, 1861; "Appendix A—Copyrights Granted by Northern District Court, 1851-1862," in Robert Greenwood, comp., *California Imprints, 1833-1862: A Bibliography* (Los Gatos, Cal.: Talisman Press, 1961), p. 501. Avery excerpted King's clock anecdote, which the reader will find in paragraphs 3 and 4 of the 1861 oration text.

60 San Francisco, 10 March, 1861, *TSK* to Randolph Ryer, New York City, King Papers, Bancroft Library-University of California (Berkeley); *Daily Alta California* (San Francisco), 9 July, 1861.

text was one thing. But when substantial numbers of loyal Unionist supporters might either stay away or demand the same refund at the gate, that dire possibility put a different light on matters for King.[61]

Three days later, editor Anthony issued a biting rejoinder to King's lecture preface. Anthony wrote from his new office on Third Street in Sacramento, brimming over with confidence at the realization his words might reach 50,000 readers (versus a non-King circulation of 16,560). Calling on what surely was not Byron's best ethical romanticism in "Don Juan," rather shaky justification for revering souls of slain troops over lost material values, especially the Spartan fare of two casks of biscuit and a single keg of butter, Anthony attempted to sever orator King from the Christian ethic. He pictured King as a willing victim of "selfish fear," enticingly stuffing his pocket with "so many hundred dollars for delivering the same oration some four or five times." Any such scheme of personal aggrandizement, in Anthony's eyes, was utterly repugnant to Joseph W. Winans, prominent in the Sacramento Pioneers and orator at Shasta on the Fourth. For Winans was one of two unnamed local citizens whose very natures, according to Anthony, "rebelled against the notion of prostituting their eloquence so far as to receive pay," above all, when lured by "considerable sums."[62]

Anthony obviously took pride in his corps of six stenographers who reported proceedings in the state legislature, one reporter actually transcribing an entire sermon by Rev. John D. Blain prior to the Fourth.[63] Blain, of course, offered up a benedictory prayer at the pavilion ceremonies. Editor Anthony indeed became so strident in criticizing King that he seemed uncharacteristically secessionist: "The people of California have not been accustomed to having Fourth of July orations peddled out to them in piecemeals, for money, and are inclined to suspect the sincerity of those whose sentiments of patriotism, however loudly proclaimed, are subordinate to their intense love of self and [are] the *root of all evil*."[64]

The Marysville *Express* jumped into the fray, recalling that King refused to permit publication of his "Union and War" lecture in the San Francisco *Call* less than two months prior to the Fourth. Yet, whatever truth there may have

---

61 *Evening Bulletin* (SFrc), 10 July, 1861. See the complete preface text immediately preceding Introduction-version *a* of the 1861 oration.

62 Sacramento *Dly Union*, 19 March, 20 May, and 12 July, 1861; J. W. Lake, ed., *The Works of Lord Byron, Including The Suppressed Poems* (Philadelphia: Grigg and Elliot, 1836), pp. 580-81. Winans signed the original petition to celebrate the Fourth with Paul Morrill, one of Anthony's partners in managing the *Union*. In fact, both Winans and Morrill served on the short-lived Citizens' Committee of Thirteen. The names of Anthony and Grand Marshal Tukey also appear closely linked as signatures on the petition. *Dly Union*, 13 and 14 May, 1861.

63 "History of the Methodist Church in Sacramento, 30 Dec., 1860—reported phonographically for the *Union*," *Dly Union*, 5 Jan., 1861; *Union*, 7 Jan., 1861. Blain served the Sixth-Street Methodist Episcopal Church in Sacramento.

64 *Dly Union*, 12 July, 1861.

been in the *Express* assertion, the secessionist innuendo brought up King's past remarks on the German question. Because of King's "thoroughly avaricious" grumbling,[65] a "sweet fountain" or rhetorical renascence had been denied uncouth "thirsty souls," who never shied away from lager beer and tobacco spittoons at their favorite saloon. Concluded the *Express*, "With a smile of contempt for the editor's greenness, the Rev[erend]. gentleman informed him that the word of God was the raw material which he coined into money, that the sermon was intended to be rehashed into lectures, and that thirsty souls that couldn't raise two bits might go to damn somebody that was fool enough to part with something for nothing."[66]

Prompted mostly by editor Anthony, the press throughout the state began to speculate about whether a fee of $150 or $200 was paid King by the Union Club finance committee on Saturday the sixth.[67] And the very day both the *Bee* and *News* in Sacramento ran the finance committee's explanation that King "unanimously" was voted $150 of a surplus in funds (not part of $2500 paid out in expenses),[68] King formally issued a card in the San Francisco *Bulletin*. Since he would not admit to reading the *Union* on his own, King specifically relied on a reprint of Anthony's reply, inserted in the *Bulletin* three days earlier, an introduction to which treated the pastor's copyright claim quite favorably.[69] King even mellowed a bit in his card when noting that on the Fourth editor Anthony rejected a synopsis of the oration, a synopsis not only prepared by the orator but conveniently containing "every position and idea" in the oration.

It was regarding the lecture system, however, that he remained quite forceful. The lecture system, for King, presuming that it was indeed becoming organized as "fast" as he thought in California, could perform "a great deal of good in various ways." Even though King never really disclosed that his claim to a copyright was invalidated by not being advertised the month preceding any "notice" sent the *Union*, he could endeavor to recover some of his ethical

65 *Daily San Joaquin Republican* (Stockton), 12 July, 1861.

66 *California Express* (Marysville) in *Dly San Joaquin Republican*, 16 July, 1861.

67 *Daily Bee* (Sacramento), 15 July, 1861; *Daily Morning Call* (San Francisco), 16 July, 1861; *California Spirit of the Times and Fireman's Journal* (San Francisco) in Sacramento *Dly Union*, 15 July, 1861; *Amador Ledger* (Jackson) in *Dly Union*, 23 July, 1861.

68 *Dly Bee*, 6 and 16 July, 1861; *Dly Union*, 8 July, 1861; *Daily News* in *Tri-Weekly Independent* (Red Bluff), 20 July, 1861. Two factors probably made the finance committee most amenable to paying King's fee. First, it met in session with Grand Marshal Tukey on the sixth. And two of the three members on the committee, Lucius A. Booth and Collis P. Huntington, were directors of the Central Pacific Railroad, a speculative project dependent on Unionist-Republican rhetoric like King's. Leland Stanford, Republican candidate for Governor, also was a director. And although an identical funding arrangement for the Presidio Band, playing half-time and only during the day, provoked minor controversy at the San Francisco celebration, the San Juan Brass Band successfully sued in 1858 over such a fee and arrangements not being met on the Fourth. *Hydraulic Press* (North San Juan), 21 Aug., 1858; San Francisco *Herald* (d), 22 June and 3 July, 1861; *Daily Alta California* (San Francisco), 3 July, 1861.

69 *Evening Bulletin* (SFrc), 13 July, 1861.

prestige as pastor by allying his role as orator with the reality of such a broadly based system. King seemed artificially beneficent as he struggled to assert: "And in the name and in the interest of other gentlemen besides myself, who are often called to speak before literary associations, I protext . . . against the right of the proprietors of the Sacramento *Union* to appropriate *verbatim* copies of addresses (whatever be their subject, [and] which may have been pledged for a score of deliveries), simply because they may decide that such appropriation in a paper is for the public good."[70]

Almost simultaneously editor Anthony reminded King about orator Winans's truly beneficent gesture at Shasta,[71] and raised the ante to $250: "We are . . . credibly informed, and we believe it is susceptible of proof, that prominent members of the Union Club, when calling on our citizens to defray the expenses of the celebration, stated that they had agreed (or intended) to give the *Rev. Thomas Starr King two hundred and fifty dollars* for the oration in question."[72] And when Anthony did reply to what he labeled as a "labored" card containing "nothing noteworthy . . . not answered before," the editor linked King's halfhearted "threat" in the *Bulletin* with the brazen tone of an overzealous supporter in some nondescript Union Club, warning that "we had better send a sufficient force to *protect our reporters*."[73] If King could muster even one such indiscreet militant, Anthony certainly possessed the initiative and resources to print at least two comments slightly more germane—one from a correspondent in Portland, Oregon, conveniently vindicating his position,[74]

70 "Card dated 15 July," *Bulletin*, 16 July, 1861.

71 Sacramento *Dly Union*, 17 July, 1861.

72 *Dly Union*, 18 July, 1861. King was offered a $250 fee on other occasions by the Northern District Agricultural Society and the San Francisco Mercantile Library Association. Indeed, some of his business acumen regarding profit-sharing and repeat performances does shine through in a letter to the lecture chairman at the Mercantile Library Association: "On the day after the twenty-second of February, some friends of mine urged me to prepare a Lecture on "The Genius of Daniel Webster, and His Relations to the American Constitution," [much] after the general scope and plan of the Lecture upon "Washington". They seemed to think that it would be interesting to the Public, and successful; and they requested me to allow them to arrange for it, so that I might receive the pecuniary returns. The preparation of such an Address would involve so much labor, that I was obliged to ask for a week to consider the proposal,-but I at once refused to deliver or write the lecture, unless some Public institution of the city should receive half the profit. After a pretty careful survey, I think that I could prepare the Address in the course of two or three weeks, and I am ready and happy to offer to your Assoc[iatio]n, for your Library fund, or for your general treasury, if you prefer, half the benefit of the Address, if you are willing that it shall be offered to the Public under your auspices. Should so unlikely an event occur, as that a repetition should be needed- as in the case of the Lecture on "Washington"-it would give me great pleasure to see that your treasury shall be even more largely favored than by the plan here proposed for the first delivery. If, however, for any reasons, you may think that the Association would be averse to such an arrangement, you are at liberty to reject the proposition without consultation; for I make it, of my own notion, without suggestion or advice from any quarter." San Francisco, 4 May and 10 Sept., 1860, *TSK* to Randolph Ryer, New York City, King Papers, Bancroft Library-University of California (Berkeley); SFrc, 4 March, 1861, *TSK* to unidentified lecture-committee chairman, SFrc, Western Americana Collection, Beinecke Library-Yale University (New Haven, Ct).

73 *Ibid.*

74 Willamette, "Letter dated 20 July," *Dly Union*, 29 July, 1861.

another from a correspondent at Michigan Bluffs, Sacramento County, relaying the displeasure of pro-British industrialists in Auburn and Placerville at King's "unjust" position.[75]

The secessionist press continued to take advantage of the controversy. In fact, the *San Joaquin Republican* in Stockton erred egregiously when asserting that King was "the only man in the state who accepted pay for delivering an oration on the Fourth."[76] Quite the contrary, Rev. Brierly at Nevada City was paid $75 as orator on the Fourth. But unlike King's repeat lecture on the ninth, no admission was charged when Brierly, the evening of the twenty-fifth, repeated his oration in the local Baptist Church. The reasons given for Brierly's repeat performance were temporary seats around the speaker's stand collapsing so as to interfere with his weak voice being clearly heard, and excessive length of the oration not being suitable for publication in any local newspaper. This despite Brierly's time of delivery on the Fourth exceeding King's hour and a quarter by only fifteen minutes.[77] By the eighteenth, the Visalia *Delta* resurrected a Sacramento correspondent's piece prepared eleven days earlier. Resurrected, of course, because there was very little, if any, merit in fanning standard anti-abolition vituperation (incendiary harangue, stale phrases, dirty agitation) into what had already become a "starred" fee controversy between editor Anthony and King.[78]

The *Placer Herald* in Auburn, staunchly secessionist as well, viewed the controversy in cutely satirical language. King really could come out "first best," if by way of benefiting from the "coinage of his own brains," he promoted his very own "copy-*right*" and conned himself into believing the miniature "irrepressible conflict" might be resolved in his favor.[79] The *Butte Democrat* in Oroville was every bit as satirical: "It seems the orator wished to gather some of the *sinews* of war, for the oration, and the *Union* wished to *make money* by publishing it, even at the cost of an infringement upon a copyright. They ought to play *quits*, for if such as they quarrel, the country may suffer by it. We cannot help feeling an intense interest in the matter, just as the old woman did, when her husband and the bear fought."[80] And the *Alameda County Gazette* in San Leandro printed the partisan rationale partly responsible for such satire, asserting that King was cunningly "(ill)starr-*ed*" enough to represent the worst brand of demagoguery. Concluded the *Gazette*, his kind ". . . look into the future and make their calculations with as much caution as the *wiry* office-seeker. They

75 Cimon, "America versus England—dated 27 July," *Dly Union*, 6 Aug., 1861.

76 *Daily Republican*, 19 July, 1861.

77 *Democrat* (tw), 6 and 23 July, 1861; *Morning Transcript*, 6 and 24 July, 1861.

78 ***, "Letter dated 7 July," *Delta*, 18 July, 1861.

79 *Herald*, 20 July, 1861.

80 *Weekly Democrat*, 20 July, 1861.

look at all questions in their various phases, and whichever tends to promote their interests the most, that they adopt. They are tenacious of popularity, and indifferent as to the particular mode of securing it."[81]

Perhaps it was somewhat ironic that when King twice delivered his "Peace" lecture at San Francisco, late in August, he incorporated a disparaging allusion from his repeat lecture of the ninth about "vile gamblers, who were willing to play as long as they could throw loaded dice that would turn up sixes."[82] King certainly did with his "Peace" lecture what he might have preferred be done with the Sacramento oration, subsequently adapted into the repeat lecture of course. In the spirit of a new lecture campaign begun in July (the fifth, for King, was the start of a "new season"),[83] he charged no fee for either "Peace" performance. Funds were raised to assist Volunteers from California, Massachusetts, and New York, a dollar a head being levied at the first performance, with free admission granted to a repeat performance much as Rev. Brierly did at Nevada City.[84] The *Alta* printed a complete text of "Peace" the day following its repetition, a manuscript and not a stenographic transcript being used, and Francis Valentine brought out a sixteen-page pamphlet edition before year's end.

Still, however, the acrimony of the controversy with editor Anthony lingered on. King's remark, in his "Peace" lecture, concerning the "serious Christian duty" of even studious ministers like himself being "willing to load revolvers for troops, and tear up their Bibles for wadding"[85] stirred up the controversy once again. Indeed, several rather poignant questions began to cut into King's image in the public mind. Was pastor King perhaps not as corrupt in his dealings as a Cheyenne Indian or one of Simon Cameron's contractors?[86] Was he not a forty-niner Unitarian refugee, as "consistent" as his father had been when rallying the masses to burn down the Charlestown convent?[87] Might he not be better off killed, as Rev. O. P. Fitzgerald tastelessly quoted from Thomas Babington Macaulay, for the heinous offense of "running into danger without any call of

81 *Gazette*, 20 July, 1861.

82 *Daily Alta California* (San Francisco), 1 Sept., 1861. Compare this clause with "shameless sharpers and swindlers, who consent to play a game only so long as the dice are loaded, and they are sure to throw sixes every time" (lecture insert after paragraph 10 in 1861 oration). King also incorporated several additional quotations from Joseph Holt in his "Peace" lecture, perhaps a second parallel relating to this same insert. However, the precise Holt quotation in the insert did not carry over to "Peace."

83 *Ibid.*

84 Mary, "Undated reply to Rebecca," *Evening Bulletin* (SFrc), 27 June, 1861; *Bulletin*, 31 Aug., 1861.

85 *Dly Alta California* (SFrc), 1 Sept., 1861.

86 *Pacific Echo* (Napa), 31 Aug., 1861.

87 Washingtonian Platform, "Letter dated 1 Sept.," San Francisco *Herald* (d), 3 Sept., 1861.

duty" like the celebrated Bishop of Derry?[88] Had King not in effect become a persecutor of Christ,[89] intent upon burying even the "star" actor in his "bigot abolition" role as sensation preacher, all the while brandishing "excessive zeal" over the heads of inhibited audiences and, in the end, "more speedily" destroying some lives?[90] Was he not, in short, tantamount to an evangelical western revivalist, whose thunderclaps belied an evanescent sort of piety and sins of the flesh?[91]

Probably *not*, such questions were mostly secessionist diatribe. But the cumulative impact of the controversy made itself felt on King. No longer did King write so confidently regarding his own role in keeping California safe for the Union. He confided to Rev. Henry W. Bellows, a member of the Committee of Arrangements for Edward Everett's Fourth of July oration at New York City: "For I honestly think that there is one percent of truth in what people here tell me of the influence of my very frequent speaking in putting California square and strong against the barbarians."[92] Although the context apparently was humorous, he more readily conceded that editor Anthony's position contained substance enough to shape a serious lecture.[93] And Anthony continued confident as ever, even on New Year's Day including a reference to his position in the 1861 chronicle of events for Sacramento.[94]

The controversy never really terminated until King, at the time the Coggins pamphlet edition of his Sacramento oration finally was published in San Francisco, rather strongly hinted that being "treated unfairly" by Anthony smacked of secessionist sympathies.[95] But editor Anthony brought personalities, not necessarily issues, to the fore, putting the controversy to rest at last: "As journalists, we considered we had a right to report and give it to the public through our columns as it had been given to the public from the speaker's lips. Mr. King, instead of acting like a sensible man, and feeling gratified at a full report of his remarks, got into a pet, threatened a copyright and also a suit against us,

88 *Pacific Methodist* (San Francisco) in *Evening Bulletin* (SFrc), 6 Sept., 1861. Fitzgerald's *Methodist* printed the ME-South viewpoint, while the *California Christian Advocate* (also SFrc) was ME-North in allegiance.

89 *Weekly Mountain Democrat* (Placerville), 7 Sept., 1861.

90 Amicus, "Undated letter," *California Express* (Marysville) in *Weekly Butte Democrat* (Oroville), 23 Nov., 1861.

91 "Letter from unidentified person,n.d.," San Jose *Tribune*, 27 Sept., 1861.

92 San Francisco, 30 Sept., 1861, *TSK* to Bellows, New York City, Bellows Papers, Massachusetts Historical Society (Boston).

93 SFrc, 28 Oct., 1861, *TSK* to N. A. Haven Ball, Sacramento, Ball Papers, California Historical Society (SFrc).

94 Sacramento *Dly Union*, 1 Jan., 1862.

95 "Extract from New Call for Patriotism, lecture delivered at SFrc on 28 Aug.," *Dly Union*, 4 Sept., 1862.

and otherwise made himself slightly ridiculous. And so the general opinion throughout the state pronounced. We had long ago forgiven and forgotten the acerbity of feeling displayed by the Reverend gentleman, but from his late remark it would seem that he still entertains a little soreness on the subject.... We trust that hereafter he will not spoil a compliment by an ill-natured remark, nor sink his strong Union sentiments to the level of selfish considerations."[96]

Anthony's "pet" reference to King's anger never made the pastor connect it sarcastically with his daughter Edith, affectionately nicknamed "Pet" by papa. Yet several random factors did tend to complicate the controversy to King's disadvantage. Four days after King delivered his oration, for example, George Van Buren, a poor black, was fined $25 in Sacramento Police Court for illegally possessing soda-water bottles, a trademark violation of law #478 passed by the current state legislature.[97] The point could well be argued in the public mind whether King, a strong advocate in the oration of guarding blacks' civil rights, did not in effect place editor Anthony in Van Buren's hapless plight by publicity on a related copyright claim. King's $150 fee was also tantalizingly identical in amount to per-diem allowances paid sergeants-at-arms at the Union Democratic State Convention in Sacramento. And if such a "pernicious" procedure of "unjust" taxation, necessary to raise Old Glory upon occasion, was rejected outright by delegates to the current Convention, Anthony's readers could well infer that, with payment already made for his patriotic seventy-five minutes upon the stage, King deserved some similar criticism.[98]

Still, King's fee raised a much broader partisan issue. With the Consolidation Act severely restricting Sacramento's financial outlays, the Union Club finance committee, it might be said, managed to hold expenses some $500 below the $3,000 ceiling requested for the San Francisco celebration in Assembly Bill #250.[99] That is, managed until, unfortunately again it might be said, King's fee ate into the committee's surplus. And the Democratic majority in the current state legislature, not in session when King gave his oration, refused to appropriate state funds for any Sacramento clergyman offering up a prayer at the

96 *Dly Union*, 5 Sept., 1862. George L. Andreini compiles an excellent checklist of manuscript items in the Boston Public Library's King Sermon Collection, but his treatment of the dialogue between Anthony and King is rather oversimplified. Andreini, "An Historical Evaluation of Thomas Starr King's Public Address with Special Reference to the Retention of California as a Union State," Diss. Southern California 1951, pp. 245-47.

97 *Dly Union—Supplement*, 15 June, 1861; *Dly Bee*, 8 July, 1861.

98 *Dly Bee*, 6 July, 1861.

99 *Dly Union*, 10 and 26 April, 1861; Capella, "Celebrate the Fourth," *Dly Bee*, 10 May, 1861. Assembly Bill #250 was "indefinitely postponed" by the Senate on 25 April, after winning approval in the Assembly on the ninth. The Committee of Arrangements for the San Francisco celebration raised some $800 more than the tabled request called for. And of the approximately $5,000 raised for the Bear Valley celebration, Union Club President Trenor Park earmarked a thousand dollars to help outfit Green-Mountain Volunteers in New England. Park's gesture, in effect, represented the charitable implication not present in King's fee.

start of each day's session. Nor would the Democratic majority permit alternative voluntary contributions, the same method supporting clergymen with the troops in military service, to introduce even a single chaplain into its sessions.[100] Under these circumstances, there was indeed considerable opportunity for Anthony's readers to overlap state monies with the twenty-five, fifty, and one hundred dollars actually subscribed by Sacramento businessmen to the finance committee.

King never could really define this perceived misunderstanding, because editor Anthony did not spell out the perception. Instead, King allowed the confused context to go unchecked, viewing the controversy somewhat complacently in terms of noncurrent events. His refusal in 1852, for example, to permit publication of his Boston municipal oration, "Organization of Liberty on the Western Continent" (he wanted to repeat it as a lecture),[101] was once again given editor Anthony. Concerned lest the *Union* text find its way as an altar cloth to some nefarious Washoe camp meeting,[102] the western nadir of Charles Sprague's 1825 oration at Boston being pirated by meetings in New York and Ohio,[103] King invalidly advanced a copyright claim quite reminiscent of John Quincy Adams's claim regarding the 1831 Quincy oration.[104]

King certainly was less than candid about personal income from the very lecture system he insisted be "broad" enough for argumentative purposes. Indeed, he had made "extra money" from the lecture circuit a prior condition for tolerating what he admitted to be a "smaller salary" in San Francisco.[105] And a few personal financial problems made him even more cognizant of this prior condition as the Fourth at Sacramento neared. King paid $900 each year to rent his house on Bush Street in San Francisco,[106] and $300 interest yearly toward

---

100 *Dly Union*, 12 and 28 Jan., 1861; *Pacific Expositor*, 2 (March 1861), 401-02.

101 William Henry Whitmore, "Preface dated 4 March, 1892," *An Oration Delivered before the Municipal Authorities of the City of Boston, at the Celebration of the Seventy-Sixth Anniversary of the Declaration of American Independence, July 5, 1852* (Boston: Rockwell and Churchill, 1892), p. 4. Indeed, King once confided to Randolph Ryer about repeating lectures: "No more of your impudence about new lectures! Do you urge people to take new goods, when they will buy old shelf-worn ones off your hands, at a profit, and count them good as new?" And much the same reason, though toned down considerably, was given at a meeting of the Board of Aldermen on 21 Dec., 1891. Boston, 18 Oct., 1859, *TSK* to Ryer, New York City, King Papers, Bancroft Library-University of California (Berkeley); Boston *Evening Transcript*, 22 Dec., 1891.

102 *Washoe Times* (Virginia City, Nevada Territory) in *Morning Transcript* (Nevada City), 9 July, 1861.

103 "Curiosities of American Literature," Boston *Evening Transcript*, 13 April, 1854.

104 *Daily National Intelligencer* (Washington, D.C.), 15 Aug., 1831; *Atkinson's Saturday Evening Post* (Philadelphia), 20 Aug., 1831.

105 Boston, 22 Sept., 1859, *TSK* to Robert B. Swain, Brattleboro, Vt, in Swain, *Address . . . in Memory of . . . King, March 15, 1864* (SFrc: Frank Eastman, 1864), p. 7; Boston, 26 Sept., 1859, *TSK* to Randolph Ryer, New York City, King Papers, Bancroft Library-University of California (Berkeley).

106 San Francisco, 4 May and 4 June, 1860, *TSK* to Randolph Ryer, NY City, King Papers, Bancroft Library.

retaining a second mortgaged house clear across the country in Boston.[107] On February 24, 1861, King's brother Edward, whose mercantile debts reportedly exceeded $20,000, arrived in San Francisco harbor aboard the *Syren*, spending some seven weeks with the family.[108] Medical bills incurred when illness ravaged King, wife Julia, and daughter Edith during the fall and winter of 1860, with Julia requiring daily medical care for lameness through the Fourth, 1861, exerted additional pressures on the family budget.[109] And, above everything else, King's concern for his health led him to decide, during the summer of 1860, that the entire church debt of $19,914.24 would be paid off no later than the spring (April 28) of 1861, a staggering undertaking requiring the treasurer of the First Church to handle over $32,000 in a year's time.[110]

Little wonder, then, King considered that "meals" digested by "paper-mills"[111] (an unauthorized version printed by the *Union*, etc.) interfered with the lecture system allowing him to cope with these personal financial problems. One question still remains, however, almost in spite of the increased benefits paid California Volunteers from King's lectures during August and September, 1861. Did King in fact plan on making a second extensive lecture tour, comparable to his northern one with "Washington" earlier, with the controversial Sacramento oration?

The question cannot be resolved satisfactorily and must be left dangling. But the texts of King's 1860 San Francisco and 1861 Sacramento orations give the reader an invaluable opportunity to evaluate the orator's Christian ethic as part of a complex revision/reporting process. Regarding the Sacramento oration in particular, the reader may want to relate the more minor revisions to possible

---

107 SFrc, 29 Oct., 1860 and 31 Jan., 1861, *TSK* to Ryer, NY City, King Papers, Bancroft Library.

108 SFrc, 25 March, 1861, *TSK* to Mrs. Susan Starr King, Charlestown, Mass., King Papers, Bancroft Library; *Pacific Monthly*, 11 (April 1864), 504; Charles W. Wendte, *Thomas Starr King, Patriot and Preacher* (Boston: Beacon Press, 1921), pp. 160-61. Daughter Edith regarded Edward M. King as a "live fat uncle" who gleefully amused her.

109 SFrc, 1 Oct., 1860 and 25 March, 1861, *TSK* to Mrs. Susan Starr King, Charlestown, King Papers, Bancroft Library; SFrc, 15 Nov., 1860, *TSK* to N. A. Haven Ball, Sacramento, Ball Papers, California Historical Society (SFrc). King specifically touched upon cause and effect when he wrote Ball: "The prospect of making $100 [per lecture], to a man oppressed with Doctor's bills etc., is truly celestial." For the complete context of this sentence, consult n. 15.

110 SFrc, 16 Aug., 1860, *TSK* to Robert B. Swain, SFrc, in Swain, *Address* (1864), p. 14; "Anniversary Discourse in San Francisco—April 28. 1861," King Sermon Collection, Boston Public Library; SFrc, 1 May, *TSK* to Rev. James Freeman Clarke, Boston, in Boston *Evening Transcript*, 28 May, 1861; "In Account with . . . By Cash Disbursements, 1857 to 1862—Cr[edit]," Treasurer's Ledger Book, Archives, First Unitarian Church (SFrc).

111 Boston, 1 March, 1861, Mrs. Jessie Benton Fremont to TSK, SFrc, King Papers, Society of California Pioneers (SFrc). Replying to a letter from King dated 22 Jan., Mrs. Fremont compared her own situation at Newburyport during the 1830's with the probable circumstances attaching to King's "Washington" lecture several years hence. Observed the wife of the Republican candidate for President in 1856, "Has it ever occurred to you, King, how soon . . . you will be forgotten, and what meals the paper-mills will make of your productions? I don't believe you'll live to be invited to lecture- in San Francisco- a quarter of a century after you orationized."

stylistic differences between oration and lecture formats. Quite obviously the extemporaneous alterations in King's manuscript, taken down as he read it by the *Union* stenographer, though from a poor seat as the phonetic errors indicate, will interest the reader most of all. An extensive table detailing King's personal income from speaking appearances, January thru September, 1861, with adaptive titles noted wherever possible, may be found after the Sacramento oration text.

"Fourth of July Address, S[an]. Francisco July 4, 1860— Episcopal S[unday]. S[chool]. Mission Celebration,—" Delivered by Thomas Starr King, King Sermon Collection, Boston [Mass.] Public Library. In paragraphs 26 thru 28 of the following text, two versions of King's clock anecdote are compared. One version obviously is taken from this 1860 manuscript, the other from an oration delivered by King on the Fourth some nine years earlier at Eastport, Maine. Since King really concludes his oration before the Sunday School gathering with one version, the reader might want to explore the possibility of word revisions reflecting a persuasive conclusion, especially since the Eastport version occurs in an introductory segment. And to enable the reader to comprehend King's process of word selection in both versions, bold type designates words retained in each version. The reader should also be prepared to fill out the abbreviation "wh[ich]." wherever King uses it.

1 Ladies and Gentlemen, Children and Friends, I welcome you, in behalf of the officers of the Sunday School who have made the arrangements for this grand Festival gathering, to a children's celebration of the Fourth of July. Our gratitude is due to them for this inauguration here of a new method of honoring and enjoying our National holiday. For the conception of this kind of jubilee, and the energy they have shown in organizing it, let us pay to them our cordial thanks.

2 Such methods of signalizing this day are not unknown in other portions of our Country. Instances could be quoted from the East in which the officers of one Sunday School have devised, year after year, a plan of celebration similar to this. And so **a** GENERAL **b** extensive ☆ has been the cooperation, and so manifest the good results, that the public authorities of the cities have at last made appropriation from the public treasury, and opened the public grounds, to endorse and strengthen their action in[1] movements which have been found, in unsectarian ways, to contribute so much to the general order and **a** JOY **b** cheer. ☆ Let us hope that this is to be only the Commencement of a series of celebrations in wh. the children of the city, without distinctions of sect and party, shall find provision made for their entertainment, and channels opened for their glee.

3 What spectacle can be more charming than this as an ornament of the public joy? The papers which we lately received from East of the Alleghanies gave us glowing **a** ACCOUNTS **b** pictures, ☆ through poems, and sermons and editorials, and letters, of the unusual splendor of the blossom-season which came to them later than usual, this year. The trees,-apple, and cherry and peach and pear,-in ten thousand orchards, were at once **a** POURING OUT **b** publishing their strength and pouring out ☆ their **a** JOY **b** gladness ☆ in the beautiful and fragrant **a** ROBES **b** raiment ☆ with wh., at the quickening touch of the sun, they

1 Words in Univers type designate non-revision process deletions made by the orator.

enrobed themselves in the poetic and jubilee week of the natural year.—This is the blossom-week of our social tree in this city. We see its boughs and branches brilliant in the efflorescence of young life [and] happiness. We see the promise of the future in the health, and grace, and beauty of these living buds on the public organism.

4 We are *all* children again on the Fourth of July. The music of the bells, to-day, awakens in the oldest of us a juvenile feeling that **a** BEARS **b** floats ☆ us back to the old playground, the earliest mates, the precious roof tree and homestead. The noise of the [fire]crackers and the Cannon rouses in the coldest of us the jubilance of emotion wh. glorious old John Adams foresaw and prayed **a** MIGHT **b** would ☆ ever be the accompaniment of **a** ITS **b** this day's ☆ celebration. We wake on this **a** DAY **b** anniversary ☆ to rejoice. When the morning sun first greets us, we think with a bounding heart of the **a** SPECTACLE **b** exultation his beams have started, and the spectacle ☆ of organised order and prosperity they have kindled in passing over the thousands of leagues wh. divide us, on our line of latitude, from the Atlantic Coast.-Call up that picture now. Freshen it in your imagination. Follow, children,-you will be able to do so with your nimble fancy,-the rays of the sun, from the moment when they dawned upon the Easternmost point of the national domain, this morning; think of the peace and plenty, the intelligence, the thrift, the power, the schools and churches and happy homes, and capitols that are the fountain-heads of equal and beneficent laws, wh. they gild, as they move westward along the track of the emigration of the last forty years; think how the wilderness has been invaded by axe and fire, and the prairies ploughed, and the marshes drained, and the rivers bridged, and the waterfalls harnessed to useful toil, and the lakes skirted by railroads- and furrowed by hurrying ships, to herald the advent and compact the power of republican civilization; and then,

draft a THINK OF WHAT THE SUNBEAMS

draft b

after illumining the central wastes over wh. the buffalo are tramping, and through wh. the wagons of the stout-hearted emigrants are slowly plodding, think of what the sunbeams

look upon in this State and city, when, four hours after they wakened Eastport, their radiance **a** IS CAUGHT BY THE HILLS **b** begins to run down from the hill-tops ☆ that overlook the waves of the Pacific. Think of the hundreds of thousands of souls whom they arouse in the valleys, and by the coasts of this beautiful infant state. Think of the harvests that are waving where, ten years ago, they saw a wilderness. Think of the bloom wh., in that short time, has supplanted the desert. Think of the cities that have sprung up, solid and prosperous, where the arid soil, not twelve years since, was only whitened with tents. Think of the noble institutions that have pushed aside and overshadowed the haunts of evil,—how, near the bar-room has **a** SP[RUNG UP] **b** leaped into activity ☆ the temperance association; near the gambling **a** ROOM **b** Saloon, ☆ the

Library hall; **a** AROUND THE **b** in place of☆houses of infamy, countless shrines of domestic affection; and, all over the face of a Country that **a** ONCE [SEEMED] **b** seemed, in its first settlement,☆to be threatened by a moral desolation more **a** DREADFUL **b** dreary☆than its summer landscape had ever **a** LOOKED **b** shown,☆ how the Spirit of religion and education has **a** UNSEALED **b** opened, by Artesian wells of the moral order,☆the renovating Streams of intellectual and of everlasting life.

5 And then remember that this spectacle is the living oration, written on the breadth of a Continent in honor of the Fourth of July. The scene wh. the sun thus kindles is, in every inspiring feature of it, a tribute to the value of the foresight and heroism wh. were combined in the passage of the Declaration of Independence.

6 We should always come together, then, to rejoice on this day. A Thanksgiving day is not for fasting; a Marriage feast is not for long faces and dismal words; and the Fourth of July is the time to **a** COME TOGETHER- **b** assemble,☆ not as Croakers or critics, but as grateful children of the past- not as partisans but as patriots- not with gloomy foreboding but with psalms of thanksgiving for historic mercies, [all these roles] leading us to the sentiment of trust.

7 There was a dark side in the aspects of the Country, yesterday, and there will doubtless be one tomorrow. It *was* well, and it *will be* well, to look at them [so] that we may be stimulated to labor, and that we may not believe we are endowed with any treasures for wh. we are not responsible, and wh. we need not guard. But to-day we will look at our privileges and gifts.-If there is corruption flowing in the arteries of government, we will rejoice that we can look back to the time when public position was felt to be a very serious trust. If there is little patriotism discernible to-day, we will cling with [even] greater fondness to the glowing story of the period when men of consummate gifts vied with each other in the zeal of their consecration to [the] public good. If there is intolerance anywhere to-day, we will be the more glad that our Empire was *founded* on the wisest religious liberty. If there is [a] lamentable lack of enthusiasm for generous principles, we will turn back **a** TO **b** with ardent gratitude to☆the Season, **a** WHEN **b** eighty-four years ago, when☆a Congress of men, representative heroes from the length and breadth of the land, staked their fortunes and lives on the truth of a noble abstraction; and by that act of faith laid the Corner Stone of the Republic.-

8 Yes, we will rejoice to-day for the more inspiring reason that we have inherited, from the blood and Spirit of these men, and that season, the forces of health that struggle with all the poisonous evils in the body corporate, and will not yield. Let us turn to the **a** FUTURE **b** centuries ahead,☆and see [some] light on **a** THE **b** their☆long vista. We will rejoice that the powers of good are fighting, in this land with the forces of darkness, now such a battle as was never before seen, on so wide a scale and for a prize so magnificent, in the [entire] compass of history.

draft a AND
draft b
We will rejoice that we do not belong to a nation whose record is closing, whose character is ripened and disintegrating, whose hands are folded over energies expended in an experience complete. And,
gathered in California, we will not despair of the future. We will heed the hopeful lesson wh. the last twelve years here emblazon. We will be devoutly and joyously grateful for the evidence **a** HERE. **b** all around us, ☆ that the forces of good in the American character, lodged there by the consecrated genius of the Fathers and the Spirit of Chris[tian]ity, are competent [enough], when left to full and free activity against wrong and evil, to organize **a** FREEDOM **b** justice, ☆ and virtue, and domestic happiness, and wide-spread peace.

9 We are joining in a *children's* celebration. And if we wish to realize, most intensely and speedily, our debt as Americans, and the prompting to joy that rises out of our history and position, we have only to look at these children, and imagine them born to the average lot of **a** THE **b** most of the ☆ prominent countries of the globe.

10 One of the mysteries of Providence, wh. can never be solved on this Earth, is the law by wh. young and innocent life is cramped by hostile circumstances, or involved with the fate of those who, it should seem, ought to **a** SUFFER **b** exhaust the penalties of justice by personal suffering. ☆ We do not see what the horror of intemperance *is*, 'til we look at the young children of the habitual drunkard, and think how *they* are doomed for [the sake of] parental sensuality. We do not appreciate the woe of chronic poverty in a city like New York, until we see the wan and shrivelled faces of the little ones, in the cheerless alleys in winter, for whom (though Nature is so bountiful) no plate seems to be laid at the feast of Nature. We cannot comprehend the horror of bondage so thoroughly, when we look at a full-grown **a** SERF **b** chattel, ☆ as when we see a little child, two-thirds white it may be, with intellect in its eyes and **a** ENTHUSIASIM **b** glee ☆ in its blood, and think that there is no development for either,-no school training, no **a** ELASTIC **b** ennobling ☆ grapple with [all the] difficulties that bar the way to success, no opportunity or responsibilities of self-development but the life of a Slave, of dependence on a Master's will and whims 'til death.

11 And what would you say to the possibility of losing your inheritance of the free American life, and being forced into the **a** AVERAGE **b** medium ☆ lot of some other country among the nations on this planet. Suppose that all the parents in this assembly should be called out with their children into separate groups, and that the **a** DOOM **b** destiny ☆ should be appointed to you, by the chance drawings from an urn in wh. the names of all the lands on the globe were mingled; what [other] Nation should [then] be your home, with its *average* condition of wealth and morals and intelligence as the limit of *your* children's hope!

12 How would you wait with **a** EAGERNESS **b** anxiety, yes with agony, ☆ to learn how the immensely freighted possibilities should dip. Suppose that to one [parent] the lot should fall of *Russia*, with no chance for any child of yours to have a better education, a nobler faith, a more powerful influence on the government of the Empire, a higher social standing, than the average Russian may aspire to now!-Suppose the paper drawn for you should have Venice, over wh. the Austrian vampire broods, inscribed on it. Suppose it should be the name of decrepit and dissolving Mexico; or Cuba, where the seeds of enterprise and thought are bruised under the heel of despotism; or Naples, wh. cannot breathe for the bayonets at its breast; or France, with its Anaconda Army pressing every noble institution of the land in its sinewy and complicated coil.

13 Nay, if the best lot- England- should fall to you, would your **a** AVERAGE **b** assumption of the average ☆ **a** LOT **b** education and possibility ☆ in that island be *comparable* with the prospect for energy, influence and fortune before your children in this State?—And what if the fate should fall to you of China, Turkey, Hindostan! I need not **a** ENLARGE ON **b** attempt any further to develope ☆ the conception.

14 You would recoil from almost any of the chances of such a hazard. The *best* of them you would account a *disaster*. The worst of them you would receive as a dreadful doom. And the intensity of your recoil is the measure of your indebtedness for the privilege of a birth on this globe, into the **a** INHERITANCE [AND] **b** history, ☆ the **a** ATTAINMENTS **b** spirit, and the prospects ☆ of the states where American republicanism finds its full expression.

15 Let that, then, be the incentive to-day to a vigorous and exuberant joy. Connect it with gratitude to the Providence who appoints by mysterious Sovereignty the earthly home of souls, and has appointed your's where labor is free and honored; where the ballot-box is open to all; where education is cheap as the sunlight; where worship is unobstructed by priestly power; where Bibles are plentiful as water; and where the path is open, and is often traversed, from the lowliest birth to the highest lines of knowledge, fortune and power. The laws and Polity that organize and perpetuate these blessings are the best things now on this globe; and, if we count them of little worth, we are insensible to the richest benefits, and have no possibility of a Fourth of July in the heart.

16 Let me call on you, also, to make *such* a joy in this day the stimulant to a more ardent *Patriotism*. A great many people feel that the possibility of such a virtue as patriotism, in a country like our's, has passed, or is rapidly passing away. "See," they say, "how corrupt every channel of public life is becoming,-how low and loathsome our politics,-how disgusting the impulses of ambition, and the qualities that often secure the most eminent success!" What [else] can a true man do, but avoid every avenue of political action and influence as debasing, and fly from its very atmosphere as [from] contamination?

17 But let us remember, to-day, that Patriotism is devotion, not to the country, with all its errors and evils, but to the *idea* and *plan* of the country, as God has drawn its outline in its geography, and hinted [at] its true Spirit in its earlier traditions and leadings. There is the Politicians' America, and God's America; the America of the present, and the America that would be, if all the noblest ideas and earlier Providential inbreathings into the land should gain full development.

18 God, we may reverently say, plainly designed our nation to be perpetually *one*, for **a** HE **b** He☆has spiked it up and down **a** WITH **b** ,from the [Great] lakes to the Gulf, with☆the bed of the Mississippi, cross-bolted it, from Georgia to Lake Erie, with the Alleghanies, and opened a path, from St. Louis to the Sierras, for a Pacific Rail-Road, wh. Congress will learn, in some day, when she studies anew the points of the compass, and finds among them a letter *W*, as well as the letters *N* and *S*. Whoever works for the disunion of our nation (and hopes to succeed) must get up, not a convention or a rebellion, but *an Earthquake* that shall pitch half of Mississippi towards the North Pole, **a** BREAK **b** snap☆the Alleghanies at the centre and turn the Ohio out of bed, and choke with ruins every pass of the Rock[y] Mountains.

19 God's America is designed to be the home of immigrants from every land,-for the first explorers and colonists of it were from every civilized European Kingdom and race.

20 And *as plainly* it is dedicated to Saxon ideas of freedom; for the French were driven, as [if] by the hand of beneficent destiny, from their whole chain of Western intrenchments, before the [onset of the American] Revolution; and the Spanish power was unravelled, [so] that Saxon principles might be laid [down] without embarrassment as the warp-lines in the **a** WIDE **b** vast☆breadth of the national loom.

21 And then, after the diagram of our true future was thus drawn, and the principles to wh. the country was **a** DEDICATED **b** pledged☆were **a** BREATHED **b** indicated☆through our Revolutionary Rhetoric and passion, the difficulties were left in our path

draft a ,THROUGH WH. WE MUST

draft b

,-[such difficulties as] the sectional controversies over a great evil; the floods of ignorant immigration; the corruptions incident to immense prosperity and power;-and in the struggle with these, and by means of these, we are to

learn the value of our whole country, be educated to understand its mission, and be trained to prize its principles, as all knowledge is tested and assayed, by passing them through the fire of controversy and passion.

22 Patriotism is devotion to the Divine Conception, wh. every land is called [upon] to realize. Our's is the noblest that is possible on the planet to-

day; for the idea of our nation is plainly the grandest, the theatre for its execution the most sublime, the preparation for its development the most careful, and the difficulties left to be removed by human consecration the most trying, that the mind can conceive [of]. It is thus that God makes true heroes and powerful states. And if we are timid because the opposing forces in our national life, to-day, are so intense,-or if we slink away from [taking any] interest in public duties and questions because there is *so much* wrong and corruption in the machinery and methods of politics,-we confess that we are not worthy of our **a** PRIVILEGES **b** opportunity, ☆ that we are not equal to our task, that we find no sense of privilege and joy in working to realize, in a mighty Empire, the **a** IDEA **b** conception ☆ of its Creator.

23 An eminent sculptor, at work upon his block, **a** EXCLAIMED **b** was asked what he was doing, and replied, ☆ "There is a noble statue buried **a** HERE **b** in this marble, ☆ and I am toiling to dig it out." **a** OUR **b** The true ☆ America is as yet only a half hewn statue. If the best men retire from interest in public life, she will [be] spoiled by the hacking of bunglers. If the best men band their energies [together] to purify the Public Spirit, she **a** WILL **b** shall ☆ come out from her mighty continental block, shapely and beautiful, the pride of the globe.—Seeing these opposite possibilities, let us, in our joy, erect the altar of a holier Patriotism in our hearts.

24 And now, before closing, a word or two of direct address to the Children. We have neglected them too long. I ask your pardon, my young friends, for spending so much time on those who are of less consequence, here to-day, than you.

25 You have not been interested [very] much in what I have been saying. You have not understood much, if anything, of the vague speech I have used. The Fourth of July is written about in your School books. The battles of the Revolution are described there so that you learn by heart, it may be, how many [soldiers] fell on each side in every [last] contest, and wh. party (British or American) remained master of the field. Yet perhaps you do not understand, through all this reading, what the real importance of the Fourth of July (and the Revolution) was to our Country and the world.

Eastport version All **the seasons of** human **history** are related to the Divine thought, and proceed according to the Divine laws of justice and order, [much] as every minute wh. is **mark**ed off by **the hands** of the **clock** is measured by the internal mechanism. But in the course of human affairs, as upon the face of **a clock**, there are some moments **more important** than others, because they **mark a**nother **hour**. The American **Revolution was** one of these transition[al] and epochal **season**s. Another **sixtieth minute** was due upon **God**'s register. Slowly and unobserved, **the** moral **pendulum** had swung, and **the** ideal **wheels** had **play**ed, carried [on] by the dead weights of the mother country's hostile legislation, 'til at last **the striking of the clock** was **heard**, and **the battle of Bunker Hill**, and **the Declaration of Independence** and **the surrender of Burgoyne**, and **the** closing military scene at **Yorktown** and **the treaty** and **Washington's inauguration** came with solemn precision, startling **the** drowsy **world** like **str**okes from the hammer in the horologe of time, pealing through-[out] the universe the change from era to era.—While we are **grateful** for **the day**, therefore, and for the blessings it has ensured, **let us be grateful** to Providence, wh. ordained that the labors of our ancestors should be thus connected with its schemes of **good for** posterity, and that so momentous an **hour** should be **struck** up**on our** shores.

San Francisco version (paragraphs 26 thru 28)
26 Let us try to get some help from an illustration. I **a** will not **b** promise not to☆detain you [very] long with it. You [all] know that **a clock** ticks and ticks, second by second, in a **a** dry humdrum **b** dull, patient☆way, 'til **the hand** reaches the **sixtieth minute**, and then it **strikes. A** new **hour** is born. What if each day should be **mark**ed, at Sunrise, by **the** louder **striking of** a **clock** to tell us that **a more important minute** was reached? What if the commencement of a New Year should always be told to us by the vibrations of some mighty bell, far up in Space, that sounded only on the morning of the first of January, touched then by the **hand** of **God**.-And now suppose that when anything very **important** was about to happen in the world, when a New Year of hope and joy for a nation or mankind was to come, a mighty time-keeper, away up among the stars, should ring out so that men could hear it, and say- "Hark,-Ah, **a** new **hour**, one of **God**'s **hour**s, has **struck** in the great belfry of the heavens!"

27 This would be grand. But **a** doe[s God] **b God** does☆**mark the** great **seasons of** the world's **history** by **a** mighty **clock**. In fact, every nation **a** is **b** has☆a huge dial-plate, and behind it are the works, and below it is **the pendulum**, and every now and then its **hands mark a** new **hour. a** It was **b** Our **revolution was**☆such a period. That is the glory of it. The English government had oppressed our fathers. It tried to break their Spirit. It was for several years a dark time, [very much] like the **season** before Sunrise. But the old time-piece kept ticking, ticking, **the wheels** kept **play**ing calmly, 'til, about 1775, there was a strange stir and buzz and clatter inside the Case,-the people couldn't bear any more,-**a sixtieth minute** came, and all of a sudden **the clock struck. The world heard the battle of Bunker hill**- one; **The Declaration of Independence**,-two; **the surrender of Burgoyne**,-thre[e]; **the** siege of **Yorktown**,-four; **the treaty** of Paris, five; the **inauguration of Washington**, six;-and then it was Sunrise, and we live in the forenoon of **the** glorious **day**.—

28 **Let us be** glad and **grateful**, on this Anniversary, that such a glorious **hour** was **a struck b mark**ed☆for our Country and the world **on our** Coasts. **Let us** hope and pray that the **good** old **clock** shall remain for centuries uninjured, and that it will **strike** many times again (but not through battles) **a** for the [cause of] **b** to **mark** new **hours for**☆humanity.

"The Two Declarations of Independence:—1776 and 1861— Oration in Sacramento, July 4, 1861—" Delivered by Thomas Starr King, King Sermon Collection, Boston [Mass.] Public Library. The following text is based upon manuscript drafts, and two additional sources: a stenographic report printed in the Supplement to the July 6 Sacramento Daily Union, *and carried again in the* Weekly Union *of July 13—and a pamphlet edition of the* Union *transcript, issued by J. G. Coggins in San Francisco during 1862. Three symbols identify the appropriate texts,* **M**-*the manuscript,* **U**-*the* Union *report, and* **P**-*the Coggins pamphlet. And, in conjunction with* **M** *and* **U**, *apparent phonetic errors committed by the* Union *reporter, in transcribing and interpreting specific words, are highlighted by* **px**—*and then* **mw**, *for actual* **m***anuscript* **w***ord, compared with* **sp**, *or the variant phoneme arrived at by the* Union *reporter. Material intended for King's July 9 lecture, and not included in the* Union *transcript or Coggins pamphlet, is set off by* **INSERT/End INSERT**. *And a minor insert within the manuscript, which does not qualify as lecture material, is designated* **ms1** ☆ *the star showing precisely where the word or group of words terminate. These editorial symbols should alert the reader to textual variations, not only between King's July 4 oration and July 9 lecture, both having identical titles, but also between King's intended manuscript version and the* Union *reporter's transcript. And as in the 1860 oration, King relies on "wh." to abbreviate "which."*

Extemporaneous preface to July 9 lecture

Ladies and Gentlemen, I intended and hoped to offer to you, and the officers of the Mercantile Library Association, an address that had not appeared in print. Having received a very flattering invitation to speak in Sacramento on the 4th, I thought that I could give *there* a large portion of the address prepared for this evening, without any prejudice to the rights of this Association. And I therefore requested the managing proprietor of the Sacramento *Union* newspaper to print only a report of the address, and not a stenographic transcript of it, as I was under engagement to deliver it here and elsewhere in the state. Though repeatedly appealed to, he refused this courtesy, which no respectable newspaper, so far as my knowledge extends, ever did before. To protect the Association here, I then obtained a copyright, and gave him notice of it. But he still printed it *in full,* in defiance of courtesy, of justice, of legal right, and of a short but comprehensive and serious sentence in a very ancient code, which runs, "Thou shalt not steal." I say this, by way of explanation, to those present who may have seen the buccaneer copy of portions of the lecture in the *Union* of Saturday last, and have found out in advance how poor is the provision for the present entertainment. It would be proper for me now to say that all persons who have read the address may retire and have their money refunded at the door, but my friend, the chairman of the lecture committee, fearing that too many would avail themselves of such a privilege, refuses to give me the right to make such an announcement.

Lecture INSERT, INTRODUCTION version a

This is one of the prominent historic days of America.

On the 7th. of June 1776, Richard Henry Lee, of Virginia, introduced into the Continental Congress a resolution of Independence on Great Britain.—On the Tenth of June, a Committee was appointed to draft a Declaration, wh. could be published at once, if Congress should vote for THE Mr. Lee's ☆ resolution.-On June 25th. the Declaration was reported, from Jefferson's pen, by the Committee to the Congress, for discussion and amendments.

On the 1st of July, the resolution of Independence was agreed to in Committee of the Whole,-two thirds of the colonies concurring,-but [with] the vote of South Carolina unanimously in the negative. July 2[*n*]*d*, the resolution WAS ADOPTED ,reported out of Committee, was adopted ☆ by the House. So[uth]. Carolina came round, and twelve Colonies voted that they were "absolved from all allegiance to the British Crown."-The Declaration by Jefferson was then taken up for discussion, and IT on the 4th. of July it ☆ was agreed to, in the shape that we find it to-day, and, with the signatures of the President and Secretary, was published to the world as the voice of the American People.

But, even then, there was *one man* who had not pronounced *for* it,-a name as important as the combined Congress,-*George Washington*. There was another assembly who had not endorsed it,-the Colonial Army under Washington in the City of New York.—

Fifty ships, laden with British troops, lay off Sandy Hook, expecting others too, while Congress were debating the Resolution. Washington had under his command 7754 troops in New York, all told. About 3000 of them had seen a year's service. Fifteen hundred were recent recruits, and *very raw*. There was one regiment of artillery. Nearly a thousand soldiers had no firelocks. More than half of THEM [NO] BA[YONETS] the troops were destitute of bayonets ☆. Fourteen hundred of the muskets were scarcely fit for use. And it was known then [that Britain would soon have AN a ☆ force of thirty thousand well-appointed veterans on the Colonial soil.-

Well might Adjutant-General Reed write, as he did, that "every man, from the General to the Private, acquainted with our true situation, is exceedingly discouraged." "Had I known the true posture of affairs," he continues, "no consideration would have tempted me to have taken an active part in this scene."-This is the PRIVATE expression in a private ☆ letter, about July 1st, '76, from the New-York Camp of a Soldier and officer, who has the full confidence of Washington.

How, then, will the Army and the Chief, receive the Declaration wh. the Civilians in Philadelphia have voted,-a document wh. will make *them all* traitors as well [as] rebels in the eyes of England, and wh. closes the door against compromise and accommodation?

Copies were sent to the Camp of Washington, and in spite of the Condition of the troops, and the discouragement of many officers, he did not hesitate. On the 9th. DAY of July 1776, at six o'clock in the Evening, eighty-five years ago *this very* day and hour, Washington ordered the great State-Paper to be read at the head of the brigades in New York. "Now," said the Commander in Chief, "let each soldier feel that he is 'in the service of a State possessed of sufficient power to reward his merit, and advance him to the highest honors of a free country.' "

The soldiers responded to it. Such bayonets as they *had*, saluted it. Their drums, though it was vesper time, rolled a moral reveille to the nation. Their rusty firelocks were grasped with fresh heroism. The Army was in chord with the civil heart, and THE Jefferson's ☆ words, adopted by the cannon of the Camp, became, if not yet the "*Te Deum*", the sublime "*De Profundis*" chant of the new nation.

The populace of New York rang all the bells of the Churches. If any Tory-priests refused, as lately [was the case] in Stockton, and their friends abetted them, I have no doubt the people then, as the true Americans in Stockton did, tried the mettle of the traitors, first, and driving them off, tried the American metal of the bell, and *proved it sound*.-There was a leaden statue of King George on the Bowling Green, in front of the fort. It was pulled down amid the shouts of the multitude, some of the soldiers assisting; and the people broke it up, and ran it into bullets "to be used in the Cause of Independence."—Thus New York, with the great English fleet at its gates, was launched upon the waves of revolution.

The Bell on Independence Hall in Phil[adelphi]*a*. rang out the signal of the adoption of the Declaration. But it was the nation itself, like a mighty Clock, that was striking a *new hour*. The musketry of Lexington, the volleys of Bunker Hill, the ballot of Independence Hall, the prompt revolutionary roar of the Cannon in New York, on the 9th. of July, at the Command of Washington, CAME fell ☆ on the ears of the drowsy world, like something *more* than the voice of a nation just reaching its majority,-like strokes from the *great* hammer of Providence in history, pealing the Change from one era to another.—Republicanism was born.

End INSERT

Oration text begins, INTRODUCTION version b

1 Fellow Citizens of California, and Fellow Americans: I congratulate you on this meeting, to-day, in the Capital of the most Western State of the great Republic. I congratulate you that we gather, not as Californians, but as *Americans*, under the protection of the Constitution of the United States, and loyal to every letter of it. I congratulate you that the American Congress assembles **M** to-day **U** IN THESE HOURS, with seats ready in each Chamber for deputies from every district of the Empire; and that California will be represented *there*

by two Senators pledged to the Constitution, **M** while **U** AND LET US THANK HEAVEN, SOLEMNLY AND MOST GRATEFULLY, THAT she will not be misrepresented in the lower house.

2 I congratulate you that the Sacramento is an *American* river, that the San Joaquin is not held by traitors; that San Diego is an *American* **px:mw** port **sp** post ☆; that the Nevada range is an *American* bulwark; that Alcatraz bristles with cannon ready to **px: mw** declaim **sp** proclaim ☆ the dialect not of Mr. Jefferson Davis but of Winfield Scott; that Shasta is an *American* summit, bearing upon its Snows, flushed with sunrise and marked with azure shadows, the Country's *Red*, *White*, and *Blue*. I congratulate you that there is no blasted heath, or desolate hillock, within our borders, that will give the black flag of the rebellion a **M** permanent **U** FIRM foothold to pollute the air; that, from the White Sierra to the **px:mw** white-edged **sp** wide-edged **P** white-edged ☆ Sea, California, by an immense majority, is loyal to the integrity of the Republic and the honor of the old Stripes and Stars; and that she is thus **Ma** TRUE **b** responsive ☆ to the appeal wh. the great fathers make to us, and to the dying **M** call **U** GLORY of him, lately the leader of the Democratic Party of the land, who poured out his last breath in the whisper to his children, heard from Eastport to Oregon, wh. shall make the name of Douglas immortal- "be true to the laws and the Constitution of the United States!"

3 Let us pause, for a few moments, upon the **M** representative **U** RIFE significance of this day.—Every nation is like a Clock. The forces at work, within it, carry forward some purpose or plan of Providence with patient constancy. But **Ma** IN SOME SEASONS **b** IN SOME SEASON **c** the season comes when ☆ a sixtieth minute is due, and a *new hour* must be sounded, perhaps not for the nation only, but for the world. Then the Clock *strikes*, and it may be with a force and resonance that startles and inspires the race. The first American Revolution was such a period. That is the glory of it.—The English government had oppressed our fathers. It tried to break their spirit. For several years it was a dark time, like the hour before the **px: mw** streak **sp** striking ☆ of dawn. But the Colonial time-piece kept ticking, *ticking*; the **U** GIANT wheels kept playing calmly; 'til, about 1775, there was a strange stir and buzz within the case,-the people couldn't bear any more.- **M** God's **U** THE sixtieth minute came,-and the *Clock struck*. The world heard The Battle of Lexington, *One*; the Declaration of Independence, *two*; the surrender of Burgoyne, *three*; the siege of Yorktown, *four*; the treaty of Paris, *five*; the inauguration of Washington, *six*;-and then it was sunrise of a *new* day, of wh. we are seeing only the glorious *forenoon*.[1]

End INTRODUCTION version b

1 Compare this paragraph with the brief clock analogy in the final paragraph of version **a** above, and also with paragraphs 26-28 in the 1860 oration text.

4 Conspirators tried to convince the world, a few months ago, that there was no further use for the old time-piece on this globe. They came near to making England believe that the machinery was worn out. There is no disputing the fact that, under the late Administration, it *ran down* utterly. With a Floyd in the War office, and a Cobb in the Treasury, and a Twiggs **M** far up on **U** UPON the Army roll,-what could it do *but* stop?-But the Cannon-roar around Sumter, **Ma** WH. TRAITORS INTENDED **b** to the Amazement of traitors/**U** BRITAIN☆, was God's method of winding it up again; and in the Victories of Gen[eral]. Scott, on Virginia Soil, over the Enemies of the Constitution and the ballot-box, we shall soon hear it strike **Ma** AGA[IN] **b** anew☆the advent of a nobler Era than that of Seventy-Six. This is the question for us to consider most seriously, today,-which party is more in sympathy with the work and the men of '76,-those who would rend, or those who are determined to save the Unity of America?

5 It would not suprise me to learn that *this* Fourth of July is celebrated with remarkable **M** fervor and jubilance in **U** FERVOR IN SOME OF the Rebellious States.-The great men of the Continental Congress *were* revolutionists and rebels. They cut boldly at the cords wh. bound them to a Constitution and an Empire. The Declaration of Independence *is* a Secession document.-At first sight, it seems as though the men and the States who have attempted to set up a new government more in **M** harmony with their passions **U** CONCORD WITH THEIR CONVICTIONS AND WISHES than the established one, and who have drawn **M** a **U** THEIR NEW Declaration of Independence, can go with the greater readiness to *those* Philadelphia fathers, and can feel the assurance of faith that *they* are in the line of succession from their spirit and their work. In fact, this has been openly claimed *by* the Apostates, and *for* them. They claim that the time has come when it is necessary for *them* "to dissolve the political bands wh. have **M** connected them with **U** CONNECTED THEM WITH **P** HELD THEM TO another people," and "to assume among the powers of the earth a separate and equal station." They affirm that to oppose this attempt is to fight against American history, and the great Charter of American freedom. They insist that their Cause is essentially kindred with the Cause of the Colonies against England. And it has been said in the public press, here and in Great Britain, **M** and **U** IT HAS BEEN SAID OVER AND OVER AGAIN in private defences of their Cause, that the North, in not allowing them to secede, is playing over again the part of George the Third.

6 Perhaps it was owing to this conviction, of the identity of the two Struggles, that the **Ma** RENEGADES **b** conspirators☆were so confident of running up *their flag* over Independence Hall in Philadelphia, after hoisting it above the Capitol in Washington. It has not been convenient to run it up yet in Washington. We have heard of no movement of Secession troops *north* of Harper's Ferry. And we shall not be likely to hear again of the American flag [being] hauled down in any American City, unless the halliards are needed to hang the leading traitors who have inflicted **ms1** immeasurable☆damage on their motherland. Let us not be afraid, on the Fourth of July, or on any other day, to meet

this claim, and fancied analogy **U** THAT HAS BEEN PUT FORWARD IN FAVOR OF THE TREASON . Let us *welcome* the discussion,-[so] that **Ma** ITS WEAKNESS **b** the audacity of the assumption ☆ may be unmasked, and that the old Declaration may be saved from the eclipse wh. partnership with the new one would surely leave.

Lecture INSERT

I invite you to consider, as broadly as possible within the proper limits of such an address, *the relations* of the two Declarations, and of the movements they represent, *to each other*. In whatever I shall have to say, *this* will be the point in view: What right has the Montgomery declaration of '61 to claim lineage from, or kindred with, the Declaration of '76? We have a right to discuss this question thoroughly, on whatever tracks it may lead us, before any literary Assembly in a loyal Community.

End INSERT

7 In the first place, look at the difference in the *methods* of the two Rebellions and attempted Revolutions. Think of the *patience* of the Colonial revolutionists, and of the events that preceded their severance of the English bonds! They did not take the steel until all legal methods were tried and exhausted. Their charters were torn up; their fundamental liberties were abrogated by the Ministry; troops were on their soil; ships commanded their harbors; the blood of their citizens was shed; the intention to break their Spirit was arrogantly promulgated, before they drew a **U** SINGLE sword in self-defence.—When they drew the sword, it was not for secession, but simply to show that they were not slaves, nor cowards; that they were in earnest in their constitutional resistance **M** and discussion **U** TO TAXATION ; and that England *must* grant them the kind of hearing wh. she had **U** SO LONG AND so insolently refused. Eighteen separate paragraphs of indictment against the Central government, in wh. the **px: mw** Colonies **sp** Colonists ☆ had no representation, containing twenty-seven specifications of acts of tyranny and outrage, are presented, in the clearest and severest phrases wh. the English tongue can **px: mw** frame **sp** bring ☆, in the old Declaration of Independence. Each of them could be, and has been, justified by facts **Ma** FURNISHED **b** laid on it ten-deep **U** FURNISHED ☆ from the fifteen preceding years of Colonial history.—[2] It was not until every **px: mw** possible **sp** peaceful ☆ method of redress, wh. British law and the Structure of the British government afforded, had been tried, that a musket was fired in protest against oppression. It was not for more than a year after Steel had been crossed,—after Lexington, after Bunker Hill, after foreign troops had been **px: mw** bought **sp** brought ☆ by thousands, after the Indians had been **px: mw** roused **sp** raised ☆ by England, after Norfolk had been bombarded by British guns, after the fruitless **px: mw** roar **sp** war ☆ of British artillery against Fort Moultrie in the harbor of Charleston, after sack and Slaughter by the

2 The *Union* reporter selects a word which King revised in the manuscript draft.

Ministry along the *whole* line of the Colonies,-that the Continental Congress could bring themselves to vote **U** ,OR EVEN TO DISCUSS, an ordinance of Secession. *Patience*, not *passion*, was their crowning characteristic.

8 How will the seceding States, or rather their leaders, dare bring themselves and their work into comparison with the dignity, this long-sufferance, this majestic self-control, wh. the Fourth of July emblazons, and wh. all the State-Papers of the Colonial assemblies represent?—Did they endure a year of military conflict with the Central government, before taking the final step of revolution? Had a hostile seventy-four [gun ship] prowled off the harbor of Charleston, or threatened the city, before the Convention of Carolina voted that the tie to the nation was cut? Had a gun frowned on Savannah, or **Ma** THREATENED **b** been shotted against **U** BEEN FIRED AGAINST ☆ New Orleans, or **Ma** BEEN ORDERED **b** turned its muzzle **U** ORDERED ☆ for any other purpose than defence, towards Mobile, when rebellion was enacted on paper, and the "chivalry" of stealing docks and arsenals and **msl** the treasure of ☆ mints, and of betraying forts, and stores, and revenue cutters, began? Had they *exhausted* legal methods of opposition to the wrongs of the federal government? Indeed, what were their wrongs? Where are the eighteen paragraphs and twenty-seven specifications, to match or echo those in the State-Paper of the immortal *Jefferson*, wh. can be arrayed against the American Congress and Constitution by the modern Jefferson, the figure-head of the new treason? (I beg pardon of the **Ma** MEMORY **b** Spirit ☆ of the great Author of the Declaration: the name of the modern Jefferson is pronounced usually in *one syllable* **msl** in this relation of syllables, representing, I presume, the relative dignity of the two Causes ☆.) It is on account of the Slavery question **M** nominally **U** AVOWEDLY that they have withdrawn. What legislation of Congress on that question have they impeached in any State-Paper yet put forth? What oppression, by any of its Acts, do they declare intolerable? Against what Bill or its Enactment, do they say that they have sought legal redress, and sought it in vain? Nay, against what Acts of Congress on that question do they complain *at all*?

9 Not one! No Act on the Slavery question has ever passed the United States Congress *but with* the consent of the States that have seceded. No action has ever been demanded by a United South **U** UP TO THIS HOUR that has not been granted. The policy of the government, in relation to it, for **Ma** FIFTY **b** NEARLY FORTY **c** forty ☆ years has been drawn and organised and enforced by their own leaders and Statesmen. Compromises have been made and broken, to suit their fancied interests; and when they **Ma** BROKE **b** tried to break ☆ up the nation, and involved [it] in an expense of five hundred millions of dollars, they held the Executive, and Senate, and a controlling **M** check **U** MAJORITY in the House of Representatives, and the Supreme Court of the Nation **msl** and 1500 000 votes for candidates devoted to every constitutional right of theirs in the free

States☆.—This is their legal parallel with the great revolutionists of '76. The Stamp-Act and tyranny, wh. they have to complain of, is, that for once in the history of the nation the ballot-box is *against* them; that, for four years, a man holding the opinions of Washington and Jefferson concerning Slavery was elected, after an honorable contest, and was to serve in the White House, while they held the Senate, the Supreme Court, and votes enough in the hall of Representatives to check any fanatic or unconstitutional Bill.

10 "But, you keep out of **M** sight **U** VIEW," it may be said, "the Personal Liberty Bills of Northern States, wh. are clearly **px: mw** contrary **sp** contradictory☆to the Constitution, and an excessive grievance to the seceded States."—Who has declared them unconstitutional? Has the Supreme Court pronounced upon them? Grant that *some* of them *are* in violation of the Charter upon wh. the South may fairly insist. Has the Central government as yet refused to put forth its whole power, to enforce the Constitution and a decision of the Supreme Court in a Northern State? We know that it has never flinched **U** WHEN CALLED UPON. When the Supreme Court shall have declared the Personal Liberty Bills of Massac[huse]tts. and New York unconstitutional and the General Gov't. shall refuse to put forth its might in making that decision sovereign within those States,-the South will *begin* to have a right to talk of revolution and Secession from the central force and authority of America. But, even then, their right would *not* be complete. They must exhaust *all legal* methods **M** through various Elections **U** TO OBTAIN REDRESS before they would have a right to violate their oaths of allegiance, strike at the flag, and inaugurate the horrors of Civil War. *Especially* if they are to claim kindred with the great Seceders from Great Britain! Our forefathers asked for not a tithe so much, in *redress* for all their Grievances, as the Secession-traitors *have always held* under the Constitution. *They* asked that *they* might not be taxed, unless by assemblies where *they* were represented. Has this been denied to any seceding State?—*They* asked only for equal representation, on the basis of numbers.—This is what the South has to *complain of* in that respect:-The North has 36 Senators, to represent eighteen millions of free people. The South has 30 Senators to represent eight millions of free people.—The North has no Congressmen to represent *its* property: the South, by the new Census, will have the right to send more than twenty such Representatives to the lower Assembly in the Capitol **ms1** and *may*, as soon as the Arms of the rebellion are grounded☆.

Lecture INSERT

Do any of you say that this picture is colored by ultra-Northern, by Abolition prejudices or proclivities? Listen, then, to what a Southern Statesman says on this part of the disputed problem. I FOUND read☆them for the first time, yesterday, since this address was written. He writes, "A more wanton and wicked war was never commenced on any government whose history has been written." Writing to Kentucky, he asks, "Could the wisest of her lawyers find the material for an indictment in any or all the pages of the history of the

Republic? Could the most leprous-lipped of its calumniators point to a single state, or territory, or community, or citizen that it has wronged or oppressed? It would be impossible. So far as the Slave-States are concerned, their protection has been complete; and if it had not been, it has been the fault of their Statesmen, who have had the control of the government since its foundation." This is not the language of an Abolitionist, nor of a Republican, nor of a Northern man; but of a Kentucky Statesman and Democrat,-a member of the Cabinet of Mr. Buchanan, Mr. Postmaster-General *Holt*,-He wrote it not six weeks ago, and published it in Kentucky,-and WORD rumor ☆ comes [to] us, wh. I devoutly hope is authentic, that he is to be appointed soon, if he has not yet been, a MEMBER OF Justice on the bench of ☆ the Supreme Court of the U[nited]. States. When this indictment can be printed *against* them, should it not seem as though the leaders of the Rebellion would have consented to stay, for *one* term, *in* the government, after losing Executive power, simply to show that they were *not* shameless sharpers and swindlers, who consent to play a game—only so long as the dice are loaded, and they are sure to throw sixes every time? If twenty millions of White People were loyal without rebellion under Mr. Buchanan, WHAT how ought six millions of White People to behave under the present President of the Republic?—

End INSERT

11 What a similarity, thus far, between the two Declarations of Independence! between the wrongs of '76 and the wrongs of '61! But even if our forefathers had not tried all possible methods of legal redress,-if there had been some **px: mw** courts **sp** cause ☆ to wh. they had failed to appeal, and some **M** avenues, promising **U** WAY OF COMPROMISE BY bloodless negotiation. wh. they had not worn smooth, they would have been justified in forcing resistance and hurrying the appeal to Arms, on the ground that *geography* was in their favor, and that Providence plainly intended them for a separate and independent government. In their Declaration, they claim the "separate and equal station to wh. *the laws of Nature* entitle them." This was a prominent and powerful Argument to dertermine[determine] Secession from Great Britain, after the affection of the Colonies had cooled to a low temperature. The Chief Justice of South Carolina said in '76, "The Almighty created America to be independent of Great Britain." He thought that "piety and political safety were blended." He thought it would be impious to hold back, and kick against the Divine suggestions of Geography.-And Thomas Paine wrote,-"Everything that is right or *natural* pleads for separation. There is something absurd in supposing a *continent* to be perpetually governed by **M** an *island* **U** a distant island." It was not until every legal method **msl** of influence ☆ was closed, that the Statesmen of that day allowed their minds to be moved by the fact that the Atlantic Ocean was the Almighty ordinance of Secession from the English throne. If the Country had been bound by physical configuration with the central power, by any isthmus or geological bond, the revolutionary movement would have been far less energetic, and, on account of the **M** moral forces **U** FORCE that would have streamed along

the U SLIGHT geographical connections, perhaps an entire failure.-The heroes of the Continental Congress were immensely strengthened by[in] feeling that God was on their side, by the structure of their continental home.

12 How is it to-day? The American Secessionists fight *against* geography as manifestly as geography fought *on* the side of our Ancestors. The Creator tells us to be *one* people, under one rule, just as plainly as He told our fathers that they might throw off the English Yoke by force. On the very day that the Declaration was adopted, before the adjournment on the Fourth of July, Dr. Franklin, John Adams and T[homas]: Jefferson were appointed a Committee, to prepare a seal, device, and motto "for the United States of America." **Ma** THEY **b** The delegates ☆ considered themselves *one* people, before they left that sacred hall. They felt that they seceded, not into independent sovereignties but into one nation. And Jefferson, on that Committee, proposed the motto "*E Pluribus Unum*-" "one out of many". This was the **px: mw** Egg **sp** aim ☆ of the Constitution of the United States. Representing only the narrow strip of the continent between the Alleghanies and the Atlantic, before Florida was purchased of Spain, while France held the mouth of the Mississippi, before population had poured in floods beyond the Blue Ridge, before the [Great] Lakes were hemmed by Saxon Settlements, before **M** the feeders of the Mississippi began to pour, into its lordly side, American wealth **U** THE WEST BEGAN TO POUR ITS PRODUCTIONS TO THE MISSISSIPPI from tropic to almost Arctic latitudes, before the Sources of the Missouri and the Columbia belonged in American charts,—**U** WHAT WOULD THEY HAVE SAID? what would have been their passion for one government, what would have been their conviction of the Divine call to one organization and *one* destiny, and the sublimest patience under the misunderstandings, the irritations, the *wrongs* even of a few years, if they could have **M** seen the geography of to-day **U** BEEN IN THE PLACE OF THE DISTURBERS OF THIS HOUR, AND HAD SEEN THE GEOGRAPHY OF OUR MAPS, WHICH THIS DAY'S SUN LOOKS UPON ? The Constitution of the United States is not written on parchment, but is stereotyped in granite ranges and river grooves since the tertiary epoch of geology. The two best lines that have been printed, since our present troubles began, are these by the Autocrat of the Breakfast Table:-"Our Union is River, lake, ocean and Sky;/ Man breaks not the medal, when God cuts the die." God *has* cut *into* the die the branches of the Chesapeake, the windings of the Potomac, and Delaware, and Shenandoah, the trendings of the Alleghanies, the mighty **M** trench and articulations **U** ARMLETS of the Mississippi, that State-lines and customs and latitudes are overruled, and it is as if the one word "*America*," and the constructive motto "E Pluribus Unum," "*from many, one*," were stamped legibly, in letters for a telescope to discern at the distance of the Moon, on the whole land from the Rocky Mountains to the Hudson.

13 Whoever works for the **U** PERMANENT disunion of our Nation, and hopes to succeed, must get [together] something more than a Montgomery Convention;-he must get up an Earthquake, that shall pitch half the Mississippi towards the North Pole, snap [off] the Alleghanies at the centre, turn the Ohio out of

bed, and choke with ruins every pass of the Rocky Mountains **U** AND THE SIERRAS.[3] The only part of the land that seems **Ma** GEOLOGICALLY **b** geographically **U** GEOLOGICALLY AND GEOGRAPHICALLY ☆ separate is New England,

Lecture INSERT

the Boundary Mark being the Hudson River and Lake Champlain. But she is geologically welded to the Green Mountains running into Canada, wh. are part of the Alleghany Chain. Before the Alps and Andes had uprisen, the Alleghanies had appeared, and were bearing a great upland stripe diagonally as far down as Georgia and Alabama, to represent, ages afterwards, an interest in free labor and free soil, in our Republic, as a physical and moral bar against disruption.

End INSERT

And she is bound, by such moral and social bonds, to the history and character and glory of the Nation, [so] that something more than an Earthquake,-the splitting of the planet itself,-would be requisite to **M** throw **U** DRIVE her off.

14 And then *see* what man has cut *into* the die to strengthen the Unity wh. Nature prefigures! What have enterprise and art done to make the work of Secession easier, or to suggest it? Have they drawn any boundaries for rival civilizations? Have they built any Chinese Walls? Have they developed any Supreme Antagonisms of natural interest, from Aro[o]stook to New Orleans?—The Red, White, and Blue of the Flag blend no more pleasantly, than the Manufactures and Shipping of the East, the grain products of the West, and the Export of the South intertwine for a harmonious prosperity and opulence **U** FOREVER . Look at the Canals, look at the Rail-roads that in two generations have been competing with Nature, to see if art could not **px: mw** overtop **sp** overtake ☆ the beneficence of Providence in binding the States into **M** perpetual **U** TERRITORIAL fraternity,-until cotton can travel north from Memphis, across Illinois and Michigan, through Canada, and down **U** ,AS I HAVE SEEN IT, by the Passes of the White Mtn's. of New Hampshire to the sea at Portland Maine, and be delivered *as cheap* in Liverpool as if direct from New Orleans.—and then *decide* what physical civilization has to say about "breaking the medal" whose die has been thus improved! Is this not sign that *Canada should come into the Union*, rather than that Arkansas or Tennessee should go *out*?

Lecture INSERT

The little girl, you have heard of recently, was not far out of the way, when they asked her the Catechism question- "What did God create?" She answered promptly: "The Earth, the Sun the moon, the Stars—*and Stripes*."

End INSERT

3 Compare this heightened description with paragraph 18 in the 1860 oration text.

The argument from Nature, that helped the old Secession movement, opposes, condemns and prohibits this one.

15 What are *we to do* when madness raves and foams to break [apart] the vital Unity, wh. tradition, and language, and nature, and art have been compacting for generations? We must rise [up] against it; we must *devote* ourselves against it; we must arm against it; we must fight against it, while steel has temper and powder will **Ma** POUR PASSION THROUGH COLUMBIADS **b** pour out passion in Paixan tones **U** POUR PASSION THROUGH COLUMBIADS . ☆—[4] Shall we listen to the Cry "*let us alone*, what have we to do with thee!" It was a *devil* that *first* made that petition,-a devil that had taken possession of the organism of a human frame, wh. is a fair type of the **M** physical Unity **U** CONFIGURATION of our Empire, **ms1** a devil like the one that came fresh from the *tombs*☆.—He thought it would be all right if the soul would just step out, and leave him in undisturbed *possession*. But, in *that* case, the only Secession allowed was the secession of the *demon*. He was *driven* out, though he rent the frame in leaving. That was the way he was "let alone". Once *his* kind were suffered to enter into swine, and make them commit suicide.—But, in our time, the government think that even swine are too noble to have partnership with the unclean Spirit in America; for an Embargo is put on the very bacon of Cincinnati **ms1** and the West☆, [so] that it shall not add strength to the "foul **px: mw** fiend **sp** being☆." The demon of Secession is *at* the old trick,-begging for pork, and *can't get it*.

Lecture INSERT

The papers tell us, however, that General Scott recently received, from one of the Secretaries of the Gov't. of el[e]ven Confederate States, an ear of green corn from a Southern plantation,-intending to signify that they should have a good harvest and *plenty of food*. I think that the result of the whole contest, the Great harvest of the Struggle, will be such that Gen[eral]. Scott can commend to them the dream of Joseph, Genesis 37.7,-"We were binding Sheaves in the field, and lo, my Sheaf arose, and stood upright; and, behold, your eleven Sheaves stood round about, and made obeisance to my Sheaf."

End INSERT

16 We must fight against the threatened rupture of the country for *our own safety*, as well as in loyalty to great traditions and in honor of the past. This whole land has been dedicated to republican government, and to immunity from European interference with our prosperity and **M** power **U** IN OUR POLITICS . Let the rebellion triumph, and how long should we be safe? How long should [we] be free from the pressure of European arrogance, and the insinuation of European intrigue? The seceding States have no Navy. As an independent **Ma** POWER **b** confederation, ☆ they could have none that would command **Ma** RESPECT **b** the fear of a fifth-rate power. ☆ Hardly a harbor that they would *hold* will float

4 The *Union* reporter transcribes words revised by King in the manuscript draft.

a **Ma** GUN-BOAT **b** bomb-ketch ☆ over its bar. One of the traitor-Commodores, whose name has been stricken from the U[nited]. S[tates]. roll for his life, and from the roll of honor forever, **ms1** and who is now in command of a magnificent rebel fleet of two river steamers without guns, ☆ lately said- "Alas! my bones will lie bleaching many a year, before the South can have a Navy!"—Allow them to go off [in search of help], and Great Britain or France, or even Spain, may have control of the Gulf of Mexico, of the mouth and the hot district of the Mississippi, and will keep us in perpetual peril, or perpetual chafe, on the great coast-line wh. has been clearly enough consecrated to American power **U** AND NOTHING ELSE . Already we are hearing mutterings, from the head-quarters of treason, that they prefer dependence on England to the old republican rule; that the monarchical system is best; and that they will take a Prince of the English stock *before* a return to the American Constitution.—That assurance has gone to England, in **U** OPEN letters to [the] London Times.

Lecture INSERT

Mr. Russell LL. D., Barrister at Law, writes home that an Ex-Governor of South Carolina said to him: "Sir, sooner than submit to the North, we will *all* become subjects to Great Britain again!"-And he tells us that, in the home of the rebellion, "the admiration for monarchical institutions on the English PLAN model ☆, for privileged classes, and for a landed Aristocracy and gentry, is undisguised, and apparently genuine."—

End INSERT

17 Now, even if we were not fighting *for* the Constitution and its impartial blessings,-could we hold back from fighting, out of self-defence, to avert the danger of British or continental control in the arteries of a Republic, purged of that peril once by Jefferson, and devoted to the Monroe doctrine by the sound instinct of **U** DEMOCRATIC Patriotism forty years ago? In fighting Secession, in this aspect, the Nation, from Maine to Oregon, is fighting *in self-defence.* No external danger so subtle and fearful can threaten us elsewhere. Keeping the integrity of our configuration, we may defy the globe.—The mountain, lifting up a great wall, acclivity and spire of granite, may defy the storms and artillery of centuries. "Roll on" it may say, to the surges of cloud and the batteries of hail. "Welcome!" it may exclaim, to the bolts and fury of the thunder. All *this* it need not dread, so long as the structure of its rock is *unseamed.* But let a crack come in it, and a *more* dreadful Enemy begins its career. Water penetrates, and the frost inserts its insidious and noiseless lever. Then the process of disintegration has begun. We can defy foreign *force* [only] so long as we offer one Polity, without fissure or crevice, from the St. Croix to the Rio Grande, from Ontario to **M** Oregon **U** THE COLUMBIA . But let a crack run along the Ohio, and down the Mississippi, and on the Eastern slope of the South Alleghanies, and *foreign* diplomacy works in; the frost is upon us, and *farewell* **U** FROM THAT HOUR to the nobleness and the peace, even of the Nation that remains

true to its past and to its trust!-We may **Ma** AS WELL **b** better ☆ fight to prevent the least line of cleavage, than fight against the **M** artful **U** AWFUL AND THE ARTFUL perils that will intrench themselves **M** there against us **U** OVER AGAINST US, AS SURE AS DIPLOMACY REMAINS WHAT IT IS.

Lecture INSERT

Reading the "Rebellion Record", the chronological annals of the Secession Movement, now publishing, by numbers, at the East, I was struck with the first entry: "Dec[ember]. 17, 1860. The So[uth]. C[arolin]a. Convention met this day at Columbia, and passed a resolution to adjourn to Charleston, in consequence of the prevalence of *the Small*-pox at Columbia, wh. was declared epidemic."—Fit comment on the movement! Admirable companionship! A brilliant Case of what our Swedenborgian friends would call *complete correspondence*! Secession is *small-pox to the Nation.*

End INSERT

18 The laws of Nature, and Providence through them, have given us the immense Republican domain, one in outline and organization to be kept *one* as the scene of a Republican scheme of civilization. The North and South, differing in character widely in many ways, are put **U** BY PROVIDENCE as two owners on a ship. According to the old story, of the Captain and Mate who owned a vessel, and quarreled about how to **U** FIT HER AND get her out of harbor, the Southe[r]n owner walks up and says, "Captain, I've anchored my half of the Ship; you may do what you like with your's!" "Don't coerce me into changing my mind. All I ask is to be let alone!"—Our national ship wasn't made to be anchored; wasn't made to have two flags floating over her rigging; wasn't made to harbor mutiny; wasn't made to be polluted with discussions in the cabin whether, or no, she should turn slaver.—

Lecture INSERT

She was built in State-compartments, but *one* Vessel,-one prow and one helm. She was built sta[u]nch.

"Timber of chestnut and elm and oak,
And scattered here and there with these,
The knarred and crooked cedar knees,
Brought from regions far away,
From Pascagoula's sunny bay,
And the banks of the roaring Roanoke!

For only what is sound and strong
To this vessel shall belong.
Cedar of Maine and Georgia pine
Here together shall combine
A goodly frame and a goodly fame,
And *The Union* be her name."

End INSERT

19 She was built for one set of officers; for a loyal crew; for free sailing on the Seas; for Cannon so *used* to the measure of "Hail Columbia," that they can't learn how to keep time with the music of "Dixie"; and for nothing but the Stripes and Stars, for the mizzen, as well as for the fore and Maintop;-nothing but this **px: mw** decoration **sp** Declaration ☆ for every *yard-arm*,-unless it be the necks of traitors who preach rebellion in the hold, and are ready to betray a portion of her deck to **M** monarchists **U** MONARCHICAL GOVERNMENTS abroad! Since the 4th. of July, '76, when she was launched, this has been her Providential destination. The Southern Shareholder can have his interest in the Ship, now as always; but he *must* haul up the anchor **U** ,AND HAUL DOWN THAT UGLY LOOKING PIECE OF BUNTING ON THE MIZZEN, or see the cable **U** AND THE HALLIARDS hacked away by Yankee Blades!—

20 In the great Secession Movement of '76, the leaders claimed that equal and separate station among nations to wh. not only the "laws of Nature," but the laws "of Nature's *God*" entitled them. They felt that their Cause was the Cause of human nature. They meant to make it such **px: mw** *publickly* **sp** popularly ☆. They stated general principles in their **M** preface **U** DECLARATION. They affirmed the rightful Equality of all men before the law. They denied that any race was created, simply by reason of its inferiority of intellect, to be serfs *perpetually* to another caste. In the original draft of the Declaration, Jefferson attacked George the Third, because he "determined to keep open a market where men should be bought and sold," and "prostituted his **M** negative for suppressing **U** POWER IN ORDER TO DEFEAT every legislative attempt to prohibit or to restrain this execrable commerce."-"He has waged," Jefferson said, "cruel war against human nature itself, violating its most sacred rights of life and liberty, in the persons of a distant people who never offended him, captivating and carrying them into Slavery in another hemisphere, or to incur miserable death in their transportation thither."—This is what the Author of the great Declaration was willing to write in '76 about the system of Slavery; this was *then* the voice of Virginia; this was the conviction of almost all the Congress; although the phrases were left out of the **Ma** ADDRESS **b** sublime State-Paper, ☆ as Jefferson tells us, partly, because a very few Southern gentlemen were not quite prepared to endorse the strength of their **M** rhetoric **U** DECLARATIONS .-But the sweep of sentiment in the Congress was in favor of **M** them **U** THOSE SENTENCES REMAINING IN , and in tune with them, and many **U** OF THE NOBLE Southerners were strongly in favor of their remaining **U** ,IN SPITE OF ALL OPPOSITION, *in* the Declaration.—

21 Now, how is it? The new Secession Movement is not only determined by the Slavery question as its Spring, but it openly takes issue with the principles of the founders of the Republic, and with the sentiments of the Southern Author of the immortal Declaration of Independence. The philosopher of the new movement is Mr. Alex[ande]*r*. H. Stephens of Georgia, *pretended* Vice-President in the Rebellion-Conspiracy. He tells us, in an elaborate speech, that

he and his associates stand on very different ground from that taken by Jefferson and the framers of the Constitution. They believed, Mr. Stephens confesses to us, that "the Enslavement of the African was in violation of the laws of Nature; that it was wrong in principle, socially, morally, and politically." They believed, he assures us, that it "would be evanescent and pass away." But "those ideas," he tells us, were "fundamentally wrong," and were a sandy foundation for a **U** PERMANENT government. "Our new government," he continues, "is founded upon exactly the opposite ideas. Its corner-stone rests upon the great truth that the Negro is not equal to the white man, that Slavery is his natural and **Ma** MORAL **b** normal ☆ condition. This, our new government, *is the first in the history of the world, based upon this great physical, philosophical, and moral truth.*" It is one thing, Gentlemen, to resist aggressions upon Slavery from without, when it is a hereditary Evil, and demands the most careful manipulation to save Society from being disorganised by **px: mw** passionate **sp(dly U)** dispassionate **sp(wkly U)** passionate ☆ attacks upon it.[5] It is another and very different thing to stand out the Champion of it; to base a State deliberately upon it; to emblazon it on one's banner; to defy the sentiment of the world upon it; to break up a vast and beneficent Government in its interest; and to flout the wisdom and insight of the fathers of a land, because they did *not* see its beneficence and beauty.

22 The Authors of the separation from Great Britain, **msl** Southern men and Northern ones, ☆ spoke words of respect for human nature. They were in sympathy with the substructure of sentiment wh. Christianity lays in the heart of the world. Oppression of all kinds they held as unnatural, temporary, wrong.—*They* said that all races have by nature the inalienable right to "life, liberty, and the pursuit of happiness."—The new Solons would rend America, and insult our **M** history **U** COUNTRY, to base their Polity on the sublime assertion that Southern white-men have the inalienable right to life, liberty, and the pursuit of Negroes. This they put forth into literature, into a **Ma** STATE PA[PER] **b** prominent speech, by their coolest thinker, ☆ sent out to stir the heart of the world with sympathy for their wrongs and their cause. Thank God that they put themselves thus at variance **U** FOREVER with the Men of the Revolution by a gulf wider than that between Lazarus and Dives, by the whole diameter of moral truth!

Lecture INSERT

There is a science now known among men as *Political Economy*. It investigates and announces the forces and conditions of National prosperity and soundness. Go to its leading volumes published in London, in Philadelphia, in Paris, in Turin, in Vienna, in Berlin, and from whatever school the pages issue, you will find them all giving one answer, through many dialects, when you ask

5 This is the only instance in which the typesetter for the *Weekly Union* alters a possible phoneme in the *Daily Union* transcript.

them what are the foundations of National permanence,-what is the substructure of material civilization?—They say- skilled labor; mind working through fingers; implements of industry shaped by Genius; thrift; homes where the marriage-bond is respected, and where intelligence and virtue, and the desire to rise are nurtured; the widest consciousness of personal worth; the freest education, and the largest privilege of studying an unbound Bible, and receiving God's unstinted benefaction of truth. And, in this answer, Political Economy is in harmony with the first Declaration of Independence.-Mr. Stephens publishes a new style of political architecture, and says "the Enslavement of labor is the basis-principle of *mechanics*." The fathers built on granite laid on the ribs of the world. The new builders hew their Corner-Stone out of *Charcoal*, and base it on a *Swamp*.

End INSERT

23 The great Continental Congress published an Address to the people of Great Britain in Oct[ober]. 1774, wh. contains **Ma** THESE WORDS **b** this sentence **U** THIS SENTENCE, AND IT IS THE OPENING SENTENCE ☆ :-"When a Nation, led to greatness by the hand of liberty, and possessed of all the Glory that heroism, munificence, and humanity can bestow, descends to the ungrateful task of forging Chains for her **ms1** friends and ☆ children, and instead of giving support to freedom, turns advocate of Slavery and oppression, there is reason to believe she has either ceased to be virtuous, or has been extremely negligent in the appointment of her rulers." Old Virginia-Statesmen readily signed these words, 87 years ago. —Where is Virginia to-day in relation to this judgment? The whole valuation of her **ms1** present ☆ property, **ms1** before the ☆ real and personal (Slaves included) six months ago, **U** EVEN AT THE MARKET PRICE THEN OF SLAVES, was **Ma** NOT SO **b** about as **U** ONLY ABOUT AS ☆ much as she has received in fifty years for the sale of flesh and blood, much of it part Saxon blood, too, from her borders. Every house, estate, public building, road, bridge, railway, mine, **ms1** pier and boat ☆ that belongs to her to-day is an funded investment of cash she has received for human **M** beings **U** LIFE ; and she has voted to leave the Nation wh. her noble children helped to found, to **px: mw** slur **sp** spurn ☆ their judgments of human nature, and to strike hands with a confederacy that says this is right; this is the true Corner-Stone of National prosperity and eminence; this is justifiable before Heaven, if only we can prove a *certain* thickness of skull, a *certain* formation of the heel, or even a *slight* percentage of taint **U** IN THE ARTERIES from Ethiopian blood!

Lecture INSERT

All Classes of rebels make this open issue with the old Charter of the Nation.—One Rev[erend]. D[octo]r. tells us that *this* is a religious war, in wh. Secessionists are contending, for the faith once delivered to the Saints, against Northern perversions of the Bible. Another D[octo]r. TELLS publishes ☆ that it is an armed protest against the Atheistic Red Republicanism of the Declaration of '76.—Another, D[octo]r. Carnes of Texas, holding the same ground, adds these words:-"Everything is going on beautifully in Texas. Opinion is universal among white and black that Texas, unrestrained by Divine Grace, can whip any two of the Northern States." I am afraid Br[other]. Carnes will have to preach yet lugubriously from Ps[alms]. 76.10. "Surely the wrath of man shall praise thee: the remainder of wrath shalt thou restrain."—

End INSERT

24 What ought the American government to say to the establishment of a State **ms1** on half its own recent soil☆, wh. thus **Ma** LAUGHS **b** scoffs **U** SCOFFS☆at the old Democratic sentiment, openly impeaches the Declaration and Constitution, and makes the enslavement of **M** labor **U** THE NEGRO the first principle of its Gospel?—

Oration-Lecture COMPARISON:
Ma/U oration

WHILE THE SYSTEM OF BONDAGE WAS UNDER THE PROTECTION OF THE CONSTITUTION, AND ITS PATRONS WERE OBEDIENT TO THE PUBLIC LAW, WE WERE BOUND BY THE COMPROMISES OF THE CONSTITUTION IN ITS BEHALF—BUT **U THE QUESTION IS,** WHAT OUGHT WE TO DO, WHEN IT THROWS OFF THOSE **U ITS** OBLIGATIONS, AND

Mb Lecture

Take notice that the question is *not* an Abolition-question. The Government under the Constitution has no right to take an Abolition-attitude. So long as States are *loyal*, and so long as the Union can be preserved or reclaimed, it ought to leave the Slave-question to the peaceful action of social forces under the Constitution.—And the very *last* thing it ought to do is to raise or encourage a rebellion of Slaves. Civilization and Chr[i]st[ianit]y. condemn this in any emergency. But suppose the disaffected States get separate, complete their disunion, and are never to be brought back. Suppose that, throwing off all constitutional obligations, and

End Oration-Lecture COMPARISON

ruthlessly tearing out more than five hundred millions from the public prosperity, it insists on rearing itself into insolence, if possible, over the ruins of the old Republic? **ms1** What *shall* we or *should* we do *then*? ☆---Some persons have said- "We ought to let these new Architects **U** OF RUIN go in peace; we ought to let them tear down what they will, and depart on such a mission, without a drop of bloodshed or the drawing of a sword." *No.* We ought to say, with all the firmness, dignity and emphasis wh. can be expressed in a Nation's attitude, and poured into a Nation's speech, when it stands up for Civilization and Chr[i]st[ianit]y., that no such Bastile **Ma** POLITY **b** Policy☆shall **U** EVER be built on American soil.-If men go out from us, to offer that insult in their first State Papers to the memory and spirit of the Revolutionary sages, **Ma** THEY GO[TO] **b** and to☆rear that black flag over the old banner on wh. *they* printed "Liberty" in letters so large as to hide **U** FROM A DISTANCE the word "Slave", they go to meet our Cannon, to dash against our bayonets, and to clear the ground for their **M** grim edifice **U** ADVANCE only over the wrecks of **M** victorious battle **U** A HUNDRED VICTORIOUS BATTLES.

25 If we do not fight to preserve the Union, to protect men still loyal in the seceded States, to beat down Rebellion and enthrone the Constitution once more;-if we could not fight with the hope of replacing the old flag over every Capitol and every fort that has insulted it,-if these States were *out* permanently and **px: mw** hopelessly **sp** hopelessly **P** helplessly ☆, then **U** MORE THAN EVER BEFORE we ought to fight them to beat down their principle. They have no right to brave modern Civilization in the latter half of the Nineteenth Century. They have no right to defy Christianity in a land that counts Churches by the ten thousand.—And the more decisively and defiantly they scream that they are *out* of the Union, and mean never to return, the more firmly should the Nation say, "You shall *never* insult Democracy and American **Ma** SOIL **b** traditions with that scheme of Government, on American soil, ☆ for we hold in trust the **Ma** CHARACTER **b** hopes and principles ☆ of the fathers,"—and the more busy **M** it **U** THE WHOLE NATION ought to be backing up **M** its **U** THE WHOLE CONTENTRATED purpose with rifled Cannon and **U** STUFFED Columbiads. Peaceable Secession is impossible. Peace, in every light, *is* betrayal of duty. We are bound to gird on armor to support the Constitution against it as rebellion, and keep the territory of the Republic intact. We are bound to draw "the Sword of the Lord and of Gideon" against any *such* new Empire as they propose to found, **Ma** AND PREVENT **b** AND BLAST **c** if they are separate, and to blast **U** FOR THEIR SUPPORT. AND TO BLAST ☆ with powder the ground where they would plant its **px: mw** ebony **sp** heavy ☆ pillars and forge its chains. That is what the American Government *ought* to say **U** —IS SOLEMNLY BOUND TO SAY to the rebels and their plans. How should they be met by foreign powers?- They must **M** plead **U** COME before the Great Court of public opinion. Is there any doubt what the verdict will be?

26 If the old Barbary States should attempt to rise again; if on the north shore of Africa, in the face of Europe, a cluster of States should attempt to confederate their power into an Empire for vilifying labor, and trading in men, would Europe suffer it [to exist]? Would Europe permit the U[nited]. S[tates]. Cabinet and Congress to recognise [it] by public decree, and by Ambassadors and by treaties, as on the level of **Ma** CHRISTIAN **b** civilized ☆ kingdons? *Not for a moment.* Their Cannon would converge **Ma** UPON **b** against ☆ its walls, and if America should support it, her fleet would run a gauntlet of **ms1** sacred ☆ warships in the Mediterranean **U** .AND IT OUGHT TO . How will it **px: mw** fare **sp** bear ☆ with such an Empire rising, or attempting to rise, on Western soil? Will Europe cry "hail brethren!," to its representatives, as they knock at foreign Cabinets, pistol in belt, bowie-knife in sheath, the crumpled American flag in one hand, and a slave-whip with Mr. Stephens' speech in the other? Will France, who first welcomed D[octo]r. Franklin as the representative of America, throw wide her Palace-hall for an Embassy of this **Ma** STAMP **b** equipment? ☆ Not until France forgets what Lafayette said with sorrow,—that if he could have foreseen that he was fighting to establish an Empire whose map was *half* Slave soil, he never would have drawn sword *for* America. Will Germany welcome

them? Five millions of Germans send back to their Parent States the entreaty and protest against it; and no **U** LITTLE Duchy will **U** EVER give them sympathy. What voice will Italy utter? Alas, Cavour is dead. But it would be a wonderful spectacle- Victor Emanuel, with the fresh Crown of united and enfranchised Italy on his **U** SOLDIERLY head, striking hands with Wigfall, **U** FRESH FROM CRAWLING OUT OF THE EMBRASURE OF FORT SUMTER, or majestic Garibaldi opening his arms to Twiggs, for any other purpose than to squeeze out his traitorous breath. **msl** No danger. Mr. Botta, a relative of the great Italian historian of our Revolution, has been writing from New York the most wise and lofty views of our struggle. ☆

27 Russia is an absolute Despotism. In its cold Capital, perhaps, their sneer at the ideas of Jefferson will find an echo. No! Russia refused to aid King George, though he pleaded and begged, when America struggled to *establish* the Declaration. And she has no **Ma** WORD **b** applause or cheer☆for those who strike at it in the interest of bondage. Entrenched in snow, she feels the pressure of the world's nobler sentiment so powerfully that she is this [day] completing the preparation for giving freedom to 22 millions of Serfs who have been in bonds for centuries. Her Monarch is ambitious to raise **M** thus **U** AGAIN from the dead the title "Alexander the Great." And she teaches to America *this* lesson out of her public law, on Slavery: *When a man is proved a traitor to the Emperor, his Slaves are free.* Gen[eral]. Butler has discovered the same principle. He has applied it in Virginia. And this Russian code will march with American armies southward to the Mississippi's mouth, before Alexander receives in Moscow a Minister from Montgomery.

Lecture INSERT

Will Holland give it countenance? In '76, she refused to contend against the first Declaration. When England asked her for men, she consented to lend a brigade, on condition that it *should never go out of Europe*! She remembers that she harbored the Puritans, and that, from her, America learned the doctrine of free public education. Austria, though she objects to Mr. Burlingame, will not help to make our Eagle, like her own, *two-headed.* Will republican Switzerland extend to their agents the hospitality of her snows? It will cool the Embassadors to learn *there* that Switzerland knows how to deal with Secession. In 1846 *seven* Cantons revolted from the federal Diet, and set up a separate league. In 1847, the Federal Army defeated the Secessionists in two battles, made them submit, and the disturbers were expelled.—Switzerland says to our Gov'*t*., "*Go thou and do likewise*!"—

End INSERT

28 What will London say? Of course the voice will return prompt and even fierce, in denunciation, from Westminster Hall. No. With immeasurable sadness we must say *no.* England hesitates: **M** Great England, haughty England, the England **U** ENGLAND whose taunts have been so bitter **U** ,AND SO BITTER TO BE BORNE, at the black **M** stain **U** BLOT on our escutcheon, on our hugging of sin

M for profit **U** SO LONG FOR THE SAKE OF THE PROPERTY!—the England who immortalized the 1st of August,-whose law, and literature, and naval batteries have **px: mw** poured **sp** pealed ☆ defiance at the Slave **px: mw** sentiment **sp**-system ☆, is the first (after Spain perhaps) to acknowledge that the Confederate rebellion is a public belligerent power! Dante, the great Italian Poet, gives an **px: mw** imaginative **sp** imaginary ☆ picture of a terrible combat between a serpent and a man, in wh. each was transformed **U** ,ERE THE NIGHT WAS ENDED, into the likeness of the other. The man's legs grew together; he sank on the ground; his tongue **Ma** GREW **b** became ☆ forked; scales covered his body; his voice turned to a hiss; and he crawled away defeated. The serpent rose, obtained feet, and speech and features, and walked [about] the Earth enfranchised and victorious.—England has long indulged in satire, at the tolerance of bondage by the Northern States of our Republic.—If now, that by striking together, its power might by crushed, she consults *her* interest solely, and not the Appeal of Civilization,-if now that the government here rises into the form of humanity, she talks only the language of selfishness, and **M** studies tariff Bills **U** CALCULATES THE INTERESTS OF THE MILLS, and the bales in Manchester, let **M** her **U** US not wonder if the world sees a new **M** reading **U** VERSION in the serpent **M** combat **U** BATTLE of Dante;-especially if Exeter Hall is willing to sink on its belly and **M** send **U** DROWN its Eloquence *into* a hiss for peace, and lick even the dirt that drops out of sanded cotton on the floor of the English Market!

29 We say this in sorrow **Ma** NOT IN INDIGNATION **b** more than in indignation **U** MORE THAN IN ANGER **P** MORE THAN INDIGNATION ☆ . Certainly not from fear. The American government can say even to England:-"*We defy the power that recognizes the Rebellion.*" And if England cannot learn that we are not a bundle of States, but one Federal Empire,-if she cannot discover that it is one central indestructible power wh. sends Ambassadors to her, and makes treaties with her, and runs up the Stars and Stripes to the mast-heads of its frigates,-if she feels bound to give a quasi-recognition to rebellious States **msl** before the Government has tried its force against them ☆,-we can and *ought* to recall our Minister, **msl** dismiss Lord Lyons, ☆ extend to *her* the same doctrine in a cup called *Ireland*, and make a strike for the St. Lawrence, while we hold on **U** WITH THE GRIP OF A CENTIPEDE to the whole Mississippi. Coming out, then, victorious, we should stand, as our Nation ought to stand, **U** NO LONGER DISGUISED IN THE SERPENT, BUT ERECT at the head of Civilization. But let us hope that nobleness as well as wisdom is to guide the action of England *yet,* and that the head of our Nation is to be greeted with cheer and sympathy from the heart of the mother-land. We wait for it. We long for it. We need it. We deserve it. And her Character is at stake and unsettled 'til it comes. Whether it comes or not, our **px: mw** cause **sp** course ☆ is clear, our triumph certain. The old Declaration of Independence will live: the new one will **M** die **U** NOT. The old was drawn by Patriots, the new by traitors. The old was written from sentiments, that well up from the pure fountains of Civilization; the new was written out of the devil's ink, in the interest of the most shameless selfishness ever uttered in the literature of State-Papers. The old was

to compact America: the new to rend it.—The issue is open. It is for us to take our part.

Lecture INSERT

In this State, we *have* taken it. Thank heaven, there is no doubt of our Geography. The Sacramento is an *American* River. The San Joaquin is not held by traitors. San Diego is an *American* Port. The Nevada range is an *American* bulwark. Alcatraz bristles with Cannon wh. Gen[eral]. Sumner has taught to declaim the dialect, not of Mr. Davis but of General Scott. Old Shasta bears up on his snows, flushed with sunrise and marked with asure shadows, the Country's *Red, White,* and *Blue.* And from the White Sierra to the white-edged sea, California, by an immense majority, is loyal to the integrity of the Republic, and to the old *Stripes* and *Stars*. In harmony with our brethren of the East, and with the tens of thousands still loyal in the South, LET US HEED THE CALL we can say ☆ that "the Preservation of the Union, the support of the Government, the emphatic punishment and solemn extinction of the traitors are the Catholic religion of us all"[1]

End INSERT

30 Let us heed the call that comes to the Nation **U** IN THIS HOUR from the heroes of the earlier time:

"Draw forth your million blades as one;
Complete the battle then begun!
God fights with Ye, and overhead
Floats the dear banner of your dead.
They, and the Glories of the Past,
The Future, dawning dim and vast,
And all the holiest hopes of man,
Are beaming triumph in your van!

Slow to resolve, be swift to do!
Teach Ye the False how fight the True!
How bucklered Perfidy shall feel
In her black heart the Patriot's Steel;
How sure the bolt that Justice wings;
How weak the arm a traitor brings;
How mighty they who steadfast stand
For Freedom's Flag and Freedom's Land!"

---

1 Compare this final assertion step with paragraph 2 in version **b** of the Introduction.

Repeat patterns by title and category in King Speaking List, January thru September 1861

Month abbreviations

Jn January
Fb February
Mh March
Apr April
Je June
Jl July
Ag August
Spt September

Place abbreviations

Msville Marysville
Nev City Nevada City
Sacram Sacramento
SF/SFrc both San Francisco
Stkton Stockton

Editorial abbreviations

anniv anniversary
app/apps appearance(s)
Ch Church
comp composed (*not* compiled)
del delivered
Gvt Government
Libr Assoc Library Association
Mt Mount(ain)
pt/pts part(s)
rev revised (*not* reviewed)
Rev Reverend
Sch School
Soc Society
swest southwest
tr translated
UC-SFrc First Unitarian Church SF, Stkton Street between Clay and Sacram
var/vars variant(s)
Vols Volunteers

Sequential tally symbols

* next to a title indicates that the item was comp and del by King prior to his arrival in California

SF/**Cal** comparative app totals by title and category—SF indicating apps in SFrc/**Cal** apps outside SFrc

prt app has been verified, but the title is a probable insert
prat app probably made based on evidence, but both title and app remain probable in this one instance

pre-**N** Apr 9-11, three consecutive "Washington" apps made prior to undertaking tour of northern California
Na thru **N**tno May 21-23, 25-Je 7, 18-20, twenty consecutive apps made by King in touring northern California, while Rev. John E. Benton of the Folsom Congregational Ch, Republican candidate for State Assembly, substituted at UC-SFrc on May 26 and June 2.

signs in margin (a thru **v**^{e}), consecutive daily apps other than covered by pre-**N** and **N**. When two apps made on same day, both signs are in bold type; when consecutive days are involved in a series, only the sign for the first day is in non-bold black; when the end of the alphabet is reached proceeding a thru z, the signs go on with the alphabet in modified reverse order (**a**^{z} thru **v**^{e}). The consecutive signs and dates for apps would read: Jn 10a 11**b**/ 27c 28**d**/ Fb 24**e** 24**f**/ 27g 28**h** Mh 1**i**/ 6j 7**k**/ 31l 31**m**/ Apr 7**n** 7**o**/ 28p 29**q**/ May 2r 3**s**/ 12t 13**u** 14**v** 15**w**/ Je 22x 23**y**/ Jl 8z 9**a**^{z}/ 23b^{y} 24**c**^{x}/ 31d^{w} Ag 1**e**^{v} 2**f**^{u}/ 4**g**^{t} 4**h**^{s}/ 11i^{r} 12**j**^{q}/ 24**k**^{p} 24**l**^{o} 25**m**^{n} 26**n**^{m} 27**o**^{l}/ 31p^{k} Spt 1**q**^{j} 2**r**^{i}/ 4**s**^{h} 4**t**^{g}/ 22u^{f} 23**v**^{e}.

def/**prp**/**np**—SF app definitely-probably-not paying a fee to King
npC/**prC**—**Cal** app(s) not-probably paying a fee to King

Tally on range of King's earnings as speaker ($150 fee per app, traveling expenses regarded as extra on all **Cal** apps)

A. 49 **Cal** paying/5 **prC** $6600-$7350 or $6950 (82.99% of **C**)

N 20 apps: 17 paying/3 **prC** $2250-$2700 or $2475 (29.6% of **C**)
N 10 "Washington" apps: 9 paying/1 *prat* $1350-$1500 or $1425 (17% of **C**)

21 total "Washington" apps: 19 paying/1 **prC**-1 *prat* $2700-$3000 or $2850 (34% of **C**

B. 23 potential/13 actual (6 **def**/7 **prp**) SF paying apps $900-$1950 or $1425 (17% of **C**, compare with "Washington" **N** above)

C. range of total, *qualified* speaking fees: $7500-$9300 or $8375 (A$6950 + B$1425), coupled with base salary of $4250 ($4000-$4500 range, dependent upon degree of "unpaid" absence during **N**)= $12,625 total personal income, Jn thru Spt 1861 ($4250 salary for nine months 50.8% of **C**)

D. strictly *unqualified* tally, based on total number of presumed paying apps over comparable ten-month periods: SF *Evening Mirror* of Mh 25, 1861, reported that the total funds generated by King's speaking apps were $12,000, the period being approximately ten months and extending from Apr 28, 1860 thru Mh 23, 1861. That is, about ten months when a month's "unpaid" vacation is allowed for. The *Mirror* tally is coincidentally similar to $12,166.67, a figure arrived at by using 23SF/ 50**Cal** and calculating a tenth month ($1216.67) on to $10,950, the *unqualified* personal income from speaking apps (versus $8375 *qualified*) earned by King, Jn thru Spt 1861.

E. Substituting $104.74 for $150 as a realistic minimum mean fee per app, derived by dividing 38 lectures/addresses into $3980 ($7960 or "nearly if not quite $8000"--a net quantity "2 for 1" compared to a personal speaking income of $3980), King in nine months (Jn thru Spt 1861) earns $5865.44, some $1885.44 more than his purported earnings over twelve months (Apr 28, 1860 thru Apr 28, 1861). King stated in his Apr 28, 1861 anniversary discourse: "During the year I have lectured and given addresses in the state thirty eight times,-sixteen times in this city, and twenty two times in the state. Many of the addresses and lectures have been given, free of all charge, for the benefit of Churches of other denominations, or benevolent assoc[iation]s. . . .And never, if I could help it, even when I received pay,-have I consented to speak under circumstances where I was to receive a larger amount than was to be given to the treasury of a public organization.--It gives me pleasure to know, and to be able to say, that for every dollar I have received by pretty hard toil in writing and travelling, more than two dollars have gone to public objects within the state. The lecturing and speaking, outside of this pulpit, with wh[ich] I have been connected, the past twelve months, has produced a nett. result of nearly if not quite $8000 to the treasuries of Churches and other assoc[iatio]ns for good within our borders." And even though King revises 34 upward to 38 total apps, and 14 SF apps upward to 16, a $150 fee would designate 26.53 out of 38 apps as paying the speaker, indicating perhaps that $150 is closer to the true mean since "many" or 11.47 apps, slightly less than one third, might conceivably be nonpaying. Two variables, however, frustrate any reliable resolution of the speculative range. Namely, the extraordinary range of single app fees earned by King--how many fees were $50 or less, how many as high as $250? And secondly, how much more than "2 for 1" is "more than two dollars?" Considering that King in his *Bulletin* card reiterated "more than two dollars" with reference to the "Washington" title, a claim qualified by editor Anthony's "only secured one dollar for himself . . . where two dollars have secured to others" (or the specific "2 for 1" benefit rule), does King's "more" increment distort those "life" or "stock" members of a sponsoring organization who might not necessarily figure in gate receipts? Particularly when only 3 of 20 "Washington" apps and 15 of 95 other apps conceivably relate to such a "more" situation, and there the lower gate receipt theory cannot be proven.

F. The Sacramento $150 or the derived mean of $104.74 clearly demonstrate that King considerably enhanced his personal income by speaking activities during these nine months. Sacram $150: $4250 salary + $8375 speaking = $12,625 total, versus Derived $104.74: $4250 salary + $5865.44 speaking = $10,115.44 total, a range of $10,115.44 to $12,625 combined personal income

(Jn thru Spt 1861) for King. Yet an extremely speculative mean fee of $135, prompted really by calculations in E above, could conceivably resolve a range of $5865.44 to $8375, the speaking component in King's income tally, into $7560 (or $4250 salary + $7560 speaking = $11,810), a total some $3310 in excess of doubling King's base salary and less than one thousand dollars ($940) short of trebling the same base salary.

King's Speaking Apps, Jn thru Spt 1861, Arranged by Title/Occasion and Organization Benefited: 239 total apps. 115 cited below—and 29 11am (Sunday + 37 12:45pm (Su) Sabbath Sch + 15 7/7:30pm (Su) + 27 8:00pm (Monday) + 16 funeral UC-SFrc apps unaccounted for (63SF/**52Cal**; 9*prt*/2*prat*)

1. Oration/lecture titles repeated **61** (SF 15/**Cal 46**)

*a) "The Life and Character of George Washington" **21** (SF 3/**Cal 18**)
Fb 22 thru Je 19 (adapted from "Washington or Greatness" lecture of Fb 20, 1852)

Fb 22 evn SF Light Guard **prp** (Washington's Birthday)
i Mh 1 evn **Msville** Odd Fellows' Libr Assoc
4 evn SF Light Guard **prp** (day Lincoln inaugurated)
k 7 evn **Stkton** Presbyterian Ladies
22 evn **Sacram** Howard Benevolent Assoc **npC**
27 evn **Auburn** Methodist Ch
Apr 5 evn SF var "Washington and His Character as a Mason" **def**
pre-**N** 9 evn **Grass Valley** Methodist Episcopal Ch
pre-**N** 10 evn **Nev City** Methodist Episcopal Ch
pre-**N** 11 evn **Folsom** Congregational Ch
r May 2 evn **Placerville**
u 13 evn **San Jose-Santa Clara** University of Pacific?! *prt* **prC** (One of two apps, see Mh 14 under 4.)
Nb 22 evn **Oroville** Brick Congregational Ch
Nc 23 evn **Red Bluff**
Nd 25 evn **Shasta** Methodist Ch *prt* west of Redding
Nf 27 evn **Yreka** Methodist Episcopal Ch ("Yreka" an Indian word for Shasta Butte)
Nh 29 evn **Deadwood** *prt* on Deadwood Creek west of Yreka
Ni May 30 evn **Rough and Ready** *prt* town of Etna in Scott Valley
Nj 31 evn **Oro Fino/Mugginsville** *prat* adjoining towns swest of Fort Jones in Quartz Valley (In a letter written to Robert B. Swain from Yreka on the twenty-ninth, King noted that Oro Fino "applies with a long petition of names" and Mugginsville "bids high.")
Nk Je 1 evn **Weaverville** Union Methodist Episcopal Ch
Nm 3 evn **Horsetown** *prt* south of Redding (King did not speak here on May 24.)

Nsno 19 evn **North San Juan** Libr Assoc (In a letter written during late May to William H. Sears, president of the local Union Club and Republican candidate for State Assembly, King postponed his Je 5 app, later settling on the nineteenth as the proper date. Although King gave bad conditions on the mountain roads as his reason for postponement, the Horsetown app on the third may have been another factor in his decision to delay the NSJ app. In this regard, see the Je 4 Red Bluff entry under "Webster" and the Je 5 Oroville entry under "Lexington.")

Repeat patterns not evident in this list:

Mh 22 **Sacram** "Washington"
27 **Auburn** "Washington"

Apr 9 **Grass Valley** "Washington"
10 **Nev City** "Washington"

Je 25 **Sacram** "Union and War"
27 **Auburn** "Lexington"

b) "The Battle of Lexington: First Days of the Republic" **10** (SF 1/**Cal 9**) Apr 19 thru Ag 26 (commemorating anniv of battle, and apparently not adapted from any pre-Cal title)

Apr 19 evn SF First Cal Guard **prp**
s May 3 evn **Sacram** Libr Assoc
v 14 evn **San Jose-Santa Clara** University of Pacific?! *prt* **prC** (One of two apps; see May 13 above, also Mh 14 under **4.**)
No Je 5 evn **Oroville** Brick Congregational Ch
Np 6 evn **Msville** Rifles **prC**
Ntno 20 evn **Nev City** Methodist Episcopal Ch (King suggested this date, in an app at SF on Mh 4, as appropriate for some commemoration of the Stars and Stripes being adopted as banner of Union forces.)
27 evn **Auburn** Masonic Lodge
b[y] Jl 23 evn **Stkton** Presbyterian Ch
e[v] Ag 1 evn **Red Dog** *prt* (King declined making an app on same day in SF at West Indies emancipation festival.)
n[m] 26 evn **Oakland** Presbyterian Ch

Repeat pattern not evident in this list:

Je 6 **Msville** "Lexington"
7 **Msville** "Union and War"

Jl 23 **Stkton** "Lexington"
24 **Stkton** "Union and War"

***c**) "The Genius of Daniel Webster and His Defense of the Constitution" **6** (SF 1/**Cal 5**) Mh 19 thru Spt 17 (adapted from 1852 "Webster" lecture)

Mh 19 evn SF Mercantile Libr Assoc **def**
Apr 12 evn **Sacram** Methodist Episcopal Ladies

Ng May 28 evn **Yreka** Methodist Episcopal Ch *prt*
Nn Je 4 evn **Red Bluff**
d[w] Jl 31 evn **Nev City** Baptist Ch
Spt 17 evn **Sacram** Libr Assoc

d) "The Union and the War" **6** (SF 2/**Cal 4**) May 12 thru Jl 24
t May 12 UC-SFrc 7:30pm var sermon "The Northern Uprising"
19 UC-SFrc 7:30pm var sermon/lecture "The Present Condition of Our Country" (rev slightly)
Nq Je 7 evn **Msville** Rifles **prC** (text substantially same)
Nrno 18 evn **Grass Valley** Methodist Episcopal Ch
25 evn **Sacram** First Congregational Ch
c[x] Jl 24 evn **Stkton** Presbyterian Ch

Repeat patterns not evident in this list:
Je 18 **Grass Valley** "Union and War"
20 **Nev City** "Lexington"
Je 25 **Sacram** "Union and War"
27 **Auburn** "Lexington"

Apr 9 **Grass Valley** "Washington"
10 **Nev City** "Washington"

*e) "Socrates: His Life, Character, and Humor" **5** (SF 1/**Cal 4**) Jn 11 thru Ag 2 (adapted from "Socrates"/"Socrates as a Religious Man," Nov 13 and 24, 1850; first del in SF, May 15, 1860)

b Jn 11 evn **Sacram** Methodist Episcopal Ch
g Fb 27 evn **Msville** Odd Fellows' Libr Assoc
j Mh 6 evn **Stkton** Odd Fellows' Libr Assoc
q Apr 29 evn SF Rev George B. Taylor **np**
f[u] Ag 2 evn **Nev City** Baptist Ch

f) "The Two Declarations of Independence: 1776 and 1861" 2 (SF 1/**Cal 1**) and 2 **Cal** apps met, but with different title and not scheduled as benefit for Vols

Jl 4 11:00am **Sacram** Union Club
a[z] 9 evn SF Mercantile Libr Assoc **def**

24 evn **Stkton** Blues/Union Guard?!
Ag 2 evn **Nev City** Vols?!

*g) "Substance and Show" **3** (SF 1/**Cal 2**) rev from Jn 7, 1852 lecture of same title; first del in SF, May 10, 1860

Jn 3 evn **Napa City** Methodist Ch
8 evn **Msville** New Presbyterian Ch
d 28 evn SF Mission Street Methodist Episcopal Ch **prp**

h) "The Confederate States: the Old and the New" 3 (SF 2/**Cal 1**)

Ag 19 evn SF Mercantile Libr Assoc **def**
21 evn **Sacram** Libr Assoc
o[l] 27 evn SF Mercantile Libr Assoc **def**

i) "Books and Reading" 2 (SF 1/**Cal 1**) apparently not adapted from any pre-Cal title

Jn 17 evn SF Mercantile Libr Assoc **def**
Na May 21 evn **Msville** Presbyterian Sunday Sch **prC**

j) "Peace and What We Must Pay for It" 2 (both SF)

Ag 29 evn SFrc Families of NY and Mass Vols **np**
p[k] 31 evn SFrc NY, Mass, and Cal Vols **np**

2. Sermon titles repeated at UC-SFrc 18 (SF 16/**Cal 2**)

*a) "The Doctrine of the Trinity" (two pts)
Jn 6 7:00pm pt 1 (first del at Hollis Street Ch in Boston, Jn 8, 1860)
20 11:00am pt 2 (again del at Hollis Street Ch, Jn 15, 1860)

*b) "The Doctrine of Atonement in the Four Gospels" (two pts)
c Jn 27 7:00pm pt 1
Fb 3 7:00pm pt 2

*c) "Substantial Christianity and the Grounds of Salvation" (first del on Apr 24, 1853)
Fb 10 7:00pm
17 7:00pm

*d) "Precious Stones" (first del in SF, Dec 22, 1860)
f Fb 24 7:00pm
Mh 17 7:30pm

*e) "Christian Thought of the Future Life" (first comp in 1854)
m Mh 31 7:30pm
Apr 14 7:30pm

f) See "Union and War" entry under 1 for two vars del on May 12 and 19.

g) "Religious Lessons from Mt Shasta"

Ne May 26 **Shasta** Methodist Ch 11:00am (impromptu, after briefly observing Shasta Butte from the stagecoach as the sun rose that same morning)

NIne Je 2 **Weaverville** Union Methodist Episcopal Ch 11:00am *prt* (del from notes or manuscript, and rev considerably after studying Mt. Shasta for ten hours on May 28)

9 UC-SFrc 11:00am (date written in by King on manuscript in his collection of sermons)

16 UC-SFrc 7:30pm

h) "Suggestions from the Comet of 1861"

Jl 14 7:30pm

28 7:30pm

i) "Secession in Palestine and Its Consequences"

h^{s} Ag 4 7:30pm the Poor

m^{n}**h**^{s} 25 7:30pm Cal Vols

3. Miscellaneous apps at UC-SFrc 19 (all SF)

*Jn 13 7:00pm "Christ's Doctrine of Human Nature and Its Depravity" (first del on Mh 20, 1853)

Fb 14 11:00am Brief eulogy at funeral service for George R. Ward (fee unknown for marriages, funerals, and baptisms)

17 11:00am Sermon on alleviating UC debt

Mh 24 7:30pm Palm Sunday Sermon (not enough data to determine whether a pre-Cal repeat)

l 31 2:00pm Brief eulogy at funeral service for John S. Mason (fee unknown for marriages, funerals, and baptisms)

o *Apr 7 7:30pm "Obstacles and Aids to Faith in Immortality" (first del on Apr 27, 1851)

p 28 11:00am Sermon marking first anniv of taking up pastoral duties at UC (Ch debt a topic here, see Fb 17 above.)

x Je 22 10:00pm Oration del at Union flag-raising ceremony, upon returning from Nev City to SF via Sacram (See Je 20 note under "Battle of Lexington.")

y 23 7:30pm Sermon advocating increase in funds for Union/National Gvt

z Jl 8 8:00pm Address commemorating eighth anniv of Ladies' Protection and Relief Soc (King apparently del sermons on a quarterly basis to benefit this organization, including 11:00am apps on Fb 10 and Je 23.)

g^{t} Ag 4 11:00am "Sentiments for Sorrows" (relating to defeat of Union forces at First Bull Run)

i^{r} 11 7:30pm Address commemorating ninth anniv of Pilgrim Sunday Sch

j^{q} 12 7:30pm Participates in debate on Sanitary Fund question--"Should administrative control over the distribution of funds for relieving families of NY Vols be centralized within NY City?"

q[j] Spt 1 7:30pm "Unity of the Moral Law" (not enough data to determine whether a pre-Cal repeat)

s[h] 4 10:00am Addresses first work meeting of UC Ladies' Aid Group

u[f] 22 11:00am Sermon on the importance of a thorough UC Sabbath Sch organization

26 11:00am National Fast Day Sermon

4. Miscellaneous apps outside UC-SFrc 17 (SF 13/**Cal 4**)

a *Jn 10 evn "Laws of Disorder" **Msville** New Presbyterian Ch (rev from 1854 lecture of same title; first del in SF, May 21, 1860)

*23 evn "Individual Power and Its Voices" **Sacram** Libr Assoc (rev from "Personal Power and Its Voices" as comp in 1858; first del in SF, May 24, 1860)

Fb 5 evn Address commemorating tenth anniv of SF Protestant Orphan Asylum **np**

e 24 2:00pm Temperance address to SF Dashaways **np**

h *28 evn "Existence and Life" **Timbuctoo** (first del on Oct 19, 1856)

Mh 11 evn Address on education at Zion Methodist Episcopal Ch for benefit of SF Livingstone Black Institute (del extemporaneously from notes) **prp**

14 evn Address at commencement exercises of the University of Pacific Medical Sch in SF (also del from notes) **np**

n Apr 7 2:00pm Second temperance address to SF Dashaways (See Fb 24 above.) **np**

May 9 12:00 noon Addresses Mai-Fest Picnic of Pilgrim Sunday Sch at Russ's Garden in SF (See Ag 11 under 3.)

w 15 evn Address on alleviating Ch debt at Parish party of UC-SFrc (See Fb 17 and Apr 28 under 3.)

k[p] Ag 24 1st evn Addresses SFrc Executive Committee in charge of gathering funds for the relief of NY Vols **prat np** though conceivably a non-speechmaking marriage ceremony **def** paying a fee)

l[o] 24 2nd evn Addresses larger, more general meeting called to aid families of Mass Vols **np**

r[i] Spt 2 1:30pm Addresses organizational meeting of UC Ladies' Aid Group (See entry dated the fourth under 3.)

t[g] 4 evn On same day state election held, drops in off street unannounced and directs impromptu remarks to SF Republican Victory Celebration for benefit of Cal Vols **np**

Spt 12 evn Address on agriculture to Northern District Agricultural, Horticultural, and Mechanics' Soc at that organization's Fair in **Msville** (King canceled a similar commitment in Msville the previous year, an app scheduled for Spt 5, because of ill health, but during a comparable period of 1862 del agricultural addresses at Stkton on Spt 11 and Oakland on Oct 9.)

20 evn SF Masonic Lecture, containing ideas of "Rev Brother Max Wolff" and tracing the importance of Masonic First Degree to biblical sources (See Apr 5 under 1; "Max Wolff" the name of a Boston editor of symbolic exegesis intended to accompany an engraving--"The Origin of the Rites and Worship of the Hebrews.") **prp**

v[e] 23 evn Addresses Grand Exhibition of SF Olympic Club for benefit of Cal Vols **prp**

*"A Sermon for The Anniversary of American Independence, July 24th 1786- [Delivered] By Samuel [Eusebius] M'Corkle [at Salisbury and/or Thyatira, Rowan County, North Carolina]- A Sermon &cc. from Esther: IX, 20-28 inclusive," Incomplete Manuscript in McCorkle Papers, William R. Perkins Library, Duke University (Durham). Quite apart from day-after or mid-month "bobolition" celebrations by free blacks in New York and other northern states, and late June Fort-Moultrie celebrations in such southern locales as Charleston and Marthasville, Georgia, both events really amounting to variant dates for the Fourth, several theories may explain McCorkle's designating the twenty-fourth as "The Anniversary" to be commemorated. Although no appearance date at all is cited on the title page, McCorkle could have repeated his sermon in Thyatira, after giving it in Salisbury sometime during the week of the Fourth. Indeed, he did repeat at least three sermons in both towns: one treating "The Law of God" (***T** *June 2,* **S** *Sept. 20, 1789), another a charity sermon (***S** *July 28,* **T** *probably August, 1793), and a third contrasting the "happiness and duty" of America and the Israelites (***S** *Feb. 18,* **T** *Feb. 19, 1795). Or McCorkle might have been cognizant of an intriguing audience factor. Many farmers in North Carolina, Maryland, and Pennsylvania, perhaps even elsewhere for that matter, preferred cutting their wheat and other grains "before entirely ripe and hard." And occasionally a committee of arrangements, rather than cancel oratory and toasts for some plowing/mowing contest, would elect to postpone a village's celebration of the Fourth until the "Harvest Home" program near the end of July. By making this consolidation, villagers might gather in their wheat, rye, oats, and hay, not only before the grain ripened excessively in the fields, but also before the onset of seasonal rains prevented them from cutting both grain and hay. In this regard, see the Philadelphia* United States Gazette *for July 28, 1828, covering the "Jubilee and Harvest Home" celebration at Valley Forge on Saturday, the twenty-sixth. A final theory merits attention, but is not nearly as direct or plausible. To mention only one example, on Monday, July 25, 1768, Silas Downer helped dedicate a liberty tree at Providence, Rhode Island, delivering an "animated" oration on such topics as terms of colonization, rights and grievances of colonists, and possible means of redress, the ceremonies being conducted from a "summerhouse" within the elm's branches. And McCorkle might conceivably have been aware of Sons-of-Liberty dedications during July and other summer months. The reader should realize the symbolic coincidence between the frame meetinghouse that served McCorkle's Thyatira and the single Greek or Christian Church remaining in the once renascent Thyatira of Revelation.*

1 And Mordecai wrote these things, and sent letters unto all the Jews that were in all the provinces of King Ahasuerus, both nigh and far.---To [e]stablish this among them, that the[y] should keep the fourteenth day of the month Adar, and the fifteenth day of the same yearly, &cc. (Esther: IX, 20)

2 The Jews, and I believe all other nations, have had their Anniversaries: or days of public rejoicing, for public and prosperous events of providence.

From Nisan to Adar, from the first month to the last in the Jewish calendar, they had their feasts, AND or ☆ their fasts, and except Tamuz, Ab, and Marchesvan, that is, except the fourth, fifth and eighth months- they celebrated some Anniversary- Festival or other, every month in the year, a sin of the Pyr[r]h[ic] Beula[h]- of envy. The Greeks and Romans had also their Anniversaries, and we have our's.

3 This day we have met to celebrate the Anniversary of our Independence. Ten years have now elapsed since we have been an Independent people, and tho[ugh] it be not, like the Jewish Anniversary, the day of our deliverance, yet it is a day that **a** IS A DAY **b** ought ☆ ever to be memorable. Let God, from above, ever regard it [so]. May all good Angels and all good men ever rejoice in it. Let no clouds nor darkness ever rest upon it. Let the day in which it was said a nation is born, let it be ever celebrated with friendly, rational, and Godlike joy.

4 Already, my brethren, have I anticipated the pleasure of joining with you, and leading your devotion thro[ugh] the exercises of the day. This pleasure is heightened by the enjoyment of public peace, and tranquility, and by that countenance which the text gives to the most scrupulous confidence, to observe it as a day of feasting, and joy, provided temperance, charity and devotion (which is also required), provided these be added to our feasting and joy.

5 It is necessary to explain this festival of the Jews. It was begun in the days of Ahasuerus, whom Prideaux supposes to have been Artaxerxes Lorgimanus, thro[ugh] whose favour Ezra and Nehemiah rebuilt Jerusalem. True he is called Ahasuerus, but this is thought to be only an honourary title, as Pharoah was before, and Caesar afterwards. They who are acquainted with the Persian language have told us, that the original word "Achashverosh" is compounded of "Achash", which signifies empire, and "thosh" the head: so that it was applicable to any person whatever, who was at the head of the Persian Empire.

6 In the reign of this prince, Haman, son of Hamadetha, of the seed royal of Amolek, was made first minister of State; and they[the] people were commanded to pay him those divine honours which they sometimes paid to the King, his master. I know that this is not expressed in the story: but it is very probable because the Kings of Persia were sometimes actually worshipped. Timocrates was put to death by the Athenians for worshipping Darius, and thereby degrading the dignity of the State. 2[n]dly, because the King commanded this respect, whatever it was. In the third chapter [Esther, verses 2 and 3], it is said that he commanded his servants to bow [down] to Haman, and reverence him. Such a command would have been unnec[e]ssary, if the respect required were no more than civil. A third reason is, Mordecai refused from the principles of his religion, no doubt, which told him "Thou shalt worship the Lord thy God, and Him only that thou serve": but did not forbid him "to give honour to whom honour is due".

7 This refusal, however, **a** WAS ALMOST **b** had almost proved ☆ ruinous to himself and [the] nation. Haman was exceedingly exasperated- meditated the extirpation of the whole Jewish race

draft a -obtained a law, not like the law of the Medes and Persians.-It was that law itself; a law that could not be reversed

draft b

—obtained a royal edict for that purpose- cast "Pur", a Persian word signifying a lot, to find an auspicious day— and after running over all the months in the year, fixed at last on the 13th day of Adar, and last month in the Jewish year.

8 This afforded to Esther, and Mordecai, the space of almost a year to defeat his nefarious design; and that time is improved by fasting, and prayer. And by their influence on the King for obtaining another decree, that the Jews should stand on their own defence, and put to death those who should rise up against them; accordingly, 800 are slain in the palace, and 75:000 through[out] the rest of the provinces, and the Jews obtain a complete deliverance.

9 Such was the occasion of the Jewish Anniversary. An Anniversary which they observe to this day, with a strange mixture of religion and riot. When they intercalate the Ve-adar, or 13th month, which is done once in three years, they superstitiously observe two feasts of Purim in the same year, the greater Purim and the less[er]: and tho[ugh] on par[t] of these days they read over the Megillah, or book of Esther: yet is the remainder spent in general riot and debauchery. And a rule of the festival is to drink untill they can no longer distinguish between the blessing of Mordecai and the cursing of Haman; so that this has been called by Arne the Jewish Bac[c]hanal, or their drunken frolic. I hope, my brethren, that religion **a** AND OUR OWN **b** in ☆ reason and interest will forbid us, in this particular, ever to follow their example.

10 When such days are not abused into superstition or licentiousness, they receive the entire approbation of my heart. They give [us] occasion to take a retrospective view of national providence, thro[ugh] the course of danger or war---and to call forward our attention to the mild and gentle arts of peace-

11 These two things should be the business of every Anniversary. Let them be the business of this day. [Therefore,] To take a retrospective view of God's national providence; and [inasmuch] as we are met to celebrate the birthday of our nation: it will not be improper to enquire into the designs of Heaven in giving existence to nations. His designs seem to be, to prevent ignorance and promote knowledge of every kind, especially the knowledge of His wisdom, power and goodness in governing the nations; to promote the knowledge and practise of justice and charity, and the principles of civil government; to extend the knowledge of natural philosophy- of commerce and trade- of agriculture and the manufactures, and above all the knowledge and practice of our most holy religion.

12 None of these great objects could be gained so easily without nations. Colledg[e]s, Schools and Universities, without national support, are [only] with great difficulty maintained. The dispute between **a** NEWTON OF ENGLAND **b** Sir Isaac Newton ☆ and Cassini of France about the figure of the earth was decided by a fleet of Mathematicians and Philosophers, fitted out at national expence. To what else do we owe the possession of this goodly land? A nation furnished the bold Columbus with that fleet with which he discovered this Western World. Nor could the knowledge or practice of morals be so easily cultivated [without national support]. Justice could not be exercised, and public spirit and patriotism would languish. Even were the government patriarchal, the [Divine] Father must be judge and executioner of His son; OR else he must die without law, or escape altogether. Was it possible that, on this account, Cain was spared? Some have suggested it. Certainly the knowledge of religion could not be so easily propagated. How long before Christianity could [it] have spread from family to family, joined by no national Union? But God raised the Roman empire for this purpose; Christianity mounted on the wings of the Roman eagle, and soon flew over all the world.

13 Far, very far am I from thinking, as some do, that God has left this world to govern itself. I believe that He has established a system of laws for the government of the natural and moral world; AND but ☆ that He reserves to himself the liberty of interposing when He pleases, and counteracting this general establishment. The natural philosopher (and astronomer) knows that God has established, in our system, the laws of attraction, and gravitation: but he knows, with equal certainty, that when planets and comets happen to come in the same direction, when some of them have begun to be drawn from their orbits by the near approach of others; he knows then that a divine interposition is absolutely necessary, and he knows that there has actually been such an interposition.

14 So also in the moral world, I believe that there are a system of laws established for the government of nations: and that God seldom departs from that establishment: but I believe that He sometimes does it. Hence IT IS [THAT] there are amongst nations, as in Nature, some appearances which can be accounted for on no human principles whatever.

15 Great and marvelous are thy works, Lord God almighty. (Revelation: XV, 3) It might puzzle some of our politicians, to tell us why this dispute was called up several years before the declaration of our independence. Why our enemies gave us time to study the debate, to learn our political Catechism, then to desist from their purpose **a** WHEN AT [THE] TIME **b** at a time when ☆ they might very probably have succeeded; and after several years to renew the attempt, when they had less probability of success.

16 It is not very easy, on human principles, to account for that almost unbounded confidence which we placed in the wisdom and integrity of the first Congress; and indeed it is not easy to account for their wisdom, unless we suppose, with Lord Pitt, that they were divinely inspired. It is not easy to account

for THE our☆growing affection and respect for General Washington, notwithstanding all his misfortunes at the beginning of the war. We all know that, in common, a General is esteemed, not according to his merit: but [according to] success. I might add some other considerations,—the state of our finances (and yet support of the war by a paper-currency)— the dis[s]atisfaction of the army (and yet their Dreadfulness in carrying on the war)— the revolt and return of the Pen[n]sylvania line (notwithstanding the proposals offered by the enemy). This is, in my oppinion, one of the most astonishing phenomenon that has ever appeared in the military world.

17 Time would fail to view, in retrospect, the whole progress of the war, from campaign to campaign, from the BEG[INNING] battle at Lexington to the fall of Col[onel]: Laurens. It is sufficient to say that the hand of God has led us thro[ugh] the war- united and supported us in it— brought it to a conclusion at a critical moment, when we appeared less able than ever to carry it on- and now gives us an opportunity **a** OF CELE[BRATING] **b** in peace and plenty to celebrate☆the Birth-day of our empire, and to turn our thoughts to peace. This is the 2[n]d thing proposed to be done, and may include the following particulars— the exercise of religion- the education of our children (and interests of literature in general)— the principles of civil government (and civil and religious rights of men)- commerce and trade— agriculture and the manufactures of [the piedmont] country. Peace has now given [us] leisure to attend to all these things.

18 I begin first with religion, not only on account of her superior importance: but [because of her] influence on all the rest. Religion promotes learning and liberty; in one word, it exalts a Nation. Religion, alas! IT has almost expired in the war, nor has she yet raised her drooping head. That Godlike man, who stood foremost in the FIELD war,☆has at the end of it, given us an example which few of us have been anxious to follow. When he took his last leave of Congress, the army, and all public life, it was in words to this effect. "I wish to retire to the enjoyment of that domestic peace, for which I have not failed to sigh thro[ugh) every stage of the war. I retire into private life, to cultivate the religion of Jesus- to follow his bright example— and to spend the evening of my days, in preparation for that blessed immortality which his religion discloses."

19 Ye Officers and soldiers, who gloried in following your leader thro[ugh] the dangers and deaths of war. Be it your glory to imitate his example when the storm of war is over, and all [is] universal peace. Here give full scope to your ambition. This is the **a** GREAT **b** most brilliant☆example he ever set before [us]. Every public action of that great man has been rising higher and higher. This last has, in my humble oppinion, surpassed all the rest.

20 My brethren, when I come seriously to reflect upon it— when I think how ungenerous it would be to suppose that it WERE was☆not a dictate of sincerity— a dictate, too, of long and deliberate reflection— a dictate of that mind which approaches near to **a** AN **b** the capacities of an☆Angel----my soul is fired with indignation at the narrow minded wittings of our Age, who without

thinking, without reading, without experience, without examination, will dare to speak disrespectfully of our most holy religion. A religion that has stood the test of almost 6,000 years, and I believe will to eternity.

21 I am therefore not concerned about the existence of our religion. No, religion is able to defend itself. When Henry the VIII had written a book against Luther, in defence of the Roman Catholic religion- when the Pope complimented him with the title of Defender of the Faith- when Henry's vanity was so pleased, on the occasion, that he could not forbear to speak of it in every company, "Defend **a** YOUR **b** me and the rest of your ☆ subjects", cries his Buffoon, "and the Faith will defend itself"! I believe that the Faith can defend itself. I am therefore under no apprehensions for its existence: but I am concerned for the happiness of those wretches who deny it. Here my indignation turns to pity. Tho[ugh] I consider them, in effect, enemies to our independence, yet I cannot forbear to pity, nor cease labouring to convince them.

22 Far be it from me to enter on this subject at all, if I did not see that dissipation and idleness, the love of sin and singularity, were making enormous strides among us: that infidelity, as usual, was closely following [in] their footsteps; and that the effort of the whole was to destroy our independence, rather than our religion.

23 I am very far from thinking that AMERICAN Independence is as firmly established as Christianity. The one is almost 6,000 years older than the other, already: and its Birth-day in paradise will be celebrated, when the 4th of July shall be forgotten forever. I do most assuredly believe that if every Soul of us were infidels, and debauchees into the bargain, the Christian religion would live to eternity: but it is a matter of doubt whether, as a nation, we would ever celebrate another Anniversary. I have heard a great deal [said] about that honour which guards our public conduct, and those fine feelings which secure our private [interests]: but I could never see the man **a** .WHO **b** ,to tell me what honour is, nor [could I ever] become security for the feelings of a man who ☆ has no feelings at all; and many such Characters have been found, in high as well as in low life.

24 Fondly would I know how we have been almost all in the wrong about religion, for so many ages [al]together. And that a few MEN whose hearts have, generally speaking, been absorbed in pleasure, who have read little else than what suited their taste,—who have never examined the doctrines, nor troubled themselves about the practice of any religion whatever: I would fondly know how such men have by mere random hit on the right, while men of sober and contemplative minds— who have devoted a life of 50 or 60 years to the study and practice of religion— have been, after all, in the wrong.

25 Come and let us reason together, if we **a** AR[E] **b** have been ☆ so long in an error we wish to be set right. If you be in the wrong, we wish to convince you; tho[ugh] by the Bye our mistake cannot be fatal, be the event as it may. If you be

wrong, wo[e] to you. This forms our apology for earnestness in persuading men: and this makes you inexcusable for attempting to oppose us.

26 We most assuredly believe the Scriptures to be the word of God- and we believe that the doctrines they contain— the existence and providence of God— the manner of our fall and recovery— the immortality of the Soul— the resurrection of the body— and a future state— are doctrines which never, to all eternity, could have entered into the heart of man, unless God had revealed them.

27 We do also, most assuredly, believe that an immediate revelation was necessary for the happiness, if not existence, of our first parents in paradise:—That God was too good to deny it— too wise not to know the best means and time to give it— and too powerful to be unable to carry these means into execution.

28 We do verily believe, that if two of the greatest infidels that ever existed were this moment created in paradise- surrounded with all the profusion of Nature, and possessed of the reasoning powers of the whole tribe of infidels, from Herbert to Hume, we do believe that their reason would be their curse- that they would be more wretched than the beasts of the field— and that they could never be happy untill they obtained a direct and immediate revelation from God.

29 "Here we are", would they say to each— say to each other! I correct the mistake. Speak, they could not at all, untill God reveal[ed] a language which each understood. "Here I am", then, might be each one's private thoughts: but how came I to be! I see nothing like myself that could have given me existence. I behold a glorious something rising in the East; I know not what it is. I see a number of objects around me, but I know not the names, nature or properties of [any] one of them. All is darkness and confusion, my creator and preserver both unknown.

30 Suppose, if you please, that sin has entered, and death by [way of] sin. Imagine that one of these persons has been struck down by sickness. He grows weaker and weaker; at last he speaks no more. His pulse beats faint. His limbs grow cold. His face looks ghastely. His lips turn pale. His Eye-balls roll in death. At last, with a deep hollow murmuring grone[groan], he bids the world adieu.

31 "What is the matter"! cries his friend. He is seized with horror, but can not tell. He sits down to think. He thinks with all the intensity of his soul: but can never, [even] if he think to eternity, reach one thought further than this---That he has lost his companion, and that his companion is totally mouldering into dust.

32 For what is there to give him any other idea? He has never had the revelation of any thing else. He has never seen a Spirit, nor ever conversed with any. He sees no bodies rising from the dead. And what is to give any idea of the

immortality of the soul- or the resurrection of the body? Or what is there to give the idea of a creating and preserving Spirit, who is infinite and eternal: unless that infinite and eternal, that creating and preserving Spirit shall deign himself to do it!

33 Certainly, my Brethren,these thoughts can come from no other source. They are as far above human thought as the heavens are above the earth, or God above his creatures.

34 The reason why we are not struck with them is because education has famelearized[familiarized] them [to us]. But let one of our modern infidels be perplexed 50 or 60 years, without these ideas, then "Deus intersit".---Let a God be introduced, and here is an occasion worthy of a God.

35 Bewildered Mortal! I, The infinite and eternal Spirit, have made, and preserved you and all flesh. I have made, of one blood, all nations under Heaven, when they grow old in Luxury and pride, I destroy them. I have formed all men for immortality-- They have fallen in their first foed[e]ral father. He has lived and died for men. He has ascended, sent down the Holy **a** SPIRIT **b** sanctifying Spirit, ☆ makes intercession now, and will come at last to raise the dead, thrust the wicked down to hell, and receive the righteous into Heaven.

36 O[h], My God! with what most surprizing force would these few short sentences strike his Soul. He would be an infidel no longer. Now would he cry, "Now I understand every thing, and all was riddles and mystery before. Now I see why God has raised nations, and how He governs empires— Now I know every principle in my Soul, why I fear annihilation and love life. What a fool [am I] to think that this thinking something, which can make such amazing progress in the knowledge of things, should at once be struck out of existence: much less that I could do it, when I cannot [even] annihilate one drop of my [own] blood. In one word, I now see thro[ugh] the whole system of creation, providence and Grace." Such would surely be the first reflections of a mind perplexed for many years.

"[Commencement] Oration delivered on the 4th of July 1818 at [the College of William & Mary,] Williamsburg Virginia, by John Mason Jr. of Geo[rge]: T[ow]n, [District of] Col[umbi]a," Manuscript in Mason Commonplace Book, Virginia Historical Society (Richmond). Indeed, at least two other academic institutions held their commencement exercises on the Fourth during the national period, namely, Bethany College and Lane Seminary. And as a notice from rector James Semple phrased the point, the William & Mary commencement convocation in 1818 would hopefully attract an audience "who feel a regard for the welfare of the college, or who are solicitous for the improvement of the rising generation, and who can do so with convenience." One of three graduates that Fourth, Mason spoke last and was awarded an L.L.B. or law degree. Junius K. Horsburgh, likewise a law candidate, led off with an oration on the "utility of legal science," and Archibald Taylor, the lone arts candidate, read an essay on "education." A correspondent of the Richmond Enquirer, *in a report on the ceremonies datelined the sixth, thought Mason's oration not only typically "animated," but "replete" with sentiments appropriate to the Fourth and "interesting" in its treatment of the apparent struggle-blessing dialectic in American freedom. And in the final paragraph of the following text, the reader can compare two draft versions and weigh whether one is necessarily more oral in style than the other. Certainly this oration was never sought after for printing purposes, however, and Mr. Randolph Hurry of New York City donated Mason's Commonplace Book to the Society during 1916.*

1 Friends and Fellow Citizens— The Birth-day of American Independence again beams upon the world. Again, the hearts and the voices of ten million of freemen unite in joyful commemoration of that auspicious day which wrested their Country from Despotism, and registered her name in characters of glory on the roll of nations.-

2 While we contemplate the rising prosperity of our Country— while we behold her happy at home- respected abroad— while we see her reap, in profuse abundance, the richest fruits of the earth— while we survey her colossal power, now reposing on the lap of honorable peace- but ever prompt to repel and avenge even the smallest aggression— while we view, with delight and pride, her ample measure of rational Liberty- the noblest and best of Heaven's gifts to social man— surely the bosom of every patriotic American must swell with pious love to that benevolent Being who rules the Universe— his heart expand with gratitude to the heroes of the revolution, whose bravery preserved our Country thro[ugh] the dread tempest of War.—

3 When we look upon this towering Republic— young, tho[ugh] already arrived at an unprecedented degree of strength and political consequence— when we contrast her short eventful history with the tedious annals of most other nations of the Earth- nations that have toiled thro[ugh] successive ages of darkness and oppression- yet still are blinded by ignorance and bigotted prejudice- still bourne down by the most detestable tyranny— we are struck with Astonish-

ment at her rapid advances from weakness, insignificance and misery to that [status] exalted of power, grandeur and happiness- now the wonder and envy of the world.-Yes, Fellow Citizens- rapid indeed hath been the growth of America.—But two centuries have passed away since wild Nature dwelt unmolested on the face of this Western continent.—Our forefathers of Britain, driven from the soil of their nativity by every species of cruelty which Tyranny could inflict, sought in the distant deserts of this newly discovered land, a relief from the weight of their woes and a Zest beyond the reach of superstitious persecution, where they might worship their Creator as their own hearts should dictate.—But what tongue can tell the difficulties that beset their enterprize! What language can convey an adequate idea of the dangers and horrors that rose continually, in dreadful array, before them! Cut off [as they were] from the civilized World— their only home, an inhospitable wild— their only hope, the sword— unsheltered from the inclemency of a rigorous climate— exposed to the incursions of ferocious hearts— and surrounded by Nations of barbarians; who, tho[ugh] they had yielded their right to the soil on a just consideration, still viewed with jealous eye the settlement of strangers among them, and marked their mistrust with bloodshed and desolation.—

4 Soon assailed on every side by hord[e]s of unrelenting savages, the colonists maintained, thro[ugh] many dismal years, an incessant, exterminating War.—Every house was a fortress.—The peaceful scenes of domestic life were invaded by the murderous din of battle, and polluted with blood.—A merciless foe spared not even defenceless females or their innocent, infant offspring.—Whole families, nay hundreds of families, were involved in indiscriminate slaughter, and their dwellings consigned to the **a** FIRE **b** frenzy of fire—☆ yet despair overcame not the survivors— such was their abhorrence of the tyranny they had fled— such their thirst for Liberty— such their unshaken invincible courage, that they chose rather to encounter every peril to which the insatiable rage of a savage enemy could expose them (and whence obstinate resistance might at length effect their deliverance), than return to the enslaved shores of Europe, [even] tho[ugh] a thousand joys of civilized life awaited them there.—But soon the scene changed.—This high-minded people encreased in number and in strength— the lapse of a few years secured a complete triumph over their old and inveterate foe.—The Indian retired, retired before their widely extended frontier— the beauties of cultivated Nature succeeded the gloom of the Wilderness.-Cities and Towns and Villages rose where before had stood the camp of the hostile native, or where the prowling heart had roamed for prey.—Agriculture, that solid basis of national wealth, filled the land with plenty, and commerce poured her rich profusion of comforts and luxuries on their shore.—[Not such acts in profusion as] Injustice, **a** VIOLENCE **b** Rapine, Violence ☆ and Murder, the horrid train that follow in the rear of Tyranny, even known scarcely by name in this land of peace, the last, distant refuge of persecuted Liberty. [But] A constant interchange of friendly offices— common fortune— a recollection of common suffering and a thousand amicable relations, men as

bonds of brotherhood that bound the several colonies to each other, and perfected a kind of moral Union between them.---Thus was founded this only Republic on Earth.-Cradled in War— inured from earliest infancy to danger— her citizens had cut their way, sword in hand, to Liberty.—

5 Could such a people crouch at the frown of Kings? Could such a people abandon those noblest feelings of human nature, which had prompted their fathers to seek an asylum in the Wilds of America? Could such a people tamely relinquish their liberties— the richest [in]heritance and best birth-right they had received— and basely entail, on posterity, degradation and misery and slavery?

6 Yet already the dark brow of Tyranny scowled upon American prosperity.—The blood-hound rapacity of haughty lordliness had snuffed the odour of the good things of our land.—They would tax American Industry to furnish [the] means of supporting their own diabolical profligacy.—They would prey upon the substance of our people, and plunge them into the deepest miseries of penury, [all] to gratify the avarice and glut the bloated magnificence of a Kingly court.----But, thanks to the vigilance and resolution of our fathers, these vile purposes of Cruelty were never carried in[to] execution.—They clearly saw that the policy of British rulers aimed at a total **a** DESTRUCTION [OF] **b** subversion of Liberty in America, and threatened with inevitable destruction ☆ the dearest and most sacred rights of Man.—

7 To soften the hearts of their oppressors, or to justify in the eyes of mankind any extreme to which they might be driven, they earnestly and respectfully entreated redress of the King.—But Cruelty is deaf and unrelenting.-Their humble petitions were spurned from the foot of the Throne.-Their manly representations and remonstrances to the Parliament and people of Britain were unheeded or despised- or, in the emphatic language of the times, "answered by a repetition of Injury."—Disciplined bands of mercenary murderors were stationed in many of our Cities, and with these fit instruments of their Will did Tyrants vainly hope to terrify our people into submission, or in the genuine spirit of despotism, determined to destroy their lives and lay waste their Country.—Resistance was deemed Rebellion, Great God!—Rebellion of Justice and Right against Rapine, Oppression and Murder.—Every hope of reconciliation fled forever— America thought not of submission.— Lexington and Bunker's hill stamped, with a seal of blood, the unalterable resolve of Liberty's last supporters to live free or to die.- The Congress of '76 proclaimed to the World that the states of America were free, sovereign and Independent.-This memorable event gave to the contest a new and more interesting character.—It was no longer the partial opposition of malcontent subjects, struggling against certain offensive measures of their Government- but a deadly conflict between Nation and Nation.—Future Ages will read, with admiration and wonder, the historic page that lays before their view the wide disproportion in strength and political CONSEQUENCE importance ☆ between the parties to this War.---Great Britian, an

Empire ancient and vast— at the Zenith of power, with an immense military force trained and disciplined by science and Experience— and half the World tributary to her public coffers.—The United States, with a few thousand of untaught recruits- badly armed- badly supplied with ammunition— a Government hastily formed in the midst of carnage and Invasion— a Treasury miserably poor, and public credit at the lowest ebb of exhaustion.—

8 But our's was the cause of freedom.-Washington, immortal Washington, whose name the latest posterity shall necrerate, led the Van[guard] of War- and discipline and order soon found a place in the American Camp.—Well assured of the courage and constancy of his Countrymen, this consummate General adopted the Fabian system of protracted warfare, and pursued it with the same vigilance and intrepidity that distinguished his illustrious Prototype.—Tho[ugh] often constrained to retreat before a victorious Enemy, he lost not the confidence of his Army.—And that Gallant band of heroes—reduced to a mere handful- without clothes- frequently without food- hunted and tracked by the blood that streamed from their naked, wounded feet— still clung with enthusiastic devotion to their Country's cause, for "Fame fired their courage- Freedom edg[e]d their swords."-

9 But these determined champions of Liberty were not doomed to everlasting suffering.-Suddenly the tide of war turns— their hopes are renovated- their efforts are redoubled.-Princeton- Trenton- Saratoga sound in thunder the American name, and triumphantly unfurl the banners of Freedom.—

10 At length, after a War of seven years checkered by every vicissitude of fortune— conducted, on the one part, with exalted magnanimity and strictest regard to humanity- on the other, but too often marked with the most deliberate cruelty, and blackened by atrocious acts of barbarity— victory declared *for* America.—

11 Thus gloriously terminated the War of '76— a tremendous storm that had darkened our Country with the gloom of death— whose dreadful thunders had shaken both Hemispheres— whose fierce lightnings had spent their fury against the Ark of our liberties, drifting on the boisterous ocean of revolutionary uncertainty.---"Sad was the year, by proud Oppression driv[e]n-/ When transatlantic Liberty arose-/ Not in the Sunshine and the smile of Heav[e]n/ But wrapt in whirlwinds and begirt with woes."-

12 The tempest was now calmed to rest-

draft a the mild beams of peace had returned.

draft b

the war-worn soldier reposed **a** FROM HIS TOIL **b** him[self] in the mild beams of peace. ☆—

The fields that so lately had yielded an imperishable laurel to his brows, now spread a golden harvest before him.—Commerce hoisted her canvass to every gale- and already opulence and elegance adorned our Cities, while content and smiling Plenty reigned throughout the country.—Science, Litterature and the liberal Arts, those happy sisters that so eminently contribute to polish and refine the human mind (long forgotten in the uproar of arms), NOW again ☆ resumed their wonted ascendancy.---

13 But tho[ugh] Independence had been achieved, and these were its glorious and happy fruits, Liberty was not yet safe.—That loosely cemented confederacy, under which affairs had hitherto been conducted, and which had been held together by the force of external pressure only, proved defective in the relaxed times of peace, and was deemed inadequate to secure the permanent prosperity of the Country.—The genius of the American People and the welfare of the Republic demanded a form of General Government, which should strengthen the executive Arm of the nation, without endangering the sovereignty of the several states- and which should effect a concentration of the force and resources of the Union, without degenerating into *consolidated Empire*, long since denounced by political experience [and] an inseparable concomitant of Tyranny.—At this juncture, the American People exhibited to the world a spectacle interesting in the highest Degree, and wholly unprecedented in the history of nations- the *formation of a Government by compact*.-That, too; a Government founded on the broad basis of Reason and Equality, where Laws, and not Men, preside.—Such is the form of Government assumed by the American People in the adoption of their present happy Constitution.-

14 This Constitution, by banishing all *hereditary Distinctions*— distinctions which Nature disclaims and which Tyrants created, in order the more effectually to oppress and debase **a** THE HUMAN RACE **b** mankind—☆ has opposed an insuperable barrier to the encroachments of criminal ambition, and filled the offices of the Republic with talent and integrity.—

15 This Constitution, by establishing competent Courts of Judicature for the determination of controversies between the different states, has removed every danger to be apprehended from that worst of national evils, Civil War—the demoniac scourge which arms brother against brother- and delights in havoc, death and destruction.

16 This Constitution, by defining with precision the offence of High-Treason, and confining it to the narrowest bounds consistent with public safety, has calmed every fear that *Constructive-Treason* (a merciless monster, thro[ugh] whose agency Tyrants have sacrificed the best friends of Liberty in other Countries) should ever rear his bloody crest in this.—

17 This Constitution— yielding no power to Rulers but by consent of the ruled- recognizing public functionaries as the servants, and not as the masters of the People- prescribing CERTAIN fixed ☆ limits to the authority of each department of Government— has so efficiently fortified the rights of the Citizen (and bound with so many massive chains the fell Giant, Despotism), that while

Americans have Virtue to preserve its purity- while they have intelligence to understand, and courage to defend and protect it, they never can be Slaves.—The Palladium of Liberty, may the Genius of America guard the sacred fane where it reposes, with a flaming sword!---

18 Thro[ugh] the lapse of thirty years, while outrageous Ambition deluged all Europe with blood- the mild spirit of this Constitution preserved the blessings of peace in America.—And during this long, uninterrupted peace, under its fostering influence, our people, far from sinking into that fatal lethargy which undisturbed repose is so apt to engender, daily acquired new strength and vigor, and prospered beyond the hopes of the most sanguine.—

19 When Britain, proud, rapacious Britain, by repeated depredations on the commerce of America, compelled her once more to unsheath the sword, under the guidance of this Constitution her armies marched from Victory to Victory, on land, while the red Cross of St.-George bowed to the star-spangled banner on the ocean.—

20 In further illustration of the advantages of [this] republican Constitution, from whose expansive, unconfined policy emanate the many liberal institutions, [of] which the United States alone of all nations can boast (and whose vivifying influence has anticipated the work of centuries), let me call your attention to the prosperous condition of our Country at this day.—

21 Internal improvements of every description are in a state of rapid advancement, adorning and enriching those stupendous, sublime works of Nature, which characterize this Continent with [all] the elegancies of Art and the useful additions of Industry, thus enhancing the value of property and augmenting, to an incalculable amount, the power and rescources of the Nation.—

22 Our wise and prudent Government, actuated by the excellent principle that peace is the time to prepare for War, appropriates the surplus of an overflowing Treasury to the erection of strong works for public defence, and to the augmentation of the Navy— of that gallant Navy so necessary for the protection of our maritime rights— and which so gloriously has broken the charm of invincibility that ONCE long ☆ hung around the fleets of **a** BRITAIN **b** Ocean's pretended Mistress. ☆—Party contention, that restless disturber of public peace- that bane of domestic felicity, now sleeps in oblivion, and prejudice is sacrificed on the altar of patriotism.—The bold, enterprizing, adventurous merchant of America explores, in triumphant security, most distant seas, and heaps upon the lap of his Country the wealth of every clime.—Already we boast a population equal in numbers to that of most states of Europe, and far, far superior to all in virtue, intelligence and love of Country. That brutish ignorance, genial soil of Tyranny's rankest weeds, so degradingly prevalent throughout the lower orders of the Ancient World, has no existence here.—To the contrary, the light of knowledge and a laudable spirit of enquiry— companions and protectors of Liberty, since they prompt the people to [make] a close scrutiny into the nature

of their laws and the conduct of their Rulers— are found in every Town, hamlet and cottage of united America.-These, and the many other eminent advantages which we enjoy above every people of the World, can be ascribed only to the influence of our free Constitution and of the just laws arising out of it.-

23 **alternate version** (oral **a**) Oh, my Country-Countrymen! ever estimate it as you ought.—'Tis this Constitution, that with a saving hand hath rent the veil of error which **the Sophistry of Tyrants had** drawn over the eyes of **mankind**!—'Tis this Constitution, that hath prostrated the **degrad**ing **belief-Doctrine that arbitrary Government was**-is indispensable **to the peace and preservation of the social order!—**'Tis this Constitution that **has opened to the world the glorious prospect of universal Liberty!**

alternate version (less oral **b**) Previously to the birth of the American Republic, **the sophistry of Tyrants had** deluded **mankind** into a **belief that arbitrary Government was** necessary **to the peace and preservation of the social order.**-But the fal[l]acy and absurdity of this debasing **doctrine**, which so often **degrad**es Man below the level of the brute. Reason has at length happily detected, and guided by her sacred light, America **has opened to the World the glorious prospect of Universal Liberty.-**

Oration Delivered by Alexander Beaufort Meek in Tuscaloosa, July 4, 1833, Incomplete Manuscript in Meek Collection, Alabama Department of Archives and History (Montgomery). Meek probably spoke at the Statehouse in Tuscaloosa, because he sketched in a structure closely resembling the capitol building on the title page of his manuscript, beneath the usual "Fourth of July" heading in capitals. An important rhetorical distinction would appear to underlie Meek's composition of this address, a distinction actually echoed in his poem before the Tuscaloosa Ciceronian Club five years later. For Meek as a lawyer and poet wanted to compose his oration so as to draw inspiration from a fancy, not momentary and unbridled, but rapt in its dedication to national worth. There simply had to be some remedy for the variables in the Fourth of July occasion tending toward demagoguery. And Meek believed that an orator speaking on the Fourth had to nurture an enduring enthusiasm, enabling him to surmount "wild ideal" words from "many a fervid" lip with "music" tone, qualities not necessarily bound to make permanent the "moon-eyed and fond" intention of "enthusiast" Hope. The reader will have to judge whether such a rhetorical purpose is attained in this address.

1 "Home of the Free- Land of the Great and Good!
Whose heritage is Glory, Hail to Thee!
Thou, oft undaunted, nobly hath withstood
Europa's best and proudest Chivalry
And conquering won a mighty destiny
First amid the nations. And thy Flag of Light
Gleams on all Climes a brilliant galaxy!"

To tell anew of that conquest bright; to celebrate again the Day on which that mighty destiny was won; to unfurl once more our banner glorious, whose folds have gleamed o'er land and sea, a starry galaxy, we've met.

2 And while we cherish the proud recollections which rise in the heart and overwhelm the soul, on this auspicious morn let us not forget the grattitude which is due to Him who guarded us in the hour of danger, and led us on to Victory.

3 Far, far away throughout this fair green land a thousand tongues are raised, to bless the memories of this Holy Day. And Gentlemen, and Respected Audience, we have gathered together for the same purpose.

4 If it be a proper enthusiasm to rehearse our glories won on many a field and hill; if it be right to sing again our anthems loud; if it will ennoble our own hearts, or our children's, to tell them of our patriot sires, and their noble deeds, and point them out examples by which a moral lesson might be learned to guide them onto duty's path, then indeed we are well assembled.

5 Years have swept away on the wings of the wind, since the Day on which the event that we are now celebrating transpired, and still as oft as its morning dawns, we greet its advent with joy and glee. On this Day we rise with feelings

differing from those of every day life. There is a welling up of the soul that causes us to forget our feeble and petty animosities, that drives away all political strifes and prejudices for the time, and [then] there is but one common sentiment among us, for we remember but one thing, that, we are all Americans. What a joyous thing 'twould be, if instead of one, an hundred such happy days could be our's in a year! 'Twould have a beneficial effect upon our People. It would bind the different Sections of this nation still stronger and stronger in the bands of harmony. Then can this Day ever be forgotten? Oh no, as long as lives Columbia's best and noblest One,-as long as— "The Child of the Sun, to whom 'tis given/To guard the banner of the Free,-/Shall hover in the sulphur smoke/And ward away the battle stroke"- and spread his plumes among the stars, it must not be forgotten. It should then be our duty and care, that it never be said again what has been said, that the Fourth day of July is dead. No, it must never be said. When it is dead, America is dead. When that day shall have arrived, the fires that have so long burned upon our hearthstones will be extinguished; the Sunlight of the Revolution will have faded away from the face of the Earth, and those Young Living Eyes that twinkled palely, during the dark hour of peril and desolation, when the Infant was struggling in the arms of the Giant, but which have since risen brighter and more glorious in the Western World, will have become dimmed and gone.

6 A Nation's Days of Jubilee should be sacredly remembered and preserved. Nothing shows in a stronger light the downward tendency of a government, than a coldness on the one hand, or a total neglect on the other, to these. As far as we are concerned, they are the very Birth and Life of our People. Every Country from time immemorial has had its days of festival and song, commemorating some event of greater or less[er] magnitude, which has been preserved in its Annals.

7 National Character and Honour, indeed, are involved to a much greater degree than we would imagine. If the victorious and glorious Acts of a people do not confer Character, what can? If we do not show honour unto ourselves, who will give us honor? A forgetfulness of these is the certain Prelude to destruction.

8 We are emphatically a people of the Future. But that Phillosophy that would teach us to take care of the Future within the Present, and the Past will take care of itself, or that we have no Past, is mainly wrong, and opposed to the best principles of the human heart. Remembering the Past learns us to act for the Present, and guides us to a better Future. To know what we have been is to know what we are, and what we may be. If we wish to preserve our well-honored institutions of old, handed down to us from our fathers, hallowed by time, and worth and glory; if we wish to see this Young Republic grow and increase, and wax stronger and stronger, and stretch its arms wide away upon the World; if we wish this "land of the brave" [to] be still the "home of the Free", then, these days- these holy days must be observed.

9 But need I urge this upon you, Gentlemen, or upon those with whom I am surrounded? Need I urge it upon those who call themselves Americans,- whether they be so by adoption or birth?-

10 Your very presence here, and the ceremonies which you have appointed for the Day, attest that I need not. Indeed why are we assembled here? Why do I see around me so many faces- the Young and Brave- the Old and Wise- the Fair and Beautiful? Is it a common occasion? Are we celebrating the Birth-day of a man? Are our rejoicings sent up to the Sky for the downfall of a Monarchy, and the erection of an aristocracy upon its ruins? Is it the shout that the Tyrant forces from the mouth of the slave, when the heart is dead? Oh No, they are the rejoicings of Freemen on the Birth-day of a Nation!

11 Sixty-Eight years ago, when darkness hung upon the land, when the soul was weary with heaviness, that Powerfull and All-hallowed Instrument, the Bible of our political faith, which has just been read in your hearing, was read before a "patriot few" and passed. But even in that hour of gloom, with enemies without and false-friend within, a sweet small voice came upon the breeze, and a song like this might have been heard to ascend, growing higher and stronger, 'til it reached the Sky, and filled the Universe;—

"Rise, ye men, if ye inherit
From a line of noble sires,
Saxon blood and Saxon Spirit,-
Rise to guard your household fires.
From each rocky hill and valley
Rise against th[e] invading band;
In the name of Freedom rally
To defend your native Land.

Foeman's feet your Soil are pressing,
Hostile banners meet your eye,
Ask from Heaven a father's blessing,-
Then for Freedom dare to die.
What, though veteran foes assail ye,
Filled with Confidence and pride
Let not hope or Courage fail ye,
Freedom's God is on your side.

To the winds your Flag unfolding,
Rally 'round it in your might,
Each his weapon firmly holding,
Heaven will aid you in The fight,
By the Mothers that have borne ye,
By your wives and children dear,
Lest your loved-ones all should scorn ye
Rise without a thought of fear.

Come as comes the tempest rushing,
Bending forests in its path,
As the mountain torrent gushing,
As the billows in their wrath,
From each rocky hill and valley
Sweep away th[e] invading band,
In the name of Freedom rally
To defend your Native Land."

When the hymn had ceased, a thousand unseen arms arose from hill and dale, and with one common voice, swore they were of right, and would be free! And on that self same night was kindled that small bright spark, which grew larger and larger and at last increased into a mighty flame, which spread throughout the land, and drove the Tyrant from our shores. May we not hope, Gentlemen, that this flame will never die, but burn brighter and fresher in every bosom.

12 While we celebrate the Day, and recount the deeds embalmed in history and song, we should not forget the Actors themselves in that Great and Sacred Drama.

"Forget?-oh never- nee'r shall die
Those names to Memory dear,
I hail the promise in each eye
That beams upon me here!"

13 But where are they?-that Spirit Band of Seventy Six! The most of them have passed away like the mist of the valley and the early dew before the morning sun. But, thank God, like the dews of Heaven their memories return again after a Season, to beautify, to freshen, and to animate. Are there any of them here to-day? Methinks I see one or two venerable forms around me, who must have acted in some of our Country's struggles- at Bunker Hill or Lexington!

14 Fearless Hearts!-with what kindling of soul and joy of Eye must they greet the coming of this day, when they look around upon this young land and see the Comfort and happiness, the work of their own hands. Would that they could remain many a year, that they might point out by their example, to their children, the path in which They trod.

"Their names shall never rest unsung
While Liberty can find a tongue.
Twines Grattitude a wreath for Them
More deathless than the diadem,
Who to Life's noblest end
Gave up Life's noblest powers,
And bade the legacy descend
To Us and Our's!"

In the name of this Assembly and of our Country, we thank them for coming up once again into the Sunlight of Independence!

15 Friends,-On this Day, while we tell and listen to the tales of our Country's wrongs, and of her triumphs,-there are lessons which might and should be learned. May I be permitted at this time to bring to your attention, for a few moments, One, the importance of which is evident to all. It is, i.e.- The influence of Mind upon Government.

16 It is a fact, the truth of which has been proven by all Time and experience, that the progress of just and correct principles in Government, has ever been proportional to the march of mind from darkness to light. All Government is and must be founded on Facts. Laws existed primarily in the Mind of the Great Existence, as a prime first cause seperable from materiality/ Secondarily, they must have been produced in Man, as inseperably connected with the material part of our being. It must be observed, however, that the Mind is made the Great Predominant Law-Actor. For it is evident to every individual, that the most complex truths, and the most elaborate deductions in any branch of Laws, when stripped of such elaborations, when explained simply, can be nothing more than so many seperate Facts. To observe then, and be benefited by those truths which have been handed down to us by the Minds of other times, as precepts and rules, and consequently to attain all the important and leading principles of Government, nothing is more necessary than, that every individual who is to be governed, who is to suffer or enjoy, should possess at least an ordinary understanding and common intelligence. If in this way he were capable of treasuring up any of those great principles, as illustrated by others, we might with propriety reason that he would be able to discover new truths himself, were he placed under appropriate circumstances. Though the march of the principles of true and just government, has in some instances been astonishingly rapid, yet because so little importance has been attached to this subject by the great body of mankind, a wide, wide field still remains for action. Laws as yet are by no means perfect. Some are recent,-in others, important principles still remain to be established by time and maturer observation. Their objects, combinations and relations are almost innumerable. Deep and laborious research is still requisite here.

17 The First Government must of a consequence have been what we may term the Father-Government. The Father was the Supreme Law-Giver. He ruled in himself, as the Head, for the rest as the Body. His mind and whole existence was the Digest, and his wishes, looks, words, and commands were the seperate Articles and Laws. The Children constituted the People. They were the Governed. They suffered and enjoyed, were punished and rewarded. Looking up to the Father as the Law, and as so of right, with his mandates and decisions they were satisfied. With no privilliges- no rights- no honors, yet they were willing to submit. How great an influence, Gentlemen, has Ignorance in enslaving Man's very Being. Then, indeed, the Parent it might be said, had "supreme dominion over the fish of the Sea, and over the fowl of the Air, and over the Cattle, and over all the Earth" so far as his own immediate family were

concerned. He was the *King*! Indeed they were all Kings then! What a time it must have been!

18 Though the Mind through its weakness may yield the Body to physical punishment, yet weak and frail as it is, our Immateriality has ever a sufficient Guard to protect it from Material persecution. This Guard is a self-saving principle. 'Tis the kinder watches of our Lives. That Spirit that never dies in the breast of Man as long as Life holds the Inner Tennement; and when at length the Living principle reaches the Threshold, and is ready to flicker off into the Unknown Void, it still clings to Man and watches with him, 'til the Soul departs. It is that which in a small "small voice", but yet loud enough to be heard through all the realms, teaches the Mind to sustain its own Intelligence, teaches us that we are wrong when we are doing wrong, and tells [us] we are right, when we are pursuing the straight onward path of Right. In a word, it is the Part of God which is implanted in Man.

19 Here we see how naturally this Patriarchal form of Government must and will resolve itself into a Despotism. The rise of long and complete control, and absolute power in one individual, is apt to produce the belief that he is not only Head, but Body and All! The Czar of Russia, at one time being told that an individual of eminence was interesting himself in some matter, petulantly exclaimed,-"There is no man of consequence in this empire, but he with whom I am actually speaking, and so long only as I am speaking to him, is he of any consequence"? Now this is what might be termed Egotistical Tyrantism. Despotism requires a step farther still to be taken. The Parent ruling the Body of the Child, supposes he has a right, also, to rule the Mind. He cannot bear a difference of opinion. Here he becomes a despot. The Child, under the influence of the principle of which we have spoken, rejects this Mental Dominion. Force, outbreak, and open collision are the consequence. Friends, retainers and relations are called in to aid the King; these in their turn combine to overthrow him. This kind of union last[s] not long. Each obtains as many followers as he can, whom he supports, and who aid and protect him. Thus arises Feudalism! The Barons attack and rob each other, and the whole in a short time grows into a Brigand! Such is the Finis of Patriarchy. What a miserable history in the way of Government! But can we wonder at this? Can we wonder at such a result, when we recollect that then the Mind of Man was shrouded beneath a foul and heavy eclipse; that then darkness, and ignorance, and superstition covered the land as a shadow. Man literally knew nothing. He was ignorant of almost all the objects around him, of the Earth on which he trod. Of that bright and never-fading canopey above him; of the Great Light Beam; of the Young Maiden Moon, and of those sweet eyes that are ever twinkling and looking [down] from the skies, upon the World below, he knew them not. He thought (and what a thought!) that they were lamps lighted up, by which he could see to wander. Aye, farther and farther into error and crime. He was ignorant of himself, and of course of others. How then could he govern?—

20 It would be an unprofitable and almost impossible task, Gentlemen, as well as an uninteresting one, to detail here a small portion, even, of those forms of Government which have existed through time, to describe their rise, progress, fall, and the causes that impelled each. They are now only known as things that have been, and are not, mere visions of a day,-"The morning Sun brought them to light,/ But they withered away with the dews of night." Let them then rest in the oblivion of ages, and if we should notice them again, it will be but as we list[en] to "A Schoolboy's tale- the wonder of an hour"- It would be unprofitable to mention more, for they teach but the same unerring lesson; it would be impossible and uninteresting from their number and nature. However, we might state here, as a generality, that the cause of the failure must have been owing to the want of a proper notion of Governmental Action, and the most profound and wretched ignorance.

21 Let us then pass on and overtake Time with centuries on his head; through a long, long night of darkness and clouds, without one little star by which to see or feel. But we must not expect, even after so long a vault, to come at once into a cloudless sky and a genial clime. No, for the night was deep, the mists were heavy, and the Sunshine was but dim. The mists of Mind are not like the mists of Heaven,-they clear but slowly.

22 Hence there will be no surprize when we say that the Rule of Tyranny and the Sway of Despotism- with iron hands- were on the World a thousand years ago. The "thinking principle" was not even then the acting principle. The "vital spark" still burned somewhat dimly. Then the strongest arm was the Law-Giver,-and that Government was the Best which ruled the Most! Now I would not wish to be understood as desiring to produce the impression, that this was as bad, or near[ly] as bad as the former. By no means. True, the Tyrannical Despotism of Power still remained. But notwithstanding all this, the passing away of the shadow had commenced; the Light which was to lighten up, and brighten the Minds of Men, though far, very far distant, had yet been kindled. Laws, Society, Life were all better. Man was better. And Government had taken up an onward march. Time rolled on, for when does he linger? No, he never stops or abates his speed, but is ever hurrying on, and will never pause or rest, 'til the circle is completed,-'til his course is finished in that Vast Ocean, the Never-Ending Life of God! And still the progress of Mind and Government was slow and frequently broken. True, there were the Republics of Greece, but they were Republics in name only; true, amid the general gloom and darkness, the sunshine would burst through now and then, illuminating the Earth for a moment, and then passing away. But though the Light did die, the night was not as cheerless as before, for a small Spark was left on which the glow was gathering. And, indeed, when we recollect the trying difficulties with which Mankind had to contend, the almost insurmountable obstacles which were overcome, and the ennobling advancement which has been made in Intelligence, Morals and Laws, the march of Mind and Government becomes a subject of pride. It was not, however, 'til some few centuries prior to the "Aera of the

revival of letters", that the light of Intelligence began, in any full measure, to arouse the Mind of Man to misrule in Government. The nearer we approach [to] the Golden Age of Leo, the nearer do we approximate correct views, and sound principles. But we must be understood as speaking comparatively here, for it would not be expected that Law could have at that time reached any great degree of perfection, when it is not by any means perfect now. During the 13th and 14th centuries there was a rapid acceleration in the Diffusion of Knowledge, and the dissemination of sound and correct philosophical principles. Art and Science then recieved that impulse which has since sent them on "conquering and to conquer". The Mind was not only expanded in the direction of an intelligent every-day existence, but to a more sensible view of those primary principles which form The basis of all just government. That Age might almost be termed the Cradle of Sound Law.

23 Indeed, Gentlemen, an examination of the History of Man will demonstrate the fact, that the pursuit of Knowledge and the progress of Civillization itself, have always been proportional. Whenever Literature and the Fine Arts have been studied, and properly encouraged, eminence, wealth, and rapid increase of National resources have followed. Great are the advantages in every way that arise from a cultivation of Polite Literature.

24 Ignorance not only deprives [us] of these, but it has an influence upon the very existence of a People. What was the cause of the dissolution of those great empires, that are now but "as things that were" so apparent in Europe and Asia? This, and that, may be given as the cause, but the only true reason, Gentlemen, was misrule in Mind- misrule in Government!

25 The Patriarchal form[s] of Government, Despotism, Anarchy, Monarchy, Aristocracy, and Republicanism, are all but different and better degrees of the same principle. They form one long chain, the links of which grow larger and purer as they grow to a termination. They are all indissolubly connected. A mere shadowing forth of difference from end to end. There is an essence of one, -the essence of the whole. It is not surprizing, either, that this likeness should exist. For as Mankind becomes more intelligent, as mental action increases in strength, sô do we expect the web of government gradually to be bettered. And these betterings run each into each. The reason of this is certainly obvious, for we have been mere beings of imitation. We watch narrowly and follow closely the tracks which have already been made. We strike not out boldly and deeply into that unknown sea where something may be that has not been, but knowing that things have been, and recognizing the doctrine that, "there is nothing new under the Sun". We (that is the World) are and have lived satisfied.

26 The Unknown Wonder, that for which the wise and learned have sought with diligence and care, that for which so many days and nights and lives have been spent in vain, and lost,-the Great Secret,-the Phillosopher's Stone, is (if it was only known) expressed in one word. And that is *New*! A New Law; A New Mind. It is not a substance by which all things material can be turned into

gold. That is but the feeble mutterings of Ignorance. However, the cause of the failure is plain. They attempted not to raise the edifice by the moral and mental forces of their Own In-Existence. The square of their judgements was but the square used by those who preceeded them. The compass of their Minds had been encompassed by others. And if in the process of time, we shall become wiser and more learned than our fathers of "Ancient memories", we will add spring and freshness to old age, and vigor to youth, and thus it is to be hoped we will form that kind of Government, which, existing New and seperate, and distinct from all others, will at last be the climax in the way of Government.

27 But, Gentlemen, some may be surprized that it should be stated, that a Monarchy and a Republic, are in any thing akin to each other. A correct examination of the true theory of these two forms of government, will justify what has been said. That there are principles involved in one, which are, and must to a certain extent be involved in the other. That there are forms and rules which extend mutually to each. There is a difference no one will doubt- that there is a similarity, no one can deny. A Monarchy is the One Man Power. One person rules- the rest obey. Take the most absolute Monarchy, and will you find one in which the people have not some power? Where will you find one in which their influence is not felt, to some degree, either in putting up, pulling down, or setting aside? In England, Russia, Prussia, France, Austria, Germany, and in fact throughout the kingdoms of Europe, have we not seen them exerting their powers in rising up against and overthrowing their rulers. When the Corsican Corporal, who built his castles in the air, so high that they burst of their own etheriality, was carrying destruction like a mad whirlwind over the Continent, who were the appealers, and the appealed? The Rulers sued to the People and they gave the power. Kings have Ministers, the Ministers have followers among the crowd, and thus it is at last the People have a portion of the Government. No, Gentlemen, There is no such Thing as an absolute Monarchy---

28 On the other hand, a Republic or Democracy is called a government of the People. Have the people, though, supreme control here? Is there no great power vested in the hands of one individual? The "I forbid it" placed in the hands of the President weighs against two-thirds of the Nation. Thus, then, it would appear from the very nature of things, Democracy or Monarchy absolutely considered cannot exist. Our form of government, however, is the last link in the great chain- the Brightest- the Purest, and the Best!

29 Though a Young People, how do we compare with Great Britain, the most powerful nation on the Globe? What impulses [are there] to noble action, fine feeling and high sentiment in a Government like her's? Her people are crushed into the dust by oppres[s]ion and Tyranny. Hundreds and thousands of families of Children are starved and beggared to pay the yearly income of a Royal Infant! Wretchedness, misery and want are on her thousand hills.

30 It is said that there are, in the city of London, over five thousand persons who do not know their own names! Was there ever such unbounded

ignorance? Here, notwithstanding her general intelligence, is seen the fault in her government. But this will not last always; there is a point beyond which endurance cannot exist,-and though the heart be dead, and the fountains of the soul be dried up in their green places, yet their hands will rise [up] to destroy the Rulers with the dreadful cry of "Bread or Blood!" We are told that we should not abuse England, that she is our Mother. We spurn her,-we call her not by that endearing title. Would a Mother treat her Child so?—

31 With what different feelings do we turn to our own dear land! The Home of the Glad and Free, "the Asylum of the oppressed of all Nations." In the words of our Declaration, we are "all born free and equal"; we do not recognise Birth-Privilliges!

32 The Freedom, Glory, and Happiness of our Country are known throughout the world. At her name the face of the oppressed lightens up with a smile, and the heart grows young with Hope again. Enthusiastic in every thing, we love our Country, her institutions, her fields and hills, her All,—

"Land of the Sunshine, and the wave,
Of dark green mount, and ocean cave,-
Land of the brave, stout heart and Good,
Of wide, wide plain, and wild wild wood,-
Land of the flowing stream and river,
My Own Good Native land Forever,
I've travelled many a weary way,
But now once more I turn to thee,
I love thee more and more on every day,
Land of the Beauteous and the Free!"

33 Cowell, the comedian, in his "Thirty Years" relates a circumstance that happened on board of a vessel, during his voyage to this country. Meeting with a regular Down-Easter, he asked him his name. The man replied- "If you're an Englishman, and I tell you my name, you'll never forget it." "I don't know", said Cowell, "I'm very unfortunate in remembering names." "Oh never mind", replied the other with a comical look, "if you're an Englishman, you can't forget mine". "There", said he, "I am." "Well", replied the Yankee, "My name's *Bunker*! will you ever forget that".

34 Fellow Citizens,-While we love to sing and listen to our Country's praise, we must not think that she is faultless. Many a dark spot still remains upon the fair face of this land. We have faults- many of them. We have candour enough to admit them; we should have firmness enough to set about correcting them. National Vanity, as distinguished from a just and correct Pride, is one. We boast of our strength, our power, our resources, our wealth, our greatness and our glory! In much we approach somewhat too nearly the character of the Brag[g]adocio! We should think well of ourselves, but not too much, if we would wish others to think any good of us. Let me not be misunderstood,-I would be the last one to deprive America of "one jot or tittle" of those deserving honors

which she has so nobly won. I am too proud of her for that. I too well know that almost every foot of ground, and every breath of air, from Maine to Louisiana-from Bunker's heights, to Orlean's plains, is hallowed by some sacred recollection. I know that she has much- much of which to be proud. But that species of vain boasting that makes us declare, that we are superior, at any time, and every time, and in every respect to any people; that a handful of Americans can cope with a thousand of Albion's braves, is bragging a little too much! In the right we will succeed; in the wrong, we are as weak as the weakest. In all of our defensive operations, we have ever been successful; when we acted on the offensive we always failed. As a Nation we want Self Respect/ It is wonderful with Vanity [that] we should lack sufficient Self Respect. Nevertheless it is true. We need a mind of our own. We have been borrowing from abroad,-and where? If our ancient enemy be so inimical to us, and we to her, why do we so slavishly follow her in matters of Mind? It is a shame and disgrace upon our People, that we look up to England for every thing great and sublime in Literature and Art. We look to her for criticism, praise, and even for the very success of our own works. We have genius here; we have phillosophers, historians, critics, poets, novelists, equal to any that have ever written or sung. Why then do we bow to others? Can we not have a standard of our own? We want an American Mind!

35 Again, we are too hasty and exciteable. Every thing that is done, is done in heat and hurry. Our political strifes and prejudices are carried beyond measure. Questions of policy- our domestic relations- whether this or that man shall be raised to the Presidential chair, all become serious and dangerous subjects of contention.

36 But, Fellow Citizens, the darkest and most fell Spirit that has yet come upon our land, has risen in the shape of a party who call themselves "Native Americans". They deserve not that name. They have brought disgrace and infamy, almost, upon our Country. They have committed riots and disturbances in a peaceful city of this Union, and have reduced her to a state almost similar to [that of] Paris during the French Revolution. They have acted as incendiaries; they have taken the lives of in[n]ocent people; they have turned helpless families of women and children [out] into the open air; they have desecrated and destroyed the temples of the Ever-Living God. As their name indicates, their efforts are directed against the immigration of foreigners, and especially Irishmen, into the United States. Our Country is called the Home of the Oppressed. We are made up of foreigners. The real Native Americans have passed away; their footsteps are dying in the forests of the far West; they are the children of the Setting Sun. The best blood, the wisest heads, the bravest hearts, the strongest arms in our land are foreigners; and the largest and best portion of them are Irishmen or their descendants. They came to our peaceful and happy Country;-they had The principles of Liberty instilled into their bosoms;-some returned again to their native land, and are now attempting to follow our path, to overthrow British oppression- to raise the flag of Freedom on Europa's shores. Our hearts and hands are with them. "Oh Erin, Green Erin, mayst thou

yet be Free,/ First Star of the World- and First Gem of the Sea!" It should be the duty of every true lover of his Country to use his best influence in putting down this self-styled "Native American" party.

37 With all her faults, we love our Country well. Nearly seventy years have passed away, and she has stood the shocks of time, amid the sneers of enemies, and the fears of friends. We have succeeded- man is capable of self-government.

38 The March of Freedom is ever onward. "Many must suffer defeat, and many must taste of death, but Freedom's battles will yet be fought and won". The time will come when the same Sun of Liberty that sheds its beams upon our own land, will extend its influence from the frozen regions of the North, far, far away upon the sunny lands of The South, "that secret shore/Where Freedom lifts her banner to the sky,/ And the Glorious Stripes and Stars below,/ Are mingled with the Joyous Stars on High!" Then there will be but One Principle, [and] that Freedom,-There will be but One Government, [and] that, The Repu[blic] of the *World*!

Oration Delivered by Darius Cadwell in Andover, Ohio, July 4, 1847, Manuscript in Cadwell Papers, Western Reserve Historical Society (Cleveland). In the following text, the reader will acquire a good grasp of Cadwell's revision process. Especially since six passages in this 1847 oration are based upon segments of an oration delivered by Cadwell, the previous year, on July 3 at Eagleville, Ohio. And the reader will note that when such comparisons are made between the Eagleville and Andover texts, **E** *designates Eagleville and* **A** *the Andover text.*

1 I regret that since I promised your Committee to address you to-day, I have had no more time, which I *could* share for the preparing of an address for this occasion. You all know that the text from which you expect me to preach to-day has been rung through all its changes, and it requires of me much time and reflection in order that my remarks may even command attention. But as we have met, to bring back from past years a day we love to think and speak of, an old day from old time, it would hardly be justice that I should leave behind, *all* old scenes and dates, and facts, for new, unbroken ground, upon which to build some wild Utopian scheme, which could only please for the moment, and fade from both mind and memory as the sound of my voice dies upon the ear. We have met, not to canvass the political character of any aspiring demagogue, nor the claims of any political party: but upon common ground, without distinction of age, party or sex, to celebrate the seventy first anniversary of our nation's independance; a day dear to the hearts of all, the birth day of our Freedom, a day which of itself is no more than any other day, but taken with the associations which crowd around, and cling to it, becomes enchantment, and then its very name, like a chain of electricity, connects and thrills at the same time every *true* American heart, and makes them all beat in unison. But why do we celebrate *this* day?

2 Now in order to answer this question, it is necessary to raise for a moment, the veil of the past. But do not suppose that I am about to enter into any lengthy details of the preliminaries which led to the revolution, nor the many interesting scenes which characterized that most notable and successful struggle. it would be tresspassing too much upon your time and patience, and questioning too seriously your intelligence. I only deem it necessary to barely glance at a few prominent features in the history of our country, familiar to us all, to be sure, but which may serve to bring more vividly before our eyes the remembrance of the past.

draft E Still I ask you to send your thoughts, with mine away over all the busy scenes to the East, until they rest on Plymouth rock, not as it is to-day, but as it was on the 22d. day of Dec[ember]. 1620. Where a little, weary band of Pilgrims had just quitted the pitiless storms of the Deep, upon that dreary, cheerless shore. Where none but savage foot had ever trod, the high waves, roaring and dashing with wild and reckless fury upon the shore. While the Winter storm rides on, and with darkened Brow and withering breath trumpets loudly the desolation that is reigning there. Yet, they are happy. There went up from that little band a sound of thanksgiving and rejoicing which reached far above the commotion that surrounded them. They had found what they sought. "A faith's pure shrine".

draft A amplified

Go then with me back through a period of 226 years and far away upon the Atlantic shore, and see what is passing there. It is a cold, bleak day in December. the huge waves of old ocean white-capped with foam, rearing high their heads, are chasing, and dashing each other, with relentless fury against the rock-bound coast, bearing upon their bosom, a ship, which nears the rock and disembarks a noble worthy few, who had left all the endearments of home and friends, all the attachments of their Father-land, encountered the pitiless storms of the deep, and now here upon this wild shore, where none but savage foot had ever trod, the Winter wind moans dismally through the tall forest trees. While the storm-god, rides on and with darkened brow and withering breath trumpets loudly the desolation that is reigning there. Yes here are the pilgrim fathers, of the Mayflower. Just landed upon Plymouth rock, and amid all the dismal scenes that surround them, strange as it may seem, they are happy. Their expectations are gratified. They have gained all they wished, all they asked, "A faith's pure shrine".

Here is no turbaned Pope to dictate. No inquisitorial instruments to torture for disobeying. Here they may *act* what *conscience* dictates, and thoughts and words be as free as the breeze that floats over New England's Hills. Here was liberty to worship God in their own way. This boon has descended to *us*, and **E** WE WILL NEVER YEIELD [YIELD] IT UP **A** when *we* give it up, it will be tendered upon our latest breath. ☆

draft E Here might have been discovered the first spark of Liberty, feeble, faint and dim, but that spark has swelled to a flame, which cannot be quenched.

draft A amplified

Here was Liberty in embryo. Yes, the first spark that ever glowed upon the Western Continent, save the wild freedom of the savage and the brute. a small spark, but it has been fed, and fanned until it has burst into a flame, which has been and we believe will be, unquenchable. Indeed how can it be otherwise?

Oh, Liberty, can man resign thee,
Once having felt thy glorious flaeme [flame]?
Can tyrants' bolts and bars confine thee
And thus thy noble spirit tame?

Never, never! Tyrants should have known this truth long ago, but sad experience has taught it them now. One colony after another sprang up, im[m]igration increased, the forest fled before the woodman's axe, and farms, towns and villages, supplied its place. The Genius of Liberty dwelt among them. The mountain range, the glen and wild-wood, the river, lake and cataract, were all congeniel[congenial] to its growth and development. The gory Eagle looks not disinterestedly from his sentinel rock, upon the soaring dove. The wolf sleeps not when a lamb skips before his den: neither could the envious jealous eye of Great Britain look calmly upon the increasing wealth and happiness of the Western world. She saw a flame increasing there, destined to melt the chain that bound us to her, and sought to keep it down by throwing over us a chain of Despotism and Tyran[n]y. It fell like a rope of sand upon the necks of the sons of those pilgrims, and the descendants of the noble hardy im[m]igrants. They knew the rights which were guarantied to them by the British Constitution, the rights which nature and nature's God gave them, and dared to resist the arm that should attempt to wrest those rights from them. Still, forbearance was not forgotten. Insult was swallowed, until injury heaped upon it, and tramped down by an iron heel, became too grievous to be borne. When they found it useless [any] longer to ask protection, where only oppression was given. Thus it was that they boldly set their foot against the rock, declared themselves independant, and enrolled their name in glaring Capitals upon the list of Nations. This was done upon the 4th. day of July 1776. That was the first day our nation had a name, an identity. In that old Hall at Philadelphia, was to be seen a band of men, worthy of their country and its cause, who were now called upon to exercise the utmost, caution, candor and judgement/ The eye of the world was upon them. The eye of Omnipotence was not hid. Upon their act of that day, hung as upon a pivot, the future destiny of the Western world. The vote they were about to record was to stand a bright monument, of their glory and fame, or a bye-word for taunting, contemptuous tyrants to scoff at and ridicule. Honor to their immortal names they dared to record it. A resolution was offered to the effect, "that the Colonies were and of right ought to be free and independant States, and all political connection between them and Great Britain dissolved."

Here we may imagine a scene of **E** DEEP AWFUL THRILLING **A** most exciting☆interest. Some hesitated in doubt, others **E** FEARED **A** trembled fearing☆the consequences of a failure. Upon one side you might have seen a **E** MEMBER **A** member rising, ☆ and with pale face and quivering lip **E** ,SAYING **A** declaring, ☆ "This step once taken can never be retraced. I shudder before this responsibility. It will be upon us. it will be upon us, if failing to maintain this Declaration, a sterner despotism, maintained by military power, shall be established over our posterity. When **E** WE OURSELVES **A** we, ☆ given up by an exhausted, harrassed, and misled people, shall have expiated our rashness and attoned for our presumption on the scaffold." Aye, that spirit was there, **E** THANKS TO HIGH HEAVEN **A** but☆it did not prevail. Every doubt was removed, every fear **E** EXPELLED **A** expelled, and every nerve quieted and strengthened, ☆ by the burning eloquence which fell from the lips of those who chose death in any of all its hideous forms, rather than **E** CROUCH AT THE FEET OF TYRANTS **A** bend their necks to the adamantine chain of a relentless Tyrant. ☆ Turn to the other side of the hall, where stands a man whose face, and words, and gestures, would have paled the **E** CHEEK **A** face☆of a Nero and nerved a dying man for war,-crying "Sink or swim. Survive or perish. I am for the Declaration. It is my living sentiment and it shall be my dying sentiment. Independance now and Independance forever." A pause, solemn as the night of the grave, when the commanding figure of John **E** HANCOCK **A** Hancock the President ☆ arose, and asks, "Shall the Resolution pass"? One unanimous Aye, resounded and reechoed, round and round that hall. the proud bird of Jove, the American **E** EAGLE **A** Eagle, catching this first loud note of freedom, ☆ leaves his lofty height, seizes the British Lion **E** IN HIS TALONS **A** by the mane ☆ **E** .THRUST HIM DOWN TO EARTH, AND WITH WIDE EXTENDED WINGS **A** ,and bearing him off in triumph ☆ utters the shrill **E** CRY **A**,clear notes ☆ of Liberty! Victory! Independance! which was echoed from every hill, and upon the breeze wafted to every Land. The declaration of Independance was **E** SIGNED **A** published, and declared that day, and shortly after signed. ☆

What must have been the wonder, astonishment and admiration of all nations, to behold the most remarkable, public paper of any nation or time, issuing from so feeble a source, and thus boldly and unequivocally reciting the long continued wrongs they had suffered, and as planily[plainly] asserting the rights that were inalienably theirs, and pledging their lives, their fortunes and sacred honor to maintain them. It has not yet ceased to be the wonder of the world. Rising Generations gaze upon it, and trace the Autographs of its signers, which of themselves, speak the language of bold determination, and conscious power. You may now hold up to your children, this "im[m]ortal littl[e] Deed of our Liberties," and point them to the "noblest richest legacy, that ever could be bequeathed." This movement was looked upon with contempt, as a puny effort, by Britain: but future events, showed them that the arm of Oppression cannot cope with the arm of right when nerved by the God of battles. Action, brave, energetic action followed, and secured to them, to us, and we trust to our posterity for all coming time, the rights which were theirs. The signers of the Declaration have long since gone to their rest, and in every true American bosom stands a monument, sacred to their memory. The shafts of death could not be turned aside from the surviving heroes of that Revolutionary struggle; but ever and anon, the funeral knell, tells us that another and another of those great hearts has ceased to beat. A few yet live to tell the t[a]l[e]. Standing, like the lightning-shrived oak, upon the mountain's brow. Their heads are bending low over the verge of the grave, where they must soon sleep, but not to be forgotten.

3 But I must not dwell [any] longer, upon equally familiar scenes, such as the first treaty of peace, the attempt made in 1812 to again subvert our rights, the triumph of our arms, and final settlement of peace. I have only alluded to what I have, to show the reason and propriety of celebrating this day. Now let us step from that past, down towards this present.

4 Friends! Whereever the Banner of Freedom waves, wherever peace and liberty prevail, there may be seen as their legitimate offspring, enterprize, industry, intelligence and boundless improvement. Mark the contrast, between this day, and the same day of the same month 70 years ago.

Had I stood then where I **E** STAND NOW **A** now stand, ☆ how different would have been the **E** SCENE. HOW DIFFERENT MY FEELINGS? **A** scene. ☆ Instead of this group of smiling faces and sparkling eyes, indexes to so many honest happy hearts, I might have seen the bear guarding her young, the panther crouching for his prey, the deer and elk drinking from yonder brook or **E** GRAZING UPON **A** eating ☆ the tender **E** HERB **A** herb that grew upon its bank, ☆ while the **E** DARK FLASHING EYE AND THE BRAWNY ARM OF THE RED MAN **A** red-browed ranger of the forest, ☆ aimed at their hearts the **E** SHAFT **A** rude instrument ☆ of death. These fields which now **E** ARE BURDENED WITH THE FARMER'S GRAIN **A** smile under the influence of cultivation, and these hard trodden roads, ☆ held firmly the deep rooted forest tree. Yes within 30 years you could scarce find here any other thoroughfare than that designated by marked trees, or the trail of the straying kine[cows], and the place, where we now seek shelter from the sun's rays, would have been shunned as the abode of loneliness and melancholy. **E** CAST **A** Direct ☆ your eye to **E** ANY **A** whatever ☆ point of the **E** COMPASS **A** compass you choose, ☆ and where **E** THEN **A** ,but a few years since, ☆ **E** WAS ONLY TO BE SEEN THE WIGWAM **A** the forest stood unbroken, in all its native wildness and grandeur, ☆ now **E** STAND **A** are blooming fields, thriving towns and villages, and splendid ☆ cities, crowded with a busy **E** THRONG **A** throng, gathered from almost every nation of the earth: ☆ Where was only the Indian trail, now are turnpikes, canals and rail-roads. **E** THE MAIL ROUT[E], WHER[E] **A** Where ☆ news **E** PLOD[D]ED **A** only plod[d]ed slowly ☆ upon a **E** HORSE'S **A** man's, or horse's ☆ back, now by means of the **E** TELEGRAPH **A** magnetic telegraph, ☆ [it] flies **E** QUI[I]CKER THAN THOUGHT **A** upon the lightning's wings. ☆ Our own **E** BEAUTIFUL LAKE **A** lake ☆ Erie, then **E** RUFFLED ONLY BY THE WIND **A** only broken save by the bark canoe, or the tempest, ☆ is now **E** PLOUGHED **A** checkered ☆ by hundreds of keels, and ornamented by **E** A THOUSAND **A** thousands of ☆ sails. When the only valuable thing afloat upon its bosom was the water fowl, now **E** FILLING OUR COUNTRY WITH WEALTH **A** bearing, millions of wealth from all parts of the earth, ☆ and **E** SUPPLYING THE WANTS OF THE NEEDY, AND BEARING INTELLIGENCE TO THE IGNORANT **A** for all conditions of men. ☆ **E** STILL THIS SPIRIT OF ENTERPRISE CEASES NOT **A** The waves of the Atlantic which rolled so wildly and uselessly to the shore, now most welcome, come familiarly home, bearing the wealth of other climes, and the people of other lands. ☆ And all these are the **E** RESULT **A** fruits ☆ of freedom **E** OF THOUGHT AND ACTION **A** ,industry ☆ and **E** AN HONORABLE PEACE WITH THE NATIONS OF THE EARTH **A** honorable peace. ☆

5 Shall these causes be continued, and these results, these priveleges, still be ours? Is a question for our consideration.

6 Peace! Yes Peace is what we all desire. For happiness is the fortune sought by all mankind, and who does not know full well that that scene in the great drama of life, can never be reached unless Peace speak the prologue. It is what nature dictates, and what God intends. For more than 30 years, (save the last) when our citizens have met to commemorate this day, the joyful proclama-

tion, could be truly made that we were at peace as a nation, with all the world. This, all did hope, might be as truly said of us forever. But a little more than one year ago, we in our fancy could hear the sullen growl of the British Lion coming over the Atlantic, rising at the North West, with a scowl upon its brow, portentous of a dire event. But its wrath is appeased. The Oregon question is settled. The partition line is fixed. The spirit of peace, is again, passing and repassing between England and America, resting upon either shore, and dipping her spotless wings in the calm blue wave. While the white flag waves in triumph over the heads of English and American, Statesmen, legislators and people.

7 Yet it cannot be said that we are now at peace with all the nations of the earth.

E FOR WHEN WE TURN **a** Turn ☆ your eyes to the South **E** WEST **A** West, far away to the plains of Monterrey, Buena Vista, Vera Cruz and Cerro Gordo. ☆ See the bright steel flashing in the **E** SUN LIGHT **A** sunlight, Armies swiftly forming for battle, and smoke and fire, and death belching from the deep-mouthed cannon. ☆ **E** THE DIN OF BATTLE, AND THE WAR SHOUT ARE HEARD **A** Hear the horrid din of Battle, the war-shout, and the heavy tramp of charging steeds. This is "the pomp and circumstance of Glorious War." ☆ But look again! Where is the field of **E** POMP AND WARLIKE **A** glory and ☆ splendor now? **E** CHANGED TO BLOOD, PAIN AND GROANINGS AND DEATH **A** Deluged with blood! Filled with, groanings anguish and death! The dying heaped up, and lying among the dead, biting the dust in bitter agony. ☆ Look at the **E** FLAMING EYE OF THE **A** eye of the still surviving ☆ soldier, but **E** A SHORT TIME SINCE **A** yesterday, ☆ kindled with vengeance and desperation, now swol[l]en with weeping and still wet with tears, his war cry turned to a sigh, as he lays the mangled corpses of his comrades, side by side in one **E** DEEP, WIDE **A** wide deep ☆ **E** GRAVE **A** grave of a foreign land, ☆ to rest 'til the trump of God shall call them.

See the Mexican females, still true to humanity, love and kindness, which ever reign in woman's heart, administering to the wants of friend and foe, but searching with streaming eyes and breaking hearts for the loved form of a brother, husband, son or lover, to take the last look, and clip a precious lock from the brow of the brave, as a treasure and remembrance of love and affection. Nor does the warrior *only*, die.

War hastens on his messengers of death.
While foe meets foe, and heeds *them* not,
Nor the Stygian ferryman, who plies his boat,
Swiftly, 'twixt shores of past and future,
The demon by enchantment sways the breast
Of every warrior, and friends and home are all forgot.
For every humane feeling of the human breast is lost,
And savage, brutal fury, reigns triumphant there.
Yet woman still the same calls out for peace,
And shrinks for safety by the thickest wall.
Yea within the walls of God's own house,
Where peace and mercy ever had been sought

And hoping still, the ball, the shot and shell
Would venture not to desecrate the sacred place.
A group of kneeling females, 'round the holy shrine
With eyes upraised to Heaven and breathing prayers
For fathers, lovers, husbands, brothers,
But all in vain! Hark! where comes
A shell, hissing as sent from hellish engine
Through the roof, and lighting on the altar
Bursts: scattering death to each of those pure hearts.
Upon that tablet, where the bread of life
Had been so often broken and dispensed,
Now shoots the death-dart of inhuman war
And all that lovely group lie dying, dead!
Oh God! what had they done to merit this?

Yet such is war. Nor is this all. There are many widowed, bleeding hearts of our country-women, far away from the scene of action, who could envy these Mexican women their sudden death. Those who have traced down the colum[n] and list of dead, till the eye rested upon the fatal risk that traces the name of the partner of her youth and her love, the father of the prat[t]ling orphan at her knee. He sleeps in a foreign land. No tear moistens his grave, no monument or stone marks where he lies. She turns with broken heart from the world, and asks for aid only at the hands of death.

8 It is true that American arms are victorious. Our national flag with its stripes and stars floats gracefully over the Capitol, but upon the late battle field it hangs at half mast, stiff and red with the blood of a Ringold, a Clay, a Hardin and McKee, while the wind, striving to toss it on high, mourns a sad requiem over the departed brave.

9 As I said before, I am not here to canvass the political acts of political men/ neither do I take it upon me now to say, whether the present war with Mexico is right or wrong. Yet I am bold in saying: that no one here wished for it, no eye here can be so dazzled and shut by the pomp and glory of war as not to behold its horrors. You cannot turn from its closing scenes: You cannot stop your ears to the wailing of widows and orphans, heralded upon the Southern gale. We would all have avoided it, if possible, although we believe the war of the Revolution to have been right, and glory in its results. And who takes pleasure in its blood/ your voices still cry out for peace. So dire a calamity as war demands it. When the war-cloud bursts, it sends a storm more scathing than the Simoom of Africa, more devastating than the tornado of the West Indies. May the breath of Omnipotence, sweep it far away and the spirit of peace rest upon the Rio Grande as upon the Columbia.

E YET WERE THIS WAR AT AN END, WERE WE TRULY

A Although, no nation can prosper, while expending large quantities of treasure and blood in war, yet were we ☆ at peace with **E** THE WORLD; **A** all the nations of the earth, ☆ **E** WHAT THEN? ARE WE FREE FROM DANGER? **A** it would not certainly follow that prosperity and happiness and our Liberties would be secured to us. ☆ Do you as individuals, while in health, look for danger from no where but without? Do you fear death only when you know that the assassin prowls about your **E** CHAMBER **A** chamber at night, ☆ **E** WHEN **A** only when ☆ death stares you boldly in the face? Or do you not **E** REMEMBER **A** know and feel ☆ that the grim monster, prostrates the strongest guard, and **E** BATTERS **A** undermines or batters ☆ down the thickest wall, to reach your citadel of life. Though no one points the dagger **E** TO YOUR HEART **A** at your breast, no tomahawk lifted over your head, ☆ yet you do not expect to live forever. Then shall this **E** NATION **A** nation look only to outward foe, and ☆ when the war cry is hushed, when no trumpet calls to arms, rest, in ease and quietude, **E** BUILDING **A** building upon sandy foundations, ☆ **E** AIRY CASTLES **A** castles ☆ of happiness, and **E** DREAMING **A** slumbering dream ☆ of future bliss? No. **E** NO! NO! **A** Never! ☆ American Citizens awake! look about you, look within for **E** EVERY PORTION/PART **A** in portion[s] ☆ of this nation, yea in its very bosom **E** ARE **A** are the seeds of death. In its very bosom, are ☆ slumbering volcanoes and **E** GATHERING **A** pent up gathering ☆ storms, which once loosed will overwhelm, and swallow up the last vestage of freedom, and **E** CRUMBLE/SHIVER **A** shiver ☆ the fabric of our government to atoms.

There are evils in our government to-day, which call to us in tones of thunder for redress, while the Chancellor of Heaven is recording the complaints and prayers of suffering humanity. Licentiousness, pollution, crime and intemperance are sweeping thousands of our countrymen to the regions of despair, and more than three millions of American born citizens are to-day groaning under the tormenting lash. Who does not tremble at such thoughts as these. Could the ghosts of our Revolutionary fathers arise before us, we should hide our faces for shame, and shrink back like McBeth before the ghost of Banquo, and beg them to return to the regions of the dead, and not open their mouths against us.

Those men fought for freedom, right **E** JUSTICE AND VIRTUE **A** and justice, ☆ and we could not withstand the rebuke, which they would give. **E** YES, THEY WERE BRAVE, VIRTUOUS, HONEST MEN AND MY BLOOD BOILS WITH INDIGNATION, WHEN I HEAR THEIR NAMES VILIFIED, AND AN ATTEMPT MADE TO BRAND THEIR MEMORIES WITH INFAMY, FOR IT HAS BEEN DONE IN YOUR OWN STATE AND COUNTY —**A** Upon beholding our degeneracy. ☆ **E** NO ONE CAN DENY **A** Now we feel, and know ☆ that these evils do exist. **E** YET DEEP AND DAMNING AS THEY ARE, **A** and the history of the past, tells us in language not to be mistaken, that although they are not like the whirlwind of beseiging armies, swift to destroy, yet their final destination, is equally dissolution and death, if permitted to continue. ☆ Must they **E** SO REMAIN **A** remain, ☆ or can they be eradicated?

Draft E They need not remain. I believe there is intelligence and virtue and moral power sufficient yet to correct them all, and I do not believe it necessary to dissolve this Union, and annihilate every thing good, all our institutions, civil and religious, in order to effect it. We the people of Ashtabula County are in a great measure free from them. There are no clanking chains here.

draft A amplified

We believe their progress can be arrested. The star of Hope is not yet extinguished. We all regret, Oh, how deeply! that when the first blow of freedom was struck, it did not break every yoke, and sunder every chain that bound man to his fellow man. That the first note of Liberty, taught to echo in that old Hall at Philadelphia, did not touch every heart, and tune every string. But of such an event we will not despair! The sun of reason shines over the whole Northern portion of our Union, and many a ray of light is striking down into the darkness of the South.

11 The little Army Temperance men, who but a few years ago, were scarcely able to bear their banner, have now swelled to a host whose tramp shakes the earth.

12 Thousands of the victims of licentiousness and crime, are being redeemed and reformed, becoming, men and women, useful members of society. Intelligence, lear[n]ing, improvement in the arts and sciences are moving on with rapid strides. And is there not virtue, and moral power yet among us, to save our country, to avert any threatened ruin. The evils of which I have spoken are scarcely known among the people of this County. Yet we are a part of the whole. It is our duty. Yea we ar[e] called upon by all that is sacred and just to put forth every effort, to preserve the Liberties we now enjoy, and extend them to every human being in our land, whatever may be his color or condition. Upon [us] rest great responsibilities/ We act not only for ourselves, but for all those around us now, and for generations who are to follow us. The great ship of life is gliding swiftly down the stream of time. She is constantly casting her passengers overboard, and when she reaches the utmost boun[d]ary of this generation and has buried its last man in the wave of death, she will still float on to futurity, yea to eternity, deeply laden with our actions.

13 When this is done, How shall be read the page of the future historian in regard to us. shall it be then said: that by our constant battling for the right: by our firm adheranc[e] to truth and justice, by our energy, prudence and perseverance, we have saved the rights bought by the lives of our Fathers, and handed them down to our posterity, a glorious inheritance: that we have preserved, unbroken, the grand structure of our Union, bound by the strongest ties of Nature, interest and consanguinity, and cemented by the best blood that ever coursed [through] the veins of man: or shall it be said, that by our negligence, rashness, imprudence and folly, we have strengthen[e]d the bonds of the oppressed, created internal dissentions, wasted our energies upon useless, impracticable theories, encouraged vice and crime, waged foreign wars of conquest, and thus wasted our inheritance, uprooted the strong holds of Freedom and demolished its temples, sundered wide the ties that hold the Union together: buried in oblivion this nation's identity, spread over the face of this fair land, the carnage of civil war: left the people in anarchy, to be collected under the banner of military despotism, or proud aristocracy, and proven the truth of the haughty boast of crowned heads, "That a Republic cannot stand."

14 Which of these alternatives you choose, I need not ask.

15 Here are the aged father and mother, who have encountered and overcome the toils, privations and wants incident to a new country/ They have converted the wilderness into a garden and led their children up to enjoy the fruits of their labor. Your heads are bowed with the weight of many years. The grave will soon be your resting place. But is it not a consoling, happy thought, that your children and grand-children have been, and are being educated in a Christian land, and are now enjoying the facilities, which guide to happiness and virtuous intelligence?

16 Here are the middle aged and the young. The present support of our country, and upon whom rests the responsibility of prompt, immediate and right, action. All these children, upon whom rests the entire hope of the future, are watching you.—Shaping their minds and actions after yours. Oh. Then how important our duty, how important that we shrink not from it. Let us then forever be found guarding our own rights, and battling bravely for the rights and happiness of our countrymen, which are truly theirs, but which they now fail to enjoy. Despair not of effecting either. The virtue and intelligence of our country, aided by Omnipotence, is sufficient to sweep away every, cloud of oppression, and the last vestage of intemperance, licentiousness and crime. God speed the dawning of such a day and may its sun never set, until the last moment of time is recorded.

Oration Delivered by Andrew Griswold Whitney in Detroit, Michigan, July 4, 1818, Manuscript in William Woodbridge Papers, Burton Historical Collection of Detroit Public Library.

Whitney probably adapted paragraphs 22 thru 32 below from the egalitarian spirit of a tribute paid George Washington by Louis Jean Pierre Marquis de Fontanes at the Temple de Mars in Paris on 9 Feb., 1800. An article in the daily *Commercial Advertiser* (NY City) for 15 May, 1826, attributes an "elegant" translation of Fontane's eulogy to Whitney during 1816, a year confirmed the next day by the semiweekly *Spectator.* Indeed, no text of such a Whitney translation apparently has survived, whether published by Francis Hall or another editorial "we" in some press source other than the *Advertiser/Spectator* or a pamphlet reprint. Yet a careful collation of sentences 2 and 3 in paragraph 27 with the final three sentences on page 11 of a French edition in the Rare Book Room at the Library of Congress illustrates the precise manner in which Whitney set about oralizing his "elegant" translation to fit not only paragraph 27, but paragraphs 24, 30, and 31 as well.

Consider sentence 2 of paragraph 27 as a case in point. Two other contemporary translations, the first by "L.M." in the Albany [N.Y.] *Daily Advertiser* for 12 May, 1826, and a second taken from pages 316 and 317 of the *Columbian Phenix and Boston Review* for May, 1800, give a literal rendition of the original French, something Whitney's amplified paraphrase fails to do, regardless of how his lost "elegant" translation may have read.

First the original Fontane version in French, then the *Advertiser-Phenix* translations, followed by Whitney's slightly modified paraphrase. Letter *F carries over to the second paradigm.

> Fontane, sentence 2: Dans les triomphes et dans (B **l'adversite**) ,il fut (*F toujours) (A **tranquille**) comme (D la sagesse) ,et (C **simple**) comme (E la vertu) .
>
> Adv-Ph: In **success/triumph** and in (B **adversity/defeat**) ,he was always (A **tranquil) like/as (A tranquil) as (D wisdom) ,and (C plain) like/,as (C simple) as (E virtue).**
>
> Whitney: [He was] (A calm *and* collected) in (B defeat *and* disaster) , (C humble *and* grateful) in victory.

Observe that Whitney amplifies ABC words to achieve greater oral effect, in each of the three instances above resorting to a pair of words linked by "and." Parallel oral amplification, perhaps as much florid as oral, occurs elsewhere relating to DE, two words Whitney excludes from this particular paraphrase. In paragraph 24, sentence 1, for example, Whitney revises to "*steady sober* (D wisdom)," two modifiers strikingly similar in paired meaning to Whitn-A though of course not linked by "and." Whitney does use "and" with word-E, however, in sentence 4 of paragraph 30, and in sentence 2 of paragraph 31. In paragraph 30, "labors *and* (E virtues) *and* sacrifices" attest to Washington's "*greatly good and goodly great*" niche among the fabled heroes of ancient Athens or Rome. And in paragraph 31, Whitney incorporates word-E into a paired possessive with "country" to achieve an oral imperative more timeless in effect. Every American citizen "that loves (E virtue) *or* his *country*," Whitney's first pair, should perpetuate Washington's name in time present and future, a projection not inconsistent with "sacred recollections" of past antiquity, "for (E virtue's) *and* his *country's* sake," the emphatic pair and possessive. Whitney's use of "wisdom" and "virtue" doubtless reverts back to his lost translation, though the amplified paired-orality accompanying either word stems, at least in part, from his paraphrase technique in sentence 2 of paragraph 27.

Sentence 3 of paragraph 27 points up a somewhat different oral adaptation, since Whitney places it in direct quotes unlike sentence 2. In this paradigm, the sign *not adpt* designates some eighteen French words not adapted by Whitney. While nine words at the start of Fontane-Sentence 3 ("Les affections douces resterent au fond de son coeur" *tr* by Adv-Ph to "His mild affections remained at the bottom of his heart/The finer feelings of the heart never abandoned him"), a clause without question not adapted by Whitney, are replaced with an ellipsis so as not to confuse the reader.

> Fontane, sentences 1 and 3:((*not adpt* Au milieu de tous les désordres des camps et de tous les excès inséparables de la guerre civile)), (D l'humanité se réfugia) (A sous sa tente) , (D et n'en fut jamais repoussée) . . . . (B même dans ces momens où) (C l'intérêt de sa propre cause semblait légitimer en quelque sorte les lois de la vengeance) .
>
> Adv-Ph: ((*not adpt* **Amid/-st** all the disorders of **the camp and/camps**, amidst all the excesses inseparable from a civil war)) , (D humanity **sought/took** refuge) (A in his tent) , (D **nor was it ever/and was never** repulsed) . . . . (B even in those moments when) (C his own interest **,in some manner, rendered the laws of vengeance justifiable/would seem to justify a recurrence to the laws of vengeance**) .
>
> Whitney: (A In his tent) , (B even when) (C retaliation might justify severity) , (D humanity) (·F always) (D took refuge and was never repulsed).

Here Whitney borrows elements from all three Fontane sentences. The emphatic "always"-·F derives from "toujours" in the previous paradigm (Fontane-sentence 2), not from any loose interpretation of "tous," "désordres," and "excès," even though "excès" at first glance logically seems capable of bringing forth "severe" degrees of "retaliation" in kind (Whitn-C). "In his tent, humanity *took* refuge *and was never repulsed*" (Whitn-AD) comes from Fontane-sentence 1 in this paradigm, and matches the *Phenix* translation except for a slight juxtaposition in word order.

The most fascinating clause above, "even when retaliation might justify severity" (Whitn-BC), orally compresses the segment inserted from Fontane's third sentence. Despite Fontane obviously speaking through the printed text of the eulogy, Whitney discards what seem written qualifiers more than anything else, phrases like "dans ces momens" and "en quelque sorte," settling instead upon an orally incisive "retaliation" (over "rendered" or "recurrence"), magnified by "severity" of degree (over "les lois de la *vengeance*"). In short, "retaliation" is heightened by "severity" in an orally emphatic manner, and specifies a more personalized application of an otherwise hypothetical and abstract "vengeance." The oral stylistic impact in sentence 3 of paragraph 27 clearly derives from some adaptation performed by Whitney, and may even represent a significant departure beyond his lost translation, problematically "elegant" though that may have been.

Whitney delivered his oration on the Fourth before a joint meeting of city fathers and lyceum members at the Detroit Council-House, as paragraph 62 amply demonstrates. Arrangements for a separate "club" celebration were made by the lyceum on 20 June, only to be joined in by a local citizens' meeting two days later. The fact that Whitney served both groups, the lyceum as corresponding secretary who would have to contact any orator chosen for such an occasion, and the city corporation as a member of a committee appointed to give dead from the River-Raisin battlefield a respectable burial within the city, may have led to his selection as speaker.

Friend Charles Larned, lyceum president-elect who read the Declaration of Independence immediately preceding Whitney's oration, probably was privy to the Fontane link when he toasted Whitney's effort in these rather flattering terms at the dinner following the joint ceremony: "The purity of his style is only surpassed by the purity of his heart." Drawing out the head-heart allusion relied on by romanticist Larned, the creative impulse for the oration could be found in a "pure" resolve by Whitney to adapt Fontane's national eulogy into a doubly "pure" native style, national purpose and oral improvement presumably diminishing any lack of cultural originality on Whitney's part.

Nor did friend Ebenezer Reed, lyceum recording secretary and editor of the Detroit *Gazette* with John P. Sheldon, another lyceum member probably attending the ceremony, mince any words in printing what he termed Whitney's "truly excellent production" in two installments on the seventeenth and twenty-fourth. By patronizing a friend's convenient specimen of "native genius and talents and learning," Reed did not seize upon the label "excellent" lightly, since he regarded it as an "excellent" opportunity for editors like himself to impart romantic "activity" and direction to community aspirations. If Whitney could favor the *Gazette* editors with a flattering report on their conduct at the lyceum meeting of 31 March, editor Reed certainly was able to return the favor when an opportunity presented itself.

A note on editorial procedures used in this oration text. Throughout the oration, bold type designates word roots and grammatical structure. Extensive editor's notes detail oral implications not otherwise evident in such rhetorical interaction. Bold type also highlights "sic." misspellings, while questionable alterations in the manuscript by the *Gazette* compositor (G) are underscored. Here are two examples of misspelling and five of compositor's alterations, to prepare the reader. First, spelling errors by Whitney: annivers**ity**[ar] and

Fan**uel**[eui]. Whitney misspells "annivers*ary*" and "Fan*eui*l," with the editor's underscoring and bracketed suffixes matching up the orator's variant. A comparable method identifies compositor's and/or orator's galley alterations. Five examples are: affect Ge, howere Gver, Gov[ernmen]ts Ggt, withe G the, and m[o]urned Gurmured. Indicating several probable variants caused by the compositor setting up "*e*ffect" over Whitney's "*a*ffect," "howe*ver*" over "howe*re*," "governmen*t*" over capital-plural "*G*overnmen*ts*," "with *the*" over single word "with*e*," and "m*urmur*ed" over "m*ourn*ed." Editor's notes will pinpoint instances where Whitney's galley proof might account for such variants in the text. The symbol "p/ps" abbreviates "paragraph(s)" in all editor's notes, and in a few instances **a**-revision alternates are posed within brackets. Whenever Whitney revises out partial words like "so-" or "dem-", for example, the rhetorical context may permit **a** SO[BER? -LE?] (i.e., sober or sole?) or **a** DEM[AND? -ONSTRATE?] (i.e., demand or demonstrate?).

Having examined the two Fontane paradigms and become better acquainted with these procedures, many readers should now be able to begin reading the Whitney oration with minimal difficulty. It is urged, nevertheless, that the more general reader pay particular attention to explanations given in editor's notes. Hopefully the general reader's few remaining queries will be answered there.

1 We are assembled, fellow citizens, to celebr**at**e the birthday of our n**at**ion:— to "call to GRATEFUL remembrance" our f**at**hers who **toiled and bled and died** to **at**chieve our independance, and to render gr**at**eful homage to the "Father of Our Spirits" who guided and supported them in its acquisition.[1]

2 A periodical celebration of events, which have produced beneficial results, have been practiced by every free and enlightened people, from the first solemnization of the Jewish festival that kept in the remembrance of Israel their deliverance from Egyptian Thral[l]dom, [down] to the celebration of the 4th of July in these United States.

3 The utility of festivals to commemorate, to **diffuse**, to transmit the knowledge, and the feelings, connected with important eras in a nation's happiness, cannot but be admitted by all who know **anything** of the nature of man, or are capable of reasoning on the details of history.-[2]

4 And what [other] nation on the records of time have had [a] greater, **a** Gor more **glor**ious **a** CAUSE **b** subject of **felicitation**- of **[con]gratulation** and of pious gratitude, ☆ than the United States?-[3] In the **annals** of what [other]

1 Compare "toiled and bled and died" with "toiled and died" in p21. And determine whether the four *at* spellings may have led Whitney to misspell "*at*chieve."

2 Relate the meaning of "diffuse" to "scattered" in p9.

3 How does "felicitation" relate in meaning to Whitney's "happiness and glory" theme (here, p7, and p33 heading)? See "cause" in p9, and plural case of same word in ps7 and 14.

nation is recorded an event more worthy of perpetual celebration and remembrance?[4]

5 Selected to address you **on this** **a** FIRST **PUBLIC** CELEBRATION OF THIS DAY IN THE TERRITORY **b** joyous and interesting **Occasion,** ☆ I should be stupid and **insensible** not to feel honored by **a** THIS **b** this **mark of**☆**attention.**-[5] Yet a stranger to most of you,- to your opinions and views,- I feel **something** embarrassed in what manner to meet your wishes on this Occasion.---[6]

6 We are all, however, Americans,- members of **one family**, having a **com**mon interest in all topics of national concern Gns, tho[ugh], as yet, we **have not all the rights and privileges of our brethren of the states**.- We have a **com**mon interest with them, also, in celebrating the day and the events **that** delivered the soil **a** THAT WE LIVE O[N] **b** on **which** we live, ☆ as well as their's, from a foreign **dominion**.[7]

7 What, then, are the **reccollections**, the **reflections**- the discussions that the morning of this day should suggest to the minds of Americans?----[8] The **causes that** led to the glorious event **it** commemorates.—**The Story** of the struggles- the sufferings- the sacrifices- the defeats- the victories,—and the manifestations of a beneficent Providence, **which** procured us the blessing;—the memory of those worthies, thro[ugh] whose instrumentality **it** was obtained and transmitted to us.—Our present **happiness and glory**, and the means by **which** IT **they** ☆ may be **a** TRANS[MITTED] **b** secured to **posterity.** ☆—[9] **These** are the subjects- **which occupy the thoughts** of all good citizens on **this** hallowed Fourth.—**These** are the topics **which, at this moment,** **a** EMPLOY **b** engage the **attention of**☆a **whole people.**[10]

8 A great nation is, **at this moment**, solemnizing the **Anniversit**y[-ar] of **its** existance.—

---

4 What word root is shared by "annals" and "anniversary (p8)?"

5 Compare "mark" with same word in p32, and "insensible" with "sensibility" in p65.

6 Determine whether there is any similarity at all between the grammatical structure of "something," the word Whitney prefers over "somewhat" apparently, and "anything" in p3. Also, see "something like" in p36.

7 Determine whether, if at all, the prefixes "com-" and "con-" relate to Whitney's desire to address "one" united celebration.

8 Relate implications inherent in these two "re-" words to the meaning of "meditating" in p9.

9 See heading identical to "Our present happiness and glory" at top of p33, confirming the pervasiveness of this theme for Whitney.

10 When combined with "occupy thoughts," is "employ" perhaps too materialistic and static a verb for Whitney? Observe that "attention of" is a slight parallel to "mark of attention" in p5. Relate the meaning of "whole people" to "public" in p5, and to "one family" in p6. Also, relate Whitney's "that-which" revision in p6 to his "it-they" revision here.

9 Each scar-honored veteran of the Revolution,- **scattered** from the Atlantic to the Missis[s]ippi- from the [Northern] Lakes to the [Southern] Seaboard,- is now **meditating** on the perils- the sufferings- the sacrifices he endured- and the battles he fought in the **cause** of Liberty,—his eye alternately gleaming with indignation at the **atrocities of a cruel Enemy**- moistening at the RECCOLLECTION remembrance☆of his Companions in Arms- brightening at the reccollection of the of the hour of victory- or beaming with honest **exultation** while reviewing the happiness his sword helped to secure in "the **times that tried men's souls".**---[11]

10 The aged Matron is dwelling with **melancholly pleasure** on the security and protection, of herself and **children**, bought by the blood of a husband or a brother.[12]

11 Assemblies of citizens are everywhere **listening to** the **tale** of American Independance,—discussing the **true** principles of Gov[ernmen]t- the sources of national prosperity- and the means of its perpetuity.—[13]

12 Youth is instructed in the rights and duties of freemen.- And even **childhood** catches,- by sympathy with the feelings of those it loves,- an enthusiasm the **reminiscence** of which shall stimulate the patriotism of manhood.-[14]

13 What **sublimer spectacle** can a nation present— a **spectacle** on which the Father of men must look down with **complacence** and **benignity**!----[15]

14 The **causes** which compelled our fathers- **more than 40 years** ago- to dash defiance in the front of England, you have **heard** read from their declaration of Independance. **This they** have delivered to us— and let **it** be kept in **everlasting** remembrance as an enumeration of the subjects of grievance to **which** a free people should never submit- and [as] a **memento** to **those that** may administer our Gov[ernmen]t, [so] that for the least of these Go offences **they** shall be hurled from the posts of honor **they** shall dare to abuse.—[16]

---

11 Compare "times that tried men's souls" with similar expression in p31.

12 Relate the meaning of "children" (and "childhood" in p12) to "posterity" in p7. And how might "melancholy pleasure" relate in meaning to "pleasantly please" in p65?

13 Compare "tale" with "the Story" in ps7 and 15, and see "listen to" revision in p22.

14 Determine the word root and meaning, if any, shared by "reminiscence," "mind," "commemorate," "memory," and "remembrance."

15 How does "sublimer" relate in meaning to "true" in p11? Compare the root and meaning of "spectacle" and "respect," "complacence" and "pleasure," "benignity" and "beneficial."

16 Observe that Whitney uses "hear" rather than "listen to," both being elements in his p22 revision. Compare "memento" with the five words listed in the p12 note. And compare "everlasting" with Whitney's revision of "last" in the final sentence of p16. How would revising "last" to "triumphant" and "glorious" render a dramatic "close" more "perpetual" than "last" alone might convey? Also, compare the "it-they" structure with Whitney's revision in p7.

15 With **the Story** of our Revolution,- its disasters- its victories- its reverses- its triumphs,- I am bound to believe you too well acquainted to need a **monitor** in me.[17]

16 You can each recall to mind the series of political events, from the **first** movements **a** OF **b** in the Cradle of☆Liberty (the Old Fan**uel**[-eui] Hall at Boston) to the Declaration of Independan[ce]- to the Act of Confederation- to the **Signature** of our present happy Constitution.—[18] You can also retrace the process of its military operations.—You remember **Lexington** where the **first** American blood cried [out] to God and our country for vengeance.—You remember **Bunker-hill** where "the chafed lion of New England leaped upon the hunter's spear that galled him."—You remember the retreat of **Dorchester**, the defeat of **Brooklyn**; you remember the disastrous march of a barefooted soldiery over the frozen roads of **Jers**[**e**]**y**,- when a pu[r]suing Enemy could trace the rout[e] of their flight by the bloody print of th[e]ir footsteps, when the weak and the wavering dispaired- when the hearts of many fainted- when Tories ex**ulted** rejoiced, and the Enemy ins**ulted.**[19] You remember the **a** REVERSES **b** glorious reverses☆of **Trenton** and **Princeton**,- you remember the fields of **Saratoga** and **Monmouth**- of **Germantown** and **Eutaw**,- and the **a** LAST **b** triumphant and glorious☆**close** of this perilous Drama at **York-town.**[20]

17 And while you review these scenes and dwell with enthusiasm on the persevering firmness, the **unwavering** constancy and the **unyielding** spirit of patriotism that supported the **actors**- you cannot but perceive, and acknowledge with grateful hearts, the **signal** interpositions of Divine Providence in their favor.-[21]

18 With re**ccoll**ections like these, we should re**call** the **consecrated** names in Our Republican **Call**endar.-[22] And as we pay them this tribute of respect and

---

17 Add "monitor" to the *mem* root comparison suggested in notes to ps12 and 14. And determine why Whitney might insert this sentence to link ps7 and 16.

18 Relate "signature" in root and meaning to "signal" in p17.

19 See "exultation" in p9, and speculate why Whitney wanted to eliminate the duplication in "-ulted."

20 Compare Whitney's itemized "field" here, repeating place names for dramatic effect, with his heightened "honor" revision in p21 that precedes itemized heroic attributes in p22, and with yet another itemized "field" in ps58, 60, and 61. Also, observe that Whitney hyphenates the closing battle name ("York-town"), while "Germantown" reads as one word.

21 Whitney continues the dramatic impact by speaking of the "actors" or players, and indeed in ps19 and 20 the various names may serve as an itemized extension of both the battle "field," and the "field" of "honor." Compare the modifiers "unwavering" and "unyielding" with "unbending" and "unspotted" in the final sentence of p22.

22 See "consecrate" as it relates to the religious image of Washington in ps30 and 32, and determine whether there is any relationship at all between Whitney's spelling of "recall," and his misspelling of "reccollections" and "callendar."

affection, [we should] endeavour to impress their **virtues** and their patriotism [up]on our own hearts.—[23]

19 As Patriot Statesmen:—Hancock- Adams- Franklin- Hamilton- Jefferson- Madison- Jay- King- Trumbull- Livingston- Henry- Pickering- Pinkney Gck- Sherman—And had not the **madness- folly and impiety** of his **latter** days obliterated the memory of his **former** usefulness, I would have added the name of PAYNE Pain[e]. ☆[24]

20 As Patriot **Warriors**:—Warren- Putnam- Green[e]- Lincoln- Gates- Sullivan- Mercer- Montgomery- Clinton- Lee- Lingan- Morgan.—[25] Nor should the names of [von] Steuben- [La]Fayette- Pulaski- Kos[c]iusco be forgotten.-

21 But besides these there are hundreds- that DECORATE adorn ☆ the **page of American history**- who labored in the same cause, in the Cabinet or the a FIELD b army,- and thousands- that tenant the **field** ☆ **of honor**- where they **toiled and died** with no other hope of recompence than the undistinguished gratitude of that country whose freedom they valued more than life [itself].[26]

22 In this Catalogue of worthies- I know you have missed the name you love to hear pronounced.- **It** comes in the **place** his own **modesty would have placed it**.-[27] Tho[ugh] he listened not to the clarion notes of his fame,- 'tis our glory to sound them.- Indeed, I a NEVER WOULD b would never ☆ consent, howere Gver often you may have listen[e]d to his Eulogy, to pronounce a discource on this day, nor would I willingly a LISTEN TO b hear ☆ one, in which the Character of this Hero- this Statesman- this Patriot- this **Man of Men** was not recalled to the **admiration** and the gratitude of his countrymen:—this **Hero**, who united the **stubborn hardihood** of the partizan **chieftain** TO with ☆ the **extended views** and the **comprehensive plans** of the **conquoror**,-this **Statesman**, whose Character

23 How might "virtues" relate in root and meaning to "Man of Men" in ps22 and 24? Taking into account the fallible and corrupt nature of many a "warrior," is it possible that a figurative "man" among "men," much less Washington in the context of a Fourth of July oration, could conceivably be as less "virtuous" as the figure is emphatic?

24 See similar use of "former-latter" in p38.

25 Unlike "Patriot," "Statesman," "Man of Men," or "Hero," Whitney does not repeat this heading of "Warriors" until p27. Are "chieftain" and "conqueror" in p22 then to be regarded as less controversial substitutes for "warrior?" Consider whether, especially for purposes of a Fourth of July oration, Whitney is perhaps reluctant to make Washington as lacking in grandeur as the average "warrior" or militiaman in the American Revolution.

26 In this rather heroic aside, directed to those lesser lights who serve beneath the names itemized in ps19 and 20, does Whitney perhaps realize that fallibility and corruption in such "warriors" may bear upon the image of their "chief?" Does he revise "decorate" to "adorn" because of some lesser distinction that might carry over to Washington?

27 One oddity of this sentence is that "modesty" and the future conditional tense, though passive and perfect, connote a heroic "last" place for Whitney. Compare the tenor of the remainder of this paragraph with "triumphant" and "glorious" versus "last" in Whitney's p16 revision.

combined the **penetration**, the **foresight**, the **acumen** of the enlighten[e]d politition and the most **unbending firmness**- **unspotted integrity** and **purity of intention**.[28]

23 This founder of a nation and father of his country- the ardor of whose patriotism burnt with [all] the fervency and purity of a **Seraph's love**.—[29]

24 This **Man of Men**, whose powerful and active intellect, enterprising and mastering Gly genius were so nicely guided by **the a** SO[BER? -LE?] **b** steady sober☆ **wisdom of the heart**,- **whose sole ambition** was **his** country- whose **sole object** was her happiness,- whose every act in public or in private life was prompted and directed by love to God and love to man.---[30]

25 This, fellow citizens, is not the mere fervency of American **partiality**.- The civilized world have judged his merit as we do.—[31]

26 A Frederick has decreed him the **palm of Excellence** over the Great Gene[r]als of the age.- A Fox has enscribed his Eulogy on th[e] **page of English history**- and **France has recorded** it in the Archives of her National Academy.-[32]

27 When I rev[i]ew the lives of those whom the partiality and Gof historians have named *great*,- when I see the **page of history** filled with the **atrocities of warriors and conquorors**— the corruption and oppressions of AMBITIOUS statesmen whose only motives were **a** THE **b** selfishness- ambition and the☆love of power,-when I see demag**auges**[-ogu] boasting [of] their services to the people [so] that they may acquire power to abuse,- when I see power uniformly corrupt the best men—when I have viewed these things 'til my heart is sick of the records of human **greatness and folly and wickedness**:—I turn to this man, who fought only for his country.-[33] I see him calm and collected in Gamid-

28 Compare "admiration" and Whitney's revision of "admirers" in p30.

29 Much as with "admiration" in p22, compare the religious aura in "Seraph" with Whitney's concluding exposition of Washington's character in ps30 thru 32.

30 See Whitney's "sole" revision in p27, and speculate whether "sole ambition" and "sole object" might be indirect revisions of an initial pairing of "sole" with an impersonal "wisdom" and "heart" ("the" versus "whose" or "his").

31 Ascertain what word root is shared by "partiality" and "partisan."

32 In the reference to France, Whitney indirectly cites his 1816 translation of Louis Jean Pierre Marquis de Fontanes' *Eloge Funebre de Washington*, an oration "recorded" in print at Paris shortly after being delivered by de Fontane on 9 Feb., 1800. See "page of history" in ps21 and 27, and compare Whitney's "palm" with "standard" in the final sentence of p29.

33 Whitney quite belatedly inserts "warriors" here, but the implications in the term are extremely perverse, certainly not patriotic, and never really are directly applied to Washington's character. To speculate a bit on Whitney's intent, compare the usage in an unfavorable "warriors-conquerors" (here) with a rather laudatory "chieftain-conqueror" in p22, and also the usage in two equally unfavorable items—"atrocities of warriors and conquerors" (here) with the "atrocities" perpetrated by the "cruel" British in p9. Is there any parallel structure between "greatness and folly and wickedness" (here) and "madness, folly, and impiety" as applied to Thomas Paine in p19?

st defeat and disaster,- humble and grateful in victory.— I see that "in his tent, even when retaliation might justify severity, humanity always took refuge and was never repulsed".—I see him, when at the head of an army that **adored** him and m[o]urned Gurmured at the neglect of their country, resign power into the hands of a people that **almost courted his dominion.**—[34] I see him accept the Chief Majestracy of the nation— himself the **a** SOLE **b** center of☆attraction that held together the masses of the Confederation— and become a Statesman,- profound- able- firm and incorruptible.- I review his whole life,- from his **first In**[**dian**] campaign on the Monogahela to its peaceful **close** at [Mount] Vernon,- and I feel my wavering faith in humanity reestablished.-[35] I catch some glimpse of its **primeval** dignity when man talked with his Maker in the Garden.- I again glory in the rank I hold in God's Creation, and thank the Almighty that I was born in the only **a** COUNTRY A[ND] **AGE b** AGE and country☆that has produced a *Washington*!—[36]

28 Our Revolution, fellow citizens, might perhaps have been **effected**, and its **objects obtained**, by the **same talents distributed in different persons.**—[37] But I esteem it a great happiness that at the outset of our national career we should have had a Character presented, as a **model for imitation**, as **nearly perfect** as humanity can hope to HAVE **reach.** ☆[38]

29 Tho[ugh] I shall not be suspected of hoping to present any new topics of **Eulogy**— yet I deem it a duty to urge upon our countrymen the importance of

34 To what degree, if any, does Whitney's inability to transform Washington into a patriotic, non-corrupt "warrior" eventually affect the credibility of Washington for the contemporaneous reader and/or audience? In p6 it was "one common family" of American men who liberated themselves from the "foreign dominion" of the British. But in this paragraph it is also American men who "almost court" the "dominion" of one of their own. In effect, the question of credibility revolves around kind and degree of power as they pertain to the American militiaman. A Fourth of July oration perhaps is not the true testing ground for such a profound question, yet two specific word antitheses can be cited. One, the "dominion" issue, has already been mentioned. The other is more a matter of degree, and can be grasped in the personal animosity implied by "murmured," and in the protracted and rather adverse impact of commercial deprivation ("amidst" versus the lesser degree of "in"). The point is not that Whitney is ineffective in this Washington portion of the text, but that now the reader is better able to make an accurate judgment on the issue of credibility, especially as the issue relates to oratory on a national holiday. Would members of Whitney's audience be apt to "mourn" and "adore" a national hero who cannot rise above "warrior" instincts in the common man? Whitney attempts to brush over such undesirable traits, perhaps rightly so on a holiday occasion, but present-day readers of this text will question Washington's credibility and true relation to the common man.

35 Compare "Indian" and "Savage" in p41, and see similar "first-close" structure in p16.

36 Relate the root and meaning of "first" and "age" to "primeval."

37 Compare this sentence with p21. Is Whitney too anxious here to set "chieftain" Washington above the fallible "warrior?" After all, fallible men are asked to "imitate" a "nearly perfect" model of statesman-like virtues, when in fact the process of imitation brings the model that much closer to less than "perfect" traits. Washington's qualities as a hero are indeed in the eye of the imitator, and such plural ambivalence as many talents possibly not reaching "different" citizens casts doubt on the democratic process. At first glance, the general terms ("same talents" and "different persons") even appear to ignore the heroic character of p27 altogether.

38 Relate the meanings of "reach," "effect," and "obtain," as used by Whitney, to your idea of the democratic process.

keeping constantly before **their** eyes the **elevated** Character of our Revolutionary Hero.—[So] that in days of political degeneracy and laxity of moral principle (and **they** may come), **they** have constantly in mind a criterion by which to judge the merits of **public men**- [and so] that in **their** choice of Rulers, **their standard of political greatness and moral excellence** may never sink to the level of **demagogues** and empirics who would **palter** with the destinies of the nation.[39]

30 Washington is now where detraction could no more disturb his peace,- but his Fame and his Character are the property of his country.- His frailties, if he had them, were not such as can sanction error or "legalise corruption". Even with his most devoted **a** ADMIRERS **b** FOLLOWERS **c** **disciples** ☆ to **consecrate** his name and memory, there Gn can work no detriment to his country but much good.-[40] The name of Washington, with **those** who know and estimate him right[ly], recalls to mind **those** men- the **greatly good and goodly great** of all **antiquity**, whose labors and virtues and **sacrifices** blessed **their** country, and whose bright example have in **aftertimes** invigorated kindred souls to emulate **their** deeds.[41]

31 The name of Washington **should** be the watchword of Americans, "in **times that try men's souls**", to rally freemen to **defend their rights**.- It is a **sacred** duty, then, of every man that loves **virtue or his country**, to **cherish,** honor and **defend this name for virtue's and his country's sake.**[42]

---

39 Explore whether Whitney's ambiguous pronoun reference "they" relates at all to the fallibility of hero Washington. Determine whether "eulogy" and "elevated" share a common prefix root. And as with the question of hero Washington's relationship to the democratic process, speculate on whether "men" gaining experience in politics necessarily become "public" enough to "palter" and qualify as "*dema*gogues."

40 Whitney is most effective when seeking to link a deified Washington with a stance emphasizing national honor. But, considering variant connotations in these three comraderie words, does he successfully brush over the "warrior" matter in ps30 thru 32? Does he successfully link religious implications in "disciples," for example, with the "-secrate" root in "sacred" (p31) and "sacrifices" (p30)? And how then does the root "vir-" in virtuous principle relate to Washington the "man?" Is hero Washington, in effect, only a "hero" because he mirrors "warrior" instincts quite "sacred" to fallible and corrupt "men?"

41 Probably as an extension of "they" in p29, observe that Whitney confuses the pronoun reference of "those," and that the two "those" references in turn cast some doubt upon precisely what two "their" references designate. "Those"-1 refers to men in time present, while "those"-2 refers to men in time past. However, there is some confusion as to precisely what men and/or time period are designated by "their" 1 and 2. "Their"-2 really could refer to either period, for example, and "their"-1 might as easily be synonymous with "her" country, not really designating either group of men. Why must Whitney attempt to consolidate hero Washington's stature in time present and time past, before using the future conditional tense in ps31 and 32? What root prefixes make "antiquity" and "aftertimes" opposites in meaning, and are both words related in any way to the pronoun references cited? And does the rather neat juxtaposition in "greatly good" and "goodly great" tend to make artificial mockeries out of "truth" and "goodness?" Did Whitney's audience perhaps desire such obvious word choices in a Fourth of July oration?

42 If Whitney had cast the ending on this sentence to read "defend this name for the sake of virtue and his country," would the connotations suggested by "man" and "virtue" be markedly different? Or would such a marked difference only be found when the ending read "defend name for sake of his virtue and his country?" Regardless of your opinion concerning these possible variations, observe that Whitney's reason for the slightly awkward possessive structure is his repetition of a "virtue-country" phrase in a single sentence. Also, why are "cherish" and "cheerful" not related in root or meaning?

32 Mark then, my countrymen, **mark** well that man among you, whatever be his rank, station, or profession of republican principles,—who **would**, even by an **in[n]uendo, insinuate** detraction from the **consecrated** Character of Washington.—And "Let no such man be trusted".[43]

Our present **happiness and glory**.—

33 ON CASTING OUR EYE, At no **period of our history** have we, as a nation, had more cause for felicitation. The **events of the late war** have demonstrated to the world that **40 years** of peace and commercial prosperity have **not** enervated the American Character: have **not** enfeebled the arm **nor** corrupted the hearts of our soldiers **nor** seamen.-[44] It has shown us repeatedly victors over the best troops of the Old World.----

34 Our naval flag has also been equally triumphant.—The Queen of the Ocean- the Tyrant of the Seas that **boasted** "to **bridge** the Atlantic"- and "that not a sail without **permission** spreads," often witnessed her ensign lowered to the "bits of striped bunting."—[45] Hull- Decatur- Jones- Bain**bridge** -LAWRENCE have demonstrated our superior skill and prowess in single ships—Macdonough and Perry that we can beat them in squadron.-[46] Europe has **a** SEEN **b** witnessed and **admired**☆the chastisements and humiliation of the PIRATIC states of Barbary- reserved [but] for Americans to inflict.-[47] And the shore Ges of the Mediter[r]anean will remember the name of Decatur as long as pirates shall dread punishment, or the captive rejoice in the deliverance from servitude. **At this moment** the "Star-spangled **banner**" is **floating**, in honor of the day, in every **port** of the civilized world.-[48] And everywhere the name of a American Ga is a pas[s]**port** to attention and respect.-[49]

---

43 Determine the similarity of degree between the designated word root of "i*nnuen*do" and "i*n*si*nu*ate." Is there any orality in the *u*'s and *n*'s of these two words?

44 See Whitney's "late war" revision in p57, complete with "forty years" peace, and compare a post-Revolution "40 years" with "more than 40 years" in p14, and with a multiple "experience of 4,000 years" in p51. Also, explore the orality in "not-nor" versus the more written "neither-nor" device, and recast this sentence to fit a "neither-nor-nor-nor" or a "neither-nor/neither-nor" structure.

45 Observe that Whitney attributes to Britain "boasting" conduct that he specifically denies in p25, and in fact equates with demagogues in p27. Determine whether "bridge" and "abridge," or "permission" and "transmitted," share a common root and meaning.

47 Compare "admired" with Whitney's revision of "admirers" in p30.

46 Whitney probably revises "Lawrence" out of this sentence because of some possible confusion between James (awren) and John (a*ura*n or awr*an*). Though John's name was spelled in the same *en* manner as James's in more than one contemporary history, the two were quite distinct individuals, John in fact dying in 1810 before the War of 1812 even began. And rather than inserting an awkward first name, Whitney preserves the heroic surname orality by striking the "Lawrence" name altogether, though not in the "lowering" posture of the British flag here. There is a very remote possibility that Whitney may have chosen "Bainbridge" over "Lawrence" as an oral counteraction of sorts to the anti-American "bridge" boast in sentence 2.

48 The "banner" of course stands for vessels in the American merchant marine, though Whitney manages some boasting of his very own here by mixing a flag "floating" (not "waving" or "flapping"

35 All our relations with foreign powers,- with the exception of **one** from [which] we have nothing to fear,- are on the most amicable footing.-[50]

36 At home, our eye is also greeted withe G the most cheering prospects. —For the year or two past, the **madness and folly** of party spirit has been fast subsiding.-[51] **Factions a** IS **b** that have rent [apart] SEPARATE/individual states are☆disappearing.[52] A more **universal** confidence and attachment to the administrators of the Gen[era]l Gov[ernmen]t, and cheerful acquiescence in national measures, is Gare fast gaining ground among all parties. And if we have not yet quite become all "Federalists, all Republicans," we have, at least, since the war [of 1812], been fast approximating to **something like** national American feelings— a National American Character.

37 Commerc[e] is recovered from the shock of losses and restrictions occasioned by the war, and, thro[ugh] all her former channels, is pouring in wealth upon the nation.

38 Agriculture is becoming, in many states, the object of legislative care and attention. Societies for its promotion are everywhere rapidly establishing,- thro[ugh] which the lights Gt of Science, the results of improvements and experiments are transmitted to the industrious and enterprising cultivator.- Immense canals and numerous public roads, either by the munificence of the National or State Gov[ernmen]ts, are progressing throughout the country.- And the surplus population of the **old** states are rapidly peopling the **new**.-[53] These **facts**— the **former** by multiply[**ing**] the faciliti[e]s of intercommunication and the **a** OTHER, BY **b** exchange of **commodities**; and the OTHER/**latter** by☆mak**ing** the distant parts of the country better acquainted with each other, and **harmonizing** their **different habits** and **modes** of think**ing** and act**ing**— are daily draw**ing** closer the bonds of the National Union,- that **sheer** anc[h]or of our safety.—[54]

---

or "fluttering") in a ship's "port" (not "part" of the world). How might altering "port" to "part" alleviate this mixed imagery somewhat? Also, see "at this moment" in ps7 and 8.

49 Does the *Gazette* compositor perhaps fib a bit here by transposing Whitney's rejected *a* to take the place of "-*can*," fashioning in effect "America" rather than "a American" or "American," the two word choices apparently preferred by Whitney? Compare the root and meaning in "port" and "passport."

50 Determine the common root and meaning of "one" and "universal" (p36), "Union" and "United."

51 See "madness, folly, and impiety" as applied to Thomas Paine in p19.

52 Compare "separate" with "separated" in p48, and determine precisely how "separate" might connote the word-insert "apart." Also, compare the root and meaning of "factions" with "facts" in p38.

53 See similar use of "old-new" by Whitney in p44, and compare "new" with "renovate," "old" with "antiquity."

54 Whitney relies on the participle-gerund ending *ing* some six times in this sentence. Compare "modes" and "commodities" in root and meaning.

Finally- our population, that **sure** criterion of a happy people, is encreasing in a ratio beyond the example of any people on the globe.[55]

39 These, fellow citizens, are some of the views of our national glory and prosperity,- some of the causes of **congratulation** on this day.—[56] Do you enquire how THIS these☆may be preserved and transmitted?---When **contemplating** an answer to this question, I took up Washing[ton]'s Farewell Address. After perusing it, I can find nothing to add- and I will not attempt to abridge [it].- Study that [address].—It contains a full answer to the enquiry.- Every American who is **able to** buy one book besides THE his☆bible **a** OUGHT TO **b should**☆have it.-[57] It **contains** lessons of practical political wisdom which, if rightly **understood** and acted on by the American people, "**Shall** bid *our* empire flourish and endure,/ Our people happy and our laws secure,/ Our **Phenix-Glory** renovate its prime,/ Extend with ocean and **exist** with time."[58]

40 **version a** While **thus** we rejoice in our own happy lot, Philanthropy would prompt us to **cast an eye on** the **world abroad.**[59] Should we do this with a view to compare **our situation** with their's, we should find, on every side, new inducements for gratitude to "Him that maketh us to differ."

version B Thus far, FELLOW [CITIZENS,] I have addressed you as citizens of the U[nited] S[tates], as members of the **great national family**. Permit me now to call your attention to **your situation and circumstances** as inhabitants of Michigan.—[60]

41 Tho[ugh] **destitute of many of the rights and privileges of your brethren** of Gin **the states**, yet I think your Territory, **at this moment**, presents a more cheering prospect than at any **period of your history**.—[61] Since the war [of

---

55 Determine the root and meaning of two oral, sound-alike words here, namely, dissimilarities between "sure" and "sheer."

56 See p4 where the editor had to insert *con* before "gratulation," and determine whether similar prefixes in "contemplate" and "contain" make Whitney join *con* with "gratulation" here.

57 Does "should" go better with "shall" in the next sentence than "ought to?" Or does Whitney revise "ought to" because of an "able" redundancy, in effect, preferring "should have" over "ought to be able to have?"

58 Compare the root and meaning of "exist" and "understood." Also, explore the concept of a phoenix bird among the ancient Egyptians, and relate that concept to Whitney's multiple of 40 and 4,000 years as noted in p33. Is America Egypt reborn, or is Whitney merely quoting the "last" act of American civilization always being perpetuated? See Whitney's revision of "last" in p16 in this regard.

59 Compare "abroad" and "abridge" in root and meaning. Also, observe that "cast an eye on" repeats "On casting our eye" which Whitney revised out at the start of p33. Does this similarity in **draft a** of this paragraph indicate Whitney's topical shift in emphasis from national-international affairs to the "happiness and glory" of Michigan Territory?

60 Compare "thus," and "world abroad" with "great national family," "our situation" versus "your situation and circumstances," in these two drafts.

1812], a respectable and permanent Military Establishment, a IN DIFFEREN[T] POINTS OF [THE TERRITORY] b at various posts, ☆ give security to the labors of Agriculture from the depredations of the **savage**, AND confidence and activity to emigration.-[62] And the **liberal** disbursements of the Gen[era]l Gov[ernmen]t encrease to a circulating medium **among you**.—

42 The first sale of Public Lands in the Territory, WHICH IS **about to commence**, is drawing the intelligence- the a ACTS b industry and the enterprise ☆ of the East **among you**, and rapidly increasing **your** population.-[63] In another year or two, we hope to be no longer indebted to THE a ☆ neighbor Ging state for the products of **our own soil**.[64]

43 Within the last year, many **objects** of public **utility** have been **effected**.-[65] Several new schools have **been established**,- **among them**, a Classical Academy.- And a Lancastrian School is now going into o**pp**eration, in which the children of the most indigent may be instructed in the most **useful** branches of Education, and in their religious and moral duties.- A University has **been established**, having the superintendance of the concerns of Education thro[ugh]out the Territory.- Other **useful** institutions have also **sprung up**.-[66] "A **bible Society**"- "The **Lyceum of the City of Detroit**"- "An **agricultural Society**"- "A **mechanic Society**" and "A **moral and humane society**." All these institutions, if conducted with common zeal and discretion, cannot fail of prov**ing** extensively and permanently **useful** in increase**ing** the general fund of knowledge- diffus**ing** **useful** information- promot**ing** industry, order and **har-**

61 Focusing a bit on Whitney's revision of "our" to "your," as just seen in p40 above, observe that in p6 "destitute of many of rights and privileges of **your** brethren of-in the states" reads "have not all rights and privileges of **our** brethren of the states." Determine whether the *Gazette* compositor revises "of" to "in" because Whitney uses "of" some five times in the sentence. Or do you see Whitney's "galley" hand in such a minor change? Also, see "period of history" following Whitney's "eye" deletion in p33, and "at this moment" in ps7-8 and 34. Observe that in p33, as in the p6 segment cited, Whitney writes "period of *our* history," not revising to "*your* history" as is evidently the case here.

62 Some contextual background regarding Whitney's use of the word "different" can be obtained from "different persons" in p28, "different habits" in p38, and "different footing" in p59.

63 Compare the usage in "among you" with Whitney's deletion in the final sentence of p41, and with "among them" in the second sentence of p43.

64 Observe that in this final sentence Whitney switches from the "your" of p41 back to a reflexive "our" pronoun.

65 Observe that in p28 Whitney refers to "effecting" the American Revolution, and that a different word ("*ob*tained") is applied to such "*ob*jects" as public utility.

66 Observe the similarity between "sprung up" here and another *up* verb used by Whitney, namely, "going up" as revised in p44. To test the orality of "sprung up," devise alternate verbs to fit this slot. Would "sprung up," or even "gone up," prove more oral than *been* words like "been built," or "been established?"

mony- AND check**ing** vice- AND improv**ing morals- and relieving the distressed.**[67] **They** are entitled to **your** fostering care and protection.[68]

44 A Bank is now **going into** operation.-[69] An Academic hall is just finished.- A superb Church- an extensive **P**rison are now **a** GOING [UP] **b building**- ☆ and a **Courthouse** [is] **about to be commenced**.-[70] Several expensive bridges have **been built**.-[71] Numerous private **buildings** are **going up**.-[72] **New** roads are **opening** and **old** ones **repairing**.[73]

45 So many undertakings of public utility and private convenience,- in so short a time, and under the disadvantages the Territory was laboring,- bespeak an attention to your interests in those that administer your Gov[ernmen]t, and a zeal and activity in yourselves, that **augur well of your future** prosperity.—

46 You have for many years labored under great disadvantages.- Among the **principal** [ones] was the delay of the **sale of Public Lands**.—This is now removed, and in its consequences will remove many other obstacles to **your future welfare**.—[74] Another **principal** disadvantage is the **form** of your Territorial Gov[ernmen]t.[75] The **mode** of passing laws is so very exceptionable

---

67 Perhaps Whitney prefers "effect" over "obtain," because he realizes that a process of public utility is involved here. In this regard, especially observe the process *ing* structure of this sentence and the manner in which "useful" relates to the root concept "utility." And in comparing the *ing* structure of this sentence with sentence 5 in p38, also observe the identical root words in "harmony" and "harmonizing,"

68 Whitney concludes this paragraph by addressing "you" as members or concerned guardians of "they" institutions. No reference at all is made to the "we-our" of p42, and observe the itemized technique of listing five institutions by title. The technique is quite reminiscent of Whitney's itemized battle "event" names.

69 Unlike the same phrase in sentence 3 of p43 above, Whitney avoids using a double *p* in spelling the "o*pp*eration" of p43. Is there any relationship at all between "o*p*eration" and the single *p*'s in such words as "su*p*erb," "*p*rison," "u*p*," "ex*p*ensive," "*p*rivate," "o*p*ening," and "re*p*airing?"

70 Does Whitney gain more process orality in this paragraph by switching away from *been* verb tenses? Compare "going into" in the first sentence of this paragraph with "going up" in sentence 3. Also with regard to sentence 3, observe that the institutional "object" Courthouse is "about to *be* commence*d*," while in p42 the more significant sale of public lands is "about to commence."

71 "Been built" is the only *been* verb in this paragraph.

72 Observe that sentence 5 repeats both elements of the revision Whitney made in sentence 3, and that the "built" of the previous sentence is here cast more in a process-mode.

73 Why is terminating construction on roads already built an unacceptable antithesis for Whitney in this process paragraph? How, for example, would this sentence read if "closing" were substituted for "repairing?"

74 Compare "future welfare" with "augur well of future" in p45. Also, compare the variant phrasing of "about to *be* commence*d*" in p44 with Whitney's concept of lesser "objects" of public utility flowing from the sale of public lands. As already suggested in a note, such lesser "objects" are to *be* commence*d* as the direct result of a primary force in the *commence*ment of selling public lands.

75 Compare "form" in root and meaning with "uniform" and "information."

that your legislators themselves tell you,- it is extremely difficult, if not impossible, **ever** to have a **uniform** and **consistent** system of Jurisprudence under the present **form** of Gov[ernmen]t, and the present **mode** of legislation.—[76] Your **form** of Gov[ernmen]t, in theory, is acknowledged [to be] bad. The very terms of its enunciation contain a deffinition of Despotism,—"a Gov[ernmen]t where the makers, the interpreters and the executors of the Laws are the same persons."- And if it has not been rendered despotic in practice, as well as [in] theory, you have only to thank the good sense, and **moderation** and patriotism, of those who have administered it, AND or☆the control[l]ing superintendence of the Gen[era]l Gov[ernmen]t.-[77] How far it is honorable OR and☆becoming [for] freemen, citizens of the One Republic, to live under a provincial **form** of Gov[ernmen]t, despotic EVEN only☆in theory, one moment longer then imperious necessity requires, is left for you to judge.[78] You have lately decided that the necessity still **exists**.- But it cannot **exist** [**for**] **long**.- Population will **a** RA[PIDLY INCREASE] **b** **increase** rapidly☆by emigration, and your resources will **increase** with it. The time cannot be [too] far distant when **you** will take upon **you** the duty of governing **yourselves.**[79]

47 In contemplation of such an event, what are your preparatory duties?---

48 The habits of thinking and acting, acquired and transmitted for so many years— **a** UNDER **b** alternately under☆the French and British **a** ,OR EVEN U[NDER] **b** Gov[ernmen]ts Ggt- under martial law, or **even** under☆American Territorial Gov[ernmen]ts,-THE your☆means of education and political information- **separated** as you **a** HAVE BEEN **b** **were**☆from the states—**have not been** such as **were** calculated to quallify **you, as a people**, for the task of **Self**-Gov[ernmen]t.[80]

49 **Your** first care, then, should be to promote the study of the political history of YOUR **our**☆common country— to diffuse thro[ughout] the people correct ideas of the spirit of **our** Constitution and **republican** GOV[ERNMEN]TS In-

---

76 Compare the root and meaning of "con*sist*ent" and "ex*ist*."

77 Compare "moderation" with "mode" in root and meaning.

78 See Whitney's revision involving "even" in p48, and speculate how reading "eve*n*" into "eve*r*" in sentence 5 might minimize time future at the expense of time present. Also, in the light of current learned use of "and/or," observe that Whitney varies between *and/or* and *or/and*, selecting the latter word in each instance.

79 Compare these final three sentences with the "you" orientation of p45, and observe how Whitney attempts to link "exist" and "increase" so as to make "you" the citizen capable of governing under present and future connotations of each word.

80 Observe that Whitney repeats both elements of his initial verb revision, the final sequence of verbs then reading "were-have been-were." Would the sentence read as smoothly if the sequence "have been-have been-were" or "have been-were-have been" were inserted in place of Whitney's revision? Determine why not. Also, determine how combining "you" with "self" and "people" in this final sentence might be a variety of oral revision, possessing an oral impact quite comparable to the written reflexive "yourselves" in the final sentence of p46.

stitutions, ☆- the nature of a **representative** Gov[ernmen]t and the important political rights- privileges and duties of citizens under such a Gov[ernmen]t.[81] Study to diffuse a relish for, and habits of punctual attention to, public affairs, when[ever the] public interest demands it.- You are now suffering [under] an evil which this attention might have prevented.- The necessity of [having] a delegate at the seat of Gov[ernmen]t is universally acknowledged. You might now be represented in the National Council, had you taken the trouble of asking for it in [the proper] season.- Do not again slumber and slumber, and slumber, over your rights and your interests, **a** AND **b** lest you ☆ again suffer a *morrow* to defeat what the exertions of *today* might secure. **Keep a steady eye on** the operations of the **neighbouring** states, AS so far as ☆ they may affect Ge your interests.-[82] Especially [the operations] of that [state] which, not content with **draining** [off] your **circulating medium** [as exorbitant payment] for the surplus of her produce, and taking her fish in your waters, seems willing to violate the integrity of your Territory.[83]

50 But your **principal care** must be directed to the rising generation.[84] Make their education, then, a matter of the first importance.

51 No republican Gov[ernmen]t, however excellent in its form, can **long exist** without intelligence and virtue in the people.[85] This position is warranted by the recorded experience of **4,000 years**.—The people must have [enough] intelligence to **a** SELECT **b** enable them to select ☆ good Rulers- and [enough] knowledge of the nature and principles of Gov[ernmen]t, and of THE **existing circumstances**- to enable them to judge correctly of their **conduct** and measures while in power.—[86] They must have [enough] virtue to **resist** corruption themselves, and to elect those only who are free from it to offices of trust,- and to enable them to make those sacrifices, TO for ☆ the good of their country, which patriotism may demand.[87]

---

81 Consult notes in ps42 and 43 for some background on Whitney's "your-our" revision here. Also, ascertain whether there is possibly any revision relationship between "*rep*ublican" and "*rep*resentative."

82 Compare the *our* variant spelling of "neighb*or*ing" with the *Gazette* compositor's variant *ing* ending in sentence 2 of p42. Also, compare "keep eye on" with "cast eye on" in ps33 and 40**a**.

83 Contrast this "draining" of Michigan's "circulating medium" with Whitney's reference to the same item being "liberally" increased by the Treasury Department in p41. Does Whitney refer here to the British influence in Canada, or to some neighbor state like New York and Ohio? To what entity does Whitney refer in the final sentence of p42?

84 Whitney here turns from "principal" disadvantages impeding citizens' rights, as detailed in p46, to "principal" responsibilities in time present that such rights be respected as statehood nears in the future for Michigan.

85 Compare "long exist" and "exist long" in sentence 11 of p46.

86 Determine the root and meaning of "conduct," "produce," and "education," "circumstances" and "circulating."

87 What root and meaning is shared by "resist," "circumstances," and "exist?"

52 But virtue in a people must be based upon religion; they are [as] inseparable as **cause and effect.**[88] "This is the cement of society; the tie that binds man to man, and man to God."—Revere, therefore, public worship,- and see that your children attend [up]on religious instruction.---

53 Let your schoolhouses be filled, and attend yourselves to the system of Education taught in them.— In imitation of some of the states, make the Constitution- the Dec[laration] of Independance- Washington's Farewell Address- and selections of American history an indispensable schoolbook.

54 Teach them yourselves **the Story** of the Revolution.[89] Make them familiar with the names- the sufferings- the sacrifices- the patriotic deeds of our fathers— from a Washington down to a Paulding and a Champ[e]. **a** AND TEACH THEM **b** Infuse into their hearts, while **susceptible,** American feelings,-and instruct them ☆ what **will be** their duty when their country **shall call** for their exertions.--[90]

55 And here, were I permitted to **address,** with freedom, that part of **this audience, whose presence** gives such additional **zest to the festivities** of the day, it would be an **easy and a pleasing task** to demonstrate of how great **importance** **a** IT IS [FOR] **b** ,in a republican country **it would be,** were ☆ every freeman, in his youth, to **receive lessons** of political morality from the lips of a Mother.--In youth, our hearts are in your hands, and you can mould them at your **pleasure.**- Not only the shape and colour of our **lives as** men are **impressed** [upon us] while under a Mother's **guidence,**- but our future **usefulness as** freemen and **as citizens** might be infinitely **enhanced** by your labor and instruction.-

56 **T'was** Spartan Mothers only that formed Spartan Soldiers.--**T'was** Cornelia that instructed the Grachii.-

57 Gentlemen of the Army, the **a** LATE WAR **b** **events of the late war** ☆ in which you were engaged has shown that *you* have not studied the deeds of your fathers in **vain.**—You have proved that their blood has not degenerated in your

---

88 There is perhaps another parallel connotation to these two logical terms. Whitney conceivably could have in mind the strident "cause" of American Independence, and the various objects "effected" as a result of the Revolution itself being "effected."

89 See "the Story" in ps7 and 15.

90 Compare "will be" and "shall call" with Whitney's revision in the final sentence of p61.

91 Whitney deletes ps55 and 56 from the manuscript, and quite obviously neither paragraph was incorporated in the *Gazette* text. Compare "t'was" or *it was* with "it is" in p55, and speculate why Whitney revises a present tense to the future conditional, reverting to a past tense in p56. Are the national statements in p56 too narrow and lacking in credibility? Is p55 perhaps too euphonious at the expense of meaning? In this regard, observe the euphonious *s* sound in "address" and "impress," "zest" and "festive," "easy" and "please," etc. And determine whether such shortcomings might account for both paragraphs being deleted from the manuscript by Whitney.

veins.[92] Under all the disadvantages arising from the habits of a **40 years** peace— from unorganized departments- with troops undisciplined in camp, untried in battle— you have repeatedly vanquished the **veterans of Europe**, the **conquorors of the Peninsula**.- You have raised the National Character, for valor, to the **a** H[E]IGHT IT HELD **b** **high ground** on which it stood ☆ at the **close** of the Revolution.—You could **not hope to do more**.---[93]

58 The destruction of American cannon, and the prowess of the American bayonet, were too satisfactorily decided at **Plat[t]sburgh**, at **Bridgewater**, at **Chip[p]ewa**, at **Erie**, at **Orleans**, for the **veteran slanderers** of American Character in the Old World to wish a second [such] experiment [upon themselves].[94]

59 Under our Gov[ernmen]t, Gentlemen, the Army is on an entirely **different footing** from that of any other country. Here, there are no invidious distinctions [made] between the **citizen** and the **soldier**.---Here, every **a** CITIZEN IS ALSO A SOL[DIER] **b** **soldier** is also a **citizen**, ☆ and every **citizen** ready, able and willing to become a **soldier** when his country calls.-[95]

60 Of these double duties of Americans as **citizen-soldiers**, you have a splendid example in the **fathers** of the Revolution,- who thro[ugh] seven years of severe duty, **under** the discipline and **sub**ordination of [their] **camps**, never lost sight of the rights and the duties of the **citizen**, but again resumed **them** the moment **their** country no longer needed **their** services in the **field.**[96]

---

92 Are "vain" and "veins" a more acceptable type of euphony, for Whitney, than that used in p55? Determine precisely how both words are complementary in meaning.

93 Beginning with this paragraph, Whitney attempts to make the "warrior"- soldier or "conqueror" more closely amenable to responsibilities of the citizen. Yet he never uses the term "warrior" in the attempt, much as was the case in his presentation on Washington's character.

94 Contrast the implications of Whitney's distinction between European military "veterans" in p57, and his mention of Europeans in the capacity of citizen "veteran slanderers" here. Is the distinction too neatly drawn, and does it in effect smack of "high" versus "low" chauvinism? If so, would such an overdrawn distinction nullify any attempt to make the "warrior" more palatable? From a sincere perspective, however, might not Whitney's revision of holding a "height" to standing upon "high ground" suggest some continuity of military-civilian resolve, especially when linked with these itemized "events" from the War of 1812? In this regard, determine how "hope" and "more" in the final sentence of p57 might mitigate any permanent sort of "close" to the Revolution, this almost in spite of "not" accompanying "hope." Would such a rhetorical impact promote a "warrior" being transformed back to a responsible "citizen?"

95 Ascertain whether Whitney in revision **b** attempts to cast the "warrior" soldier more in the role of the responsible "citizen." Also, observe that the "citizen"-to-"soldier" word order of revision **a** continues in the second segment of this final sentence, and throughout p60. But, in p61, Whitney's word order becomes slightly more complex as the military-civilian topic concludes. In p61, for example, revision **b** order begins the paragraph and two revision **a** couplings complete it.

96 P60 of course begins with Whitney spelling out the citizen-soldier duality, and observe his revision **a** word order in "fathers" to military "camps," as well as in "citizen" to "field." Also, how does "under" relate to "sub-" in root and meaning? And is Whitney's use of "them" and "their" a confusing pronoun reference? Or is "their" an acceptably loose gender usually assigned to one's homeland?

61 While, therefore, you study the duties of your profession (the rules of honorable **warfare**)- and cherish the ancient sentiment "**Dulce** a EST b **et decorum est** ☆ **pro patria mori,**"- cultivate, at the same time, the social and political duties of the **citizen**, and keep in remembrance your rights and privileges as such.- And when our **country shall call** us, also, to ASSIST **join** ☆ you in the **field**- a IT SHALL b IT WILL BE [OUR DUTY TO] c we will bring valor and **patriotism** with us, and ☆ learn discipline and **tactics** of you.[97]

62 Gentlemen of the Lyceum of the City of Detriot, in pu[r]suance of the duty which **you**, sometime since, charged upon me as a member of a YOUR BODY b the Lyceum, ☆ I was engaged in preparing a discource for this day, adapted to the An[n]iversary of a **scientific and literary body**, when **you** consented to celebrate **your** Anniversary in **conjunction** with the **citizens** en masse, an[d] attend [upon a joint ceremony featuring] an address suitable to the events this day commemorates.[98]

63 Even under other circumstances than these, the importance and utility of your institution a DEM[AND? -ONSTRATE?] b **would** require ☆ that it **should** not be passed over in silence.---[99]

64 Your Society, Gentlemen, has, I think, **some features peculiar** to itself.- Other **Societies** of this nature confine their views to certain subjects of **Science or Literature**. [Yet] your constitution contemplates, at **some future** period, to **embrace them** all.- Their sittings are usually **private**,- your's are public.— Their's are a kind of Aristocracy in **Literature**,- every **feature** in your institution is **republican and popular**.-[100]

65 You know, GENTLEMEN, there are **some facetious** gentlemen among us— whose a SENSI[BILITY? -TIVITY?] b **susceptibility** to the **ridiculous** ☆ is peculiarly

---

97 Note the Latin quote heroically attributed to Joseph Warren at Bunker Hill, and compare the root and meaning of "join" with "conjunction" in p62. Also, compare Whitney's use of "assist" with "affiliation" in p66. Determine the root prefix shared by both words.

98 Why does Whitney revise "your" as a modifier of "body" out of the manuscript? Is it merely to remedy a developing "you" redundancy? Or does Whitney perhaps realize that "your" versus "scientific-literary" might suggest a lesser relic or "body" of faulty valor on the part of American citizen-soldiers? Of these two alternative explanations, why might "your" mortal death remove some enduring value from the Revolutionary experience, and even detract from Whitney's ethical appeal as orator on such a ceremonial occasion?

99 Observe that Whitney continues to revise time present to the future conditional.

100 Compare "literature" in sentence 5, following so closely as it does upon "science-literature" (here) or "scientific-literary" (p65) with Whitney's revision of "Society" in sentence 3 of p66. Determine what parallel structure there is, if any, in Whitney's recasting that "society" as "literary." Also, explore the possible root relationship between "peculiar" and "private." Does Whitney's rather polarized meanings for these two words ignore any such root structure? Evaluate what would appear to be euphony in "feature" and "future," "embrace" followed immediately by "them." And determine whether "republican and popular," as used by Whitney here and in p66, heightens orality at the expense of written brevity.

exquisite- and their tact in ascertaining precisely the **Golden Medium in all things, no doubt,** equally so— who seem to feel "an immense **ridiculosity** in the idea of a Philosophical, **Scientiffic and Literary** Society's being established" on what they **pleasantly please** to call,- "this verge of the Creation."-[101]

66 But, Gentlemen, I know [of] no reason why intellect should not act as vigorous[ly]- fancy shoot as creative[ly]- the affections **glow** as warm[ly]- and **patriotism** thrill as exquisite[ly] in the **a** ATM[OSPHERE] **b pure atmosphere** ☆ of the Northern Lakes as in the smoke of An Atlantic City,- on the banks of the Detroit[River] as [on] those of the Connecticutt, the Hudson or the Potowmac.[102] Your principal[-le] of **affiliation**, which is deemed a kind of **quiz[z]ic novelty**, by **quiz[z]ical** gentlemen, is **by no means a new thing under the sun.**—[103] There are and have been,-for a long series of years- in each of the New England Colleges,- a **a** SOCI[ETY] **b Literary Society** ☆ called the **a** P.B.K. **b** Phi Beta Kappa, ☆- each [one] in affiliation with all the others. **And** the principle, in the extent it stands in your constitution, was borrowed **immediately** from a **similar** Society in Phil[adelphi]a.[104] Preserve it, then,- it can do no harm,- it is a good **republican and a popular** feature.- It may hereafter be the source of profit and **amusement** to you when abroad- **and** yield the **same** to strangers who may visit you.[105]

67 Finally- listen to **a** THIS PLEASANT FACETIA **b the pleasant** facet**iae** ☆ of th**ese** gentle**men**, **a** AND **b** for your **amusement,**- and ☆ pursue your own course.—[106] You have organized classes of Original Essays- of Criticism and of Oratory. In

---

101 "Pleasantly please" is perhaps Whitney's holiday wordiness and euphony at its most obvious. But regarding orality versus written substance see "pleasant" in p67, followed by "pleasure" in the next paragraph. Also, see "susceptible" in sentence 3 of p54. And, really to do nothing more than satisfy your curiosity about orality and euphony, compare these three items from ps64 and 65: "some features," "some future," and "some facetious."

102 "Potowmac" is quite obviously a proper spelling for Whitney's era, but can you discern any relationship at all between "Atlantic city" or "Detroit" and his apparent doubling of the final *t* in "Connecticut?" Also, despite the editorial addition of *ly* to make this first sentence read a bit more smoothly, you might want to try reading Whitney's sentence without the *ly* insert. Assuming that you have the proper grammatical structure in mind, does Whitney's original version contain more orality even though it may not read as well?

103 Observe that Whitney's second "quizzic" has the same *al* ending as his misspelling of "principle," and that "novelty" has the same root as "new." What parallel structure, if any, is there in "by *no means* new *thing* under *sun*" and "*Gold*en *Med*ium in all *thing*s, *no* doubt" in p65? Compare "means" and "Medium," "gold" and "sun" and "glow" for related figurative connotations. If "*new* thing under sun" indeed borders on being labeled as a colloquialism, following so closely as it does upon "*no*velty," how then might both the expression and "quizzic," combined with "ridiculous" and "facetious" from p65, allow Whitney to play seriously with an undercurrent of oral humor here? Determine whether "pleasantly please" in p65 would, even in some small way, fit into any such humorous context.

104 Compare "immediately" with "Medium" in root and meaning.

105 Observe that Whitney specifies humorous "amusement" in this final sentence, and twice in p67. Also, note the minor parallel structure in "and similar" and "and same."

th**ese** exercise**s**, you are already conscious of much improvement to yourselv**es**.- And th**e** constant attendance of th**e** public at your sitting**s** show that th**ey** have received- if not instruction- at least **amusement**.—Go on then, Gentle**men**, with th**ese** pursuit**s**, 'til increase of number**s**, of talent**s** and of mean**s** shall enable you to extend your view**s**— to th**e** various class**es** of Science and Philosophy— to a Library- Reading Room- a Museum and **eventually** a Philosophic and Chemical Apparatus.[107]

68 Your **motives are pure**,- your object**s** are [those] of public utility.[108] And, in good time, th**ey** are all practicable. Th**ey** are th**e** cause of Science- of morality- of th**e** extention and diffusion of knowledge and virtue. Let th**e** **consciousness** of th**is** be your [only] reward.- And leave it to th**e** good **pleasure** of the community [as to] **whether they will, or will not**, bestow support and **patronage** on such object**s** **OR NO**.[109]

106 Determine precisely how the prevalence of a plural case in ps67 and 68 induces Whitney to revise "this" to "the," in line with revising a singular "facet*ia*" to the plural "facet*iae*." Consult a possible precursor of Whitney's revision in "facetious" (sentence 1, p65), and speculate whether he was revising simultaneously here, using this revision as a topical device of sorts for the plural grammatical structure in these two concluding paragraphs.

107 All plurals are marked, with special emphasis being placed upon Whitney's pronoun ending to *th*. Also, ascertain whether "eventually" and "event" share a common root and meaning.

108 Compare "pure motives" with the "pure atmosphere" revision made by Whitney (sentence 1, p66).

109 Do not add a final *t* to "no" at the conclusion of Whitney's text, since "whether or no" was a rather customary expression during the nineteenth century. Observe, however, that at least in this single instance Whitney prefers "not" over "no," probably because of excessive duplication in the two words. Also, observe that Whitney follows through on revision **a** (sentence 1, p67) in a limited manner, using a singular "this" only once (sentence 4, p68). And that instance really might be termed more generally plural than singular, consolidating as it does a plural number of "events" for the audience's "consciousness." There is indeed a key question to ponder in evaluating the effectiveness of ps67 and 68. Should Whitney have ended his oration on a "grand" note, attempting to link the Lyceum "club" in voluminous fashion with a citizens' resolve carrying over from the Revolution and War of 1812? Or should he have played down such "grander" principles of patriotism and civilization, focusing instead on the "club" listeners and their practical humanistic gadgets (sentence 5, p67)? Consider how the *Gazette* reading audience and "club" listeners might be at odds on such a question. Or has Whitney attempted to compromise these two points of view for his oral-written audiences? In this regard, compare the root word "patria" in p61 with the scope and meaning of "patronage" (sentence 5, p68) and "patriotism" (sentence 1, p66).

Selected Reading List for Further Study of Fourth of July Orations

I. Appendix follow-up, five oration manuscripts relating to revision process, 1798-1832:

A. Rev. John D. Blair, 1798 oration at Richmond Va., Henry E. Huntington Library (San Marino, Cal.). Minimal number of non-complex revisions, probably indicating a prior draft not now extant.

B. Cyrus King, 1802 oration at Saco Me., Butler Library-Columbia University (NY City). In the absence of newspaper coverage, cataloger bases place of delivery (since not specified by orator) upon contemporaneous items of correspondence.

C. Joseph S[ain]t: Leger d'Happart, 1814 oration at Robb's-Town [West Newton] Pa., Darlington Memorial Library, University of Pittsburgh. Includes "To the Auditors" page, with Leroy d'Happart underscoring and making numeral-plus-"X" notations between lines ca. 1934.

D. John H. James, 1825 oration at Cincinnati Ohio, Public Library of Cincinnati and Hamilton County. Alludes to the Marquis de Lafayette's 19 May visit to ceremony at Grand Lafayette Masonic Lodge in town, with Theodore A. Langstroth making favorable evaluation ("Very good") on first page.

E. Caleb Cushing, 1832 oration at Newburyport Mass., Library of Congress (WDC). The Manuscript Division holds Cushing's inventive "memoranda" notebook (reading sources, oration outline, and minor clause composition), as well as a draft of his letter on the tenth to chairman Ebenezer Moseley of the local Committee of Arrangements, his galley proof ("Copy for Correction") of the oration pamphlet published locally by T. B. and E. L. White, and his distribution list of some 171 persons (except #41, the institutional Boston Athenaeum) designated to receive pamphlet copies.

II. Chapter follow-up, eight units partially defining review context of specific orations, 1821-1859:

A. John Quincy Adams, 1821 oration at Washington D.C.

1. Compare commentary in Philadelphia *National Gazette* (d), 16 thru 18 July, incl. WDC, 27 Jl, *JQA* to Robert Walsh Jr., Philadelphia, and Walsh to JQA, 30 Jl, Adams Family Papers-Massachusetts Historical Society, with that in Boston *Dly Advertiser*, 24 thru 25 Aug.

2. Compare commentary by "Brief Reviewer" in Richmond [Va.] *Enquirer* (sw), 17 and 27 July, with that in *Dly National Intelligencer* (WDC), 20 July.

3. Compare commentary by "Servius Sulpitius" (*Remarks of SS, on an Address . . . , taken from the Alexandria Gazette* [Alexandria, Va.; John Shaw Jr., 1822], pp. 22-30 of review no. 3 from *Gazette* issue dated 8 Aug.) with "Valerius Flaccus" in Washington [City] *Gazette* (d country), 26 July, and "Mutius Scaevola" in Alexandria *Herald* (tw), 13 Aug.

4. Compare review by attorney William Jones Spooner (Boston: Wells and Lilly, ca. 7 Aug. 1821) with Jacob Bailey Moore's "vindication" rejoinder (Concord, N.H.: Hill and Moore, 1821), and with the not-so-flattering treatment by "Vindex"-Philip Ricard Fendall (New York: G. L. Birch, ca. Jan. 1822).

5. Miscellaneous—"Commentator", New York *Commercial Advertiser* (d), 16 July; Portsmouth [N.H.] *Journal*, 21 July; "Seneca", *Southern Patriot and Commercial Advertiser* (d. Charleston SC), 24 July.

B. Rev. Hooper Cumming, 1824 oration on the fifth at New York City

1. Compare commentary by "New-Englandman" in N-Y *Evening Post*, 15 July, with parallel "epistle" by "Friend to Modest Merit" (Bridgeport, Ct.: Lockwood and Sterling, 1824), pp. 13-18.

2. Compare orator's explanatory letter to editor William Coleman in N-Y *Evening Post*, 16 July, rpt. in *New-England Galaxy* (Boston), 23 Jl, with "postscript" reply by "Friend to Modest Merit," pp. 19-20.

C. William Emmons (Orator, "Fredoniad" printer-salesman, and sometime professor), 1826 oration at Boston, 1827 oration at Providence R.I., and 1828 oration at New York City

1. Compare 1826 Boston oration (pamphlet printed by WmE) with "eulogy" on John Adams and Thomas Jefferson at Salem Mass., 27 July (WmE printer), Boston oration repeated at Salem same day as eulogy delivered (*Essex Register* (sw), 27 Jl; Salem *Gazette* [sw], 28 Jl), and at Exeter N.H. on 22 Aug. (*Rockingham Gazette*, 22 and 29 Ag).

2. Compare 1827 quasi-libel skirmish over the Providence oration, allegedly spurred by editor Sylvester S. Southworth (*Literary Cadet and R-I Statesman* [sw, Providence], 4 thru 11 July), with minor incident on steps of City Hall in New York, stemming from the second of two orations there on the Fourth in 1828, and involving High-Constable

Jacob Hays ("Punning in High and Low Life," N-Y *Enquirer for the Country*, 3 July, 1827; N-Y *Spectator* [sw], 11 July, 1828).

3. Compare orator's 1826 "national poem" (pp. 10-16 of Boston oration pamphlet) with two versions of brother Richard's 1828 "Independence" poem (version 1—NY *Morning Courier*, 4 July, verse sequence 1 thru 6; version 2—N-Y *Enquirer* [d], 4 July, rpt. in *Courier* [d], 29 Jl, verse sequence 1-2, 5, 3-4, and 6. Verses 346 completely recast, with following revisions to 125: v.11.4 phrase, "This, the grand hour of freedom's" to "The day that hail'd a nation's" [birth]; v.21.2 "proclaim" for "exalt"; v. 21.4 "heavens" for "clouds"; v.51.2 "note" for "notes"; and v.51.3 clause, "With us, the hallow'd strain begun" to "The anthem, first, Columbia sung").

4. Miscellaneous notoriety—compare "Sublimity", NY *Sun* (d), 28 Dec., 1833, with "An Important Error," NY *Evening Signal* cited in Troy *Dly Whig*, 24 July, 1840; also, see "Pop Emmons," Syracuse [N.Y.] *Star* in Boston *Museum*, 22 Nov., 1851, and lithograph of orator gesturing in *The Inaugural Speech of WmE, Delivered on the Morning of General Election, May 31, 1826, by Particular Desire of His Fellow Citizens* (Boston: WmE, 1826).

D. George McDuffie, 1827 oration at Hamburg S.C.

1. Using commentary on oral animation by "A." as a guideline (Augusta *Chronicle and Georgia Advertiser* [sw], 14 July), compare texts of two Hamburg orations. One delivered to a Mechanics' Society dinner in B. Picquet's warehouse on the second, and the other at a banquet hosted by E. W. Harrison in the Farmers' Hotel on the Fourth (texts in *Chronicle-Advertiser* [sw], 7 and 11 July).

2. First oration—compare commentary in Charleston *Southern Patriot* (d), 24 July, with two critiques by "Philo-[William Jones] Lowndes" in *Dly National Intelligencer* ("Standard of Intellect," rpt. in Lynchburg *Virginian* [sw], 17 Sept.; "What Constitutes An Orator," rpt. in *Virginian* [sw], 4 Oct.).

3. Second oration—compare commentary by "One of McDuffie's Constituents" in *Chronicle-Advertiser* (sw), 28 July, with reply by "Citizen" in same title for 1 Aug.

4. Miscellaneous background—Augusta Ga., 12 July, unidentified person to *Cadet* editor, Providence, in *Literary Cadet and Rhode-Island Statesman* (sw), 1 Aug., rpt. in *Chronicle-Advertiser* (sw), 18 Ag;

"Unhappy Occurrence," *Virginia Free Press and Farmers' Repository* (Charles-Town), 29 Aug.; Baltimore *Marylander* (sw), 9 Jan., 1828; "Hamburg sale and advertisement, dated 11 Aug.," *National Banner and Nashville* [*Tenn.*] *Whig* (sw), 2 Sept., 1830.

E. William Foster Otis, 1831 oration at Boston

1. Huntington Library copy of Carter-Hendee-Babcock 1831 pamphlet edition, with contemporaneous reader's marginal comments in quotes and word underscoring duplicated—compare reader's favorable symbols on pp. 21 ("good", ll. 13-23, *under Oliver*[Cromwell], *ever had an*, and *our* [importance]), 22 ll. 4-5, *our* and *fellow*), and 24 (ll. 17-19, *host of angry consequences*) with otherwise hostile comments, especially those on p. 11 ("You are a miserable tool," ll. 17-18, *miserable tools*) and p. 29 ("John Bull's word," l. 9, *so called*). For the reader's objections to Otis's florid style, see the specific instance of Europe on pp. 14 thru 18 ("poor Europe," 14:ll. 13-22; 15:l. 3 compared to "covered with Leprosy," 18:ll. 7-8). Also, see 13:ll. 22-29, 14:ll. 1-4, 15:ll. 15-19, 16:ll. 4-7, 17:ll. 1-14, and 18:ll. 2-4 (*iconoclasts*). For other objections regarding floridity in the printed oration, see "horrid" (31:l. 17, *extortions*) or 30:l. 10, *eviscerate*, and "[overly] fine" (36:ll. 1-4). Together with 5:ll. 17-18 (*exultation* and *waving*); 6:ll. 20-24; 7:ll. 1-3 (*that it*[*principle*] *lacks husbandry*), l. 15 (*quiring*), and ll. 27-30 (*our firesides next perish*); 8:ll. 23-32; 9:ll. 7-17 (*too solely*); 10:ll. 13-28; 11:ll. 4-20; 19:ll. 17-21 (*choir of civilization, glories*, and *gorgeousness*); 20:ll. 1-14; 23:ll. 15-23; 28:ll. 16-30 (*imaginary phantom*); and 29:ll. 1-2 (*strong insinuations*).

2. Compare initial 1831 Boston *Review* pamphlet with pp. 12-29 of *Reviewer Reviewed* rejoinder, published same year by Carter, Hendee, and Babcock.

3. Miscellaneous—"V.L.Q.," *Independent Chronicle and Boston Patriot*, 9 July; *New-England Palladium and Commercial Advertiser* (Boston), 22 July; Boston, 13 Aug., *WFO* to Allyne Otis, London Eng., Harrison Gray Otis Papers, Massachusetts Historical Society.

F. Edwin Forrest, 1838 oration at New York City

1. Ghostwriter question involving William Leggett—NY *Evening Post* cited in NY *Evening Star*, 6-7, 9, and 20 July; *New Era* (d, NY City) and *New-Yorker*, 7 July; N-Y *Commercial Advertiser* (d), 20 July; "Newspaper excerpt" and Philadelphia, 17 Oct., *EF* to George Seaman, John A. Morrill, and Edmund J. Porter, NY City, in William Rounseville Alger, *Life of EF, the American Tragedian* (Philadelphia: J. B. Lippincott, 1877), I, 348-50.

2. Repeat recitations on nineteenth and twenty-first by friend W. R. Blake, manager of Franklin Theater, done concurrently with publication of oration pamphlet—"Undated correspondent's report," *New Era* (d), 21 July; *Sunday Morning News* (NY City), 22 July.

3. Miscellaneous commentary—*New Era* (d), 6 July; "Report by editor J. Palmer," Boston *Columbian Centinel*, 7 July, rpt. in Boston *Commercial Gazette*, 9 Jl, and Cincinnati *Dly Whig and Commercial Intelligencer*, 16 Jl; "Opifex", *New Era* (d), 11 July; NY *Evening Star*, 23 July; "Publisher's preface, dated 10 May 1876," *Gem of the Century* centennial edition (St. Louis, Mo.: A. Wiehusch and Son, 1876).

G. Edmund Bellinger Jr., 1851 debate with Alfred Proctor Aldrich at Clinton S.C.

1. Compare commentary by "Union" in Charleston *Courier* (d), 10 Sept. 1828, with "Charleston a Second Moscow" article in Charleston *Southern Standard* (d), 10 July, 1851.

2. Compare commentary in Charleston *Southern Standard* (d), 8 and 14 July, with "Aqua Fortis" in Charleston *Mercury* (d), 12 July.

H. Rev. George W. Taylor, 1859 oration at Washington Grove near Marysville Cal. (text in *Dly California Express* [Msville], 6 July)

1. Compare editorial commentary in *Dly National Democrat* (Msv), 7 and 9 July, with that in *Dly California Express* (Msv), 8 and 11 July.

2. Compare commentary by "Timbuctoo" (datelined pseud. town-7 Jl) in *Dly Express*, 8 July, with "Friend" (datelined Timbuctoo as well-9 Jl) in *Dly Democrat*, 9 July.

III. Chapter follow-up, thirty-nine numbered critical references, 1808-1860:

1. Tristram Burges, *An Oration, Delivered in the Baptist Meeting-House, in Providence, on the Fourth of July, 1801, In Commemoration of American Independence* (Providence, R.I.: John Carter, 1801), copy with marginal comments by contemporaneous reader in Rare Book Room-Library of Congress. Reader's comments/revisions placed in quotes, and underscoring of words by reader duplicated. Attitude toward orator—p. 4:ll. 5-12, "not true," 4:ll. 14-20, "weak", and 4:ll. 22-31, "It ought to be done;" 5:ll. 4-7, "Yes we have;" 7:ll. 3-9, "Witness the present day;" 13:ll. 11-21, "This fits you exactly," and 13:ll. 32-39 thru 14:l. 1 (compare with 12:ll. 1-8), "again at your demagogues;" 21:ll. 1-36, "What hast thou to do with American

liberty, thou pleader of a British cause;" and 22:ll. 1-8, "Why not then bury your Tory hatchet." Diction General—3:ll. 6-22, "flat and dogmatical" (compare with *today* under Diction Specific); 6:ll. 23-30, "false logick," and 6:ll. 30-38, "turbid and broken;" 8:ll. 10-16, "abusive nonsense," and 8:ll. 31-39 thru 9:ll. 1-25, "oratori[ca]l rant;" 12:ll. 25-39 thru 13:ll. 1-4, "absurd misrepresentation;" 13:ll. 4-11, "pityfull"; 14:ll. 24-34, "turgid *little* figures;" 18:ll. 25-39, "false reasoning;" and 22:ll. 8-18, "puff". Diction Specific—5:l. 14, substitute "to oppose" for *lingering in*; 6:l. 6, *today* termed "flat"; 7:l. 38, *fiery element* labeled "absurd"; and 14:ll. 6-7, contrast between *solitary* and *millions* termed "wonderfull small."

2. *juvenile, by mature writer. Gabriel Nourse, *The Glorious Spirit of '76, Being A Collection of Patriotic and Philanthropic Addresses on the Anniversary of American Independence; To Which Is Added A Funeral Oration, On the demise of our dear departed Friend and Hero, Gen[eral]. George Washington, Concluded by A Solemn and Pathetic Dirge, Delivered by a Youth of nine years old.—with an Address on the Present State of America, The Whole of Which are Particularly Designed for Schools* (Hagerstown, Md.: Jacob D. Dietrick, 1806), copy at Clements Library-University of Michigan (Ann Arbor). Nourse published a second juvenile title the same year: *The Youth's Instructor, or Student's Companion, Being a collection of words the most useful and elegant, selected from Bayly, Johnson, and Sheridan—with an explanation, where any is necessary, agreeable to those justly celebrated authors.* Nourse, "Proposal datelined Sharpsburg Md.-10 Jan.," *Maryland Herald and Hager's-Town Weekly Advertiser,* 10 Jan., 1806.

3. Hext M[c]Call, *An Oration, Delivered in S[ain]t. Michael's Church, before the Inhabitants of Charleston, South-Carolina, on the Fourth of July, 1810, In Commemoration of American Independence, by Appointment of the American Revolution Society, and Published at the Request of That Society, and Also of the South-Carolina State Society of Cincinnati* (Charleston: W. P. Young, 1810), copy with marginal comments by contemporaneous reader in Ford Collection-New York Public Library. Reader's comments/revisions placed in quotes, and underscoring of words by reader duplicated. Diction General—p.8:ll. 5-6, "Here is not a happy coincidence, [as] sacred and profane allusion ought not to be so immediately blended;" 10:ll. 30-31, "handsome [epigram];" and 15:ll. 14-25 and 16:ll. 2-13, "very[overly]fine." Diction Specific—7:l. 8, revise *swelled the full chorus of freedom* to "swore to be free;" 9:ll. 20-21, revise *wonder of the world* to "form of the beauteous wonderer;" 10:l. 11, *deceitful* labeled "idiom"; 13: l. 22, *wall three thousand miles thick* termed "not a very correct figure;" 14:ll. 9-10, revise *((we were)) entitled, ((and))* to "that state was [entitled];" 15:l. 14, revise *their grave* to "its den," since "not fair

to make this Hydra sprung out of the graves of those great men;" and 19:l. 22, revise *plains* to "mountains".

4. Ross Wilkins, "Oration in Academian Grove to Pittsburgh Quintilian Society," Pittsburgh *Commonwealth*, 12 July, 1817.

5. Hugh S. Legare, *An Oration, Delivered on the Fourth of July, 1823; before the '76 Association, and Published at Their Request* (Charleston, S.C.: A. E. Miller, 1823), pp. 5-9.

6. Timothy Pickering, *Observations Introductory to Reading the Declaration of Independence, at Salem, July 4, 1823* (Salem, Mass.: Warwick Palfray Jr., 1823), p. 3.

7 *juvenile speaker. Anonymous pupil, "Oration to scholars of Newville Seminary," Lancaster [Pa] *Intelligencer*, 9 Aug., 1825.

8. William Hunter, *Oration Pronounced before the Citizens of Providence, on the Fourth of July, 1826, Being the Fiftieth Anniversary of American Independence* (Providence, R.I.: Smith and Parmenter, 1826), pp. 5-7 and 27.

9. "Review of 1826 oration by Josiah Quincy at Boston," *Literary Cadet and Saturday Evening Bulletin* (Providence RI), 19 Aug., 1826.

10. Peter P. Lowe, *1826 Semi-Centennial Oration on American Independence* [*at Dayton Ohio*], rpt. during 1843 by *Miamian and Manual of American Principles* (Dayton), notice in Hamilton *Intelligencer*, 10 Aug., and during 1876 by Dr. Thomas Hill, acting as editor for Centennial Publishing Company of Portland Me. Manuscript note by J[ohn] W[aterman]. T[refethen].? on p. 4 of copy in Newberry Library-Chicago attributes "Preface" and collation of text to "Rev. Dr. Hill of Portland, Expr[esident]. of A[n]t[ioc]h. Col[lege]."

11 *juvenile speaker. Master Edward P. Tabb, "Oration at Norfolk [Va.] Town Hall on 20 July to association of youthful townsmen," *Carolina Sentinel* (New Bern NC), 5 Aug., 1826.

12. Q[uerist]., "Recipe for a 4th of July Oration, dated 3 July" (with editor's preface), Boston *Evening Bulletin*, 5 July, 1828, rpt. without preface in *New-England Galaxy* (Boston), 11 Jl.; New-York *Enquirer for the Country*, 18 Jl; and Charlottesville *Virginia Advocate*, 19 Jl. *Bulletin* editor's preface —"Were we not certain that our *physical* correspondent intended to be entirely general (and not at all particular) in amalgamating the ingredients of the subjoined composition, sent to us on Thursday, we should

by no means consent to serve it up. As it is, those who do not take it (and nobody should, except in desperate cases) will find it exceedingly harmless." A second piece by correspondent "Q.", titled "The Governor's Ghost: A Legend of the Last Century," appeared in the *New-England Galaxy* two issues after the reprint (25 Jl). For three other recipe-format references, consult "A Recipe for making a Fourth-proof Dandy," *Morning Chronicle and Baltimore Advertiser* in Edenton *Gazette and North-Carolina General Advertiser*, 20 Aug., 1821; "Character of General Summary," *Berkshire American* (North Adams Mass.) in *Virginia Free Press and Farmers' Repository* (Charles-Town), 22 July, 1829; and J.E.D., "Recipe for a Modern Concert—1834," *New England Galazy*, 26 April, 1834.

13. "The Era of Eloquence," Salem [Mass] *Observer*, 19 Jl, 1828.

14. Jeremy Diddler (pseud. from British character role in "Raising the Wind," 1803 James Kenney farce), "A Lecture on Lecturing," New York *Enquirer* in *Central Watchtower and Farmer's Journal* (Harrodsburg Ky.), 16 May, 1829.

15. Valmonser (pseud. possibly connoting citizen of French locale in "Foundling of the Forest," 1809 William Dimond play), "Commentary addressed to editor," Columbia [S.C.] *Telescope*, 10 July, 1829.

16. Ichabod, "The Fourth of July—Revolutionary Veterans" (poem), Providence [R.I.] *Journal and General Advertiser* in Utica [N.Y.] *Sentinel and Gazette*, 25 Aug., 1829.

17. "National Jubilee"/"Fourth of July," *Yeoman's Gazette* (Concord Mass.), 3 July, 1830, and *Yeoman's Gazette, Mechanic's Journal, and Middlesex Advertiser* (Concord), 30 June, 1832.

18. "Printed excerpt on satin for Kentucky drawing rooms, from 1829 Tristram Burges oration at *Clay*ville R.I.," *New-England Weekly Review* (Hartford Ct.), 12 July, 1830.

19. Maria Pinckney ("Lady, for Her Goddaughter"), *The Quintessence of Long Speeches, Arranged as a Political Catechism* (Charleston, S.C.: A. E. Miller, 1830), pp. 14-15, quoting 1830 oration on the fifth to Beaufort Volunteer Guards by Charleston-*Mercury* editor John A. Stuart.

20. "Review of 1832 oration by Charles Jared Ingersoll at Philadelphia," *North American Magazine*, 1 (Dec. 1832), 122-25.

21. "Fourth of July," *Morning Courier and New-York Enquirer for the Country*, 21 June, 1833.

22. "The Fourth of July," *Western Monthly Magazine*, 1 (Aug. 1833), 375-78.

23. Alexander H. Stephens, "Diary entries dated 20-24, 26-27, and 30 June, 2-3, 4[incl. n.], and 7 July, 1834," ed. James Z. Rabun, *Georgia Historical Quarterly*, 36 (March 1952), 92-94, together with *An Address, Delivered at Crawfordville, on the Fourth of July, 1834* (Augusta, Ga.: *Chronicle* and *Sentinel* Office, 1864).

24. "Description of Fourth of July celebration in a Yankee village" (under plain "Fourth of July" heading)/"Fourth of July" heading for second reference, Cincinnati *Mirror and Western Gazette of Literature, Science, and the Arts*, 25 June and 2 July, 1836.

25. N., "American Multiloquence," *Harvardiana*, 4 (April 1838), 270.

26. Anonymous critic, *Some Remarks upon an Oration by Asa Child, before the Citizens of Norwich* [*Ct.*], *July 4th, 1838* (n.p.: publisher/printer not specified, 1838).

27. Charles W. Upham, *Oration Delivered at the Request of the City Authorities of Salem, July 4, 1842* (Salem, Mass.: Chapman and Palfray, 1842), pp. 5-8.

28. Horace Mann, *An Oration, Delivered before the Authorities of the City of Boston, July 4, 1842*, 4th ed. (Boston: publisher/printer not specified, 1842), pp. 1-3, rpt. as "Go Forth and Teach" centennial edition by National Education Association in 1937.

29. "The usual Fourth of July Procession in New-York—extending from the Battery to Fourteenth street" (pictorial sketch), *National Jubilee: A Holiday Salute, and Fourth of July X-Pounder* (NY City), 1844 pictorial issue at Beinecke Library-Yale University, New Haven Ct.

30. W[illiam]. Gilmore Simms, *The Sources of American Independence: An Oration, on the Sixty-Ninth Anniversary of American Independence; Delivered at Aiken, South-Carolina, before the Town Council and Citizens Thereof* (Aiken: Town Council, 1844), pp. 5-9.

31. Citizen of Boston, *Remarks upon an Oration* ["*True Grandeur of Nations*"] *Delivered by Charles Sumner before the Authorities of the City of Boston, July 4th, 1845* (Boston: William Crosby and H. P. Nichols, ca. 20

Oct. 1845), together with "Letters Responding to Sumner's Oration," ed. Worthington Chauncey Ford, *Proceedings of the Massachusetts Historical Society*, 50 (April 1917), 249-307.

32. A., "Patriotic Citizens before Tory Priests," Hamilton [N.Y.] *Student and Christian Reformer*, 14 July, 1847.

33 *juvenile, by mature speaker. B[enjamin]. F[aneuil]. Porter, "A Fourth of July Address to Sunday School Children [at Tuscaloosa Ala.]," *Schoolfellow*, 1 (July 1849), 217-21, and (Aug. 1849), 227-31.

34. Reuben T. Durrett, "Galley-proof columns of 1852 Louisville city oration, text printed as corrected in Louisville [Ky.] *Dly Courier*, 17 July," Filson Club-Louisville. Durrett's Collection of Fourth of July oration pamphlets is located at Regenstein Library-University of Chicago.

35. "Club Literature—review of Charles P. James's 1853 oration, 'American Man of Letters,' to Cincinnati Literary Club," *West American Review*, 1 (Oct. 1853), 205-07.

36. Thomas Vester Moore, "Excerpt from 1854 oration at Richmond [Va.] African Church" (under "Fourth of July Orations" heading), *Dly National Intelligencer* (WDC), 15 July, 1854, rpt. in Green/IV6/*a*314-15 and *c*130-31.

37. Stephen A. Douglas, "Sketch of thirty-five minute oration in 1858 at grove near mother's Clifton Springs residence," Syracuse *Standard* in Rochester [N.Y.] *Democrat and American*, 12 July, 1858.

38. James Russell Lowell, "Review of 1858 oration by Rufus Choate at Boston," *Atlantic Monthly*, 2 (Aug. 1858), 374-82.

39. "The National Birthday," New-York *Tablet*, 7 July, 1860.

IV. Miscellaneous numbered critical references, 1918-1969:

1. Frederick Tupper, "The Fourth of July Oration," *Nation*, 107 (6 July, 1918), 10-11.

2. Edmund Lester Pearson, "Unfettered Eagles," *Scribner's Magazine*, 76 (July 1924), 61-67, revised as "Making the Eagle Scream" (chapter 2) in *Queer Books* (Garden City, N.Y.: Doubleday Doran, 1928), pp. 19-39.

3. Cedric Larson, "Patriotism in Carmine: 162 Years of July 4th Oratory," *Quarterly Journal of Speech*, 26 (Feb. 1940), 12-25.

4. Loyd Haberly, *The Fourth of July: Or An Oregon Orator* [poem] (St. Louis, Mo.: Haberly Press, 1942).

5. Frederick H. Lawton, "Fourth of July Orations," *Journal of the Rutgers University Library*, 17 (June 1954), 63.

6. Fletcher M. Green, *a* "Listen to the Eagle Scream: One Hundred Years of the Fourth of July in North Carolina, 1776-1876," *North Carolina Historical Review*, 31 (July 1954), 313-17, adapted into *b* "The Spirit of '76," *Emory University Quarterly*, 11 (June 1955), 65-82, version *a* rpt. as *c*-chapter 5 of *Democracy in the Old South and Other Essays*, ed. J. Isaac Copeland (Nashville, Tenn.: Vanderbilt University Press, 1969), pp. 129-33.

7. Howard Hastings Martin, "Decline of the Fourth of July Oration" (subhead), part of chapter 7 ("Summary and Conclusions") in "Orations on the Anniversary of American Independence, 1777-1876," Diss. Northwestern 1955, pp. 341-46.

8. Martin, "The Fourth of July Oration" (adapted from diss. chapters 3 thru 6: 3-"Themes before 1789," 94-145; 4-"Themes after 1789," 146-94; 5-"Speakers' Purposes," 195-265; and 6-"Oration as Part of National Literature," 266-329), *Quarterly Journal of Speech*, 44 (Dec. 1958), 393-401.

9. Leo M. Kaiser, ed., "Stephen F. Austin's Oration [at Potosi Mo.] of July 4, 1818," *Southwestern Historical Quarterly*, 64 (July 1960), 71-79.

10. Frances Lea McCurdy, "The Genius of Liberty," *Missouri Historical Review*, 57 (July 1963), 337-43, adapted into chapter 3 ("Blessings of Republicanism") of *Stump, Bar, and Pulpit: Speechmaking on the Missouri Frontier* (Columbia: University of Missouri Press, 1969), pp. 47-67.

11. Orville A. Hitchcock and Ota Thomas Reynolds, "Ford Douglass' Fourth of July Oration [at Framingham Mass.], 1860," chapter 9 in *Anti-slavery and Disunion, 1858-1861: Studies in the Rhetoric of Compromise and Conflict*, ed. J. Jeffery Auer (New York: Harper and Row, 1963), pp. 133-51.

12. Patricia G. Bowman, "Frederick Douglass: Fourth of July Oration [at Rochester N.Y.], 1852," *University of Rochester Library Bulletin*, 19 (Spring 1964), 42-48.

13. Phineus Donan (orator), "A Scream from the American Eagle in Dakota [Territory], 1885 [pamphlet edition of purported Fargo oration]," *American West*, 5 (July 1968), 45-47.

14. Barnet Baskerville, "19th-Century Burlesque of Oratory," *American Quarterly*, 20 (Winter 1968), 727-39.

15. Robert Pettus Hay, "Freedom's Jubilee: The Fourth of July in Charleston, 1826-1876," *West Virginia History*, 26 (July 1965), 209-12.

16. Hay, "A Jubilee for Freemen: The Fourth of July in Frontier Kentucky, 1788-1816," *Register of the Kentucky Historical Society*, 64 (July 1966), 176-80.

17. Hay, "What Ever Became of the Fourth of July?" (epilogue), in "Freedom's Jubilee: One Hundred Years of the Fourth of July, 1776-1876," Diss. Kentucky 1967, pp. 289-302. Compare with Martin/IV7 above.

18. Hay, "Providence and the American Past" (revised from diss. chapter 8- "Providence", 172-202), *Indiana Magazine of History*, 65 (June 1969), 79-101.

19. Hay, "The Liberty Tree: A Symbol for American Patriots," *Quarterly Journal of Speech*, 55 (Dec. 1969), 414-24.

INDEX